STRINDBERG

STRINDBERG

A Life

SUE PRIDEAUX

YALE UNIVERSITY PRESS
NEW HAVEN AND LONDON

To John, Kate and Sam

Designed by Sarah Faulks

Printed in China

Library of Congress Cataloging-in-Publication Data

Prideaux, Sue.
Strindberg : a life / Sue Prideaux.
      p. cm.
Includes bibliographical references and index.
ISBN 978-0-300-13693-7 (cl : alk. paper)
1. Strindberg, August, 1849–1912. 2. Authors, Swedish–19th
century–Biography. I. Title.
PT9815.P75 2012
839.72'67–dc23
[B]

                          2011038050

A catalogue record for this book is available from The British Library

Endpapers: *View over Slussen* by Carl Tholander, ?1898. Stockholm City Museum. Slussen, the central area of Stockholm where Strindberg grew up while the Industrial Revolution advanced.

Pg. i: Sketch of Strindberg by Carl Larsson, 1885.

Frontispiece: Strindberg, c.1869 when he gave up his medical studies for the stage. Kungliga biblioteket, Stockholm, Strindbergsrummet, Bilder, Kartong 3, 1870_1.

CONTENTS

PREFACE

During the writing of this book it became apparent to me that outside Scandinavia Strindberg is best known for two things: *Miss Julie* and alarming misogyny.

At the time he was beginning as a writer, Scandinavia was preoccupied by the Woman Question on which Strindberg set out his position in a manifesto advocating that girls and women should have equal rights to education, jobs, votes, money and sexual promiscuity. Hardly misogyny, but such a degree of emancipation seemed like denigration to a generation that put frills on its furniture legs and its women on pedestals. It earned him the enmity of the feminists, led by the Queen of Sweden, who did not have quite such radical changes in mind for her sex and arranged for him to be prosecuted for blasphemy.

As for *Miss Julie*, had he written only that one play his fame would have been assured but he wrote another sixty plays, three books of poetry, eighteen novels and nine autobiographies. Some ten thousand letters survive, along with a lot of journalism. There is also the Green Sack in which he hauled drafts and notes and jottings that might one day come in useful, now reduced to sixty-nine box files in the Royal Library of Stockholm. If more of this vast agglomeration had been translated he would surely be more widely valued as one of the founders of modern literature and enjoyed as an irreverent commentator on the ideas of half a century.

The English-speaking world does not think of Strindberg as a humorist but in *The People of Hemsö* he wrote Scandinavia's great comic masterpiece. *The Red Room* and *Black Banners* were gaspingly accurate satires that like Swift's or Pope's were deliciously *à clef* at the time, but the *clef* does not date them and they remain politically sharp and funny. His twelve history plays earned him the title 'Sweden's Shakespeare' and he deserves the title for the clear shape he brings to the huge subject and the electrifying psychological duels between historical characters. He wrote the first modern history to tell the story of his nation through its ordinary people rather than through kings and battles. Today a commonplace way of writing history, in those days it was both new and feared, being seen as certainly subversive and probably anarchistic. During his time in France in the 1880s, he again went against the political grain, this time taking up an essentially conservative position against the march of the machine to write a historical record of the fast-disappearing ways of agrarian France, which still harvested by the moon and ploughed behind the horse.

As surely as the plough horse was being replaced by the mechanical plough, Strindberg was living in perplexing times. During his time at university, Darwin's *Origin of Species* was translated into Swedish and a greater intellectual, moral and political upheaval could hardly be imagined as the Protestant Swedish state fought the new pieties of evolutionary science. Though a naturalist and a scientist, Strindberg could never, in his words, be satisfied with ending up as no more than a barrow-load of shit to spread over the garden. He was extremely close to two painters, Munch and Gauguin, during the time that led up to each man painting his masterpiece questioning the idea that the physical world exhaustively describes reality and the self is merely an evolutionary result. When Edvard Munch's *The Scream* was first exhibited in Paris in 1896, Strindberg described it as 'A scream of fear as nature prepares to speak to the bewildered little creatures who, without resembling them at all, imagine themselves gods.' He was also close to Paul Gauguin during Gauguin's last period in Paris before he returned to the South Seas to paint *Who are We? Where do we come from? Where are we going?*

Strindberg's own quest to answer these questions has given us the well-known image of Strindberg the alchemist hunting down the hobgoblins of the occult as he brewed gold, captured the spirits of the dead in the Cimitière du Montparnasse, recorded dreams, injected apples with morphine to see if they had nervous systems, experimented with electricity and magnetism and absinthe and everything else that Paris of the 1890s knew as *Le Rêve*, as he worked on identifying the source of that mysterious entity which, though invisible and non-provable, undoubtedly exists: the self. Less well known is his approach to the quest for self through reason: his interest in the work of Charcot, Pierre Janet and Bernheim, the teachers of Freud, and his friendships and correspondence with pioneering scientists like Carl Ludwig Schleich whose discovery of local anaesthesia raised new questions about the brain, consciousness and self.

As a playwright, Strindberg was far less interested in social situations than his great contemporaries Ibsen and Chekhov. His growing interest lay in revealing the unconscious through the language of the conscious. Arguing that literature ought to emancipate itself entirely from art and become a science, he called himself a vivisector, writing a series of autobiographies with the purpose of 'dissecting the corpse of the person I have known best and learning anatomy, physiology, psychology, and history from the carcass.' As a consequence he wrote outside the mainstream of his time, continually seeking novelty and invention in a completely personal way. The results are best known in two sorts of plays: his murderously claustrophobic domestic *danses macabres* that deal with the force-fields of submission and control pulsing between characters in the plays such as *Miss Julie*, *The Father*, *Comrades*, *The Dance of Death*, *Playing with Fire* and *The Stronger*, plays whose influence was openly acknowledged in the following generation of playwrights by Eugene O'Neill, Arthur Miller and Sean O'Casey and did not stop with them. Tennessee Williams's *Streetcar named Desire* can almost be read simply as an updated *Miss Julie* and the turbulence and psychological violence in Edward Albee's *Who's Afraid of Virginia Woolf?* and *The Goat, or Who is Sylvia* owe much to *The Dance of Death*. O'Casey wrote in one of his letters: 'Strindberg, Strindberg, Strindberg, the greatest of them all . . . Barrie sits mumbling as he silvers his little model stars and gilds his little model suns, while Strindberg shakes flames from the living planets and the fixed stars. Ibsen can sit serenely in his Doll's House, while Strindberg is battling with his heaven and hell.'

The later, more difficult category is the dream play or ghost play which found its heirs in film and in the Theatre of the Absurd, embracing irrationality and doing away with the old Aristotelian unities of sequential time and conventional space, and with them the unity of self. No coincidence that Strindberg was doing this in 1907, the same year that Picasso's Cubist *Les Demoiselles d'Avignon* fragmented the picture plane, Schoenberg shattered music's tonal framework with the first performance of his *Chamber Symphony* and Einstein had his 'happiest thought' that would lead to the theory of relativity. Strindberg introduced flashbacks and re-runs to show that there is no such thing as a single, immutable self. Older and younger selves exist on simultaneous planes of time, dead men speak and the 'I' is so fragmented that it is like the bits at the end of the kaleidoscope endlessly forming and reforming, a concept that runs close to the alchemical principle that there exists a prime matter that is common to all matter, a universal particle: matter's self that can take almost limitless shapes. As tricky to stage as gold is to distil in the alembic, the dream plays are seen by some as impossibly difficult nonsense and by others like Max Reinhardt and Ingmar Bergmann as the summit of dramaturgy.

André Breton referred to Strindberg's *A Dream Play* in his second Surrealist Manifesto of 1929. Surrealist Theatre and Expressionist Theatre are a direct legacy though many other lines have been drawn: to Pirandello's *Six Characters in Search of an Author*, to Brecht's *Good Woman of Szechwan* and to Samuel Beckett who denied being influenced, though parallels have often been remarked between *A Dream Play* and *Waiting for Godot* and between *The Roofing Feast*, Strindberg's 1906 stream-of-consciousness novel in which a dying man reviews his life, and *Krapp's Last Tape*. Strindberg was one of Kafka's favourite authors.

Never afraid of the difficult, he loved to experiment in every direction, literary and scientific. He frequently failed, often because he refused to believe accepted truths until he had verified them for himself, such as trying to prove in a Berlin street that the world really was round, an experiment that nearly got him arrested. Photography was an enduring interest and the self-portraits are another facet of the self-examination. Characteristic mistrust led him to make his own cameras, often lensless, lest the lens stealthily insert some distortion between the eye and the truth. He also drew and painted rather well. The highest price for one of his paintings currently stands at $4,168,160, not that he enjoyed the fruits of his success in his lifetime. Watching aghast as his contemporaries slid with apparent ease into wealth and celebrity, he stumbled from one fiasco to another, defiantly refusing to play anyone's game. He is comical and unsparing in his accounts of his mistakes and his infinite capacity to alienate people with influence.

At the end he was celebrated in spite of himself by the people of Sweden who, insulted that he had never been awarded the Nobel Prize, collected their own money to award him the People's anti-Nobel. Ten thousand lined the streets to follow his funeral procession.

A hundred years after his death I cannot help feeling it is a shame that he did not write in a more widely accessible language. His careless flair that left a trail in many directions of influence might then have been better understood. I hope that this biography might help to make August Strindberg more approachable. Even more than most, he is a writer whose life illuminates his work.

* * *

It is traditional to reference quotations from Strindberg's letters by their numbers in the Swedish edition of the *Complete Letters* but as one purpose of this book is to make Strindberg's writings more easily accessible to the non-Swedish-speaker, I have simply referenced the letters by date so that they can be looked up in the Swedish edition or in the English (or any other) translation. Equally, I have not followed the tradition of referencing quotations from either the old or the new edition of the *Collected Works*, except on the few occasions when I had no alternative. Instead, I have quoted from English-language translations and given the source in the note. The free translations of the poems are inadequate and they are my own. The titles of Strindberg's works in English translation have varied over the years. I have used the titles as they appear in the Modern Humanities Research Association bibliography compiled and edited by Michael Robinson.

* * *

I have received enormous help from the scholarship of others, some alive, some dead: Harry G. Carlson, Torsten Ecklund, Olof Lagerkrantz, Frederick J. and Lise-Lone Marker, Michael Meyer, Elisabeth Sprigge, Evert Sprinchorn, Mary Sandbach and Egil Törnquist, to mention a few, but my deepest thanks go to Professor Michael Robinson, the outstanding Strindberg scholar and translator, who has been generous both in his encouragement and his permission to quote freely from his translation of the letters. In Denmark, at Skovlyst where the book was born, my thanks to Bjørn Mortensen, Preben Hald, Helle Nebelong, Jens Henrik Tiemroth and to Johnny Møller Jensen of Den Gamleby Museum Århus.

In Austria, thanks to Irene Hauer-Karl and Helene Stangl-Kullinger at the Strindberg Museum, Saxen, to Graf Carl Philip Clam at Burg Clam and to Luise Verey who helped with arrangements. In Sweden, Pelle Floden at Berns Salon, Gurli Malmsten at Dalarö and Kymmendö, and Dan E. L. Sundberg, sure pilot through the skerries. In museums and libraries, Anna Höök of Kungliga Biblioteket and Erik Höök of Strindbergsmuseet, as well as helpful librarians and archivists at Modernamuseet, Nationalmuseum, Nordiska Museet and Albert Bonniers Förlag. In England, Christopher Sinclair-Stevenson, Dr Tom Rosenthal, Professor Neil Kent of Cambridge University, Professor Gerald Libby and Dr Tim Cutler who brought expertise on psycho-medical matters and Sir Richard Lambert who gave invaluable insight into *A Dream Play*. Most important, Gillian Malpass, Sarah Faulks and Sophie Sheldrake of Yale University Press. Thank you all.

1 MISS JULIE'S KITCHEN

During the winter of 1887–8 August Strindberg and his family took up residence in the smartest district of Copenhagen, living well beyond their means in the Hotel Leopold just round the corner from the Royal Theatre.[1] Always fond of a good address, Strindberg was inclined to be optimistic, not to say unrealistic, where future prospects were concerned and throughout this winter he was nourishing hopes that Denmark might prove more profitable than his native Sweden where his plays were not being performed, his books were not being published and he had seven manuscripts lying around that nobody wanted. His latest play, *The Father*, was to be given its world premiere at Copenhagen's Casino Theatre. Although he had only just arrived in Copenhagen, Strindberg was already well known to the city. His waxwork figure topped with human hair stood in the Panopticon,[2] an object of horror to all traditionalists who knew that he represented the Modern Breakthrough, a literary movement extensively heralded in the radical press. Copenhagen looked forward to being shocked.

The Father tells the tale of a man in the clutches of the demons of dread and mistrust as his doubts grow about the true paternity of his child. It reflected Strindberg's own fears following his wife Siri's thunderbolt revelation that five years earlier she had an affair when she was away in Finland acting in *Jane Eyre*. From the very start of their marriage there had been rumours of Siri's promiscuous behaviour with both men and women but Strindberg had always pooh-poohed them. People always said such things about actresses, he would respond confidently, serene in their love. He himself had always been faithful to his adorable 'little lioness' but now he had discovered that she had broken the condition of trust on which the marriage was founded. She had made a fool of him and turned the last five years of their marriage into a sustained fiction. Worse, she had raised the tormenting spectre of uncertain paternity over the children who bore his name. As their childish features ripened into maturity over the coming years, what lover's face would he see emerging?

The course of intermittent embraces and continuous verbal battles between the husband and wife onstage in *The Father* reflected the current state of the playwright's own marriage. Strindberg and Siri were figuratively and on occasion literally at each other's throats. Sometimes they threw knives and forks at each other.

'Seeing them in the hotel at meal times, nobody would imagine them a family', observed Axel Lundegård who was translating *The Father* from Swedish into Danish.[3] The two men were sharing a meal in the hotel dining room when 'through the empty room came a blond-haired, tall, thin lady followed by three children and a nursery-maid. Strindberg, who was in the middle of his pudding, said nothing. He didn't even look up but I [Lundegård] was curious.

"My God, who's that?" I asked.

"My former wife", he answered gloomily . . .

"Are you – you're not divorced?" I stammered.

He gave me a most unfriendly look but as we were both living in the Hotel Leopold, he couldn't get out of giving me an answer.

"Well," he said, "there's been no legal divorce but that's not necessary. I no longer regard my wife as my wife but as my mistress. She must be content with that. I will not be seen with her in public." '[4]

Strindberg would be thirty-nine in January. He had been married ten years to Countess Siri von Essen, a Finnish-born aristocrat not overly intellectual but resourceful, intelligent and pretty. When they married, Siri had been on the plump side with abundant blond hair and china-blue eyes, a spirited and indulged young woman with ambitions to go on stage, but now she was thin, as Lundegård observed, and carried herself with the graceful melancholy of the disappointed actress. Siri had not set foot on the stage for four years. The three children following her into the hotel dining room were uniformly pale and blond, they had pleasing manners and were so charmingly dressed that only the gimlet-eyed might spot Siri's economical refurbishments. The eldest daughter Karin[5] was a well-behaved seven-year-old fresh from education in Paris, her spontaneity curbed by a precocious sense of responsibility as a result of the emotional switchback of her parents' marriage. Next Greta, aged six, less blond and less eager to please. While Karin invariably smiles charmingly at the camera, Greta scowls. Finally, three-year-old Hans who looked like everyone's dream of a son, a chubby angel, but he had arrived too late in his parents' turbulent marriage to merit wonder and celebration, even though he belonged to the more important sex.

Siri and Strindberg occupied separate bedrooms in the Leopold, the hotel where actors and writers congregated in Copenhagen. Among their fellow guests was thirty-eight year-old Victoria Benedictsson,[6] a feminist writer of great intelligence and long-faced Virginia Woolf-like beauty. Benedictsson was a casualty of her parents' battle of the sexes: her mother raised her as a girl and her father as a boy. As a writer she used a male pseudonym. Like Strindberg, Benedictsson had been discovered by Georg Brandes,[7] the most powerful literary critic of Northern Europe. Georg Brandes could, and did, make and break authors. He was immeasurably important at the time, not only in Scandinavia but in Germany, Russia and England where he became a friend of John Stuart Mill; indeed, his translation of Mill's 1869 essay *The Subjection of Women*[8] had a great effect on the feminist movement in Scandinavia during the time Ibsen was writing his major plays. Brandes's influence extended as far as the United States where a triumphant lecture tour led to him being crowned with laurel wreaths symbolising the everlasting immortality of his genius and scholarship. Few outside Scandinavia remember him today. Brandes coined the term Modern Breakthrough[9] to describe the literature of the future that he saw emerging in the work of Balzac, Zola and Ibsen, a literature emancipated from art, based not on historicism or romanticism or on imagination but on the writer's present and direct experience, a literature in which, as Strindberg put it, the author took the corpse of the person he knew best – himself – and learned anatomy, physiology, psychology and indeed the whole history of the world from the carcass. In 1879 Brandes had discovered Strindberg's first novel *The Red Room*, after which he had never ceased to declare Strindberg a genius, tirelessly and faithfully promoting and supporting him through difficult times. The two men had not actually met until this Christmastime in Copenhagen where Brandes was directing Strindberg's play *The Father* at the Casino Theatre.

'I value this man's [Strindberg's] talent highly', Brandes wrote to a friend during this week. 'It is sad that an unhappy marriage of the most peculiar kind – he clearly feels the strongest physical attraction to her together with the greatest spiritual loathing – makes this great talent almost monomaniac. He belongs to the not inconsiderable army of the unpredictable. But he is a man of genius.'[10]

Brandes's home was in Copenhagen so he was not staying at the hotel alongside his two literary protégés, Strindberg and Victoria Benedictsson. One of Brandes's peculiarities was that he refused to review the work of women authors, such were the misogynistic times. However, in 1885 when Benedictsson published her sexually frank novel *Pengar* (Money) under the male pseudonym of Ernst Ahlgren, he had praised it highly, hailing it as part of the Modern Breakthrough. Critic and author met. They had an affair. Now she had written her next novel, *Fru Marianne* (Mrs Marianne) and Brandes had dismissed it as *Damenromanen* (women's fiction), a word she described as her death sentence and she had come to the Hotel Leopold to be close to him while she killed herself.

In the middle of the night between 7 and 8 January 1888, Strindberg was woken by a knock on his bedroom door. He started up from his sleep to see his eldest daughter, seven-year-old Karin. She told him that earlier in the night Benedictsson had come to her bedroom wearing a white nightgown:

> Her face was so pale it shone out of the darkness. She told me she had taken poison and was terribly afraid. (It was morphine.) She still wanted to die, she said, but she was overwhelmed by terror and asked if I would watch over her.
>
> I followed her into the big bedroom and she got back into bed. How the time passed I don't remember. Nothing was said.[11]

While Karin kept watch by the bed her thoughts 'went round and round'. Suicide was one of the few mortal sins that could never be forgiven by God and she was greatly troubled lest she was damning her soul for ever by keeping company with the suicide. Legally, suicide was a crime. Some years earlier her father had been charged with the crime of blasphemy and it had been a terrifying episode that had etched itself deep into the family consciousness. Strindberg himself had been panic-stricken at the time and now Karin was terrified that, like Papa, she would be tried in a court for a crime against God. 'The law punished you with prison if you failed to hinder a suicide', she fretted, 'there seemed no other course but to take my punishment.'[12]

At last Benedictsson told her to leave the room.

I fumbled my way through the corridor to Strindberg's door. When I went into the room he started up from his sleep and stared at me wildly. I told him why I couldn't bear to be alone and why . . . I told him Victoria Benedictsson's story. I'll never forget the expression on his face. He was so interested. Not a smidgen of human sympathy or compassion crossed his features, just naked curiosity; he was fascinated.[13]

Fascinated indeed: the writer in the workshop had taken over from the sympathetic papa. Strindberg was a naturalist writer of experience-based literature and here was a positively gothic experience being delivered first-hand. Memory, Strindberg pointed out, is our capital[14] and Karin was giving him the first piece of capital to store up in the depository of his memory to be used in his next and most remarkable play, *Miss Julie*. The rest of the mental capital for the play would not come to him until they had left the Hotel Leopold but he had not long to wait.

The Father failed despite Brandes's support, generally good reviews in the papers and warm applause in the theatre. After eleven performances the theatre's actor-manager Hans Riber Hunderup went bankrupt and that was the end of the run. The Hotel Leopold was now out of the question. Strindberg and his family must give up the glitter and vivacity of the snowy capital and move to affordable outer darkness. They found a cheap house belonging to a policeman, on the coast some eighteen kilometres north of Copenhagen.

'We moved to a horrible little house in Klampenborg surrounded by empty summer villas with boarded up verandas and somewhere a yowling cat that Siri rescued.'[15]

In February they moved even further out to Taarbeck,[16] a fishing village overlooking the sound separating Denmark from Sweden. Here they rented the Villa Maud which was, and is, a comfortable, unpretentious seaside dwelling with its front door conveniently giving onto the main coastal road and a quiet back garden with lilac trees shading a grass lawn sloping down to the seashore. Had there been money for heating, the Villa Maud might have been charming but it was a particularly harsh winter and so it came to be remembered as one of the worst places they had ever lived. Strindberg slept alone in a freezing bedroom where the ice was as thick inside the window as out. When his bitterness became too great, he would raise his arms and fling foul curses across the narrow sound at the stretch of his native Swedish shore visible through the window. Locals recalled Siri as a thin, neurotic woman always occupied with the children. They also recalled the lighted windows often illuminating Strindberg chasing his wife round the table.

With the failure of *The Father* there was very little money for the family to live on. Yet there were prospects. André Antoine[17] wrote from Paris that he wished to put on *The Father* at the Théâtre Libre, the leading avant-garde theatre in Paris. Poland wanted a translation of his debut novel *The Red Room* and Berlin intended to perform one of his early plays, *Lycko-Pers resa* (*Lucky Peter's Journey*) but none of this amounted to ready cash. Until the payments came, the family crept together in the two rooms they could afford to heat while Strindberg wrote his next book *Le Plaidoyer d'un fou* (*A Madman's Defence*) in French with furious rapidity, hoping that Antoine's interest might indicate a lucrative new market in France. 'Sparks fly out of the brain freely, superbly, when the right word is born in an alien language',[18] he wrote, flooded with exaltation as he finished the book during a snowstorm.

In the village of Taarbeck, there was a garrulous old crone who used to go from door to door selling vegetables. With her brown skin, hooked nose, glistening black eyes, greasy kerchief and insinuating manner, Strindberg was of the opinion she was of gypsy blood. The children were convinced she was a witch.[19] Just as summer was knocking on the year's door, she arrived like the wicked witch from fairy tale offering them 'a palace' to live in at the suspiciously cheap rent of 50 kroner a month (he had been paying 300). Such an economic offer borne by a quasi-magical bearer had enormous appeal for Strindberg. The palace was charmingly named Skovlyst, 'Delight of the Forest'.[20] It had been a royal dwelling, the vegetable-seller told them, but now it belonged to the Countess Frankenau. The vegetable-seller's son, Ludvig Hansen, was the countess's servant. He would come and collect them in the countess's carriage. With the arrival of Ludvig Hansen came the rest of the drastic adventure that fructified in Strindberg's imagination to become *Miss Julie* with Ludvig Hansen metamorphosed into the servant Jean and the Countess Frankenau into Miss Julie.[21]

> The carriage arrived at twilight, considerably later than had been arranged, a dilapidated old thing from Frederick the Seventh's time

drawn by two rake-ribbed, mangy horses. Down sprang the servant, a fine fellow with lustrous black moustaches. An enormous diamond pin sparkled in his bright red tie but his black eyes shone even brighter than the diamond. On the box sat his adolescent brother Charles in a faded livery much too large for him with many buttons of silver that were tarnished and dirty but each button bore the family crest.

The party set off through the spring-green forest while the twilight fell gently over the landscape and the coquettish gypsy entertained the gentry in the carriage and played gallant cavalier with the ladies.[22]

Siri laughingly enjoyed Hansen's facetious gallantry but their banter annoyed Strindberg who became increasingly irritated by the macabre theatricality of their progress as the skeleton nags pulled the ludicrous carriage down the noblest allée in all Denmark, Kongevej (the King's Road), connecting the royal castle of Copenhagen to Hamlet's Elsinore. Broad enough for several carriages abreast, Kongevej was punctuated by monuments and obelisks and ran through splendid woods of thick-trunked beech and paper-white birch, at this time of year unfurling their canopy of fresh young leaves. Ferns brushed the wheels of the cart, the first pale stars of evening freckled the sky. In the last of the daylight, the squat silhouette of the castle's stubby towers showed as mere stumps against the dark trees. 'By the time we got there, it was pretty dark', Karin's narrative continues,

The carriage swung through the entrance down a short avenue of chestnut trees past a lake with a little pavilion in the middle and there we were at an enormous front door under a portico supported by pillars . . . The Countess stood on the step curtseying . . . [she had] a round, sunburned cat's face, fish-eyes and poor front teeth. She was wearing an ancient costume in the fashion of the previous century, a pale blue crinoline dress with a tightly laced bodice and bare shoulders. Her hair was smooth, parted in the middle from forehead to nape, with two little plaits like earmuffs wound round her ears. Siri asked if this was a fancy dress party.

'No', came the answer that surprised us all. 'This is my usual attire.'[23]

They were shown into the salon, a well-proportioned room running the length of the house, elegantly embellished with plasterwork. The furniture, so far as they could see, really was as fine and antique as advertised by the witch-like vegetable-seller, but it was difficult to judge detail since none of the candles had been lit in the candelabra. What muffled light reached the room leeched in through the line of west-facing windows overlooking the lake which was now flushed ruddy with the sun's last afterglow. The Countess clamoured and yammered over how cold they must be after the journey. The servant Ludvig Hansen had been quietly standing in the shadows. Now he stretched out his hands. A silver chalice materialised out of thin air. He set it down in front of Siri, covering it with a piece of lint that smelled strongly of pure alcohol. He invited Siri to set fire to it. This she did and the astonished guests saw the blue-flamed lint floating up into the air and in its place – abracadabra – a goblet of wine stood in front of Siri who laughed delightedly. The servant proposed the same to Strindberg but he was agitated and refused to take part, pursing his lips and making his disapproval felt.

Siri then said that she would like to see the apartments before it became completely dark but this suggestion only led the Countess and her servant to enquire with elaborate concern after their guests' health, stressing their need for a rest before further exertions. This stupid fiction irritated Strindberg and Siri who were in rude good health and did not appreciate being treated as invalids. Clearly their hosts were playing for time. Presently, the Countess disappeared with her servant. They heard whispering.

' "Let's run", said Strindberg, casting a glance at the door; but despite his words he remained sitting in his chair.'[24]

A minute or so later, the Countess appeared with a hurdy-gurdy clutched to her breast. Throwing herself to her knees she launched into her limited repertoire on that least musical of musical instruments. Before the guests could say anything, the door to the salon flew open once more, this time revealing Hansen who made a theatrical entrance in a faux-medieval get-up with a squashy velvet beret ornamented with a cock's feather, a wig made of horsehair and two shiny, black-lacquered staves, one held firmly in each hand. Behind him came a new character in this drama: his sixteen-year-old sister Martha Magdalena, a girl whose colouring and complexion could not have contrasted more greatly with his. Her eyes were pale and her hair was luminous, gold or red. She was dressed in what is described as a 'circus costume' of grubby satin with a tight-fitting bodice showing plenty of décolleté, with long sleeves wide at the wrist and a full skirt rippling to the ground.

By now the glow from the salon windows was minimal. Everything had faded to degrees of mouse-brown so that it was difficult to distinguish what was substance and what shadow.

> The black staves were placed upon the floor, the young girl was lifted by her elbows and there she was, suspended in the air with one elbow resting on each stick. Once more, Strindberg's eyes darted uneasily towards the door. Hansen performed a series of 'magic passes'. One stave was taken away. The young girl now rested only on one elbow – more magic passes – the servant heaved her body so she was lying straight out into the air. The whole time the Countess was lying on the floor churning out one dreadful melody after another and the gypsy [Hansen] was chattering at us ceaselessly with his explanations of how his magnetic influence and magic passes were rendering the swaying maiden stiff and unconscious. Siri was having trouble stifling her laughter. But Strindberg suddenly stood up and demanded the carriage. Now there was uproar.[25]

While Siri was able to giggle at this farrago of amateur theatricals and conjuring tricks, Strindberg was discomfited by a superstitious half-belief that there might well exist a reordered world where such things as swaying maidens suspended in mid-air were possible. It was part of the built-in paradox of the period that scientific rationalism's advances (Darwin's *Origin of Species* was available in Swedish translation from 1872) had over the years suggested nothing so much to Strindberg and many like him as that if every species was in a state of permanent evolution, it was perfectly logical to suppose that part of this *perpetuum mobile* actually encompassed a breaking down of the boundaries between the biological and the extra-biological, between the natural and the supernatural. In 1872 he had assisted in translating Karl Eduard von Hartmann's *Philosophy of the Unconscious*[26] into Swedish and in 1886 he was among the thousands in Europe reading two quasi-scientific best-sellers which fed the public's growing wish to believe in spine-tingling impossibilities. Hippolyte Bernheim's *De la suggestion* and Max Nordau's *Paradoxes psychologiques* dealt with the shadowlands of the human psyche: hypnotism, magnetism, psychomancy, somnambulism, mesmerism, the divided personality (with impeccable timing, in that same year Robert Louis Stevenson published *Dr Jekyll and Mr Hyde*) and the ability of one human mind to influence another and control it completely.[27]

Demonstrations of 'suggestion', 'electrification', hypnotism, séances, mesmerism and magnetism were enormously popular in theatres, circuses, fairs and private parlours. Just down the road from Skovlyst there was a dentist called Dr Odhal who gave public performances of hypnotism in his surgery.[28] However, there were various specific factors that contributed to Strindberg's captivated unease. The first was obvious: the Countess and her servant had the wit not to charge money. This seemingly lifted them out of a certain realm of charlatanry. Then there was the curious completeness of the experience: the magic show was part of an almost supernatural narrative that had been unfolding since the brown, wrinkled finger of the vegetable-seller had pointed Strindberg's steps towards the enchanted castle. Finally, there was the willingness to believe. With the material world so difficult – lack of money, failed books, failed plays, his failing marriage to Siri – and his mind in thrall to Edgar Allen Poe, he was ripe to suspend belief, to enter a world in which he said he felt free, isolated, like a cosmic sliver floating in the ether, straining to see clearly into this half-penetrable half-world. He was ready and willing for the supernatural to materialise like a developing photograph; ready to take up tenancy in a world of enchantment, to rent rooms in a world where 'the plausible can be imperceptibly transformed, drifting subtly into the amazing'.[29]

At last the Maiden came out of her enchantment, ceased her peculiar horizontal swaying, jumped down to the floor from her black-lacquered staves and lit a couple of candles in the magnificent candelabra. The family were invited upstairs to view their apartment. A jumble of bottles, paint pots and vessels cluttered the staircase. Siri saw only normal household muddle but Strindberg saw 'bottles and retorts such as alchemists use'.[30] Determined on the fairy-tale character of the adventure, he describes a journey of magic, riddles and transformation. He is conducted through a sequence of 'chambers' rich in furnishings and treasure inhabited by sleepy maidens, menacing hounds, a stuffed eagle with a snake in its claws and so on. Strindberg's elaborate description swarms with symbols and is pregnant with symbolic numbers.

Martha Magdalena in her grubby circus dress played Eurydice, lighting their way through this underworld with the guttering candelabra clasped in her solid young hand. They were not allowed to see their future bedrooms which were said to be under restoration but they were promised three rooms running almost the full length of the first floor, including a panelled salon and a balcony overlooking the lake. Strindberg demanded, and got, a tour of the garden.

Skovlyst's neglected garden had progressed, like its carriage horses, beyond the picturesque into the ruinous but there was a heart-stoppingly beautiful orchard of cherry trees whose polished auburn trunks rose from a snow of fallen blossoms. Throughout his life, horticulture was more than a whim for Strindberg. It was to him what farming was to Tolstoy, an activity of profound importance spiritually, scientifically, allegorically and symbolically.

'If you would know the invisible', he wrote at the opening of his *Occult Diary*, 'look carefully at the visible.'[31]

During the long-drawn shadow of his deprived youth, the cultivation of white pelargonium had stood for beauty and the possibility of freedom. As he aged and his vision widened, the potting bench had become the crucible of creativity that simultaneously demonstrated God's immutable rules for the natural order of things and his own ability to overcome at least some of them. For years he tried to grow tea, coffee and magnolias in his native Scandinavia. To date, only magnolias have succeeded.

In Skovlyst's 'charming greenhouse' he found luxurious melon plants spiralling their tendrils through his beloved pelargonium and jasmine. The sight of the mist bench 'set him afire'.[32] If gardening as an art of transformation was a branch of alchemy, the mist bench and the greenhouse were the alchemist's tools — the retorts and alembics that enabled the gardener to overrule natural laws.

While Strindberg toured the garden, Ludvig Hansen hovered with the contract conveniently to hand. Lest he lose the client, at the last minute he threw in the free use of the southern tower. Strindberg signed. With a last waltz from the hurdy-gurdy, the Countess waved them off.

On 3 May Siri and the children arrived in advance to prepare the quarters for Strindberg who could not spare the time from writing; his pen was the family's only source of income. The advance party discovered things to be different in daylight. The splendid front door was barred. Instead, they were shown to a narrow side entrance where the eight dogs that had been concealed on their previous visit burst out, leaping and barking so fiercely that little Hans ran away screaming. Siri wondered what on earth to tell Strindberg who was terrified of dogs.

Worse, Skovlyst was not a castle at all. With its white-stuccoed façade and stubby twin towers each end, by daylight it looked like one of those

48

Italianate villas that sprout ten a penny on the Riviera or the Swiss lakes. It had originally been a royal hunting lodge dating from the 1600s. Its twin towers were, in fact, hunting towers and its long lines of windows did not betoken a ballroom *à la* Versailles but were designed for royal guests to poke their guns out. The lake, originally designed to lure water-fowl to the gun, was by now purely ornamental and housed a little island crowned by a crumbling neo-classical pavilion. Nor was Countess Frank-enau any more genuine than her castle. Her parents were a cadet branch who had assumed the title on buying the royal property from the king. As for the Swaying Maiden, that was a trick taken from an illustrated book on conjuring tricks and illusions recently translated into Danish.[33] A strong metal corset fastened round Martha Magdalena's torso with rods running down her arms was attached to hooks on the end of the black staves; hence the need for dim lighting, long sleeves and a trailing skirt to conceal the ironwork.

The twilight had also concealed the animals. Now daylight showed the Countess's love of animals as boundless as it was out of control. Adored, neglected and dilapidated animals had the run of the place. As well as the eight jut-ribbed dogs that terrorised the Strindberg family, there were chickens, ducks, geese, peacocks, turkeys, horses, cows, rabbits, twenty-two sheep and lambs, a pair of nanny goats named Caroline and Mathilde after the queen who, in the episode of Danish history that most resembles *Miss Julie*, took her physician as her lover and as a result of sexual congress with a social inferior was disgraced, jailed and exiled. There were also pigs, cats feral and domestic, and 'an especial pet, a blind cock of eighteen years that Miss Frankenau used to scrub with a scrubbing brush'.[34] Sick duck-lings and orphaned lambs were stuffed down the bodice of the old-fash-ioned blue gown. It was, as she had told them, her normal, everyday dress. Strindberg's daughter Karin remembered how the hooped skirt of the Countess's gown stood up like a blue balloon when she milked the cows.

'Yes,' says the servant Jean in *Miss Julie*, Act 1 Scene 1. 'Miss takes a pride in some things, in others she demeans herself . . . Happiest in the kitchen and the stables but never driving with just *one* horse . . . Cuffs dirty but the family crest on every button.' Karin had already noted the crested buttons on the dirty and ill-fitting livery during the two-horse carriage drive.

Countess Frankenau and her half-brother provided the inspiration for the two main characters but it was the happenings at Skovlyst and in Copenhagen between May and August that provided the inspiration for

many of the events in the play, which Strindberg wrote with great rapidity at Skovlyst during July and the start of August.

* * *

Anna Louisa Frankenau was forty when the Strindberg family arrived.
She was the last pillar in a noble line that since 1692 had propped up
Denmark's church, law and literature. When she died, the title would
die with her.[35]

A genuine title ran down the family, though not through her parents.
Whether Anna Louisa was aware that her own right to the title had been
bogusly assumed remains opaque but what is certain is that, carrying the
heavy responsibility of the last of the line, Anna Louisa was brought up
more as a boy than a girl. This was not unusual for an only daughter heir
to an important estate in Sweden at the time (we remember Victoria
Benedictsson's male/female upbringing). This pretend-boy status was an
accepted convention to overcome misogynist prejudice against a woman
in power. Miss Julie describes this form of upbringing in a long speech
after she and the servant Jean have made love in the play. She tells him
of her training in all the masculine and earthy arts of running an estate,
including the slaughtering of animals. This applied to Anna Louisa Frankenau. More accustomed to keeping company with animals than people,
her social and intellectual education had been neglected and as a result
she was a kind woman but headstrong and eccentric; her understanding
was simple, her responses naïve.

Anna Louisa knew that her father had a bastard son eleven years her
junior by the gypsy vegetable-seller. She also knew that her mother was
in ignorance of the bastard boy. As soon as her parents were both dead,
she wrote to her unknown half-brother, offering him a home. At that
moment Ludvig Hansen was a member of a fairly profitable gang of
thieves so he ignored the invitation. She invited him again in 1884 and
this time she came in person: 'Two small arms closed about my neck,
she placed her soft cheek against my own and cried a little. I don't know
if it was charity, sentiment or love that compelled me to join her.'[36]
Whatever it was, the terms included money and, most importantly, the
condition that his parentage remain concealed. He did not want to be
known as *horebarn* (whore's child) and so he suggested he should be
known as her servant. Anna Louisa readily complied, happy to protect

her parents' posthumous reputation. It is important to remember that throughout his time at Skovlyst, Strindberg had no idea that the servant was in fact the Countess's half-brother.

Ludvig Hansen was probably twenty-nine when Strindberg arrived at Skovlyst but when it comes to hard facts about him it is always difficult to feel completely confident.[37] He started stealing from his mother almost as soon as he could walk but he waited until he was seventeen before he was first in trouble with the police for thieving. Ladies' man, musician and brawler, before he came to Skovlyst his occupations included swindler, petty thief, mountebank, illusionist, hypnotist, conjuror and very briefly actor: 'But I had to turn up at the theatre every day! Slavery!'[38] In all these pursuits, he was considerably helped by his looks, charm and exceptional talent for lying. Three years into employment at Skovlyst, things were already disastrous. Grand designs of throwing out new agricultural projects, doubtless imagined in good faith, had necessitated a big loan against the security of the property. Hansen employed vague friends and feckless relations such as his adolescent brother Charles and his sister Martha Magdalena in jobs they were clueless to fulfil. Like his half-sister the Countess, Hansen was prepared to love animals much more than people but to minister to their everyday need for food, drink and hygiene, that too was slavery and so the pathetic beasts 'chewed the walls or their mangers'[39] and stank. A new phrase entered Strindberg family code, 'the Skovlyst smell', apparently a mixture of old washing-up water, dirty clothes, rotting meat and wet dog.[40] Neighbours were already sending Anna Louisa anonymous complaints denouncing her servant, complaints that would soon lead to lawsuits, the sale of the property and the death of the noble line wound in shrouds of debt and dishonesty but, meanwhile, the tenancy began.

When Siri and the children arrived on 3 May, they were at last allowed to see the rooms that supposedly had been under restoration. They were in a state of indescribable squalor and filth. This was where the eight half-starved dogs had been kept and Siri's worst problem was how to deodorise the floorboards after she had scraped away the mound of dog excrement from beneath the bed. She demanded Martha Magdalena's help and between them they cleaned everything, even unpicking the feather beds, boiling up the feathers and sewing them up again. Cleanliness was extremely important to Strindberg and Siri set up a bathtub for him in the pantry adjoining the semi-basement kitchen and there it stayed until the 1980s when builders stripped it out.[41]

Strindberg arrived a week after Siri and wasted no time in beginning the first page of a new novel, dating it 10 May. After the failure of *The Father* he thought it wiser to put away all pretensions towards the Modern Breakthrough and revert to a genre that had been successful two years earlier in a rumbustuous and irreverent comedy, *The People of Hemsö*, a sort of *Cold Comfort Farm* set in the Swedish skerries. Now he hoped to repeat the lucrative trick with *The Romantic Sexton of Ranö*, a novel based on his memories of a youthful stay with a clockmaker at Årdala. The project chimed with his carefree mood and circumstance. Warm weather had come and here he was living cheaply with the time and the space to write while Siri taught the children to read in both French and Swedish and peeled the potatoes.

He always preferred to write in small, claustrophobic spaces. The southern hunting tower that had been thrown in at the last minute was one such; the other was the decayed neo-classical pavilion that sat in the middle of the lake. His writing day kept a strict routine:

'I am up at seven . . . boil my coffee (for no one else but I can do that, just like Balzac and Swedenborg). Then I go out for a walk . . . the morning possesses something that makes one feel young at heart, reborn, a feeling that evaporates with the dew . . . after an hour and a half I am back home.' People who saw him during his walk said he was purblind to the external world and incapable of responding even if a well-loved friend wished him good morning.

> By now I am wet with sweat and loosen my clothes all the way down to my belt. And so it begins: on yellow, uncut Lessebo Bikupa paper, with Sir Joshua Mason's 1001 nib and Antoine Fils's *violette noir* ink it breaks out, accompanied by continual cigarette smoking until 12 o'clock. Then it is over. I am extinguished; I go and lie down to sleep, wake up renewed, read, write letters, sleep, but am too tired to eat . . . then I eat dinner [at 3] take a good after-dinner nap (which I have done since I was twelve years old); get up at 6 and have to solve the terrible problem of what to do with the evening . . .[42]

A problem solved by his new friend Ludvig Hansen. Come evening, the two of them would carry candles, bottles, glasses, tobacco, Hansen's *batterie de magie* and Strindberg's guitar across the drawbridge to the crumbling pavilion in the middle of the lake. Pulling the drawbridge up behind them they were safe to carouse as long as they liked, free from women, children and dogs. We know that Hansen practised mesmerism on Strindberg in the little water-girt folly and we can only imagine further occult experiment. On 15 May they listened to the nightingale in the currant bushes. It was the first time Strindberg had heard a nightingale and it soon prompted an entire chapter in a book.[43]

Hansen's servant status and gypsy blood ought to have precluded this sort of intimacy in those overtly racist and class-ridden days but Strindberg genuinely enjoyed his company. Strindberg has a well-justified reputation as a racist but this was only after someone of a different 'race' or class had offended him. Then, as we will soon see with Hansen, Strindberg would exercise his full mastery over words with maximum prejudice and minimum mercy but meanwhile a robust friendship flourished between the two men. Strindberg was always credulous about spook-dabbling and he was entirely deceived by Hansen in that department while, however, retaining the author's precise evaluation of the sorcery with which Hansen's quick-witted conversation contrived to slide from truth to lie, from the plausible to the frankly incredible. 'There'll be a novel in this!'[44] Strindberg wrote in a letter gleefully.

At this time, Georg Brandes (for whom Victoria Benedictsson had attempted suicide) was giving a series of Tuesday afternoon lectures at Copenhagen University. 'There is a German philosopher living in Italy, whom I am studying', wrote Brandes. 'His views correspond closely to my own . . . he has an ill-sounding name, and he is still unknown. He is called Friedrich Nietzsche.'[45] Strindberg followed the lectures in the newspapers and visited Copenhagen during the lecture series. He was sitting on a bench in Kongens Nytorv watching the world go by when Brandes walked past. They fell into conversation. 'This is the man for you', said Brandes but Strindberg could not afford to buy Nietzsche's books so Brandes lent him *Beyond Good and Evil* and *The Wagner Case* and Strindberg was immediately overtaken by one of his wholehearted enthusiasms. He was just coming out of a period of socialism. Now socialism was *humbug* (a popular word in Scandinavia at the time, probably because of Dickens[46]) and, for a limited period, Nietzsche's 'Aristocratic Radicalism' set him on fire. One may say that if Brandes discovered Nietzsche, this park-bench meeting resulted in Strindberg becoming Nietzsche's first international disciple.

'Here's evolution!' Strindberg wrote in June, having plunged headlong into correspondence with Nietzsche. 'The strongest and wisest to the fore, the lesser go under!'[47] 'Liberty? Equality?' asked Brandes. 'It is clear as daylight that Liberty and Equality are mutually exclusive. Equality is not possible without constraint. Continual constraint.'[48] Democracy was crapulocracy.

Nietzsche sent Strindberg *The Genealogy of Morals* and *Twilight of the Idols.* Strindberg, who all his life questioned anything put in front of him, interpreted Nietzsche's aristocratic radicalism paradoxically. He topsy-turveyed its theories of pure blood and master/slave races on which later the Nazis built their repellent theories. Instead, in an age when, largely, class and lineage were destiny, Strindberg took Ludvig Hansen with his 'slave' blood (ditto the servant Jean in the play) to represent the *übermensch* thoroughly capable of changing the world through their will to power, whereas the Countess Frankenau (ditto Miss Julie), those two last weak dribbles of pure blue blood, were the *untermensch*.

Despite his congenial evenings with Hansen, it was improper that the women of the house should keep familiar company with a servant and Strindberg was shocked to see the servant and the Countess drinking from the same cup. This and further easy intimacies gave Strindberg the idea that drives *Miss Julie*, the idea of sexual intercourse between mistress and servant. 'Hansen's employment', he decided, 'had begun chastely, he had risen to servant and become her lover.'[49]

Strindberg blushed that his family should be living in such an irregular household. In a family context he could be correct to the point of prudery and his embarrassment at the sound of Frankenau and her servant's drunken dinners next door turned to fury one day when Hansen took an axe to the communicating door and burst blind drunk into the family dining room, waving his revolver and terrifying the children.

It was the turning point in the relationship. 'The righteous man [Strindberg means himself] whom we at first think superior and controlling is in fact being manipulated through his honesty and reasonableness. The gypsy has turned him into a false witness by cunning',[50] he wrote and went off to Frederiksborg to buy a revolver of his own. Now things deteriorated rapidly.

June and July saw a spate of break-ins and burglaries in nearby properties. A band of gypsies had arrived in the area. Racism and paranoia ran rampant. The local paper advised the good citizens of Taarbeck to lock their doors and keep an eye on their blond Aryan children whom the gypsies wished to kidnap for unspecified sinister purposes. At Skovlyst a peacock disappeared along with other animals and small articles. Hansen publicly accused Strindberg of being the Thief of Taarbeck and stealing the peacock and other things. Peacocks had not been a feature of Strindberg's writing but from now on they strut intermittently in and out of his literature and we can judge how traumatising he found this accusation by the fact that a full eighteen years later he mystified a bookseller by suddenly and incomprehensibly blurting out, 'I have never stolen a live peacock!'[51]

Strindberg's pride had been injured. In formerly trusting Hansen, he had made a terrible misjudgement. His work was nothing if it did not reflect psychological truth and we see how he copes with the mental shock of his own misjudgement in the novel he had begun at Skovlyst, *The Romantic Sexton of Ranö*. He could not afford to abandon the book which was almost finished but the last three chapters have always perplexed the critics by taking a sudden deep dive from cheerful pastoral to sinister. We discover that the sexton's father killed his mother after which he co-opted the sexton, then only a young boy, into bearing the mother's body home. It gradually dawns on us how the charming opening of the novel has been fantasy, an evasion of reality and conscience all along.

Once Strindberg had come to this moral conclusion about Hansen, the gloves were off and the relationship between the two men turned into a sort of re-run of *The Father*, a horrible fight for mental ascendancy as each man clutched his revolver either side of the communicating door. Strindberg's liberal political attitude towards Hansen, his former drinking companion, changed radically. Now Hansen was 'the gypsy' and 'the Pariah' (Nietzsche's word for the lowest of the low). 'Every word he speaks is a lie', he said, adding that he was going to 'squash him like a flea.'[52]

'Horribly nervous and with mild persecution mania after stormy days and sleepless nights! Go about with a revolver and a lead-tipped stick to protect my fair-haired boy from the Gypsy's kidnap plans!' he wrote to Edvard Brandes in a letter jocular in tone but paranoid in undertone.[53]

As for Hansen, without Strindberg's friendship to live up to, he reverted to his previous bad behaviour. He did not even pretend to fulfil any duties about the estate but stayed out all night tomcatting, returning at dawn to sleep away the day. He broke into Strindberg's quarters, disarranging his possessions without stealing anything but perturbing him by infinitesimal but deliberately detectable disruptions. It was a war of psychic demoralisation using strange weapons that show Hansen to be every bit as familiar with the snakepit of psychological torment as the playwright.

'He sets his dogs on me', wrote Strindberg, 'has infected the latrine, is drunk and riots every night, breaks into my apartment and terrifies my family, shoots his revolver beneath my window at three o'clock in the morning, performs Indian dances outside my door at the same time rattling sheets of zinc . . . enters my apartments with an illegally copied key, not to steal but to seek out family secrets so he can blackmail me at his leisure.'[54]

Finding no material for blackmail, Hansen's next weapon to hand was his younger sister, Martha Magdalena.

> I never had any designs on her but Hansen sent her on errands to my room in the evening after I had gone to bed and in the morning when I was getting up. I only went with her once, and then with a sheath so I am (almost) sure she didn't get pregnant. If she is, I shall assume the child's upkeep, though I think another is father to the child. In any case, nothing before a doctor has certified she is pregnant.[55]

He was right that another was more likely to have fathered the child (if there was a child); Martha Magdalena was sleeping with the gardener on a regular basis while the hasty sexual liaison with Strindberg occurred on Midsummer Eve, the evening on which the action of *Miss Julie* takes place – in the very tower room in which a few weeks later he wrote the play – and when Miss Julie describes her congress with Jean as bestiality we have the original in Strindberg's description of his coming together with Martha Magdalena: 'Her hair fell unruly about her face which wasn't pretty but it was young, a mouth like a deer, a plebeian nose and little blue button eyes that looked startled', he wrote in a letter that included a sketch of the girl.[56] When he used the episode in a novel he put it this way:

> The ugliness in her eyes, the filth that clung to everything about her, these things his mind suppressed. There stirred in him the desire to take her roughly like an animal, like a dog takes a bitch; but at the same time there came a firm resolve never to kiss her . . . He and she would simply come together as animal with animal and afterwards they would part . . . That is how he thought it would happen and that is how he dreamed of it that night.[57]

Martha Magdalena gave him body lice: 'I got both scabies and scandal though I was only with her once!'[58] and her dirt recalls Jean, the servant in the play who 'knows how to wear a tailcoat but beneath it there is no guarantee he is bodily clean.'[59]

Afterwards, Strindberg was ashamed. No matter that he and Siri had not made love for half a year, he had dishonoured her and the children by making love under the same roof that sheltered them. When he confessed to her, his shame was far greater than Siri's chagrin.

Now Hansen had found the material to blackmail him with: rape of a minor. In fact Martha Magdalena was not underage, as both she and Hansen alleged. She was not fifteen, as she and her brother said. Nor was she eighteen, as Strindberg protested he thought her. She was sixteen, turning seventeen on 18 September of that year. Strindberg suffered months of anguish until the true facts came out in court during the trial in October. That the sex had been consensual was also revealed when Martha Magdalena naively told a journalist:

'I went with him because I rather liked him and I thought it was a pity we did it only once.'[60]

Strindberg was cowardly in many ways. He was frightened of dogs and of the dark but he was not a moral coward. Falsely accused, he refused to submit to Hansen's blackmail but took the rape charge straight to the police. In fact he took it to the very same policeman whom Hansen, a prolific and imaginative extortionist, was trying to blackmail for police brutality after Hansen had punched the policeman on the nose.

On 2 July Strindberg finished *The Romantic Sexton of Ranö*, the novel that had changed from comic to tragic as life at Skovlyst dissolved into chaos. Strindberg was in dire need of money and about ten days later he started to write *Miss Julie*, true fruit of this episode in his life, writing it in two to three weeks. Except for the character of Kristin the cook (whom in the introduction to the play he describes as an abstract commentator, 'laden with morality and religion . . . a subordinate figure'[61]), the happenings at Skovlyst seem to have furnished him with all the main ingredients for the play except the episode of the fiancé and the whip, but this might have been suggested by the well-known photograph taken six years earlier of his new friend Nietzsche, with whom he was maintaining a correspondence throughout this Skovlyst period. Side-by-side like a couple of carriage horses, Nietzsche and his rival in love Paul Rée pull a wooden carriage in which sits Lou Salomé, a famous man-eater and Nietzsche's fiancée, eagerly leaning forward as she brandishes a whip over the two men.

Strindberg's correspondence with Nietzsche became increasingly strange until at last he received a letter signed 'Nietzsche Caesar' so peculiar that he wrote to Georg Brandes 'I know I am pestering you with letters, but I now believe our friend Nietzsche is mad.'[62] He was indeed. Five days after Strindberg's letter to Brandes, Nietzsche's friend Franz Overbeck[63] bundled the poor, demented philosopher off to Basle where he committed him to an asylum.

The final ingredient for the play is the razor that Jean gives to Miss Julie so that she can take her own life. This was provided during the period of the writing of the play when, on 21 July, Victoria Benedictsson again booked herself into the Hotel Leopold in Copenhagen for the purpose – again – of dying for Georg Brandes's sake. Her first attempt had taught her the uncertainty of poison. This time she took up a razor and, gazing into a mirror, slashed at her throat several times. Her carotid artery was severed and she died in a welter of blood.

The day following Benedictsson's suicide, Georg Brandes wrote a letter to his brother Edvard, the editor of the newspaper *Politiken*:

> Miss Benedictsson killed herself last night. She cut her throat in four places with a razor . . . If you can avoid it, please ensure *Politiken* does not report the how and why she killed herself . . . I have my personal reasons for not wishing this suicide to cause a sensation or for enquiries as to the reason for it . . . She left a very long letter to me. As early as January she made an unsuccessful attempt to kill herself with poison . . . The sight of her corpse was dreadful.[64]

This was merely the final paragraph of Georg Brandes's letter dated 22 July. The earlier paragraphs had dealt with the more important subject of his injured feelings: reviewers had objected to his overuse of the personal pronoun in his new book.[65] 'I do not think I write "*I*" more often than is strictly necessary', he wrote.

Twenty days after Benedictsson's suicide, the play *Miss Julie* was finished and sent off to Strindberg's habitual publisher Karl Otto Bonnier. 'This play will be remembered in history!' Strindberg wrote prophetically in the accompanying letter but Bonnier replied with an unambiguous rejection. The play was probably prosecutable and certainly unstageable, he wrote.

This was the heaviest of the blows raining down on Strindberg at the close of this summer. The trial for rape was hanging over his head. His new form of naturalistic playwriting born in *The Father* and continued in *Miss Julie* was rejected. Antoine wrote from Paris to say he had dropped *The Father* in favour of Ibsen's *Ghosts. The Father* had not brought him any money. *Miss Julie* was unsaleable. The summer had started full of hope but Skovlyst, the castle in the air that had embodied high metaphysical expectations, had proved a grotesque chimera of his own imagination. The fairy tale was ending horribly. He must find somewhere cheap for his family to live and, in order to support them, he must write something quickly for the Christmas trade. So he moved just up the road to the Nyholte hotel and churned out a charming little pot-boiler, *Blomstermåln-ingnar och djur-stycken (Flower Pictures and Animal Paintings)*, a book of gardening hints and tender reminiscences of his attempts to grow the exotic plants that enchanted him. The animal anecdotes are maybe a little less lyrical.

In September with the trial imminent, the press sharpened its claws for a little fun. A cartoon in *Punch* on 22 September and a humorous piece in *Københavns Posten* on 27 September wondered whether Martha Magdalena was pregnant and if so who the baby might look like. Then there was the question of the Thief of Taarbeck. Might it have been Hansen, or even Strindberg, all along? The paper reminded its readers of the notorious 'Jekyll-and-Hyde Burglar of Blackheath' whose London adventures had thrilled the Danish press. The burglar of Blackheath was apparently respectable by day and wicked by night. Might he and the Thief of Taarbeck be one? Strindberg was certainly respectable by day . . . From here it was a short step to the press's final terrifying suggestion. The summer of '88 had been the summer of Jack the Ripper's Whitechapel murders. Might either Hansen or Strindberg be Jack the Ripper, asked Edvard Brandes's *Politiken*.[66] With his friends asking such questions, a climax had been reached in the summer's mixture of nightmare and farce. Unable to take any more, on 18 September Strindberg simply jumped onto a train for Sweden, leaving the muddle and mess and his family behind him.

But before leaving Skovlyst altogether there is one final thread connecting the place to the play. The servant Jean who seduces the daughter of the house is reduced to a state of slave-terror by the sound of the Count's bell and the sight of the Count's boots:

'I only have to hear that bell ring and I jump like a frightened horse – and when I see his boots standing there so straight and proud, I cringe', Jean says in Act 1. Yet Hansen was afraid of no man, he cleaned nobody's boots. This boot-and-bell terror was not gleaned from Hansen's behaviour. It was more probably an autobiographical component, a recollection of childhood that maybe had risen like a soap bubble as Strindberg lay in the bath that Siri had installed for him in the servants' basement quarters. The bath used to stand in the larder adjoining the kitchen and anybody lying in the bath gazed directly at the gaping mouth of the dumb waiter that occupied, and still occupies, a corner of the Skovlyst kitchen. An open-fronted wooden box suspended on ropes, when the ropes are pulled the dumb waiter shuttles up or down between the basement kitchen and the master's quarters above. The arrival of the master's muddy boots from the superior heights could hardly be a more obvious symbol of the grinding of the servant beneath the heel. As he was growing up, Strindberg's father's boots used to take the same journey at home and in the early pages of his autobiography one of the first things he tells us about his father, who beat and terrorised him, is that his manservant had to wear gloves when he cleaned his boots because a servant's hands must not touch the lining.[67]

53

2 THE SON OF A SERVANT

'I always regarded my father as a hostile power, nor could he tolerate me.'

From the speech given by Strindberg on his sixtieth birthday.

2
    Father was of the reserved nature which often betokens a strong will. He was an aristocrat by birth and upbringing . . . He lived a lonely life at home, cutting himself off from society . . . He called the man servants and the maids by their first names and they addressed him as 'Sir'. He was an aristocrat to his fingertips in appearance and in his habits. He had a patrician face, beardless with a delicate complexion, and he cut his hair like Louis Philippe. He wore glasses, always dressed elegantly, and insisted on clean linen. His manservant had to wear gloves to clean his boots because his hands were too dirty to touch the lining.[1]

Strindberg's *The Son of a Servant* is one of the few autobiographies to begin by detailing the class system at the time of its subject's birth, so all-pervasively did its static, impenetrable and (to a child) mysterious structure dominate his country, his home and his emerging consciousness. Class functioned as an interpretive code providing his young mind with a map for how the world works. Together with religion, class-consciousness became part of the lining of his mind which he could never entirely decorticate, even during his most enthusiastic period as a socialist.

On the walls of the family home hung a family tree. No matter that it took a full three hundred years for the veined branches of the bloodstream to flow back to a noble source, the connection was all-important to Strindberg's father, Carl Oscar Strindberg, though it made no difference to his position in society where he remained inescapably trapped in the status of burgher, however aristocratic his mien, manner and Louis Philippe haircut.

In the wake of the French Revolution, those countries that had not altogether abandoned the system of Estates retained three but the Kingdom of Sweden retained an archaic Four Estates: nobles, clergy, burghers and peasants. The representatives of the descending Estates had descending voting rights in the Riksdag (Parliament) which might or might not be called at the caprice of the king who had absolute power. Thus the country was provided with an iron corset fastened round the body of society, holding it rigid and rendering it inflexible during this most changeable century while democracy and the Industrial Revolution advanced inexorably through the rest of Europe. It was not until 1866, when August Strindberg was a rebellious youth of seventeen, that Sweden was cautiously set on the road to real democracy with the Riksdag being replaced by a bicameral system of elected representatives. Even then, only about 5.6 per cent of the population was entitled to vote.[2]

Sweden's perverse adherence to outmoded forms and structures reflected the country's drastic lack of self-confidence during the first half of the nineteenth century. To understand the Sweden of Strindberg's time and the psychological insecurity that made it vulnerable to Strindberg's political criticism and frightened of him as a firebrand and effective force for political change, one must go back to the time of Sweden's rapid decline from world power to domestic backwater in the Napoleonic wars and their aftermath.

In 1800 Sweden, Denmark and Russia attempted to keep themselves out of the Napoleonic wars by signing a treaty of union of unarmed neutrality. The purpose of this was to protect their shipping from attack by either side in the war. Britain, however, interpreted their alliance as a veiled move to undermine the British blockade of France, so in 1801 Nelson sailed against Denmark, destroying the Danish fleet and bombarding Copenhagen. He intended to sail on and do the same to Sweden but the lucky timing of the assassination of Tsar Paul 1 (1754–1801) created a pause in hostilities for Europe to regroup. Paul's successor, Tsar

Alexander I (1777–1825), wished for peace with Britain and dissolved the union of armed neutrality. This left the Swedish king free to follow his own inclinations which were, unfortunately, eccentric. King Gustav IV of Sweden was personally convinced that Napoleon was the Beast of the Apocalypse described in the Book of Revelations. This being the case, it was obviously his sacred duty to vanquish him. The plans he concocted were full of misjudgements, delays and discords. There was an exhausting and pointless march to Pomerania and back that caused one of his own generals to suggest that the king should be put aboard a ship bound for India, and Napoleon to suggest that he should be put in a madhouse.[3] Russia grasped the chaotic moment to seize what had once been Sweden's territorial possessions on the Russian border and in 1809 the disastrous peace treaty of Fredrikshamn signed Sweden's vast empire, and its greatness, away. A third of its territory was ceded to Russia, along with just over a quarter of its population. Stockholm, which since the Middle Ages had lain at the centre of empire, now became a border town. Sweden lost Lapland, Estonia, Latvia, the Åland islands, Finland, parts of Russia including the land on which St Petersburg stands, the coastlines of the Gulf of Bothnia and the Gulf of Finland running right down to the city of Riga, as well as the strategic territories controlling both sides of the narrow entrance to the Baltic Sea.

As if losing the empire was not exasperating enough, the Swedish king was caught trying to flee with the Bank of Sweden's reserves. His nobles called time on their foolish king, who was deposed and exiled to live out his life wandering pseudonymously about Europe, eventually dying in a Swiss inn. His uncle Charles who had been placed on the throne in his stead was aged and childless. Charles appointed as his heir Prince Christian August, an unpretentious stocky little man given to falling asleep on sofas. Finally, in May 1810, he fell asleep for good, collapsing and dying on military manoeuvres. There was then no obvious heir to the decrepit king. Civic unrest broke out over the loss of empire, the parlous state of public finances and the general loss of leadership encapsulated in the question of succession. The old king Charles XIII was still alive but who was to succeed him? One party, led by the Marshal of the Realm Axel von Fersen (who had been such a success as Swedish envoy to the French Court that many suspected he was the father of Marie Antoinette's son, the Dauphin Louis-Charles), wished to place Gustav IV's son on the throne but the idea was so unpopular that it resulted in von Fersen being kicked to death by the mob in front of Stockholm's House of Nobility on 20 June 1810. The other candidate was a Danish duke but the idea of being ruled over by the ancient enemy was repugnant to many Swedes. Two couriers were sent to Paris, it being both prudent and polite to consult Napoleon whose appointments already sat on a number of European thrones. Such envoys were always sent in pairs (like Rosencrantz and Guildenstern) to spy on each other and to keep each other honest but one of the couriers, Carl Otto Mörner, simply disregarded proper procedure and offered the throne to Napoleon's Marshal, Jean-Baptiste-Jules Bernadotte (1763–1844). In 1810 Bernardotte became the Crown Prince of Sweden and in 1818, on the death of Charles, he acceded to the joint throne of Sweden and Norway, taking the name Karl Johan XIV and reigning until 1844, five years before Strindberg was born. He was a conservative king who succeeded in blocking almost all attempts at domestic reform. However, as befitted his Napoleonic past, he was alert to Sweden's defensive needs and while the country was adapting from a roomy empire to a small country with long borders, money and men were lavished on two defensive *grands projets* worthy of any French president. The first was a plan to build three Brobdingnagian fortresses, designed as refuges in time of future wars when, it was envisaged, they would house the royal family, the government, the national bank, currency reserves, the royal regalia and gold stocks. The Karlsborg fortress[4] was the only one of the three ever completed. A construction the size of a Soviet hotel, its five kilometres (some three miles) of walls encircled minefields, hospitals, shops, generous royal quarters and sufficient accommodation for more than six thousand people. Like many building projects, it overran. Instead of taking ten years to complete it took ninety by which time advances in artillery had rendered the impregnable fortress very pregnable indeed. The second project was the Göta Canal, another eternal endeavour positing a bottomless budget. Ten regiments were set digging from Gothenburg to the Baltic coast and they kept on digging for twenty-two years while the rest of the world installed railways. Sweden stubbornly hampered its own industrial progress by sticking to its glorious dream of becoming the Promised Land of Canals and as a result the railway was installed later than in India, Cuba and the majority of European countries.

While the money poured into these two white elephants, domestic reforms moved forward at a glacial pace. In 1849 when Strindberg was born in Stockholm, the city was one of the more backward and unhealthy capitals in the whole of Europe, a small and smelly place with about 70,000 inhabitants. The city that during the Enlightenment had rejoiced in European importance and harboured credible ambitions to become the Paris of the North,[5] these days was most often compared to Constantinople. This was no compliment. Contemporary Europeans found Stockholm unhealthy, unsafe, old-fashioned, chaotic and dirty. The fine baroque palaces of King Charles XII (a king so greatly admired by Voltaire that he wrote a biography of him)[6] had failed to spread the universal enlightenment they pioneered and remained jigsawed into a largely unimproved medieval higgle-piggle. Piped water was unknown. Citizens pumped their drinking water from communal wells. Water for household tasks was drawn straight from the rocky shore. The city boasted one public bathhouse containing twelve baths. Night-soil was emptied into open drains that ran down the street to be cleansed by rain or, during the winter months, frozen where it lay. Strindberg is not the only writer to describe the tremendous stench associated with the spring thaw. Households fortunate enough to have privies had them emptied by drunken gangs lurching and slopping towards refuse tips and dung heaps in the middle of town. In wintertime the vagrant and homeless slept on the iced-over dung heaps for warmth. Citizens were obliged by law to carry torches after dark as protection against brigandage. The unpaved roads were unlit apart from a few strategically placed oil lamps which, the quaint saying went, 'made darkness visible'.[7] The average man died aged forty, women at forty-four. Cows and pigs meandered the streets. The Kornhamn quay, just round the corner from the palace, was known as 'bluebottle quay' because of the cloud that buzzed and swarmed above it. Time was not standardised throughout the country until Strindberg was twenty. Any citizen found walking outside his own town or district without the proper papers might be arrested as a vagabond and forced into labour. Gallows featured at important crossroads. There were public stocks and chain pillories.[8]

Strindberg wrote how thoroughly frightened he was when, as a five-year-old, he was taken into a church where criminals were undergoing public punishment:

Everything white and gold. Music as if from a hundred huge pianos singing over his head but he couldn't see any instruments or any players. The benches form a long avenue and at the end of it is a picture – out of the Bible probably . . . the people are leaning up against the benches as if they are asleep . . . the boys take a look around and they see a strange stool painted brown. On it are two men in grey robes with cowls over their heads. They have iron chains on their feet and hands and guards are standing next to them.

'Thieves' whispers Uncle. It is hateful there. Strange, inexplicable, cruel, harsh, and so cold'.[9]

Strindberg left nine volumes of autobiography which are a complex mix of sticking closely to the action of his life and veering into the wildest imagined scenarios, thus nicely raising the question of the nature of truth and whether a writer's lived action is more truthful than his thought. Although he left instructions that these nine volumes should be known as his autobiographies, he did not write them in the first person. His main protagonist is not 'I' or even 'August' but 'Johan' (the first of his two baptismal names). He never used the name Johan in everyday life but he takes it as the name of his alter ego in the running series of autobiographies. He obviously found this to be a useful device but the continual use of the third person makes it difficult for the biographer, as will be seen in the passages above, below and throughout this book, where the biographer must meet the challenge of implying the first-person nature of the narrative without resorting to cheating by altering pronouns. Here is another memory from the same year:

For many nights he lies in bed, without getting up by day. He is tired and sleepy. A harsh-voiced man comes to his bed and says that he must not lay his hands outside the coverlet. They give him evil-tasting stuff with a spoon. He eats nothing. They whisper in the room, and his mother weeps. Then he is sitting up again at the window in the bedroom. Bells are tolling the whole day long. Green biers are carried across the churchyard. Sometimes a dark mass of people stand round a black coffin. Gravediggers with their spades keep coming and going. He has to wear a copper plate tied by a blue silk ribbon on his chest, and chew all day on a root. That is the cholera epidemic of '54.[10]

The copper plate tied to the chest and the medicinal root are interesting remnants of medieval witchcraft offering superstitious protection against the epidemics of dysentery, cholera, yellow fever, smallpox and even malaria that swept through Stockholm until piped water, sewerage and vaccinations were properly organised. He remembers sulphur burnt in his room as a disinfectant turning the mirrors yellow.

The quarantine hospital was an important terror of his childhood which resurfaces repeatedly in his literature.[11] Quarantine hospitals were often built on the small rocky islands that pepper the Swedish coast. Grim waiting-rooms for death, each had its disinfecting house, mortuary and cremation furnaces, often on separate islets connected by draw-bridges that could be raised for complete isolation. In later life the quarantine hospital became the perfect *mise-en-scène* for Strindberg the playwright to create a hermetically sealed world in which any rules at all might pertain – or none. 'The world of illusions. Life as a dream, a prison. The world of folly.'[12] Best known in *The Dance of Death* and *A Dream Play*, the quarantine station becomes, like the peacocks of Skovlyst, a recurrent symbolic motif. The place itself symbolises a kind of secular Hell and Limbo rolled into one, while the forty-day period of the *quarantina* becomes a period that he takes as significant throughout his life. Within the context of religion and mysticism the forty-day period is an accepted interval that marks milestones on the roads to Christian salvation and alchemical enlightenment (the only two beliefs to endure Strindberg's numerous forays into different religions and peculiar beliefs). Forty is the number of waiting, of preparation, of testing and of punishment; it comprises the mystical cycle of being and non-being; it is the number of weeks the child takes to grow in the womb and the number of days Christ was tempted in the Wilderness. When he tells the story of his own life Strindberg is not above extending or compressing events to lend them greater spiritual weight and probably the greatest example of such spiritual self-aggrandisement is the period he came to call the Forty Days during his marriage to Harriet Bosse in 1901,[13] which were not forty days at all but, like any good symbolist, Strindberg occasionally tweaks reality to invest it with greater significance.

August himself took less than forty weeks to grow; he was a seven-month baby and in that age of high child mortality his survival was almost miraculous given that he arrived two months premature to a mother who made no secret of the fact that she did not want him.[14] Nora already had a favourite son. Nothing August could do would ever be good enough to budge Axel the eldest son from the sunny and forgiving beams of his mother's favouritism or Oscar the second son from his father's. Four of

August's eleven siblings died in infancy but right from the start he demonstrated the toughness and tenacity that would irritate many in the years to come. Although Carl Oscar Strindberg and his wife Ulrika Eleonora[15] already had two sons, August was the first born in wedlock.

When Carl Oscar Strindberg met Nora, he was a spice merchant. It was not an aristocratic occupation and he was not an aristocrat anywhere except in his own imagination. Life had come easily to Carl Oscar, the considerably younger, and considerably indulged, sibling of an exceptional brother and brother-in-law who had each managed to make such a difference to the Swedish economy that they had leapfrogged straight out of trade into the best drawing rooms in the land. Both were regular guests of the king and in the shadow of their glory Carl Oscar had become accustomed to the idea that he, too, was superior and entitled to a higher social standing than had been delivered to him at birth. His illustrious elder brother Ludwig, seventeen years his senior, had taken over their father's modest spice business, bought ships to move the spices and soon he controlled the Swedish spice trade, becoming one of the richest men in Stockholm. Carl Oscar's sister Elisabet was the wife of another man who importantly transformed Swedish society, Samuel Owen, an English engineer and inventor who had been brought over in 1804 to install Sweden's first steam engine. With the Stockholm archipelago composed of some thirty thousand islands, rocks and skerries and the construction of canals rushing on apace, the need for efficient shipping is obvious. Samuel Owen built Sweden's first paddle steamer in 1817, transforming commercial efficiency and social intercourse at a stroke. No longer was shipping at the mercy of wind and weather. Timetables could be made and reliably met. A street was named after Owen and a godlike bust draped in the order of Gustav Vasa joined the family pantheon. By the time August was born there were almost twenty small paddle steamers flying the Strindberg flag. It was both Carl Oscar's fortune and his misfortune to have two such successful relatives. Their success stood in the way of him having to forge his own way as he moved through the family businesses on the wash of their glory. He started in his brother's spice business when he was twenty-six and he did not like it. His nostrils flinched from the acrid smell of the spices; the dust-puff flour bags clouded the mirror polish of his boots and he was particularly repelled by 'the dreadful stickiness of syrup on my fingers'. So he moved to the steamship ticket office dealing with nice, clean bits of paper but he had

2, 3

not the quip and twinkle to make him popular on the dockside. The words contemporaries most often used to describe him are 'handsome' and 'overbearing'. The physical features he shared with August were piercing blue eyes and an abundance of springy, fair hair but while August allowed his mane the freedom of the raging lion, Carl Oscar's was clipped as close as a box hedge. He led the bachelor life of his class and income, spending long evenings slaking his needs at the waterside cafés where the waitresses had only one way to supplement their wages. Three quarters of the adult female population was unmarried at this time and a husband was more than a girl in such a situation could expect.

When he met Ulrika Eleonora Norling (he always called her Nora), she was a waitress at the Liljeholmen Inn. A small, doll-like creature, she was twelve years younger than him. Her father, a tailor and caretaker, had died in the great cholera outbreak of 1834 that killed more than twelve thousand Swedes. When her mother was fortunate enough to secure a second husband, Nora was sent away to make her own way in the world at the age of eleven. First she worked as a nursemaid and then she became the servant of a prison officer in Långholm prison. She was fifteen when she started work at the Liljeholmen Inn.

The couple drifted for six years in a loose relationship that produced first a child who died, then August's two elder brothers. It would have been entirely predictable for Carl Oscar to desert Nora: women in her situation had no bargaining power. Yet he went on to marry her. The answer perhaps lies in Carl Oscar's strong sex drive, a quality widely attested. Carnality certainly oozes off Nora's photograph. While the average wife of the time poses for her photograph half-obscured by a prestigious mess of jewels and draperies and an air of statuesque detachment, Nora faces us with an almost sneering air and a well-composed simplicity of dress. The puritan-plain bodice sweeps sinuously down the ski-slope figure. A band of black silk encircles the flesh of the bare neck. The shiny hair is parted down the centre like a modest young Queen Victoria but the tilt of the head is challenging, the lips full and sulky. Sleepy, sensual eyes stare directly at the camera; Nora gives herself to the stranger who took the photograph in a way that today is the everyday currency of model and photographer but then was shocking, so shocking that some thirty years later when he wrote *Creditors*, August took just such a come-hither photograph of a wife as the device on which the play turns and the marriage is destroyed. Nora's advantages lay all in her body.

She was sensuous, stubborn and implacably stupid. While she was perfectly acceptable as a mistress, Carl Oscar's decision to marry her put him outside society. His brother ceased to speak to him and his sister kept up the connection only guardedly, for the sake of the children.

Nine months before August was born, Carl Oscar, Nora and their two sons moved to a tiny flat above the steamship office on the quay at Riddarholmen (Knights' Island), the smallest of the four islands that comprise the city of Stockholm. Riddarholmen was the seat of aristocratic power during Sweden's glory days and although world power had become a thing of the past, the little island still bristled with the palaces of the noble families and retained its mystical position at the apex of Sweden's class structure. As he went about his daily business Carl Oscar walked the narrow streets between lovely palaces designed as stone expressions of autocratic power, and when he took his family to Riddarholmskyrkan (the Knights' Church) they worshipped surrounded by the imposing sarcophagi of royal tombs. The church served as a kind of stone Almanach de Gotha: around the walls were displayed the escutcheons of every family belonging to the highest order of chivalry – more than three thousand of them – and when a noble line ran out the escutcheon was broken, a solemn custom Strindberg refers to in *Miss Julie.*

Living and working on Riddarholmen within sight of everything Carl Oscar aspired to and could never attain, his domestic circumstances became more and more chaotic as the connubial bed produced child after child.

'The furniture', August remembered, 'consisted mostly of tables and beds. Children on ironing boards and chairs, children on tables, in cradles and beds. The father had no room for himself, although he was at home most of the time. He never accepted invitations from his many business friends because he could not return them.'[16]

Money troubles mounted. Eventually in 1853, when August was four years old, Carl Oscar was declared bankrupt and his unloved son August became the whipping boy for his disappointments.

Hungry and afraid, afraid of the dark, of spankings, of upsetting everybody. Afraid of falling and hurting himself, afraid of being in the way. Afraid of being hit by his brothers, slapped by the maids, scolded by his grandmother, caned by his father and birched by his mother . . . he could do nothing without doing wrong, utter no word without disturbing somebody. Finally, the safest thing was simply not to move.

His highest virtue was to sit on a chair and be quiet. It had effectively been dinned into him that he had no right to exist.[17]

He used to conjure himself into what he hoped was a state of invisibility. His brothers remembered him creeping into cupboards to undress and his sisters seem hardly to remember him at all; 'an unremarkable child' with 'nothing special about him at all'.

The spiderweb of ennui hung over his parents' marriage and there is no doubt that they colluded in bullying their least loved son, nor did any of his siblings step in to comfort or defend him. When a sin had been committed in the family, his brothers fought back against the parents' accusing finger but August was too frightened or too proud to refute an accusation and then he would be beaten. The other children were probably only too relieved that it was him and not them. 'The ugliest kind of untruthfulness in children occurs when they accuse one another', he later wrote. 'They know that somebody must be punished and it makes no difference who.' August was a quiet, gentle child and he hated the treachery and injustice meted out to the meek within the family, a double treachery in an ostentatiously Christian household. 'Blessed are the meek', Jesus had said and August's childish inclination was towards meekness but it earned him years of victimhood.

A typical incident, one that can stand for many, blew up from nothing more than Carl Oscar regarding the level of wine in the flask on the dining table, thinking it lower than it ought to be:

> 'Who drank from the flask?' he thundered.
> Frightened, he blushed.
> 'So it was you?'
> 'No. No.'
> 'And now you're lying as well. I'll see you after dinner.'
> 'Come with me', said his father. They went into the little
>   bedroom. Mother followed them in.
> 'Ask father for forgiveness', she said.
> 'I didn't do it, I didn't do it', he was screaming now.
> 'Ask father for forgiveness.'
> His father had brought out the whip from behind the mirror.
> 'Please, dear Papa, forgive me', cried the innocent child. But now
>   it was too late. He had condemned himself by his words. To

ask for forgiveness was tantamount to a confession. His mother
assisted at the execution of punishment.

He crept into the kitchen to find comfort. He told the servant he
had not done it.

'Are you still lying?' came his mother's voice. She had been
eavesdropping and she hauled him in again to be punished a
second time for what he had never done in the first place.[18]

Time and again outbursts of unjustified accusation would let him know
he was in for a beating whatever line of defence he took and he would
be thrashed into confessing to something he had not done. His continuous bewilderment at his inability to do right left him with a strong feeling
of the helplessness of the child and an abiding pity for the condition of
childhood which never left him. It made him into an exceptionally kind
and sympathetic parent when the time came for him to have children of
his own: even in today's climate of the involved father, there are few who
write affectionate letters to the baby while it is still *in utero* or who are
happy to take care of the children while the mother is pursuing her acting
career in a foreign land. Such was the after-effect of his youth, when he
was frightened of practically everything and there was nobody to defend
him.

Once Nora had caught her husband, she took the opportunity to
abdicate responsibility. 'Wait till I tell Papa!' was the means by which
Nora controlled her children.

When the cry was heard, 'Papa is coming!' all ran and hid themselves,
or rushed to the nursery to be combed and washed. At the meal table
there was a dull routine of fear and a deathly silence: father said hardly
a word. He lived in his own house as if on sufferance – the provider
for all, the enemy of all . . . the children considered the mother small-
minded and mean when she squealed to Papa; she could be unjust and
violent and could administer punishment wholeheartedly.

Looking back, he concluded that his father loved his mother and that
'she loved him but whether as rescuer, as husband or as family provider,
one cannot say. Always difficult to decide that sort of thing.'[19]

'What will the neighbours say?' was a refrain that rang around the
house. Many decisions, both moral and practical, were taken on the basis
of what the neighbours might say and this raised the question of self in

Strindberg's young mind and led him to ponder the question of identity and to wonder how he could be himself if his behaviour must depend on the unpredictable opinion of others.

The superstitious and uneducated maids played the active part in his early upbringing. In Stockholm you are never far away from the sea and although later he took great inspiration and delight in the laughing waters of Stockholm, as a child they addressed him only in the subliminal snarl of death:

> On quiet winter evenings, it was not unusual to hear cries of help from drowning people. They would be sitting round the lamp in the nursery. One of the maids would say, 'Hush!' They would all sit and listen. Long, continuous cries would be heard. 'Now someone is drowning', one of the girls would say. They would listen till all was quiet. Then the maids would relate a whole series of stories about people who had drowned.[20]

In the nine years following his birth, Nora gave birth to four more children who survived and several who died. Christening, burial, christening, burial. Memories of tiny corpses lived on in the black papers that had been wrapped round the funeral candles and were afterwards pasted onto the nursery walls.

They moved to a larger flat in Klara, a five-minute walk away over the Vasa Bridge. Here, the tall apartment building illustrated Sweden's social hierarchy in microcosm. On the ground floor, in the finest apartment, lived a baron. Above him a general, above him a Supreme Court judge and so on. Social status declined as the stair ascended until finally it reached the top wing housing a Madame with her bevy of girls. August knew that the general reported to the king and the king reported to God and so he was always frightened at the entrance to the building where stood the general's orderly with his spiked helmet and sabre, for his report on August's behaviour was likely to reach God himself.

He was allowed to play outside in the central courtyard where there was an interesting corner by the refuse bins but it was unfortunately also the favourite place of the local dogs who gave him the terror of dogs that would last all his life.

From the windows of the apartment the nave of Klara church rose like a mountain and on the mountain sat a giant with a copper hat who kept up a never-ceasing clamour to announce the flight of time. He sounded the quarter hours in a soprano voice and the hours in a bass. He knelled in the middle of the week for funerals – and that was often during the cholera epidemic. And on Sundays he rang so much that the whole family was nearly reduced to tears and no one could hear what anyone was saying. The chiming at night when he lay awake was terrifying. But worst of all was the tolling when a fire broke out. The first time he heard that deep, dull bong in the middle of the night he fell into a fit of shivering and wept . . . 'There's a fire', someone whispered. 'Where?' . . . in the morning, the servant girls read in the papers that two people had been burned to death. 'It was God's will', said his mother.[21]

Nora was ferociously religious. Shunned socially, and unable to control her children, she was happiest in the company of the uneducated servant girls who shared her ignorance and superstition. She used to like staying in bed late gossiping with the servants and telling fortunes in the coffee cups. Nora was a Pietist and she revelled in the hellfire sermons of the rabble-rousing preachers[22] who at that time had a great hold over Sweden's ill-educated and poor. The Lutheran state church looked on Pietism with suspicion as a dangerous, privatised Christianity doctrinally unsound because it preached faith and redemption by personal revelation rather than through the church. This threatened the considerable hierarchy of priests who had a stranglehold on redemption as long as it was only possible through priest and church. Pietism was perceived as subversive and a danger to the stability of society and the fact that the urban poor made up a large proportion of the congregation compounded the establishment's unease and caused it to suspect Pietism as a potential rallying point for social revolution. This was a mistaken perception. Pietism gave the poor some self-respect. It gave them glamorous preachers to follow. It banned all the luxuries they could not afford and by making a virtue of their poverty and ignorance it engendered smugness, always a static quality, rather than rebellion.

Pietism distrusted books and book-learning. The Bible was the only book allowed and even then Holy Writ should preferably be read aloud by a Pietist leader rather than read privately. The Bible should not be subjected to questioning or to intelligent reasoning. Inquiry implied doubt and doubt was blasphemous. So, with independent thought mistrusted to the extent that it was a sin, Nora could be perfectly justified in seeing August's fondness for book-reading and intellectual inquiry as a punishable offence. A Pietist believed that no man could ever earn his own salvation however virtuously he strove. It was a matter of divine grace who was saved and who was not. The soul could battle all its life to win redemption but it could never win the fight if it had not been pre-ordained for salvation by God himself. This was a devastating argument in the mouth of a not very bright mother who knew that she was one of God's chosen and told her son he was not. However badly she behaved, Nora knew she would fly straight up to Heaven while August would go to Hell. Strindberg puts Nora's pitiless Pietist argument into the mouth of the cook Christine in *Miss Julie*:

> Miss Julie: Oh, if only I had your faith! Oh, if . . .!
> Christine: But you can't have that except by God's special grace, and that isn't granted to everyone.
> Miss Julie: Who has it then?
> Christine: That's God's great secret, Miss Julie.

3 BASIC TRAINING

In 1842 Sweden had introduced compulsory education for its children and fourteen years later, in 1856, August Strindberg started school, aged seven. At this time Sweden had a population of 3.5 million. Thirty years earlier it had been 2.5 million and in the space of Strindberg's lifetime it grew to 5 million.[1] He was part of a population explosion brought about by 'Peace, vaccines and the potato which brought us health, wealth and proletarians', as a contemporary bishop noted.[2] Crown Prince Oscar (the future Oscar 1) gave thought to the vastly increased number he would have to rule over and became a moving force behind the 1842 Education Bill that made it compulsory for all boys and girls in Sweden between the ages of seven and thirteen to go to school. The Crown Prince's attitude was atypical of the ruling class who largely saw no point in giving the poor an education that would only give them access to the miasma of revolutionary ideas floating in from Russia and France. Why pay to educate servants to subvert their own splendid position in society? However, under Oscar, liberalism marched on. The first Poor Law followed five years after the Education Bill. The two were not unconnected. Now, for the first time, each parish was obliged to look after its poor; no longer could they pursue their age-old policy of simply flinging human flotsam over the parish boundary. The idea behind the Poor Law was to restrain the fast-growing human mass from roaming the roads and countryside in vagabond bands, begging, stealing and posing a danger to the security of the state and a personal threat to every law-abiding citizen. (We hear the echo of this fear ringing down the years in the rumour of the roving robber band supposed to have stolen the peacock and Strindberg's overcoat in the Skovlyst robberies.) The new state schools were to teach reading, writing, arithmetic and the Lutheran state religion, the idea being that education would produce an obedient and stable domestic workforce happy to mind the machinery while Sweden cranked itself into the Machine Age. All too variable state schools were set up, one in every parish, while fee-paying schools continued to flourish beside them. The sexes were segregated. Soon after his seventh birthday, August started at the Klara state school, though by this time the family had moved from Klara, which was in the heart of Stockholm, to a less public arena.

'Father's dislike of meeting people after his bankruptcy, and the unfriendly verdict of public opinion regarding his marriage, had induced him to retire to Norrtullsgatan. Here he had rented a house with a large garden and wide-stretching fields with a pasture, stables, farmhouse and greenhouse.'[3]

If you look at a map of Stockholm today, Norrtullsgatan is a fairly central thoroughfare in the north of town but in those days it was an unmade road surrounded by tobacco fields, orchards and pastures grazed by the model herds of dairy cows recently introduced to improve native stock.[4]

The walk from Norrtull to Klara school on seven-year-old legs in decent conditions took half an hour but somehow it always took longer than the time allowed. Most of the year he would have to get up in the dark before the rest of the household and make his way by the occasional lantern hung in a tree. In winter the snowdrifts reached high up his legs, gripping his boots in their frosty clutches. In the spring thaw the road was furrowed with little watercourses and encumbered by boulders and fallen branches. In the summer there were wild strawberries to hunt for beneath the cow parsley parasols that swayed in the northerlies blowing down the luminous surface of Brunnsviken bay where the boats described silver curves in the water and gulls in the air. Invariably he arrived late and invariably he was beaten for it but if Klara school was, as his class-mates agreed, 'a preparation not for life but for hell',[5] its brutalities were counterbalanced by the enchantment of living in the countryside. Nature produced absolute happiness in his heart for the first time and he compares his discovery of the natural world to the idyllic education Rousseau describes in *Emile*. When he came to write about this time in his life, Strindberg was going through a phase of ink-slinging atheism but had he been in softer mood he would surely have described Norrtull as Edenic, his utter delight as pre-lapsarian and the quality of his feelings as intense as a religious conversion. Nature was the first thing to stir his soul to its depth and the love that was kindled in his seven-year-old heart would move and motivate him for the rest of his life. It was, as we remember, the garden and greenhouse of Skovlyst that persuaded him to take on the lease of that fateful place.

His first spring in Norrtull was

> a wonderful time of surprising discoveries. The garden that surrounded the little two-storeyed house was very spacious. Avenues of apple trees, enfilades of berry bushes. Here and there clusters of lilac and jasmine and a huge old oak in the corner. There was plenty of shade and space and just enough of the air of decay to make the place seem romantic. East of the garden rose a wooded hill crowned by a Classical temple. The back of the hill had holes like a cheese where they had tried unsuccessfully to extract gravel, they made picturesque little dells and hollows, filled with osiers and thorn bushes . . . To walk in the garden when the freshly turned earth lay black under the apple trees' pink and white canopy, and when the tulips blazed their oriental colours seemed more solemn than sitting an exam at school and more glorious, even, than church on Christmas morning.[6]

His response to nature's lavish beauty was not confined to the inchoate swelling wonder of the Romantic. Right from the start, he wanted to investigate and to understand, to ferret things out, dig and delve, stroke and sniff. The father set the three elder boys to garden tasks: hoeing, weeding and watering, raking the paths and scratching the moss from the tree trunks with ships' scrapers. As his muscles swelled and his limbs grew longer, he discovered that he could be useful and with a sense of usefulness his spirit grew braver. He, who in the overcrowded flat had known his highest achievement to sit stock still for hours on end hoping to evade notice and escape punishment, became aware of the joy of activity. He shinned up the steep ladder in the hayloft for the pleasure of the fall onto the moon-pale pile beneath. He plunged into the water of the fjord, parting it noisily with his body and flinging himself on a parching rock to dry. He learned to mount Bruno, the farm horse, at a run. He shot at small birds with a bow and arrow. He read *Robinson Crusoe*, 'an epochal event',[7] and the games got wilder and wilder. 'All this activity', he says, 'made us a little uncivilised.' Nora decided that the boys were getting beyond her control so she took up the sword of the avenging angel to cut off their pleasures and expelled her sons from this Eden to a strict summer camp where his brothers bullied him. 'I cried buckets', he wrote, and he cried even more when he went back to school.

As a grown man, his worst nightmare was to dream that he was back at Klara school. His first teacher looked like the ogre in the picture book of Tom Thumb and his approach would be presaged by the dreadful squeak of his boots coming ever nearer; when finally he appeared he told them he would beat them to a pulp if they did not know their lessons. He flogged them and made them crawl on the floor to humiliate them. Another, who always began the class with the words 'Bring me the cane!',[5] hanged himself when his brutality was exposed in a newspaper. Klara school was a theatre of injustice, a citadel of tyranny where an attack could come from any quarter with a rush of feet and a roar and a shout. Dread kept the boys in such a constant state of transcendental cowardice that when they were at home they did not dare venture out of doors for fear of meeting their teachers who expected them to spend all their time preparing the next day's lesson. He felt continually guilty and later thought of Klara as a place of punishment for Original Sin, a penal institution for crimes committed before he had been born.

Most pupils came from the upper classes and wore velvet jackets. August wore coarse clothes and moved in a stinking aura of the cheap fish oil that was used to waterproof his boots. The boys in velvet jackets did not like sitting near him because of the singular smell. Bullied at home, bullied at school, valued in neither place and tormented in both, Strindberg's behaviour must have frightened his fellow pupils. He was physically strong for his age, the manual labour in the garden and the daily journey to school saw to that, but he would never join the fights by which hierarchies were decided and alliances made. His contempt for violence and indignation at injustice kept him loftily apart. Later, when Strindberg was the school's most famous pupil and his contemporaries were asked for their memories of him, on the whole they had difficulty remembering him at all; at school, as at home, he employed the trick of invisibility but there were times when he could not repress sudden fits of high physicality and his habitual fear of exposure would leave him. Then he would break out into madcap exaggerated naughtiness: lighting fires or sliding down hills on his leather breeches to show off to the other boys, invariably getting caught and punished. Fear alternated with recklessness, exhilaration with anxiety and young as he was, he was acutely aware of himself swinging from pole to pole without moderation or balance.

That this frenetic imbalance might be a mirror of the unpredictability and brutality he met both at home and at school could hardly occur to him for he knew no different until, miraculously, moderation and civilised behaviour broke out during the French lessons at school. Reason ruled the class. The reason for this reason? It came in the shape of the nine-year-old daughter of the rector who attended the lessons along with the boys. She sat on the bench at the back so as not to be seen and it was deemed a great misdemeanour to look round at her, but she was there and he felt the change her presence made. None of the boys wanted to be humiliated or flogged in front of her and even the teacher had a smile on his face when he spoke to her. August fell in love and was aware of a kind of collective breath of tenderness exhaled by the boys and men in her presence, a soft breeze that dispersed the habitual atmosphere of horrid, institutionalised vindictiveness. Some of the boys managed to show their love by speaking to her but he never dared. He merely watched her and yearned and daydreamed of rescuing her from dramatic catastrophes. Being without experience of tenderness, he felt helpless in the face of the persistent pain and despair love brought him and eventually he simply longed to be dead and one day at home he surprised everybody by seizing a knife and saying he was going to cut his throat. His parents decided he must be ill. Strindberg remembered this desperate childhood reaction to first love and he used it in *Miss Julie* when the servant Jean tells Julie how as a small boy he stole into Julie's garden (which Jean refers to as Eden) and spied her for the first time. Jean says he was so overcome with hopeless desire that he determined to die

> but I wanted to die beautifully and pleasantly without any pain. And then I remembered it was dangerous to sleep under an elder bush. We had a big one, in full flower. I stripped it of its treasures and bedded down on them in the oat bin . . . I fell asleep and woke up feeling really very ill. But I didn't die, as you can see. What did I want? I don't know. I had no hope of winning you of course.[8]

The presence of the little girl in the French classes had another important effect on Strindberg. It led him to become an early advocate of co-education which he concluded would civilise males and spare them a deal of trouble in later life: 'Innocent friendships would be formed, the electricity carried off and Madonna-worship brought within its proper limits . . . false ideas of woman as a separate and mysterious species would not have followed him and his contemporary males through their lives.'[9]

He tells us that he was not particularly gifted as a schoolboy but he seems to have been a year ahead of his schoolfellows and by the time he had completed his first year of schooling his father had the humiliating experience of being unable to help him with his Greek and Latin home-work. August had an excellent memory. He was good at organising large chunks of information. He was particularly fond of practical subjects such as geography and the natural sciences. He set up a herbarium, made collections of insects and minerals, forced himself to learn the names of all the plants in the Stockholm area, learned to distinguish birds by their notes as well as by their feathers and their eggs but this clerk's talent for cataloguing was able to co-exist with unusually strong flights of imagina-tion. When the teacher showed coloured pictures of plants and animals he saw the whole classroom, whose normal state was a submerged and dirgeful gloom, shine and glow and he writes about this not as a metaphor but as a vision. He was blind to the beautiful patterns of mathematics but he did well enough in arithmetic by the simple strategy of deciding to learn it by rote. Geometry he actively disliked, not that it was difficult, but its very existence aroused an unaccountable fear in him. It claimed too vast a kingdom. Linnaeus, his great countryman, had invented the botanical classifications that up till now had satisfied Strind-berg the list-maker as a kind of material imperialism ruling over a section of the visible world but geometry, a science that drew patterns in the invisible, claiming rule over unseen laws governing the abstract and infi-nite, that was a concept that disturbed his imagination. It was not until a surveying book came into his hands that the subject engaged, then overtook, him. The book set him scurrying about in a frantic phase of 'measuring everything in sight. Trees, houses, gardens, avenues – any-thing, everything – distances were surveyed, volumes calculated, card-board models constructed.'[10] Geometry's magical key to unlocking invisible laws, at first instinctively feared, turned out to be the very key to unlocking Strindberg's life-governing idea, the idea of an underlying esoteric order, a discoverable formula that ruled over the abstract and the infinite, waiting to be uncovered by the persevering scholar. Once he had glimpsed the splendid reach of geometry's invisible empire, he was on fire to discover what lay behind everything he could see. He was, he says, as full of amazement as a chicken just hatched, staring at the world and trampling the eggshell that had shut out the light for so long.

'There was nothing new in the world. Plato had already proclaimed this truth before Christianity came! The world, reality, the visible, is only a semblance, a shadow play of ideas. That is to say, material reality is something base, secondary and accidental. Yes, indeed!'[11] No wonder he had instinctively feared the power of geometry when it had the capacity to teach him such a lesson. Now he ceased to compile lists. Instead, he investigated everything that came into his hands to see what was really behind it. Toys, watches, household goods, all were taken to pieces and sometimes put back right, sometimes not. He was as destructive as a cuckoo in the nest. He found an old galvanic battery in the attic

> and made so many experiments with sulphuric acid that he ruined a pile of handkerchiefs, napkins and clothes. After he had galvanised everything possible, he stopped playing around with that and turned to gold- and silver-plating. During the summer when he was alone he studied chemistry like a madman. He dreamed of having enough money to buy a chemistry set. However, he did not want to carry out the experiments described in the books, he wanted to make new discoveries.[12]

He tried to make an electric generator using bits from the family spinning wheel, the whalebone spokes of an umbrella and strings filched from a sibling's violin. He drove the family mad with tearing their useful things apart. When his father told him there had long existed a reward for the person who could invent a perpetual motion machine, he set to work with parts of the coffee percolator, a soda-water bottle, bits of a birdcage, a hanging lamp and planks that he had made by smashing a chest of drawers to bits. When the machine did not work, he hurled it against a wall in a fury. However, he succeeded in making a Leyden jar, a primitive electrical device whose ingredients included the skin of a dead black cat[13] he had found in the road on the way back from school and brought home in his handkerchief, and some home-made electro-phosphorus. This established his reputation as a scientist and after this triumph he laid chemistry aside for the time being.

He read everything that fell into his hands. In his free time the eleven-year-old boy could be seen in a dressing-gown and cap with a long tobacco pipe in his mouth (smoking was perfectly usual in the young; Sweden was full of tobacco fields in those days and the poor households with numerous children found it extremely useful as an appetite-suppressant). Pipe in mouth, fingers stuck in his ears, he would blissfully bury himself in a book and when his brothers deliberately disturbed him reading, he would jump up and threaten to strike them. Adventure stories, classics, theology, his reading included a German guide for midwives and the *Thousand and One Nights*. Previous to his adventures in geometry and chemistry he had no interest in either poetry or fiction both of which he had found tedious but, following his extensive investigations into what lay behind the tangible matter of the world, his tastes in reading changed to match and he would read poetry aquiver with the most wonderful sensation, 'as if he were floating on air'.[14] He tried fiction again and now this too was transformative. Here were people with an inner life. He understood what they thought, he recognised why they were saying what they were saying. He was not yet reading plays but poetry and fiction taught him that as in geometry, so in words: the esoteric underlies the exoteric if you will only open your ears to the subtext the author has imprisoned in the text. He realised for the first time that 'my soul had been imprisoned and now understood how long it had in fact been fledged but they had clipped its wings and put it in a cage. Now [I] went to father and wanted to talk to him properly, about real things. But father only withdrew.'[15]

Nothing had improved between father and son. With his wide range of interests, August was treating the walk to and from school like a scavenger hunt, picking up all sorts of interesting bits and pieces (such as the dead cat). There was a phase, appropriate for a future alchemist, when he was particularly drawn to metal. Every day he might find a couple of horseshoe nails, a wagon pin, or at least a screw nut, and sometimes a horseshoe. He liked the nuts the best and in the course of two months he collected half a bagful. One evening he was playing with them when his father came in.

'What have you got there?'
'Nuts.'

'Where did you get them?'
'I found them.'
'Where?'
'On the street.'
'All in one place?'
'No, many places. You walk down the middle of the street and keep your eyes on the ground.'
'You're lying. Come here. I want to talk with you.'
The talk was with the birch rod.
'Now will you confess?'
'I found them in the street.'[16]

The thrashing followed the usual pattern. His father made it known he would only stop when August confessed. Eventually he gave in and made a false confession. It hurt to be beaten like a dog but pain was transitory; not so injustice. He found it absurd that he could only quench his father's thirst for the truth with a lie before God. Now he was branded a thief and often reminded of this. He was furious with God, with his parents and with his brothers who, as so often before, had known the truth and had not spoken up for him and yet when his brothers were being bullied he would throw himself at the bully, 'shouting "Don't hit him! Don't hit him!" He couldn't bear to see any of his blood punished or suffer in any way. He felt it in his own body. Always this feeling of dependence, of being tied with the insuperable bond of blood, the umbilical cord that could never be cut off, only chewed painfully.'[17] Later when they were all grown up, his brother Axel described August as a preternaturally shy boy[18] and maybe the words conceal the worm-squirm of Axel's bad conscience, for his sisters Anna and Nora said more straightforwardly that as a boy August had a deep-rooted fear and distrust of everyone and everything.[19]

After four years at the hated Klara school, he moved in January 1860 to Jakob,[20] a school for the poor children of the working class where his coarse clothes and smelly boots caused no alarm. At eleven, he was well grown, tanned from his outdoor life and handsome with his blue eyes and the mane of ash-blond hair flopping over the exceptionally high forehead that gained him the nickname 'professor'. After a year at Jakob, he was outshining his elder brother. Carl Oscar found it offensive when he was put above the better-loved boy and so in 1861, August was removed to the Stockholm Lyceum,[21] a private, fee-paying school or *gymnasium* where, August observed,

> Since the existence of private schools depended upon the goodwill of the pupils, the latter enjoyed great freedom and were treated like human beings. Corporal punishment was forbidden, and the pupils were allowed to ask questions, to express themselves, to defend themselves against accusations, and, in a word, were treated as if they were capable of independent thought. For the first time it seemed as if he had some rights. If a teacher had his facts wrong, he could not simply insist he was right by the virtue of his position.[22]

In these circumstances, learning was a delight. He learned to speak French, German, Greek and Latin. His parents became proud of his learning, if not of him, and they began to boast to others that their son would 'wear the white cap', the badge of the university student. Like a flower unfolding, he responded to their pride in his learning and when he came back from school he would explain what he had learned that day. His mother would listen with the awe of the uneducated and for a little while he would bask in her wonder until a certain point was reached when Nora would take up the Pietist sword to cut him off in full flight. Her weapon was irrefutable illogic. August's knowledge was of no account because what mattered was his soul and his soul was in complete spiritual darkness. Look what had happened to Adam when he ate from the Tree of Knowledge! The only knowledge worth having was the knowledge of Christ. The road of intellectual pride was a certain and sure road to damnation. He was as sounding brass, a jangling cymbal and a cracked fool's bell.

'Why did they bother sending me to school', he asked himself bitterly, 'if education was nothing compared to the mysterious, irrational doctrine of Christ's Atonement?'[23]

His mother's temper worsened with every year that passed. His twelfth Christmas was marked by Nora becoming embroiled in such a disagreement with her brother about her favourite hellfire preachers that she collapsed in hysterics.[24] A dramatic haemorrhage followed during family prayers. Nora was suffering from tuberculosis of the lungs. On 22 March 1862, August wrote to his brother Oscar who had left school the previous year and was now in Paris studying languages:

Stockholm

My Good Brother Oscar,

   Now we no longer have a mother. She died on the night between Wednesday (19) and Thursday (20); we were all in her room, but she was unconscious so she didn't recognise us . . . We are very sad but Father has calmed us by telling us that it was God's will. Schoolmaster Bohman[25] said that to me, too. She is going to be buried on Tuesday, Annunciation Day. The mother of Herr Carlsson, Father's former book-keeper, died very suddenly not long ago. Falk the butcher died last night in the house next door. . . . Don't cry too much or despair, for it was God's will, but calm yourself and take comfort in the word of God, as we have done.

Your affectionate and grieving brother,

August

Nora left a chilling farewell letter warning her sons against the vices of drunkenness and whorehouses. For a few months August reproached himself with lack of real emotion at losing his mother but soon a new emotional turmoil swept the house: a new wife was arising from the ashes of the first. Just as August himself, when his time came, would never put away a wife without soon finding a replacement, so Carl Oscar replaced Nora with indecent haste and August, who had apparently recently seen *Hamlet* (it does seem rather too good a coincidence), had plenty of opportunity to cast himself in the role of the melancholy prince wronged by a parent's re-marriage. Like Nora, Emilia Charlotte Petersson had been Carl Oscar's servant. She was *Mam'selle*,[26] the governess brought into the household to look after the children during Nora's final illness. Like Nora, she was considerably younger than Carl Oscar, like Nora she was the daughter of a caretaker and again like Nora she was appallingly parsimonious and unpleasantly pious, wielding religion as an even stricter weapon of discipline than her predecessor. Where Emilia Charlotte differed greatly from her predecessor was in her pretensions. While Nora paraded her humble origins and lack of education as a yardstick of virtue against which her supposedly over-privileged children could never measure up, Emilia Charlotte had given the boys the impression that she looked down on them ever since taking up her position in the household. She had previously worked in a titled household and somewhere along the line she had Frenchified her good old Swedish

4

names of Emily Charlotta to Emilia Charlotte. In photographs she looks just as a wicked stepmother should, marvellously gothic, with a strong jaw and a sinister, hollow-eyed beauty crowned by masses of elaborately arranged dark hair. She was thirty years younger than her bridegroom and not much older than his children. Carl Oscar marked the occasion with a speech telling his children that the marriage was prompted purely by concern for their future. His time for passion, he said, was past. The following year, she bore him a son.

When Carl Oscar announced his intention to marry Emilia Charlotte, August went into a Hamlet-like sulk, decided she was his enemy and behaved very rudely towards her. The two elder boys had a rather uncomfortable matter on their consciences as they were keen masturbators and Emilia Charlotte, only four years older than Axel, was one of their night-time inspirations. August had been joyfully and bucolically introduced to the habit by some boys on a bathing party the year before his mother died. As he had made no connection between this simple pleasure and religious, reproductive or moral issues he enjoyed himself freely until shortly after his mother's death when a notorious book in a yellow cover came into the household, bringing with it an enormous burden of guilt and fear. *A Warning against the Enemy of Youth by a Friend of Youth* by the German Pietist Karl von Kapff[27] galloped through Sweden like the Four Horsemen of the Apocalypse spreading terror and misery. Possibly unique in extending the consequences of masturbation to politics, von Kapff suggested that this favourite practice of revolutionaries spread their poison through society. The picture of revolutionaries launching, maybe in concert, their deadly emissions to spread the miasma of revolt like a ghostly nimbus through bourgeois society is truly a wonderful one but it is not entirely laughable. Indeed it has a tiny claim on the prophetic when one thinks how violently Swedish society and state was later revolutionised by Strindberg's crusade for sexual freedom and sexual equality. Meanwhile, von Kapff's book terrified the fourteen-year-old Strindberg who thought himself

condemned to a lingering death or lunacy as his spine took ten years to crumble and his brain to rot. His face would turn into a death's head and his hair would fall out. Horrible. And the cure? Christ! But Jesus could not heal the body, only the soul. His body was condemned to death at twenty-five; the only thing was to save the soul from eternal damnation.[28]

He took to spending hours in church. He, who had complained that two hours in church every Sunday turned his feet into blocks of ice and his mind into soup, now spent so long in church that he put the rest of his pious family to shame. This galled them but Carl Oscar soon found opportunity for revenge: August longed to be confirmed. Carl Oscar ought to have welcomed the dawning of long-awaited religiosity in his son but instead he turned it into a new way to make August miserable. He said that August was not old enough. Emilia Charlotte added unpleasantly that while August remained unconfirmed his religious convictions were of no importance anyway. Heaven became a battleground. August could read the Gospels in Greek but he swallowed his pride and joined a confirmation class of much younger children and when he eventually achieved his goal and the bishop conferred the power of the Holy Ghost by laying his hands on August's unruly locks, the boy felt nothing and despaired. Truly the Pietists must be right: salvation might not be won, it could only be granted and it had not been granted to him.

The dependence of youth had now become excessively painful. He had reckoned on leaving school when he was fifteen but he had to wait until he was eighteen. As luck would have it, in his last year when he could see the door of the prison opening, he was kept in for another year by a new rule that forced the students to remain in the highest class for two years. He was tired of living and sought comfort in heaven but heaven being notoriously deaf he found a greater degree of comfort in what he describes as the first time he fell in love as an adult. He was fifteen and the object of his love was the landlord's daughter Edla Heijkorn, a pretty woman of thirty. It was an elevated amour conducted in French. It was also wordy. He wrote compositions in French which she returned adorned with her comments. They wrote love letters in the same language. 'What were the love letters about? Everything – Jesus, the fight against sin, life, death, love, friendship, despair.'[29]

He himself described it as a sexless love. Maybe it occupied some vestibule of mourning, a space in which he could confront the perplexing memory of his dead mother, safe from mockery and unkindness. Edla was a Pietist. She carried the authority of a mother but unlike his mother she did not feel that religion was logically so weak that it needed to shut the door on intellectualism because it could not stand up to intelligent scrutiny. 'Pietism was then', he wrote looking back on this time, 'what spiritualism is now [1886] – a cut-rate philosophy claiming to offer a higher knowledge of hidden things, which was therefore eagerly taken up by women and the great uneducated and finally even made its way into the royal court.'[30] Edla was the first adult to take both his faith and his intellect seriously and to present the possibility that each, while growing, might nourish the other.

Their habit of conversing in French infuriated Carl Oscar and his new wife who must have been further angered at the age gap between August and Edla, containing as it did an inescapable element of mockery of the even greater age gap between themselves. Edla was only three years younger than the new Mrs Strindberg. Consciously or unconsciously, August had found a splendid way to discomfit his father and stepmother. Perhaps in this tense four-hander one can glimpse the first rehearsal for the murderously claustrophobic domestic *danses macabres* that were to become his great plays.

It was a time of fluctuation: between religion and scepticism, between his chaste love for Edla and flirtatious liaisons with waitresses with whom he was re-running his father's early life. To earn money he took up private tutoring. He also taught at a girls' school where 'the big ones wandered around and showed their stockings which attracted him' but he dared not do anything about it which was probably fortunate. In 1866 he was contemplating going into Holy Orders and preached his first sermon in church. The following January he led a classroom rebellion against school religion. Later that year in the summer, he slept with a girl for the first time. 'So that was all it was!' he wrote, a reaction similar to his reception of the sacrament of Confirmation. Each had failed to supply the expected transfiguration.

In May 1867 he became the first of his family to matriculate, albeit without great distinction. His only A was for industry, with AB for religion, French, natural history, history-and-geography and composition, B for maturity, Latin, German and philosophy, C for mathematics. When autumn came, he set off for Uppsala University. By now his father had rebuilt his fortune and was running about forty-one ships, roughly a third of all the steamships plying the waters of Stockholm and he was earning a handsome salary of about 7,000 riksdaler (rdr) per annum. He gave August nothing but a handful of cigars and told him to fend for himself, so he went up to university with the 80 rdr he had earned from his tutoring together with a gift of 15 rdr from the old cook Margaret, who called it a loan so that he should not feel ashamed of accepting her charity.

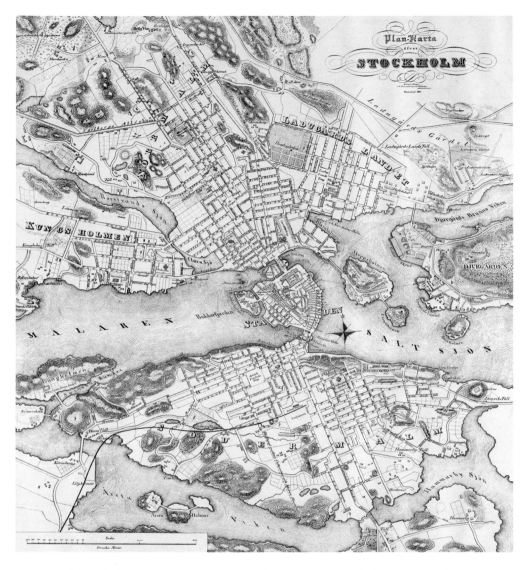

1   Map of Stockholm. C.F Ström, 1861, original reproduction made by Jarmo Sundman,
Stockholm City Archives, Sweden.

2   Strindberg's father, Carl Oscar Strindberg. Kungliga biblioteket, Stockholm, Strindbergsrummet, Bilder, Kartong 10, cos_1865.

3 Strindberg's mother, Ulrika Eleonora Strindberg. Kungliga biblioteket, Stockholm, Strindbergsrummet, Bilder, Kartong 5, UES_odat_2.

4 Strindberg's stepmother, Emilia Charlotte Petersson.

5   Strindberg, aged about 15.

6   Edla Heijkorn, his first love.

7   The Royal Library, Stockholm where Strindberg was employed between 1874 and 1882.
Kungliga biblioteket, Stockholm, Maps and Pictures Sv. Uts. Sthlm Österm. B.7/2.

9   Gustaf Klemming, the Chief
Librarian, by Strindberg. Kungliga
biblioteket, Stockholm,
Strindbergsrummet, vf 196 d 16.

8   The Reading Room in the Royal Library.

10   Strindberg, *c.*1869 when he gave up his medical studies for the stage.
Kungliga biblioteket, Stockholm, Strindbergsrummet, Bilder, Kartong 3, 1870_1.

11   Berns Salon, model for *The Red Room*.

12   Georg Brandes, literary critic who discovered Strindberg.

13   Edvard Brandes, newspaper editor.

14 (ABOVE)   The Wrangel Palace, Stockholm. Copperplate produced in the 1660s by Erik Dahlberg in *Suecia Antiqua et Hodierna*.

15 (LEFT)   Strindberg in 1874, shortly before meeting Siri. Kungliga biblioteket, Stockholm, Strindbergsrummet, Bilder, Kartong 4, 1874.

16   Siri as Jane Eyre, 1877. Kungliga
biblioteket, Stockholm, Strindbergsrummet,
Bilder, Kartong 9, SVE_1882_2.

17   Siri's first husband, Baron Carl
Gustaf Wrangel. 'That inert mass
she calls her husband.'

18   Dalarö in 1892.

19   Fashionable promenade outside the Dalarö hotel.

20 Strindberg's love letters to Siri were written in several languages and sometimes cast them as legendary lovers: to Cleopatra from 'Tuus Antonius' in Latin, to Juliet from Romeo in Swedish and here, both written in the same day in June 1876, to Thérèse from Léon in French and 'Darling, My Love Ophelia' from Hamlet in English. Kungliga biblioteket, Stockholm, Strindbergsrummet, SGNM D 68:89.

21   'I am fat as a pig!' Self-portrait on Kymmendö, May 1882. Kungliga biblioteket, Stockholm, Strindbergsrummet, sgA, Staaf 1882.

22 (LEFT) Siri in the title role of *Sir Bengt's Wife,* Nya Teatern, Stockholm, 1882.

23 (BELOW) *Lucky Peter's Journey*, Acts II and III, Nya Teatern, Stockholm, 1883. The Music and Theatre Library of Sweden.

24   Invitation to Greta's baptism on Kymmendö, 20 July 1881, drawn by Carl Larsson. Strindbergsmuseet, Stockholm.

25 Looking from Dalarö towards Kymmendö which became the fictitious island of Hemsö in Strindberg's popular novel *The People of Hemsö*.

26 The writing hut that Strindberg built for himself on Kymmendö.

27   Susanna Berg who owned the island of Kymmendö and appeared thinly
disguised as Madam Flod, owner of the fictitious island of Hemsö.

28 Jonas Eriksson, the ambitious steward who became master of the real island of Kymmendö by marrying Susanna Berg. In Strindberg's book *The People of Hemsö* the rascally steward Carlsson takes the same shortcut to social elevation by marrying Madam Flod. Strindberg was not welcome back on the island after publication.

29 Ingegerd, daughter of Albert Berg on whom 'Gusten' in *The People of Hemsö* was based.

30   Self-portrait from the Gersau album, 1886. Strindbergsmuseet, Stockholm.

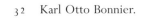

31   Hotel Hof, Gersau, where the family lived in 1886.

32   Karl Otto Bonnier.

34   Verner von Heidenstam, from a painting by J.A.G. Acke, 1911. Nationalmuseum, Stockholm.

33   Albert Bonnier. Kungliga biblioteket, Stockholm, Maps and Pictures Alb. 24:67.

35   Siri and Strindberg playing backgammon at Gersau, the only photograph of them together. Strindbergsmuseet, Stockholm.

36 and 37   Marie David (left) and Siri
(below) both photographed by Herman
Turnell in Stockholm in 1893 when they
were living together. Kungliga biblioteket,
Stockholm, Strindbergsrummet, Bilder,
kartong 25, sgKB Smirnoff 17:43, 21,
17_39_18.

38   Pages from Strindberg's 1886 notebook for *Among French Peasants* which aimed at documenting French peasantry and its way of life before it was destroyed by industrialisation. Kungliga biblioteket, Stockholm, Strindbergsrummet, sgNM D 74:1,50.

39 Self-portrait with daughters Karin and Greta, Gersau, 1886. Nordiska museet, Stockholm.

40   Hans, photographed by Strindberg, 1886. Strindbergsmuseet, Stockholm.

41   Greta, photographed by Strindberg, 1891.

42   Self-portrait, 1886. Strindberg set great store by this romantic portrayal of authorial despair. Strindbergsmuseet, Stockholm.

43 'Every hat flew up and a great cheer rang forth.' Strindberg returns to Stockholm to stand trial for blasphemy, 1884.

44 Courtroom in Stockholm's Old Town Hall.

45 'The anarchist blows up Stockholm's Castle with Infernal Machine', a = steel plate, b = dynamite, c = steel weight, d = hemp yarn, e = electrical wires, f = hemp to burn so steel weight drops down on dynamite, g = the king, h = Piccadon wine, i = Strindberg. Sketch by Strindberg in letter to Jonas Lie, 2 December 1884. Kungliga biblioteket, Stockholm, Strindbergsrummet, EPS 53 Lie, Helvetesmaskin.

46 Bishop John Personne, author of *Strindbergian Literature and Immorality among Schoolchildren* which denounced Strindberg as a corrupter of youth.

47   The hypnotic gaze, 1886.

48   Skovlyst, home of Anna Louisa Frankenau where Strindberg spent the summer of
1888, writing *Miss Julie* in the room behind the top three windows on the right. Historisk
Arkiv for Rudersdal Kommune.

49   Hotel Leopold in Copenhagen, scene of Victoria Benedictsson's suicide.

50 (ABOVE) Playbill for the premiere of *Miss Julie* on 14 March 1889, with Siri in the title role. The Royal Library, Copenhagen.

51 (LEFT) Viggo Schiwe created the role of Jean in *Miss Julie*. The Royal Library, Copenhagen.

52 (LEFT) Ludvig Hansen, Countess Frankenau's steward; the model for the servant Jean in *Miss Julie*, photographed in 1938, aged about 79. Historisk Arkiv for Rudersdal Kommune.

53 (BELOW) Plan of the kitchen at Skovlyst, showing the bath that Siri installed for Strindberg. While writing *Miss Julie*, set in a kitchen, he took his daily bath looking straight at the bell and the dumb waiter which he uses in the play as the symbols of the Count's authority that reduce the servant Jean to a state of slave-terror.

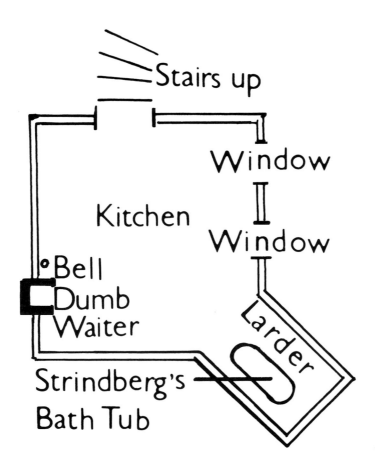

The term's rent was 15 rdr, the midday meal cost 12 rdr a month and there were books, clothes, tutorial fees, wood for heating (a small bundle cost 4 rdr) and evening meals to buy. It is not so surprising that from time to time in Strindberg's plays and stories one finds the characters who wield the power offering their victim a cigar while administering a life-crushing blow.

4 THE FREETHINKER

I've been reading like mad and had tutorials with two old crones and a half-crazy old college hack – who now needs paying – so I haven't time for thought and I am still enjoying an absolutely shameless sense of calm – I've scrounged the odd shilling here and there and so I've kept hunger at bay. At length, weary of sleeping half-clothed on settees, I rented a room – a closet I should say – with what my friends call a marvellous suicidal atmosphere . . .

Strindberg wrote to his cousin shortly after arriving at Uppsala in September 1871. 'Directly opposite me is an attic room – somebody told me a young girl was coming to live there', the letter goes on:

at length some furniture was carried in – Pow! I thought, now she's arrived – Slaves lugged in one thing after another – but there was no sign of an owner – I ran my eyes over the stuff – unusually fine furniture – it can't be a student – a pianoforte – impossible – a sewing basket – Hey! It *is* a woman! But perhaps it isn't a sewing basket? – An umbrella – anyone can have one of those – Underpants – oh hell, I've got some like that too . . . There's a thick book. Women don't read thick books – there's a ball of flaxen yarn and a pair of scissors on the table . . . Torn by raving doubts and every devilish torment I went out.
Returning home that evening I saw a light in her room – Pow! Only a half-lowered blind – what carelessness – after a few minutes wait I saw a pair of legs – stout – well, could go either way – shirt or shift, that is the question – I bent down – dammit he's got hairy legs – there goes another dream the way of all the rest –[1]

Throughout his time at Uppsala University, the dominant tone in his writing is one of self-mockery in the face of comic adversity as he plunged with more enthusiasm than dignity into whatever this new world had to offer. Sometimes priapic, sometimes cod-suicidal, sometimes loud, impatient and demanding but always having fun, his experimental university prose demonstrates the vigour that made both his writing and himself so attractive.

He started enthusiastically enough, attending all the free lectures, but he soon noted, with only gentle exaggeration, that at this rate it would take him forty years to cover the philosophy course and ten years to cover a single Shakespeare play. The way to get on as a student was to put on a frock-coat, call on professors and negotiate terms for private lessons. It was Klara school with its velvet-coated aristocrats all over again. He did not own a frock-coat, had not money for private lessons and thought the system both absurd and immoral. A friend offered to lend him a frock-coat but he was damned if he would play any part in the charade. He had expected the brilliant Uppsala of Descartes, Linnaeus and Swedenborg but the university had fallen into a period of provincial mediocrity and timidity.

'There was something pettifogging in the way the professors fought for advancement by means of pamphlets and newspaper articles', he wrote,[2] noting what a pathetically large number of the professors were addicted to alcohol and snobbery, licking the neck of the bottle and the boots of the nobility. Well-born students had *nobilis* written by their names and it was remarkable how much more could be achieved by the noble than by the intelligent. 'The way to the degree examination was not easy; one was compelled to seek out secret ways, bribe door keepers, creep through holes, run into debt for books and much, much more besides.'[3] However, adversity always brought out the fighting best in him and he was not idle. He discovered a system for borrowing books rather than buying them. He read widely and he made his first acquaintance with Swedenborg, who later became enormously important to him but now struck him as 'crazy, an arrogant Swede who had lived in retirement and fallen prey to megalomania, the special disease of solitary people.'[4] He taught himself the bassoon, the guitar and backgammon and he experimented with writing, often testing out styles and points of view through comic critiques of his own situation.

By the end of the first term, his riksdaler were spent. When Christ-mastide was passed, his father made it plain that no money would be forthcoming for a return to Uppsala next term and if he indeed wished to resume living in the family home he would be expected to pay rent. Strindberg cast about for a means of support. A friend recommended schoolmastering and soon he found himself in the absurd position of teacher at Klara school where his own schooldays had been 'hell on earth'. Carl Oscar, who could perfectly well have afforded to lend his son the money to go back to Uppsala, made it known that he was morti-fied by this fall in his son's social standing: becoming a schoolmaster was 'like being a sergeant', he said, and he would only permit it if August continued to study for his university examination from home. It seems as grotesque that his father should put him in such a position as that Strindberg should become a teacher at Klara of all places, but so he did. As a schoolmaster he was a bad disciplinarian who simply left other teachers to administer punishment while he took the coward's way out, using the old excuse that he was only obeying the rules. While the horrors were taking place around him he would bury his head in a book, as if that would bury his conscience.

With his salary of 900 rdr per annum, he could afford to buy books. Schiller and Byron became favourites for their ability to combine ideal-ism with beautiful language and their trick of disguising revolutionary politics as literature. Byron's *Don Juan* he found 'merely frivolous' but he greatly admired *Manfred* because 'all his denunciations of men were really criticisms of society'.[5] He revered Schiller's definition of art as that which ennobles us by pointing towards the ideal. He tried to emulate his heroes by writing poetry but found it simply would not come. He formed pas-sionate opinions on everything he read and fired them off like rockets to his friends. His criticism of the literature of his own time is not startling to readers today but it was original for a young man of his time. He deplored its preoccupation with self which he described as 'A mental malady reduced to a system by Fichte who taught us that everything took place in the ego, and through the ego, without which there was no reality. It was the formula for romanticism and for subjective idealism.'[6]

Aware that his own hypocritical refuge from schoolmastering into books was producing the very self-absorbed egotism that he disliked, he knew himself just as mutinous, wavering and petty as the prototype Fichtean romantic. He took to declaiming poetry (other people's – he still could not write his own) believing, for some reason, that it might be a cure. His disgust at everything, including himself, continually increased and he thought of fleeing to Algiers to enlist in the Foreign Legion. Did Ibsen's *Peer Gynt*, published a couple of years earlier, play a part in this fantasy? Fortunately, he was rescued from this spiritually arid stretch by a friend who recommended him for the post of tutor to two girls in a rich, cultured family of idealistic freethinkers.

> The Sandahl house was one of the finest in Stockholm with a porter, Pompeian staircases and painted windows in the hall. In a handsome, large, well-lighted corner-room with flowers, bird-cages and an aquarium he was to give lessons to two well-dressed, washed and combed little girls, who looked cheerful and satisfied after their dinner. Here he could give expression to his own thoughts. The catechism was banished, and only select Bible stories were to be read, together with broad-minded explanations of the life and teachings of the Ideal Man, for the children were not to be confirmed but were to be brought up after a new model. They read Schiller and were enthusiastic for William Tell.[7]

Summer came and he was invited to join the family at their summer house. All the joys of the nineteenth-century extended summer house party were his: sitting around on sunny lawns discussing art and literature, singing quartets and dancing, teaching the children, botanising, sailing, riding and swimming. It was, he says, a place where 'everything could be said and everything could be true; it all depended on the point of view.'

As the summer approached its end he says that he looked forward to the beginning of the autumn term at Klara with dread but his feelings must have been mixed because he was plainly an unusually inspirational teacher who was loved by his pupils. His history lessons stuck in his pupils' minds for his fierceness that they should remember dates and use language accurately. His excitement in physics lessons was infectious, especially concerning electricity, and they looked forward to his nature lessons when he used to bring in stuffed animals which he had probably borrowed from museums.

'I had several good history teachers later', a pupil recalled, 'but never one whose lessons were so vivid as well as so informative . . . Strindberg was one of the teachers we adored. When I had to change school, my chief regret was that I would lose Strindberg as a teacher.'[8]

Casting about for an alternative to teaching, Strindberg only knew that what he wanted was 'not to be enrolled as a regular member of society. It was not from dislike of work, for he worked strenuously and was unhappy when unoccupied, but he had a strong objection to being enrolled. He did not wish to be a cipher, a cog-wheel or a screw in the social machine.'

As the summer house party was drawing to a close, one evening there was a knock on his door and Dr Axel Lamm, a fellow guest, stepped in. ' "How are the moods?" he asked, and sat down with the air of an old, fatherly friend.'[9]

Dr Lamm had observed the unhappy, directionless youth. He put forward a proposition. Why not study to become a doctor? Strindberg had, in fact, turned over the idea already. Doctors ran in and out of the Sandahl house and their lives did not much resemble cog-wheels. But a medical degree took eight years. Impossible. Lamm came up with a peculiarly generous offer: Strindberg could live rent-free, not as tutor or a servant, simply as companion to Lamm's two sons while Lamm supervised his medical studies.

There were no Pompeian staircases in the villa Stora Trädgårdsgatan 19 but it was a comfortable enough house that overflowed with generosity of spirit. The Lamms were a Jewish family who ran an open, liberal and cosmopolitan house where many languages were spoken and a merry-go-round of visitors passed through with gossip, fashion and politics from all corners of Europe. Strindberg's memoirs of his time in the household turn into panegyrics and his admiration of the Lamms overflows into praise of Jews in general. 'Men who are wanderers', he writes in this context, 'have to watch unceasingly, observe continually, and gain new and rich experiences, while those who sit at home become lazy and lean upon others'.[10]

He admired such a family in which nobody was afraid. How gently parents could behave without fearing to lose their authority! The children were treated as equals. Philanthropy and tolerance were instinctive. The housemaid was a Pietist who, feeling her faith unthreatened, good-humouredly adopted the cheerful, jesting tone which reigned in the house.

Strindberg's admiration of Jews was not typical of his countrymen. The history of the Jews of Sweden was not a happy one. Before 1775 they had not been allowed into the country at all, with the exception of a few outstanding individuals who could be useful to Court or State. In 1782 a set of regulations was drawn up admitting Jews to the country, while strictly limiting their liberties. They might settle in only three cities, Stockholm being one. They might not marry Christians, become civil servants or sit in parliament. They might only pursue crafts that were not organised by the recognised guilds. This did not leave them much obvious room for manoeuvre but the upper tier soon established themselves as engravers, gem-cutters, grinders of optical glass, cork-cutters, financial dealers and calico printers, all of whom slipped through the net controlled by the guilds. The lower tier of illegals was lumped with 'Savoyards, Acrobats, Comedians, Clowns, Tartars and Gypsies'[11] to be hounded from pillar to post. Widespread anti-Jewish sentiment is vividly attested in sixteenth-century books, pamphlets and written references.[12]

Between 1806 and 1809 immigration was again prohibited altogether while Gustav Adolf IV was fighting Napoleon whose assimilation of Jews as equals in French society only confirmed his status as the Enemy of God in the eyes of the king. This prohibition was lifted after the disastrous king had been deposed and there followed a period between 1815 and 1875 when legislative reforms increasing Jewish rights and liberties were matched by the growing paranoia of a populace which feared, and on occasion rioted against, the growing establishment of Jews within their society, though the numbers were small. When Strindberg entered the household of Dr Lamm in 1868 there were only about six hundred Jews in Stockholm.[13] The previous year, most posts in the civil service had been opened to people outside the Swedish Church and this was seen as a great step towards emancipation. Strindberg describes the atmosphere in the Lamm household as buoyant: it was assumed that the sons would have brighter prospects within Swedish society than their father.[14]

Strindberg's medical studies under Dr Lamm included zoology, anatomy, botany, physics and chemistry. Laboratory work was a mystical and imaginative pleasure. He derived the same exaltation from mixing and analysing, from overseeing the fire-driven journey of chemicals and liquids to distillate or crystallisation as he had experienced during his childhood experiments with chemistry and he uses the same joyous phrase: 'penetrating nature's secrets'. When he was alone in the laboratory he made private potions and soon he had concocted a little phial of prussic acid. 'To have death enclosed in a few drops under a glass stopper in his jacket pocket was a curiously pleasant feeling',[15] he wrote; his hand would creep secretly to his pocket to close round the glass.

The practical side of medicine did not appeal so much: 'He used to think of Faust while examining yet another specimen of urine'.[16] Ailing flesh was unlovely. Cauterising venereal sores was repellent, as was holding the patient's head and feeling it twitch while Dr Lamm tackled an infected tonsil by thrusting a fork down the patient's throat and removing the organ with a quick twist. Unappetising certainly, but the medical round alongside Dr Lamm provided the passkey to a network of bedrooms interconnected by illness and revealing every aspect of the human condition. Doors swung open on countesses in silken four-posters and pathetic cases in malodorous slums, on heroic stoicism and stark terror. All this was invaluable material for Strindberg the writer but possibly even more valuable was the experience of sustained kindness and generosity extended towards him, together with the chance to observe and be part of life in a happy and functioning family between autumn 1868 and January 1870 – the only time in his life that this happened. He could never have become such a convincing writer had not this short period given him a thorough understanding of the other side of the coin: the real nature of disinterested benevolence.

He also discovered theatre, going two or three times a week to the Royal Theatre which at that time was showing mostly French comedies. Intoxicated with the idea of becoming an actor, he worked out his own method of training himself for the profession, a method as poignant in its high-mindedness as startling in its ignorance. Visiting the National Museum, he would take up poses in imitation of antique statues; when out walking, he practised moving as Goethe prescribed with his head high, his chest out, arms hanging freely and hands loosely clenched, 'fingers falling in a beautifully rhythmic pattern', which must have been a surprising sight to meet. He did gymnastics every day and fenced but it was impossible to work on his voice in the house without giving the game away, so he declaimed out of doors. When the autumn season opened at the Royal Theatre, Strindberg presented himself as ready to take on leading roles. After a blustering interview, the arrogant boy was offered non-speaking parts – take it or leave it – and of course he took it.

He informed his father in a stiff letter and he told Dr Lamm in a more relaxed fashion. The benevolent Lamm anticipated financial insecurity and pulled strings to set up some journalism jobs that might bring him a little money.

Theatre life as a supernumerary was not glamorous. Soon he was bored and he began to feel thoroughly foolish. How could he retire from this fiasco honourably? He plucked up courage, demanded a speaking part and was allowed to try for a part with a single line in Bjørnson's *Mary Stuart in Scotland*. 'The lords have sent an envoy with a challenge to the Earl Bothwell', he declaimed and even in his own ears it sounded like a rant. After the rehearsal he was taken aside and tactfully steered towards acting lessons. He wept for rage, went home and took an opium pill that he had been keeping for emergencies. Then a friend took him out and they got stupendously drunk.

The following morning he woke up 'in a complete state of collapse' and was overtaken by misery and remorse over his breach with his father and stepmother which he felt had 'cursed his life'. He wished to be reconciled, to put what he generously called 'the petty troubles of childhood' behind him and he longed to get to know his sisters who were strangers, so separately had they been brought up.[17]

While thus lying on the sofa he felt an unusual degree of fever, during which his brain seemed to work at arranging memories of the past, cutting out some and adding others. New minor characters entered; he saw them mixing in the action, and heard them speaking, just as he had done on stage. After one or two hours had passed, he had a comedy of two acts ready in his head . . . But now he had to write it. In four days the piece was ready. He kept on going from the writing table to the sofa and back; and in the intervals of his work, he collapsed like a rag. When the work was finished, he drew a deep sigh of relief, as though years of pain were over, as though a tumour had been cut out. He was so glad, that he felt as though someone was singing within him. . . . that same evening he sat down to write a note of congratulation to a relative. When he had written the first line, it seemed to him that it read like a verse. Then he added a second line that rhymed with the first. Was it no harder than that? Then with a single effort he wrote a four-page letter in rhyme and discovered that he could write verse . . . It seemed to him like a visitation of the Holy Spirit . . . someone or something seemed to be there which, or who, was not there before . . . he fell on his knees and thanked God for the gift of poetry. His communion with God had been very irregular; it was a curious fact that on occasions of great necessity he would rally his own powers within himself and he did not cry to the Lord at all; but on joyful occasions, on the other hand, he involuntarily felt the need of at once thanking the Giver of all good. It was just the contrary to what it had been in his childhood . . . His idea of God had developed into the Author and giver of all good things, whereas the God of his childhood had been a God of terror whose hand was full of misfortunes.[18]

The doors of perception opened by the opium pill and drinking bout did not close once the drugs were out of his bloodstream. The gift remained and he went on to write more poems and plays. When one looks at this early clutch written in the inspired rush, it must be conceded that however divine the intervention, the resulting art was of dubious merit but the fact that words continued to glimmer and swell on the God-given tide was perhaps more important than the words themselves. At last he felt chosen, blessed, directed. He related the bestowal of the gift directly to the gift bestowed on Jesus's disciples by the Holy Spirit at Pentecost: the gift of tongues, the ability to be heard and understood in any language; surely the dream gift for any writer. Maybe it took a force as great as the conviction that God himself had bestowed his blessing on Strindberg's intellect finally to oust the anti-intellectualism of the Pietism that had oppressed and inhibited him all his life. It was the foundation of an entirely new relationship with God, a direct relationship, mediated by nothing and nobody. From then on, he never doubted the value of his own intelligence or wavered from the conviction that he was a writer.

The first play *A Nameday Gift* is lost to us. It dealt with the family reconciliation he yearned for. He probably burned it. He went on to write, in quick succession, *The Freethinker*, a modern play based on his own crises of faith, a tragedy set in antiquity called *Greece in Decline* (later reworked as *Hermione*) and a history play about Erik xi, the unfortunate Swedish monarch who unsuccessfully wooed Queen Elizabeth i, murdered his barons and then was himself murdered. It is interesting that a history play should have come to Strindberg right at the start of this showering of gifts. In time he became Sweden's Shakespeare in terms of history plays, with a cycle of twelve major plays as important in Sweden as they are unrecognised outside, based as they are on historic Swedish episodes little regarded in the wider world. (He burned this early version of *Erik XI*; the one we now know was written nineteen years later.) Finally, he wrote *In Rome*, a play in verse concerning the neo-classical Danish sculptor Bertel Thorvaldsen whose opulent, indeed vulgar, museum Strindberg had visited on a cultural expedition with the Lamm boys.[19] In the play, Thorvaldsen has completed his first masterpiece. It is unrecognised. The sculptor's father commands him to abandon his art for an honest calling. Thorvaldsen agonises. A *deus ex machina* enters his studio in the shape of a rich Englishman who buys the piece, enabling Thorvaldsen to sculpt happily ever after. There is some good writing in the play but the autobiographical element does nothing for the balance of the father–son conflict at the heart of the piece.

Strindberg sent these early efforts to the distinguished dramaturge and head of the acting school at the Royal Theatre, Frans Hedberg,[20] who came back with his opinion that Strindberg's talent lay in writing rather than acting. Perhaps seeing that the young man needed more time to mature, Hedberg suggested that in an hierarchical world, Strindberg would gain more success if he had a solid qualification behind him. In short, he advised him to complete his degree at Uppsala. Hedberg accepted *In Rome* which was premiered on 13 September 1870, performed eleven times and earned the playwright a respectable 258 rdr, a sum that together with the 180 rdr due to him under his mother's will and now belatedly paid, funded his return to university. The two years between January 1870 and March 1872 he spent between Uppsala and Stockholm, experimenting with literary forms and pursuing a wide and eclectic course of studies. It was a fruitful time.

At Uppsala he made many friends who he tended to keep in separate compartments. There were the medicos, atheists and scientists with whom he discussed matters material, peered through microscopes and measured God against Darwin; a priest and a law student with whom he played cards late into the night and a wide and more diverse circle among whom he formed a tighter inner circle, the first of many clubs into which he would organise his best friends throughout his life. He found it a convenient and congenial way of structuring friendships so that the group was always actively focussed on progressing their common intellectual interests rather than just socialising. This first was called the Runa club and it had nine members, all aspiring writers who read their work to each other. Many members of the Runa club would remain friends throughout his life. One recalled how Strindberg

> would charge in and shake me awake at 4 or 5 in the morning crying, 'Up, lazybones, let's get to work!' He wore old clothes with such elegance one didn't notice they were old . . . he had a guitar which he sang to . . . Strindberg's way of life was very simple [compared to the rest of us] . . . I remember one term he limited himself to drinking a toddy once a week, other evenings he had bread and milk . . . His figure was elegant, his head interesting and his bearing attractive . . . Strindberg was a great favourite with the ladies. His chief attraction was his attitude towards them. He was always respectful, attentive and warm without ever being condescending . . . He did not flirt but was certainly no misogynist and he respected women . . . Fragilely sensitive, he won sympathy by his capacity for sympathy.[21]

Strindberg continued to demonstrate his remarkable facility for difficult languages by learning Icelandic whose sagas and rhythms grafted themselves to his writing bones. He found he had a talent for composing songs that he sang to his guitar. He learned to paint by borrowing an easel, colours and a brush and 'when he had conjured up green bushes and grass he felt unspeakably happy, as though he had eaten hashish'.[22] Profligate maybe but such diversity would be of lifelong practical use to him. Both painting and music would serve to rebalance him when the stresses of writing became too great. Strictly against his father's commands, he also wrote three further plays. Carl Oscar had contributed some money towards his son's return to university on condition that he did not write any more plays but now Strindberg could balance disobedience to his father against obedience to God and Hedberg.

August 1870 heralded a rush of glory. His play *The Freethinker* was published under the pseudonym Härved Ulf, a thrilling moment in any writer's life even if the publication was paid for by his cousin Oscar. A month later *In Rome* opened at the Royal Theatre and he stood at the back of the gallery to watch his own play being performed. The experience horrified him; he found it so bad that he could not believe the applause was genuine but thought it was a put-up job organised by his friends. 'The actors were good,' he wrote, 'the staging more atmospheric than he had dreamed it could be. Everything was good except the play. He ran down to the water and wanted to drown himself.'[23] Fortunately, his friends came looking for him, told him the play was good and forced him to come with them to a restaurant to celebrate. Still he did not believe them and was amazed the following morning when he went to the grocer's and bought the papers to find that the critics had given the play excellent reviews. All his life Strindberg would be unable to watch any of his plays without the same excruciating sense of embarrassment and shame.

At Christmastime *Hermione* (the re-worked *Greece in Decline*) won an honourable mention in the Swedish Academy's play competition and in October 1871 *The Outlaw* was premiered at the Royal Theatre. A 'Viking play' in the fashion seeping in from Norway at the time,[24] the rather stiff piece is a long argument for and against God translated to twelfth-century Iceland and written in the stylised phraseology of the sagas. It was not a great success. *Aftonbladet* reported not one hand clapping but the Royal Ear heard and was gratified. A summons arrived from the Lord Chamberlain commanding him to appear before the king. Suspecting a practical joke, Strindberg spent a restless night tossing between hope and fear. Morning enquiries brought the unlikely confirmation that it was indeed the king who was summoning him.

> Accordingly he travelled to Stockholm and was received in audience with the king. The latter was just now very ill, and looked so emaciated as to make a painful impression. He stood with a benevolent aspect smoking his long tobacco-pipe, and smiled at the young, beardless author walking awkwardly between the rows of young aide-de-camps and chamberlains. He thanked him for the pleasure which he had derived from his drama, adding that he himself when young had competed for an Academy prize with a poem on the Vikings and was fond of the Old Norse legends. He said that he wished to help the young student to take his doctor's degree and closed the interview by referring him to his treasurer [who gave him the king's gift of 200 rdr].[25]

Giddy stuff for a twenty-two-year-old. Encouragement watered the bloom and the result was his first masterpiece, *Master Olof*, though, like the sculptor hero of Strindberg's *In Rome*, his masterpiece would moulder unrecognised for years. Ten wasted years he later considered them, which was not entirely true for both play and playwright underwent a good deal of development in between.

On 3 March 1872 he left Uppsala University for ever, in the middle of a term and without a degree. He did not leave as though shot from a cannon; the reasons simply accumulated. He had made an idiot of himself in a public debate on Dante's *Divine Comedy*. The literary club had descended into disunion and lethargy. His wanderlust had been ignited by a group of travelling players. Money had run out. He wanted to be a useful member of society. All these reasons contributed to his discontent and he borrowed the train fare to Stockholm from his room-mate. In Stockholm he borrowed more money from friends (it is notable how throughout his life, friends dipped into their pockets to support Strindberg's restless genius). He rented a room in a police constable's home at 7 Grev Magnigatan across the street from the barracks of the Second Life Guards whose training for war he compared to his own preparation for life's battle. The painter Carl Larsson lived in the same block and their miserable descriptions of the place might have been more cheerful had they become acquainted but Strindberg remained existentially aloof, not wishing to know the people behind the names on doors but icily judging whose spiritual children they were by the morning newspapers stuck in their letter-boxes.

Thanks to Dr Lamm's thoughtful introductions he was earning a small living as a journalist though he considered it a humiliating position. Like many an aspiring *littérateur*, he chafed at the need to throw off rubbish in order to write serious plays but he turned his hand to 'novelettes' for a ladies' magazine called *Svalan* (*The Swallow*), art criticism and think-pieces for *Stockholms Aftonpost* and translations for the distinguished publishing house of Bonnier and he eventually secured a regular income by becoming the editor of an insurance magazine, *Svenska Försäkringstidning*. At first he toed the line, writing puff pieces for insurance companies and uplifting stories starring those who were fully insured and survived disaster with a smile and a purse full of money but soon he jettisoned these little fairy tales for investigative journalism, printing revelations that focussed on scandalous scams in the marine insurance business. It was a time when merchant ships were woefully unseaworthy and scant regard was paid to sailors' safety or, indeed, their lives. In taking up this crusade Strindberg, the son of Stockholm's chief shipping agent, was slipstreaming Samuel Plimsoll, 'the sailors' friend', whose vigorous campaigning resulted in the British Merchant Shipping Act and the ubiquitous Plimsoll line.[26] Strindberg achieved some publicity for the good cause, further antagonised his father, made powerful enemies including his employers and managed to fold the insurance magazine in six months. Further assorted jobs followed but two years was enough of failing to make an adequate living by his pen. He needed a salaried job that would permit him time to write. He applied for a job as the assistant librarian in the Royal Library and, though he was eventually appointed in December 1874, the appointment was not without its humiliation because he still had no academic qualification and so needed special permission. In a rush of excitement he had some smart visiting cards printed which he could not afford: as a schoolmaster he had earned 900 kronor (kr) per annum (in 1873 riksdaler had changed to kronor), as a freelance writer earnings had been unpredictable and as a librarian he could at least depend on 180 kr, though his rent cost him 200. Like the Russian functionary in Dostoevsky's novels, the Swedish functionary typically pursued many nominal posts within the gift of his patron, flitting from desk to desk, mosaicking a living wage while enlarging his patron's sphere of influence. Unfortunately, Strindberg only had the one job but it had two advantages: plenty of spare time to write and all the resources of one of the great libraries of Europe.

The Royal Library occupied one wing of the Royal Palace. With its hundred thousand volumes, Strindberg thought it resembled 'a geological deposit of unfathomable depth where, as in a pudding stone layer was piled upon layer, marking the successive stages arrived at by human folly or human genius.'[27] He also compared it to a gigantic brain but a more prosaic observer compared the library to 'a store room where it is totally impossible to order the chaotic masses; consequently, it is rather difficult to gain admittance to this sanctuary of learning.'[28] Strindberg was later part of its move to new quarters in Humlegården when he likened the undignified spectacle of the books trundled through the street to a man with his inner organs spilled out to public view.

One of the library's special treasures was the *Gigas Librorum* (the Giant Book) also known as *The Devil's Bible* or *Black Book*, a most unusual Bible containing a number of exorcisms and spells in a section entitled 'Experimentum de Furto et Febribus'. It had long been an important text for occultists. Written on 300 parchments, each the entire hide of an ass, it was penned by a monk in a single night, helped by the Devil who as usual demanded his soul in payment and less usually inserted his own likeness into the sacred text. We see an odd, black-faced fellow with red horns

7, 8

and a froggy body wearing only a polka-dot nappy. The library held many occult volumes and texts and the chief librarian Gustaf Klemming was a noted mage, a spiritualist and Swedenborgian who was so terrified of being buried alive that he kept a coffin of open-weave willow in the basement and instructions that he was to lie there thirty days before interment. When the time came for the Royal Library to move, Klemming considerably intensified his mystical aura by escorting the *Gigas Librorum* down the street on a huge sledge. Although at the time Strindberg was enough of a sceptic to hold a larky evening in the library to spook his friends, we may take the years he spent at the Royal Library to be a period in which he made his first acquaintance with arcane and occult texts and, though they held no special interest for him at the time, Klemming's extraordinary personality exercised a powerful hold over his imagination for many years to come.

Since 1873, Strindberg had been supporting a mistress. Not much is known about her except that her name was Ida Charlotta Olssen and the relationship looks uncannily like a re-run of his father's relationship with his mother. Ida Charlotta was a 'waitress' from the class one did not marry – unless one was Carl Oscar. By the time Strindberg joined the Royal Library in December 1874, he was already bored of her and had tried to do the honourable thing and pass her on to a friend. Foolishly, she sought to reawaken his passion by being unfaithful, thus giving him the perfect grounds to break off the relationship, which he did in April 1875, but Ida Charlotta had become pregnant in March. The earliest she could have discovered would have been late April, more likely May or June, and by then she had already provided him with the reason to deny paternity and he abandoned her. The son who was born in December was given his first name, Johan and we can only conjecture what pathetic hopes lay behind the naming.

Strindberg's guilt lingered and he refers to the incident in two autobiographical novels: *The Son of a Servant* (1886) and *Inferno* (1890). The real legacy was his lifelong horror of the man's uncertain position towards biological paternity. It surfaced throughout his life whenever he became suspicious of one of his wives (with some justice in the case of the first two) and it made him obstinately convinced that he had written a much better play in *The Father* (1887) than Ibsen's *A Doll's House* (1889). In Strindberg's play the father is so tormented at never finding the answer to the true paternity of his daughter while his clever wife torments and teases him that he ends up in a straightjacket and she gets what she wanted all along: control of the household and the money.[29] This, he felt, was both more ingenious and more psychologically truthful than Ibsen's Nora. Would Nora, a woman of a certain age and untrained for any occupation except manipulating men, walk out of the doll's house slamming the door on her family life when she could only be walking into a future of prostitution? The wife in *The Father* achieved her independence more thoroughly and with greater wit. It never ceased to rankle with him that Ibsen's play achieved the greater success.

Storms must have raged in Strindberg's breast that summer. As he was learning of the unwanted paternity, he met the woman who was to become his first wife, Siri von Essen. He described their meeting in a poem entitled *Sailing*:

> It was in Drottninggatan
> One burning June day
> On the narrow pavement
> That we met, you and I.
>
> You disappeared into the current
> Flowing past the shop windows.
> The clack of your small boots
> Faded with the rustle of your skirt.
>
> Your blue veil floated
> Above the hats and parasols.
> Then it sank slowly
> Into the human river.
>
> I sought it,
> That pennant topping your mast.
> Now, whenever I brave the storm
> I hoist it.

He was twenty-six when they met and she was twenty-four and married with a two-year-old daughter. Siri was born Sigrid Sofia Mathilda Elisabeth von Essen on 17 August 1850, the only child of the Finnish Baron Reinhold von Essen. Finland had been subsumed into the Russian Empire in the war of 1808–9 and Siri grew up on Jackarby, a country estate near what is now Porvoo. Her mother, Elisabeth (Betty) Charlotta In de Bétou, was a Swedish aristocrat who found country life 'horribly provincial'[30] and bloomed during the social season when Helsinki's balls imitated St Petersburg's. Betty liked to coquette and shock in small, well-judged ways like smoking cigarettes, behaviour that would draw attention to herself while never threatening her social position. Siri grew up with her mother's engineered impulsiveness and her father's past military glory.

The baron had contentedly retired to country pursuits, living off his estates and investments which were sufficient to support a large number of indoor and outdoor servants. Steeped in past von Essen glory, he ruled his little empire from his 'Voltaire chair' in the library. He adored his women and though Siri was the only child there was no question of her being brought up as a boy, though after dark to prove her courage, her father would send her on errands across a reputedly haunted courtyard.

> 'Are you a coward?' he would ask her. 'I cannot believe General von Essen's granddaughter is a coward.'
>
> She was not, as he discovered when she was three years old and he came to punish her after she had rampaged through his study, leaving the place a heinous mess.
>
> 'Well, I suppose I shall have to give you a little smack', he said.
>
> Up flew her fists as she advanced on him; 'If you hit me, I'll hit you.'[31]

Discipline had dissolved and the baron sat back in his Voltaire chair to enjoy the rest of his life as the willing pawn of his lively wife and daughter.

When she was thirteen, Siri was shown the social splendours of St Petersburg and she went on to Paris where she attended a convent school. She spoke French to her mother and Swedish with a Finnish accent to her father. 'All her mother's dreams revolved around Siri making a good marriage'[32] but Siri returned from Paris with the one ambition calculated to shipwreck those dreams. She wished to become an actress. This would make her completely unmarriageable. Betty von Essen, who seldom needed to raise her voice to get what she wanted, steered Siri towards the perfectly respectable occupation of becoming a singer instead.

By the time Siri was eighteen, the family could no longer defer payment for the Chekhovian idyll. Betty was the one with the strength of character to take the axe to the cherry orchard; the baron could no more face the emotional shock than he had been able to face the bills all those years. He was sent on ahead to Stockholm leaving Betty and Siri to oversee the sale of the manor house with all its dependencies: land, livestock, sawmill, distillery, the furniture and even the books.

In 1868 Siri and her mother joined the baron in Stockholm where Siri dutifully studied singing with her aunt, Mathilde In de Bétou. The following year she was accepted by the Academy of Music in Stockholm but an infection of her vocal chords put paid to her training. Maybe she did not miss her studies too much as she joined her mother in full pursuit of a suitable husband from the higher echelons of society. It was not quickly forgotten that the Crown Prince (later Oscar II) once invited her to dance that year. Siri was extremely pretty. In photographs her eyes look brown but they were dark blue. Their darkness contrasted shockingly with her abundance of platinum hair. She was lively, flirtatious and willowy with a graceful neck, a feature much prized in those days when people were still beheaded in Sweden. A sculptor told her he 'would like to cut off her head and keep the neck'[33] but perhaps the attractions of her neck became secondary to the attractions of her fortune when, in 1870, her father died in his chair while she was reading aloud to him. This improved her chances by 25,000 kr which she would inherit on reaching her majority at the age of twenty-five.

That summer she met Baron Carl Gustaf Wrangel,[34] a popular Captain of the Swedish Life Guard. To this day it is a moot point whether the most splendid building in Stockholm is the Royal Palace or the Wrangel Palace. Carl Gustaf was a pretty distant offshoot of the famous family but nevertheless he bore the splendid name and a title. He was eight years older than Siri and a good catch. The fact that he had neither money nor country estate could be glossed over by an anxious mother with a rich daughter.

Carl Gustaf was passionately fond of the theatre. He was wont to start an amateur dramatics society wherever his regiment was posted and this was how the two of them met. He showed well on stage. Society girls swooned over his looks and nicknamed him Phoebus for his Apollonian beauty; her mother described him as 'solid' and he was about as animated as a statue of the god. 'He's very pleasant and I like him very much but I'm not in love with him, at least not desperately. Just swooning', Siri wrote girlishly to her best friend Constance Melins.[35] The baron's letters to Siri also show a notable lack of passion but passion was not expected

17

14

in the marriage market and Betty, at least, was passionately delighted at having secured such a son-in-law.

They married on Siri's twenty-second birthday. Their daughter Sigrid was born ten months later. As a society wife, Siri had to put away all thoughts of an acting career but she might have floated along on the illusion that she had met her soulmate as the young marrieds indulged their shared passion for amateur dramatics in the drawing room. She made a point of keeping up with matters theatrical and by the time she met Strindberg on Drottninggatan she had already seen his brief appearance on stage in *Maria Stuart in Scotland* and read his play *Hermione*.

When they looked back on that meeting, it seemed as if fate was making doubly sure they met, for each had received a letter guiding one towards the other. Siri's letter came from Constance Melins, who wrote asking her to be kind to Ina Forstén,[36] a young Finnish pianist who was coming to Stockholm to give a programme of concerts. Strindberg received a similar letter from Ina Forstén's fiancé, Algot Lange,[37] one of Strindberg's friends from Uppsala who had become an opera singer. When Siri heard that Ina had an introduction to the promising young playwright she was eager to be introduced but Strindberg had no interest in meeting Stockholm's queen of amateur dramatics. Then Ina introduced them on Drottninggatan.

Siri invited him to visit them and it seemed as if this was the second signal sent by fate, for she lived at 12 Norrtullsgatan and as he stood on the doorstep he realised he was standing at the entrance to one of the homes he had lived in as a child. Dazed by superstitious dread and half expecting to come face to face with his iron-souled father, he was overcome by nausea and almost fled but in this keyed-up moment the maid opened the door and he had no choice but to take the symbolic step over the threshold.

'Of Byzantine slenderness, which allowed her dress to fall in simple, noble folds, like the dress of St Cecilia, her body was of bewitching proportions, her wrists and ankles exquisitely turned.'[38] If fate had played a part, it had no further work to do. Never were there more willing lovers, though lovers was exactly what they did not become for more than a year. During the summer and autumn he presented himself almost daily, becoming 'Uncle Augis' to Siri's child, boon companion to Siri's husband and mentor and spiritual adviser to Siri herself. 'Henceforth this woman represented to me a soul incarnate, a soul pure, unapproachable . . . woman as both virgin and mother . . . I worshipped her.' Conscious that his very presence re-ignited Siri's acting ambition, his role began as stern prohibitor. It was as unthinkable to him as it was to her mother that Siri should ruin her reputation by becoming an actress. He embarked on turning her into a writer. So began her sentimental education. Their two fair heads bent together over the books that he decreed she should read. He wrote her long and valuable letters concerning the craft of writing. These were precisely the subjects that interested him throughout his life and as he awakened her interest, he deepened his own. Seized by creative excitement, 'my brain twitched like a polyp in vinegar'[39] and he flung off a new version of *Master Olof*, the obstinate play that no one would publish and that would not leave his imagination alone.

His advice to Siri encompassed the usual advice given every writer: write what you know. 'God preserve us from writers who regurgitate from books. It's the secrets we want to know – the natural history of the human heart that we have been trying to put down for a thousand years . . . Note also that you have the freedom to cheat!'[40]

He encouraged her to begin a novel based on her days in the Paris convent and to write it in the manner of a sensational French novel: 'Make it a nunnery and you'll be irresistible!' So far, so ordinary, but Strindberg was never niggardly with his secret recipes for his success and, just as he later gave away his alchemical formula for making gold to another wife, so now he revealed to Siri the special twist that was the secret to the vigour of his writing, a technique that Stanislavsky would call the use of emotional memory: the ability to conjure a particular emotion by recalling an incident that occasioned that emotion and then to act (or write) in the strong grip of that emotion. To sharpen up her style and divert her from too much Fichtean self-absorption, he recommended translating foreign novels into Swedish but this did not get far as he chose *Madame Bovary*, a book she refused to finish because she found it shockingly immoral. He borrowed George Sand's epistolary novel *Elle et Lui* from the Royal Library and lent it to Siri. They took to writing each other long, serious letters with more than half an eye to publication. Later he used them as the base of an epistolary novel called *He and She*. He wrote equally long and serious letters to her husband the baron. Often he wrote to them jointly. Men of Strindberg's generation were much given to Madonna-worship and the bachelor admirer was an accepted role. Strindberg the *preux chevalier* added greatly to the gaiety

20

of Carl Gustaf's life. Not many indolent barons had a lively playwright running in and out of the house and enlivening domestic longeurs.

> As soon as dinner was over she went to the piano and began to entertain us with some songs, and after that the baron and I discovered that we possessed a hitherto unsuspected talent for Wennerburg's duets. The hours passed rapidly. Finally we amused ourselves by casting parts and reading a short play that had just been performed at the Royal Theatre.[41]

Quite soon, Strindberg decided to pretend he was in love with Ina Forstén. Maybe he realised that he was falling in love with Siri and wished to disguise the fact. Maybe he was piqued at taking the castrato supporting role. Maybe he simply wanted to fling a *deus ex machina* into the static triangle in order to provoke some sort of change. Had the playwright in him taken charge? We know that when at work, he took fiction for reality and often created experiences in order to write about them but to do so they had to be so inextricably combined as to fuse: his deliberately manufactured experiences were worthless to his writing unless he completely believed them while he was living them. 'The lie', he wrote of his sham love for Ina, 'originally a mere whim, took shape and form. Full of apprehension and shame, I told myself fairy tales that I ended in believing. In them I played the part of the ill-starred lover, a part that came easily enough, for with the exception of the object of my tenderness, the fairy tales agreed in every detail with reality.'[42]

His letters to Siri and Carl Gustaf concerning Ina read like one of the novelettes he wrote for the women's magazines. 'Oh, if only you knew how my heart still bleeds', he wrote in October: 'how black I shall appear to you – but have mercy and hide my secret [his supposed passion for Ina] . . . Forget me! Do not let your home be infected by an unclean spirit! Close your door upon my sorrow!'[43]

He played the part so successfully that Ina's father called to interview him as a prospective son-in-law and Ina's fiancé Algot Lange wrote him a furious letter suggesting that as duels were no longer fought, Strindberg should shoot himself. Strindberg realised he had taken things too far. Terribly confused and emotionally overwrought, he knew that he had got in too deep and the only solution was to get away.

'Buy me; living!' he proposed to Rudolf Wall, the editor of *Dagens Nyheter*. 'I come very cheap. This is my idea. Send me to Paris for a month.

If by that time I haven't sent you some excellent articles you can get rid of me as you please'.[44] Wall responded positively and on 5 October Strindberg invited Siri and Carl Gustaf to a farewell dinner at his lodgings.

All his life Strindberg was preoccupied with setting the scene. Even when he had no money he arranged his rooms with great originality and élan. This evening his room

took on the appearance of a temple. A porcelain chandelier looking like leaves and flowers – a type often seen in churches that I had picked up in a junk shop – was suspended from the ceiling. The cracks were skilfully concealed with swags of artificial ivy that I had found some time ago at my sister's. Beneath the three-armed chandelier stood the dining-table. A basket filled with roses, which glowed red amongst the dark foliage, was placed on the white damask tablecloth and the roses, reaching up and mingling with the drooping ivy shoots, gave the effect of a flower show. Round the basket that held the roses stood an array of wine glasses, red, green and opal, which I had bought cheaply at a sale, for each had a flaw. The same applied to the dinner service: plates, salt cellars and sugar bowl of Chinese, Japanese and Swedish porcelain.

When he opened the door to Siri, 'The Baroness, dazzled by the lights, clapped her hands as if she were admiring a successful stage setting.' When, at last, the time came to rise from the table

to say goodbye perhaps for ever. The Baroness burst out sobbing and hid her face on her husband's shoulder . . . And with an outburst of affection at once pure and impure, passionate and full of angelic tenderness, she put her arms around my neck and kissed me in her husband's presence. Then she made the sign of the cross over me and turned to go. My old charwoman who was waiting on the threshold wiped her eyes and we all shed many tears.'[45]

5 PLAYING WITH FIRE

18

Strindberg never reached Paris. As the steamboat passed the little island of Dalarö, some thirty miles south of Stockholm, he was seized by a fit of suicidal despair and jumped ship.

> A sudden terror of this long and senseless journey seized me . . . a pain like a toothache began to torment me, but in my confusion I could neither describe nor locate it. The farther the steamer advanced into the open sea, the greater became the strain. I felt as if the umbilical cord that bound me to the country of my birth, to my family, to her, was tearing asunder.[1]

19

He took a room in the Dalarö hotel where over an absinthe and a cigar he decided to kill himself 'by contracting pneumonia or some other fatal disease, which would keep me in bed for weeks. I would be able to see her again, kiss her hand and say goodbye for ever.'[2] He dashed down to the shoreline and flung himself into the icy October sea. When he felt he could swim no longer, he turned back. The moment of greatest importance had arrived. According to all instructions given to bathers, the real danger consisted in remaining naked too long out of the water and so he sat in the freezing wind until his skin felt as if he had been scorched all over by a red-hot iron, then he returned to the hotel, sent a telegram to Carl Gustaf and called for a doctor. The hotel sent up a none too intelligent priest instead. This made Strindberg furious. On the threshold of the hereafter, he felt himself at least entitled to a good, strong theological debate but his fury gave way to soaring barcaroles when the Wrangels arrived post haste. Much sentiment was shed. In his fictionalised account, Strindberg says he lay in bed feeling 'like the wolf who has devoured grandmother and now lies in bed about to gulp down Red Riding Hood as well.' And so confused are we at this suicide attempt, at once deadly serious and a complete sham, that we are as unable as he to sort the theatre from the real. Carl Gustaf, whose naivety is always difficult to evaluate, invited Strindberg to come back to Stockholm and live with them while he recovered. In terms of etiquette, this was a grossly improper offer. Siri's reputation would have been utterly compromised by the presence of a bachelor under her roof and Strindberg, careful of her good name, refused. The Wrangels returned to Stockholm and Strindberg followed soon after, returning to his old rooms and his job at the Royal Library. Next month, the Wrangels took in another guest, Siri's eighteen-year-old cousin, Sofia In de Bétou, whom Siri describes as a healthier, stronger, calmer, everyday version of herself.[3]

That winter deceptively smooth seas laquered rumbling depths. In December, Ida Charlotta Olssen gave birth to her son. In January 1876 Strindberg and Siri began to meet secretly in cafés and museums. He thought that Siri had 'the smallest feet that ever wore shoes in Sweden' and he derived indescribable pleasure from walking in step with his beautiful baroness 'like a four-footed animal'.[4] The same month saw Ina Forstén finally married to Algot Lange so that complication, at least, was out of the way. The correspondence between Strindberg and his father during this time is incomplete but it suggests that Carl Oscar might have accused his son of fortune-hunting or social climbing through his close association with the Wrangels; maybe the father was jealous of his son running in and out of aristocrats' houses. There was a more concrete dispute about money when Carl Oscar decided to leave the shipping agency solely to his favourite son Oscar. On 8 January Strindberg and his brother-in-law Hugo von Philp,[5] who had just married his sister Anna, visited Carl Oscar in militant mood. There was a tremendous row. Strindberg and von Philp returned the following day when, according to his father, they physically assaulted his wife. If true, this must have given a delightful release to years of pent-up rage. Strindberg made an attempt at reconciliation the following Christmas through his brother Axel, regretting such a family in which 'distance has bred monsters and silence given birth to ghosts',[6] but this effort met with no success. He never spoke to his father again and seven years later when Carl Oscar died Strindberg did not attend his funeral though he was in Stockholm at the time.

In February Sofia In de Bétou again came to stay with Siri and Carl Gustaf. Soon there was no doubt what was going on. Come March Carl Gustaf asked Siri's permission to spend the night with Sofia and Siri consented. Strindberg was disgusted and poured out his feelings in a long, passionate letter to her:

> Are you to going to be your husband's procuress? . . . Rise, young lioness shake your golden mane and send thunderbolts from your lovely eyes to make the idiots tremble . . . Come! Fulfil your high ambitions! Become an actress – I shall give you a theatre of your own . . . Are you afraid of becoming my wife? Are you afraid of the prose of the everyday? Oh, don't you know I wield a magic wand that can strike water from rock – poetry from dirt – I can work a coffee-grinder and make it sound like music – I shall go to the market to buy us potatoes but I shall always put a flower on top of the pile.

From offering potatoes he went on to offer her a *liebestod*, then fashionable: 'Die with me – oh, in your company I will gladly give myself up to those eternal, unknown spheres where our souls may embrace one another and we need be ashamed of nothing, ask permission of no one but God. Re-read all my letters – can't you hear how they tremble with love for you, my queen?'[7]

His queen, however, was frightened. Divorce was a scandal that would expel her from society for ever but things had gone too far, Stockholm was a small goldfish-bowl and a rumour went round that Carl Gustaf had purchased a quantity of saffron (believed to be an abortifacient), the implication being that Sofia was pregnant. Siri was never a jealous woman and she did not care if Sofia was pregnant or not. What she did care about was that people were talking: her husband's career would be ruined along with the reputations of all concerned if his affair were to become known, which of course it did. When Siri's mother learned she immediately told her brother, Sofia In de Bétou's father, thus precipitating exactly what she wanted to avoid for her daughter: scandal and divorce. The whole family was in an uproar. 'Think of her honour! Think of her finances! Think of the scandal!' her mother wrote to Strindberg.[8]

During the months of March and April, Siri veered between bravado and cowardice but at the root of everything (she later told her daughter) lay the absolute certainty that she loved Strindberg 'boundlessly'. This was no repetition of the lukewarm, manageable love she had felt on her marriage to 'that inert mass she called her husband'[9] and it was this certainty that lay behind the declaration of independence that she wrote at the end of April to her

Darling, darling Mummy

I am not made for a peaceful home and the scent of roses. I thrive on struggle. I have tried hard to find satisfaction in a loved and loving man, a cosy home, good friends, an adorable child . . . I have tried to be completely contented but I have never succeeded. Battle and progress is my motto – Peace is not for me – I wasn't born a Woman – I was born an Artist! . . . As Carl's wife I could never become an actress – I had no right to destroy his name, his reputation, his position . . . As August's wife I can live quietly, training as an actress until the day when my glorious Goddess takes me in her arms and I am worthy to be called her daughter.[10]

On 4 May, to preserve everybody's honour and make sure Carl Gustaf was not expelled from his regiment, Siri travelled to Copenhagen where she spent two weeks with her aunt Augusta[11] playing the part of the stage-struck wife who had deserted her husband for the theatre. He took the case to court on 16 May and on 20 June the marriage was dissolved. The whole thing was finished only three months after Carl Gustaf's first adultery with Sofia. Both emotionally and practically it was too short a time for such enormous change.

Siri had given Carl Gustaf their three-year-old daughter as part of the bargaining process. Money was her other weapon. Despite the marriage settlement, she still remained a considerable heiress and Strindberg, always fastidious over points of honour, was determined not to be seen as a fortune-hunter. The normal procedure would have been for her money to become his on their marriage, particularly as she had no bargaining power; as a divorced woman she was an outcast from society who could only be rescued if Strindberg married her. He held all the cards but he had no ambitions to turn into the typical nineteenth-century money-grabbing despot-husband; he wished to live up to his ideals which included equality within marriage. A marriage contract was drawn up that would give each control of their own property (his was precious little).

Betty von Essen and Carl Gustaf were not so scrupulous and the period between the divorce and Siri's remarriage saw the two of them wrangling over control of the money that Strindberg was busy signing away. To her mother's chagrin, Siri outmanoeuvred her and the rift that had opened between mother and daughter at the start of the scandal deepened when Siri transferred the bulk of her fortune to her daughter Sigrid, to be managed by Carl Gustaf until the child came of age. For herself, she retained a large shareholding worth 13,000 kr in a company called Guillemot and Weilandt. She calculated that this shareholding would yield the investment income she required to support herself while she trained as an actress. It would bring her in 3,000 kr. Quite a sum. Carl Gustaf only earned 570 kr a year and Strindberg's salary was about a quarter of that.

There followed a summer of love and uncertainty as the two lovers navigated between the poles of their real desires and the ideals that they had hastily agreed between them during those few scrabbled weeks of spring. Their agreement included the condition that they would not marry for the period of a year so that people truly would believe she had left her husband for the sake of her career rather than for him. During that year it was his responsibility to write plays for her to star in and hers to train as an actress. When they did marry it was to be an alliance between equals. As well as maintaining financial independence they would occupy separate bedrooms and bathrooms; in no way would he tyrannise over her just because she was a woman. They would not make love until they were married lest she become pregnant. But they were in love and in lust and repeatedly they ran the rim, only to withdraw at the last moment until one day

> Damnation! She was wearing black silk stockings. Her leg was a little fuller than it had been, and the whiteness of her knees shone forth through this black veil of mourning. Those black legs moving in a cloud of skirts were the devil's temptation . . . Tired of her constant fear of pregnancy, I lied to her. I told her that after much diligent research in the library I had learned how to cheat nature. I suggested certain preventative techniques to her and alleged that I had an organic defect which made me, if not sterile, at least less dangerous.[12]

Their lovemaking was a source of joy to them both and they revelled in its repetition.

While Strindberg remained in Stockholm, Siri rented a cottage in obscurity, Upplands-Väsby by name. Here she took lessons with drama teachers and worked hard on her voice; her Finnish accent was not an advantage on the Swedish stage. As she attempted to cut this natal inflection from her vocal chords, the symbolic deracination emphasised her alienation from her 'darling, darling Mummy' for the first time in her life. Siri had never been so vulnerable. She was anxious concerning the health of her daughter Sigrid who was manifestly unwell and she attempted to persuade Strindberg into marriage ahead of the agreed timetable. This was a mistake. It would invalidate the legend of the spotless divorce and endanger her reputation, an issue that mattered to Strindberg. As to her daughter, he wrote, as many a stepfather-to-be has written both before and since, 'Why must everything be sacrificed for your love for your child? What has that to do with me?'[13]

Quarrels alternated with ecstatic reconciliations. At this important time when each should have been increasing a real understanding of the other, they were not free but bound by a level of public interest in their lives that precluded any purely private actions. They lived apart and each lived a part. Stockholm gasped at the young and beautiful couple, he such a promising iconoclast and she so bizarrely hell-bent on social suicide. They were fooling nobody. 'The son of the people had carried off the alabaster beauty, the commoner had won the aristocrat, the swineherd had mated with the princess! But at what a price!'[14] What would happen next?

Siri was not the only one straining at her part of the bargain. Strindberg was not writing the star parts for her that he had promised but had returned to work on *Master Olof*, the play that obsessed him and that never had a decent role for Siri. It was rejected yet again by both the Royal Theatre and the New Theatre and he fell back on journalism, flinging himself into founding *The Stockholm Gazette*, a magazine which folded after the first issue.

In the autumn he took a rest from public failure and private turmoil by reinstating the Paris trip he had dramatically cut short the previous year. He went to Paris as a sort of roving cultural reporter for *Dagens Nyheter*. The sight of the burnt-down Tuileries engaged his republican fervour but it was the great Christian bulk of Notre Dame with its overwhelming spiritual presence and its literary connection to Victor Hugo that moved him most deeply. On the Paris stage, he found himself bowled over by the acting of Sarah Bernhardt which he found 'utterly truthful' but disappointed by the plays, old warhorses by Sardou and Dumas which lagged far behind Ibsen and the Northern consciousness in terms of politics and psychology. Art criticism was to become an important and enduring branch of his journalism and he would later become a particularly close friend of Gauguin. On this visit Strindberg was seeing the new art called Impressionism for the first time; perceiving its importance, he wrote three articles for *Dagens Nyheter*, in which Strindberg's journalism once more unintentionally alienated the establishment as he wrote truthfully what he saw and felt. Earlier that year, the secretary of the Swedish Academy of Fine Arts had given a speech to the Academy dismissing the new art as 'sloppy improvisations' unworthy of attention[15] but Strindberg's articles took both the art itself seriously and his readers' right to be as adequately informed as possible. Although Strindberg in fact found Impressionism unsatisfying and its psychology as empty as French plays (an attitude typical of many Scandinavian artists who saw Impressionism as something of a pretty incident on the road leading from Realism to Expressionism and Symbolism), his report is interesting for its impartiality and its success in describing a vivid mind-picture in a few simple words for his newspaper readers who had never seen anything like it.

'In a word – simply a moment's impression; like a photograph when the subject has moved, or like trees photographed in a high wind' (interesting that he should assume his readers so familiar with photographs that he could make the reference) and his description of Sisley bears the test of time: 'The whole canvas is painted in a colourless white, light red and light blue, matte and bloodless – the effect is, as it were, albino. It is meant to be a summer landscape but it looks as though snow or frost lay over it.'[16]

This was the first time he had been abroad, apart from the brief trip to Denmark with the Lamm boys when he had visited Thorvaldsen's studio, and he was homesick. At home, things were going well for Siri. Dramaten Theatre offered her a year's trial. She was to make her debut as the tragic heroine Camille in *A Theatre Piece* by Leroy, due to open on 27 January 1877, but on 13 January her daughter Sigrid died. Sigrid was four years old and according to the autopsy she died of tuberculosis of the brain. Siri's mother suggested that it was a punishment from God for her immoral behaviour. Relations between mother and daughter, already cold, now froze. They ceased to speak. Siri's stage debut went ahead as planned, a mere two weeks after Sigrid's death, and the additional notoriety of monster mother was added to her tarnished reputation. No wonder that *Dagens Nyheter* reported that her debut was received 'with greater interest than is normally given an actress making her debut . . . It is impossible from this performance to prophesy whether Mrs von Essen will become a great actress but it is certain she made a great impression and awoke the public's sympathy.'[17]

Siri never became a great actress, hardly even a good one. On 13 April she opened as Jane Eyre in a stage adaptation of the book by Charlotte Birch-Pfeiffer. Reviews were lukewarm but she had every excuse, for her aunt Mathilde had contacted her to say that her mother was not expected to live long. Siri rushed to the mother she adored and they were reconciled before Betty died on 29 May. In the space of a year, Siri had lost her marriage, her daughter and her mother.

Strindberg had never really liked or respected Siri's mother whom he described as 'a modern Cassandra'[18] and though he gave Siri plenty of acting advice at this time he did not give her exceptional emotional support, indeed he could not while they were living apart. Things might have been different had they been together because it was during this, her time as an actress, that his alabaster Madonna, his pure princess, his gentle, motherly Siri turned into – an actress. She drank like a man and smoked and swore. She treated male members of the company like equals. Casting off her aristocratic propriety, she revelled in a bohemian mess of powder puffs, greasepaint, dirty coffee cups, cigarettes and unbuttoned bodices. Strindberg was appalled. He was always a fastidious man, physically as well as morally. Dirt, drink and disorder held no romantic appeal for him, they belonged to the early poverty that had scarred his mind; besides, he was not championing the idea of female equality so that women could behave as badly as men. The understanding in his mind had been that the elevation of women to equality would generally elevate standards. He, who had found it shocking during his acting career to be required to *dance* in the forenoon, was discomfited by Siri's abrupt moral change. Rows were followed by reconciliations that often began with him frantically covering the button boots of his 'little leopard' with ravenous kisses and went on to their logical conclusion. Strindberg was not exceptional of his generation in finding ladies' boots overwhelmingly erotic but in view of the fact that in his writing boots often play a part in the force fields of submission and control that pulsate between characters, it is reasonable to point out that during his marriage to Siri his letters refer again and again to her boots rendering him helpless. After they had parted (by which time his father had died) boots figure considerably less often in his love letters. Whether this signifies that the boot is specifically conjoined with the two themes of his sexual conquest of the upper class and the son's struggle for conquest over the father, one may conjecture. Maybe the object had simply lost its potency for him.

On 1 July Siri was given a year's contract to act at Dramaten on a basic salary of 2,100 kr plus 3 kr per performance. During the summer she discovered she was pregnant and they agreed to marry on 30 December. They married in their flat in order to avoid attention but as the wedding guests included Siri's ex-husband whose birthday it was, as well as Ina Forstén, Algot Lange and Sofia In de Bétou's mother, the occasion hardly went unnoticed.

The following month, Siri's ballooning silhouette was an object of interest as she played Fru Lynge in Ibsen's *The Pillars of Society*. On 24 January she gave birth to a girl whom they named Kerstin for the good reason that it was a name with no family connections on either side. They handed her over to the midwife and a day later she was dead. Speculation has always surrounded Kerstin's death. It might have been perfectly natural. Infant mortality ran at about thirteen per cent at the time. Or they might have been following the old tradition of allowing the baby to die by a nod and a wink to the midwife who would simply not feed the child.

One would imagine Siri might have felt cursed under a heavy judgement, as if the lives of two daughters and a mother were the Faustian price for the bright twinkle of her stage success, but she talked of this time as a happy period in her life and one may believe her for she was a straightforward woman who was not given to blighting everyday life by shadows and dread.

Strindberg put the death of a baby in the book he began the following year, *The Red Room*, a bracingly unsentimental critique of Swedish society whose pity lay in the pathetic death of a baby and in the portrayal of Sweden's children, 'as they try further to embitter their sad lives by teasing each other and calling each other names'. One can almost hear memory sliding over him in shivers as he pleads the case for a more humane treatment of children in society.

Ten years later he was still thinking about their dead child when he wrote his only straightforward account of the sad incident in a letter to a cousin. The peculiarly cold tone of the letter is because he wrote it from Skovlyst at the time when his marriage was over in all but name. 'When Siri and I married,' he writes,

she was pregnant, as you perhaps noticed. She had been my mistress since her first marriage was dissolved, but not before, for all parties behaved properly throughout, which is why we could not go on seeing each other afterwards. At the end of January 1878, or the beginning of February, accounts differ [he might well be fudging the date on account of the shameful fact that the baby had been conceived out of wedlock], a girl was born three months prematurely, and immediately removed to the midwife's where she died, two days later [according to the register she died the same day]. The midwife gave it emergency baptism and the child was called Kerstin, according to our wishes. It was buried in the New Cemetery and recorded in the register at Jakob's church (christening or death) as 'parents unknown'. The reason why the child was given to the midwife was to protect the delicate position of its mother and father, both of whom were royal civil servants; our intention was in due course to adopt the child.

Then, as events, work and struggles unfolded, the whole matter was forgotten. Yet time and again I heard Siri accuse herself of cowardice in giving the child away . . . Later on, Siri sometimes doubted if the child really had died; she regretted that Fru Johansson had never revealed the number of the grave, in spite of repeated reminders, and now and then she dreamed that the child was still alive.[19]

Remorse was for a much later stage. At present, Strindberg and his little leopard lived happily, glamorously and extravagantly, entertaining generously and enjoying the best of food, clothes, wine, parties and Siri's little button boots in an apartment on Normalmsgatan furnished with von Essen portraits and family heirlooms. The following year the company in which Siri's money was invested suddenly went bankrupt. Everything was gone at a stroke. Strindberg's monetary affairs were a Byzantine labyrinth of loans to and from banks, ious to and from friends, and possessions jumping in and out of pawn shops. On 9 January 1879 he declared himself bankrupt, as his father had done some twenty years earlier. Necessity makes an excellent whip and on 15 February he set about his first novel, prefacing it with a quotation from Voltaire, *Rien n'est si désagréable que d'être pendu obscurément* ('Nothing is so painful as to be hanged in obscurity'), which about summed up his desperation as a writer at this point in his career.

The Red Room takes its title from a private dining room where Strindberg met his friends within Berns Salon,[20] Stockholm's version of a Paris *bal* or *salle de danse*, a popular bang-up-to-the-minute, glass and iron pleasure palace looking like nothing so much as a Mississippi paddle steamer washed up on the green grass of Berzelli Park. Tiers of lacy wrought-iron balconies surrounded the central atrium where young working-class women danced and caroused with men from every walk of life.

Here Stockholm's artists, radicals and *demi-monde* could imagine they were Paris bohemians as they waxed garrulous over absinthe and upstairs, in a little private dining room, Strindberg followed his customary pattern of forming a club of his male friends. All were ambitious, talented and terribly poor. They gave each other impressive nicknames after the Norse gods, maybe to buoy themselves up until they achieved the god-like status their talents deserved. The Red Room where they met was a cod-medieval gloom of arches, vaults and stained glass with murky murals of knights and maidens and yet the novel that bore its name was the utterly revolutionary first modern Swedish novel. In it Strindberg created the first anti-hero whose deadpan comic helplessness in the face of circumstance takes up exactly the tone of his early self-mocking letters from Uppsala.

A breakneck romp without much plot, *The Red Room* held up a mirror to Swedish society. Its vast cast includes slippery press barons, corrupt politicians, venal vicars, conmen evangelists, stout businessmen whose wives chisel the housekeeping, cheating insurance companies, crawling civil servants, a deaf opera critic, philosophers who debate by a dunghill, a hunchback much in demand to model for the Descent from the Cross having the natural physique for it, prostitutes, artists in various stages of selling out the Muse to money, a group of starving idealists who assuage their hunger by reading aloud from cookery books, a baroness, a journalist whose moustaches hang down 'like stalactites' and many more. The text crackles with Strindberg's characteristic fireworks: the journalist digs his pen into the inkwell 'as though he were fishing for the serpent of Midgård', the evangelist bites and tears at his cigar and spits out the fragments 'which whirl around like flies before settling on the backs of the religious tracts', the philosopher 'flicks through the philosophical card pack and turns up an ace' and Falk (the hero) retaliates by 'throwing fistfuls of philosophical snuff into the eyes of his opponent', Pompeian frescoes 'remind one vividly of the path that does not lead to salvation' and an entire chapter on absinthe contains a brilliantly extended metaphor in which café tables are the horses on which one gallops out of the stable in all sorts of directions. The tipsy actress (how the public must have nudged and winked) puts her feet up on the sofa and, growing too warm, unbuttons her bodice as unconcernedly as a man unbuttons his waistcoat after dinner, 'her voice grown gentle and her eyes dropping slowly like the curtains after a death scene'.

For a young man writing with his back to the wall of bankruptcy it is peculiarly understanding and forgiving of the human folly necessary both for society to survive and for every individual to survive within it. The artist requires just as much selfishness to achieve his aims as the banker. Most individual achievement initially depends on a drilling determination entirely devoid of social responsibility. It is impossible to live without suffering or inflicting suffering, however high one's ideals. Death is the only utterly pure, uncorrupted state. At the end of the book one of the young Turks has killed himself but the others have all made their compromises. We laugh, recognise ourselves, feel ashamed but also forgiven.

Publication of The Red Room coincided with the moment when Sweden was bitterly disillusioned with the reforms of the 1860s by which, at last, the king's powers had been limited and government remodelled into the long-awaited two chambers. To what end? The king remained on top of the heap while the farmers in one chamber and the bureaucrats in the other bickered over budgets. A succession of disastrous harvests in the late 1860s led to waves of emigration to a far-off promised land the very existence of which, alongside the standardisation of time throughout the country, introduced a feeling of reality-slip and a general feeling that the importance of individual communities was being sacrificed to a system of political reforms that was not working and that cared neither about the individual nor local issues. In the 1870s the average worker had eleven öre a day to feed himself (100 öre to a krone) while prison inmates, hardly in the lap of luxury, were fed for twenty-five öre.[21] During the time Strindberg was writing The Red Room, Sweden experienced its first big industrial strike. In 1880, the year following publication, the Marxist firebrand August Palm, who later transformed Sweden into a socialist democratic state and spent six years in prison while doing so, arrived on Sweden's shores and began his agitations. Strindberg's bang-on satire pointing out the shortcomings of Sweden's government and the real squalor and poverty of the lower classes turned him involuntarily into John the Baptist to Palm's Christ. *The Red Room* which had started as a comic novel had made him, whether he wanted it or not, the popular hero and champion of Sweden's proletariat.

Published in November 1879 by Seligmann & Co,[22] the book was an immediate popular success. Four swift reprints earned him more than 2,000 kr. Reviews were predictably mixed according to the politics of the papers they appeared in but that only added to the chatter. Few books engage the whole spectrum of the reading public but the poor read it for laughs and for encouragement and the rich read it to unlock the *roman à clef* and shriek at their friends. The two Scandinavian intellects that counted, Henrik Ibsen and Georg Brandes, praised it highly and this conferred on it the imprimatur of literature. Strindberg was widely hailed as a genius but it was characteristic of him that once he had won the coveted laurels he could barely endure their pressure on his brow.

He loved his ideas being taken seriously but they must stand alone without him. Just as he hated being in the audience for his own plays, Strindberg found it intolerable to be the centre of attention and instead of building on the remarkable literary and financial success of *The Red Room* he hid himself away in the Royal Library to lose himself in obscure scholarship. He taught himself Chinese and Japanese. He researched early Swedish travellers in the Far East and Siberia. He charted the dialect names for the ladybird throughout Sweden (garnering his information through a network of travelling salesmen) and concocted links between these common names and the ethnic origins of the Swedish people as suggested by Dr Olof Rudbeck, a previous polymath from Uppsala University whose interesting contribution to science was a theory that all the world's peoples had originated in Sweden.[23] Strindberg wrote a playful piece on the history of aquavit in Sweden, a paper in French on *Relations de la Suède avec la Chine et les Payes Tartares* which won him election to France's La Société des Etudes Japonaises, Chinoises, Tartares et Indo-chinoises and he discovered a long-lost map of Central Asia which won him the silver medal of the Imperial Geographical Society of St Petersburg.

He also began writing for the theatre again. *The Secret of the Guild* (1880) was put on at the Royal Theatre with Siri playing the part of

Margaretha, the wife of one of the two stonemasons who vie to rebuild Uppsala cathedral. In terms of a play centred on the allegory of architecture, *The Secret of the Guild* is not a patch on Ibsen's *Master Builder* written twelve years later, though the characters of Strindberg's two rival masons have all the complicated character traits that made Strindberg's later plays so absorbing. He wrote *Lycko-Pers resa* (*Lucky Peter's Journey*) (1882), a coming together of Ibsen's *Peer Gynt* (1867) and Dickens's *A Christmas Carol* (1843) in which a Scrooge-like old man curses both Christmas and his son Per, an archetypal innocent abroad who is set on a journey with a lucky ring and a good woman. After many adventures, Per discovers that a lucky ring only buys you treachery but the love of a good woman is pure gold. Characters include rats, an elf, a shadow, talking brooms and statues and to this extent a certain interest lies in *Lucky Peter's Journey* foreshadowing the late, mystical plays that break the bounds of realism. The play bowls along and it was a popular success but Strindberg was always rather ashamed of it, considering it a pot-boiler.

23

At last he wrote the big part for Siri, the name part in *Sir Bengt's Wife* (1882). The two of them had worked out the ideas in the play together, partly in reply to Ibsen's *A Doll's House*. The love of Sir Bengt's wife for her husband proves stronger than her need for independence and the play has a sentimental ending whose only excuse is the honeymoon happiness Strindberg and Siri were enjoying at the time. Seven performances earned him about 166 kr and good notices for Siri whose voice, thanks to coaching, had become less grating.

22

On 26 February 1880 their daughter Karin was born and this time Siri took two months before returning to the stage. Strindberg was enchanted by the baby. Home life was idyllic. Siri's pet name for him was *Grisen* (the pig) and she found him 'absolutely adorable when he was in a good mood, particularly if he had taken a little wine, just a little.'[24] Now that they had money from his writing it ran through their hands in a stream of delights. Each was as ungrudging and profligate as the other. They loved to spend freely on themselves, on friends and on nice clothes. He makes sketches of his own outfits and writes to her, 'Don't you need a smart spring coat like this one? [sketch] In men's trouser material, checked, brownish-green with lapels, which I see are in fashion, and suit everyone! Do!'[25]

They were generous to anyone who asked and they loved to entertain. He formed another club, *Klubben* (The Club), whose only aim was 'Pleasure' but this was no orgy of degeneracy but the domesticated pleasure of young-marrieds meeting for dinners, going on outings and shore-side picnics and putting on shows in a little marionette theatre they built at home. Siri made the costumes and Strindberg made a fool of himself; 'Mr Strindberg will debut in the role of the Horse' reads one play-bill.[26]

They waited three months to christen Karin until the return of the *Vega* under the command of the polar explorer Nordenskiöld from its triumphant exploration of the north-east passage round Asia.[27] The expedition's zoologist Anton Stuxberg[28] was to stand godfather to Karin. 'Stux' was a friend of long standing who had been a member of the Red Room and now he joined The Club. He and Strindberg called each other Stux and Strix and wrote each other slangy, boyish letters that made Strindberg feel clever and happy as they mixed masculine joshing with serious scientific speculation and observation. During the voyage of the *Vega*, Stux arranged, at Strindberg's request, the purchase of various Chinese books and no less than 1,050 Japanese books and artefacts intended for Strindberg's attention at the Royal Library. On the *Vega*'s return to Stockholm, Stux borrowed Strix's formal suit for the reception at the Royal Palace to welcome the successful explorers home. Strindberg was not invited; King Oscar who had ascended the throne in 1872 had literary ambitions himself, and envied him.

6 A SHORT SWEDISH HONEYMOON

In the spring of 1881 Siri was again pregnant and Dramaten termi-
nated her contract. Strindberg was indignant and urged her to
contact a new supporter in his life, Ludvig Josephson,[1] the director at
Nya Teatern (the New Theatre). Josephson was a brilliant director
whose first stint in Stockholm's Royal Theatre had ended because the
Swedes refused to take direction from a Jew. He then moved to the
slightly less anti-Semitic Norway, taking over direction at the Christiania Theatre where they merely shouted 'Foreigner' at him which
covered both his Swedishness and his Jewishness. He brought Ibsen's
'unactable' *Peer Gynt* successfully to the stage in a legendary production
with music by Edvard Greig and sets by Frits Thaulow but in 1879 he
was forced to return to Stockholm where he worked outside the establishment at the New Theatre. In January 1881 Strindberg sent him
Master Olof, the play that for the last ten years had hung round his neck
like an albatross. Josephson had already rejected *Master Olof* in one of
its many revisions but this time Strindberg sent the play in its first,
prose version and Josephson responded: 'I have not for many years read
a play that has made such an overwhelming impression on me. I say
plainly that there can never have been a more short-sighted, insensitive,
lazy and un-Swedish theatre board than that which refused this piece
for production.'[2] He promised to produce the play but he was less
enthusiastic about employing the pregnant Siri. She, however, showed
her mettle by taking on her husband's overspill newspaper work and
writing three articles for *Morgenbladet*, one on the need for universal
education, another reporting on a strike and a third attacking the institution of monarchy.

Since the publication of *The Red Room*, Strindberg had received many offers to write in newspapers and magazines. He rejected most of them through libertarian fastidiousness. To voice his point of view independently was one thing but to become a voice in other people's publications was a sacrifice of individual conscience he could not countenance. He was doing himself great damage by this idealistic attitude which caused offence to many influential and sympathetic liberals who were merely presenting him with writing opportunities, not trying to bind him in chains.

He was in the grip of one of his periodic fits of what he called *knappologi* (buttonology), a word he coined for the pedantic classification of some particular branch of knowledge. His last buttonological moment had been the ladybird survey but this time he was afire to write the complete history of the Swedish peoples, no less. Not a history from the point of view of kings, generals, battles and great men but the history of the common man. The two best publishers in Sweden, Seligmann who had published *The Red Room* and Isidor Bonnier, both rejected the idea but, strangely, the conservative publisher Fritzes, whose bookshop had the equivalent of the Royal Warrant, commissioned him to write this potentially socialist history for a fee of ten thousand kr. The book eventually ran to more than a thousand pages and took eighteen months to write, a remarkably short time considering that the spadework was no slavish bookworming. Humankind, not the printed word, was his tutor and the city of Stockholm was his library. A friend of his, Artur Hazelius,[3] was embarking on a similar but even more ambitious project compiling a museum that would present a complete picture of Sweden's past – from peasant dwellings to fish-hooks – the result would be Skansen, the world's first open-air museum. The two young buttonologists went for walks together exploring, scavenging and investigating Stockholm's historical layers, carrying a miner's lantern, a mountaineer's rope and a ball of twine through cellars, crypts, underground tunnels and rooftop walkways like Theseus in the labyrinth. It was enormous fun.

In early summer, Siri and Strindberg left Stockholm, taking baby Karin and a midwife for the approaching confinement. First they stopped at Dalarö, the island where he had jumped ship on the way to Paris and made his melodramatic suicide attempt, but Dalarö had become a fashionable summer resort for Stockholmers; here they would be the focus of gossip and attention. Nearby was a far smaller island, Kymmendö,

25

reachable only by small, private boat. The same family had owned and 27, 29
farmed the little island for the last two hundred years during which time
its size and position had made it exactly suited to sustaining one manor
farm on the medieval pattern. It remained unchanged and as Strindberg
was finishing his history *The Swedish People* he travelled deep back in
time.

> Away they went, out into the open sea where the lighthouse of Huvud-
> skär was blinking. They swept past a broom beacon; a little later a
> white sailing mark, looking like a spook, appeared. One moment they
> saw the remains of a snowdrift, shining like linen laid out to bleach;
> in the next, herring buoys rose out of the blackish water and scraped
> against the keel of the boat as it passed over them. A seagull, startled
> out of its sleep, flew up dazed and frightened, rousing mews and sea
> swallows. The screeching birds made an infernal row. And far in the
> distance, where the stars descended into the sea, could be seen the
> two eyes of a fair-sized steamer, one red and one green . . . And now
> the boat ploughed its way leeward into a narrow channel: the sail had
> to be taken down and they took to the oars. It was not long before
> they had reached another small channel; and then they saw a light
> shining from a little cottage set between alders and pine trees.[4]

Kymmendö's violet-shadowed shoreline rimmed a generous shelter
belt of woods floored with moss and ferns, and all the wild mushrooms
and berries that would be harvested in season and preserved to sustain
the family through the winter. This protective ring of woodland was
pierced by azure inlets that could be sown with decoy ducks and lobster
pots and curtained with fishing nets. Emerald meadows fed generations
of tough, short-legged cattle, wiry sheep and well-muscled workhorses
through the archipelago's short but intensely hot summers and yielded
hay towards the long, iced-in winters.

Strindberg describes the kitchen in the novel he wrote based on his
experiences on the island:

> The kitchen looked like a sailing vessel with its keel turned up as
> though it were floating on its cargo, which consisted of everything
> imaginable under the sun. Away up high, under the sooty roof-truss,
> fishing nets and fishing tackle hung from the beams; and underneath

boards and boat planks were stowed away to dry. There were coils of hemp and flax, grapnel, grappling iron, pieces of forge-iron, bunches of onions, tallow candles, hampers, baskets and boxes for provisions. On a cross beam freshly stuffed decoy ducks were laid out in a long row; sheepskins had been flung over another, and from still another beam dangled sea-boots, knitted jerseys, shirts, underwear, socks and stockings. Fastened between the beams were bread-spits on which – through holes in the centre – were threaded round loaves of bread . . . In the interests of modesty all lights were extinguished at bedtime, because the girls also had their beds in the kitchen . . .[5]

This was the real Sweden, free from asphalt, priests and politicians. There was a timber mill with its pleasant smell of carpenter's glue and pine sawdust and a smithy in which stamping feet raised sparks; in the farmhouse the old peasant ways persisted, such as putting a dried fish-skin into the coffee pot to give a clear brew and counting window-panes to make your dreams come true. All this was grist to *The Swedish People*.

They rented a simple cottage. Strindberg always loved to write in the smallest possible spaces and he built himself a tiny wooden writing hut in the woods. The idea was that he would write there in perfect peace but, almost uniquely among writers, he hated to write without the sound of children's voices in his ears and so he marked a path to the hut with pebbles and other signs for the children to follow alone – without grown-ups. (He decided to call his new-born daughter Greta after the girl in the fairy tale *Hans och Greta*, the English Hansel and Gretel.)

The twenty-eight-year-old painter Carl Larsson[6] had been commissioned to illustrate *The Swedish People* and he joined them on Kymmendö. Four years younger than Strindberg, a solid-looking man with a high-cheekboned face criss-crossed with laughter lines, Larsson's ginger moustaches and goatee beard outdid Strindberg's in baroque curls but his hair never attained comparable volume so he took to theatrical hats: the fez and the velvet beret. The friendship that developed between them led to a correspondence written not so much in their shirtsleeves, Strindberg observed, as in their underpants. They had much in common. Larsson was born in Stockholm's Old Town; his parents had been part of the wave of peasants that moved to the town for work. He felt intimidated and disliked at home. School too was brutal. To support himself through the Academy of Fine Art, he worked as a photographic retoucher and he had spent the last few years scraping by: illustrating books and journals and newspapers, the painter's equivalent of Strindberg's jobbing journalism. He and Strindberg understood each other's strategies. Larsson's weapon in battling life-long depression was to create happy, feel-good art though private self-portraits might include his alter ego, a grotesque and sinister clown doll. For Greta's christening, he drew a big placard to be carried round as an invitation. The christening party lasted two days with music and feasting and dancing. Just as in Stockholm, Siri and Strindberg entertained magnificently, far beyond their means. Crayfish and guests were shipped in from Stockholm and Dalarö. Formal dress was the order of the day. 'Stux' failed to pin his many medals to his lapel and Strindberg took umbrage. His infant daughter was being insulted. Unlikely as it may seem for such a journey, Stux had in fact packed his decorations. The suitcase was broached, medals were pinned and peace was restored.

24

The four summers that Siri and Strindberg spent on Kymmendö were happy, probably because Strindberg could exercise complete control over human contacts, thus enabling him to use his working time efficiently, exclude annoyances and party on his own terms. Kymmendö summers became the holiday branch of The Club with Strindberg, Stux and Larssen addressing each other as Literature, Science and Art, and Siri was Music.

Siri was the greater sailor of the two; she took long sailing trips alone and was not frightened to sail as far as Dalarö to pick up guests. Siri and Strindberg used to go sea-bathing *à deux*. This was most unusual at the time – husbands and wives did not do such things together. After swimming they would lie basking like seals on what is still known as Strindberg's rock and when the sun-slant left the rock they would gather up their things and walk back to the cottage to settle on the porch where he would play his guitar and she would sing as the sky changed from scarlet and gold to the milky tones of advancing night.

This is the romantic recollection of the locals but equally characteristic is an edgy incident when a group of them were bathing:

We used to jump into the water from a rock. Once when Strindberg, naked and ready to jump, looked down into the clear, green water through which one could see the bottom many metres down as distinctly as through a glass, Strindberg hesitated and said to Carl Larsson, 'You lack the moral courage to show your fear and get dressed and go home', which he [Strindberg] then did.[7]

This was a typical example of what Strindberg called his vivisections. It was not enough for Strindberg the anatomist to dissect his own living corpse; he must investigate the living corpses of others as far as he possibly could. The shifting points of entry into such investigations were often small; they might merely involve recognising a sub-threshold impulse common to all, such as the splinter of irrational fear before jumping into the sea. Such synaptic connections are the language of the common unspoken and as such pretty banal and commonly ignored, but it was Strindberg's great genius as a writer committed to exploring the whole truth of every layer of consciousness that he would explore the leap across the synaptic gap even if it resulted in him offending his friends by offering them impossible moral choices (cowards if they jumped and cowards if they did not). It was all part of his compilation of a mental dictionary of common, non-rational impulses running beneath the visible tip of the iceberg of human behaviour, a subliminal subtext threading through his plays, poetry and fiction.

'This inexorabilty', said one of his friends who during their long friendship experienced many vivisections, 'was indeed the final consequence of his ideas, which were pursued to the bitter end, where others would have tempered the light of truth for our poor human eyes, making it at once more attractive and more beneficent . . . Strindberg enquired into the mysteries of motive forces, mechanisms, transformations, and permutations, as an engineer might have done.'[8] Or as he himself put it, he allowed his thoughts to run riot like calves let loose in spring, leaping tail in air over all restrictions, all enclosures. It gave an unusually demanding aspect to his friendship but if your pride could stay the course it was unusually interesting too.

On Kymmendö he would be up before everyone else, working on his history of the Swedish people until it was time for the children's breakfast which he would give them, dandling the little ones on his knee and feeding them so that Siri could sleep long into the day. He made a garden, as was his habit wherever he lived, and to this day he is remembered as a wizard who pushed the bounds of horticulture further than they have been pushed on Kymmendö before or since, magicking melons and globe artichokes and other exotics from the ground. Months before the summer journey, the windowsills in the Stockholm flat would sprout wooden seed-boxes that would accompany them down on the ferry. He planted *Narcissus poeticus* 'beloved of Ovid in his metamorphoses', tulips between cabbages, which he 'thought looked very elegant', and white pelargonium that he thought 'looked like a swarm of white butterflies with purple wings alighted on their dark leaves' and he observed that in his childhood 'there used to be three colours [of flowers] without mid-tones. Now there are all manner of colours so we can write a whole sonata or imitate an artist's palette.'[9] Hybrids were all the fashion.

Siri was restless to resume her acting career. Offers were not forthcoming but in the spring of 1882 Nya Teatern in Helsinki opened its arms to its native daughter with the offer of a guest appearance in *Jane Eyre*. Strindberg made no objection to her going to Finland while he stayed at home with the nursemaid and the children. He had argued for the complete freedom of women to pursue their own career in his chapter on women in *The Swedish People*, and he meant it but that did not mean he could not interfere. While he stayed at home he bombarded her with acting advice: 'Don't be sloppy! Energy! No slacking! Give them full face. Don't act in profile!' but mostly his letters were tranquil and domestic.

Sthlm. 5 May 1882

Dear Siri,

I'm sure you'd like to hear from us at home even though nothing particular has happened I'm writing again.

The little ones are bright and well. Greta can go out today. We're off to Kymmendö next Saturday. . . . Spent several evenings with Josephson. Very friendly. I'm invited to dinner with him on Sunday together with Norman [the composer Ludvig Norman] and several others. When I'd had a few drinks the other evening, I told him that if you didn't act in his theatre I'd create a theatre of my own for you. He looked thoughtful!

I've succeeded in borrowing some money so we are debt-free (even at the Grocer's) and needn't worry all summer! If you need 100 marks, I'll send them! If you don't, that's fine! I've bought some new clothes and now look very smart! . . . Now I've rattled on about everything I know. Greta's hat (Karin's old grey one) is half-finished but there's a piece missing! Eva[10] wants to know where it is! . . .

Come home soon to

Your own

August

'Don't stay there too long', pleads another letter and 'Have you received my last four letters and telegram?'

He never complains about looking after the children; that duty seems to be a constant interest and delight: 'Greta is so clever. She crawls and stands up, supporting herself on furniture!'[11]

Money was beginning to surface as one of several worries. Anxiety always went to his stomach and he complained of 'stomach catarrh'. The patent remedies he took probably did not help. He also started to take tranquillisers that year and to drink heavily. Greta contracted pneumonia and fortunately recovered, and his sister Elisabeth[12] suffered her first bout of mental illness. He was fond of Elisabeth who was sensitive and intelligent. It must have taken bravery on her part to write to him as she was still living with their father; she told Strindberg she felt hopeless and life was pointless.

He responded tenderly: 'It normally takes a long time before people discover their purpose in life though I believe everybody has one, great or small . . . If one can see no point in working, which has happened to me many, many times, then one feels pretty miserable, for then it is only dire necessity which brings the machine fitfully to life.' He recommended she read Dickens and he gave her a job helping with the illustrations to Old Stockholm and The Swedish People. 'Tell me', he ended, 'if you need some modest financial help and I'll let you have it. I know just how soured life can be by money.'[13]

Siri was an extremely poor housewife. Had it not been for her acting career he would have classed her among the abominable parasite women who unjustly enslaved other women to do their proper work but her acting made it all right that she had a cook and a nursemaid. However, one of her duties was to oversee the household accounts and economy was not one of her strong points, as can be seen from the question marks and desperate notes that meander the margins of the account books. 'What has happened to that 4.04 kr?' reads a typical despairing scrawl.

Troubled both by their poverty and her distress he took the opportunity while she was working in Finland to suggest a tactful solution:

Siri, Do you wish for a peaceful summer? Let me take care of the housekeeping! Not because I can do it better than you, but because we can cease to squabble over such trivial things and escape that endless row about there being no money and you having to ask me for more; and because I have learned the worth of money and taught myself economy, but first and foremost because our relationship shouldn't be spoiled by such bagatelles . . . You'll have your own pocket money and you can do what you like with it! Believe me, it'll work. But if you don't want to, just say straight out and that's fine, you can take over the housekeeping again. You mustn't believe there's any ulterior motive behind this – only the ambition for our great happiness!

She allowed him to take over but he was no better at bookkeeping. Much too free-handed with loans to his friends and love of parties, food and fun, the money ran through his hands just as fast.

The Swedish People was proving as burdensome as Sisyphus's stone and he had to take a further eight months' unpaid leave to work on it. Finally, in August 1882, he gave up the post at the Royal Library altogether in order to finish it, sacrificing his only steady income. On 30 December 1881 Ludvig Josephson had put on *Master Olof*, as he had promised. With a running time of five hours, it tested the audience but the reading of the historical episode it was based on was uncontroversial, the characterisation intriguing and the story-telling as lively as Shakespeare. Even the right-wing critics conferred stately approval and there was an air of the establishment lowering the gangplank if he wished to come aboard and he finished *The Swedish People* in April 1882 in a warm glow of confidence and expectation. He had written a thousand pages in eighteen months. Even Klemming, the occultist Chief Librarian at the Royal Library to whom the flesh was pretty unimportant, remarked on how thin and ill-looking he had become. Strindberg himself dared not go out in company for his brain 'felt like a spinning wheel'. Nor did he dare take a holiday from writing which was now their only source of income. *Master Olof* had earned him a mere 750 kr and he reckoned he needed 6,000 a year. *The Swedish People* was first published in instalments. On the back cover of the first instalment he wrote a trailer for his history which tore into Sweden's best-loved historian Erik Gustaf

9

Geijer whose history he hoped to supplant. Geijer's histories had done much to shape Sweden's consciousness of its identity and provide it with some self-confidence during its fragile immediate past. Strindberg claimed that while Geijer 'counted only the King's lackeys as the Swedish people' he, Strindberg, would tell the real story from below, from the view of ordinary people 'in the small circumstances of their quiet lives.' This was seen as politically inflammatory and culturally insulting; certainly, it demonstrated recklessness for his own future prospects in the literary establishment of Stockholm.

Strindberg was an amateur historian writing from his own observation and his wide-ranging narrative contained innumerable mistakes. The experts who had been insulted by the book's provocative trailer before they even opened it, jumped on his every inaccuracy with glee. He had mis-dated a bronze razor and so on. Carl Larsson who had produced illustrations to Strindberg's detailed briefs was dragged down with him, the illustrations being more imaginative and atmospheric than historically precise. Larsson and Strindberg's view of history was mercilessly unpicked.

Surprised but defiant, Strindberg re-named Kymmendö the den of nihilists and settled down to write his next book in cut-throat mood. 'When one goes into battle, impartiality is a crime', he wrote to Edvard Brandes,[14] and into battle he went with a new satire, *The New Kingdom*. *The Red Room* had been an affectionate satire on the theme of youth's aspirations, a book that was easy to love and that immediately became beloved. *The Swedish People* had been an attempt at an extremely interesting and timely idea but was over-extended, hurried, under-researched and finally far too personal. Whatever interested him had been given too much space and whatever did not, had not. The history had not fully conveyed the strength of his passion as a utopian and a reformer, his outrage at the lack of social progress in a time of peace and prosperity, or his intense anger at the transparent strategies exercised by the government and the middle class in order to preserve their own comfort at whatever price but this he would do in his new book, *The New Kingdom: Satirical Sketches from the Era of Assassinations and Jubilees*. It let rip in ten shatteringly direct chapters which did not spare church, state or big business. This new kingdom was ruled by crooks who support and protect one another. The chapter on the nobility for example was named 'After the Shining Example of our Forefathers', taking its title from part of the inscription on the portico over Stockholm's House of Nobility, and it was narrated by a bedbug who had lived in the House of Nobility for the last hundred years, burrowing about in its hidden corners. In each chapter, Strindberg named names – as if he needed to make more enemies. A chapter called 'Moses' did not spare those Jews whose money supported Sweden's crooked establishment. Knowing the response this chapter would elicit, he wrote to his Jewish friend Edvard Brandes:

I am regarded as an anti-Semitic and have satirised the Jews in my new book. I do not hate the Jews, only *our* servile, medal-greedy, despotic, oppressive Jews who with all the power of wealth (they have found it easy to cheat the stupid Swedes of their money!) work, in their ruthless way to support the reaction against us. Thus they are your enemies as well as mine.

Uppsala University has three docents in Swedish literature, for example [Karl Warburg, Henrik Schück and Ernst Meyer], all smallminded, stupid conservative Jews who carp at everything new. All (virtually all) our publishers are Jews who sell the works of Luther and the New Testament in order to appear liberal, but if one really wants to be liberal in politics or literature, just try! It's simply their misfortune to be Jews and I'd like them as little if they were Swedes! They are foreigners and behave in a hostile, foreign manner towards us; well, that is their right, but I am also within my rights when I defend myself.

So this isn't a question of Jewry, nor even of Jews, but of *our* Jews in Sweden who act illegally as a syndicate.

Let us stick together and not part company over a detail. You're no Jew because you have publicly forsworn Jewry [the Brandes brothers were free-thinkers; their family name was Cohen but they had taken up the more neutral name of Brandes], that's why I have felt able to speak to you about this and I'm surely above suspicion of being so narrow-minded as to be an intolerant religionist or racist.

Your brother would have been given a chair at Stockholm University by now if the Jews weren't so afraid he'd compromise their syndicate. The loss is more ours than his![15]

The book had as great an effect as he could have wished. Reaction in the corridors of power was shock and a sort of surreptitious delight at the audacious truths he had dared speak. Karl Warburg, one of Strindberg's three 'small-minded, stupid, conservative Jews' at Uppsala University, proved not so small-minded as he defended the book on libertarian grounds in *Handelstidningen*. Count Snoilsky, one of Sweden's great poets but never its staunchest moral hero, did not dare express his sympathy directly but conveyed a message of support via Klemming.[16] The right-wing press hoped to crush the book under the weight of silence but the rest generally felt that truths had been told, though it was a pity that the arguments had been robbed of their essential weight by Strindberg's persistence in naming names. To which he, maybe with a regretful look back over his shoulder at the mess he had made when publicly debating Dante at Uppsala University, replied that they need only look to Dante for the great example of satire which is all the more powerful for naming names.

An unpleasant pamphlet attacking him was published pseudonymously[17] and his friend Pehr Staaff leapt to his defence with a counter-attack. So great was all this tumult that Strindberg started to talk about leaving Sweden. He asked his publisher Claës Looström to advance him two thousand francs 'so I can travel and get out of here' but it was not forthcoming. He rented a studio, ostensibly to have somewhere to work in peace but also as a bolt hole. Siri was left to deal with the considerable fallout at home. She, fortunately, felt *The New Kingdom*'s satire was lively and fresh if a little childish, and she took the bracing view that if he as a writer felt that the attacks against him were too personal, those were the rules of the game he had set up and it did not behove him as a civilised being to take the game further by answering personal attacks with more personal attacks.[18]

At this moment two of his Jewish supporters came to his rescue. Josephson commissioned the play *Sir Bengt's Wife* which solved the immediate vacuum in Siri's acting career and Karl Otto Bonnier,[19] the young sprig whose father Albert had founded the immensely influential and progressive publishing house of Bonniers in 1865, took the boat from Stockholm to pay Strindberg a visit on Kymmendö. Strindberg had already done some small things for his father, including translating the English nursery rhyme *Baa Baa Black Sheep* into Swedish. Now the bright and charming son came with a generous offer: Bonniers wished Strindberg to become one of their authors. As they discussed the proposition, young Bonnier followed Strindberg round his vegetable garden where the author seemed much more concerned for his melons than his next book, snipping a stem here and tying up a tendril there as Bonnier's terms became increasingly generous. Eventually, agreement was reached. Bonniers would publish his next book (of poems, as it happened, a Bubo in his brain had burst, he said, and nothing but poetry was gushing out) and they would pay off his debt to Looström. Somehow 2,000 francs turned into a letter of credit for 3,500 francs and on 12 September 1883 with money in his pocket and the next book sold, August, Siri, the two children and the faithful nanny Eva left Sweden for France. Strindberg was thirty-four, with a spring in his step and a world to conquer. Siri was thirty-three and dispirited, she knew she was looking at the end of the illusion. Once upon a time he had written to her in the maelstrom of love: 'Beloved! Come! Fulfil your high goal! You can be an actress. I shall create a theatre just for you . . . You have a great crime on your conscience! You wanted the reward of genius without risking the martyrdom – oh it's a sweet martyrdom! Fulfil your calling, become the greatest actress or author in the land!'[20]

She had only half undertaken the martyrdom. She had enjoyed playing the actress rather than working at her acting. The babies had come; the great roles never had. She could not blame him. He had encouraged her, used his contacts to beg for roles for her and he had been generous with technical advice. Despite Strindberg's later great fame as a playwright who portrays the scorpion dance involved in marriages whose two protagonists are doing everything to undermine each other, not even his most hostile critic has cast doubt on the straightforward intention in his heart that she should succeed. Her love of partying had turned into a fondness for the bottle that was becoming remarked, even among friends. It had cost Strindberg the friendship of his beloved Stux who now had married Helga Franckenfeldt,[21] an actress he had met through the Strindbergs. Helga was a good sport who joined in the merriments of The Club where she was never too proud to act as waitress but at some point she decided that Siri's 'loose morals' would tarnish her reputation and she could no longer afford to associate with her. Strindberg took offence. Stux and Strix ceased to speak to each other. The feud lasted ten years. Other men friends like Strindberg's cousin Dr Edvard Selander had remarked on Siri's embarrassing behaviour. Selander described a morning drinking spree when,

> To interrupt the bacchanal was impossible because of Fru Strindberg's obstinate opposition, and towards the end of the morning the party

was more than merry, with the young lady and Frithiof Kjellberg completely drunk. When I mentioned this unfortunate situation to Strindberg, he said it didn't help to cause a scene and that he couldn't absolutely forbid her or she would drink in secret and it would be worse.[22]

When they left for France, Siri was pregnant again. She knew that when they reached their destination she could not hope for a career on the French stage. They stood on the platform, smartly dressed as always, with their children, their nanny Eva, their trunks and cases of books and the blue and white pram with its milk-stained top. Siri's career as an actress, apart from her creation of the role of Miss Julie in Denmark in 1888, was over.

'Next summer we will be back on Kymmendö', he promised, but six years would pass before they came back to Sweden. First they would live in Grez, Paris, Lausanne, Pegli, Genoa, Lausanne, Chexbres, Geneva, Lausanne, Paris, Luc-sur-Mer, Paris, Grez, Othmarsingen, Weggis, Gersau, Issigathsbühl, Copenhagen, Klampenborg, Taarbeck and Skovlyst, and the time abroad would transform him from an essentially Swedish writer into a European voice.

7 RABBLE ROUSER

Being the filthy-minded writer I am I have made a special study of the water closets in the hotels [on this journey to France]. The most dazzling invention was the one I found in Hamburg. There, one excreted into something that looked like a soup tureen, and on looking down there was nothing to be seen, despite the fact that one could have sworn to the deposition of a couple of metres; the bowl was still shiny enough to serve genuine turtle soup in and no splashing of water had been heard as it had in Stralsund, where the seat activated a stream of water as soon as one sat down. It was quite magical.[1]

The water-closet at the end of the journey was situated in Grez-sur-Loing where the Scandinavian artists' colony included Carl Larsson. Following the criticism of his illustrations to *The Swedish People*, Larsson had returned to Paris and put all his efforts into a large narrative history painting swarming with carefully detailed objects in the genre beloved by the coagulation of worthies that formed the jury of the Paris Salon – and they rejected it. Without either admission to the Salon or a scholarship, all avenues seemed closed to him. Weakened by poverty and hunger, Larsson fell ill and became suicidal. He cut up the painting and gave the pieces to his friends in a gesture so redolent of the farewell suicide note that the friends became alarmed.[2] Karl Nordström, a fellow artist, coaxed him to move to Grez on the edge of the Forest of Fontainebleau where he might recover his health and spirits in the little village that had inspired Henri Murger to write *Scènes de la vie de bohème* on which Puccini based *La Bohème*. Robert Louis Stevenson, the Goncourt brothers and Corot had all found solace from *Paris intense* in Grez's unpretentious landscape of soft meadows and orchards floating on violet-tinted river mists that Strindberg lyrically describes in his book, *Among French Peasants*. Larsson joined the group of Scandinavian and American artists practising the fashion for painting *en plein air*, and it was the making of him. Just as Strindberg in writing *The Red Room* and *The New Kingdom* had heeded those great prophets of modernism Zola, Baudelaire and Georg Brandes and ignored the fictitious merit attached to histori-cism, instead portraying modern life and concerns, so now Larsson was painting to the same principles, and finding his métier.

When Strindberg and Siri descended from the train, Larsson was on the platform to meet them. Sweden's Zola was descending to join Swe-den's Gustave Doré, Larsson proclaimed, and they fell into the old pattern of parties. Strindberg refers ironically to orgies but although the Finnish sculptor Ville Vallgren[3] observed that Siri sometimes drank too much, they hardly sound the height of depravity as Strindberg describes them:

> [I] put together an orchestra made up of Trumpet, Flute and Guitar (Vallgren, Aug Sg. and Spada[4]) and discovered there was smoked herring and a pale Eau de Vie that smelled of *brännvin* [Swedish brandy] in the village store; I had just bought a perch rod and carried out some preliminary research into the habits and diet of French fish when, as I said, the cold arrived and we took refuge in Paris.[5]

Here he made the acquaintance of two Norwegian writers: the famous Bjørnstjerne Bjørnson[6] and the amiable Jonas Lie[7] who acted as a benevo-lent father-figure to the Scandinavian colony abroad and was unfailingly kind to everyone including the disgraced Oscar Wilde during his Parisian exile. Bjørnson was another matter. Fifty-one years old, he was a literary lion more famous than Ibsen, a man with many attitudes, few beliefs, fewer unselfish impulses and enormous influence. They called him the uncrowned king of Norway and Bjørnson was not shy of acting the part. In winter he wore a wolf-skin coat and a Scottish tam-o-shanter to write at an open window for all to see. He was a successful novelist, poet and playwright who would be awarded the 1903 Nobel Prize for literature. His journalism was influential and his politics effective but not so radical as to impede the progress of his ambition that moved forward as smoothly as a train on shining rails. Bjørnson was a powerful figure in the nationalist movement that won Norway independence from Sweden in 1905 and he wrote the words to Norway's National Anthem. In short, he occupied exactly the position of respected revolutionary in relation to Norway that Strindberg longed to occupy in relation to Sweden.

Following the publication of *The New Kingdom*, Bjørnson had written an encouraging note to Strindberg and, on meeting, the two men straight away took a passionate liking to one another. Wearing his mantle as Scandinavian sage, Bjørnson advised Strindberg to stay away from Sweden where his energy would be squandered in parochial battles with petty minds. His considerable talents should, instead, be exercised on the international stage. Strindberg replied that they must get back to Sweden soon: Siri wished to resume her acting career. Whereupon in January 1884 Bjørnson wrote to Ludvig Josephson:

> His wife doesn't want to stay abroad long as she wants to go home to act in comedies. Swedes here say she can't act, that she hasn't the grace or the voice (too dry) for the stage. If this is so, why don't you tell him, Josephson? Firmly, strongly, incessantly. He thinks she has a considerable acting talent and has made a great hit. He thinks it's the King and his friends who want to block her career and that she's being persecuted for her husband's sake.[8]

Bjørnson told Strindberg straight out that Siri ought to be content to be the wife of a famous man, it was vocation enough for a woman and she should devote herself to the role but Strindberg disagreed, he still believed in Siri's talent and he still wished their marriage to be one of two equal working partners.

Strindberg was homesick. Bjørnson and Lie were applying too much pressure and as they tried to seduce him into becoming a spokesman for their international radicalism, their efforts were achieving the opposite effect. His thoughts turned ever back to Sweden. He and Siri were finding it difficult to settle in Paris. He felt self-conscious speaking French and Siri found it difficult to manage domestically. She did not find motherhood the all-consuming bliss that Strindberg insisted a proper woman ought; instead, the ghost of her career haunted her brain and she wanted to go back to Sweden to act. She was lonely, it was difficult to heat the apartment, the nanny could not speak French and so Siri had to go out and buy fuel and food. As for French food! When a friend sent them a bag of Swedish dried peas they seized on it with pathetic joy, telling all their friends and immortalising the peas in prose before finally eating them in a ceremonial feast seasoned with sentiment and nostalgia. When Christmas came, it was made as Swedish as possible. Between October and the New Year they moved apartments three times, their physical restlessness demonstrating the restlessness within Strindberg's soul as he wrote a long and beautiful cycle of poems called *Somnambulist Nights*. It tells of the journey undertaken by the poet's soul over five nights as it flies like a bird over Sweden and Paris, each night alighting on a high vantage point and surveying a different cultural landscape. The first night he lands on the cross of the church in which he was confirmed, and we are hardly surprised to find him examining organised religion and finding it cruel, unforgiving, irrelevant to daily life and unworthy of its founder, the pure Christ whom he loves. The second night atop the National Museum, he rummages through the great world of ideas and develops a thought that will tear at him and cause him great confusion in the coming months: the idea that any man-made art is infinitely inferior to the naturally created. By implication the very poem he is writing and we are reading has itself no value, nor can any of his work have value, and yet writing is all he knows, his only means to mend the broken society he surveys. The third night atop the Royal Library, he argues that all the wisdom in books cannot make our lives better because they only advance endlessly contradictory theories:

> What progress Kant and his pure reason
> Since he denies us air and freedom?
> Fichte with his precious ego,
> Hegel with his endless nego,
> Schelling's absolute identity,
> What a heap of contradictions.
> If only two agreed together
> Then we might have dared believe.
> But when each screams the *only* truth,
> The beating soul can only grieve.
> Mired in theory, ever hoping,
> Ever ready to believe,
> Pilgrims progress,
> Darkness deepens,
> Books can never heal our pain.

Lighting on the Observatory, it is not the stars above that catch the eye but electricity's spreading light below. 'Holy twilight' has been outshone by science's glare. He enters a church where a choir of high-pressure steam machines conducts a hissing song of praise to the glorification of electromagnets. Steam pumps invade the rhyme; scientists take over; the church houses new gods:

Now upon the church's altar
A new Lord of power and might
Face as rigid as a Psalter,
Illumined by electric light –
Hail our god Denis Papin!
[the inventor of all sorts of steam-related wonders such as the
    condensing pump, safety valve, steam piston, etc]
Hail Papin, and Hail your cauldron!
This is your time – now, today.
But the world will barely hymn you
Ere another grabs your throne . . .
Edison is toiling up that
Glorious hill to steal your bone . . .

Seeking solace in Nature's empire, he wends his way towards the Jardin Zoologique only to find that humankind has turned the natural world into something spurious and artificial, a 'nature improvement company' for its own gratification.

Finally as the somnambulist awakes he paints the image of himself at his desk as he thinks these thoughts and records them, painting a picture of the poet's lair replete with symbolic objects: walls hung with pictures, a ticking clock; a lamplighter passing outside the window illuminating the world outside by the new means of gasoliers. The poet turns to face us. His eyes are large as teacups and as we meet them we see they are the sightless orbs of a dead man. As his pen moves over the white paper we remark the movement of his arms, we hear the scratching of the nib but we see that the paper remains unmarked. 'Look,' he says, 'I'm starting to write in white!'

This desperate negation went deeper than exile, deeper than Siri drinking and dreaming of the stage, into a terrible internal divide and contradiction. Tired of books' eternal fuss, he nevertheless had an absolute need to believe in an idea, a religion or a philosophy. All was hollow and meaningless if an intellectual shape could not be imposed upon the purpose of existence. The poem indicates that he felt able to divine purpose, beauty and truth only through the natural world. Logically, with his great talent for horticulture, he should have exchanged his pen for the spade then and there, to spend the rest of his life digging for truth in his garden but naturally he did not take this route. Instead, he opened the books of the great nature-centred thinkers, Jean-Jacques Rousseau and Tolstoy. He also read Max Nordau's recently published *The Conventional Lies of Civilisation*[9] and *What is to be Done?* (1863) by the Russian anarchist Chernyshevsky,[10] a book that greatly influenced Lenin. Chernyshevsky advocated revolution in order that society might 'return' to a contented rustic socialism that had never in reality existed, proposing a system based on traditional peasant structures that would provide everyone with guilt-free food and church-free virtue.

In January 1884 Strindberg moved the family to Switzerland, land of Rousseau and Liberty. He needed to sort his own ideas from those of the gentle and persuasive Lie and the attractive steamroller Bjørnson. He wrote a combined letter to them both:

> I'm collecting my many new thoughts, awakened, dear friends, in your company. But I'm trying to sort out mine from thine, for you gave me such a going over that I came away with a great deal that was yours . . . Imagine! I've never seen the Alps before! . . . We thought at first they were clouds, but when it dawned on us they were mountains our minds turned somersaults and we were so overwhelmed that my wife wept and I scampered about the train compartment like a squirrel so as to see out of both the windows at once . . . The spirit of Rousseau pervades this wonderful neighbourhood . . . Were I to strain my eyes I could see the nihilists in Geneva![11]

They settled in Ouchy by Lake Geneva where Byron had written *The Prisoner of Chillon*, that great political poem hymning the liberty which Strindberg now hoped might be realised through Chernyshevsky's rustic socialism.

Strindberg had dedicated *Somnambulist Nights* to Bjørnson and Lie and they responded generously to the stream of letters that poured from his pen over the coming months as he tried to 'sort out my old rat's nest of a soul. My aversion to art as falsification has taken on a kind of fanatical religious character . . . Bonnier pressed me all autumn to write a novel, because novels sell'. (He had, instead, been sending Bonnier a series of political pamphlets that certainly would not sell.)

> Now come the consequences! People no longer read me! I really am dying. My words fly off into empty space! This is my dilemma! To be useful, I must be read! To be read I must write 'art', but I consider 'art' immoral. So: whether to die with a pure soul or carry on with what is for me an immoral activity! Solve that! And then, when I've pondered and fought, along comes that black devil who dwells in my heart, and mocks everything: the epicurean spirit of art awakens in me, and I long for the pleasure that producing works of art affords. And it is tremendous pleasure, which is precisely what makes it immoral.[12]

Over the next period he often compares writing fiction to masturbation. Fiction was for 'little pussy poets who write masturbatory books', he wrote, and 'the deliberate conjuring up of hallucinations at one's desk seems to be like masturbation . . . It is this struggle against my new calling which is undermining my health.'[13] He resolved to eschew fiction with its specious artistry. Yet how could he be unaware that the money they lived on was supplied by the Christmas run of the fairy-tale fantasy *Lucky Peter's Journey* which had earned 30,000 kr from fifteen performances and his publisher was begging him for more of the profitable stuff?

Unfortunately for literature there was a young editor of a small-circulation political magazine happy to take Strindberg's political pieces. Hjalmar Branting[14] then editor of *Tiden*, was to be one of the great politicians of the century rising to become Sweden's first Socialist Prime Minister in 1920 and the architect of Europe's most successful Socialist state. Branting never ceased to value Strindberg as a political thinker and even when they were old men together they were still debating politics over a game of skittles. Now in the youth of the relationship, while Branting was publishing Strindberg's political pieces and Strindberg was loudly eschewing fiction, he was simultaneously badgering Branting for material on which to base his next piece of fiction:

> I now want to do a Nihilist story, set in Geneva! Send me, on loan s.v.p., photographs of two of the most sympathetic Russian nihilists you have, a young man and a woman, along with a couple of Nihilist

books, beautiful but not savage! I already have *Unterirdische Russland*. Send a novel and a pamphlet on their doctrines as well as something on the wretched situation in Russia – to borrow! Do it now, straight away! But they must be beautiful. What are the most beautiful Russian things in this line?[15]

The hero in Chernyshevsky's book slept on a bed of nails and ate only meat to build up his strength for the Revolution. It was part of anarchist-nihilist discipline to purify the body to prepare it for action. Strindberg fell short of the bed of nails but he began to take unusual care of his body, drinking nothing stronger than red wine, taking cold baths, fencing lessons, riding lessons and long walks in the countryside around Geneva that he thought 'as beautiful as heaven'.[16] One day, during a carriage ride together with Siri and a Swiss lady and her brother, he jumped down and asked the brother to keep the horses at full clip while he ran behind.

To this day I can see him running after our carriage covered in dust, his curly hair sticking to his temples. 'Aren't you getting tired my beloved piggie?' his wife called to him, but he only shook his head and kept on running, keeping up with us all the way. We stopped at a crossroads, and he swung himself up, breathless but proud and contented, onto the driver's seat again.[17]

His bent for buttonology surfaced once more in a mighty plan to study the peasantry of Europe and write a comprehensive record of its languages and ways before they disappeared for ever beneath the standardisation imposed by galloping technological progress. 'I intend to spend a few summers of my life discovering Europe the way Stanley discovered Africa', he confided to Carl Larsson with an eye to Larsson and his sketchpad keeping him company. The book was to be called *Through the Continent of the Whites*, a play on Stanley's *Through the Dark Continent*. But first he must take a look at Italy. Siri was eight months' pregnant but he would not dream of travelling without her and the children and the nanny.

'God, what a disappointment!' he wrote to Larsson from Genoa:

The oranges had me fooled for a day, but then! The Mediterranean? The Jungfrufjärden is far more beautiful! It's just a straight line like this! _____ The olive trees are horribly grey. The countryside looks like a garden and uglier than the oil paintings. The pine trees look pretty much the same. And the people? Moleskin and slouch hats! Not at all picturesque, old man![18]

Later he put his personal disillusion with the long-idealised Italian landscape into *A Dream Play* and, practically verbatim, into the mouth of Jean, the valet in *Miss Julie*.

By April 1884 they were back in Switzerland and on 3 April Siri gave birth to their third child. They called him Hans after the other child in the creepy fairy tale *Hans och Greta*. In May, with his head full of fatherhood, Strindberg began a new book. Money had run out and he was writing at breakneck speed to pay off the hotel in which they were staying. The book was called *Giftas* (*Getting Married*).

The question of marriage was intimately bound up with *den store nordiske krigen om seksualmoralen* (the great northern battle on sexual morality) or the Woman Question as it was also known. It covered the changing role of women in industrialising societies, education for women, votes for women, property rights, the right to a career; in short all the issues of gender asymmetry that commanded attention, debate, legislation and varying degrees of procrastination throughout Europe. Sweden's women, for instance, achieved education far earlier than many of their European sisters but they had to wait until 1919 to vote – which was early compared to their Swiss sisters (1971) but late compared to Finnish females (1906). In 1873 the Swedish Society for Married Women's Property Rights had been formed with the objective of giving the woman rights over any property she brought to the marriage as well as any property she inherited during the marriage and any income she earned as a married woman. This was not fully achieved until 1921. A married woman was at the mercy of her husband financially unless a marriage settlement had been entered into and so a woman must decide between marriage, which would make her dependent but give her a social position, and becoming an old maid in which case she might keep her property but be stripped of social standing. Morally, marriage also presented an appalling compromise for the wife who must not betray an improper enjoyment of sex but remain frigid but fertile, a sort of fecund virgin, while tolerating a husband with a priapic member whose whopping needs were respected by society. These double standards offended Strindberg who as a husband rejoiced in Siri's enjoyment of

40

the marriage bed. Since their marriage he did not dream of visiting brothels like the majority of his fellow husbands: 'that collection of semi-cretins who lived like dogs in secret but respected each other so long as there was no scandal . . . while society with all its hidden vices, sat there dealing out social status according to a scale of values that put honesty far below nil. This community was nothing more than a tissue of lies', as he put it in *Getting Married*,[19] twelve short stories dealing with the conundrums of how to achieve a successful marriage within society's structure of hypocrisy and inequality.

Since his schooldays when the parson's daughter had taken up her silent position at the back of the classroom, Strindberg had championed sexual equality. On marrying Siri he had taken legal steps to preserve her financial independence and with it her dignity and self-esteem. His pro-women stance, seen as left-wing in political circles and idiotically treacherous by most men, had been most comprehensively set out in *The Swedish People* (1881) in which he devoted a whole chapter to the position of women throughout the ages, praising the strong women of Scandinavia who had taken responsibility for power and used it wisely and well, such as the great Queen Margareta who founded the Kalmar Union,[20] but his admiration changed to exasperation when it came to the affected manners of the eighteenth century when, as he saw it, women were seduced by the snobbery and materialism of court society into selling their independence for a mess of gallantry. He raged at them for conniving at gyniolatry, as he called it, presiding over their own degradation as they willingly ascended the pedestal, trading real power for the currency of the boudoir and the jewel-box and falling in with the charade of the gallant and the helpless coquette. The chapter concerning women ends with his hopes that modern woman would put this gyniolatry behind her and work to pursue her own career while fulfilling her duties as wife and mother.

Now, three years after writing *The Swedish People*, he was a married man with three children, an inadequate income and a wife unwilling or unable to pursue her career. His wife and children gave him the greatest possible domestic delight but he also understood that his needs had brought Siri a degree of unfair imprisonment and frustration; in the preface of his new book *Getting Married* he set out a feminist manifesto so scandalously progressive that it won him many new enemies:

WOMAN'S RIGHTS

Which the laws of nature would grant her, but of which, thanks to our perverse social system (and not as a result of male tyranny) she has been deprived.

1. The right to the same education as men . . . *etc.*
2. Boys and girls shall attend the same school . . . *etc.*
3. The girl shall have the same right to 'run wild' and choose the company she pleases.
4. There shall be complete equality between the sexes which will do away with that revolting form of hypocrisy called gallantry . . . *etc.*
5. Women shall have the vote . . . *etc.*
6. Women shall be eligible for all occupations . . .
7. The above laws will mean the moral code will become less rigid, for a mother has to learn tolerance . . . no one knows better than she how patient and unexacting you must be with the erring children of man.
8. Women shall be exempt from military service. Anyone who regards this as unjust should take into consideration the fact that nature extracts compensation from her in the form of heavy maternal duties.

And on it goes into a second list of another fourteen points that include:

9. Deeds of Settlement and the judicial divisions of property shall be obligatory on all married couples.
10. When he marries a man shall be obliged to take out a life insurance . . . this is more especially his duty if he takes a woman away from a gainful occupation.
11. A woman should keep her own name on marriage rather than taking her husband's title in its feminine form.
12. Separate bedrooms shall be the rule from the beginning. A practice so offensive to decency as a common bedchamber brings its own punishment and gives rise to confusion, distaste, satiety, and even worse. This rule will make a woman's position freer and will give her the right to possess her own body.
13. If a woman is solely her husband's wife . . . she should receive an allowance for clothes and recreations . . . she shall not receive clothes as presents for which she has to say thank you. Moreover, she shall have the *right* to pay for her amusements herself, even

when she is out with her husband, and thus be spared from always being *treated*.

14. If a married woman is gainfully occupied and does not run her own home, she shall be obliged to contribute from her earnings as much to the household as her husband does. . . .

Finally, he attacks 'the people who have made woman what she is [in our society], the marriage that is sanctioned by the Church and the form of emancipation invented by man, namely "gallantry" which in the author's opinion is the silken thread by which women are enslaved.'[21]

Some of the stories in *Getting Married* end happily, some not. Sometimes the man has the upper hand, sometimes the woman and sometimes it is circumstance that dictates fate. They are stories of subtlety and insight. In the story called 'Bad Luck', for instance, the entire balance of power between the newlyweds turns on a discussion concerning the recipe for salad dressing:

> At dinner all the food was sweetened with sugar. He hated sweet food but he did not want to upset her. However, he did ask if it was her idea or the cook's. It was hers; it was the way they did it at home. The salad was dressed with cream, egg and sugar. He blurted out another question. Wouldn't she prefer it dressed with oil? No, oil didn't suit her. But of course they could prepare a salad dressed with oil especially for him. No indeed, he didn't want to make a fuss. Better leave things as they were.

He sent the manuscript of *Getting Married* to his publisher, nervous that it might attract prosecution for obscenity. Bonnier felt confident that they would not be prosecuted but he felt a little anxious about the sexual frankness and the relaxed, colloquial language that Strindberg used to tell these undramatic little stories in which nothing happens but everything happens. Strindberg had a different concern. Almost as soon as he had delivered the manuscript it dawned on him that he might have presented his enemies with opportunity to ban the book on the grounds of blasphemy. In the first story, 'The Reward of Virtue', he had referred to the Christian rite of Holy Communion as 'the impudent deception practised with Högstedt's Piccadon [wine] at 65 öre the half gallon, and Lettström's maize wafers at 1 kr a bag which the parson claimed to be the body and blood of Jesus of Nazareth, the political agitator who had been executed 1800 years ago.'[22]

33

54   Strindberg painted by Christian Krohg in Berlin, 1893. Henrik Ibsen bought the picture and
hung it in his writing room, once remarking; 'He is my mortal enemy, and shall hang there and
watch while I write.' Norsk Folkemuseum, Oslo, NF. 00327.

55   Strindberg sometimes tuned his guitar haphazardly, to allow chance to play a role in composition. Nationalmuseum, Stockholm (Photo: Hans Thorwid).

56 (ABOVE) Edvard Munch's 1892 exhibition in Berlin's Equitable Palast. Strindberg's portrait stands on the easel. Munch Museum, Oslo.

57 (LEFT) *Stanislaw Przybyszewski* by Edvard Munch, 1895, charcoal and oil on cardboard. The watermarks caused by a leaking studio were welcomed as illustrating Strindberg's theory of the role of chance in artistic creation. Munch Museum, Oslo.

58 (LEFT)   Edvard Munch, *c.*1894 when he and Strindberg were close friends. Munch Museum, Oslo.

59 (BELOW)   Dagny Juel, standing at the piano.

Auch ein Kompromiß.

Der Papst hat gegen die Aufführung von „Salome" in Rom sein Veto eingelegt. Um sein Bedenken zu
zerstreuen, hat sich Salome entschlossen, den Kopf des Modernisten Haeckel auf der Schüssel zu präsentieren.

60 (ABOVE) The Civic Hall at Jena
set up for a lecture by the Monist
Ernst Haeckel in riposte to
Darwin's godless evolutionism. By
courtesy of the Ernst-Haeckel
Museum, Friedrich-Schiller-
University Jena.

61 (LEFT) Salome offers the Pope
Haeckel's head on a platter.
Drawing by F. Juttner from Lustige
Blatter, no17, p.8. c.1900.

62   Frida Uhl, aged 18, two years before she met and married Strindberg.

63   Mitzi Weyr, Frida's elder sister.

64 Strindberg at Varmdö, summer 1891. Strindbergsmuseet, Stockholm.

65   The Inferno walk up the gorge from Dornach to Burg Clam.

66   Strindberg as alchemist in the 1906 edition of *Antibarbarus*. Kungliga biblioteket, Stockholm.

A STINDBERG

67   Lithograph of Strindberg by Edvard Munch, 1896. Insulted by the misspelling of his name and the gratuitous inclusion of a female nude, Strindberg threatened Munch with a revolver. In later versions of the lithograph Munch included the 'r' in Strindberg and excluded the naked lady. Munch Museum, Oslo.

68 (LEFT)   In 1896, during the Inferno crisis. Kungliga biblioteket, Stockholm, Strindbergsrummet, Bilder, Kartong 4, 1896.

69 (BELOW)   Munch's cartoon mocks Strindberg whose alchemical experiments landed him in the ward for syphilitics in the Hôpital de Saint Louis. Munch Museum, Oslo.

L'exposition d'Edward Munch

> Quelque incompréhensibles que soient vos paroles,
> elles ont des charmes.
> BALZAC. — *Séraphita*.

Edward Munch, trente-deux ans, le peintre ésotérique de l'amour, de la jalousie, de la mort et de la tristesse, a souvent été l'objet des malentendus prémédités du critique-bourreau, qui fait son métier impersonnellement et a tant par tête comme le bourreau.

Il est arrivé à Paris pour se faire comprendre des initiés, sans peur de mourir du ridicule qui tue les lâches et les débiles et rehausse l'éclat du bouclier des vaillants comme un rayon de soleil.

Quelqu'un a dit qu'il fallait faire de la musique sur les toiles de Munch pour les bien expliquer. Cela se peut, mais en attendant le compositeur je ferai le boniment sur ces quelques tableaux qui rappellent les visions de Swedenborg dans les Délices de la sagesse sur l'Amour conjugal et les Voluptés de la folie sur l'Amour scortatoire.

Baiser. — La fusion de deux êtres, dont le moindre, à forme de carpe, paraît prêt à engloutir le plus grand, d'après l'habitude de la vermine, des microbes, des vampires et des femmes.

Un autre : L'homme qui donne, donnant l'illusion que la femme rende. L'homme sollicitant la grâce de donner son âme, son sang, sa liberté, son repos, son salut, en échange de quoi ? En échange du bonheur de donner son âme, son sang, sa liberté, son repos, son salut.

Cheveux rouges. — Pluie d'or qui tombe sur le malheureux à genoux devant son pire moi implorant la grâce d'être achevé à coups d'épingle. Cordes dorées qui lient à la terre et aux souffrances. Pluie de sang versée en torrent sur l'insensé qui cherche le malheur, le divin malheur d'être aimé, c'est dire d'aimer.

Jalousie. — Jalousie, saint sentiment de propreté d'âme, qui abhorre de se mêler avec un autre du même sexe par l'intermédiaire d'une autre. Jalousie, égoïsme légitime, issu de l'instinct de conservation du moi et de ma race.

Le jaloux dit au rival : Va-t-en, défectueux ; tu vas te chauffer aux feux que j'ai allumés ; tu respireras mon haleine de sa bouche ; tu t'imbiberas de mon sang et tu resteras mon serf puisque c'est mon esprit qui te régira par cette femme devenue ton maître.

Conception. — Immaculée ou non, revient au même ; l'auréole rouge ou or couronne l'accomplissement de l'acte, la seule raison d'être de cet être sans existence autonome.

Cri. — Cri d'épouvante devant la nature rougissant de colère et qui se prépare à parler pour la tempête et le tonnerre aux petits étourdis s'imaginant être dieux sans en avoir l'air.

Crépuscule. — Le soleil s'éteint, la nuit tombe, et le crépuscule transforme les mortels en spectres et cadavres, au moment où ils vont à la maison s'envelopper sous le linceul du lit et s'abandonner au sommeil. Cette mort apparente qui reconstitue la vie, cette faculté de souffrir originaire du ciel ou de l'enfer.

Trimurti de la femme.   Une autre.

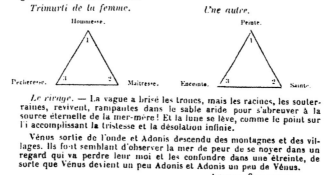

Le rivage. — La vague a brisé les troncs, mais les racines, les souterraines, revivent, rampantes dans le sable aride pour s'abreuver à la source éternelle de la mer-mère ! Et la lune se lève, comme le point sur l'i accomplissant la tristesse et la désolation infinie.

Vénus sortie de l'onde et Adonis descendu des montagnes et des villages. Ils font semblant d'observer la mer de peur de se noyer dans un regard qui va perdre leur moi et les confondre dans une étreinte, de sorte que Vénus devient un peu Adonis et Adonis un peu de Vénus.

AUGUSTE STRINDBERG

71 (LEFT)   Paul Gauguin, at the time of their friendship. Private collection / Roger-Viollet, Paris / Bridgeman Art Library.

72 (BELOW)   Madame Charlotte in her *crèmerie*, where she accepted Strindberg's and Gauguin's pictures in return for food and drink.

73   The Hôtel Orfila, where Strindberg was tormented during his Inferno crisis. Kungliga biblioteket, Stockholm, Strindbergsrummet, Bilder, Kartong 29, SGNM_53_4_26.

74   'Papus', Gérard Encausse, leading French occultist and editor of *L'Initiation*.

Le Petit Journal

SUPPLÉMENT ILLUSTRÉ

Huit pages : CINQ centimes

DIMANCHE 31 MARS 1895

La nouvelle rotonde des fauves au Jardin des Plantes

75 (LEFT)   The Jardin des Plantes, where Strindberg found solace from Inferno's anguish and experimented on plants, injecting them with morphine to discover whether they had nervous systems.

76 (BELOW LEFT)   Kerstin aged six, his guide through Inferno.

77 (BELOW RIGHT)   Cover of *Inferno*, 1912 edition.

Auguste Strindberg

INFERNO

STOCKHOLM
ALBERT
BONNIER

78   Strindberg in Lund, towards the end of the Inferno crisis. Nordiska museet, Stockholm.

On 13 September he wrote to Bonnier, 'Do you think there'll be a prosecution about the Piccadon?' Bonnier dismissed his fears. On 27 September he published a first edition of four thousand copies. Six days later the city bailiff appeared in his office to confiscate the entire print-run but he was able to seize only 320 copies because the edition had almost sold out. As Strindberg had suspected, the book was in violation of the law against blasphemy.

'I assume you will wish to return to defend the case', Bonnier wrote. 'I think it very likely at the very worst you will be fined.' The prospect of a fine was hardly appealing. Nor was the alternative, a maximum sentence of two years' hard labour. He wrote to Bonnier on 6 October: 'I shall of course come home if you are threatened with prison. Otherwise not.' Strindberg did not know what to do and was bombarded with conflicting advice from all and sundry. He had by now moved from Chexbres to Geneva which amused and amazed him with its '100 millionaires out of population of 60,000!'[23] as well as an openly anarchist bookshop-cum-lending library where he often spent his mornings among the discontents and dissidents. The bookshop was owned by Mikhail Elpidin,[24] a political refugee from Russia who printed much of the dissident literature himself but somehow was also managing to make money as a double agent for the Russian secret police. When Strindberg sought his advice on whether to go home and face prosecution, Elpidin assured him that going to prison was just idealism and tantamount to admitting guilt. However, Strindberg was not entirely convinced either way. The very day after he wrote to Bonnier telling him he would return if Bonnier was threatened with prison, he wrote to Carl Larsson:

I want to show my active contempt for this idiotic law by not returning home. Home? What home have I in Sweden? The worst of it is, Bonnier may get put in clink. In that case, I must come back and go to gaol. This is mortifying; I don't like those demonstrations on quaysides and station platforms, and don't intend writing any vainglorious proclamations. But still worse, my wife is crying and my son is ill. How can I drag them out into the October cold? . . . P.S. The worst of it is my friends have telegraphed to say I must return and win popularity for myself by making a speech at the station! God, how old fashioned![25]

Bjørnson sensed an opportunity to turn Strindberg towards internationalism and pressed him to take the course that would, in effect, make it impossible for him to return to Sweden. 'This prosecution is the biggest and best advertisement for the book', he wrote. 'Don't go back to Sweden! Face your exile like a man and create a kingdom for yourself.'[26]

Three days later Bonnier wrote saying that if he did not return he, Bonnier, would be arrested. At the same time, Bonnier wrote to Bjørnson urging him to encourage Strindberg to come back to Sweden. On receipt of Bonnier's letter, Bjørnson revised his previous opinion and wrote urging Strindberg to go back and face the charges. It would be a great advertisement for the book as well as advancing the cause of liberty, Bjørnson now urged.

Strindberg replied to Bjørnson the next day:

Your Majesty! I am in receipt of your Imperial decree and will have the honour of completely ignoring it! . . . I don't want any more immoral advice about returning home and making a spectacle of myself in order to advertise my writings, which need no such assistance!

Your former friend,
August Strindberg.[27]

War had broken out. Strindberg had made a powerful enemy just at the time he should have been grappling every possible friend to him with hoops of steel. A characteristic of Bjørnson's politics was that he was never afraid to trim to the wind of public opinion. Indeed, his popular success depended on it and the truths contained in Strindberg's letter made him uncomfortable. He went on the attack, writing to a Swedish journalist, 'He [Strindberg] is a wretched coward! Attacking me in the coarsest most swinish letters I have ever read . . . he is a craven, lying creature . . . In all my long experience I have never met anyone so repulsively self-worshipping, perfidious and cowardly.'[28]

It was always dangerous to trade insults with Strindberg whose slurs were unlike Bjørnson's in that they did not thunder grand moral judgements but more resembled Shakespeare's in painting verbal pictures that had a comic edge, a technique at once more entertaining and more memorable. Bjørnson was 'a spiritual cannibal who wanted to eat up all souls that came within reach' and 'a boa constrictor who wanted to devour me, and Siri as well'.[29]

While Strindberg continued to vacillate, Albert Bonnier was facing up to persecution, prosecution and the possible ruination of his publishing house if Strindberg did not come back to face the charges. Anti-Semitism did not run far beneath the surface and Bonnier and his family were being cold-shouldered, threatened and insulted. He was a Jewish publisher who had published a Christian blasphemy – a gift to avid Jew-haters.

Bonnier decided to send his son Karl Otto as emissary to plead with 32 Strindberg, just as earlier he had sent Karl Otto to Kymmendö to secure the author for his publishing house. Karl Otto found a far different Strindberg from the man who had out-negotiated him during their tour of the vegetable garden. Strindberg was nervous at this time, his daughter relates, and he was short of sleep because baby Hans was teething, Siri was not well and Strindberg was moody and up-and-down.[30] Karl Otto arrived on the same day that Strindberg wrote the crushing letter on moral consistency to Bjørnson that began 'Your Majesty', knowing as he wrote that he was burning his boats with the most senior and influential Scandinavian voice that might have spoken up for him in the coming trial. When he looked up from his writing desk he must have wondered if the figure in his study was indeed Karl Otto Bonnier or some joke or figment produced by his overheated brain.

Karl Otto pleaded with him. Strindberg said he would not come back to Sweden. Karl Otto retreated to his hotel downcast and prepared to return to Stockholm alone. The following morning, early, he received a visit from Strindberg who had changed his mind. He would come home to Sweden: he would not be called a coward.

During the train journey, Strindberg was miserable, depressed and apprehensive and, unusually, bad company. They took the night train to Hamburg and when they arrived it was a beautiful, clear morning. They had to wait some hours for their connection to Kiel where they would catch a boat to Stockholm. As they sat beneath the awning of the station platform Strindberg was quiet. Suddenly he took his handkerchief out of his pocket and began to weep.

'I'm sorry,' he said, 'I can't help it. It's my nerves.'

He soon ceased weeping but he was wretched all the way to Kiel. On arrival, while Bonnier saw to their suitcases, Strindberg looked out of the train door and caught sight of the steamboat that was to take them to Denmark.

'I was just organising our luggage', wrote Bonnier, 'when Strindberg yelled: "Look at the boat! *Omen accipio!*" Understanding nothing, I gave him an enquiring look. "Can't you see what it says? Auguste Victoria! Victory! August!" '[31]

The name of the boat had transformed his mood. Misery was abandoned and throughout the rest of the journey he was his usual self, a charming and voluble companion.

The two men arrived at Stockholm's Central station on the morning of 20 October. The platform was crammed. As he stepped out of the carriage the huge crowd flung their hats up to the sky and their cheers rolled round the air like thunder.[32] He knew that the moment had come, the clichéd moment he dreaded. He must make a speech, the speech of the political exile at the railway station. He hated being the centre of attention, knew he spoke badly in public, felt shy and too embarrassed to make a fine job of it but it did not matter; he might have said almost anything and be cheered to the rafters.

'I thank you', he said. 'It is good to see you. It makes me happy that we can get some clean air into our lungs. When I left Sweden, it was barely possible to breathe the air. Whatever the outcome, I will do my duty.'[33]

The crowd bore their idol to the Grand Hotel where they remained beneath his window until he appeared and acknowledged their cheers.

'That a private citizen should be received and acclaimed as though he were a monarch,' wrote *Aftonbladet*, 'that a thousand people should gather merely to set eyes on this man and comfort him by assuring him of their sympathy is, in such a case as this, of the utmost significance and well worth the notice of the authorities. For it is an expression not merely of sympathy for Strindberg but above all of disapproval of this prosecution.'[34]

That evening Josephson took the opportunity to put on a special performance of *Lucky Peter's Journey* at the New Theatre. 'Thalia's temple ablaze with a thousand gaslights seemed to triumph over the dark protestant church next door', says Axel Lundegård. Time and again waves of applause greeted libertarian lines. At the third act the entire audience, which included a large number of women, 'turned, in the orchestra stalls, towards Strindberg's box while applauding, or leaned over the sides of their boxes or balcony seats and cheered the slight, pale man as an occasional flicker of pleasure lit up his careworn, melancholy features, called forth by the festive event and a triumph the like of which few people have ever experienced.'[35] When the curtain fell he was called on stage and presented with a laurel wreath. The people took off their coats and waved them like toreadors. Yet all was not jubilation. While he waited for the trial he also received hostile letters, some enclosing excrement.

To strengthen himself for the coming trial he decided to give up drink: 'As from today I only drink water. The future will therefore be formidable!'[36] but he discovered that abstinence weakened his resilience and blunted his brain so he took it up again. The trial began on 4 November. 44 He conducted his own defence, presenting a thoughtful case based on points of theology, a subject on which he was as knowledgeable as any judge or pastor. He confounded one of his prosecutors, the chairman of the court, by a reference to one of his own publications which upheld Strindberg's case. Throughout the trial, which continued for thirteen days, Strindberg was, 'when among his friends, exactly the same as usual, possibly a little more serious. But every now and then that beautiful smile shines through', Gustaf af Geijerstam wrote to Siri, going on to assure her further that 'He won't be imprisoned. There would be Uproar . . . apparently the King himself gave orders to appoint liberal jurors so the trial can be finished with minimum fiasco.'[37] When the jury retired to consider their verdict they were closeted for four and a half hours. At last the knock came on the connecting door. Strindberg stood up, calm and pale. One newspaper reports a crowd of ten thousand waiting out on the street. When the jury found in Strindberg's favour thousands of throats let out a great roar and thousands of hats flew skywards, darkening the air. A police escort was required to get him to the Grand Hotel where he gave another brief speech:

'I thank you for your acclaim but I do not take it as directed towards myself personally. I see in it an expression of joy over the victory for free thought and free speech.'

That evening, his friends gave him a victory banquet at which they rejoiced uproariously but Strindberg felt awkward. 'No, I'm just not cut out to be "a great man" ', he wrote. 'Can never bring myself to believe in those cheers. They cheer me today; tomorrow they'll boo.'[38]

The following morning, he left for Switzerland. He had decided beforehand that if the verdict went his way and he was a free man he would shake the dust of Sweden off his boots as soon as he could. 'I don't want to bestow another night upon this country unless I have to', he wrote to Bonnier. 'Ovations hold no appeal for me, and I place no trust in popular favour. My thanks for the good will you have shown me, and for all your kindness. My respects to your family, both old and young.'[39]

His pessimism about the trial and its aftermath was well placed. A medal was struck showing his head in profile encircled by noble words taken from *Master Olof*, 'The Truth is always Audacious'. Strindberg's audacious victory benefited many in terms of freedom of speech down the years to come but in terms of his own life it acted like a slow puncture. Bonnier proposed a new edition of the book, anticipating sales of thousands but only on the condition that the story that had been the subject of prosecution was omitted. Strindberg could not possibly agree to such a morally craven suggestion. For what had he stood trial and risked prison? To win free speech and wear a gag? Bonnier fell from the ranks of idealised Jews to the ranks of the unjust.

'It would be asinine to hand over one's weapons to the enemy when he chooses to ask for them. I won't change my way of writing and opinions just because I've been abused',[40] he wrote to him in words in which we recognise the iron will of the small boy who refused to bow to the system of discipline imposed in his childhood, when his only hope of escaping a whipping had been to tell lies confessing to crimes he had not committed. Whether it cost him a whipping or lost book sales or lost friendships or any other sort of material advantage, whatever the consequence nothing was worth a moral compromise.

8 UNDER THE ICE

Had Strindberg been found guilty and condemned to the two years' hard labour that justice demanded for the crime of blasphemy, he might have had any number of vociferous supporters but once the fight had been won, Sweden preferred to forget its troublesome martyr.

'At the very moment when I'd gone under the ice, the reactionaries were hitting out at my fingers with their boathooks every time I tried to clamber up', he wrote to Georg Brandes.[1]

Bonnier remained resolute in his refusal to republish *Getting Married* unexpurgated but Strindberg was in desperate need of money.

'Can you see if I've any way out apart from turning into a hack, or shooting myself?' Strindberg wrote to him, ending the letter, 'With greetings and good wishes for a good end to this hellish life.'[2]

The need for money together with the need to explain himself led him to dash off a short book which he called *The Sequestration Journey*[3] dealing with the whole episode of the trial. It made fun of everyone including himself and it made lively reading. The book would have sold had it come quickly to the market but again Bonnier failed him; he told Strindberg it was unworthy of him as a writer[4] and refused to publish it, probably because he wanted to bury the whole uncomfortable episode. Bonnier was not finding it easy being Jewish and at the centre of a Christian blasphemy scandal when he was trying bring up a family and build a publishing business in Stockholm. Strindberg gave him one more chance by an oblique retaliation in a newspaper article entitled 'My Anti-Semitism' in which he warned Jews against becoming conservative and chauvinistic and went on to explain his vision of Jewry's unique role. The Jew's glory, he said, was precisely his lack of fatherland. This was what enabled him to become the international arbiter, high-minded, above nationalism, a superior being above those who claimed a mere, limiting nationality. It was the Jew's role to be 'free from all national prejudices, unfettered by the deadening dogmas of Christianity, brother to all men . . . the most intelligent race in Europe', and so on.[5]

While the article was a gauntlet flung at Sweden's discriminatory society, it was also aimed at Bonnier to slap his courage into action but it failed on both counts: within the mainstream of society it only confirmed Strindberg as an uncompromising and awkward voice and it did not change Bonnier's mind either.

'What kind of tactic is turning the other cheek when one gets a kick up the arse?' he asked Bonnier. 'That's just plain rotten Christianity!'[6] But Bonnier was not to be cajoled into publication.

'My view now', Strindberg wrote, 'is everything is shit! My journey to the land of the Mastodons was frightful. Archaeology as far as I'm concerned. But people wanted Strindberg crucified.'[7]

As time went by he gradually learned that among the people who particularly wanted Strindberg crucified were the feminists of Sweden. Considering the plea for women's rights that he had rather long-windedly listed in the introduction to Getting Married, it was a shock for him to discover that the prosecution of the book had been instituted by the very sex he had been championing. It seemed that two feminist groups were behind the trial: the Society for Married Women's Property Rights, made up mostly of upper-class women with a great deal of property which they could afford to pay lawyers to protect, and the Federation, a Pietist group that aimed to abolish prostitution.[8] Siri supported the Federation and subscribed to their journal and this had already been a source of friction between her and Strindberg who loathed Pietism and who, besides, believed that prostitutes could fend for themselves if treated fairly. The Federation was centred round the queen and the rumour, probably true, was that she was behind the prosecution.

Not only the queen was his enemy but also the king. Having rigged a liberal jury to avoid the spread of civil unrest, the monarch had mingled with the crowd thronging the street outside the courtroom awaiting the verdict of the Strindberg trial. He had been jostled, separated from his protectors and thoroughly frightened when the crowd burst into their riotous jubilation.[9] Strindberg had frightened a king! He drew a cartoon of himself blowing up the monarch by means of an Infernal Machine which involved string, dynamite and a Communion cup of Piccadon wine.[10] It was something to laugh at and there was little enough of that. Strindberg was finding it terribly difficult to write and this had not happened to him before. Normally he would dash off words in his study, never re-reading, flinging down each sheet onto the floor as it was finished and gathering them up when the piece of work was complete but now, for the first time the words would not come. He had planned a collection of stories called *Utopias in Reality* exploring social ideals and he was struggling with them when he received a timely invitation to a sightseeing trip. He accepted the diversion with alacrity.

His host was a new friend who had contacted him with messages of support during the trial. Verner von Heidenstam[11] was a Swedish aristocrat ten years his junior, a budding poet of delicate health and a deep purse who had studied painting in Paris and Rome and travelled as far as Egypt, Palestine and Syria. Von Heidenstam invited Strindberg to join himself and his wife on a tour of the Tyrol, Venice and Rome. Strindberg was not the first traveller to discover that Venice in February resembles cold porridge but few tourists are as horrified by Rome. He could only see its grandiose splendours as bloodstained monuments to an oppressive society founded upon slave labour. On his return, he hymned the simple pleasures of the birds that had begun to sing again in the Swiss trees and he became so homesick for the Swedish archipelago that when he thought about it his legs began to itch.

May 1885 found him in Paris where he had the opportunity to contemplate the degree of his own professional failure at Victor Hugo's funeral. Hugo was given a state funeral but his will stipulated that he should be sent to his grave in a pauper's coffin. Down through a sea of mourners rolled the humble ship of state, saluted at the Arc de Triomphe by a guard of honour of young poets, and down the Champs Elysées by the whores of Paris who had decided to honour the dead man by offering their services free on the broad margins of that great thoroughfare.

In June they moved from stifling Paris to Luc-sur-Mer where the sea 'turned one stupid just by looking at it' because it was not the sea of Sweden but however much he yearned for home there was no question of returning to the Kingdom of Lies. He was still finding it difficult to write and when he received a commission from a new and potentially promising source, he made a bad job of it. The editor of *La Nouvelle Revue* (a lady) politely and quite rightly turned the piece down and this did not improve his view of her sex.

> It seems to be women and that damned Christ who rule this over-civilised world and its book market. Since I'm on the way to becoming an atheist (the world is run by idiots = God is an idiot) I shall probably henceforth attack God too. What effect this will have on our relationship and my tellurian existence we shall doubtless discover.[12]

It was not easy to switch sides. Atheism only meant something to him as a negative, a denial. Once plugged in to Christianity, he observed, it was impossible to unplug. An ex-Christian could not take up any position except by a fixed reference to heaven: 'I live in an eternal feud with my former self, a feud that is destroying me. I am split quite in two.'[13]

The unexpurgated version of *Getting Married* was at last brought out in November 1885, a whole year after the trial. Public interest had waned and sales were small. Albert Bonnier had stuck by his decision not to publish and this caused a breach of trust between them that was never entirely healed though Bonnier continued to be his publisher, off and on, for many years. The book was in fact brought out by Bonnier's nephew Isidor who published it anonymously so the family should not suffer further persecution. Isidor also commissioned a second volume[14] but the writing went slowly. His heart, Strindberg confessed, was not in the Woman Question any more. Women, whom he had always thought reasonable beings in need of reasonable championing, had acted ridiculously against him. Unreason begat unreason. 'A reaction to extremes can only occur by means of being extreme. So I really pile it on in *Getting Married II*',[15] he told Georg Brandes, and indeed the introduction to the second volume could not have been in greater contrast to the first which had started with the long and rather wearisomely detailed list of women's rights. The second volume began instead with a scattergun volley of misogynist quotations taken from Rousseau, Aristotle, Schopenhauer and even Annie Besant whom he detested. The stories themselves are more fairly balanced than the introduction suggests but there was one story, 'The Breadwinner', that was particularly thrilling to his ill-wishers in Sweden and particularly hurtful to Siri.

It begins:

He wakes in the morning after harrowing dreams of overdue bills and undelivered manuscripts. His hair is sweaty with anxiety, his cheeks quiver as he dresses. But he hears the children in the next door room and he dips his burning head into cold water and drinks his coffee that he makes himself to spare the nursemaid from having to get up at such an early hour.

The husband gets down to 'his terrible job of writing' while the wife fritters the morning away. When they meet for lunch she smells of cognac. The nursemaid seems to spend most of the day on the garden seat keeping one eye on the children and the other on *True Women* magazine which she has borrowed from the mistress. Friends observe the marriage and gossip: ' "I've good reason to believe that she reckoned at one time that he'd make her name for her as an artist . . ." ' and so the story goes on, describing the negative side of their marriage pretty undisguised and with a pitiless eye. It ends with the work-weakened husband dying of his burden and of a broken heart.

This was too much for Siri who 'for the peace of the household' asked his permission to cease reading what he wrote. This dealt a terrible blow to the marriage. No longer could they share the illusion of intellectual collaboration, no longer laugh or argue over the absolutely central component of his life – his writing. It was, in fact, the second great blow to the marriage roundabout the time of the trial. The first blow was sexual: Hans's birth had left her with protracted gynaecological problems which her daughter describes as haemorrhages, pain and uterine bleeding. Siri consulted a specialist in Geneva but her problems persisted and she continued to visit doctors and midwives and to go to the pharmacy to purchase alum, a home remedy against bleeding. There can be little doubt this was a devastating development in the marriage. Sex had been an important mutual joy from the start of the relationship, even before they married, and indeed his propensity to describe marital sex as healthy, natural and thoroughly enjoyable to both parties was one of the reasons that a large number of people, including many of the libertarians who had supported his right to free speech during the trial, nevertheless found his writing (and by association, Strindberg himself) offensive and embarrassing.

It was a widely held belief at the time that if a man had no natural outlet for his sperm it might go to all sorts of places in his body, even his brain, and cause 'deleterious congestion'. According to the contemporary experts Drysdale and Nordau whose books Strindberg had on his shelves, sexual need was worse than hunger and abstention was a sin against nature. Siri's sexual inaccessibility during this time caused him to worry for the state of both his bodily and mental health.

The first volume of *Getting Married* had been written by a happily married man and the stories within the volume often concerned the psychology of how love finds solutions for problems. This second volume was written by a man lonely within his marriage who had taken a courageous step and won a noble victory in a ruthless place that then had turned its back on him. No wonder the stories addressed questions of social justice in a society based upon marriage: the questions, in fact, that had come into sharp focus in his own marriage over the last year. Not only the questions but the answers were cruelly personal.

The Woman Question begged the Worker Question. Women who did not work seemed to need a great many servants to run their houses. He summed it up: 'To attack the Saucepans is reactionary. How can a wife be rescued from the saucepans if some maid or slave isn't saddled with them instead?' In Siri's case, their faithful servant and nursemaid who travelled with them wherever they went.

The Religious Question was now an urgent and personal issue between them: Siri wished baby Hans to be christened; Strindberg would not condone the Church's idea that children were born wicked and must be 'saved' by christening. He doted on the innocent condition of childhood and now he wrote an admirable article[16] putting forth children's social rights and obligations that stands scrutiny to this day.

His daughter Karin's recollections of her parents at this time were uncomfortable. She says that he had changed greatly since the trial; in its ghastly aftermath he was sombre and moody, spoke softly with an over-controlled voice, flinched when they kissed him goodnight and when he looked at them it was with a penetrating gaze that made the children uneasy. The children were constantly aware of tension between their mother and father though they did not argue openly in front of the children: they had made an agreement that they would not do that.

Siri was neither happy nor healthy this year. On top of her gynaecological problems she had developed respiratory troubles and toothache that turned into a long-running saga of pain and surgery. A brutal dentist fractured her upper jaw during the extraction of a molar and eventually she had to have a metal plate inserted in her jaw.

'Her fire burns lower, the age of maturity begins! What sorrow, the day she broke her first front tooth!' Strindberg wrote. 'She weeps, clutches me in her arms, begs me not to stop loving her! She is in her thirty-seventh year! The hair grows pale, the breasts subside like waves after a storm, the stairs grow tiring for her little foot and the lungs no longer function strongly as they did before.'[17]

The 1880s saw a fashion of experimental co-operative communities. In what he called this new age of maturity in his marriage, Strindberg's thoughts turned towards rescuing his defeated spirit by thinking about broader solutions, not to his own but to society's problems by working on *Utopias in Reality* (1885). He pleaded with Bonnier to send him the books he needed but could not afford to buy: de Tocqueville's *Democracy in America*, Jacoby's *Hérédité*, Hartmann's *Philosophy of the Unconscious*, Junius's *Carl XV*, Maudsley's *The Pathology of Mind*, Buckle's *History of Civilisation* and 'the best logic and psychology textbooks used in Swedish schools.'[18] Bonnier was alarmed by this reading list and tried to encourage him back to fiction by sending him *War and Peace* but Strindberg responded that he far preferred the *Confessions* in which Tolstoy who, like Strindberg, could never completely sever the umbilical attachment to Christianity, worked out his own church-less version of that faith.

In October 1885 he took Siri for a little holiday to a famous model co-operative community, the Familistère at Guise which had been set up and paid for by the vastly rich cast-iron stove magnate Jean-Baptiste Godin. To Siri's distress, no church had been built within the community but at least it did not deny marriage. She was pleased to see there were plenty of married quarters and a nursery to look after the workers' children while their mothers and fathers were blissfully engaged in the manufacture of heating appliances in the vast adjoining factories. According to Strindberg, he and Siri returned more in love than ever.

Social zeal rekindled, and struck by the sea-change that mechanisation was bringing to French society, he became smitten by the need for a comprehensive documentation of France's peasantry and agriculture before the advancing tide of industrialisation drowned the old ways. He decided to travel through *La France profonde* gathering material for a book on the subject; the trip took some time to plan and finance and it was not until August 1886 that he set off. He had hoped his old friend Carl

Larsson would be his travelling companion but instead he went with an admirer from his Royal Library days, Gustaf Steffen, a future Professor of Economics and Sociology who was rumoured to be the son of Gustaf Klemming and a cloakroom attendant at the Royal Library who was popularly supposed to be a witch. This added excitement to the prospect of weeks in Steffen's company.[19]

'If you could drum up a thousand kronor now, we might make a start right away. Let's go!'[20] Strindberg wrote, taking the tone of master to Steffen's servant.

A week later he was charging his dear Herr Steffen to

get hold of one of the photographic revolvers you can get in Paris which you carry in your pocket and shoot off like a gun. Two of them would be better for we must be careful of our equipment. You know they're obsessed with spies [in France] . . . I fear there's a French spy here in the pension. He calls himself Commandant Rapp and pumps me unmercifully. No doubt they believe I'm spying on their fortifications! Or else they resent the fact that I portray their domestic situation in German. I'm longing to make this journey and all may yet go well! P.S. Where can I get a French passport?[21]

From any normal point of view the journey was a disaster but each had a taste for fiasco. Antipathy swung between the two men like a compass needle. Steffen was a Marxist:

'Are you sure that industrial socialism is not really the latest offshoot of the idealism which miscarried in the French Revolution?' Strindberg asked suspiciously. 'Can you swear that the mind of Karl Marx, who was born in 1818, really bore no trace of this?'[22]

Steffen was an industrial socialist wedded to the idea of mass production:

'Over-production of luxury!' Strindberg exclaimed, adding sensibly, 'One can't eat telephones or sewing machines.'[23]

Thriving on the difficulties thrown up by good, hard physical setbacks, they travelled third class, got off at small stations, walked miles carrying their baggage and in order to record any interesting building in a time-saving fashion Strindberg sketched the right-hand side and Steffen the left: the two could later be put together by the publisher. They interviewed peasants, read local papers, fired their photographic revolvers, suspected they were being spied upon. And they fought. At last Strindberg had a bodily adversary to fight rather than flailing, as he had been all year, at that amorphous mass, the whole of Sweden. Strindberg eventually accused Steffen entirely spuriously of stealing money from him and they parted furious enemies.

Strindberg came home completely refreshed and boasting like a small boy of his tough achievements. They had travelled 3,880 kilometres by train and, as Siri remarked, the journey had cost 1,900 francs and resulted in no book but it did, the following year, result in a splendidly unsettling account of Strindberg's side of the story in which he triumphs over his travelling companion by trumping Marxism with Hegelianism in an excellent story called 'The Battle of the Brains', a Poe-like tale of a battle of nerves between two travelling companions that spins out of the railway carriage into a nightmare of delusion.

Strindberg's loss of judgement and confidence since the trial, amply demonstrated by the patchiness of his last two books, had moved the family's finances into acute crisis. In the autumn of 1885 he arranged for the property they had left behind them in Sweden to be put up for sale and Siri had the melancholy experience of letting go the last of her family furniture. Strindberg sold his most valued possession, his library. After their outstanding debts had been paid off they had only raised 660 francs, a slender month's expenses. Almost worse was the public statement that the sale made about the state of his finances, advertising the poverty that was the humiliating consequence of his failure as a writer. In December a sympathetic Swedish journalist Emil Hillberg[24] opened a fund to provide a stipend for him, the idea being to raise sufficient funds to provide an income of three to four thousand kronor a year for ten years. The Swedish public might or might not approve of what Strindberg wrote but Hillberg thought it shameful that they should let their country's leading writer starve.

Now that longed-for support from Sweden had arrived, Strindberg was appalled and embarrassed. 'Hillberg surely knows that after such a revelation the victim can never have a happy moment, never have a glass of wine, never ride in a carriage, never visit a restaurant. Who wants to accept an invitation from a pauper?'[25] He also worried that his impartiality would be compromised if some mediocre author or rabid feminist contributed to the fund; he would have to be polite about them in print.[26]

The appeal for the fund went ahead, with the unintended consequence of calling all his old enemies to their desks. Siri and Strindberg who 'aroused the deepest indignation and disgust in all right-thinking people'[27] were the focus of newspaper articles and gossip at home in Sweden. Scurrilous pamphlets attacking Siri accused her of unbridled promiscuity and questioned the paternity of the children. In great distress, Strindberg wrote privately to his friends in Stockholm begging them to track down the authors so that he might cut the hydra heads from the monster rumour.[28] He resolved not to read such filth but was helpless to push it out of his mind where it festered, leading him to question the paternity and subsequent fate of their first child, the daughter who had died while Siri was making her debut on the stage. Was the child actually his? Was she actually dead? Might she still be alive? Had Siri hidden her away somewhere? Was this why the money always ran through their hands so fast? Was Siri sending the money away to pay for the upkeep of this concealed daughter of doubtful paternity? This was torture enough but another old rumour from her acting days was also being circulated. Her short stage career had been dense with gossip that she had lesbian inclinations and ran after fellow actresses. At the time, Strindberg had leapt to her defence on the gallant grounds that the same was said of all actresses who refused to give themselves to the first man who came along. To have the charge of lesbianism against Siri resurrected roused deep terrors at this moment when their sex life had collapsed.

Lesbianism was a comparatively modern neurosis; it had been criminalised as recently as 1864 when Strindberg was fifteen years old. That it was taken seriously was demonstrated by the fact that it carried a sentence of between two and eight years' hard labour. It was probably no coincidence that this new law coincided with the early stirrings of feminism; the public sphere was dominated by an all-male establishment who mostly found it difficult to distinguish between lesbianism and feminism, who felt threatened by any notion of female emancipation and who had long been angered by Strindberg's tireless campaigning for women's rights. But Strindberg was not a spokesman for lesbianism, nor was he immune from fear of it when accusations were levelled against Siri.

Apprehension always preyed on his stomach and he sought to still his nausea with absinthe which he had not drunk since the trial. But absinthe only fertilises paranoia, particularly when taken with stimulants, stomach medicines and sleeping draughts of belladonna. He decided to give up on the Swedish market and write his next book in French. Meanwhile, they would move.

Siri wants to go to Neuchâtel and start a pension for the many Scandinavian gentlemen who go there to study French because the place is cheap. I shall go with her and take up gardening; my doctor has explicitly stated that unless I exercise or do some kind of manual work, the fire in my brain will never be quenched. On his advice I have taken up drinking and billiards, playing cards and being sociable. It helps for a little while but is seven times as bad afterwards . . . [but just now] we're stuck here because we owe 2,000 francs, and our debts mount up like an avalanche.[29]

9 MADNESS AND MODERNITY

The pension in Neuchâtel proved no more than a castle in the air but the book written in French was to become a very real construction; French has always been a good language for books driven by despair.

The homesick little family moved as close as they could to Sweden, huddling back into the Scandinavian artists' colony in Grez-sur-Loing where they had spent the first light-hearted weeks of exile in the days when all was promise. Many of the same artists were still there and life centred round the two *pensions* Chevillons and Laurents. Strindberg settled his family into Laurents which extended longer credit.

'Sterile! Sick! Nothing done! Moved. The summer has gone without my accomplishing anything and without rest. Where will it end?' he wrote to Verner von Heidenstam whom he tried to lure to Grez with the promise of orgies.

> Old friends come out from Paris on Saturdays and last Sunday we held a very respectable orgy which went on for two days with singing, guitars, tambourine and wild *joie de vivre* . . . it was almost Decameronian (without the screwing, at least in public, that is still regarded as a private matter) . . . we had everything you and I wrote about (except naked women) . . . my existence has never been so precarious as it is right now. One dances with the noose around one's neck.[1]

Christmas came and they were still in Grez, Strindberg in ominously high spirits. At this time he was fond of 'my Flying Dutchman cloak' of black velvet and as he flitted about he seemed to be trying to recreate the happy days of old on Kymmendö: organising charades, singing to his guitar, making sentimental speeches as they sat down to table (usual for

34

55

Scandinavians but unusual for him) and directing a *tableau vivant* of Rembrandt's *Anatomy Lesson* which nearly froze to death the sculptor Ville Vallgren who was playing the naked corpse. Among the party were two Danish girls: Sofie Holten, a pretty, pliant artist of twenty-seven who sometimes wrote for Edvard Brandes's *Politiken*, and Marie David who was twenty, Jewish and red-haired with a square determined face and a mysterious character. Her mother had been a well-known adventuress and Marie David's paternity was shadowy. She said Georg Brandes was her father. He denied it.

The girls were thoroughly modern; they crackled with youth. Strindberg would be thirty-seven in January and Siri was a year younger; they were not yet ready to be old. Ever since Marie David and Sofie Holten had arrived in the gossipy artists' colony, everyone said they were lesbians but Strindberg fairmindedly defended them. He enjoyed a gentle flirtation with Sofie Holten; they sang duets together to his guitar, she painted his portrait and he contemplated a bicycle tour with her to observe French peasants. The other girl, Marie David, was largely disliked by the community who found her impudent and strident but Strindberg at first found her extreme feminist views amusing and they enjoyed hammer-and-tongs arguments. Marie David made no secret of the fact that she found him old and his opinions old-fashioned and he enjoyed the challenge but as time went on he grew to dislike her. She was the first real friend Siri had made since their exile had begun and he felt she was a bad influence. Marie was a heavy drinker and she encouraged Siri, who needed little encouragement in that area. The more Siri drank the coarser she became. She took to smoking cigars which impressed nobody and she embarrassed him in front of his friends. Ville Vallgren observed Siri's pokes at eternal youth with distaste. He found it undignified and sad to hear her parroting Marie David's opinions with all the eagerness of the Past taking dictation from the Future.

Marie David thought it monstrous that Siri should be forced into exile from the theatre for the sake of her husband's failed writing career. Was this the freedom and equality Strindberg preached, Marie David asked, and encouraged Siri to believe she should go back to the Swedish stage for a last attempt to realise her dream. At her age, with a metal plate in her mouth and breathing difficulties, it was possibly unrealistic to expect great success from a stage comeback but Strindberg was helpless against the argument. How could he point out the truth? Siri seemed to think she could earn 2,000 kronor a year if she went back to the stage. Strindberg could only silently resent Marie David's undermining of his marriage while pleading with Siri not to leave them.

The artists' colony included Karl Nordström,[2] a fine landscape painter who immediately took a great liking to Strindberg. Nordström wrote gossipy letters to his fiancée Tekla Lindeström, detailing the ins and outs of the interwoven relationships. While he observed Strindberg regaining some of his sexual confidence through his gentle flirtation with Sofie Holten, he viewed Siri's friendship with Marie David with disgust that deepened when Marie David started to give Siri massages. Marie David had taken an anatomy course and maybe she was trying was to relieve some of Siri's medical symptoms but Nordström saw only one explanation. The way Siri and Marie David carried on made him feel nauseous, he told Tekla: 'And do you know, it was so damned heart-rending for me to hear and see that I was ready to weep with him – as he revealed to me all the bottomless misery and wretchedness of his married existence.'[3]

At the end of the Christmas festivities an American let fly with his revolver and Strindberg crept through the darkened *pension* shielding his children behind a mattress like a human tortoise. The American later shot himself.[4] It all had the air of desperation but in February 1886 things got better. Albert Bonnier cancelled Strindberg's debt of 8,000 kr to the publishing house and by March the public appeal which Strindberg had been unable to stop had raised 3,680 francs. This enabled him to pay off the mounting debt that had trapped them in the *pension* with the rest of the overheated community.

Since they had left Sweden they had spent two years moving between hotels and *pensions*, running up debts and moving on when the bill could be paid. Siri was weary of this and when Strindberg rented a little house on the high street in Grez and put down six months' rent, she prepared to be happy. They hired curtains, a stove and a piano and he engaged a boy to help him in the garden. They put the girls into school where Strindberg insisted they wear clogs in solidarity with the peasants, and Hans sat in the pram while his father worked in the garden. He was such a sweet, solemn baby that they nicknamed him the 'Philosopher'.

Two months later, despite the rent he had paid, they were off.

'I can't stand travelling. But after I've been sitting in one place for three months my eye finds everything repulsive and I have to move on. If only somebody would invent movable landscapes!'[5]

The rest of the year saw the family hectically flying from one picture-postcard Alpine *pension* to another while he conducted a damned soul's flight through the mountain peaks in his Flying Dutchman cloak with his senses wide open and brain afire, creating a new literature of psychology and introspection. His writer's block was ended, the divine gift had come back to him but in a new and uncontrollable form that convulsed his whole existence. He wrote four books and a play in under a year.

'I'm tired!' he wrote to Albert Bonnier in the letter that accompanied the manuscript of the first book.

> And I walk around with a six-shooter in my trouser pocket. But then I think it might be amusing to see how things turn out. I've read too much lately: psychology, ethics, psychiatry, sociology and economics so that my head is like pulp. I regard myself and my talent as dead, and am now writing the story of my life in a curious form (secret!). I believe this will enable me to analyse myself and discover what makes me tick.[6]

'You doubtless ask yourself: what is this? Is it a novel? No. A biography? No. Memoires? No! My reply is the book is precisely what it claims to be: the story of a soul's development between 1849–1867'.[7]

The Son of a Servant is an account of his life from birth to university. The language is plain and colloquial, the focus is sharp, noticeably sharper than Zola's naturalism which was then the ultra-modern literary form.

'The psychological material is the most important element (that is why there are no descriptions and the anecdotes have only been included to shed light on character)', he wrote in the same letter to Bonnier, which goes on to point out the difference between his own psychological and subjective naturalism and that of the 'photographic' naturalism of Ibsen and Zola which relied heavily on social context to portray the dislocation of the individual within it. In a year or so Strindberg would be able to say he had written a play that required no other furniture than two chairs and a table; meanwhile, this year's work was clearing away the furniture. 'Trivialities such as whether he washes himself after having intercourse for the first time are omitted, as is detailed discussion of the whore's furniture.'[8]

The plot is recognisably Strindberg's life and the hero/anti-hero is given his own baptismal name, Johan. A walking case-study in late nineteenth-century psychology, Johan is constantly aware of the fluctuating and contradictory impulses that make up *la multiplicité du moi*. Profoundly alienated, stretched thin by the conflicting tensions within himself between social man, intellectual man and natural man, he lays bare an utterly modern soul: inconsistent, spiritually turbulent, often unkind, arrogant and cowardly. Strindberg was writing for a reading public who were pretty well acquainted with the ins and outs of his life from newspaper columns and who on the whole found him unsympathetic. In the circumstances one might expect explanations, apologies, self-justification or even a whitewash, but the book was hardly ingratiating. He emerges as a roaring boy with a sex drive as strong as his spiritual drive. It is obvious that he is driven more by this spiritual intensity than the more conventional urges of ego and ambition. His spirituality fuels his rage as well as his pure vision of certain virtuous things (women, children, Jews) and he does not allow the tiniest disappointment of expectation to go unchallenged or unpunished. 'When I see something go haywire, or some stupidity or injustice make headway, I get all twisted up until I can straighten the matter out.'[9] Genuinely believing that he has the power to straighten things out, he takes the seeds of injustice (real or perceived) and waters them with paranoia until he is hacking at a hostile jungle of his own making. It is a remarkable self-portrait.

Strindberg had started writing the book in French but it soon reverted to his native language. He sent the manuscript to Albert Bonnier without great confidence, telling him that if he did not want to publish it he might send it on to Isidor but Albert Bonnier was delighted. Here at last was the successor to his early best-seller *The Red Room*. Bonnier sent him a good advance though not large enough to wipe out all his debts. Poverty was, Strindberg observed regretfully, the one great misfortune that destroyed both one's life and one's honour.[10]

Bonnier's delight at *The Son of a Servant* led him to start its sequel, *Time of Ferment*, telling of his time at Uppsala and his brief acting career. He completed the book in a month. Bonnier was again enthusiastic and Strindberg promised the next tranche of 'my interior history' but a few days later he had changed his mind: 'I'm going to start writing *two* pieces for the theatre! So I'm returning to literature after all. What is one to do? One can't practise what one preaches, and one preaches for the world to come.'[11]

Twelve days later he changed plans again: 'Since life is short but art is long, I'm going to complete the celebrated account of my life. This has the great advantage of enabling me to get to the bottom of myself before I return to literature. Am therefore starting on volume three.'[12] This was *In the Red Room* and it told the real story behind his first successful novel, *The Red Room*, when he was a member of Stockholm's rackety bohemia, working as a teacher and a jobbing journalist. He completed it in seven weeks.

Two weeks later he was sending Bonnier the outline of the next book, *He and She*. This was to be an epistolary novel based on the love letters between him and Siri written when she was still married to the baron who was then conducting his affair with her cousin Sofia In de Bétou. Bonnier recoiled. He could not agree with Strindberg that the letters were 'so interesting and so beautiful and reflected so much credit on all concerned that for the sake of his wife and his children they should be published'.[13] The lawsuits consequent upon publication would be giddying, Bonnier calculated, and tried to discourage him but Strindberg could not stop and he sent him the completed book in August, the third month of this conflagration of the brain.

This prolonged psychiatric self-examination was producing a sublime exaltation but he realised the real danger of a sustained period of such intensity. He began to question the boundaries between such morbid acuity of self-knowledge and insanity. More curious than frightened, he turned to books for the answer to this latest and deepest dive into the human condition. He read the most recent publications on extreme psychological states: Henry Maudsley's *The Pathology of Mind* (1879), Théodule Ribot's *Les Maladies de la volunté* (1883) and *Les Maladies de la personalité* (1885) and Hippolyte Bernheim's extremely important book *De la suggestion et ses applications à la thérapeutique* (1886), a book that took a whole creative generation by storm with its pseudo-scientific validation of 'suggestion', the idea that one mind might gain power over another in the battle of the brains. This was a process separate from hypnotism and mesmerism, both of which fascinated people at the time. In hypnotism and mesmerism the two protagonists were in the same room but suggestion could be made from far, far away. The weak will became an instrument of the more powerful will, in other words a zombie. Suggestion travelled on the ether, the mysterious medium filling all empty space whose identification and analysis was a Holy Grail for nineteenth-century scientists. Suggestion was an important and enduring idea for Strindberg that featured largely in his thoughts and work over the next years, changing and developing in his mind as he related it to Nietzsche's divisions of power, which he soon encountered.[14]

'I now have a whole library on madness, from which it transpires that everyone is crazy apart from the doctors',[15] he joked to Verner von Heidenstam, but privately he consulted a doctor on his sanity and he wrote a note instructing that if he was to go mad 'like Tolstoy', he should be killed or sent to a particular asylum in Belgium where they reputedly treated the inmates with humanity.

Siri was also doubting his sanity and she consulted a certain Dr Oltramar[16] in secret but Strindberg discovered and became suspicious of her and frightened. He thought she was plotting with the doctors to have him locked up in a lunatic asylum, an idea that even after their confrontation and her denial, he never totally relinquished. He could not fully trust Siri after this; once you were in one of those places you never got out.

He had not yet brought his biographical self-examination completely up to date but he could not calm his exalted brain until he had written the two plays that had been pestering him since June. The first was called *The Marauders*, a play that underwent several transformations after this first version which he dashed off in eight days and sent to Albert Bonnier proudly announcing that it was his answer to Ibsen's *Ghosts*, the play that every modern playwright had been trying to eclipse since it had come out four years earlier.

The Marauders (later reworked into *The Comrades*) was not yet the hoped-for step beyond *Ghosts* but it did take feminism some steps further out of Nora's *Doll's House*. Its title came from the husband's comment to the wife: 'It seems you women are marauding the territory we have plundered and fought over so long while you were sitting at the fire.'

The play asks the question whether a marriage can accommodate two careers and it obviously relates to Strindberg and Siri's failed attempt. The husband, Axel, the latest in a line of breadwinning patriarchs, knows that a job is a job. The newly emancipated wife, Bertha, tramples every human value in pursuit of her right to work. Both are artists. Each has submitted a picture to the Salon. Bertha pulls all sorts of tricks to have her picture accepted. She is outwitted by her husband whose honourable double bluff achieves his undeclared aim – to have Bertha's picture accepted rather than his own. Professional success will, he hopes, give Bertha a chance to become more balanced. Bertha's painting is accepted and she continues just as foul. In the final twist we discover that Axel, knowing his painting was much better than his wife's, has switched the paintings they sent to the Salon. It is his painting that has been accepted with her name attached. Refusing to put the record straight, Bertha plans to build a career on the deception.

Albert Bonnier did not like the play and refused to publish it but he generously offered to print ten copies for Strindberg to submit to whichever theatres he chose. None of the Stockholm theatres would touch it.

The wife in the play drinks too much and she suffers, as Siri suffered, from gynaecological problems. Her great friend is a lesbian girl of illegitimate birth who encourages her in a ruthless pursuit of her rights and ambitions. It was not difficult to see Siri and Marie David. Since Siri had 36, 37 ceased to read his writing or talk about its subject matter, Strindberg had no need to worry how deeply his writings might hurt her but his guilty conscience found her mute hostility unbearable. Whether she read it or not, his writing was driving an ever-widening cleft between the two of them.[17]

In December 1886 he sent Bonnier the latest volume of the autobiography, *The Author*, covering his life since 1877, and Bonnier, true to his impulse to keep his head down concerning anything to do with the blasphemy trial, refused to publish it.

New Year's Eve saw Strindberg still hyperactively volatile and denying the obvious setbacks of the last year.

'It may well be', he informed Bonnier, 'that my comedy [*The Marauders*] will take off, if not this year then next year (like *Ghosts*), and it will most assuredly be a monument or a milestone marking a stage in my literary development.'[18] He also promised Bonnier two more plays to complete the *Marauders* trilogy. The first would tell the story of Bertha's childhood with particular reference to her relationship with her father and the final play would tell the story of her destiny as a mother and the wife of a pork butcher,[19] an idea of peculiar potential brutality. The final play was never written though one may take his next play, *Miss Julie*, as a semi-realisation of it, with the excruciating cruel servant Jean taking the place of the pork butcher.

He went on to tell Bonnier that he was going to start the New Year with a new life as a human being. To this effect he was moving to Bavaria where, as usual, hope sprang eternal that he would be able to live far more cheaply than to date and he also proposed another enormous study, this time of the German people and peasants.

By February 1887 he had installed himself and the family in Issigathsbühl on the Bodensee (Lake Constance). They had taken the floor of a
country house which was close by an army barracks and he fell victim
to excited admiration of everything German and martial.

> In Germany! Patriarchy and male discipline, recruits three ells tall with
> plump cheeks. France was absinthe and self-abuse. Switzerland matri-
> archal slop. Here there are males with lively pricks. I admire Bismarck's
> speech [Bismarck had just suggested France and Germany might go to
> war]. . . . In Germany women aren't permitted to study at university.
> In England the medical association is discussing their fitness for higher
> study. A book attacking their emancipation has appeared in Paris. Reac-
> tion on every side. I have a keen nose, you see![20]

More important than these old songs were his political comments in
the same letter: 'If we are to have State and Society, well, dammit, let's
do things properly. If there are to be nations then let there be guardsmen;
if there are to be guardsmen then let them live in barracks and drill from
five in the morning till eight in the evening! Oh, we antiquated old
idealists!'[21]

Strindberg had ostensibly changed in a short month from freedom-
loving supporter of feminism to contented citizen under the Kaiser. Fired
by Bismarck's speech he proposed himself to Albert Bonnier in a new
capacity as a war correspondent but only on certain conditions:

> Firstly, I don't want to send in despatches that have already been more
> accurately reported . . . Then I don't want to comment on military oper-
> ations which I don't understand . . . But if war breaks out, will you
> publish a book in instalments and equip me at your expense? The costs
> won't exceed more than half of what the book will bring. 2,000 marks
> maybe, 1,000 for a horse . . . my kingdom for a horse! I am frightfully
> keen and am going to see it through even if it costs a little red blood.'[22]

The letter goes on for a long time and asks Bonnier to wangle a press
pass before signing off with a flourish in German. As the war was largely
in Strindberg's head, Bonnier had no reason to respond with any practical
measures.

One may understand Strindberg's rather surprising immersion in
testosterone-rich Prussian militarism by going back to the early time in
their courtship when Strindberg was teaching Siri to write and remember-

ing that he gave her two important rules. First: write what you know. Second: achieve emotional authenticity by writing in the grip of powerful emotion.

He had plenty of emotional memory to draw on for the new play he was writing which tells the progress of a mental breakdown. Breakdown was the subject he had been researching over the last year, and this crucially was when he realised what he was doing and described the past months as having taken the corpse of the person he knew best [i.e. himself] and learned anatomy, physiology, psychology from the carcass. However, in order to make the progress of a breakdown truly interesting, the character who breaks down could hardly be Strindberg's own wavering self. It makes a far more gripping story if the fall comes from a great height of self-belief and self-confidence. The stronger the man, the greater the fall. Who, in the whole continent of Europe, was the strongest man? The Prussian officer. Hence Strindberg's immersion in Bismarckian bellicosity: he was shrugging himself into the skin. The play begins with this fine man swaggering around the stage in his uniform, with spurs jingling on his highly polished riding boots, and it ends with him voluntarily resigning himself to the straightjacket held out to him: he has broken down and his wife has had him certified insane.

The Father is much tougher than Strindberg's previous plays and finally it makes the breakthrough he had been fumbling towards. At last he had put the devastating process of self-analysis that had nearly driven him mad into practice and had written a new sort of play that elbowed itself ahead of Ibsen and Zola, the shock of whose naturalism had been to write plays about recognisable individuals firmly planted in the present. This meant loading their characters with circumstantial detail, such as where they lived, family history, occupation, where they fitted into the class system and so on, making them real and believable to the modern playgoer who could then be swept away by empathetic identification. By and large, these plays had a decent number of supporting characters who served, like the foundations of a building, to root them realistically within the recognisable community context. Strindberg's previous play *The Marauders* had followed this formula. It was awash with social framework and extraneous characters. *The Father* is minimalist in comparison.

All the better for deserting polemic, it is a technical experiment in simplification to the extent that in the cast list the main character is not even given a name, simply 'the Captain'.[23] There are also characters called the Pastor, the Nurse, the Orderly and the Soldier (who is given a quality for a name, Nöjd, meaning a sort of bovine, mindless contentment) and of course the daughter Bertha is named, this being the back story of Bertha in *The Marauders*. The issues are simplified to the drama growing inside the captain's head where a mere shadow, a suggestion planted by his wife, leads to a wrestling match with phantoms and the eventual smothering of the man by his own terrors.

Strindberg also simplifies the stage setting. Not yet two chairs and a table, but in contemporary terms its simplification is radical. He gives only the mental furniture needed for the play: a coat rack where military uniforms can be donned or discarded with mental attitudes, and a few other symbolic objects such as a clock, a lamp, weapons on the walls, rifles and game bags and a round table that holds the latest science book through which the captain, a competent amateur scientist, escapes to the infinite world of scientific conjecture before eventually surrendering himself to the even more seductive world of insanity. The plot of *The Father*, such as it is, tracks the man's growing paranoia concerning the paternity of his daughter. The real subject of the play is how a tiny idea can grow to take over a life. It could be staged inside a skull.

Strindberg wrote the play at great speed and when it was finished in February 1887, he was too dejected by Bonnier's recent rejections even to send it to him. He tried other Swedish publishers but just as his manuscript was landing on their desks, Stockholm was being rocked by a book called *Strindbergian Literature and Immorality among Schoolchildren* written by a famous Swedish educationalist and future bishop called John Personne.[24] The book denounced Strindberg as the corruptor of Swedish youth. His writing was a cesspool of iniquity that was spreading filth, ordure, immorality and indiscipline through Sweden's coming generation, corrupting youth and promoting false and pornographic values. Personne particularly blamed Strindberg for masturbation in the young: 'the evil which can lead to the spiritual and bodily ruin of our children . . . I refer to the secret sin which has been called the most dangerous enemy of youth'. As well as masturbation, Strindberg was blamed for schoolboys going to 'houses of vice' after school and even using their lunch breaks for the same purpose. After plenty more accusations of sexual corruption, Personne urged the public prosecutor to take action under the provisions of the Swedish penal code against the dissemination of Strindbergian literature.

It seemed that in Sweden there was no other issue that spring and summer of 1887. Newspapers and preachers drove a moral crusade whose moralising fervour the writer Oscar Levertin compared to the spread of the Black Death throughout the land[25] and it is apparent in letters and newspapers how parents with children who were the slightest bit out of control seized the opportunity to blame Strindberg rather than their own shortcomings. For a whole generation of anxious parents he had become the scapegoat for their children's sins. A petition was got up demanding greater censorship; six thousand citizens signed it and presented it to the Ministry of Justice.

The second strand to Personne's book was anti-Semitic. 'In *The New Kingdom*,' he wrote,

> Herr Strindberg devoted a whole chapter entitled *Moses* to the ruthless satirising of the Jews. In his later filth-writings, however, published by Herr Bonnier, things are quite otherwise. In these he not only writes most favourably of the Jews but even represents them as fellow-enthusiasts and fellow-campaigners in the great new cultural movement seeking to remove the boulder which holds us down . . . One hears of a kind of agreement between Herr Bonnier and Herr Strindberg by which the former agrees to act as the latter's publisher, allowing him more or less uninhibited freedom to write what he will. Provided he leaves Moses in peace . . . For my part I cannot see the moral distinction between such a publisher and someone who hires thieves to steal for him, or runs a brothel.[26]

Bonniers survives to this day as one of the great publishing houses of Sweden, but Albert Bonnier was later to write in his memoirs that the book sparked such hostility against himself, his family and his business that the publishing house was almost brought down. Prized authors deserted him and five leading publishers resigned from the Union of Publishers which Bonnier chaired. Strindberg's books were sent back from the bookshops to Bonniers' warehouse where they gathered dust in dispiriting piles. Looking back on this time, Bonnier said that it started an unprecedented persecution of both family and firm from which it took ten years to recover and the same might have been said by many Jews in Sweden. As for Strindberg, nobody spoke up for him and he was more alone than ever.

Nothing had changed in the six years since Strindberg had published his first novel, *The Red Room*, when Georg Brandes had written:

The situation here is really terrible. The reactionaries are powerful and triumphant, the people spineless and old-fashioned in their ways; the bestial instincts of the masses are being let loose in the form of gross hatred . . . the reactionaries are vicious all along the line . . . we suffer from the fact that the writers most *en vue* here combat narrow-mindedness with a certain coarseness of expression which frightens people off and back into narrow-mindedness. And then, as you rightly feel, we suffer from this intellectual syphilis called Protestantism. It gradually robs people of their confidence, their voice, their strength, and is passed on like the physical ditto. And nowhere does it wreak havoc as in Scandinavia.'[27]

10 EXPERIMENTAL THEATRE

From about 1850 when the paper negative was invented, certain prophets of the self-conscious such as Baudelaire and Mallarmé did not neglect the importance of being photographed. The image had become an integral part of modern, self-centred literary work and while previous generations had been prone to have their portraits cluttered up with historical references, the men at the cutting edge of late nineteenth-century culture were making statements about themselves as modern men who neither wanted nor needed cultural context. Strindberg could see the importance of this. He bought a camera, rigged up a cable release and took a series of self-portraits that he sent to Albert Bonnier with the suggestion that he publish them in a book of photographs to accompany the autobiographies.

The photographs were taken in Gersau towards the end of 1886 but they might have been taken anywhere. Location plays no part in the story. He is in his study writing, or playing his guitar or playing backgammon with Siri (this is his only photograph of the two of them together and we only see her back view) or he is in the garden with a wheelbarrow and the children, all wearing straw hats. There is one unsuccessful attempt to show himself as a fiercely sophisticated *boulevardier* in evening dress with top hat, cigar and a hard stare but usually he is a countryman in a tweed jacket buttoned to the chin and his face is gentle. However hard he tries (and in one photograph he flexes a fencing foil) he hardly looks like a man intent on corrupting a whole generation. We may take two contemporary accounts to judge how representative these photographs are, the first from Verner von Heidenstam and the second from Strindberg's elder daughter Karin. Von Heidenstam recalls him as well built,

30, 39, 42, 47
35

34

slim, on the tall side, with a high, intelligent forehead, curly upbrushed hair, well-tended moustaches, perpetually melancholy eyes, pronounced cheekbones and deep lines round a full, well-shaped mouth. His habitual expression was so severe, said Heidenstam, that if you met him on a mountain path you would hand him your purse before he asked for it but in conversation he would first be shy, then warm up to a courteous, unaffected charm and finally become so involved as to forget himself, at which stage you might be lucky enough to be rewarded by his exceptionally beautiful smile. Von Heidenstam said he never heard him laugh. His daughter Karin also says she never heard him laugh and she confirms his shyness and his rather formal gravity. She also says he was a gentle, patient, kind and indulgent parent who loved to share any activity with his children. During this photographic phase the children found it thrilling when he allowed them into the darkroom where they had to stand quiet as mice and still as grass for ten minutes in the ruby glow of the red-shaded lamp watching foggy swirls become indistinct ghosts become sharp images of themselves, or Papa.

39, 40, 41   'We were photographed by Papa while he hid his head under the black cloth and counted the seconds out loud. His apparatus consisted of a big yellow-varnished camera which was mounted on a tripod and his gentle pleasant way of treating children meant that I literally gaped with absorbed interest, as can be seen from my portrait.'[1]

He also welcomed the children into his study while he was writing. 'Come here, children', he would say softly and take little Hans on his knee while the girls stood either side of him. He would show them the pressed flowers in his herbarium or his illustrated books on natural history and when the children made their innocent and often naïve observations he did not laugh, they remembered, but would widen his eyes while amusement crept over his face.

They had moved to a manor farm in Lindau on the eastern shore of the Bodensee in Bavaria. It must have reminded Siri irresistibly of home, and Strindberg of her high status and wealth when they had first met, for it was much like Jackarby, having been in the same family since the 1400s and containing all the generational accumulation that he and Siri had just had to sell by auction in Stockholm. Its lime-washed white walls, green shutters and pastoral context conjured the white house with green shutters on Kymmendö where they had spent their happiest times. Strindberg rejoiced to be in a proper context of rural self-sufficiency with herds of all the right beasts to supply milk and a variety of meats, a neat log shed, a well-run kitchen garden and useful and beautiful orchards.

Even his new atheism was powerless to inoculate Strindberg against Easter in the mountains with thousands of resurrected flowers pushing towards the sun through the most unpromising sludge of mud that only the day before had been sugared with granular spring snow. Come summer he sent for crayfish just as he had on Kymmendö and they feasted under the stars, overlooking the silvery Bodensëe, and let off fire-works.

He wrote in a little tower room from which, he never tired of boast-ing, he could look across the lakes and mountains into a Kaiserdom, a kingdom and a republic. Here, disregarding all politics, he wrote a zesty, bawdy comic novel of peasant life which he himself compared to a Breughel painting. He called it *The People of Hemsö* and it takes place on the imaginary island of Hemsö in the Swedish skerries, a thinly disguised Kymmendö. Cognac and Swedish *punsch* flow day and night and there is sailing, fishing, hunting, farming and harvesting, lust both requited and unrequited, food and feasting and a plethora of farm hands and milkmaids who all work for Madam Flod, the widow who owns the island. Carlsson arrives to take up the post of farm manager. He proves to be a windbag, and he lays siege to the gullible widow. There is quarrelling on the third Sunday of the Banns when it comes to light that Carlsson has been both a railway bum and a Bible pedlar, that he has been discharged from three jobs and left another without proper notice. All this is revealed to the widow Flod but the flame of love burns in her breast. At last the wedding day arrives. The widow Flod pays a brief visit to the grave of her late lamented husband while Carlsson steps behind a gravestone to answer a call of nature.

> And then the bells started to ring again bingbonging like anything and it was time for the congregation to crawl inside but the Hemsö folk had no pew since it was burned to the ground so they had to stand in the aisle. It was frightfully hot and they felt ill at ease in the sizeable interior. They began to sweat out of sheer embarrassment and looked like culprits in a line-up.

The wedding is accomplished. There follows tremendous feasting as the long summer twilight settles over the sea and the skerries in a melon-coloured haze. The midges do their nocturnal polkadotting and the parson crawls into the bridal bed in such a drunken stupor that he cannot be wakened and they have to winch him out with block and tackle.

Carlsson's ship is now well launched on the Sea of Fortune. He becomes a homebody and sits in his chair spouting Holy Writ. The farm hands, unsupervised, snooze under hedges. The neglected farm is overgrown and the animals riot impiously. Some German mining prospectors arrive with promises of untold wealth. Carlsson's dreams have come true! No need for all the hard work of farming. The Germans pay Carlsson for mining rights with worthless share certificates, wreak havoc dynamiting for feldspar, and vamoose. Winter comes. Snowflakes spin down endlessly, grey as moths and big as chicken feathers. Carlsson at last gets his wife to sign her will in his favour. Unknown to them both, her son Gusten is spying through a hole in the panelling. Carlsson, now secure, makes a tryst with one of the young farm girls. The widow follows their footsteps through the snow and she observes them fiddle-faddling. She falls into an ice hole, crawls home, flings the will onto the fire and turns her face to the wall as all good Vikings do when it is time to go home to Valhalla. Now there is a problem. The island is iced in. The body is starting to stink and they must get her to the graveyard on the mainland. The creek lies frozen, the bays and inlets and channels and coves are iced over. They put the coffin in a boat and set off. Sometimes they push the boat like a sledge and sometimes they row it and sometimes they cut channels in the ice. The boat capsizes. Coffin and body are lost down an ice hole in the sea. Carlsson and Gusten are stranded on the ice. They hear roaring. An ice storm is coming. An onrushing wall of snow is behind them. The air is loud with the crackshots of breaking ice as the sea approaches.

'Keep going with the wind and you'll come west. You'll find land there', Gusten's voice comes fitfully on the wind through the darkness ahead of Carlsson, but Carlsson has grown fat sitting by the fire and the sea behind him is screaming and groaning like a wild beast ravening for prey on this dreadful night.

Gusten arrives at the parsonage and shouts the parson out of bed: 'We've lost mother!' Cue for much drinking.

When the storm has come to an end, a rescue party is mounted. They row through the ice floes. They salvage the boat that had carried the coffin. Gusten says it is useless to continue the search as the currents have probably carried the coffin out to sea. All are mightily relieved.

Nobody wanted to see the dead woman floating into sight. The parson leads the men in a hymn around the ice hole. As Gusten rows home to become the master of Hemsö, the fishermen line up their boats and raise their oars in a salute.

The People of Hemsö is the great comic masterpiece of Swedish litera-ture. It is Strindberg's happiest and most popular book and while he was writing it he assured his friends that he and Siri were living in Lindau like newlyweds, drinking beer, playing backgammon and singing student songs. He was a woman-hater only in theory, he assured them, and he had never been happier than he was here and now living with six women.[2] However, this was not the whole truth. Siri was terribly unhappy. She felt humiliated that they were living on the money from his books that she felt belittled her in the world's eyes. They quarrelled constantly and Strindberg started taking little trips to escape from her and to investigate the rumours against her which he could not entirely dismiss from his mind. In April he was in Vienna where the newspaper *Neue Freie Presse* was going to publish his psychological pieces *Vivisections* and while he was there he took the opportunity to probe his friends back home for the names of her lovers. Those pamphlets that had been circulated round Stockholm, did they name names, he asked on the pretext of protecting Siri's reputation and he put forward names of candidates he suspected, including actors she had once acted with and doctors who had treated her complaints, but nobody had any names to give him. Without a male lover, his mind became fixed on the alternative. Siri was still in corre-spondence with Marie David who was encouraging her to think of herself as a woman deprived of her human rights and shut up in a doll's house of Strindberg's making. Marie David was actively urging Siri to leave Strindberg and urging her to divorce.[3] Maddened by this interference, in June Strindberg wrote a letter to Edvard Brandes saying that he had heard that Marie David and Sofie Holten had seduced a servant girl in Grez whom they had driven to her death and that the police were plan-ning an arrest. A few days later he wrote to Carl Larsson demanding information about the case. All that was needed was an accusation from the mayor of Grez to condemn the two girls, Strindberg said, as if Larsson could procure the accusation from the mayor or would wish to even if he could. The letter added that 'The worst of the two ladies is still pestering my wife with love letters urging her to abandon her husband and children'.

35

Hoping to get at the truth, he tried to trip her up in conversations and to bend her will to his own and force her to confess by the power of Bernheimian suggestion and by the mind-games that Huysmans called 'fluidic fisticuffs', such as out-staring her in a mirror.[4] The tension between them grew until finally she confessed that she had been unfaithful. It had happened in the early days of the marriage, in 1882 when she had gone to Finland to act in *Jane Eyre*. He had been left behind looking after the children on Kymmendö and, desperately in love as we remember from the tumble of affectionate letters he wrote containing little pieces of news about the children and suggesting fashionable clothes that might suit her, as well as proffering advice and encouragement on her acting. All the time he had been conducting himself as the perfect husband of a modern, emancipated wife, trustingly fulfilling his side of the bargain by looking after the children so as to enable her to pursue her own career, she was being unfaithful. It was a terrible betrayal of his ideals and of their love. Kymmendö was his favourite place on earth and now he could never go back there; she had corrupted their Eden. As if that were not grounds enough for misery, he had plenty of time to think what a fool he had made of himself over the last five years as, believing in her, he had repeatedly sprung to her defence against the continuous rumours of her promiscuity and attacks on her reputation. How many people had known the truth before him? She had made him utterly ridiculous. At first she told him that an engineer had forced himself upon her on the Helsinki boat. Later, according to her own unconfirmed version of events, she told him a different story that there was no engineer and no force but an actor called Eric Dahlström, a member of the company at Nya Teatern in Helsinki who had been staying at the same hotel, and they had enjoyed a brief affair which had ended on her return to Stockholm. Later still she told her daughters that she had never been unfaithful to their father at all.[5]

Whichever version was true, actor, engineer or pure provocation, it was enough to send him into a vortex of misery, jealousy and instability. Siri's heinous crime, as he called it, was bad enough in itself but its consequences defied dread. How was he to know that she had not been unfaithful on other occasions? He now suspected her of whoring with all the world, men and women, and he brooded on the legitimacy of his children and the further horror that he might unbeknownst be brewing syphilis from one of her connections.[6]

He hit Siri, knocking her to the ground. With one of his knees on her chest he began pummelling her with his fists. Maybe Siri had thought it safer to confess in the presence of the children for Karin remembers looking down on her mother lying on the floor, her face framed by her spilling blond hair. Siri did not scream but simply lay without saying a word, staring up at Strindberg with widening eyes. The children started crying and shouting 'Papa! Papa!' and Siri was released. All sources agree that he attacked her only once but it terrified the children who were present and from then on Siri began to be wary and afraid.

'Provoked to the very root of my testicles' and typically wishing to ascertain provable fact, Strindberg went to a brothel in Geneva, pausing only to pick up a doctor on the way. Here he had his penis measured in its excited state (16 × 4 centimetres) and after a performance that the whore said was entirely creditable though not *cum laude*, as he recorded with heartbreaking honesty, he had his semen examined and pronounced fertile. 'I wasn't a *big* man in a passive state but normal when aroused.' It may be gathered between the lines that he had been suffering from anxiety concerning the size of his organ for some time. Siri had let him know that Wrangel was 'a giant capable of satisfying her, her cousin, and whores all at the same time' but it is not known how long before she had told him this or how often. Once furnished with the medical proof of satisfactory measurements he was able to tell her with icy dignity that 'the screw is not necessarily too small because the nut is too big.'[7]

After this there is a burst of letters to his intimate men friends recounting that their sex life is now flourishing as never before. He says he has put aside his gentle dealings and good manners and taken to beating her as a prelude to intercourse. Aroused by his brutality, she is sexually satisfied as never before. It sounds unlikely. Beating did not play a part in any of his later sexual relationships or in his subsequent literature even when its subject is the battle of the sexes. Had flagellation come into it, he would surely have valued the insights the activity afforded the human condition and used it accordingly. It seems more like the club-room boast of a humiliated man.

At nearly forty he thought he could not bear a future of 'masturbation and charity' and he begged the long-suffering Pehr Staaff to find him a peasant woman with good breasts and hips who had recently had a child 'by an unknown father who had slunk off'. Not over twenty-five. Clean and particular about her appearance. Head not too full of socialist ideas.

He would bed the mother and bring up the child. He could neither work nor contemplate a future without the sound of children's voices around him.[8] In the same letter that charged poor Pehr Staaff to find this ideal peasant duo he charged him also to find a publisher for *The People of Hemsö* in place of Albert Bonnier who had written to him in July 1887 with the devastating news that he would neither publish the book of photographs nor *The Author*, the fourth volume of autobiography. Bonnier felt that these books would only aggravate Strindberg's 'regrettable and quite unprecedented unpopularity'[9] and in fact the books remained unpublished until shortly before Strindberg's death. Having failed with Albert Bonnier he tried his nephew Isidor who, eventually and anonymously, had republished the unexpurgated *Getting Married*. Isidor turned him down as well and June saw Strindberg selling his only remaining asset, his life insurance policy. This was a desperate act that in the plays of Strindberg and Ibsen signifies the last resource of the rascal as it will leave his family destitute in the event of the breadwinner's death.

Strindberg could not forgive Albert Bonnier for telling him he was unpublishable in Sweden and it unleashed a torrent of paranoid fury that reads like any author raging against his publisher in such a situation except that it was exaggerated and worsened because Strindberg had finally turned against Bonnier as a Jew. The Jews were out to get him. Marie David was Jewish and she was trying to steal his wife. Albert Bonnier was trying to kill him as an author by keeping him poor so as to torture him to death. Jews did not believe in friendship or gratitude. They were reptiles who had spread poison against him in a filthy pamphlet that had been circulated in Germany; its authors were a cabal of publishers intent on destroying his career, consisting of Albert and Isidor Bonnier and another of his former publishers, Claës Looström.[10] This was not true. The filthy pamphlet existed but neither Bonnier nor Looström had anything to do with it as Strindberg might have discovered; if he had used his common sense he would have known that it was most unlikely that Looström would have collaborated with the Bonniers on anything. Looström was no lover of Jews.

Karl Otto Bonnier sent him a private gift of 500 kr. Strindberg's letter of thanks was thorny: 'That you have saved the Strindbergs cannot be denied, perhaps, but considering how various Bonniers have been saved by Swedish writers, the opportunity of paying a small debt of gratitude should not have been too disagreeable to you. Besides, had he enjoyed a little more freedom of expression, Strindberg would not have required your charity.'[11]

'Now I have sold everything that could be sold,' he wrote to his brother Axel, 'there remains only my corpse (and above all my cranium) to sell to the Karolina Institute.'[12]

All was not anti-Semitism, self-mockery and despair, for he was hatching a promising scheme with another Jew, his loyal supporter Edvard Brandes who told Strindberg about an amateur experimental theatre newly started in Paris by André Antoine[13] who worked for the Paris Gas Company by day but by night was transforming the Paris repertoire, which for the past decade had clung to proven successes and profits delivered by the illustrious trinity of Dumas, Sardou and Augier and now the audience was ready to grow out of them. *Crime and Punishment* had just been published in French and Paris was afire for Russian radicalism, for Dostoevsky and Tolstoy. Antoine was putting on plays by Tolstoy, Zola and the brothers Goncourt in borrowed spaces with minimal props and naturalistic acting. Strindberg became so excited that he immediately wanted to become part of this new movement. He quickly translated *The Father* into French and sent it to Zola, hoping that he might forward it to Antoine with a recommendation that it be put on at the Théâtre Libre. He also travelled to Copenhagen to visit Georg Brandes and discuss the possibility of setting up a similar experimental theatre in one of the Scandinavian capitals. He decided to approach Scandinavia's leading actor–manager August Lindberg[14] who was an old friend from the Royal Theatre days when Strindberg had made his brief foray onto the boards. Lindberg was a lean, dark, hawkish, analytical man, three years older than Strindberg with a good profile and excellent theatrical judgement who had managed to make a career of playing pieces he believed in. He had premiered many of Ibsen's controversial plays and created many of the great Ibsen roles including Osvald in *Ghosts*. Strindberg wrote to Lindberg suggesting that they create a new experimental theatre together, starting on a small scale with a touring company. He would write five new plays for the first year's programme: a tragedy, a comedy, a burlesque and two one-acters. They would be so pared down to psychological interest that there would be no need for the expense of costumes, sets or props. Writing from the country of Elsinore, he was proposing a rather lovely reversion to the old idea of a company of strolling players. He outlined a company of eight players including two girls (one blonde, one brunette) and two lovers (one idealistic, one realistic and ugly) and he proposed they raise the capital by subscription. To calm Lindberg's nerves he promised plays that were only interested in 'artistic aims': no politics, sex or social agenda. This last proposal, betraying as it did Strindberg's lack of confidence, must have killed Lindberg's interest at a stroke. What was modern theatre without sex, society or politics? Lindberg's fears must further have been stirred by the unusual addendum that if Lindberg wanted his own wife to be part of the company, Siri should be as well for she was 'a great actress' but Lindberg must keep this proposal a secret for Siri had no idea of it.[15]

Lindberg politely declined but another opportunity bobbed up most unexpectedly when Hans Riber Hunderup[16] wrote to Strindberg proposing to stage *The Father* in Copenhagen. Hunderup was less reliable than Lindberg: a brilliant, careless thirty-year-old actor–manager with a reputation for being sketchy about budgets, he was such a quintessential energiser that things usually worked out in the end. He had just taken over the management of Copenhagen's Casino Theatre which was a popular venue for light comedy and easy fare. Hunderup was out to make his reputation. He too had read about Antoine's venture in Paris and he was determined to try something of the same. He had the influential backing of both Brandes brothers, Edvard who would give it a fair wind in *Politiken* and Georg who was sufficiently interested to volunteer his help in directing the play. This was enormously encouraging to Strindberg who was now back in the Alps finishing *The People of Hemsö* and playing silent cat and mouse games of paranoia and suspicion with Siri. Finally he filed a petition for divorce against her in the Swedish Consistory Court and this was probably another cat and mouse game because you could not be granted a Swedish divorce unless one or both parties were resident in Sweden. He also wrote to the editor of *Dagens Nyheter* informing him of the divorce 'to pre-empt false rumours'.[17]

This left Siri in a hopeless position. Strindberg was about to move to Denmark to oversee the play and he planned to take the family with him as usual, though Siri would only be travelling in the capacity of his mistress and the mother of his children, not as his wife, a position she had dishonoured. As he was taking Siri back to Marie David's native land, Strindberg took the precaution of making Siri promise not to contact her. He also wrote to Siri's two aged aunts suggesting that they charge

Marie David and Sofie Holten with homosexual conduct. This must have come as a severe fright to the old ladies who had no reason to accuse the two women of anything.[18]

On 4 November 1887 they set off for Copenhagen. Now, more than ever, Strindberg was wary that Siri was working with her allies to have him certified and he stopped at Roskilde to get a certification of sanity from the most famous Scandinavian doctor in the field of mental health, Knud Pontoppidan,[19] a charismatic and wonderfully beautiful psychiatrist with ice-blue eyes and a record of success in treating writers and artists suffering from nervous breakdowns. Controversially, Pontoppidan believed in the supremacy of the nervous system over organic functions of the body and he tackled his patients through talking and listening rather than the freezing baths and other physical shocks that then comprised cures for madness. His response to Strindberg's request was reasonable: he could not possibly say if Strindberg was sane or insane without a period of observation.

Strindberg had no time for that. He was speeding to Copenhagen to meet Axel Lundegård who was translating *The Father* from Swedish into Danish and this was when they all foregathered at the Hotel Leopold, where young Karin was summoned in the night by Victoria Benedictsson asking her to keep her company while she made her first attempt at suicide for love of Georg Brandes.

Hunderup's finances stood eleven performances of *The Father* before he went bankrupt and the Strindbergs vanished into the gothic grotesqueries of Skovlyst whence they emerged with *Miss Julie* written and Strindberg found innocent after yet another trial, this time for sexual intercourse with the purportedly under-age Martha Magdalena.

Before they went to Skovlyst, on 12 November, having that day watched the dress rehearsal of *The Father* he wrote an informal Last Will and Testament, addressing it to his translator Lundegård. First he listed the practical affairs he would like Lundegård to put in order should he commit suicide. He does not know if he will or not. He is balanced on the edge, having been driven there by the ghastly experience he usually avoided, watching his own play on stage. Sitting in the audience listening to the witches' brew that his mind had made of the scraps of experience, lived or imagined, what he called the jumble of bus tickets, newspaper reports, old clothes cut up and re-made, the thoughts and counter-thoughts that made up his fictional works, he saw for the first time what

49

48

he had done to Siri. He realised that she had been vilified in the piece; he also saw for the first time that the character of the father is, in a way, insane. He had not seen this before because insanity can only be written convincingly from inside when the real world has slipped away or been dismissed and the mind finds itself in a different place. Face to face with this truthful but untruthful account of the past year, the long letter he composed to Lundegård charged him to see that Siri was rehabilitated and asked him to assure people that Strindberg was sane, after which he went on to explain the confusion between reality and imagination during the process of creation, referring to himself as the hypnotist-writer who if he is successful hypnotises the audience but this can only be achieved if he too enters the dream through a degree of self-hypnosis:

> It seems to me as if I were sleepwalking. As if life and invention were inextricable. I have no idea whether *The Father* is a work of the imagination or if my life has been that; yet I feel that at a given moment, probably quite soon, I will know which and then I will collapse, either into madness and remorse or suicide. Constant work on my writing has made my life a shadow existence; I feel as if I were no longer walking on this earth but rather floating, weightless in an atmosphere not of air but of darkness. If light penetrates this darkness I shall collapse crushed. A strange thing is a frequently recurring dream at night, I feel I'm flying weightless and find that quite natural. Gravity has been dissolved and with it all notions of right and wrong, true and false have ceased to exist, and that everything that happens, no matter how strange, is exactly as it should be.[20]

Under this spell of unreality he wrote the final volume of autobiography in French, bringing the story of his life up to date. The book was written between September 1887 and March 1888 and it recounts the story of his marriage. Siri's name is changed to Marie, surely not by chance. When Siri read it she was dismayed and said it was all true and yet all completely untrue.[21] He called the book *Le Plaidoyer d'un fou* (*A Madman's Defence*) and it was while he was writing it that he discovered Edgar Allen Poe with whom he felt such an instant affinity that while devouring Poe's *Tales* he flirted with the idea that Poe's soul had migrated into his own. Poe's story 'Eleonora' contained a passage that is similar to the one he had just written, quoted above, on the conjunction of insanity and creativity.

'Men have called me mad', Poe wrote,

but the question is not yet settled whether madness is not the loftiest intelligence – whether much that is glorious – whether all that is profound – does not spring from disease of thought – from *moods* of mind exalted at the expense of general intellect. They who dream by day are cognisant of many things which escape those who only dream by night. In their grey visions they obtain glimpses of eternity, and thrill, in waking, to find they have been on the verge of the great secret . . . they penetrate, however rudderless or compassless, into the vast ocean of the light ineffable.[22]

These days *Le Plaidoyer d'un fou* reads like nothing so much as *Metamorphosis* by Kafka, who was himself a great admirer of Strindberg's writing. The 'I' character, the husband, is split in two like Kafka's Gregor and his monstrous alter-ego beetle. Sometimes one sees the marriage from Strindberg's rational everyday self who is perfectly capable of walking neatly suited down the street and sometimes one sees it from the deep, invisible chasms of paranoia and insanity that lie unsuspected but equally precisely tailored beneath the neat suit. The genius is the seamlessness between the two. In terms of contemporary works the book relates more strongly to paintings than literature and even so it is a few years earlier than its closest equivalent paintings, Edvard Munch's *Anxiety* (1894) and *Evening on Karl Johan* (1892) which illustrate exactly that same interior panic within the conformist exterior. Shortly after Strindberg had finished writing *Le Plaidoyer d'un fou* he realised that it was not for publication and sent it to his brother Oscar 'as head of the house of Strindberg', asking him to deposit it in the family archive.[23] It was not until 1964 that the book's greatness was truly recognised when it was republished in Paris and the *soixantardiste* intellectuals hailed it as a modern masterpiece prefiguring both Freud and existentialism: 'Schizophrenia, the disease of our own century is here. Here, too, is the modern game of ambiguity: who is lying? Who is mad? Who is wrong? Which one the executioner and which the victim?' wrote Roger Grenier in the *Nouvel Observateur* on 17 December 1964.

After the Skovlyst period, Strindberg returned to thoughts of divorce and of experimental theatre. He offered Siri a divorce on the grounds of his adultery with Martha Magdalena but she refused, saying she did not want to make use of something she no longer cared about. She was fair-minded and defended him from the scandalmongering newspapers. She moved in with her aunt Augusta Möller in Copenhagen while Strindberg, who knew that in *Miss Julie* he had finally created the revolutionary play that released him from the shadow of Ibsen or any other playwright who had gone before, set about getting it staged. Bonnier, who had grudgingly agreed to publish *The People of Hemsö* subject to fussy cuts, was far too frightened to publish *Miss Julie* but Strindberg badly needed it to be published to bring the script into the new experimental theatres. He approached Seligmann who had made good money out of publishing *The Red Room* and he consented to publish it with certain prudent cuts to get it past the censor, such as the omission of Julie's comparison of her intercourse with Jean to an act of bestiality. It is a measure of *Miss Julie*'s shocking modernity that it was not published uncensored in Sweden until nearly a century later, in 1984.

On 14 November 1888 Strindberg founded the Scandinavian Experimental Theatre. He advertised for actors through *Politiken* and he wrote to everyone he knew for money. Siri, who now went under the name Siri Essen-Strindberg, was appointed general and artistic director. She was also the leading lady and bought herself a fine white dress with a bustle. They were set to open on 2 March 1889 to perform three of his most brilliant and enduring plays, *Miss Julie*, *The Stronger* and *Creditors*, the last also written at Skovlyst, but disaster struck in the middle of the dress rehearsal the day before they were due to open when they were raided by the police delivering the censor's ban on performing *Miss Julie*. Bravely they went ahead with the opening, substituting *Pariah* for *Miss Julie*. Nevertheless, Siri was given the chance to create the most important female role her husband ever created for the stage as they got round the censorship by mounting a private performance of *Miss Julie* at the Students' Association in Copenhagen on 14 March. This was nearly sabotaged by another confusion between art and reality when Strindberg succumbed to the idea that Siri was having an affair with Viggo Schiwe, the actor who was playing Jean, and Strindberg subjected the two actors to a storm of jealousy and suspicion that was entirely appropriate, given the nature of the play. In such circumstances it was maybe not surprising that the critics found Schiwe's Jean 'polite' and too gentlemanly and Siri's Julie 'cold, much too cold, and one gets no idea of the kind of woman who would seduce a man like Jean'.[24]

Although the play aroused horror and disgust, his revolutionary staging elicited praise. Later, when finally *Miss Julie* was staged at the Théâtre Libre in 1893, he set down his ideas on staging in a preface to the play. It was of the utmost importance that the piece be played right through so there should be no break in the intensity. 'I have eliminated the interval', he wrote in the introduction, 'which gives the spectator time to reflect and thereby withdraw from the suggestive influence of the author-hypnotist.' The introduction goes on to propose a revolution in make-up and lighting. In those days the actor still went on stage in character make-up. 'Suppose an actor – to achieve an irascible, choleric look – applies a couple of bold, black lines between the eyes and that he looking wrathful with his ineradicable expression has to smile in response to somebody's remark! What a horrible grimace!' and with this proposal for more subtle make-up came the suggestion that the harsh glare of the footlights which turned the eye sockets into black pits either side of the wedge of shadow cast by the nose should be eliminated. If softer side lighting was used to illuminate facial expression it would also illuminate psychology. He deplored tennis-match dialogue, such as written by Sardou, when characters feed each other lines and 'everyone talks as if they are editors of comic magazines'. He also deplored painted flats. The audience's imagination should not be wasted on believing in painted saucepans, he wrote, and for the performance of *Miss Julie* he hired real saucepans from the kitchen of Siri's aunt and put them on real shelves. The critics were particularly taken by this and while they were so shocked by the piece that one critic recommended Strindberg be deported, the saucepans came in for general praise.

The Experimental Theatre gave only three performances, two in Denmark and one across the Sound in Sweden. Siri had set foot again in Sweden! Strindberg found the pull so strong that in April 1889 he put his own feet back on Swedish soil again, but timidly and out of sight on a small island in the archipelago where he could avoid the bear pit. He bombarded Siri, who was still living with her aunt, with letters, some threatening, some cajoling but all begging her to bring the children and join him so that they might live as a family again.

'I'm dying bit by bit – and yet I cannot hate you! Why didn't you shoot me a while back . . . I've two cottages on an island more beautiful than the verdant isle of our salad days, and you and Karin and Greta and Putte [Hans] will live in one of them which is as fine as a castle, and I'll live in the other.'[25]

She came quickly.

This was the last period they were to spend together as a family and they spent it in Strindberg's beloved Swedish skerries. They could not go back to Kymmendö where the natives felt that they had been mocked in *The People of Hemsö* but they lived on Värmdö and Runmarö. That summer, the children remember, he was fascinated by snakes. He used to catch quite large adders in his net and play his flute to them whereupon the charmed animals would get up on their tails and perform a swaying dance. He also wrote two beautiful books, *Life in the Skerries* and *By the Open Sea*, a haunting novel dealing with a man's descent into love and thence into madness, which particularly fascinated Kafka.

In December 1890 they would soon have lived long enough in Sweden to qualify for divorce and on 19 December they visited the Pastor on Värmdö to apply for one based on 'a year divorced from bed and board'.

Siri, short of money, wrote a begging letter to Marie David and one January evening the nursemaid Eva Carlsson said, 'There's a man at the door.' They looked up to see a cigarette glowing, an upturned collar and short clipped red curls.[26] It was Marie David and she moved in with Siri and the children.

This ignited Strindberg's fury and the divorce proceedings became ugly. Both women drank more heavily when they were together and he wrote a letter to the Church Committee on 29 January saying that Marie David was a famous lesbian known to be addicted to alcohol who drank cognac with her breakfast coffee, absinthe before lunch and cognac throughout the day and that she had tried to seduce his wife and children from him.

'Now Froken David is living with Fru Sg and my children at Lemshaga. I am condemned by the court to pay for a tribaidic *ménage* until I die; and the children! whom I'm not allowed to see! And no one can help them! *No one!*'[27]

The Church Committee ruled that Marie David should cease all contact with Siri and the children and on 10 June 1891 Marie David sued Strindberg for libel. Marie David and Siri were then living in Sandhamn and on Midsummer Day Marie went to visit a lithographer called Petersson who had known her in Grez-sur-Loing and had agreed to act as character witness for her. Unknown to her, Petersson lived in the same house as Strindberg on Runmarö and when she rang the bell, Strindberg came to the door. Seeing who it was, he pushed her roughly down the stairs, giving her grounds for an action for assault. He countered with an action for trespass. Later that summer, he wrote two excellent plays, *Leka med elden* (*Playing with Fire*; 1892), a lustful comedy of social observation and *Bandet* (*The Bond*; 1892), a touching courtroom drama based on the devastating experience that is divorce where nobody ever really wins and each parent sees clear-eyed the future tragedy to which they are dooming their children by the turning of their love to hate.

The cases brought against him by Marie David were heard on 8 September and the following July the court found Strindberg guilty of both libel and assault but sent a clear signal where their sympathies lay by fining him a derisory amount.

On 21 September 1892 their marriage was finally dissolved. Siri and Strindberg never saw each other again.

The following spring Siri and the children went to live in Helsinki 36, 37 with Marie David who supported them all on her private income and they continued to live together until she died some five years and several spells in hospital later. She and Siri both converted to the Roman Catholic faith together and after this Marie David changed, becoming strait-laced, puritanical, giving up drink and disapproving of the smallest frivolity, according to the children, who confirmed that she was an alcoholic but thought that there was no more than loving friendship between her and their mother. Marie David was thirty-two when she died of tuberculosis, the same disease that had killed her mother at a young age. In her final months she had determined to join an order of nuns but she died before she could take her final vows. Shortly before entering the convent she burned all of Siri's letters, so we will never know.

11 THE BLACK PIGLET

Eight days after his divorce Strindberg took a train to Berlin, disembarking at the exuberantly vaulted Stettiner Bahnhof on 1 October 1892, carrying a small suitcase of clothes and an enormous, bulging green sack that was his filing system and his archive and all his literary work in progress.

A small group of admirers formed a welcoming committee at the station. He gave them, one said, 'the smile of a child who is headed straight into the woods of fairyland', another noticed how small were his feet, how precise his steps and how this added a quality of remoteness and dignity to his figure. Another, a Satanist who saw auras, clutched his neighbour's arm and hissed, 'I see the placenta still attached! He'll never free himself from Woman. He'll never cut himself loose from the womb!'[1] The members of this observant crowd were mostly ten to twenty years younger than Strindberg and part of an artistic and literary circle that did not lack confidence. They saw themselves as future immortals and Strindberg as an important signpost to their future. From afar they already knew his intellectual incisiveness, critical ruthlessness and unpredictable brilliance. Now that they were greeting him in the flesh, it was a considerable help that he had style, presence and an attractive degree of shy reserve.

He had been invited to Berlin by the thirty-two-year-old Swedish poet and novelist Ola Hansson,[2] a rather wispy man with a nervous manner, fair moustaches and a sufficient number of neuroses to provide him with an accurate vision of the importance that would be played in the literature of the near future by the psychology of sex. Strindberg and Hansson had corresponded over the previous few years. Strindberg introduced

Hansson to Nietzsche. Hansson had written the Nietzschean short story *Pariah* on which Strindberg based his play of the same name but it was Hansson's volume of erotic case histories, *Sensitiva Amorosa* (1887), which he referred to in Strindbergian manner as 'anatomies of the soul', that had been received with such hostility in his native Sweden that it had driven him into exile in Berlin where he lived with his older, German-born wife Laura, who wrote under the name Marholm. She looks very presentable in photographs; it must have been her psychiatric difficulties that caused her contemporaries to describe her as coarse, ugly and masculine. She was widely disliked. A raging persecution complex would lead her to end her days in an asylum but meanwhile she and her husband delved into the psychology of sex and she, more forceful than he, promoted his writing. The Hanssons took Strindberg to live in their house in the wooded suburb of Friedrichshagen where he could enjoy the dawn walks that were necessary to kick off his writing day. Evenings were spent discussing the topics that had been the subject of his correspondence with Ola Hansson: split personalities, *doppelgänger*, abnormal psychology and the topic Poe had raised in Strindberg's mind: the relationship between genius and insanity. Hansson was interested in a slightly different angle: the idea that artistic genius was close to criminal genius, supporting his case by phrenology (porcelain phrenology heads were all the rage) and Lombrosan eugenics.

Soon after Strindberg's arrival, the Hanssons held a party for him to meet the group of admirers who had been at the station. Strindberg did not speak copybook German but they said he expressed himself clearly and precisely even on obscure subjects, though in broken phrases, rolling his r's and prolonging his s's.[3] The party lasted all night and he impressed them by carrying his drink with inexorable dignity. The writer Adolf Paul[4] attended the party and was so smitten by Strindberg's extraordinary originality and genius that he became a devoted disciple, taking it upon himself to report for posterity everything Strindberg said and did.

Strindberg talked the whole evening, dazzled us with his astounding paradoxes, impressed us with his scientific theories, turned hitherto accepted scientific principles on their heads . . . and he spoke of his private life with such frank openness that we looked at each other in some embarrassment. At length — it was morning — he took his guitar and, standing on one leg, sang Swedish songs.

Some time after this, walking with Paul towards the corner of Neue Wilhelmstrasse and Unter den Linden, Strindberg spotted a tavern whose sign was a Bessarabian wineskin suspended by chains. As it squeaked in the wind, Strindberg playfully mistook it for a piglet hanging up there.

'Hey', he said. 'That piglet's squealing a welcome. Let's go in.'[5]

The place was immediately rechristened Zum Schwarzen Ferkel (the Black Piglet) and became Strindberg's clubroom, the latest in his series of clubs like the Red Room and The Club. A new circle clustered round him for a night's conversation, fellowship, hard debate and inspirational speculation. 'By six o'clock in the evening, once Strindberg had begun frequenting the place, it was impossible to find a square inch.'[6] The sun rose and set through alcohol. Outside light filtered in through rainbow-coloured liquor bottles cramming the windows, like stained glass in a church and it became both their cathedral of ideas and their theatre of fantasy where they kept masks and swords and theatrical costumes and their musical instruments.

'Explain the riddle of the universe, my children', the evenings would often begin. When the riddle was proving elusive and the room looked as if demons had run riot, Strindberg would pick up his guitar which he kept deliberately un-tuned to illustrate the importance of chance in the creative process.[7] He would play duets with the twenty-five-year-old Polish philosopher Stanislaw Przybyszewski (pronounced Shibishevsky)[8] who 'improvised on well-known themes but only in the grand manner, and his control of his listeners was so complete that resistance was impossible. It ceased to be music, the piano was forgotten. It was a gale, a waterfall, a thunderstorm, which turned souls inside out.'[9] A favourite piece was Schumann's *Aufschwung* which he played like a soaring acoustic manifesto but in less exalted mood he and Strindberg would launch into the duet they called 'The Dead Russian's Funeral', the piano becoming ever more *doloroso* while Strindberg hopped about on one leg improvising Aeolian discords on the un-tuned guitar. One night, Strindberg, Doctor Carl Ludwig Schleich[10] and a Japanese sea captain sang folk songs till dawn to determine which nation should be awarded the palm of poetic genius.

Any accepted truth raised the rebel in him. For instance, why should he believe the world was round just because everybody said so? Back to first principles. He set up an experiment with the German poet Erich Hartleben[11] and Schleich, who takes up the story:

With some trouble we managed to buy, from an old Jewess, a badly frayed broom and the three of us strolled along . . . it was arranged that Hartleben should plant himself in the middle of the roadway with the broom planted bristle end upwards. Strindberg and I were prepared to sacrifice our clothes to science, and laid ourselves down on the asphalt . . . Hardly had we assumed the position from which our observations were to be made when a policeman ordered us to get up and clear off, uttering the most insulting suspicions and casting doubt upon our scientific qualifications. 'This', he said, 'is not a night refuge!' With a great expenditure of scientific argument we at last succeeded in persuading our policeman of the importance of our experiment, and it is an affecting instance of the scientific spirit of our police force that he was almost ready to lie down beside us in order to prove once for all that the earth is not round. But all this had taken so long that Erich Hartleben had begun to feel bored, and he suddenly appeared, broom in hand, puffing and gasping that 'it was altogether too tedious a business!' So our beautiful experiment fell through, and we continued to question the spherical form of the earth.[12]

Strindberg was now calling himself a Providentialist. He had decided that writing was a shameful profession because 'a writer flays his friends and offers their skins for sale and expects them to buy them. . . . this is to behave like a Croat, to chop, defile, burn and sell. Fie, for shame!'[13] Instead, he wanted to be blown about by fate, to take wing on the ideas offered by the Berlin group with the notion of possibly alighting on a new career in science, the subject that had interested him in his youth before he became a writer.

The group saw themselves as part of a great renaissance of the soul against the intellect, part of the mystical underground current running as a counter-culture to Darwinian certainty. They were not rising up against science – but against scientism, the attitude that all phenomena were explicable. Science, they felt, had stepped into the shoes of religion. Scientists were the new keepers of priestly certainty; they were accorded papal infallibility and permitted to maintain a moral blank while mechanisation marched on and spiritual needs were ignored.

They were not particularly interested in debating God versus Darwin. That was no longer the issue, with Nietzsche having famously declared God dead, continuing with the observation that 'considering the state the species Man is in, there will perhaps be caves, for ages yet, in which his shadow will be shown.'[14] Scientism seemed to be one of these shadows. They wished to restore validity to the invisible and the irrational, 'the disorderly confusion of our senses, the endless, boundless journeys of our hearts and minds, the mysterious operation of the nervous system, the whisperings of our blood, the prayers of our bones: the whole sub-conscious life of the soul.'[15] They aimed to find a technique to tap the unconscious processes for art: to master and control that elusive process 'inspiration'. To this end they studied the structure of the brain, optics, psychiatry, mysticism and symbolism, they paid attention to dreams before Freud made it routine to do so and, notoriously, they sought to unlock the doors of perception through excessive use of drink, drugs and sex.

It might have been just another pleasure-fest for self-indulgent artists were it not given validity by the calibre of the brains involved and the number of seriously respected medical men and scientists in the circle. The most notable medico was Doctor Carl Ludwig Schleich, who had been part of the unsuccessful experiment to prove the earth round. Schleich was an enormously distinguished physician and surgeon whose claim to fame was to discover a reliable means of local anaesthesia by injection. When he joined Strindberg's circle in the Schwarzen Ferkel, Schleich was coming to the end of his long experiments in perfecting the technique which began to be applied clinically two years later. Up to this time, the parts to be anaesthetised were sprayed with an ether spray which formed a numbing coat of ice: always painful, often dangerous, sometimes fatal. Schleich's research into the brain led him to concentrate on the role that glial cells played in the functioning of the nervous system and to experiment until he found the correct strength of injectable solu-tion of cocaine and married it up to the delivery network of glial cells.

Schleich was not the only pioneer in brain research. Przybyszewski, he who 'saw' the placenta attached to Strindberg when he arrived at the railway station, had written a distinguished study of the microscopic structure of the *cortex cerebri* and was the author of *Zur Psychologie des Individuums* (*On the Psychology of the Individual*; 1892) before he turned violently against structured methods of study and left medical school to study mysticism, Satanism and the power of black magic. He was a fore-runner of Wilhelm Reich in the heavy emphasis he placed on the power of sex as the motor driving the heart, soul and intellect of every man,

woman and child. 'In the beginning was Sex' is the first sentence of one
of his books but he was very charismatic and got away with such things.
He had two children by a downtrodden mistress, and when he felt particularly affectionate to one of his men friends he would say, 'I give you
Martha as a present, go and have sex with her.' Strindberg did not avail
himself. Przybyszewski was thin and blond with a quizzical, aggressive
manner and pale blue eyes permanently screwed up against the rising
smoke from the cigarette glued to his lower lip. According to contemporary viewpoints he looked like either a Slav Christ or Satan incarnate – we can decide for ourselves from the portraits Edvard Munch
painted of him. Przybyszewski knew demonological literature inside out
and to this extent he was a successor in Strindberg's mind to Klemming
at the Royal Library. For all Przybyszewski's posturing as a Magus it was
his neck-or-nothing exploration of heightened states of consciousness
that made it possible for Strindberg's work to pass further from naturalism to modernism.

Another doctor, Max Asch,[16] was a leading Berlin gynaecologist whom
they nicknamed 'Priapus'. Asch brought authority on female hysteria and
any other sexual matters to their debates and he commanded their
respect in another way, too: whenever he entered the Ferkel he usually
had a new mistress on his arm.

These were the scientists but there were writers and poets including
Richard Dehmel, taste-makers, artists, art critics, historians and magazine editors including Julius Meier-Graefe who produced the magazine
Pan that became their mouthpiece, and any passing Scandinavians who
arrived in town, including the great writer Knut Hamsun and the Norwegian painter Edvard Munch[17] whose birth as a graphic artist is largely
owing to Meier-Graefe who saw graphics as a way for Munch to make
money by selling popular editions. Munch immediately produced a book
of graphic masterpieces including *The Scream*, *The Sick Child*, *Death and
the Maiden*, *Vampire*, *Harpy* and *Madonna*, which Przybyszewski used as the
cover of his novel *The Vigil* which he presented to Strindberg. The musical
side of things might have been even more interesting had the Finn Jean
Sibelius joined the group; he was in Berlin at the time and he visited the
Ferkel once but never came back because his sensitive ears found the
noise level too high.

The important thing, Strindberg wrote, was that they were all chasing
something inexplicable, something more difficult to catch than a greased

pig, the unconscious part of the brain that neither pathology nor psychiatry could fully explain.

'The artist works unconsciously, creating like nature herself by trial and error with incredible waste', he wrote:

> When I create, I lose contact with my surroundings. I fall back to the level of instinctual life. But for my undeveloped brain the effort is too great. It hesitates; it draws back. The messages I receive are much too often left at the threshold of my unconscious without being arranged according to the laws of time and place. And as for what lies on the other side of that threshold, it has been stamped in our time with the cheap label Madness.[18]

Before laughing at some of their more ludicrous attempts to catch the greased pig, one may remember that they were just a piece of the great jigsaw quest that some twenty years later resulted in the formation of the Vienna Psychoanalytical Society (1908) and the publication of Freud's major books on dreams and sexuality (1910). Ten year later still, came Jung's *The Psychology of the Unconscious*.

Inspired by all this scientific investigation, and nervous that he might need 'a sideline to keep myself afloat for the time being', Strindberg turned the kitchen of the Hanssons' flat into a darkroom and became obsessed with solving the problem of colour photography. He made his own camera from a cigar box and a piece of paper with a hole in it. A thirty-second exposure was just right. The colours, he found, had the obstructive habit of remaining invisible on the exposed plates but he was certain they were there. All that was needed was another experiment or two to make the breakthrough. 'Developing with liquids must be the mistake', he decided; 'I shall now use gases!'[19] But gases got him no further. He was building up quite a science lab in Laura Hansson's kitchen.

The same month he had arrived in Germany one of the popular celebrity scientists had given a lecture at a scientific congress in Berlin. Ernst Haeckel,[20] the highly regarded Vice-President of the University of Jena, was a natural scientist who made it his mission to illustrate 'nature's soul', bringing the Divine back into Darwinism and the standards of beauty and symmetry found in classical sculpture and architecture to evolutionary biology. Haeckel built up his case by taking the recurring patterns in nature to construct a religious narrative of evolution. Nature as design became nature as designed. His enormously popular and beautifully illustrated books, *The Natural History of Creation* (1868), *Monism as connecting Religion and Science* (1892) and *Art Forms in Nature* (1899), revealed to readers the diversity of the world through the microscope. It was micro-cosmology, a journey into a world so exquisite that the readers who bought the books in their millions were comforted by the nobility of spirit conveyed by these hitherto unseen patterns in nature. Haeckel's illustrated books did much to inspire the organic nature-based forms of Art Nouveau and Jugendstil and they influenced Strindberg who began to call himself a Monist and painted emotionally charged paintings of 101, 104, patterns in nature, mostly trees, the sea and clouds. Haeckel also started 109 Strindberg on a long road of scientific experiments concerning the elements. Haeckel's Monism proposed that there was no such thing as a chemical element, it being the nature of things that everything obeyed a natural cycle of birth, maturity, death and decay; elements were no exception to this rule. Elements were unstable and they might be unpicked by careful work in the laboratory. Strindberg began to try to unpick the element of sulphur in the Hanssons' kitchen.

Laura Hansson was not amused. Her husband had encouraged Strindberg to join them in Berlin to further both their literary careers and Strindberg, who was supposed to be the blue touch paper for cultural revolution, spent his time shut up in a kitchen cooking up experiments like the Sorcerer's Apprentice. In addition, sulphur smelled terrible. Laura had organised a programme of introductions to the right literary people but Strindberg would not cooperate: networking was not, and never had been, of the slightest interest to him. He felt that he was being organised, something he always disliked, especially by a woman. He started to call her Laura the Mortician and Lady Bluebeard. Threatened by her energetic efforts to manage his career, he decided she was 'A dangerous woman, stealing the spermatozoa from men and passing them off as her own. Bit by bit she'll box me up and put me away in the nuthouse'[21] and he did a midnight flit, leaving the Hansson house without a word and showing up at Przybyszewski's with the precious Green Sack. Laura the Mortician had been spying on him, he told Przybyszewski, he had found the Green Sack gaping open and the letters from Nietzsche were missing. She had stolen them for unnamed purposes. Later he remembered that he had left the letters in Sweden for safekeeping but meanwhile the feud raged.

Edvard Munch had arrived in Berlin a little after Strindberg and he lost no time in seeking him out. They became firm friends. Munch was highly intelligent, a mathematician, linguist and a gifted writer who, like Strindberg, wrote a running autobiography throughout his life. He had grown up in a home just as cold and disapproving, steeped in poverty, misery and grim Pietism. Munch's mother, like Strindberg's, had died when he was young. Both men had nearly died in their infancy (Strindberg of cholera, Munch of tuberculosis) and Munch's childhood had been dominated by his father who did not spare the whip. When he arrived in Berlin he was a spiritual Puritan who had endured years of loneliness, destitution and vilification for the sake of his art which was then so radical that, like Strindberg, people said he was mad, so that when he painted *The Scream* he wrote the words 'Can only have been painted by a madman' along one of the painted striations in the sunset sky.[22]

Munch had been invited to mount a one-man exhibition by the Berlin Society of Artists, the Verein Berliner Künstler. Its traditionalist leaders had not yet caught up with Impressionism and when, on 5 November, Munch's strong Expressionist works were unveiled they caused such panic that a vote was held to close down the exhibition immediately. The Kaiser himself was moved to make a speech against modern art; now Munch had even more in common with Strindberg as his art, like Strindberg's literature, became the target of the violent antagonism of all respectable people. The art gallery where Munch's shocking show had been safely shut up behind locked doors became the battleground between conservatives and progressives. There was fighting in the streets and the young artists formed a human battering ram and charged the locked doors. By midnight the progressives had broken away from the Verein and formed themselves into the Berliner Secession. A new location was found to re-open the exhibition, by which time Munch had quickly painted Strindberg's portrait and sat it on an easel at the entrance so it was the first thing you saw: Cerberus at the gates of Hell.

Munch's portrayal of extreme psychological states was understood and appreciated by the Berlin intelligentsia as the pictorial equivalent of Strindberg's psychological naturalism. Munch was considered to 'paint souls' and Strindberg to write about them; together they slaked the great thirst for the acknowledgement of the metaphysical. They found themselves for the first time in their lives understood, lionised and making money. In a coming together of minds they began to paint together, something Munch never allowed to happen before or after. Munch was producing his best-known masterpieces during this time – *Vampire*, *Madonna*, *Self-portrait with Cigarette*, *Dagny Juel* – and he was building up to *The Scream* which he painted when he went back to Norway in the summer. In terms of painting styles, Munch and Strindberg agreed on finding Impressionist technique too careful and the subject matter too domestic. Strindberg, who had enjoyed painting since university, had already exhibited his paintings the year before in Sweden to critical incomprehension: one critic likened a canvas to dirty bed sheets hung out to dry. He had sold eight canvases, unfortunately all to the same purchaser who failed to pay. He was painting semi-abstract landscapes 101, 108, which are completely original and often compared to Turner, though they 109, 111, are rougher, less misty and more muscular, the paint often being applied 112, 113 with a palette knife. Skilful mood paintings, they show the powerful rhythms and patterns of nature: trees, waves, clouds, coastlines and seas either hectically stormy or radiantly tranquil. The heightened mood and narrative drive of the paintings relate to the dramas of his plays and stories, though only one painting shows a human figure. While Munch and Strindberg enjoyed painting in each other's company, each retained a strong independence within the companionable relationship. Munch seems to have brought surprisingly little to Strindberg's paintings. Strindberg's influence was stronger on Munch as he convinced Munch of the role that chance can play in artistic creation if the artist is willing to relinquish total control and allow fortuitous events to intervene. One can see this very clearly in two great pictures of Munch's. First, the portrait *Stanislaw Przybyszewski*[23] which shows the watermarks from a leak 57 in the studio. Munch allowed the watermarks to remain across the portrait which would not be half so powerful, haunting or other-worldly if he had painted them out. The second triumph of fortuitous chance and irrational impulse is described by Adolf Paul who entered Munch's studio while Munch was painting a red-headed model: ' "Kneel down in front of her and put your head in her lap!" he [Munch] called to me. She bent over and pressed her lips against the back of my neck, her red hair falling about me. Munch painted on and in a short time he had finished his picture *Vampire*.'[24]

On 3 April 1892 *Miss Julie* had received its German premiere at the Freie Bühne in Berlin, the experimental theatre that had already shown *The Father*. These were the first performances of Strindberg's plays outside

Scandinavia and it was this interest in his plays that had led Hansson to invite him to Berlin. On 21 January 1893, the day before his forty-fourth birthday, *Creditors* opened in Berlin's Residenztheater.[25] It was a great success, both artistically and commercially; it had a tremendous run of seventy-one performances and was given a gala in Vienna. A brilliant play written, like *Miss Julie*, during his time at Skovlyst, it concerns a divorced husband who begins, ostensibly benevolently, on a relationship with his ex-wife and her new husband. Seamlessly the relationship darkens until finally he kills the husband by *envôutement*, psychic murder. A tensely strung psychological thriller, it appealed to the popular audience who could not get enough of mesmerists and hypnotists, as well as to the high-flown who saw in it the all-important *états de l'âme* rather than *états des choses*.[26]

The play brought in both money and notoriety. Munch and Strindberg bought matching raincoats of a modish cut and the two of them became one of the regular sights at fashionable openings. Frida Uhl,[27] the young journalist who later became Strindberg's second wife, describes her first sight of them at the opening of Hermann Sudermann's play *Heimat*:

> Eleven o'clock. I have left the theatre. The snow is white and thick in the moonless and starless night. . . . A long, well-lit vestibule. Right at the end of it, in the shadow of a door, three men about to say goodbye to the hostess a bit early. . . . A slim blond man transfused by spirit. A thin, pale face with marvellous blue eyes, a person who is shy in life but risks everything in his art: Edvard Munch, the painter whom I had wanted to meet for a long time. But I look past Edvard Munch. Behind him, in the shadow, a tall, grim creature appears. He wears a dark grey raincoat over his shoulders. Like a rugged grey rock he grows out of the floor. Stone-grey is the colour of his coat, stone-grey his hair. Like stone his mighty head. Grey his roving eyes, grey his hollow cheeks.
>
> The flying Dutchman! I can't take my eyes off him . . . He steps out of the shadow . . . The eyes are like doors of eternity. Deep sapphire blue, like the skies above my native mountains. I never knew or imagined that so much light could radiate from a human being.[28]

Frida Uhl was twenty. She was Austrian, the daughter of a rich, powerful Court Councillor Friedrich Uhl who was a friend of the Emperor Franz Josef and the editor of the official Hapsburg court newspaper

Amtliche Kaiserliche und Königliche Wiener Zeitung. A clever and influential man and a handsome one, Court Councillor Uhl dressed like Richard Wagner with flowing locks, a velvet jacket and a big, soft romantic bow tie. He spent most of his time in the capital where discreetly he kept a mistress. He had separated from Frida's mother shortly after Frida was born but the couple maintained the hymeneal fiction for the benefit of Austria's strait-laced society. For the same reason they concealed the fact that one of Frida's grandparents was Jewish. Frida was possibly still a virgin but she had come to Berlin in pursuit of the newly married author of the play *Heimat*, Hermann Sudermann with whom she had enjoyed a flirtation in the sheltered confines of her home where Sudermann had come to take advice from her father. Frida had followed Sudermann to Berlin but he was disinclined to take things further and took shelter from Frida behind the skirts of his wife. Undeterred, Frida remained in Berlin unchaperoned, pursuing a career as a journalist. In reply to her father's repeated pleas for her to come home, she sent him arts reviews for his newspaper. With Sudermann putting up the barriers, she had set her sights on Munch but it was Strindberg who transfixed her interest. A month passed before they met again.

Meanwhile Strindberg's international reputation grew. On 16 January 1893 *Miss Julie* was at last performed in Paris by André Antoine's Théâtre Libre. The circumstances were not ideal. It was given as part of a triple bill along with *The Brazilian Household* by Coolus,[29] a play and playwright that have sunk almost without trace, and Edmond de Goncourt's *A bas le progrès*. As a prelude to his own play, de Goncourt stepped onto the stage to deliver a bellicose denunciation of Nordic literature urging that Strindberg and Tolstoy's 'Slavic fog' should not be allowed to cloud the 'lucid French intellect'[30] after which de Goncourt hid at the back of Daudet's box to observe the reaction to his play and to watch *Miss Julie* to which he gave fewer words in his diary than the problem of finding a cab to take him home.

Miss Julie played for eight days. A long time in Paris, as a delighted Strindberg observed. The critics were vehement, their opinions divided more or less evenly for and against, while de Goncourt's play provoked yawns and comments about old-fashioned attitudes that led de Goncourt, most uncharacteristically, to doubt his cultural immortality. Antoine himself, whose opinion was of supreme importance, felt *Miss Julie* made 'an enormous sensation' and was something 'quite new'.[31]

On 5 February the editor of *Das Magazin für die Literatur*, Otto Neumann-Hofer and his wife Annie invited Strindberg and Frida Uhl to a dinner party. Frida anticipated the party with enormous excitement but when Strindberg arrived he had forgotten they had already met and he greeted her as a stranger. They sat opposite each other and he did not think she was beautiful. 'Her eyes were large and well-shaped, like those of the children of the south, and her nose seemed to have changed its mind as it grew up, for it took a sudden turn in the middle, and in a trice became Roman. This unexpected bit of levity on its part gave charm to the profile which reminded [me] of a cameo.'[32] At the end of the evening as he helped her on with her coat she asked,

'Who is going to escort me home?'

'I am of course', he replied and as they strolled through the darkness, the youthfulness of her voice made him think of forests and lakes, of Gainsborough hats and hay-rakes so that when she invited him to dine in her boarding-house rooms the following evening, her youth excused her impropriety and he put it down to innocence. Her fellow lodger would, she assured him, be present.

When he arrived the following evening there was no sign of the fellow lodger but a large basket of glorious roses caught his eye. Just as a servant entered with wine and cigarettes, she broke off a spray of roses and knelt to fasten them in Strindberg's buttonhole. Still kneeling, she drank his health. She confided her life story: the convents that had so tormented her with religion that she had thrown it all overboard; now, it was true, she was sometimes aware of a vacuum but like everyone else she was expecting something new to come into the world. For the time being she was chiefly interested in raising humanity out of poverty and freeing it from oppression. Talk turned to Nietzsche in whom, she said, she had taken a superficial interest but she had put him aside when he had disappointed her hopes for achieving universal equality.[33] She went on to talk about theatre and offered her assistance and contacts. Her tumbling talk reminded him of the early days with Siri when they had hoped to solve Sweden's problems though socialism and shared long, passionate talks about books and theatre. For a moment it struck him that perhaps he was the object of a practical joke. Had he been set up? Had one of his mischievous Ferkel chums briefed this young girl to say such sympathetic things and make a fool of him? He scrutinised with suspicion a curtain that hung before a door but no feet were sticking out from beneath.

However, the possibility of an eavesdropper kept him in a healthy state of uncertainty so that by the time he left he had managed to keep them both from being compromised by incautious flirtatiousness. He walked home confused, with guilty feelings for having suspected his hostess first of loose morals, then of evil designs and lack of trust.

He had left behind the rose she had given him. The following day he sent her a note: 'I did not forget the rose, but left it behind on purpose, so as to have an excuse for calling to get it the next day but when the time came, I lacked courage.'

Maybe he lacked courage or maybe inclination. He did nothing to encourage her. She invited him to the theatre. He refused on the grounds that this would compromise her (it would also compromise him). She countered that it would do no harm if they 'went out on the spree' and she invited him to dinner on 11 February. He called for her at the first address but the landlady who did not approve of gentleman visitors had moved Frida on. When he called for her at the second address she no longer reminded him of Gainsborough hats and hay-rakes. Hunched in her fur coat as they walked to the restaurant, he thought he had never known such a Loki, such a shape-shifter. A little witch walked by his side with a stooping way of walking and a headscarf over her hair. Reluctantly he accompanied this aged and unappealing silhouette to the fashionable restaurant in the Zoological Gardens where she seemed to be suspiciously well known; once more he must give her naïveté the benefit of the doubt. Strindberg takes up the story to describe the dynamic of a *coup de foudre* first hand, and the description is surely important for the illumination it betrays on his instinctive reactions in the sexual battlefield.

When they entered the brightly lit premises, and she took off her fur and scarf she was suddenly transformed into a youthful beauty. A simple, close-fitting moss-green dress revealed the figure of an eighteen-year-old, and her hair, which she wore brushed back, made her look like a grown-up schoolgirl. He could not conceal the effect this magic had on him, but let his eyes sweep over her whole person, as if he were seeking for some enemy with a hidden searchlight.

'Eros! Now I'm lost!' he thought, and from that moment he was.

She very well saw the effect she had produced and she phosphoresced, sat as if enveloped in light, sure of victory, her expression triumphant. The woman-hater was conquered.

Fright took hold of him. She had his soul in the pocket of her dress; she could fling it into the river or the gutter, and this added hatred to his feelings for her. He saw his only hope of salvation in the influence his flame might have in kindling hers, so that she became as surely bound to him as he was to her. With this half-formed aim in view he did what any man in his position would have done; he crept close to her, made himself small as a child, roused her compassion but the noble compassion of a merciful being towards a broken human soul, a soul condemned that saw no hope of bliss. She listened and received what he gave as tribute, listened calmly, majestically, maternally but not spitefully like a coquette.[34]

At the end of the evening, he left the table for a moment. When he came back he discovered that she had paid the bill. It was an unspeakable insult. He summoned the waiter and rearranged the situation. They parted coldly but his thoughts turned endlessly back to the moment when her youthful loveliness had crept out from the animal skin of her fur and he had felt both attracted and repelled.

By now there was talk. Otto Neumann-Hofer, feeling perhaps responsible for his part in bringing them together at the dinner party and perhaps also, as editor of *Das Magazin für Literatur*, unwilling to offend Frida's more powerful father, took her to Zum Schwarzen Ferkel for a dose of aversion therapy.

'Bottles line the walls', Frida described the Ferkel.

Tables and again tables. Thick cigarette smoke and loud voices. Then, suddenly, silence. I see Strindberg sitting behind a big table and talking. I cannot catch his words, his voice is low and quiet. He holds himself erect, his head high, sitting squarely and heavily, almost majestic . . . A dark slim young man jumps up. 'That's the insurance agent Richard Dehmel', Otto smiles. 'He does accounts in the morning and composes poems at night.' . . . Dehmel's cane lashes through the air, cuts off the golden neck of a green bottle. The guests are jubilant. Champagne sparkles in the glasses, champagne streams across the floor . . . Strindberg is presiding over this Witches' Sabbath as calmly as if it were a committee meeting. The handsome young Pole Stanislaw Przybyszewski is sitting to his right in the attitude of the favourite disciple at the Last Supper. He is the only one who has not a wine glass but a water glass standing in front of him. This large glass is full to the brim with cognac. He is bent forward, his eyes riveted on the glass; greyish-blue, slanted half-closed eyes, a greyish skin a thin blond Henri IV beard; on his blood-red finely chiselled lips is a voluptuous and tortured smile. Now he comes closer and slowly kisses the hands of August Strindberg who, surprised, and with a blush, withdraws them.

'What do we want here?' I ask, and turn away, sad and depressed.[35]

When next they met she affected a great interest in Strindberg's children. He showed her photographs and so moved was she by his son Hans that she begged she might keep a photograph and she besought him that the next time his thoughts were straying towards the Ferkel he would renounce the sink of iniquity – for the sake of little Hans. He obviously remained undecided. At the end of the evening she let down the veil of her hat and, before he had time to guess what she was doing, pressed a kiss on his lips through the veil. Their first kiss, and delivered in such a way. By the time he stretched out his arms to embrace her, she had disappeared through the doorway and closed the door.

She was a girl of good family. They had kissed. In normal circumstances he was duty bound to propose to her. Were these normal circumstances?

Frida never lacked push. She took it upon herself to be his business manager. On 4 March he received one thousand marks in advance on a German edition of *A Madman's Defence*. He kept one hundred, sent five hundred to Siri in Finland and let Frida keep the rest safe. The following day he proposed by letter and after some prevarication Frida consented to an engagement 'without rings and without witnesses . . . As regards independence, my dear friend, of course you will always have that – without limit.' The idea of such moral permissiveness within marriage made him furious. That evening he presented her with one of his paintings which he called *Night of Jealousy*, a scumble of grey-black which carries the date 9 March, probably the date their love was consummated. In the morning she left for Munich and Strindberg went straight back to Zum Schwarzen Ferkel. He was having his bust sculpted by Max Levi and his portrait painted by two Norwegian artists, Severin Segelcke[36] and Christian Krohg, the elderly and conventional leader of the Norwegian naturalist school of painting who came to Berlin with his wife Oda, who danced naked in the Ferkel with lobsters in her hair. Two years later Ibsen bought this portrait of Strindberg by Krohg and hung it in his study to write the rest of his plays beneath Strindberg's 'demonic eyes' and this was the closest they ever came; Ibsen and Strindberg never met.

A few days after Frida had left for Munich, Edvard Munch brought his beautiful compatriot Dagny Juel into Zum Schwarzen Ferkel. They called her Ducha, the Polish word for soul, and she seemed to have about her the absolute receptivity of a wax tablet, a woman who received any impression a man wished to impress on her. Some described her as a poison swamp-flower who exuded decadence and invited evil behaviour; others saw her as pure, yet others simply found intellectual inspiration in her. Before she arrived in person she sent her photograph to the Schwarzen Ferkel 'to awaken interest' and when she at last appeared, the arrival of a beautiful, well-bred young girl, the niece of a Norwegian Prime Minister who publicly declared her belief in free love confounded them. This was a hitherto unknown type of woman; before her arrival the only women seen in the place were prostitutes, mistresses or inquisitive wives but when Dagny entered the Ferkel on Edvard Munch's arm she was claiming her place as an equal.

Frida, no friend of hers, described 'A beautiful figure. Tall and sophisticated. Dressed in dignified, colourless grey. Curly blonde hair above her brows. Below protrudes a fine Grecian nose. Her lips are narrow and sensual, her teeth white. Her most beautiful features are her aristocratic hands, the well-groomed feet, and her lack of weight.'[37]

Dagny was enigmatic, drawling and languid.

> She drank absinthe by the litre without getting drunk . . . there was a piano by the door, an extraordinary instrument which one could shut off by means of a handle, so that if Stachu [Przybyszewski] started hammering away on it nobody else in the building would be disturbed . . . One man would dance with Dagny, while the other two sat at the table and watched: one would be Munch and the other, often as not, Strindberg. The four friends there were all in love with Dagny, each in his own way but they never let it show . . . Przybyszewski would hold forth on pathological eroticism and Strindberg on chemical analysis while Munch just sat and listened . . . A couple of years later Dagny went to Tiflis [Tblisi] where she met her end: a wild young Russian held a revolver to her forehead, and when she burst out laughing he calmly pulled the trigger killing first her then himself.[38]

79   Harriet Bosse, as Strindberg first saw her as Puck in *A Midsummer Night's Dream*, 1900.

80   In his study, holding 'the eagle pen' made from a feather from Harriet's hat, 1902.
Kungliga biblioteket, Stockholm, Strindbergsrummet, Bilder, Kartong 13, 1902_5.

81   The Intimate Theatre,
Stockholm, 1907–10. Stockholm
City Museum.

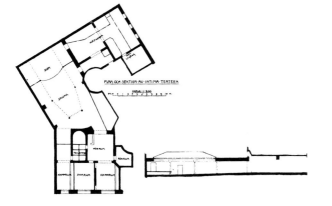

82   Ground plan and section of
the Intimate Theatre.

83   Interior of the Intimate
Theatre, Arnold Böcklin's *Island
of the Living* and *Island of the Dead*
on either side of the curtain.
Stockholm City Museum.

84   August Falck, beside the bust of Strindberg by Max Levi in the foyer of the Intimate
Theatre.

85   *The Father*, performed at the Intimate Theatre in 1908. Kungliga biblioteket, Stockholm, Strindbergsrummet, Bilder, Kartong 29, Fadren 1908.

86   Harriet Bosse, as Indra's daughter in *A Dream Play*, 1908. The Music and Theatre Library of Sweden.

87   Harriet Bosse and August Palme, in *To Damascus I*, 1900. The Music and Theatre
Library of Sweden.

88 (ABOVE)   Strindberg
castigates the Swedish Academy,
Söndags-Nisse, 17 September
1903. Kungliga
biblioteket, Stockholm.

89 (LEFT)   Strindberg as
naturalist, Darwinist and
Symbolist, caricature by Oscar
Andersson, *c.* 1900. Nordiska
museet, Stockholm.

90 (LEFT)   The Blue Tower,
Stockholm, Strindberg's final home.
Stockholm City Museum.

91 (BELOW)   'The modern Hercules
cleanses literature's Augean stables' by
Edvard Forström in *Puck*, 16 July 1910.

92   Photomontage of Strindberg among some of the roles he created, 1908. Kungliga biblijoteket, Stockholm, Maps and Pictures sv.p 5.

93 A triple exposure photograph of Stockholm, 1907–8, typical of Strindberg's creative approach to photography which aimed at transcending the objectivity of the medium. Kungliga biblioteket, Stockholm, Strindbergsrummet, sgNM_Exprerimentfoton_xx.

Bosse—Wingård gifta.

Harriet Bosse.   *Gunnar Wingård.*

Fru Harriet Bosse och hr. Gunnar Wingård gifte sig den 24 maj — utan att någon människa mer än de två bröllopsvittnena visste av det. Jo, naturligtvis även kyrkoherde S. A. Fries. Det var nämligen hemma hos honom — i hans bibliotek — som vigseln ägde rum.

94   Announcement of Harriet's wedding to Gunnar Wingård, 24 May 1908.

95   Anne-Marie Strindberg, Harriet's daughter.

96   In the Blue Tower, autumn 1908. Kungliga biblioteket, Stockholm, Strindbergsrummet,
Bilder, Kartong 3, 1908_4.

97   Fanny Falkner, as Judith in *the Dance of Death* (part II), 1909 at the Intimate Theatre.

98 (ABOVE) His study in the
Blue Tower, 1911, showing the
telescope that Fanny Falkner
was looking through when he
proposed to her. Kungliga
biblioteket, Stockholm,
Strindbergsrummet, Bilder,
Kartong 29, sgNM_53_1_31g.

99 (LEFT) In the last year of
his life. Strindbergsmuseet,
Stockholm.

100   Over ten thousand people lined the streets of Stockholm for his funeral procession, 19 May 1912. Stockholm City Museum.

The fourth man was Dr Schleich who would take Dagny over from Strindberg when Frida came back from Munich but until then Strindberg was the envy of all as he enjoyed three weeks with Dagny as his mistress. Adolf Paul writes with envy how she fulfilled every man's fantasy, wanted every man and when she had had him, like Bizet's Carmen, threw him away,[39] but her importance to the circle was more than being merciless and emancipated. Everyone in the group was on the watch to see who could find the new formula for the artistic and literary works of the future and Dagny in her strange hieratic silence had the gift of inspiring new thoughts in them.

The Austrian critic and dramatist Hermann Bahr thought it would be a good joke to file a story that Strindberg was engaged to Frida. The story was published in the *Deutsche Zeitung* on 22 March where it was read by Frida's father, a crony of the Kaiser and nominally a Catholic. He was far from pleased to read that his daughter was to marry an older, penniless, divorced Protestant with a notorious past. 'First Miss Julchen, then comes Ulchen', was his cynical Viennese response. However, convention demanded that after such a notice in the paper she should marry Strindberg or her reputation would be ruined. Her father sent her back to Berlin, promising a dowry of three thousand marks. She arrived on 1 April, a day on which Strindberg was already extricating himself from a double booking with Dagny and another mistress, Gabrielle Tavastjerna, the wife of a Finnish poet. He could think of nothing better than to pretend to be ill and spent the day cowering in bed while Schleich fended off Dagny, probably taking her over in the process. Frida took up position at the bedside with a bag of bonbons and news of the dowry.[40] On the 11th they exchanged rings. The very next day they broke it off after she had sent him a letter discussing the physical side of marriage; he was shocked by such forwardness. Things might have ended on this stumbling block of her lack of maidenly behaviour but for the arrival of Frida's sister Mitzi, a woman of both sense and glamour married to the well-established sculptor Professor Rudolf Weyr.[41] It was Mitzi's job to save her sister's reputation by making certain the marriage went ahead. To this end, she was the physical bearer of the promised dowry.

Mitzi reported back her first impressions in a letter to her husband:

He lives here in a furnished room, has nothing to call his own except a trunk – gave all his furniture to his first wife, cannot bear the

63

thought of settling anywhere for any length of time, never knows if he has any money or how much . . . Blushes like a young girl, this happens quite often, and makes his face flower into a bewitching beauty. His mouth and eyes are wonderful, the latter blue like a clear morning at sea. His hair is already much greyed, his face deeply lined – a figure of catastrophe. He worships flowers – is starving but buys a plant. . . . When he and Frida have a misunderstanding, he says, 'I can't bear this', and runs away without his hat. Then when he comes back he asks, 'Was it you who wounded me or I you?' He does not remember next morning what he has done today: no longer knows even what he has written; creates everything under hypnosis. When it is down on paper it has, as far as he is concerned, disappeared. By contrast his head is always full of lucid and detailed plans of what he is to write.

A few days later Mitzi wrote again to her husband:

And Strindberg – he could drive people like us quite insane. I have never before in my life met such a person, no one like him exists among us, thank heaven! . . . He looks much better and creates a much more favourable impression than his photograph. Often he looks much younger, too. But then suddenly his face changes to that of an old man when he suddenly, as often happens, begins to brood and right in the middle of a sentence forgets that someone is with him and for quarter of an hour doesn't say a word and doesn't hear a thing that is said to him. When I am with him, I can't for a moment rid myself of the fear that at any instant he might go mad, but simultaneously more and more I feel that he is a true genius . . . Frightening, absolutely frightening! I cannot understand how Frida has the courage to entrust herself to such a person. But one can no longer keep the two of them apart; on the contrary one must do everything to join them together. I am afraid his love for her is mainly of a sensual nature, for intellectually and spiritually Frida cannot satisfy a man such as him – no woman could, for that matter . . . Generally speaking he is rather shy and completely sufficient unto himself . . . Her love for him is, in contrast, nothing but literary admiration and idolatry for his genius . . . I can do nothing, absolutely nothing, except to give her some sensible advice on what to buy, suggestions on her trousseau, and to support her in her wish to marry him as soon as possible.[42]

There remained one stumbling block to the marriage: Strindberg's divorce papers. The banns could not be called without these official papers which were stuck in Sweden. However, a heroic solution was found: different laws pertained on Heligoland, an island in the North Sea which had recently been exchanged with the English for Zanzibar.[43] Here, marriage still conformed to English laws. Banns were not necessary.

On the eve of their departure for Heligoland, Frida and Strindberg walked down to the Lehrter Station to pick up their tickets. Suddenly Strindberg ran off after two gentlemen with whom he remained in conversation for some twenty minutes and on his return to Frida he was pale as parchment. Grim auguries. One of the men was Baron Wrangel, Siri's first husband: 'He said exactly the same as the last time when I married Siri. He wished me all the luck in the world. This will never work out. I'm damned and doomed again.'[44]

They had known each other three months when they were married on 2 May, Strindberg wearing a new outfit, a soft light-beige English suit with matching sailor's hat and a wide black silk cravat with dark green stripes. Two sailors acted as witnesses as well as Mitzi who was there to see the deed was done. The wedding involved answering twenty-three questions put by the priest and when he asked the question, 'Do you solemnly vow never to bear another man's child?' Strindberg with his left hand on the Bible and his right hand raised, answered, 'I solemnly vow never to bear another man's child.' Frida started laughing hysterically and could not stop. Strindberg and the cleric were appalled. Mitzi said Frida was crying with emotion and pretended to wipe away her tears with a handkerchief, telling her to calm herself, which she eventually did.[45]

For their honeymoon they rented a cottage in Heligoland surrounded by the things Strindberg loved best: a profusion of flowers and the glittering North Sea. The first night in bed he tried to strangle Frida in his sleep. He explained that he thought she was Siri and it did not happen again. Later, again in his sleep, she heard him say, 'She would not believe I could get such a young girl!'

Frida had a great taste for the melodramatic and where other brides might have found such a first night a setback, she found it thrillingly exciting. Both she and Strindberg described the honeymoon as extremely happy.

12 FRIDA, NO STRANGER TO DRAMA

After three weeks in the pretty, flower-girt cottage in Heligoland with Strindberg pottering about his scientific experiments and Frida trying to sell both his and her own articles to German newspapers, she suggested a visit to England. He was reluctant. He found the English language more impenetrable than Chinese but Frida, who had been at school in England, pointed out the importance of three literary figures who were showing interest in his work. The critic Justin Huntley Mac-Carthy had written extremely perceptively on *The Father* in the *Fortnightly Review*.[1] William Heinemann[2] had expressed interest in publishing a translation of *Somnambulist Nights* and Jack Grein,[3] London's equivalent of André Antoine, had earlier offered to stage *The Father*, though it would have to be a private performance because of the English censor. Grein's Independent Theatre, now three years old, brought the avant garde across the Channel. He was called 'the most abused man in England' for having premiered Ibsen's *Ghosts*; he was also the first man in London to stage a play by George Bernard Shaw.[4]

'If I go to England', Strindberg fretted, 'she'll have the upper hand as she can speak the language. I'll be herded about like a deaf-mute, and feel like an idiot among my literary colleagues while she pops them straight into her pocket! I don't like the idea of that at all! The very fact that she's acting as my protector with these German newspapers is humiliating enough!'[5]

Nevertheless, they left Heligoland on 20 May 1893. Frida described Strindberg embarking with 'One green and white striped footbath which accompanied him like cleanliness itself from one hotel to another, a small case of clothes and a green flannel sack about one yard in length, with gentle billowing valleys and summits and fastened by a cord. It contained all his manuscripts. It contained his theory that plants have nerves. It contained the theory that elements can be split. It contained theories that refute Newton and God himself.'[6]

Frida was horribly sea-sick and while she was recovering in Graves-end[7] he received the first copies of the German translation of *Le Plaidoyer d'un fou*, the book he had written in French telling the story of his marriage to Siri. He knew it was 'a cruel book, as cruel as life'[8] and had sent the manuscript to his brother with the intention that it should remain in the family archives, unpublished until his death. However, circumstances changed during a drinking bout with his fellow Swede, the author and publisher Gustaf af Geijerstam, who let fall that he was planning a book on Strindberg's marriage to Siri. Appalled at this news, Strindberg felt it important that his own version should be heard. Interest in Strindberg was so great in Germany that a translation was quickly produced under the title *Die Beichte eines Thoren*. His conscience tormented him over the book and he had strictly forbidden Frida to read it but with Frida recuperating in bed in Gravesend while Strindberg took healthy walks along the banks of the Thames, how could she resist lifting the lid of Pandora's Box? Never a stranger to drama, Frida says she read it during a thunder-storm, shuddering as she wondered which chamber of Bluebeard's castle she had entered, while Strindberg (who was always afraid of thunder, as well as the dark) cowered on the floor behind a table.

His version is that she immediately punished him by announcing that they must economise. She had a word with the cook who thereafter only gave him horrid, cheap food to eat and she telescoped their living accom-modation down from two rooms to one. This was war. In order to feel free to think and work, he always had to have a room to himself, however small. She had effectively stopped him writing. The Green Sack remained unfattened and Strindberg became sulky. As they walked along the banks of the Thames he harboured violent fantasies of pushing her into the river or of the rough dockers ravishing her; he became frightened that he could have such thoughts and 'he realised what might make a man a murderer and determined to flee. But first he must have some money.'[9]

After ten combative days in Gravesend, Strindberg and Frida at last moved to central London where they took up residence in Grein's flat in Pimlico.[10] Grein had gone abroad for the summer, the theatre was closed and there was no question of a production of *The Father*. Maybe his generosity in lending the flat was some expression of a guilty conscience over disappointed expectations. The flat was adjacent to a market (now Tachbrook Street market), a place of garbage, vice and crime whose stink of rotting produce infused their every inhalation. The bedroom offended Strindberg's prim sensibilities with its 'lewd, English double bed' and he sulked. Nothing could please him. He might have derived real pleasure and profit from seeing Turner's paintings while he was in England but although his own paintings are most often compared to Turner's, it is not known with any certainty whether he saw them or not.

Frida, on the other hand, was in her element. She would make a career of trying to organise famous, if often unwilling, men and now she bustled about making contacts, assiduously pursuing William Heinemann who, while he greatly enjoyed having lunch with her on a regular basis, never had any serious intention of publishing Strindberg's poetry.

Financial expectations were raised by news of a Swedish translation of *Le Plaidoyer d'un fou* to be published in the newspaper *Budkaflen*, but quickly lowered as the newspaper argued that it did not feel the need to pay Strindberg because the text had already been published in German. None of the projects that had brought them to England were bringing them any money at all, Frida was taking control of affairs and Strindberg felt like a child stranded in the mental darkness of uselessness in a country whose language he did not understand.

'This is how things stand', he wrote to Frida's sister Mitzi.

After a month of happiness and work on Heligoland, we conceived the idea of going to England to see how the land lay regarding my plays, etc. Frida, our treasurer, with her head fairly up in the clouds of married bliss, assured us we had the necessary means for our journey; thus we set off.

In England we fell into the clutches of genteel robbers, and after a month we were cleaned out . . . We therefore decided I should go ahead to Rügen to rent a flat for the summer. Frida was to follow me in a week or two. So off I went! But then I received a letter from Frida about a theatrical venture in London too grand to make any sense . . . Now she declares it her firm intention to remain a whole year in London to launch a theatre'.[11]

To Frida he wrote: 'Well, for your part you have been treating me like an idiot, at first playfully, then from habit, and finally in earnest.'[12]

Six weeks after the wedding, on 17 June, leaving Frida in London he took a coal freighter to Hamburg and thence to Rügen, a beautiful island in the Baltic, the German equivalent of his beloved Swedish skerries. Here Adolf Paul and Karl August Tavastjerna,[13] both members of the Ferkel circle, were spending the summer. They must have been delighted to have the great moving spirit of the Ferkel descend on them but the sentiment was not reciprocated. Neither of them had any brilliance of thought. Paul was useful as adoring disciple, recorder of events and greaser of palms and wheels but he was universally disliked and acknowledged to be an unpleasant man. Tavastjerna, a Finnish poet, was a dull man made duller by his poor hearing. The Berlin bohemians put up with him because he had a lively wife, Gabrielle, with whom Strindberg had some sort of affair in Berlin before and during his entanglement with Dagny Juel and his engagement to Frida, but whether consummated or unconsummated is unclear.

Strindberg suffered a guilty conscience over Tavastjerna's wife while he endured Tavastjerna's stultifying conversation and a midsummer heatwave. The scorching sands of Rügen made him think of the burning beaches of Dante's *Inferno* where the blasphemers, among whom he counted himself, lie outstretched. He was working on his scientific studies according to the Monist principles of Haeckel and he was yearning for the more stimulating members of the Berlin circle as he tried to prove the theory postulated by Haeckel: that the chemical world obeyed the same cycle of eternal transmutation as the natural world. Haeckel had suggested that elements were evolutionary products generated by combinations of varying numbers of primal atoms (the atom was a half-known entity; atomic numbers had yet to be discovered). Haeckel's proposal was that as combinations of atoms, the elements might not be immutable but transmutable. This gave new encouragement to the old alchemist's proposition that all matter had life and that everything could be transmuted into everything else. As a schoolboy scientist, Strindberg had ambitiously tried to make a perpetual-motion machine from bits of a coffee grinder cobbled together with violin strings and the spokes from an umbrella and in the same spirit of scientific derring-do he continued his quest to split the elements.

Like a new Doctor Faustus he had begun with the element sulphur – the element that conjured Hell and the Devil, the occult and the forbidden; and as he continued his studies he wrote to Richard Dehmel in Berlin, begging him to send the necessary chemicals and equipment, assuring Dehmel he would be able to prove the presence of carbon in sulphur in eight days – a fortnight at most! (Eventually he did, to his own satisfaction, taking rather longer than a fortnight but as the traces of carbon he found in the sulphur might well have come from the ash of the cigars he smoked during his labours, the successful experiment could not reliably be replicated. Nevertheless, Strindberg maintained a steadfast belief that he had succeeded.)

Parallel with his experiments he began writing a scientific book which he called *Antibarbarus*. In the introduction he proposed the dawning of a new era, a new chemistry that scientifically demonstrated the complete unity of nature, 'the prevailing monistic theory of nature's all-pervasiveness and unity, as applied by Darwin and Haeckel to the other natural sciences', as he says on the first page of *Antibarbarus*. The book was certainly revolutionary in reversing the conventional procedures of empirical science: first came belief in a statement he wished to be true, next came the experiments designed to prove it.

While immersed in burning sulphur in Rügen's hellish heat, he fired off letters to Frida who was still in London and to his main scientific consultant, Bengt Lidforss,[14] a friend from the Schwarzen Ferkel. Blond, sharp and bird-like, with small eyes and a stammer, Lidforss would rise to great heights as a scientist, becoming the first to verify the Mendelian laws in a single plant family. He would publish important books on subjects such as the physiology of plant cells and be appointed the Professor of Botany at Uppsala University and a member of the Swedish Academy of Sciences. While taking his own more conventional route through verifiable research, Lidforss none the less placed a real value on Strindberg's intuition-led attitude to scientific proposals. Lidforss had first met Strindberg while he was still a student in Lund in 1892 and he had become fascinated by the way Strindberg's mind worked in its illogical, quicksilver intuitions. He often addressed Strindberg as 'Lord and Master' and Strindberg reciprocated with 'Amanuensis'. The two men were important to each other and fond of each other. When Strindberg and Frida left Berlin for their marriage in Heligoland, Lidforss was one of the two friends who saw them off at the station.

Lidforss was a legendary drinker in Zum Schwarzen Ferkel but he held back from the general promiscuity because he was infected with the syphilis that would kill him. He had met Dagny Juel while he was a student in Lund and he was already helplessly in love with her when she made her dramatic entrance to the Ferkel. He yearned, envied and abstained, while she conferred her favours on Edvard Munch, Strindberg and Schleich. There is a story that when Strindberg had lost interest at the end of his three-week affair with Dagny and he was panicking that Frida was coming back to Berlin, he tucked a handful of condoms into the lovesick Lidforss's pocket and told him to help himself – everybody else had. If this is true, it might explain the revenge that Lidforss was storing up and soon would wreak upon Strindberg.

In May, while Strindberg was still on honeymoon, he received the news that Lidforss had returned from Copenhagen to Berlin to find Dagny 'sleeping with just about everybody'.[15] Lidforss embarked on an epic drinking spree and was in danger of arrest. He must be sobered up and bundled back to Lund in time to receive his doctoral degree from the king. If he missed the ceremony it would cause such scandal that his future career would be irreparably blighted. Strindberg stepped in and organised a rescue party. Lidforss was decanted onto a train to Lund where his father vented his fury by slapping his face before tidying him up for the king. The day had been saved but Lidforss was furious with Strindberg for interfering in his life. Back in Berlin, Dagny flayed the skin off Lidforss's top hat and hung it like a trophy beneath the portrait of Strindberg on the wall in Zum Schwarzen Ferkel and then she gave herself to Przybyszewski as his mistress.

During the writing of Strindberg's scientific treatise *Antibarbarus*, he ran his speculative theories and formulae past Lidforss, relying on him to weed the jungle of primitive intimations from the sunlit glade of reason. Lidforss took his role seriously and expressed encouragement and enthusiasm.

At the end of July, Strindberg accepted an invitation from Frida's mother to visit her at the magnificent family villa in Mondsee where Frida's father and mother came together annually to perpetuate the legend that they were still a happily married couple. There was a fine view of the lake and the mountains, plenty of servants and a drawing room the size of a ballroom where both Wagner and Brahms had given recitals. Strindberg was hoping that Frida would join him. She was still in London but evidently disenchanted now that Grein had returned from his trip abroad and they were both living in his Pimlico house in an improper situation which would have fired the jealousies of hell had it been Siri living in a house with another man but when Strindberg writes about his marriage to Frida he often expresses the idea that the whole thing felt unreal and disconnected, like a numbed limb, or a mind overcast by a dream. As for Frida, both before and after her marriage to Strindberg, she was known as a man-eater who never passed up a meal and it must be likely that something personal happened between her and Grein in the house in Pimlico which resulted in her writing to Strindberg that Grein was a fraud and a confidence trickster, his maid was a part-time prostitute and his secretary was desperate to escape from such a rackety set-up and had asked Frida if he could work for her instead. Letters and telegrams flew. Frida wished to rejoin Strindberg but she refused to visit the house in Mondsee. She hated the house and she had a shrewd idea that her mother, a vague religious mystic given to enigmatic spiritual utterances, might enchant Strindberg – which she duly did on first meeting, inviting him to call her Mama because 'Mother-in-law has such a horrible sound'. The two of them fell into a deliciously consolatory, undemanding mother–child relationship and Marie Uhl expressed her admiration that her daughter had managed to marry such an advanced soul. Strindberg threatened Frida with divorce if she did not join him but she would not come to him there so they met up in Berlin, surprisingly joyfully. No accusations were uttered, no questions or explanations, only:

> 'Do you have a lot or a little money?'
> 'Why do you ask that?'
> 'Because I have a lot and I want a festive dinner in Berlin.'[16]

They took two adjoining rooms in Albrechtstrasse and stayed there two months, their happiness clouded only a little by the smell of his experiments which were making Frida feel sick. During his morning walks he would take a box of morphia and a syringe in his pocket to conduct research en route. He thought he might be able to prove whether plants had nervous systems by injecting them with morphine. Once he was arrested when injecting apples hanging from a tree but he explained his scientific quest to the policeman who thought he was a madman and let him go.

Frida was again busy trying to promote his work. Her promotion might have included the anonymous complaint of immorality lodged against the German edition of Le Plaidoyer d'un fou: the complainant signed herself 'a German mother' and there are competing theories that the 'German mother' was either Marie David trying to get the book banned[17] or Frida (in her memoirs she says that it was a friend of hers) trying to get it more publicity. If Frida, it backfired. The book was confiscated under the *Lex Heinze* and Strindberg found himself with a prosecution for obscenity hanging over his head.

In early October 1893 Frida discovered that she was pregnant. She wanted an abortion and she fled to Vienna to her sister Mitzi, leaving a note saying she wanted a divorce. If he wished, he might charge her with desertion or, if he preferred, she would divorce him for cruelty. Strindberg was distraught at the idea of an abortion; pregnancy and motherhood were sacred states. He sent telegram after telegram to Frida and to Mitzi. Frida at last consented to be reunited on the condition that they lived somewhere other than Berlin where Przybyszewski, Dagny and Lidforss were living in an unholy trinity. Przybyszewski had left his common-law wife with whom he had two children and had married Dagny. Lidforss was hanging round the home of the newly married couple, yearning.

Frida and Strindberg were reunited in Brünn, the capital of Moravia, at the end of October. Soon afterwards they accepted an invitation from Frida's maternal grandparents, Cornelius and Marie Reischl, to stay in their large, stark mansion on the northerly bank of the Danube in Dornach.[18] Cornelius Reischl was a rich man, now over seventy, with an honourable and lucrative career at court stretching behind him. Dornach was his hunting estate and in the ornamental garden he had already built his mausoleum which he enjoyed showing off to visitors. While he waited to occupy it he spent his time killing and eating the game that swarmed over the large estate. Strindberg's delicate stomach soon revolted at the quantities of strong meat and his mind at Reischl's right-wing conservatism but he had resolved to behave respectfully to the old man, 'While', as Frida observed, 'he waited for the child as a naïve and pious person awaits the perfect completion of life.'

Strindberg and Frida were given their own small set of low-ceilinged rooms on the ground floor between the covered carriage entrance and the Danube, so close to the river as to be almost in it. He painted some lovely oil paintings of the view through the bedroom window, paintings that show that if he had seen any Turners while he was in London they had not changed his style.[19] Behind Haus Reischl the wooded land sloped

110

steeply up towards a high crag crowned by a grey, turreted tenth-century castle, Burg Clam. The discovery that Paracelsus had pursued his occult studies in the castle's library gave renewed energy to Strindberg's chemical researches and at this point one might begin to call them alchemical studies for he began to dabble with trying to make gold from copper mixed with sulphate of iron. Instinctively, and despite his much trumpeted atheism, he felt that this was a transgressive activity. He writes of the peasants of Clam coming to stone him 'the Protestant magician' but this only happened in his conscience; it was what he felt he deserved for his poverty, his abandonment of creative writing, his bizarre, dislocated marriage to Frida, his failure as an alchemist and his heretical dabbling in forbidden and occult matters.

While the peasants did not actually stone him, they held him in superstitious awe, making the sign of the Cross on catching sight of him and asking, 'Have you made gold yet?' They were Roman Catholics. So was Frida's family. So, now, were Siri and his children. He was surrounded by Roman Catholics all possessed of the certainty that only they might enter the Kingdom of Heaven while he would be excluded. Catholicism had taken the place of the Pietism of his youth and there was no doubt that consciousness of his recent loose living in Berlin, taken with the moral indifference of lightly entering into marriage and the deliberate sin against Christ that must weigh down the conscience of any alchemist, was burdening him with guilt.

He writes about

> a feeling that life was not quite real, that it was a dream state and actions, even the basest of them, were performed under the influence of a strongly hypnotic force outside ourselves. For this reason he did not feel himself to be entirely responsible. He did not deny the bad in himself, but he knew that deep down there was an upward-driving spirit that suffered humiliation at being clothed in human flesh.[20]

Even if he wished, he could not cut the spiritually contaminating Berlin connection because Bengt Lidforss was continuing to play an important part in the genesis of *Antibarbarus*. Lidforss wrote that the landlord of Zum Schwarzen Ferkel had smartened the place up and raised the prices and it had become fashionable. They had to find a new place. Call it, Strindberg responded, Zum Schwarzen Strindberg, furnish it with a real human skeleton – a woman's, showing her supernumerary vertebrae. Place a bible on the altar with a condom as a bookmark. At the same time that he was proposing that Lidforss follow this childish route he was suggesting something quite else to one of his oldest friends from his Red Room days, Leopold Littmansson[21] who was assuming a new importance as he came to represent the pull against the Berlin Satanists, the pull of the upward-driving spirit.

'Let me tell you my dream', he wrote to Littmansson, and went on to outline a new monastic order.

An order of superior beings seeking new paths . . . Particular stress shall be laid on fostering a collaboration between philosophers, scientists and historians in order to seek the solution to the riddle of life, which must be solved. Those inventions in most urgent need of discovery so as to liberate the spirit from its bonds and raise it over time and space are: the one-man aeroplane . . . not the airship. The telescope (without lens and reflector) etc., (see my *Antibarbarus*); the art of making gold and diamonds (it's already possible to make silver although people think it's only 'reproduced' and silver has thus lost its value). Hence money will be overthrown! . . . this is my dream! When we've trained ourselves to produce the highest form of human being, then and only then shall we reveal ourselves!. . .We'll build a white Viking ship painted in gold and other colours; dress ourselves in white ceremonial attire and row down the river Aisne playing new instruments which I'll invent, and let nature (chance) invent new melodies, singing songs in new scales and quartertones and in eighths which no one's ever heard before, so we'll sail into the Marne and up again to Aisne, our home![22]

This typical fin-de-siècle cod-religious, cod-medieval fantasy was part ideal dream escape and part designed to loosen the purse-strings of Littmansson who was inclined towards the airy-fairy. Strindberg asked Littmansson to send him two books which were being read by the alchemists and mystics of Paris: *La Vie et l'âme de la matière: études de dynamochimie* (The Life and Soul of Matter: Studies in Dynamic Chemistry) by Fr Jollivet-Castelot and *Les Métamorphoses de la matière* (The Metamorphosis of Matter) by Claude Hemel, both books following the monistic track of trying to apply scientific methods to arrive at a synthesis of matter and spirit. He was humiliated that he had to ask Littmansson to send him these books from Paris but he could not afford to buy them himself.

Indeed, he often could not afford the stamps for his letters and had to wait days to post them. He hated being so poor. He was already in trouble with Grandfather Reischl for ordering a piano without being able to pay for it. To Strindberg it was inconceivable to live without a piano but Grandfather Reischl took a different view when the instrument was delivered and he was expected to pay. Strindberg was genuinely surprised at such an attitude from a man who had the money to pay for plenty of pianos but he pledged to repay the debt, which indeed he did when he had accumulated enough money to pay it off two years later.[23]

Strindberg's differences with Grandfather Reischl over their attitudes to money, Jews and pianos finally volatilised in March 1894 because of Strindberg's attitude to the impending obscenity charge looming over the German edition of *A Madman's Defence*. When he had stood trial for blasphemy in Sweden the ordeal had almost been too much for him. It had wrecked his first marriage and his mental health. He simply decided not to undergo such a thing again and he ignored the summons on the grounds that as a Swedish author he was under no obligation to answer to a Prussian court for a translation of his work. Grandfather Reischl felt differently. There was a confrontation in the courtyard conducted across the bloody body of a roebuck the old man had shot and was cutting up. Grandfather Reischl ordered him to attend the court or cease to darken his doors. Frida's mystical mother, who continued to adore Strindberg, pleaded for clemency and a compromise was reached by the rather biblical solution of evicting a donkey from its stable and installing Strindberg and the heavily pregnant Frida. They were much happier in the little whitewashed Haüsel where Strindberg cooked his gold and sulphur in his alembics upstairs where the rising fumes could not trouble Frida downstairs as she neared her confinement. He made a paradise for them, decorating the little cottage inside and out with beautiful paintings and he planted roses, clematis and a walnut tree. During the tranquil nights he took evocative and mystical photographs of the night sky. He called them 'celestographs' and they show swirling, patchy patterns in browns and blues that might well be galaxies in microcosm or dust swirls in macrocosm. He used his own invented technique that required no camera, no shutter and no lens, simply facing sensitised photographic plates towards the night sky and leaving them to expose. He liked to play with the fanciful idea that the stars might simply be points of light shining through pierced pinholes in the firmament of the sky.

With the writing of *Antibarbarus* coming to an end he needed to visit Lidforss in Berlin where he found things far different from his arrival less than a year ago when the welcoming committee had called him 'Master' and kissed his hands. Now the bookshops were bursting with his books and books that other people had written about him; he was famous to a greater circle but the Ferkel circle had collapsed without him at the centre. Fellowship disintegrated on his departure and they were writing squalid books and plays disparaging each other. Dated in tone, often their slurs pretend to respectable roots in Darwinism: Ola Hansson's book says that Strindberg is 'among the earthworm group of animals. He lacks a governing brain. The spinal brain gets longer and longer but no brain develops.' Strindberg's mind is 'a chaos where all thoughts are jammed together, scuffling, elbowing, somersaulting, – an orgy of ideas, a carnival of contemporary thought, a battlefield where armed masses of notions fight without leaders.'[24] In her valediction Hansson's wife Laura Marholm called Strindberg the product of his Finnish-Lapp blood and a degenerate Mongol type. Dr Wilhelm Hirsch published *Genie und Entartung* in which the author analysed Strindberg as suffering from paranoia and pathological jealousy. Adolf Paul wrote the first of his books on Strindberg, *With False and True Eye*, a sort of extended bruised love letter, and there was also a volume of eulogistic essays that redressed the balance called *A Book about Strindberg* with contributions from Georg Brandes, Knut Hamsun, Bjørnson and others. Przybyszewski had also written a book called *Requiem* which was extremely hostile to him; this he could not understand at all but he rationalised it: 'That Poland hates me because I mounted his Juel before she knew him, I can understand but on the other hand, I really can't take all his future marriages into account every time I have intercourse!'[25]

Even more puzzling than Przybyszewski's hostility was that of Lidforss who had called him Master and had encouraged and supported *Antibarbarus* through the writing process, acted as scientific advisor and helped translate the finer points into German. In December Lidforss had written gushingly that the book was 'intense and overwhelming', going on to say, 'Every line so clearly bears the noble imprint of genius that the whole work, in spite of a few things that will be anathema to the professionals, must be a splendid success.'[26] In February he intimated that he was going to include Strindberg in a work he was planning on modern natural scientists but in April he wrote a scornful newspaper review publicly

66

damning not only the book but Strindberg as a scientist. 'Strindberg's old opponents', he wrote,

> will no doubt take this excellent opportunity to make capital out of Strindberg's many eccentricities, while the trained professional will mostly dismiss it with a shrug of the shoulders and a few words about genius and madness . . . *Antibarbarus* proves one point: Strindberg is neither a reformer nor a philosopher but purely and simply a poet . . . in whom the boundaries between fact, hypothesis and fantasy have been obliterated.[27]

Perhaps Lidforss was taking his revenge for what he saw as the wrongs Strindberg had inflicted on himself and Dagny, or possibly he was making a statement about himself to the scientific community as he emerged from bohemian student to career scientist and felt the need to distance himself from unorthodox scientific speculation. Strindberg's initial reaction was at first creditably gentle and understanding: 'Lidforss isn't dangerous; he's pathological',[28] but soon he was calling him 'a disgusting person' and threatening to erase him from the face of the earth and he persuaded Schleich to write to Haeckel asking for a testimonial that Strindberg was not mad to which Haeckel responded with a letter saying that he had found nothing in the book that could be called absolutely irrational or insane, a grudging endorsement which irritated Strindberg enormously.[29]

The baby was born on 26 May, a girl. They called her Kerstin. Unexpectedly and horribly he found himself unmoved. He had been anticipating the same glorious paternal bliss that had swept him with the highest waves of emotional pleasure when Siri had given birth. Instead, he felt he was being degraded by the physicality surrounding the event, overwhelmed by 'the animal side of things, food and excrement . . . the rooms all looked as if demons had run riot. Food, kitchen utensils, and babyclothes strewn all over beds and sofas.'[30]

He wrote to his eldest daughter Karin who was now fourteen, inviting her to Dornach to help look after the baby girl and to teach Frida Swedish so that the new mother could spend her time translating his work from Swedish to German. Karin replied, 'I really cannot understand how Pappa can afford to offer me 200 francs a month with clothes and all expenses paid when he cannot afford to provide 200 francs maintenance for the three of us.'[31]

Baby Kerstin did not thrive, she cried all the time. The peasants, and probably Frida's family too, blamed her feeble health on his impiety. The Reischls insisted she be christened lest she die unclaimed by Christ and float for ever in limbo. Strindberg and Frida resisted.

He was still writing to Littmansson who shared the dream of setting up a monastery, 'a beacon against materialism at a time when industry and finance had pushed themselves so much to the fore.' If this did not work out he thought about becoming a lighthouse keeper which would allow him plenty of time for writing, or a telegraphist. Neither idea is entirely absurd. He had always been mystically drawn to lighthouses and he was trained as a telegraphist. What is obvious at this time is that all his thoughts seemed tending towards escape. Frida's too. One day she made a charade of running away to Munich with the baby but he merely waited in the Haüsel unperturbed, and she returned. The way out became clear in June.

During the season of 1893–4, the Northern Lights dazzled the theatres of Paris. Eleven plays by Scandinavian authors were put on, admittedly most by Ibsen but on 21 June Lugné-Poë's Théâtre de l'Oeuvre had a notable triumph with the premiere of *Creditors*.

'This is happiness', Strindberg wrote,

> this sense of power, to sit in a cottage by the Danube surrounded by six women who regard me as a half-wit, and to know that at this very moment in Paris, the headquarters of great minds, 500 people are sitting in a theatre quiet as moles, and foolish enough to expose their brains to my suggestions. Some may revolt, but many will leave impregnated with the seeds of my intellect, and they will give birth to my spiritual children.[32]

Next, *The Father* was scheduled for production and *Le Plaidoyer d'un fou* would soon be published. His celestographs were lectured on in Paris. The French press was prepared to make him their next Polar star.

'I've Paris dangling on a hook!' he crowed[33] and Littmansson offered his home in Versailles as a base from which to complete his conquest of the city. Strindberg crated up his paintings (Littmansson thought he had a good chance of selling them in France), his store of favourite yellow, uncut Lessebo Bikupa writing paper and his winter overcoat. Frida suspected he was planning to flit, leaving her behind. He sensed her watchfulness and began to believe that she was interfering with his post.

113

Suspicion and jealousy slipped into silent battles. He wrote to Littmansson of his shame and despair and terrible feelings of guilt, having two wives and four children and failing to support any of them. He had sent no money to Siri for ten months.

'I feel a terrible discord between what I am and what I am thought to be by those about me; the disproportion between my abilities and what I do; my shame over unfulfilled obligations; the unjust hatred, persecution, nagging, the eternal harassment, the encroachment of material things. I'm sick, nervously sick; hovering between epileptic attacks of furious work and *paralysie générale*'.[34]

The following day he left for Paris, having delivered a homily on motherly duty to Frida who pleaded to come with him. The baby who was now being fed by a wet-nurse would, she said, be just as happy staying in Dornach being looked after by her family and servants. This was undoubtedly true. Frida told him that she yearned to resume her profession as a journalist and he told her bluntly that her journalism was useless because German papers could pick up French news by translating from French papers and as for reviews, no one learned anything from them anyway (he certainly had not). They parted with some pain on both sides on the morning of 15 August. Before a month had passed, he wrote to her:

Dear Little Martyr,
Even though:

You, at 22, entered your twenties just two years ago,

You, instead of vegetating there, spent sixteen hours daily aestheticising your novels,

You have experienced the most beautiful thing of all – childhood and motherhood.

I have never worked, thought, suffered, and, at the same time, had such pleasure as I have had, from your beautiful state as a young mother,

Everything that you bring out in your [last] letter is false,

I am telegraphing you 250 francs so that you can come here to torture me and make me happy.[35]

13 FRENCH VIVISECTIONS

'Never has Paris, in the shrill voices of the newspaper boys, in the evening, in the tangle of carriages, in the busy bustle of the people, in the brutal jostling of the passers-by, struck me so forcibly, as the capital of madness, inhabited by lunatics', wrote that hardened Parisian Edmond de Goncourt in his journal of 1894.[1] The same year, Félix Valloton published his harsh graphic series *Paris intense* showing the sharp-elbowed savagery of the pickpockety pavements. Pointillists, Impressionists and Divisionists honed their understanding of optical sciences in capturing the sense of movement of the whirling boulevards. Baedeker describes the city as 'long in evil odour' and Strindberg, terrified of the rush and the crowds, panicked lest the 'poisoned, evil air' rise to his brain and drive him mad. He felt peculiarly vulnerable:

> By the Avenue de Neuilly
> There's a slaughterhouse nearby
> And when I go into the city
> I always pass it by.
>
> The big wide-open shop window
> Glistens blood-red onto the street,
> Presenting a white marble tableau
> Reeking of new-butchered meat.
>
> Today there hung on the glass door
> A heart — a calf's heart I think,
> Wrapped up in pleated paper,
> In the cold it seemed to shrink.

Then my thoughts flew [back home to Sweden]
To the old Norrboro bazaar,
Where the glistening rows of shop windows
Are goggled by kids and mamas.

There in a bookshop's window
Hangs a thin calfskin-clad book.
It is a piece of torn-out heart
That dangles there on its hook.[2]

He took up residence in the fresh air of Versailles with the Littmans-sons who were helping him with translations for publication in French. When he had to go into the city for his meetings with publishers and journalists he was as timid as a child, but ten days after his arrival he forgot his fears when he received a letter from Zola offering to shake his hand, an offer he never bothered to take up, and an invitation to a supper party for him to meet Albert Langen,[3] a twenty-four-year-old German millionaire who was proposing to become his publisher in France. Langen's father was the sugar-beet king of Germany and Langen was married to the daughter of Bjørnstjerne Bjørnson, the grand old man of Scandinavian literature who had taken such a tremendous liking to Strindberg when he had first arrived in Paris with Siri, but then become a spectacular enemy during Strindberg's blasphemy trial in 1884. This posed no obstacle between Strindberg and Langen who was establishing a publishing house that was taking advantage of Paris's passion for Scandinavian authors. He had already signed up Knut Hamsun and Georg Brandes. On the evening of their first meeting things might have gone wrong as Langen brought along the playwright Henri Becque.[4] Strindberg had written a scathing review of one of his plays but 'Becque proved a jolly fellow, witty and amusing and said some charming things about *Creditors*. Like everyone else, he'd gone to hiss the Scandinavians but confessed himself won over. He knew exactly what I'd written about him and laughed over it. He's invited me to *La Plume* [the Symbolist journal which held literary evenings].'[5]

Langen's right-hand man was a diverting twenty-five-year-old Danish painter with a limp, called Willy Grétor.[6] The men enjoyed a lavish dinner at Laurent's fashionable restaurant in the Champs Elysées and by the end of the evening Strindberg not only had the entrée to literary Paris but an agent for his paintings as well. Grétor, a relentless networker, promised him an exhibition, told him he must exhibit at the Champ de Mars and straight away sold four paintings to a collector who would, however, pay later. Grétor guaranteed Strindberg a steady income of 900 francs per month if he could churn out pictures at a steady rate. He was caught in a whirl, feted by a circle of literary men twenty years younger than himself. It was like his arrival in Berlin all over again, except that these young men had money and inclined towards commerce rather than ideas. Two days later, Grétor offered Strindberg his apartment rent-free until the beginning of October. After all, you could hardly lay siege to Paris from the suburbs. If Strindberg was serious about making his mark, he must move from Versailles to be in the centre of things. The apartment was on the ground floor in 51 rue de Ranelagh, the long, straight street that runs between the Seine and the Bois de Boulogne. It was abominably overfurnished with ormolu clocks, crystal chandeliers, brilliant mirrors, gleaming parquets, oriental rugs, pictures by Boucher, Leonardo, Rubens, van Gogh and a Cézanne that had been purchased from Gauguin. Luxury always made Strindberg uneasy. He did not want to inconvenience Grétor, he muttered. No question of that. This was just a little place he kept for his mistress who was on holiday at the moment. Grétor himself lived in a far better place on the boulevard Malesherbes which was so noisy that not only Marcel Proust's rooms were cork-lined but Grétor's as well.

Strindberg set up his easel among the gewgaws and at the end of the first week he had sold 900 francs' worth of paintings. It was giddying, but although he saw the bills and receipts, he never saw the money. From the outset he instinctively distrusted Grétor. 'Listen!' he wrote to Frida, 'There's something rotten here – about Langen too! A demi-mondaine atmosphere . . . I live in a cocotte's flat that still stinks of perfume – Tomorrow I'll have ten paintings ready to go off . . . the pictures were bought a week ago. I've seen the letter myself. The money was to arrive the following day! Then a day later. Then . . .'[7]

He had become one of the work-horses in Grétor's stable of painters and forgers turning out old masters and antique furniture. Grétor was taking Strindberg's paintings, signing them himself and sending them to Germany for sale as his own work. He was an impressive confidence trickster who lived for years on a network of mistresses, using the richer to pay for the poorer. The current rich mistress, the Baroness Rosa Pfaeffinger, was paying for the apartment Strindberg was living in which was usually occupied by his Italian mistress while Grétor and the baroness lived in her even more resplendent apartment in the boulevard Malesherbes. Just now the baroness was on holiday and the Italian mistress had moved in with Grétor to the better apartment. Grétor was laying waste to the baroness's fortune with astonishing rapidity and doing his best to make sure that Langen's sugar-beet millions went the same way. He was a talented forger with particular skill at faking Italian Renaissance paintings and he covered Langen's walls with Michelangelos, Mantegnas and Leonardos, and scattered his parquet floors with astonishingly pedigreed antiques. Strindberg was right to suspect Langen as well as Grétor; Langen did not have Grétor's need of other people's money but he was just as amoral. The only sin Langen recognised was bad business, to paraphrase Frank Wedekind, the young man Grétor hired to be Langen's secretary and whose entertainingly unprincipled central character in *The Marquis of Keith* was based on Grétor.

On 12 September Frida gave in to family pressure and allowed the baby to be baptised as a Roman Catholic, after which the sickly child recovered her health and Frida made her escape to Paris, leaving the child in Dornach. In Paris she was met at the station by Langen's liveried butler with a bouquet of roses. This was the life! Langen engaged her as a translator and she was soon spending long hours and evenings alone with Langen or Grétor or Wedekind while working on articles and translations. Frida says she was attracted by them all and later she admitted to Grétor's daughter that she was ready to fall to any or all of them. 'I was quite fascinated by Willy Grétor that autumn, and did everything to gain his friendship, like suggesting I should come to his studio to take lessons – but I was met by a constant and demonstrative coldness, so I struck up a close friendship with Frank Wedekind instead, in order to make Grétor jealous. But even that failed.'[8]

Langen and Grétor cooked up a publicity stunt to bring together the famous woman-hater Strindberg and the famous hater of Scandinavian plays, Sarah Bernhardt. The divine Sarah indubitably remained the queen of the well-made play and she would sit on her throne for years to come, hissing at what she witheringly referred to as *La Norderie*. The plays of Ibsen, Tolstoy and Strindberg with their intimate play of psychology, together with the newfangled fashion of pioneering directors such as Antoine and Lugné-Poë to mount plays in studio spaces at the top of rickety stairs, aroused the irritation and ire of the great actress who hated the thought that the world was moving on from the art of declamation statuesquely delivered from behind the proscenium arch. Bernhardt was acting in *La Femme Claude* by Dumas, and Strindberg was put up to reviewing the play in *Le Figaro*[9] as a curtain raiser to a public meeting between Strindberg and Bernhardt on stage during the interval of the play.

The prologue to the evening was a splendid dinner party in Langen's apartment. Strindberg and Frida had to leave for the theatre before the rest of the party and they were escorted downstairs by a servant to a waiting taxi. Strindberg, who felt he was being manipulated and put on show like a zoo animal, quickly grabbed Frida's arm and rushed her away. They walked the streets in silence for what seemed hours to Frida until her feet hurt and she said, 'J'ai soif.' They stopped for a drink and spent the rest of the night giggling in cafés like naughty children.

News came from Dornach that the baby was ill again and the wet-nurse departing. The day Frida left for home, Strindberg had a dinner engagement and they said goodbye on the street outside the Printemps department store, waving and blowing kisses to each other with no idea that they would never see each other again.

In Dornach, her family were anxious for the great fortune she would inherit. They pressed her to part from Strindberg. She need not even be divorced; the Catholic Church had never recognised the marriage and it could simply be annulled. Frida wavered. She received showers of letters from Strindberg: sometimes sweet and entertaining, sometimes foully insulting. He accused her of behaviour inappropriate to a wife while she was in London and Paris, suggested she had not been a virgin when they married (which was perfectly possible), accused her of being a prostitute and finally provoked her into sending him the papers necessary to institute the annulment. By the beginning of June 1896 she had started an affair with Frank Wedekind. The following February the marriage was annulled and by this time she was carrying Wedekind's child, a boy born in Munich on 21 August 1897. She named him Friedrich after her father and gave him the surname Strindberg. Wedekind was never a man for babies and he had lost interest before the baby was born. Frida never became a writer. Like Siri, she failed to apply herself to the career that she said she burned passionately to pursue. Nor did she live up to the fate of her other rival Dagny Juel who was the genuine *femme fatale* of that set, and paid the price. Two men shot and killed themselves for love of Dagny – and one shot Dagny herself. Frida seemed incapable of committing herself fully, either to art or to love. Following the break with Strindberg she led a directionless, privileged, peripatetic life that was given some shape in 1908 when, following a scandal, she had to leave Europe for England. There, described as sexually ravenous, unreliable, yet magnificently fearless, she continued her pursuit of famous men. After a brief fling with Augustus John he used to duck to avoid her, describing her as the walking hell-bitch of the western world: 'The sight of Madame Strindberg bearing down on me in an open taxi-cab, a glad smile of greeting on her face, shaded with a hat turned up behind and bearing a luxuriant outcrop of sweet peas – the sight, I confess, unnerved me.' She opened a nightclub off Piccadilly called the Cave of the Golden Calf, [10] after the idol that had proved the downfall of the Israelites. Ezra Pound used to go there together with a handful of artists whom Frida employed to decorate the place: Wyndham Lewis designed the posters, Jacob Epstein took time from designing the tomb of Oscar Wilde to let his erotic imagination run riot on the club's pillars and Eric Gill made the fine sculpture of the Golden Calf itself. Decadence had moved on since Ferkel days. More Weimar than W.1, homosexuality flourished in the super-heated Vorticist garden of gesticulating figures, dancing and talking, while the rhythm of ragtime throbbed through the wide room. As usual, money was a problem and the club closed just before the outbreak of the First World War whereupon Frida went to America to bask in Strindberg's reflected glory. She lectured on him, put on one or two of his plays and tried to make films.

When Georg Brandes asked her if, given her time over again, she would still marry Strindberg, 'Oh yes,' she replied, 'Through him my insignificant existence was raised to a higher sphere. I would marry him again without a moment's thought or doubt. At any price.'[11]

She never married again and she never called herself anything but Strindberg. Eventually, suffering from Alzheimer's disease, she died in 1943 in the family villa in Mondsee where she is remembered as an eccentric recluse hauling up baskets of food through upper-storey windows.

* * *

The merry-go-round of Grétor's mistresses propelled Strindberg out of the over-furnished apartment to the Hôtel des Américains near the Jardin du Luxembourg. The break with Langen and Grétor was an easy shedding of an assumed skin. There had never been any intellectual or emotional involvement, only opportunism on both sides. Negligible in itself, the break marked another moral step, confirming the end of compromise with money and emotional dishonesty. No more puppet masters, no more ridiculous apartments, no rich young wife.

> A free man once again, I felt a sudden release of the soul's energy and was sent soaring . . . I had decided to attain the summit of knowledge . . . Back once more in my wretched student's rooms in the Latin quarter, I dug deep into my trunk and drew out from their hiding place six fine porcelain crucibles. A pair of tongs and a packet of pure sulphur completed the equipment of my laboratory. I then proceeded to build a fire as hot as a blacksmith's forge, to lock the door, and to draw the curtains. Three months after Casiero's execution, it was still not wise to be seen handling chemical apparatus in Paris.[12]

Casiero had assassinated the French President on 24 June 1894 in the most successful of the anarchist attacks that held bourgeois Paris to ransom in the mid-1890s. Since the suppression of the Paris Commune in 1871, spontaneous attacks of terrorism – bombings, shootings, stabbings and attacks by *les vitrioleuses*, women who threw vitriol at unfortunate innocent passers-by – demonstrated the vulnerability of the bourgeoisie and the frailty of the institutions they believed in. Strindberg was prudent to draw the curtains. Anyone spied through a window cooking up chemicals might be suspected of bomb-making. Three hundred suspected anarchists had been arrested on just such wispy evidence.

While Strindberg withdrew to his private occupation behind closed curtains, sometimes standing all day over his crucibles in a room as hot as hell and stinking of pitch and sulphur, dressed only in a nightshirt and slippers with a belt round his waist and a straw hat on his head, the world continued to take notice of his more conventional work. On 7 November an exhibition of his paintings was held in Gothenburg. This was not thanks to Willy Grétor but to a more honest admirer, Algot Colander. The critics were respectful. Realising that they had an international figure to deal with, they did not compare his paintings to dirty bed-sheets as they had last time, but little money came of the exhibition. In December Lugné-Poë mounted *Creditors* at the Cercle St Simon and *The Father* at the Nouveau Théâtre, changing the ending which he thought was too strong for the Paris audience. Instead of the Captain (the father) dying at the end of the play he was supported out through a door. Strindberg never minded actors or directors making even drastic changes to his texts; he was quite without authorial vanity, always urging actors or directors to cut or change what they felt did not work.

Christmas was coming and the Scandinavian colony was clustering round William and Ida Molard. William was a French civil servant whose passion was music; he played the piano fluently if inaccurately. He was a close friend of Frederick Delius[13] whose musical imagination was currently taken up with American and Scandinavian folk tunes. Delius was far from immune to the centrality of occultism to Parisian life and culture; he had just finished writing a ponderous book on musical instruments equating each instrument in the orchestra with an occult personality or force which had co-authored with the leading French occultist Gérard Encausse, alias 'Papus'.[14]

When Gauguin came back from his first visit to Tahiti in 1893, he had settled in the apartment above the Molards in 6 rue Vercingetorix. He and Strindberg rapidly became close friends and from January until the following June when Gauguin embarked on his next and final voyage to Tahiti they saw each other almost every day. Gauguin played his mandolin and Strindberg played his guitar and they planned a South Sea musical entertainment which sadly came to naught. It was an easy-going household where artists and musicians went in and out and a party might develop at any hour. Boundaries blurred between the Molards and Gauguin's ateliers and their social life and Gauguin's weekly 'at homes'. When he had taken his earlier trips to the South Seas they had stored his paintings and sculptures, taken care of his affairs and sent him the French newspapers. Molard's wife Ida was an acquaintance of Strindberg's from the old days. The couple bore a superficial resemblance to the Hanssons with whom Strindberg had lodged in Berlin, in that William Molard seemed the more feminine: a silvery little man immensely kind and unassuming. His wife Ida was a muscular sculptress who adopted the feminist uniform of the day: short hair, man's suit and tie. But she did not become one of the 'hermaphrodites and tribaides' who had roused paranoia in Strindberg when Siri's sexuality was in question, for he had quickly realised that Ida's strict jacket clothed a maternal bosom tender enough to mother him and Gauguin and, indeed, the entire Scandinavian colony in Paris. Strindberg long cherished fond memories of 'Rue Vercingetorix,

74
71

where many fates were decided . . . Ida Molard, absinthe, *Merlan frit*, *du Blanc*, *Le Figaro* and Lilas!'[15]

When Strindberg and Gauguin met, Gauguin was trying to raise money to return to Tahiti. He was a year older than Strindberg and, like Strindberg, he was a husband with a bad conscience, having deserted his Danish wife Mette and their five children. Gauguin's letters to Mette are remarkably similar to Strindberg's letters to Siri, though posted from more exotic locations. Guilt wars with self-justification and boasting with self-pity. And money. There is always money and an excuse why it cannot be sent.

'How can I send you money?' he writes from Martinique. 'At the moment I am in a Negro hut lying on a seaweed mattress, and without the wherewithal'.[16]

Mette was Edvard Brandes's sister-in-law (both Georg and Edvard Brandes owned paintings by Gauguin), Strindberg had met her in Copenhagen in 1887 and disliked her on account of her feminist haircut – he was in the midst of his paranoia over Marie David at the time.

Lugné-Poë's production of *The Father* was premiered in Paris on 13 December. Strindberg was far too nervous to attend but it was a brilliant affair with Rodin in the audience, and Gauguin's long goatish face taking in every nuance beneath an astrakhan hat. Reviews were excellent. *L'Echo de Paris* pronounced it 'the first unquestioned and indisputable victory for Scandinavian literature in Paris', a view echoed by Camille Mauclair in *La Revue encyclopédique*: 'The Scandinavian theatre's first unquestioned success in Paris. We have had excellent evenings before, Antoine's *Ghosts*, *A Doll's House* at the Vaudeville but these were successes for the actors or for tragic effects. Strindberg had achieved his triumph through his ideas, through the irreconcilable violence of his piercing and brutally realistic genius.'[17]

The play was given ten performances and Strindberg should have been rejoicing but a friend who visited him on Christmas Eve found him hunched in an enormous overcoat at his writing desk, with a revolver and a photograph of his children. Suicide was always at the back of his mind, he said, and Christmastime away from his children was particularly bad. He was swept off to the Molards where the motherly Ida enfolded him in her recreation of Scandinavian Christmas (he describes this in the first chapter of *Inferno*). The fragrant tree, traditional meal, Swedish *punsch* and familiar old carols beautifully played and sung were more than he could bear. Overcome with nostalgia and remorse, he fled to the Brasserie des Lilas to drown his regrets in absinthe.

His new friends realised that he was suffering from more than misery: he was ill. His hands were covered in sores that bled when he tried to write or button his clothes. Ida Molard set about raising funds, channelling them through Nathan Söderblom, the Swedish pastor in Paris, so that he should not be embarrassed.

Sufficient money was raised to pay for Strindberg to be admitted as a patient to the Hôpital de Saint Louis on 11 January 1895. This was the only time in his life he spent in any hospital or institution. He remained until 31 January under the care of the director of the hospital, Professor Henri Hallopeau,[18] who treated him for psoriasis, a burningly uncomfortable bleeding skin rash that often makes its appearance following a severe shock. He had been suffering from it since 1888,[19] the traumatic year when he was in Denmark writing *Miss Julie*, separating from Siri, being persecuted by Ludvig Hansen and prosecuted for the alleged rape of Martha Magdalena. Stressful incidents make psoriasis flare up and the misery of suffering from it will often induce depression and social isolation. Alcohol makes it worse. For years he had been drinking absinthe. He had also been subject to the fiery fumes from toxic chemicals such as mercury and sulphur and sulphuric acid. His treatment is not recorded but the standard treatment would have been exposure to sunlight, application of coal tar, Goa powder and doses of arsenic taken orally. Arsenic is a cumulative poison which cannot be excreted; it often leads to cancer and may have contributed to the stomach cancer that killed him.

Psoriasis had long been assumed to be a form of leprosy and though the two diseases had been distinguished from each other in 1841 by Hebra in Vienna, the distinction had not registered on the public mind where it still carried the stigma of the Outcast and the Unclean, a biblical punishment of malefactors. Strindberg himself suspected it a judgement on his denial of God and his Faust-like usurpation of the Creator's role in his occult and forbidden activities as an alchemist. 'Swedenborg explained to me the reason for my stay in the Hôpital de Saint Louis thus', he wrote. 'Alchemists are attacked by leprosy which produced itching scabs like fish-scales – my incurable disease in fact.'[20] The Hôpital de Saint Louis treated only dermatological and venereal diseases and the two were inextricably linked in the popular mind (the destruction of the

69

nose by syphilis was sometimes called leprosy of the nose). It was a shame and a disgrace to go into the Saint Louis; people inevitably assumed the worst. Twice he obtained doctors' statements that his skin rash was not of a syphilitic nature but written statement has never been much help against rumour.

Mournfully he described his hospital companions, a syphilitic lot:

> One had a nose missing, another an eye, yet another had a lip hanging loose, another a rotting cheek . . . and around this banquet table of criminals and condemned men moved the good Mother, the matron in her austere black and white garb, handing to each his poison draft. I clinked glasses with a death's head, and we drank each other's healths, I in arsenic, he in strychnine [strychnine was given for syphilis].[21]

The angelic Matron became as devoted to him as he to her. She allowed him to smoke in his room, even offering to roll the cigarettes for him, and he was allowed out to drink at cafés. He enjoyed long scientific talks with the pharmacist in the hospital laboratory and soon they were great friends and boiling up experiments together in the hospital crucibles.

Two journalists came to interview him in hospital and wrote respectful pieces but another implied it served him right for his misogyny and another said he had damaged his hands making a bomb. 'Pretty typical reporting', Strindberg commented, 'in this tin-can-anarchist era.'

On leaving hospital he issued a dignified statement thanking everybody, and went straight round to Gauguin's studio where Gauguin was organising a sale at the Hôtel Drouet to raise money to get back to Tahiti. Strindberg's name would attract attention and so he asked him to write the preface to the sale catalogue. However, Strindberg had never really liked Gauguin's paintings, so he wrote a letter, starting: 'I cannot understand your art and I cannot like it.'

The letter goes on to describe how, when he first came to Paris, he had understood what the world considered modern art, the art of Manet, Monet and Puvis de Chavannes. He had till now dismissed Gauguin's vision because it was so new and so particular:

> I saw trees which no botanist would recognise, animals which Cuvier had never dreamed and figures which you alone could have created. A sea which might have flowed from some volcano, a sky in which no God can dwell . . . No, Gauguin is not a rib from the side of Cha-

vannes, or from Manet, or Bastien-Lepage. Who is he then? He is Gauguin who hates a burdensome civilisation, something of a Titan who, jealous of the Creator, makes his own little creation in his spare time, the child who takes his toys to pieces to make new ones. Someone who abjures and defies, preferring to see the heavens red rather than blue, as the crowd does. Indeed, now that I've warmed myself up by writing, it seems to me I'm beginning to get some idea of Gauguin's art.

A modern writer has been reproached for not depicting real human beings, but for *simply* constructing his figures himself. *Simply!* Bon voyage, Maître! Only do come back to us and look me up again. By then perhaps I will have reached a better understanding of your art which will enable me to write a real preface to a new catalogue for another show at the Hôtel Drouet. For I too am beginning to feel a profound need to be mad and to create a new world.[22]

Gauguin was delighted with the letter and simply printed it as the preface to the exhibition catalogue, but Strindberg's new-found understanding of Gauguin's work was before its time and sales were disappointing. Only nine of the forty-seven paintings were sold, two of them to Edgar Degas.

Strindberg, too, had little money and in March the Scandinavians living in Paris appealed for funds to support him.

'He is living here most insecurely', wrote Knut Hamsun, one of the signatories of the appeal,

now and then writing an article which may or may not get accepted. He is ill paid too. *Figaro* paid 40 francs for his latest article on sulphur, of which his translator got 20, so that Strindberg only received 20. He is in debt at his lodgings, he has lived there on credit the whole time and doesn't know how long he will be allowed to stay. He has one tiny room, where he also has to sleep. He lacks clothes. This winter he has been walking around in a light grey summer suit which, reasonably enough, embarrasses him. He cannot visit people dressed like that, not even editors . . . One evening we went out for a meal. We stopped outside a place which didn't look too smart and where other shabbily dressed people were going in. But Strindberg said, 'No, this is too bright for me, this is too expensive – let's go somewhere else.' But the way he said 'This is too bright for me' moved me deeply. He said it without complaint, simply as a statement.[23]

Strindberg was less meek when Hamsun tactlessly left the first instalment of the appeal in his lodging while Strindberg was out. Charity so ungraciously delivered was an insult. 'Keep your thirty pieces of silver' read his thank-you note, 'and let us be finished with each other for life.'[24] Undaunted, Hamsun arranged for the Deutsches Theater in Berlin to put on a benefit performance. Strindberg refused this charity too, telling them to send the sum to his daughter Kerstin in Dornach but this merely continued the domino fall of fury and hurt pride, with Frida's father and grandfather feeling grossly insulted by the gift and raging at Strindberg for publicly humiliating them. It was an outrage for a Uhl to be named as the beneficiary of charity.

That spring Strindberg finally withdrew from public life to commit himself totally to science. He was at the height of his celebrity and might have used the publication of *Le Plaidoyer d'un fou* to slide with apparent ease into the comfortable role of *cher maître*, existing on well-meaning handouts, but fame's puppet-show alarmed and disgusted him. He left the smart Latin Quarter where he was well known and slouched off to anonymity in Montparnasse where he plunged into his lonely spiritual quest to become an alchemist, to distil gold from base matter and purity from his own sinful soul, and finally run down the hobgoblins of magic and the occult to see if there really was anything there.

Alchemy is a double journey, a paradoxical synthesis of contemplation and action. Transmutation of metal cannot be achieved without the virtuous transmutation of self. A central tenet is that all things are living and thus able to change from one shape to another. Just as the acorn is waiting to change into the oak, so lead is waiting to turn into gold. There are twelve stages in alchemy running from calcinations to dissolution; each stage is associated with a particular symbol and a particular colour. Many alchemists believed that the philosopher's stone was compounded of pure sulphur and mercury, the 'chemical wedding' representing the union of the sun (Sol) and the moon (Luna), which is the union of Hermes and Aphrodite. The cooking process of alchemical transmutation involves a steaming and hissing laboratory of bulbous alembics, where the raw material is heated until it passes into a pipe that is prettily named 'the swan's neck' whence, as the temperature rises, the aromas and distilla-

66

tions rise into a rounded receptacle called a Moor's head where it is forced through more tubes, airy passarelles, bulbs and cylinders and receptacles in which transformations take place and impurities are shed. There are no instruments to guide the process except a thermometer and, though alchemical literature might fill several libraries, there are no accurate recipes; each alchemist must throw his stone without knowing where it will land, how close to the unknowable and unreachable. Each makes his own journey through the mystical world. The chemical journey being a metaphor for the spiritual journey, neither will succeed without the other. In occultism there is a tradition that drugs used in measured doses lift the veil. Baudelaire used hashish and Strindberg used absinthe, the mind-altering alcohol which is distilled, appropriately enough, by a journey through retorts and alembics that is similar to the alchemist's distillation apparatus. The chief ingredient of absinthe is wormwood and this suited Strindberg's positioning of himself as sinner and outcast of a vengeful God, condemned to wormwood and gall. Absinthe's side effects may include nervousness, stupors, convulsions, hallucinations, insanity and blindness.

'I will be mad', he had written to Gauguin, just as he had written years before to Nietzsche, but this time he was not simply being polite to a philosopher but declaring the intention to plunge himself into the Dionysian journey of submerging the conscious in the lava of the unconscious, thus continuing the journey that had started in Berlin with Schleich and Przybyszewski, the journey Jung was still travelling as late as 1926 when he stressed the role that alchemy played in constructing a bridge to the future, to the modern psychology of the unconscious.[25]

It has been recorded that there were no fewer than fifty thousand alchemists in Paris in 1883.[26] There is no specific statistic for 1895 but the number can only have grown with Symbolism engulfing the arts and occultism the city.

Towards the end of the nineteenth century a tide of mysticism swept across the world . . . a reaction against the all-powerfulness of science which had ruled Europe in the second half of the century. Tables turned, spirits revealed themselves by means of slates and chalk. They tapped at us with chair-legs or spoke through the creakings of old chests of drawers – all our nursery tales were re-awakened under another name . . . Thus was announced the reaction against naturalism. It expressed itself through a distrust of science, and through a penchant for the subject, romantic and fantastical, for what was called 'The Dream' . . . In Paris, all these tides and eddies, all these attractions to the occult and the mysterious, to what was forbidden, miraculous, and terrifying, spun around like some spiritual whirlpool. Like ghosts emerging from their graves, astrology and the Kabbala, fortune-telling, incantation, magic and alchemy suddenly marched out of obscure corners and joined in the whole dance.[27]

Occult publications sprang up like dragon's teeth: *La Revue spirite*, *Le Spiritualisme moderne*, *L'Isis moderne*, *L'Etoile*, *L'Ame*, *Le Cœur*, *Le Sant-Graal*, *Le Voile d'Isis*, *Le Lotus bleu*, *La Résurrection* and *L'Initiation* which carried ten articles by Strindberg in 1896. It had been founded by two of France's great occultists, 'Papus', a medical doctor, Mage and alchemist, and De Guaïta, an avid occult scholar who built up a library of more than two thousand books on the subject and was a morphine addict for whom Papus supplied prescriptions. Strindberg's faith in 'Papus' was apparently limitless, if what he wrote to a friend is true: 'I have suggested to Papus that I should "kill" myself with cyanide and he recall me to life following my prescription; but he's reluctant to do so because a medical commission would only say: "All right, but, as you see, he wasn't really dead." '[28] Another correspondent was François Jollivet-Castelot, the president of the society of alchemists whose book *La Vie de l'âme et de la matière*, declaring a belief in the unity of matter and in the capacity of elements to be transmuted, had captivated Strindberg the previous year. Jollivet-Castelot's monthly magazine of alchemy and hermeticism *Hyperchimie* also published Strindberg's articles.

74

He was permitted to work in the analytical laboratory of the Sorbonne. His work on the nature of sulphur was reported in *Le Petit Temps* on 30 January 1895 and several professional chemists wrote commentaries on his researches. When he published an article claiming to have discovered the true formula for iodine as well as a means to manufacture it from coal-tar derivatives, he wrote it up in *Le Temps* of 14 May[29] and it attracted great attention, even causing a tremor on the Paris *bourse* because a cartel that had cornered the iodine market feared a crash. He became, for a time, respected by the scientific community who, let us not forget, were themselves finding it as slippery as gliding eels to untangle genuine science from the paranormal, with so many new and invisible rays and forces being discovered. Pierre and Marie Curie were among the famous scientists in thrall to spiritualist beliefs; they were so hoodwinked by a stout medium who went by the name of Eusapia Palladino that they published a report on the means by which they had scientifically verified that her tricks were indeed not tricks but genuine paranormal occurrences. They were willing to swear to the genuineness of Palladino's great bulk levitating in the air and floating light as a feather, to the invisible hands that pulled Marie Curie's hair, the stool that crawled up Pierre Curie's leg and the table that floated prettily over his shoulder.[30] The Curies' fine analytical minds were not the only ones to confuse boundaries. Sir William Crookes,[31] who discovered the element thallium and isolated helium and was a giant of early atomic theory and spectroscopy, testified to having met ghosts in the flesh. Crookes believed in levitation and automatic writing, saw phantom figures and attended séances. Sir Oliver Lodge,[32] knighted for his services to science and a pioneer of wireless telegraphy, believed that communication was possible with the dead who were merely in a changed state, lurking about. With so many genuine scientific discoveries of the hitherto invisible making reality so fluid, it was not a great leap for genuinely scientific minds to entertain the idea of parallel realities existing in the sphinx-like ether from which that year alone had emerged the Lumière brothers' cinematograph, the electro-telegraph and x-rays, which particularly excited theatre-goers as rumour spread that they might be incorporated into opera glasses.

Strindberg was living in a family-run *pension* at 12 rue de la Grande Chaumière, an elegant stone building with pretty round-headed windows on the same side of the street as Filippo Colarossi's art school. On the other side of the street stood a modest house made remarkable by swirling Art Nouveau maidens either side of the door and sinuous script above the door advertising it as a *crèmerie*. It served up nourishing meals cooked by Charlotte Futterer, a cosy Alsatian lady who understood about credit and was happy to take artworks in lieu. Gauguin and Strindberg made it their local, as did Mucha who was keeping up a correspondence with the dead through automatic writing, and Frederick Delius, who wrote a recollection of Strindberg at this time:

> Strindberg lived in a *pension de famille* just opposite at No. 12. Among the habitués of the Mère Charlotte at that time were Strindberg, a Polish painter named Slivinsky [Wladyslaw Slewinski]; Mucha, a

Tcheque designer of decorations and *affiches*; Paul Gauguin, the great painter; Julien Leclercq, a poet; the *maître de ballet* of the Folies Bergère, also a Tcheque, and myself . . . I generally took my meals at home but occasionally lunched or dined at Madame Charlotte's to meet Gauguin and Strindberg. Or sometimes I would fetch Strindberg for a walk in the afternoon. It was at that time Strindberg wrote his pamphlet *Sylva Sylvarum*. He certainly was extraordinarily superstitious, for often on our walks he would suddenly refuse to go up a certain street on the pretext that some accident or misfortune was awaiting him there. Or I would sometimes fetch Strindberg for a walk in the afternoon and we would go through the Luxembourg Gardens and around the Panthéon, up again the Boulevard Raspail, and down the Boulevard St Michel, turning down the Boulevard St Germain, towards St Germain des Prés, then up again through Rue de Tournon, the Galeries de l'Odéon, and back though the Luxembourg Gardens.

While wrestling with the problem of the sins he had committed and continued to commit, Strindberg was also going alone to the church of St Sulpice to sit for hours in contemplation of Delacroix's *Jacob wrestling with the Angel*. Both Gauguin and Strindberg identified themselves with Jacob's struggle against the angel as each man struggled with God. Gauguin painted the struggle in *The Vision after the Sermon*. Strindberg wrote *Jacob Wrestles*.

'Another favourite walk at that time was the Jardin des Plantes', Delius's recollection continues.

Strindberg seemed extremely interested in monkeys at that time. He had a theory that the gorilla was descended from a shipwrecked sailor and an ordinary female monkey. One of his great proofs of this was the similarity between the inside of the paw of a gorilla and the palm of the hand of an old sailor. He showed photos of both, and indeed there was a great resemblance.

Strindberg was also greatly occupied with alchemy, and claimed to have extracted gold from earth which he had collected in the Cimitière Montparnasse, and he showed me pebbles entirely coated with the precious metal. He asked me once to have one of these samples analysed by an eminent chemist of my acquaintance. My friend examined it and found it to be covered in pure gold. He was hugely interested and expressed the desire to make Strindberg's acquaintance. So I arranged a meeting in my rooms for a certain Wednesday afternoon at three o'clock. My friend arrived quite punctually but we waited in vain for Strindberg. At a quarter past four a telegram arrived with these words: 'I feel that the time has not yet come for me to disclose my discovery. – Strindberg.' The scientist went away very disappointed, saying to me: 'Je crains que votre ami est un farceur.'

Strindberg also professed to have extracted pure carbon out of sulphur, and in fact I found him sometimes in his room stooping over an open coal fire stirring something in a retort. At the time he did not tell me what he was doing, but afterwards it dawned on me that the carbon probably came from the coal smoke of the open chimney . . .

He was much interested in spiritism at that time. Paul Verlaine had just died and Strindberg had in his possession a rather large photo of the poet on his death-bed. He handed me the photo one day and asked me what I saw on it. I described it candidly, namely, Verlaine lying on his back covered with a rather thick eiderdown, only his head and beard visible; a pillow had dropped on the floor and lay there rather crunched up. Strindberg asked me did I not see the huge animal lying on Verlaine's stomach and the imp crouching on the floor? At the time I could never really make out whether he was quite sincere or trying to mystify me. However, I may say that I believed implicitly in his chemical discoveries then. He had such a convincing way of explaining them and certainly was very ambitious to be an inventor. For instance, Röntgen rays had just been discovered and he confided to me one afternoon over an absinthe at the Café Closerie des Lilas, that he himself had discovered them ten years ago.

His interest in spirits caused me and Leclercq to play off a joke on him. I asked them both to my rooms one evening and we had a spiritistic séance in the form of table-rapping. The lights were turned down and we joined hands round a small table. After ten minutes' ominous silence the table began to rap and Leclercq asked it what message the spirits had for us. The first letter it rapped out was 'M', and with each letter Strindberg's excitement seemed to increase, and slowly came the momentous letters M E R D E. I do not think he ever quite forgave us for this.

. . . Edvard Munch, the Norwegian painter, had just arrived in Paris and came to see me in my rooms in the rue Ducouedi, and I asked him to accompany me to see Strindberg, who he had already met before, and who now had removed to the Hôtel Orfila in the rue d'Arras [actually the rue d'Assas]. We found him pouring over his retorts, stirring strange and evil-smelling liquids and after chattering for five or ten minutes we left in a most friendly manner. On fetching Munch the next day to go to lunch he showed me a postcard just received from Strindberg, worded something in this wise, as far as I can remember: 'Your attempt to assassinate me through the Müller-Schmidt method (I forget the real names) has failed. *Tak for sidst.* [Thanks for the visit.]' It appears that the method to which he alluded consisted in turning on the gas from the outside so as to suffocate the person within, or some such proceeding. And this was not the only time he suspected that an attempt had been made to assassinate him. Some time before, when Przbechewsky [*sic*] and his wife, old friends of his, arrived in Paris, he confided in me that they had only come to kill him.'[33]

Delius wrote this reminiscence in 1920, twenty-five years after the event, and he was making himself the centre of events as the recollections of a distinguished middle-aged man entitled him to, but the recollection is inaccurate. In fact, Delius was on a concert tour of Norway during the time that the situation between Munch and Strindberg became so agitated that Strindberg accused Munch of trying to murder him.

14 INFERNO

In February 1896 Strindberg ceased to live in the sociable hurly-burly of the Molard circle, though he continued to take his evening meal in Madame Charlotte's *crèmerie* where three of his canvases hung on the walls alongside Gauguin's. The motherly Madame Charlotte cherished hopes of marrying Strindberg who was unaware of her ambitions. He was intensely attracted to an English sculptress called Miss Lecain whom he met at one of Gauguin's Thursday evening parties. She looked ravishing dressed in a kimono and little else is known about her except that Gauguin warned him off, saying she was a notorious man-eater. Strindberg was still married; guilt overcame him and he broke off the relationship.

He used to browse the second-hand book stalls along the Boulevard St Michel and on discovering a volume by the chemist Mathieu Orfila,[1] he opened it at random and read: 'Sulphur has been included among the elements. Nevertheless, the ingenious experiments made by H. Davy and the younger Berttolet seem to prove that it contains hydrogen, oxygen and some special base which no one has succeeded in isolating.'

'Judge of my ecstasy, my religious ecstasy I would say, when faced with this revelation amounting to almost a miracle!'[2]

Further ecstasy gripped him on seeing the writing above the door on a modest family *pension* named the Hôtel Orfila[3] in the rue d'Assas. He must move in. Dark, labyrinthine and creaky, Strindberg thought its atmosphere mystic and he uses the Orfila in his novel *Inferno* where it becomes his *locus poenitentiae*, a cross between a religious seminary ruled over by a shadowy abbot and a ghost train in which all sorts of inexplicable psychic and physical horrors leap out of the dark to attack and punish him. He stayed there five months in a small room with a marble fireplace, an iron bedstead and his retorts and alembics lined up on the window sills. His bills were being paid by an art patron named August Röhss and though he had enough money for absinthe at the Closerie des Lilas every evening, he had only one pair of trousers – and they had a hole in them. He decided that he had succeeded in making gold, or maybe he was simply bored of the quest; the main ingredient was green vitriol and the recipe produced some sort of gold-coloured flakes which had the annoying habit of losing their lustre over time. The fact that gold is incorruptible and never loses its lustre was a detail; he was generous in sharing the recipe: 'If the specimens have faded, freshen them up over a cigar!'[4] he urged his fellow scientists. There are always wry and ambiguous strands in Strindberg's commitment to alchemy and indeed all things occult and at this time one begins to wonder how wholeheartedly he was actually plunging into this chymical wedding, whether in the same spirit as he had plunged into his other weddings: with one eye on total commitment and the other on what fascinating material it might produce for a book. Just as each marriage had in its decline been transmuted into literature so now he began preparations for the next volume of his autobiography, calling it *Inferno*.

At that time there was much literary seeking of a Zola of the occult.[5] Although there had been numerous mystical, Symbolist and decadent poets and writers such as Baudelaire and Mallarmé, artists such as Moreau, mystics and mages and founders of new religions such as Madame Blavatsky, there had still been no great novel, no literary successor to Poe. Huysmans came close.[6] Balzac had attempted it with Gauguin's favourite book *Séraphita* but he had got carried away by Swedenborgism and a large chunk of the book was simply an explanation of its doctrine. Strindberg saw the challenge, not simply to tell fairy tales of angels and hermaphrodites, as Balzac had in *Séraphita*, or spine-shivering horror stories of Black Masses, as Huysmans had told in *Là-Bas*, or even to update the fantastic and grotesque beauty of the Master himself, Edgar Allan Poe, but to find the story within himself, to write a record of his life as he surrendered himself completely, without reservation, to the Occult within himself, exploring the shallowness of sanity by giving priority to the deeply irrational within the mind and the psyche. He would tell the tale as he moved through everyday life surrendering himself to superstition and allowing himself to be guided by signs and omens.

At the start of February, he moved into the Orfila to begin the experiment. He bought a huge, blank-paged book so hefty that it weighs nearly four kilos. Bound in rose-red cloth, the colour symbolising enlightenment for alchemists, damnation for some, for others erotic love and for himself the colour of disappointed love. Also, as he notes, the colour of Sweden's torture chamber in the old days which was known as the Rose Room. Altogether a suitable colour for recording his journey through inferno. On the cover, in black ink, he wrote its title, *Occult Diary*, and when he ceased to keep it, in 1908, he wrote on the cover 'This diary must never be printed! This is my last will! Which must be obeyed!' For fifty years it lay inviolate, an object of superstitious awe, sealed with a double seal in the Royal Library where first he had encountered occultism as a young man working under the odd, haunted mystic Gustaf Klemming.

Inside, on the first page he wrote quotations from the Bible, Shelley, Eliphias Levy and the Talmud – 'If you wish to discover the invisible, pay great attention to the visible' – and above them all in bigger letters, possibly added later when he repented of this dangerous flirtation with magic, the words 'Ne fais plus cela!' The diary records dreams, strange coincidences, correspondences such as Swedenborg recorded (the resemblance between a crab's shell and false teeth, for instance) and inexplicable events, recording the peculiar journeys of the subliminal mind when released from conscious control. Soon he realises that 'From my former atheism I had relapsed into the deepest superstition.' At which point nothing is too banal to become an omen. As he moves through a world of omens and symbols, it is but a short step for them to become messages from 'the powers'. The mission then becomes one of interpretation, a decoding of messages to see where the powers want to send him and in this way to show him the meaning and purpose of his life.

He visits the occultist Papus, finds that the maid is in bed with scarlet fever and some unknown creature has killed their best duck. Next day he finds a nine of spades in the street. The card of death! He hears that the Shah of Persia has been murdered and a Swedish nobleman has died in Paris.[7] He sees the resemblance between the face of pansies and those of certain people. He notes the similarity between the walnut and the brain and the death's-head marking on the wings of a moth that haunts graveyards at night. Like Hamlet, he takes notes of the shapes of clouds. Pebbles shaped like hearts are a good omen but twigs lying in his path forming the shape P—y (Przybyszewski) signify evil. A rooster weather-vane flaps its wings, soot falls into his absinthe, an indentation on his pillow takes a curious shape; nothing is too great or too insignificant to be a message from the powers. What does it all mean? Dreams, mostly dreadful, are recorded.

> May 14. I had a dream last night. An amputated head had been stuck onto a man's trunk, making him look like a drunken actor. The head began to talk. I was terrified and knocked over my folding screen, trying to push a Russian in front of me to protect me against the furious creature's onslaught. This same night I was bitten by a mosquito and killed it. In the morning the palm of my right hand was covered with blood. May 17th (and subsequent days). Absinthe at six o'clock outside the Brasserie des Lilas, just behind the statue of Maréchal Ney, is now my only vice and my last remaining pleasure.

Cuttings from newspapers, butterflied inkblots, random connections, *frottage* and sketches and scientific speculations pepper the pages of the *Occult Diary*. It is notable that however puzzling the words, the thoughts are clearly expressed and his handwriting remains as neat, controlled and legible as it always is (apart from the time when he was in the Hôpital de St Louis and writing with bandaged hands). He was fond, during this time, of employing the words exoteric and esoteric. 'I must find a way of splitting myself in two, become a sober, well-behaved working man and alongside him, if I'm able, let a silent, esoteric *Übermensch* grow up at the edge of the field.'[8] With Darwin and literary realism having swept heroes off the face of the earth, and life reduced to mere matter, Strindberg was replying with a Monist blurring of all distinction between the animate and the inanimate: a twig or a lump of coal might deliver a message to him that is more important than someone's words. Looking for the hero within himself allowed the imagined to become real and reality to assume the character of a dream, a *mis-en-scène*, the mere frame for the eloquent imagination. The *Übermensch* keeps the diary while the exoteric story is told in the letters and by the accounts of those everyday friends who perceived nothing abnormal as they ate their meals with him or accompanied him on his long daily walks about Paris. His sister Anna and her husband came to visit him and found him his usual courteous, rather over-formal self. He was, Anna said, 'unusually harmonious in his behaviour.'[9] His other friends found him equally well balanced and in

June when they learned that he would be leaving Paris for a short trip to Sweden, the Molards and others organised a series of farewell parties for him with coloured lanterns strung from house to house and dancing overflowing into the streets, Strindberg joining in the dancing with evident pleasure. Gauguin was among the revellers and it was the last time the two of them met. By the time Strindberg came back to Paris, Gauguin had made his final departure to Tahiti where he followed Strindberg's progress through the articles and newspaper cuttings that the Molards used to send him.

In contrast, Edvard Munch was exposed to the full force of Strindberg's paranoid suspicions when he arrived in Paris in February 1896. Munch had been in the city about six weeks before the two men met up with each other. Strindberg felt slighted at this delay in renewing the friendship and doubted Munch's friendship. However, Munch's only brother had died tragically and unexpectedly just before Christmas and he was in no mood to revive the excesses of the old Schwarzen Ferkel days. Munch was also extremely busy bringing *The Scream* to Paris, knowing that its exhibition would make or break him in the city. He had painted it in 1893 and it had immediately created a sensation in Berlin but it was not until 1895 that it was seen in Paris, when the lithographic version was reproduced in *La Revue blanche*, causing such a sensation that he was invited to mount an exhibition at La Maison de l'Art Nouveau.[10] This was the most exciting invitation that could be extended to any contemporary artist and Munch was determined to make the most of it. La Maison de l'Art Nouveau was the new gallery opened by Siegfried Bing,[11] the Charles Saatchi of those days. Taste-maker, market-maker and gallery owner, Bing had already launched the fashion for Japonisme and Art Nouveau.

Although Munch was famous, he was impecunious and in order to exhibit his pictures at the Salon des Indépendants[12] he had to throw them out of the window so the landlord could not take them in lieu of rent. He was thirty-three, emotionally unapproachable, drinking like a whale and only growing more handsome with age. Munch features large in the book Strindberg wrote about this period in his life, *Inferno*, in which he inexplicably turns Munch from a Norwegian into a Dane and calls him 'beautiful Henrik'. Maybe Strindberg envied more than his classical good looks, for Munch possessed the intense self-containment born of a single purpose, whereas Strindberg endured all the cloudy uncertainty of the polymath.

They had been close friends at the start of the Berlin period but the friendship had cooled as Frida monopolised Strindberg and acted as a wedge between him and his friends. Munch had found Frida uninteresting. He did not even make a sketch of her, which speaks for itself as he made portraits of almost all the others.

Munch brought news of Dagny Przybyszewska, concerning whom unfinished business lay between the two men. Munch honoured Dagny for her reckless integrity in the cause of emancipation and sexual equality in contrast to the feminists who talked emancipation while clinging like vines, as Siri had when she was married to Strindberg. Dagny, by contrast, now that she was married to Przybyszewski, was doing her best to support him and the children by giving piano lessons; to Munch she embodied the spirit of Brave New Woman but Strindberg nursed a hatred of her borne of his bad conscience over his affair with her while he was newly engaged to Frida. Dagny was 'that woman who broke up families' and 'a whore who fucked four nations in four weeks'[13] (Sweden, Norway, Poland and Germany: Strindberg, Munch, Przybyszewski and Schleich). He had already written an essay inspired by her, *La Genèse d'une Aspasie* (1894) and she became the model for the emotional executioner Henriette in his play *Brott och brott* (*Crimes and Crimes*) written three years later in 1899.

When Strindberg went to visit Munch in his studio it was like entering the Schwarzen Ferkel all over again and being confronted by his debauched past which was shameful to him now that he was purifying his soul as an alchemist. Munch's pictures of the Berlin crowd stood stacked against the walls and among the pictures he had brought with him to exhibit were many ravishing pictures for which Dagny had posed, including *Madonna* (then called *Conception*) showing her naked at the moment of sexual consummation, *Jealousy* showing Munch and Dagny bound by love and Przybyszewski consumed by the corrosive emotion, and *Vampire* for which Adolf Paul had modelled. There was also the painting of *The Scream* which would be exhibited at Bing's. The image has been interpreted in innumerable ways over the centuries but this is what Strindberg wrote about it when he was asked to review the exhibition for *La Revue blanche*:

'A scream of terror before nature, turning red with fury, which is making ready to speak on behalf of the storm and thunder to the tiny, heedless creatures who, without resembling them, believe themselves to be gods.'[14]

The first time Strindberg went to visit Munch, he found his way barred by a Great Dane of monstrous proportions lying stretched across the threshold of the *porte cochère*. Thereafter in Strindberg's big, pink, secret *Occult Diary* Munch is always accompanied by this diabolic familiar, a hound of hell which terrifies Strindberg. In real life, Munch had no dog at the time, only a troublesome cat but in Strindberg's mind his sightings of Munch and his Cerberus would be accompanied by an auditory hallucination, music on the air: the strains of Schubert's *Aufschwung*, the piano piece Przybyszewski used to play over and over again in Berlin and, in view of the careful attention to the signs and symbols through which the powers were communicating to him, this was enough to convince Strindberg that Munch was a remote agent for Przybyszewski who had sent Munch to Paris to murder him as revenge for being Dagny's lover.

In June news reached Munch from Berlin that Przybyszewski was in prison for the murder of his long-term mistress Marta Foerder and their children who had died of gas poisoning. At this news, Strindberg's terrors multiplied. Przybyszewski was going to kill him by *envoûtement*, that hybrid between primitive witchcraft and the imperfectly understood properties of electricity and electro-telegraphy to carry thoughts, voices and intentions through the ether. Strindberg was far from alone in believing such irrational things possible. The part played by electricity in mental manipulation such as mesmerism and hypnotism was the subject of newspaper articles and popular science books including *Les Etats profonds de l'hypnose* and *L'Extériorisation de la sensibilité*[15] and now Strindberg joined the debate with an essay linking this train of speculation with Dr Charcot's experiments at La Salpêtrière, calling it *The Irradiation and the Extension of the Soul* and it was published in *L'Initiation* in 1896. *Envoûtement* was not only talked about but occasionally practised, a well-known case being an attack on Huysmans which resulted in first one duel being fought between Jules Bois and the Marquis Stanislas de Guaita in which, magically, two shots were fired but one bullet never left the barrel, and a second duel involving Bois and 'Papus'. Strindberg was in Paris during these events and learned about them from Georg Brandes. Earlier in the year Strindberg had tried to cast an *envoûtement* on his daughter Kerstin so that she should become ill and Frida would summon him to her side for a reconciliation but the spell had misfired: it was not Kerstin who became ill but another of his daughters, Karin, his eldest. Racked with remorse, he became terrified that he had lost the upper hand over the hounds of Hell. He began to hear voices in the walls of people who were plotting to kill him and he resorted to exorcisms.

In the *crèmerie* where he still continued to take his meals and to appear perfectly normal among his friends, Madame Charlotte discovered him in her kitchen one morning having arranged all the saucepans in a circle and, wearing nothing but his shirt and his underpants, performing a dance of exorcism around them. Madame Charlotte reported affectionately:

> He explained he was doing this to chase away the evil spirits which might poison the food. During the hot weather he would usually climb in through the window, since evil spirits stood watching the doorway; and one day everything in the kitchen exploded just before lunch was to be served. This was a consequence of Strindberg trying to make gold in a saucepan, and the whole meal was ruined.[16]

He also practised subjugating Munch to his will. His diary of 4 June reads:

> I went to see the Danish painter who lives in the rue de la Santé. The huge dog had gone. We set off to get some dinner at a pavement café in the boulevard Port-Royal. My friend was cold and felt indisposed. I put my coat over his shoulders and he became most amenable, I could do what I liked with him . . . Then suddenly he had a nervous seizure, he began to shake like a medium under the influence of the hypnotist . . . what could this mean? A tunic of Nessus? Was my garment impregnated with my nervous fluid? . . . Had I become a magician without being aware of it?

Munch merely had a chill.

The truth concerning Przybyszewski gradually unfolded. He had not gassed his mistress or his children. He and Dagny had spent some time with her family in her native Norway and when they returned to Berlin they were accompanied by their eight-month-old baby. The existence of the child reduced his mistress to despair; realising she had lost Przybyszewski for ever, she committed suicide by gassing herself. Przybyszewski's guilty ramblings led the police to hold him for two weeks on suspicion of murder after which he was released from custody, if not from guilt.

Strindberg continued to be convinced that Munch was Przybyszewski's infernal agent and he was wary of the painter but he wanted another portrait of himself. The earlier portrait Munch had made of him in Berlin was coloured and subtle. While it masterfully conveyed the ambiguities inherent in his personality, it was not the image Strindberg wished to go down to posterity. Munch was making strong lithographs at the time and this was the medium he chose. Lithography involves drawing on the surface of a stone from which the image is printed. Strindberg's superstitious horror must have been complete when he discovered that the financially embarrassed Munch was re-using an old stone, drawing his portrait on the back of a stone whose other side contained the drawing for the lithograph *Jealousy* whose subject was the triangle of love, hate and envy between Munch, Przybyszewski and Dagny. At this time, Munch liked to draw symbolic borders round his pictures. Round the strong image of Strindberg's head he drew a border of a slim nude woman whose hair extended in zigzag thunderbolts all the way round the edge. Maybe the thunderbolts were inspired by Strindberg's current obsession that he was the target of persecution by people wielding electrical machines. In the bottom left-hand corner Munch followed the old tradition of writing the name of the sitter. Unfortunately the name was misspelled STINDBERG. Munch had missed out the R. Strindberg was tremendously insulted. *Stind* means stout, swollen or replete. Strindberg also objected to the incorporation of the naked lady in the border: he did not wish to go down to posterity branded a satyr. At the next sitting, Strindberg arrived wordless, laid his revolver on the table between them and stayed silent throughout the session. Munch eventually got rid of the naked lady, converting her narrow figure into a continuation of the wavy lines of the thunderbolts. She only appears in the earliest versions of the lithograph. He also corrected the misspelling, which was probably a mistake rather than an insult. Munch was not yet expert at lettering in the back-to-front process required for lithography, as can be seen in the earlier *Self-portrait with Skeleton Arm* where he drew one of the letters in his own name (the N) back to front. Or it might have been that Strindberg sitting there reminded him of a fragment of poetry from *Peer Gynt* for which Munch was designing a poster for Lugné-Poë's production in which Toulouse-Lautrec's morphine-addicted muse Jane Avril danced an unforgettable Anitra. Strindberg had expressed a wish for a hierarchical portrait, one to go down immortalising him for posterity, and there is a passage in *Peer Gynt* that connects with the Ozymandian vanity of such notions:

Han, Memnon, faldt det mig bagefter ind,	He, Memnon, it occurred to me later,
Lignet de såkaldte Dovregubber	Looked like the so-called Dovre kings,
*Slig som han sad der stiv og **stind***	Sitting there so stiff and **stout**
Med enden planted på søjlestubber.	With his bottom planted on broken columns.[17]

Munch's conciliatory corrections failed to mend the breach, and Munch vented his annoyance in an unflattering cartoon, *Strindberg in the Clinic*,[18] which shows him looking miserable and covered in sores. For his part, Strindberg's paranoia concerning Munch grew greater until one day following a visit from Munch he wrote in his diary:

> I heard a stranger go into the room next to my bed. Then silence. For three hours I remained awake, unable to go to sleep which I normally did very quickly. Then I felt an alarming sensation glide all through my body. I was the victim of the electric current flowing between the two rooms on either side of mine. The tension finally increased and though I fought it I finally left my bed obsessed with the single idea:
>
> 'They're killing me! I don't want to be killed!' I went out to look for the serving boy in his cubby hole. But alas, he wasn't there! Obviously got out of the way, bribed, a secret accomplice. Waking the proprietor I alleged that the fumes from the chemicals in my room made me feel unwell, and I asked him if he could let me have another room for the night. By a chance which must be ascribed to the wrath of providence, the only available room was situated below that of my enemy . . . As I drew the curtains around my bed I heard my enemy in the room above climb out of his bed and drop some heavy object into a trunk, the lid of which he then closed and locked. Which meant he must be hiding something. The electric machine, perhaps?[19]
>
> Next day, a Sunday, I packed my bags and pretended I was taking a trip to the seaside. I shouted, 'Gare St Lazare' to the coachman. But once we had reached the Odéon, I told him to take me to the Rue de la Clef near the Jardin des Plantes. I shall stay here incognito long enough to finish my research before leaving for Sweden.

He was hiding from 'Edvard Munch and everything related to Juel-Przybyszewski'[20] but he was also hiding from the police for he had new worries to fuel his paranoia. Willy Grétor had been arrested and many of his art forgeries had been unmasked. Strindberg, who had painted for Grétor, was terrified that the police might be after him, suspecting him to be an art forger, and that Grétor and Langen themselves might also be looking for him to kill him to suppress the evidence he might give against them.[21]

This was when he sent the postcard that Delius remembered, the card accusing Munch of trying to murder him by 'Pettenkofer's method',[22] shooting gas through a wall which was the same method by which Przybyszewski was suspected of murdering his mistress. The postcard led to them parting for ever in just such an abrupt and illogical way as he had parted from Frida and Siri, never to see each other again. Just as with his wives, the thunderclap parting was to be followed some months later by the friendliest of letters, as if nothing unusual had occurred between them, the letter invited Munch to join him on a little holiday if he was free but Munch was not free and that was the end of any exoteric relationship between them though each lived in the other's thoughts, referring to each other in their diaries and paintings until their deaths.

By summertime he had finished stimulating the experiences for his novel *Inferno* but psychosis and paranoia by no means took their leave. The hounds of Hell refused to be ordered back to their kennels and it was obvious that his alchemical experiments, being unholy, had brought down an unstoppable persecution by the powers. The persecution by unknown forces together with the auditory and optical hallucinations he experienced are typical alcoholic delusions. In fact, they read remarkably like Munch's diary accounts of his own alcoholic crisis some years later. Strindberg himself wavered between wondering if he was enduring the punishments of a sin-hagged Faustus for straying into God's prerogative, a place men should not go, or if he were simply experiencing the physical reaction to the hair-raising catalogue of chemicals that he was in contact with on a daily or near-daily basis. He lists arsenic, chlorine, cyanide, mercury, nicotine, sulphur, vitriol, absinthe and the sleeping drug sulphanol.

Fleeing Munch and his other persecutors, he left 'the unclean atmosphere' of the Orfila for the comparative peace of a small rented room close to the the natural world he loved, the Jardin des Plantes where he spent every day in that veritable Garden of Eden, deriving consolation from the beautiful plants that turned their faces to him like his own innocent children and the melancholy animals in the extensive zoo, whose speaking eyes told him a different story from that told by their skeletons in the evolutionary galleries which taught that each was simply a collection of atoms all struggling to assert their own experience at the expense of all the others. Martin, the bear in the zoo, aroused his greatest pity and twice a day the impoverished writer with holes in his trousers would buy the bear a handful of cherries for his breakfast and supper.

The cemetery at Montparnasse was another favourite haunt and both places became the subject of beautiful, reflective essays.[23] In the cemetery he felt that his body and his senses and his spirit took on the properties of a great sounding chamber receptive to what he called the psycho-magnet of world history. He tried to capture the emanations of the dead in test tubes and subject them to chemical analysis.

Throughout this period he practised bibliomancy and in July when he opened his Bible at random it opened at Isaiah 54: 'The Lord saith "For a small moment I have forsaken thee but with great mercies I will gather thee. In a little wrath I hid my face from thee for a moment; but with everlasting kindness will I have mercy on thee, saith the Lord thy Redeemer." '

Taking this as a promise of redemption and hope, 'At 11 [the following morning] I packed, and fifteen minutes later fled, giving my address as Dieppe. And now I lie on a bed in a garden pavilion on the ground floor, the doors stand open; hollyhocks outside and acacias. It is the first feeling of summer that I have had. And now I am waiting for something new or the end or some persecution.'[24]

Lest the new end awaiting him was death itself, he made suitable arrangements:

> If I die here I have no one to take care of things. I beg you to telegraph and reclaim my body, for I regard it as a punishment to be cut up in the anatomy hall and have the janitor sell my pieces to shops. The cheapest method is burning (50 francs). Otherwise, I have had a child-ish wish, since I was young, inexplicably to be buried in Montparnasse. It costs 500 francs but that could surely be got from Bonnier as an advance on my Collected Works.'[25]

Strindberg's host in Dieppe was the successful Norwegian landscape painter Frits Thaulow[26] who made enough money to exercise his natu-rally benevolent nature. When, the following year, Oscar Wilde was released from Reading Gaol he went straight to Dieppe where Thaulow was not embarrassed to be seen with him and often invited him to dinner at the Villa des Orchidées. His wife Alexandra was equally magnificent. During Strindberg's stay at the Villa des Orchidées she was at first puzzled to discover dribbles of candle wax about her well-kept home but she soon discovered that Strindberg was getting up in the night and tapping the walls and ceilings with a broomstick to check for hidden machines. She suggested that they go round the house with a compass which would detect any untoward electrical activity. This pacified him for a while but when Strindberg saw a man peering through binoculars, a sight not uncommon on that or any coast, he was not to be mollified. People were spying on him and on 28 July 1896 he left Dieppe for Ystad in southern Sweden to take the medical advice of Anders Eliasson,[27] a doctor he had briefly visited the previous year. Eliasson was not one of the distinguished doctors of Strindberg's acquaintance who made great leaps in medical science. He was a loner, an introvert and an autocrat with a firm conviction of his own high worth but his happiness lay in supporting those he considered greater intellects and he counted it an honour to be one of Strindberg's financial supporters. In return, Strindberg used him as a sounding board, writing him about a hundred letters throughout the Inferno period.

When Strindberg arrived at Eliasson's large, desolate property, the omens were not good. The building was constructed in the perfectly innocuous Swedish vernacular style but in his imagination it became transformed into a Buddhist monastery. The little domed edifice in the centre of the courtyard which in real life was maybe a bread oven, or a well, or a privy, became in his eyes a sinister recreation of the tomb of Tamberlaine at Samarkand. An apathetic tortoise dragged itself across the flagstones and plunged into the tall grass nearby, and he imagined it an exotic terrapin lost in a green nirvana that merged with eternity itself.[28]

Eliasson examined his body and found it 'sound and strong'. But bodily strength was little comfort. 'During our first interview after my arrival from Dieppe, he fixed me with an observant eye and then said, "What's the matter with you? Depressed? Yes! But there's something else underneath. There's an unhealthy look in your eyes I've never seen there before. What have you been up to? Debauchery, secret vices, lost illusions, religion?" '[29]

The words spoke to his conscience. He had never ceased to fear God, and he had defied him. Like Faustus, he had been possessed of the certainty that he was clever enough to sign up to the contract without having to pay the price. He had thought that his superior self could remain above moral laws; keep the upper hand over Mephistopheles and manage to cheat him out of the payment of his soul at the end of the contracted period. Now doubt overwhelmed him. He had conjured the powers and was paying the price. Where hubris entered nemesis was never far behind.

> Is it possible, I ask now, that the evil principle is dominant in me? I have evil in me and I hate it . . . We are forbidden to pry into the Creator's secrets. . . . I regarded my researches into the hidden as criminal activities for which I should be punished . . . my occultism cost me my health and almost my personal freedom and I regard it as criminal to continue . . . I suddenly realised that I was no Job; no righteous man who must be tested but a robber who has ended on the cross because his deeds deserved it and who had to be punished.

Doubt and terror poured out in a succession of letters to Hedlund while his suspicion of Eliasson increased. The doctor prescribed a calming regime of cold showers, bland food and large doses of sulphanol, a common soporific. He also gave him strophanthin, a cardiac stimulant. Over-use of sulphanol was known to produce a morbid state of mind known as sulphanolism. Combined with the heart stimulant the effect would be unpredictable. One of the doctor's patients who used it had woken from the drug-induced sleep quite mad and leapt out of a window. He took away Strindberg's Bible and Missal and allowed him only innocuous books, to calm his mind. Unfortunately the bed he gave Strindberg had big brass knobs at each corner 'like the conductors of a machine for generating electricity' and a wire-sprung mattress like the coils in a generator. Eliasson had apparently also placed an enormous coat of chain mail in the attic directly above Strindberg's bed, turning it into machine of death should there be an electrical storm. He decided that the doctor's so-called medicines were probably poisons and he was trying to kill him on account of his success at making gold which was going to imperil the entire world's economic system. His paranoia boiled, but never boiled over: he was evidently perfectly capable of dissembling, for Eliasson found him excellent company on their walks during which he was a fund of knowledge, good sense and good humour. The complicated strands of this time can be examined, if not unpicked, in chapter seven of *Inferno* and in the fine play *To Damascus* that he wrote the following year.

Who knows how long this silent battle of fluidic fisticuffs might have continued had he not received a letter from Frida on 15 August, saying that she pitied and loved him. She invited him to Dornach. It was time that he as a father should get to know his little girl. 'Recalled to life' by the letter, he hastened by train to the big house on the banks of the Danube.

76   I had said goodbye to a baby six weeks old and I returned to find a little girl two and a half years old. At our first meeting she gazed into the depths of my soul, her manner not severe but very serious, apparently looking to see whether I had come for her or her mother. Reassured, she allowed herself to be kissed, and clung with her little arms around my neck. It was Doctor Faust's return to earthly life.[30]

15 OUT OF INFERNO

When he arrived in Dornach everyone was there but Frida, who was in Munich. Unbeknown to Strindberg, she was the mistress of Frank Wedekind and both of them were working, more or less, for Albert Langen on his satirical magazine *Simplicissimus*. Strindberg had thought Frida's invitation to Dornach was a first step towards reconciliation and as she was not there he conjectured that she wished to be cajoled. He wrote her beautiful letters, to no effect. Her mother Maria Uhl, however, clasped both Strindberg and his spiritual crisis to her bosom. Frida had always found her mother overly fey and monumentally credulous, and Marie Uhl now told Strindberg how she too had been persecuted for studying forbidden texts. She too had been tormented by sleepless nights, mysterious happenings, mortal anguish and nocturnal attacks but, she confided, she had found salvation in Swedenborg. Mother- and son-in-law bathed in mystical rapture for three days. This was as much as Grandmother Reischl could stand. She might be old and the mausoleum in the garden waiting with gaping door, but she remained owner of the house and she ordered Strindberg out. He moved up the hill to a large house belonging to Marie Uhl's twin sister Melanie in Saxen, a little hamlet in the flowery meadows half-way between grand-mother's house on the banks of the Danube and the rocky promontory crowned by the castle of Clam.

He was given a charming bedroom with a four-poster bed and pinkish wallpaper. It immediately became the Rose Chamber, symbolic of the torture chamber in Stockholm as well as the tortures and betrayals of passionate love, and it can be traced in his letters and literature, notably in the play *To Damascus*. With Marie and Melanie dancing attendance on the questing sage and little Kerstin to act as innocent guide through the spiritual realm, he applied himself to reading the great Swedish mystic and visionary Swedenborg, who had an enormous influence on many Symbolists and visionaries including Balzac, Maeterlinck and William Blake. Swedenborg had been one of the leading physicists and anatomists of his time. He had invented the first mercurial air-pump and conducted valuable scientific research into the brain and spinal cord before giving up science for visionary mysticism in his fifties. The parallels are obvious. Swedenborg had been weaving his way in and out of Strindberg's life since his student days at Uppsala University where Strindberg had first encountered his books and found them 'daft'. He had next encountered Swedenborg when he worked at the Royal Library under Klemming, himself a Swedenborgian. Next, during his short but intense friendship with Gauguin who was awash with enthusiasm for Balzac's Swedenborgian novel *Séraphita* and it became an important link between them when Gauguin recommended it to Strindberg who read it over Easter in the year they spent together, but now it was time for him to read Swedenborg's own texts, of which there are many volumes.[1] The complications of the mystical doctrine have no place here but the essential element for Strindberg at this time was Swedenborg's idea that Inferno (or Hell) is not another place. It is not a judgement upon the earthly life, not a state to be endured in the hereafter. Inferno is a state we may encounter in this mortal life. If we recognise it for what it is and allow the mills of God to grind us up exceeding small, we may pass through to a consciousness of redemption and perfect happiness on earth. Heaven and Hell are not located elsewhere. They are internal and spiritual states. Heaven may be achieved by anybody and it may be achieved before death because it is an opening of an interior consciousness. In this sense, Swedenborg offered the perfect antidote to Strindberg's mother's Pietism, allowing him at last to shed the burden of original sin that had been such a heavy one since childhood when his mother had encouraged him to believe that his actions, good or bad, could carry no spiritual power to influence the outcome because that had been decided before his birth.

Swedenborg gives Inferno a specific landscape with particular geographical features. Fortuitously there was a remarkable similarity between Swedenborg's description of Hell and the physical features of the walk from Grandmother Reischl's house on the banks of the Danube up to the castle of Clam.[2] The path through Hell, the path that purified him, can

65

still be taken today. Like all penitential and expiatory walks, it offered trials by Earth, Air, Fire and Water and plenty of symbolic features. The narrow path that Strindberg took becomes a *locus classicus* in Strindbergian literature. It is the gorge in *To Damascus* and *Inferno* (he allots little Kerstin the role of Beatrice) and it is a path we can take today, finding it virtually unchanged since his time. Starting at the bottom, the hidden entrance to the gorge is difficult to discover. Then a scramble up a steep hill, the climber bent to forty-five degrees. A change of direction along the slippery rim of a hurtling watercourse that opens into a crashing, boulder-strewn stream. Stepping stones. To the right the spume-slippery path is overshadowed by birch and fir and to the left by the huge, threatening form of overhanging granite resembling a gigantic human head: the frowning gods. Next, a great v-shaped cleft four times the height of a man, a rocky vulva reminiscent of Peer Gynt's entrance to the underworld. From here the devil beckoned Strindberg but he passed on, drawn by the gleam of a placid mill-pond whose pearly peace is violently sucked up into the noisy repetitions of the water-wheel's rotation: the cycle of eternal suffering. Then a little habitation for pigs: a sty with six doors which became the doors to Dante's red-hot sarcophagi. A step or two further on, the flames of the blacksmith's shop symbolised the heat of hellfire. Salvation, after such a journey, came almost at the top of the steep gorge where a small wayside shrine, easily missed, stood at the edge of the forest. Just a modest Madonna with downcast eyes and a few wild flowers at her feet, tributes from the passing faithful. From here he could look down on the Danube's wide plain as Christ looked down on the world when tempted by the devil. It was sufficient. Strindberg felt forgiven.

Although his delusions of harassment and persecution did not immediately disappear, they dwindled. More importantly, he felt that he was no longer in their thrall. They had been reduced from sanity-threatening terrors to mere annoyances. He renounced Black Magic but still dabbled a bit in alchemy every now and then, walking uphill to the castle to smelt a bit of gold where Paracelsus had done the same. Down in the ancient town square of Grein he found a printing press and published a tract on gold-making. Marie Uhl reported an incident when he grabbed a knife and stabbed the empty air in order to fend off hostile spirits, and once she found him lying on his bed dressed in black as if lying in state but she had her shrewd suspicions that he was play-acting. 'My sister and I have often wondered', she wrote, if these dramatic and frequently theatrical events were not so much expressions of an occasional abnormal idea but rather experiments designed to create a good theatrical effect and, also, to test its impact on an audience, i.e. ourselves, for whom these scenes were performed. It is difficult to decide how much is fantasy, how much reality, hard as it is to imagine how Strindberg really saw the real world. It is certain that, despite all the moments of anxiety we lived through because of him, he also provided us with many amusing and even pleasing ones, by means of his talent for natural comedy.[3]

Winter came. Snow fell. The Danube lay like a corpse in a winding sheet. It became clear, even to him, that Frida had no intention of joining him. His father-in-law, who would rather have shot himself than see Frida's marriage re-ignited, indicated that Strindberg had outstayed his welcome and on 27 November 1896 he left for Sweden 'to face the fire of the enemy' as he gloomily grumbled, 'I'm ruined, for I've lost all aptitude for writing. And I can't sleep at night', but in fact his mind was seething with new ideas for books and plays. The last five years had seen Strindberg occupied by a vast range of scientific exploration as he sought to employ a unifying vision and to put up a fight against the contemporary trend towards fragmentation of knowledge into separate disciplines: 'the specialisation which has brought about our own Babylonian confusion where things are so far gone that a mineralogist can't understand a zoologist', as he put it.[4] The great idea behind his scientific essays, which sometimes he called scientific poems, was the inextricable interrelation between all matter. All, in their way, were hymns to unity.

Having eschewed Black Magic and worked his way back from atheism in which he was never comfortable, he had constructed an adaptation of Christianity which suited him for the present.

> Impossible to believe in a God in whom I was part owner, for then I'd be able to make slight changes in my own destiny . . . God in us, yes, in so far as we are emanations of His being, that is one thing, but God as a fixed point outside us, by which alone we can accomplish anything, the Creator above us, and we his creations with traces of his being, under him, that is how I understand the matter.[5]

In December 1896 he arrived in Sweden's southernmost province Skåne. It had become his custom on moving home to stay a few days with a medical doctor for a consultation on his general health. He no longer trusted Eliasson with his Buddhist monastery full of tortoises and electrical machines so he stayed with Dr Lars Nilsson[6] whom he had met a few years earlier. He hoped Nilsson might cure his insomnia but he only prescribed a different dosage of sulphanol. It might have helped if he had altered his drinking habits but he found he had to go to bed every night half-drunk so as to manage to get to sleep at all. After five days he moved on to the city of Lund where he soon became the centre of a sociable circle who vied to make life easy for him. When it came to domestic matters, he was helpless as a child and grateful for the smallest acts of domestic kindness, observed Waldemar Bülow, the gossipy and agreeable editor of a local paper, *Folkets Tidning* (*People's News*) who lent Strindberg his housekeeper to cook and clean his lodgings in 8 Grönegatan, a street neatly connecting two of Strindberg's interests as it ran between the Cathedral and the Old Observatory. Lund is the second university town in Sweden, rich in Romanesque and Gothic architecture, a place where quaint student traditions are scrupulously observed and Strindberg was delighted to be hauled out of his lodgings on 1 May by the students to join their May Day revelries. He described his outfit in a letter to Kerstin: Papa wore 'a white student's cap with a black band and yellow and blue cockade – felt back in my youth again, and drank punch for 14 hours.'[7]

78

Åke Hans Tavern became the meeting place of an evening. No Schwarzen Ferkel, it was far calmer and, on Strindberg's side at least, free from the passions and rivalries of sex though fate had thrown his old rival Bengt Lidforss into the circle. Lidforss had grown up in Lund where he was now a docent at the university. Like many graduates of the Schwarzen Ferkel, he had remained a polymath and he was particularly valued for his popular explanations of current scientific theory. The two former rivals for Dagny's favours put their differences behind them and became friends. Strindberg enjoyed being known as 'den Store' (the Great One or the Master) in Lund where he stayed three years comfortably and fruitfully, showered with friendship, money from his plays which were suddenly being put on again, and once again writing novels and plays.

A new beginning required new clothes. He had become interested in ancient Swedish history and he decided he would take up cycling again, to gather material for a series of articles pulling together Swedish history, biology, agriculture and culture. The project was initially to be one of his grandiose national surveys but it became *Scanian Landscapes*, a series of charming articles for *Malmö Tidningen* (the *Malmö Times*). His dark hair had turned a becoming white at the sides and he had a cycling suit made with a jacket and knickerbockers of dark grey tweed flecked with white dots, like the plumage of a sparrow-hawk. (*Ornen* or the eagle had long been one of his alter egos with which he sometimes signed letters.) Argyll socks, yellow shoes and a shirt with a button-down collar completed the striking outfit in which the eagle would pedal through the countryside.

In February Frida made a new application for a divorce. He had no idea that she was expecting a child by Frank Wedekind. She was also expecting Wedekind to marry her but by April he already had a second mistress: 'I am playing a double game – which of us doesn't?' By June she and Wedekind had parted and their son, Max Friedrich, was given the surname Strindberg when he was born on 21 August.

He made no objection to the divorce application which felt, like many events connected with Frida, not quite real and certainly meaningless in the greater scheme of things. A legal process had no power over the consciousness of their inextinguishable connection. He continued writing letters to 'Mother' Uhl full of concern and affection for Frida. He also wrote a charming series of more than a hundred letters to little Kerstin, sometimes addressing her as 'Dearly Beloved Child', sometimes 'Dear Little Glow-worm' and sometimes she is a princess, the daughter of the Emperor Napoleon whose identity he assumes on the wonderfully fanciful grounds that Napoleon also had an Austrian second wife. Father and daughter never saw each other again but this outpouring of enchanting letters was to have its effect on Kerstin who left Austria when she was grown up to live in Sweden in order to learn her father's language and read his writings. She ended life in a mental institution and here she was visited by Strindberg's publisher, the faithful Bonnier, who came away pondering how a being who was not in full control of herself, who grimaced, twitched and sometimes screamed, managed to communicate such great charm.

Whether it had anything to do with renouncing Black Magic or not, Strindberg's fortunes took a turn for the better on his arrival in Lund. *Lucky Peter's Journey* was put on in Stockholm by Molander, the first time a play of his had been performed in Sweden for seven years. It ran for sixty-five performances and he was able to send a large sum of money to Siri and the children. *The Father* was put on in Venice and Milan, and was a great success though the Italians paid him nothing. He was also approached by Gustaf af Geijerstam who wished to become his publisher. Geijerstam was an old friend who had been a great support during the trial for blasphemy though Strindberg never really liked him, describing him as 'born bald with glasses, a pot belly and the eyes of a rabbit in need of a piss'. He was now the literary editor for Gernandts publishing house and wished to publish any new work.

Happy, prosperous and calm, Strindberg began to write his autobiographical novel *Inferno* which skilfully conveyed his near-madness during the previous three years in France. Hoping it would make him the Zola of the occult, he wrote it in French, and he had high hopes it would win him the Nobel Prize for literature, a prize he would never win, any more than would Zola, Ibsen or Tolstoy. He was once more writing at his old, blazing pace: sweating with the rapidity of his thoughts, flinging each completed sheet to the floor, neither correcting nor revising. He began the book in May and finished it by 25 June when he sent it to Gustaf af Geijerstam who enthusiastically accepted it, promised a thousand kroner for the first edition and set about finding someone to translate it into Swedish. In August Strindberg went to Paris to find a publishing house for the French edition. This was more difficult than he had expected as Paris had lost interest in things Scandinavian.

It was a great shock and disappointment when the many French publishing houses that printed occult matter rejected *Inferno*. It was a book before its time. Plot-less, meandering and entirely subjective, it forms a headwater to the stream of consciousness literature but it is unlike Woolf or indeed Proust or Joyce who use the beauty of words to suck or seduce us into their stream. Strindberg uses almost childishly plain language. He is not trying to prove a case; the book shows him as work in progress and he beckons us to have a look, to explore with him. Strindberg was greatly admired by Kafka and if *Inferno* resembles any book it is *Metamorphosis*, with Strindberg's exoteric self as Gregor Samsa and his esoteric self as the monstrous beetle. The point of the book or journey is to find a locus of meaning. What is science? What belief? Where precisely is the absurd located? When does thought become knowledge become belief become superstition? He planned to end the book with 'What a joke, what a dismal joke life is!' but changed it to:

Here then is what my life adds up to: a sign, an example destined for the improvement of others: a laughing stock set up to demonstrate the vanity of celebrity and fame: a laughing stock to teach the young what ways of life they should avoid: a laughing stock that believed itself a prophet and found itself unmasked as an impostor . . . And there, brothers, you have the fate of one man among so many others. Now admit that a man's life may bear every appearance of a practical joke.

It was not until he met up with Marcel Réja,[8] a peculiarly interesting young poet, art critic and psychiatric doctor, that his luck changed in Paris when Réja made the introduction to a willing publisher. Réja's dominant interest was in the link between insanity and creativity. He had studied under Charcot at the Salpêtrière and he published the first serious book on the art of the insane, *L'Art chez les fous, le dessin, le prose, la poésie* (1907). The first psychiatric doctor to try to understand and establish the clinical connections between creativity and abnormality, a subject that had long interested Strindberg, Réja later set up a museum of madness in Paris to try to educate the public on the taboo subject.[9] Réja managed to place *Inferno* with his own publisher the *Mercure de France*, though in fact the Swedish edition came out before the French because Geijerstam had the work speedily and brilliantly translated by a close friend of Strindberg's[10] and the Swedish edition was published on 1 November 1897 to a flurry of puzzled disappointment. Commonly the critics mistook his depiction of a mental crisis for the crisis itself and the general tone was one of lamentation for a noble mind o'erthrown: 'a seething mind crumbling into pieces', 'the suicide of his talent', 'a spiritual bankrupt who stares appalled at the dregs of his misery', 'an unpleasant and ridiculous book'. But Henrik Ibsen wrote that he admired Strindberg's 'very great talent . . . I have read his work with *great* interest. Not least, his latest book *Inferno* has made a powerful impression on me.'[11]

Despite reviews, the book sold well. Within a fortnight Geijerstam offered him good terms for a second edition. This unfortunately encouraged him to write a sequel, *Legender* (*Legends*), an occult pot-boiler that sank, and *JacobWrestles*, a symbolical description of religious struggles that the author himself acknowledged a chaotic failure.

That summer Andrée's balloon expedition set off for the North Pole with Strindberg's godson Nils Strindberg[12] on board but a muddled rumour got about that it was in fact the writer going on board and that he had chosen this original way either to commit suicide or to get rid of his wife. Siri's children in Finland received an alarming telegram from somebody signing himself 'Daddy' asking them to come to Stockholm immediately for a farewell banquet but the muddle was easily cleared up as Strindberg was in closer communication with his children these days, having cleared his conscience by sending them money. Now that he was no longer ashamed, he felt able to write them much more natural letters and he was able to tell them that the telegram had not come from him.

Greta was becoming an actress. 'I always imagined it would be Karin who would go on stage, and Greta who would be the domestic one', he wrote. 'But I was wrong, as you see!'[13] Karin was adopting the Roman Catholic faith. Strindberg was also veering in the same direction. Swedenborgianism was too prescriptive. The written body of work was massive and ridiculously detailed. The *Arcana Coelesti* alone runs to thirteen volumes and there are numerous other volumes dealing with visions and symbols and correspondences, and a whole system of the significance of colours and of numbers that imposed Swedenborg's system of imaginings on the fantasy and imagination of the faithful. Strindberg was never going to be a slave to anybody else's imaginings or symbols. Inner meanings meant nothing if they were not born within his own heart and head. Karin's conversion to Roman Catholicism led him to write to her that he was content that she was returning to

The faith of our fathers . . . and the Protestants now seem to be returning to it in droves after having lost their way and dissolving into as many sects as the philosophers, both past and present. But a piece of advice: never reason about religion, Karin. If anybody brings the subject up, then, politely but firmly, interrupt them and don't be afraid of confession: 'I am a believer and do not discuss these sacred things.' The truths of religion are axiomatic for me and thus cannot be proved and do not need to be proved, and if one attempts to prove an axiom, one gets tangled up in the absurd. Religion is thus as exact a branch of learning as mathematics, which is predicated upon unproven and improvable axioms which must, nevertheless, be taken 'in good faith' if the whole of mathematics is not to come tumbling down.[14]

This was at the heart of his preference for Catholicism over Protestantism. 'Protestantism seems to me the religion of the rebel, the freethinker's endless reasoning about faith, dogma, and theology, but not religion.'[15]

Karin, Siri and the other children had been brought to the Catholic faith by Marie David who died in December 1898 aged thirty-two. With Siri long out of his life, Strindberg had ceased his paranoid hatred of lesbians and the opening chapter of the novel he wrote that year, *The Cloister*, contains a description of a homosexuals' ball that is affectingly sympathetic and displays great compassion.

The following year his second daughter Greta came to Stockholm to be confirmed into the Catholic Church. She was eighteen. Father and child had not seen each other for seven years. Both were apprehensive, but the first visit on 24 July was quickly followed by a second. Each found only kindness and joy in the visit which marked the beginning of a tender and blossoming friendship.

Blessings rained down. 'I seem to have regained the grace of being able to write for the theatre', he wrote in March 1898. 'The religious battles are over, and the whole *Inferno* saga has come to an end.'[16] After six dry years without writing a play, a stream poured from his pen. He wrote twenty plays between 1898 and 1901, mostly completed with his usual rapidity. The first two, written in 1898, were *To Damascus* (Parts I and II) and *Advent*. *To Damascus* is the larger, more ambitious work. It was only completed in 1901 in a final, third part that made the play come full circle, each part corresponding with the parts of Dante's *Divine Comedy*: Inferno, Purgatorio and Paradiso. What makes the play seminal is the combination of the entirely modern idea of the multiple-faceted personality with the medieval form of the pilgrimage play. It deals with the domino-fall consequences of the first action a man takes against the dictates of his conscience. Founded as usual on his own life, the story starts with a famous writer who feels damned and persecuted, meets an unhappily married woman and imagines that the right thing to do is to rescue her from her unhappiness. This first action sets up the duality between absolute good and our limited vision of goodness. Following an accident, the hero finds himself in a monastery that is also a madhouse. He becomes split into the Beggar and the Stranger, each the dream self of the other. The play ends unresolved, with the Stranger drawing with a stick in the sand. It is a beautiful and haunting play. Strindberg found himself weeping while he wrote parts of it and when he sent it to Gei-jerstam he had no idea of its value: 'If you find it good, chuck it at the theatre. If you find it impossible, chuck it away.'[17]

He began on Part II a little later in the summer. By now The Lady had transmuted from being Siri to being Frida. She is pregnant and in labour. The emphasis shifts to a study of guilt and the workings of the conscience. The stranger has been successful in his scientific labours to make gold and has been invited as the guest of honour at a banquet at the Academy. He arrives to find some of the diners in full evening dress with decorations, some are in suits and yet others are dressed as tramps. The well-dressed guests gradually disappear and he is left among the tramps who mock him. Honour is turned to humiliation. Unable to pay for the banquet, he is confined in a cell with his *doppelgänger* the Beggar. Released, he is desper-ate to discover the health of his wife and child. He is amazed to be told by his mother-in-law that the baby has not yet been born. Everything that has been seen on stage since he left her has taken place over a few minutes in his mind. The baby is born and the audience is left with no idea which world he will opt for, the real or the imaginary, esoteric or exoteric, and indeed which is which. Well ahead of its time, *To Damascus* had an enor-mous influence on modern theatre and film, on Beckett, Kafka, Ingmar Bergman and even Hitchcock. It is an intricate play composed like Wag-ner's *Ring* cycle as an endless circle. Geijerstam at once understood its significance and offered a thousand crowns for the first edition. One or two critics recognised it as something extraordinary but most wrote it off as confusion. It caused Georg Brandes to declare that he had now lost all interest in Strindberg. The original title for the play had been *The Mauso-leum*, after the mausoleum in the garden in Dornach built for the über-worldly grandmother and grandfather Reischl in their garden and the self-righteous, disapproving old couple provide at least part of the model for the malignant couple in the next play he wrote that same year, *Advent*, which also combines realism with fantasy. The old couple are portrayed in all their venality and one follows the neatly satisfying Swedenborgian idea that crime is its own punishment. The devil appears, lightly disguised as a schoolmaster. A nightmarishly bizarre ball, recalling the homosexual ball in *The Cloister* and the Academician's banquet in *To Damascus*, shows how Strindberg was enjoying his new-found talent for writing set-pieces. Finally the couple are given hope of redemption but it is a pretty small hope. A play with less power to enchant than *To Damascus*, it is fascinating in its own right but the greater play eclipsed *Advent* which suffered accordingly and was not performed until 1915.

The concept of the monastery, lay or religious, had long haunted his imagination. The pull of the monastic life had been particularly strong throughout his Inferno period and it had been making frequent appearances in his recent fiction. Now the time had come. In August 1898, feeling spiritually strong and full of idealistic expectations, he visited the vast Benedictine monastery of Maredsous in Belgium with the intention of staying. He stayed one night. The fathers drank wine with their five-course evening meal! They took snuff! This was a deal too worldly. Quite sufficient to extinguish any idea that the Roman Catholic Church might become his home. In fact the visit had exactly the opposite effect. It opened the possibility for the spiritual quest to continue beyond Roman Catholicism, and one may suspect that this was his real intention all along, for he sabotaged his own visit by arriving at Maredsous on, of all nights of the year, St Bartholomew's Night. On the same night in 1572 the Catholics had massacred between five and thirty thousand Huguenots during the French Wars of Religion. 'But I was not afraid', he wrote, 'since I had attended night mass and was forced to accept the consecrated wafer and even make the sign of the cross. Otherwise they would have killed me as a Huguenot.'[18]

The 22nd of January 1899 marked Strindberg's fiftieth birthday. 'Nothing would be more natural', ran the leader in *Folkets Tidning* on the 21st, 'than that our leading writer August Strindberg should tomorrow be the object of congratulations that would unite the nation in enthusiasm, overlooking his weaknesses and seeing only the greatness of this great man. But Swedes are envious, and patriotism runs thin.' *Svenska Dagbladet* published an untidy half-page of bitty tributes that looked like an office leaving card. *Dagens Nyheter* referred to him as Sweden's greatest writer. The Swedish Theatre put on a performance of *Master Olof*, a choice of play that stoked bitter conjectures of how different his career might have been if this play had not eaten up much of his youth and his self-confidence in rejection and rewritings. Old friends from his youth, Carl Larsson, Gustaf af Geijerstam, Hjalmar Branting, Pehr Staaff and others gathered in the gothic room in Bern's salon where he had set his first successful novel *The Red Room*, but he refused to join them. Instead he dined quietly with Waldemar Bülow, wearing a black frock-coat and a rosebud in his buttonhole. He was not forgotten in Germany where a *Festschrift* cele-

101 *Palette with Solitary Flower on the Shore*, 1893, oil on wood. Private collection. The solitary
flower emerging from the impasto may be seen as symbolising the artist's lonely striving.

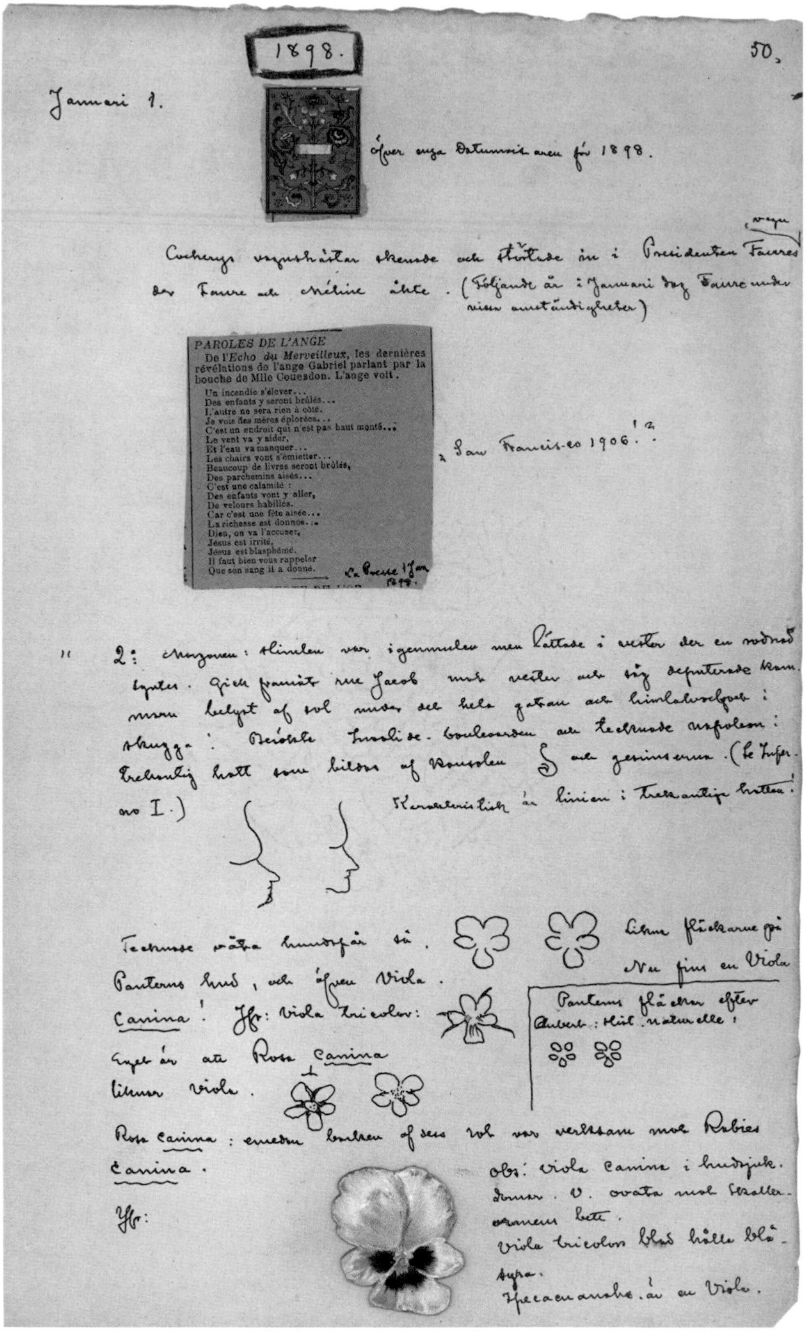
1898.
50.
Januari 1.
PAROLES DE L'ANGE
De l'Echo du Merveilleux, les dernières révélations de l'ange Gabriel parlant par la bouche de Mlle Couesdon. L'ange voit.
Un incendie s'élever...
Des enfants y seront brûlés...
L'autre ne sera rien à côté.
Je vois des mères éplorées...
C'est un endroit qui n'est pas haut monté...
Le vent va y aider,
Et l'eau va manquer...
Les chairs vont s'émietter...
Beaucoup de livres seront brûlés,
Des parchemins aisés...
C'est une calamité :
Des enfants vont y aller,
De velours habillés.
Car c'est une fête aisée...
La richesse est donnée...
Dieu, on va l'accuser,
Jésus est irrité,
Jésus est blasphémé.
Il faut bien vous rappeler
Que son sang il a donné.
La Presse 1 Jan 1898.
San Francisco 1906.

102 Page from the Occult Diary, 1 January 1898, with notes on his visit to Les Invalides, profiles of Napoleon, observations on flower forms and a newspaper cutting reporting the Angel Gabriel's revelations to Mlle Couesdon. Kungliga biblioteket, Stockholm, Strindbergsrummet, SGNM D 72.

103 (LEFT) *The Night Sky*, celestograph, 1894. Distrusting the camera's distortion, celestographs were produced by laying unexposed film towards the subject, which produced, he maintained, a truer image than if the film had passed through a lens. Kungliga biblioteket, Stockholm, Strindbergsrummet, Celestografier, bild 7A.

104 (BELOW) Photogram of crystallisation, 1890s, another cameraless technique developed to record mineral structures as his interest in chemistry grew ever greater. Kungliga biblioteket, Stockholm, Kristallationer, bild 1A.

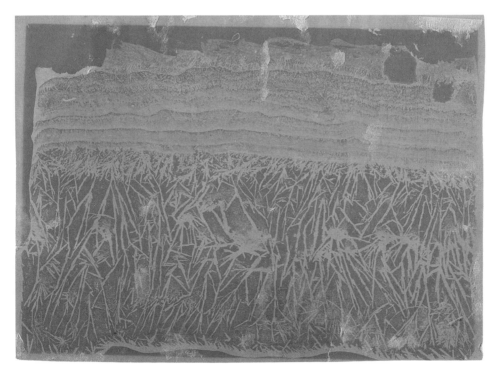

105   *Beach, Kymmendö II*, 1873, oil on wood. Örebro Konsthall, Sweden. His beloved Swedish archipelago was often the subject of his early naturalist paintings. Courtesy of Örebro Konsthall, Sweden.

106   *Storm after Sunset at Sea*, 1873, oil on canvas. Private collection.

107 *Eclipse and Polar Light,* 1891, oil on cardboard. The Royal Library of Sweden, Stockholm.
Kungliga biblioteket, Stockholm, Strindbergsrummet, sgNM 19:13,17.

108 *Double Picture*, 1892, oil on cardboard and collage. Private collection. Strindberg claimed that he was the first to paint symbolic landscapes and certainly the double pictures echo his written insistence that everything has a double significance: estoteric and exoteric.

109 *Night of Jealousy* 1893, oil on cardboard. Strindbergsmuseet, Stockholm. Given to Frida on their engagement, the dedication on the reverse reads; 'To Miss Frida Uhl from the artist (the Symbolist August Strindberg). The painting depicts the sea (bottom right), clouds (top), a cliff (on the left), a juniper bush (top left), and symbolises: a night of Jealousy.' Rough surface treatment and dark colouring reflect the tempestuous emotion.

110   *The Danube in Flood*, 1894, oil on panel. Private collection. Strindberg painted this view of the swollen waters from their window in Dornach, while Frida's belly swelled with their child. The bloodless pastel colouring is uncharacteristic of his work.

111   *The Wave VII*, 1901, oil on canvas. Musée d'Orsay, Paris. Waves breaking in the open sea were a recurring subject and an ideal symbolist vehicle to convey almost any spiritual message (© RMN (Musée d'Orsay) / Hervé Lewandowski).

112 *Mysingen, 1892*, oil on cardboard. Bonniers Portrait Collection, Stockholm.

113   *Wonderland*, 1894, oil on cardboard. Nationalmuseum, Stockholm. One of the
pictures Strindberg sent to Littmansson in July 1894, describing its double meaning:
'Exoteric: A dense forest interior, in the middle an Exot. Hole opens out into an
idealised landscape . . .Esoteric: the Wonderland, the battle of light against darkness. Or
the opening of the realm of Ormuzd and the exodus of the liberated souls to the land
of the sun . . .' (Photo © Erik Cornelius).

114   *The Child's First Cradle*, 1901, oil on paper. Private collection. Painted while Harriet was carrying their unborn child. A poem accompanying the painting began; 'And you, child of the South and the North, were carried in the light green beech woods by the blue sea.' (Letter to Anne-Marie Strindberg, 4 September 1901.)

115　*Inferno*, 1901. Private collection. Similar in its 'glimpsed through' composition to *Wonderland* and *The Child's First Cradle*, this landscape of the unconscious reveals a much darker place.

116   *The Town*, 1903, oil on canvas. Nationalmuseum, Stockholm. By now he and Harriet had reached a loving solution to living in Stockholm: separate houses and frequent visits (Photo © Erik Cornelius).

117   *The Avenue*, 1905, oil on canvas. Thielska Galleriet, Stockholm.
One of his last paintings, the avenue suggests life's relentless march
towards death but there is hope in the breaking light on the horizon
(Photo © Tord Lund).

118　*The Island of the Dead* by Arnold Böcklin, 1886. Museum of Applied Arts, Leipzig. Strindberg's favourite painting, it hung in the Intimate Theatre and appeared at the end of *A Ghost Sonata* (© akg-images / Erich Lessing).

brating his work along with that of Edvard Munch was prepared in the shape of an issue of the magazine *Quickborn* devoted to his writing and Munch's graphics. Well intentioned and beautifully produced, it roused Strindberg to fury. He tore into the 'horrible masterpieces' Munch had produced, criticised Munch for not having one new idea in seven years and his letter of thanks to the unfortunate editor reads: 'Many thanks for the copies of *Quickborn*. The name was not a happy choice, the colour on the cover is unsympathetic and the reproductions are not first class.'[19]

A week after his fiftieth birthday he summoned up the courage to set foot in Stockholm itself for the first time since the blasphemy trial. A brief visit was all he could endure. He walked the streets like a ghost, loving the ancestral echoes but flayed by the personal memories and regrets. He soon returned to Lund and began a new play that had possibly been stirred up by *Quickborn* with its greetings from Berlin. *Brott och brott* (*Crimes and Crimes*; 1899) is set in Paris. Its main characters are a painter Adolphe based on Munch, a playwright Maurice based on Przybyszewski and a sculptress Henriette based on Dagny who goes from one man to the other, captivating them erotically and destabilising them psychologically. Maurice lives with his mistress Jeanne and their child. A success with his new play makes him attractive to Henriette. He wishes the child dead (*envoûtement*) so he can marry Henriette. The child dies. Maurice is arrested on suspicion of murder and his play is taken off. He is disgraced. It turns out that the child has died a natural death. His play and his reputation are revived but his conscience has been stirred. He gives up Henriette to support his mistress Jeanne but she will not forgive him and Maurice turns to the priesthood. Strindberg later called it his 'boulevard play' and said he found it facile, a judgement perhaps driven by his disgust and regret over the Ferkel years that had inspired the piece; he said that he far preferred the mystical pieces that had preceded it but to this day it is often performed and remains cliff-hanging entertainment. When it was put on in February 1900 it was rightly and enormously popular. King Oscar, who was in the audience, was observed to clap it heartily, though his dislike of Strindberg was well known.

Few things apart from a fiftieth birthday have the power to galvanise artistic activity like the dawn of a new century and 1899 saw a tremendous burst of artistic activity in him. During the next three years he wrote no less than seventeen full-length plays and it is surely significant that this rebirth took place during the time that Strindberg at last found the courage to go back to live in Stockholm. History plays were back in vogue, the revival of *Master Olof* had been a great success and in April he began his late cycle of history plays with *The Saga of the Folkungs*, the story of Magnus the Good who ruled from 1319 to 1365. Magnus ascends the throne aged three. During the first part of his reign, Sweden experiences a golden age. The Russians are repulsed. Sweden is sufficiently prosperous to free its slaves. Magnus's reign is lauded but he is aware that while he is a lucky king, he is not a strong king. The Black Death comes, the people look to him and he cannot change their fate. His wife and son plot against him. He is deposed and they take the throne. The plot, well known to every Swede, uses Strindberg's instinctive understanding of psychology to humanise history and tell a gripping tale; but these history plays contain far more than bare psychological tales. Maybe it was his new-found skill in portraying crowd scenes, balls and banquets that gave him the confidence to spill into the epic, writing enormous set-pieces that would not disgrace *Aida*. There is a march of Mongolian prisoners, a madwoman dumping a pillow-full of feathers from a balcony, a scaffold scene, a Golgotha-like tableau and a festive procession that collides with a band of frenzied flagellants.

Two days after finishing *The Saga of the Folkungs* he began on *Gustav Vasa*, the king who ruled between 1523 and 1560 and in 1518 was carried off to Denmark as a hostage. He escaped to lead a peasant rising against the Danes, captured Stockholm in 1523 and drove the enemy from Sweden. The play opens when he has been on his throne for ten years. Like Magnus the Good, he is considered the fount of all goodness but unlike Magnus the Good, Gustav Vasa is a skilful politician and has his share of ruthless opportunism. Master Olof, now older, wiser and an accomplished courtier, supports his master but his heart is touched as his son, afire with youth's uncompromising idealism, wants to expose every compromise and 'tear down like Luther'. 'Begin with yourself, then', Olof tells him, 'the universe will always be there . . . When I was your age I thought I knew and understood everything. Now I know nothing and understand nothing, so I limit myself to doing and patiently enduring.' Two days later, Strindberg began *Erik XIV*. This is the last play in the Vasa Trilogy of *Master Olof*, *Gustav Vasa* and *Erik XIV*. Erik XIV was the son of Gustav Vasa; he might have been schizophrenic or his mental instability might be explained by the large amount of arsenic found in his body on exhumation. The opening scene sees him behaving like the

Red Queen in *Alice*, liable to throw things and to demand executions on a whim. A complex plot of court politics and the dynastic marriages of Europe, the play ends with Erik being outwitted by his brother Johan, who seizes the throne. Like all the history plays, *Eric XIV* is an excellent play with strong characters and a speedy plot but interest in Swedish history being what it is, they are seldom performed outside Sweden.

On 15 June 'I was serenaded by the students [of Lund University] . . . I wept and was seized with a terrible longing for Stockholm.' He left Lund for good but there was no point in going to Stockholm at midsummer when it was intolerably hot and everyone would have left for their summer houses. Instead he went to join his sister Anna and her husband Hugo von Philp who had a summer house in Furusund in his beloved Stockholm Archipelago.

'I'm writing every day', he wrote to Karin on 8 July 1899,

> to get lots of money for your brothers and sisters; young ladies need beautiful clothes, and young Hans has got a bicycle . . . I am now living in the most beautiful scenery in Europe . . . young people and children wander about in light clothes, beneath oaks and birches, in green meadows, lawns, groves, woods and by the shore. And the sun shines hot. The sea is quite warm. In the evenings I sit on the veranda with my sister. Steamers and sailing ships pass by on their way to Russia, Finland and Lapland, which enlivens the picture. My sister often plays Beethoven, for me the summit of music, while my brother-in-law and I smoke and drink punch . . . My brother-in-law, a Doctor of Philosophy and a well-to-do man (consequently no Strindberg but a Philp) is a director of the bathing society, where I never go. I am now writing a tragedy *Erik XIV* taken from Swedish history. Gustav Vasa's son, Erik wanted to marry Elizabeth of England; later he wanted to marry Mary Queen of Scots and ended up marrying a corporal's daughter from Stockholm (who sold nuts in the market). He ended his days in prison, poisoned by Johan III. A fine story! Now you know more of my secrets than anyone else. But you are never satisfied and demand to know still more (like a jealous woman), you would like to know more than I know myself, you little tyrant!

> But enough ticking off, and peace! Kiss of peace and all's well . . .

> Your Pappa August.

He finished *Erik XIV* in Furusund on 1 August and on the 5th he wrote to Geijerstam that he had a Swedish saga play in his head. He burned to write it but knew that he must take some rest. All his energies must be summoned for him to go and live in Stockholm. Crabwise he approached the city, gentling himself towards the centre via a hotel on the outskirts, then settling into what one of his friends described as pathetically modest furnished rooms in Narvavägen 5, close by the first rooms he had occupied as an independent young man on leaving Uppsala University. By October re-entry was complete but still he was not going to enter society, become respectable, win a social position or hold his tongue. He moved to Banérgatan 31, close to the old deer park where he could take his morning walks before settling down to work. It was not as traumatic to be back as he had anticipated for 'it doesn't matter where I am, for I can't get away from myself!. . . yes, this is the milieu in which I grew up and I am rediscovering myself here and there every day!. . . Mostly alone although I have at least 1,000 acquaintances here.'

He had been on the move since 1883. Now Stockholm and its environs became his frame for the rest of his life.

In October his new publisher Gernandts lived up to their promises and published the Vasa Trilogy. *Gustav Vasa* was accepted for the Swedish Theatre by 'Stockholm's Theatre King', Albert Ranft,[20] and Strindberg was once more in the happy position of walking down the street of his own city to attend play rehearsals and give directorial advice to the excellent director Harald Molander, who had the sense to take it. Together they built a production that ran for two and a half years and brought him in 15,000 kr. Strindberg as usual attended only the dress rehearsal. He was far too nervous to be present at the premiere or he might have caught sight of Harriet Bosse, an oriental-looking twenty-two-year-old actress in the audience who greatly admired his work.

The following month Strindberg's plays continued to take Stockholm by storm. The Swedish Theatre put on *Erik XIV*, again directed by Harald Molander, and it achieved thirty-seven performances. His writing room sprouted Shakespeare's *Complete Works* as well as a portrait and a bust of the Bard. Aged fifty, with no home of his own and only other people's furniture to sit on (the landlady's desk bore offensive stains of her late husband's 'awful cyanide blue ink'), he was able at last to assuage, if not to shed the enormous burden of guilt at having been unable to support Siri and their children over the years. His Christmas letter to the children reads:

Today I am sending you 500 marks . . . and this means that since last December you have received 8,375 marks. I have also repaid large debts this autumn. You should know that everything I owed my brother Oscar Sg., 2,300 has been repaid, also my debt to Eva Carlsson [their former maid] . . . so it has been a good year though there is no reason to suppose that next year will be as good for writing cannot be driven like factories or workshops.[21]

Strindberg did not make much of the evening of 31 December 1899 when the old century gave way to the new but Harriet Bosse remembered how she was driven to a symbolic gesture. She was spending the evening in Stockholm with her brother

who was then a cadet in the Norwegian army. I remember that I spoke a good deal about Strindberg with him. I told him I had never met Strindberg – and then I suddenly had the impulse to wish him, unseen, a happy New Year. We wound our way to Banérgatan, where Strindberg lived at the time. His apartment was situated on the ground floor. It was dark and silent there. No doubt he had already gone to bed. With our noses pressed against the window pane, we stood there – my brother and I – and then I waved a happy New Year to him through the closed window.'[22]

16   HARRIET BOSSE

During the spring of 1900 Strindberg was Stockholm's darling. His plays swept the theatres. With the history plays and *Crimes and Crimes* such a success, the Royal Dramatic Theatre known as Dramaten decided that it would premiere the difficult Symbolist play *To Damascus* later in the year. The male lead of the Stranger was to be played by August Palme, a good friend of Strindberg's and an excellent actor. There was no obvious candidate to play the Lady who is a complex mixture of Siri, Frida and Redemption. Palme suggested Strindberg take a look at Dramaten's production of *A Midsummer Night's Dream* where three leading actresses were showing off their talents. Strindberg hated to see other people's plays, even Shakespeare's, but he went and was enchanted by Harriet Bosse who was playing Puck. He was particularly taken by her 'sweet legs' and thought her 'a perfectly magical apparition of charm and roguishness, the essence of poetry, and more!' He sent her a message inviting her to call on him.

'Visit from Miss Bosse', reads the entry in his *Occult Diary* for 3 1 May. It is the only underlined entry so far that year.[1]

'When I saw Harriet's beauty,' he wrote in the *Occult Diary*, 'I shuddered.'[2] She entered his life in the manner of a Symbolist heroine, a Séraphita or a Mélisande. She was the thirteenth child of her parents' marriage, a powerful number in the symbolism of numerology. 'You were to me', he said, 'not a human being but an apparition.' She was twenty-two, small and slender with an almond face, dark eyes, well-marked eyebrows and long black hair. 'Her movements', he wrote, 'the wonderful play of her body, that most captivating childlike smile on her little face, with its two rows of milk teeth, the youthful proportions of her slender figure . . . like music for the eye.'[3] She had lost her mother when she was fifteen and had supported herself since she was sixteen. Her chief characteristics were hard work and real talent. She did not trade on her beauty though it was obviously of great importance to all who beheld her. She looked, he thought, like a tiny, exquisite Javanese temple dancer. 'You are from Java', he would often say to her.[4]

When she was sixteen she enrolled at the Conservatoire in Stockholm, where Siri had studied twenty-four years earlier. Here she studied solo singing and piano and lived with a sister who had a glove shop. Another sister, Alma Fahlstrøm, had her own theatre company in Oslo. In need of a Juliet, she had sent for Harriet who became an overnight sensation but soon her brother-in-law's attentions became improper and she found the need to leave.[5] In 1898 she went to Paris where she studied acting for six months at the Conservatoire under Maurice de Féraudy.[6] The old-fashioned, declamatory style of acting still dominated the French stage but Harriet was interested in the new plays and as an actress she was instinctively finding her way towards the quieter, allusive delivery of roles that better conveyed the psychological element of the plays that she read and saw at Lugné-Poë's Théâtre de l'Oeuvre and at Antoine's Théâtre Libre. After she saw *Miss Julie* at the Théâtre Libre, she read everything she could of Strindberg's writing.

> Here I found all the newness and freshness which I had been yearning for – here I felt an irrepressible, untamed, uncompromising force, reminding me of the Norwegian literature . . . but the equal of such unique genius, such originality and brilliance in modern dramaturgy I had never before experienced – and as I sat there among the audience, comprised solely of actors, chills ran down my spine and I trembled with admiration and awe.[7]

On receiving Strindberg's invitation, Harriet approached the house where she had blown her new year's kiss with excitement mixed with trepidation.

'Strindberg himself opened the door with a sunny, radiant smile. He invited me into a room in which a table – heaped with wine, fruit and flowers – was set. No one could radiate charm as Strindberg if he felt like it, and I was completely under his spell.'[8] Conversation touched on 'everything upon heaven and earth' including alchemy. He showed her a piece of metal and she agreed that it was gold though later she commented that if had shown her a dog and said it was a cat, she would have agreed to that too.

When the time came for her to take her leave, he asked for a feather from her hat that he might fit it with a steel nib and use it to write plays for her. He did not see her again that year until December,[9] but by then he had planned or written six magnificent new plays with her feather between his fingers and her self in his mind as the heroine in *Easter*, *The Dance of Death*, *The Crown Bride*, *Swanwhite*, *Queen Kristina* and *A Dream Play*.

The day after Harriet's visit, he travelled to Furusund to spend the summer season with his sister Anna and Hugo von Philp, but last year's Isle of the Blessed had become the Isle of the Damned. Hugo was no longer the cheerful, easy man of summer 1899. He had become seriously ill, querulous and inclined towards emotional stock-taking and accounts. Hugo and Anna had been married twenty-five years; they were approaching their silver wedding anniversary and there were skeletons to take out of cupboards and examine. Anna Philp said that she found joy banal and was never happy unless conflict was crashing around her. Philp and Strindberg quarrelled, probably over literature and certainly over the rights and wrongs of his conduct towards Siri all those years ago. Strindberg stormed back to Stockholm. He did not speak to the von Philps for four years and he drew a merciless picture of their marriage in one of his greatest plays, *The Dance of Death*, taking the von Philps for the model of Edgar and Alice who perform the scorpion dance of just such a marriage whose energy and delight comes from mutual torment.

Back in burning Stockholm, Strindberg found himself in a cauldron of summer heat and smells. The city was deserted by everyone who could afford to leave it, and he was in another circle of Inferno with the von Philps' spite ringing in his ears as he rode in a cab through the streets peopled by left-behinds, 'cripples, drunks and demonic-looking children. A dog which wanted to jump up on the driver's seat; the driver chattered about revolting subjects; finally I found myself driving behind two harlots, one of whom seemed to be in love with the other; one was dressed like a nun, all in black, with a tall, white collar.'[10]

Over the previous couple of years his other sister Elisabeth had been losing a terrible struggle with her sanity. He had been helping financially and sending her bracing letters of advice. Her delusional and paranoid symptoms were ostensibly similar to those he had suffered during his

Inferno crisis: she was being persecuted and people were trying to poison her. He briskly recommended the course of action that had quieted his own psychological problems: spiritual and psychological self-examination and reading. But Elisabeth was not August. She had not his mental resources, his spiritual drive or his underlying belief that he was an *übermensch* braced by the thought that battle with the invisible demons, if it did not kill him, would only make him stronger. In 1900 Elisabeth was certified insane and admitted to a mental hospital. Her incarceration led him to reflect on the purity of vision of the insane and he made this the central point of *Easter* which became one of his best-loved plays and is often put on in Stockholm at Eastertide. The play revolves round a simple-minded girl, Eleonora, a holy innocent who acts according to the uncompromising dictates of virtue. Compromise being a machine for oiling human intercourse, her honesty has a profoundly unsettling effect and the play raises the question whether absolute goodness and social justice can co-exist. It shows how complex his vision was of Harriet that he wrote this part for her. There must have been much pure gold, not only that of his own making, in their first long meeting.

That hot and lonely summer saw the death of Albert Bonnier, the publisher who had made him. In his *Occult Diary* he wrote down a list of those who had died. They included Eliasson, he of the tortoise and the Buddhist monastery. 'Shall I die now?' Strindberg writes.

Rehearsals for *To Damascus* were to begin in December. He prepared himself to see again the Puck-sprite that had put a girdle round his imaginative earth since May. In November, as if in preparation, he re-read his love letters to Siri. In December he began to feel overwhelmed by telepathic communication with Harriet and she invaded his sleep and overtook his dreams. Passages written in Greek in the *Occult Diary* become a secret code in an already secret document.

'First dress rehearsal of *To Damascus*' reads his entry for 15 November.

> The inexplicable scene with Bosse. This is how it happened! After the first act I went up on stage and thanked [Bosse]. Made a remark about the final scene in which the kiss is given through the lowered veil. [He had taken Frida's peculiarly memorable gesture of lowering her veil before bestowing her first kiss on his lips.] As we stood there in the middle of the stage, and I was speaking seriously about that kiss [Har-

riet's] little face became transformed, grew larger, assumed a supernatural beauty, seemed to approach mine, and her eyes were ensnaring
me with black lightning flashes. Then, for no reason, she ran off, and
I stood there crestfallen as after a miracle, with the impression that I
had received a kiss that intoxicated me. Then [she] haunted me for
three days so that I felt her presence in my room. Later I dreamed
about her, like this: I was lying in a bed; B came in her costume of
Puck; she was married to me. She said about me: 'Behold, the man
who created me', gave me her foot to kiss. She had no breasts, absolutely none.

The foot-kissing may easily be traced back to Siri and the kiss though
the lowered veil to Frida but the moment that was so electrifying for
Strindberg held no special significance for Harriet. According to her
written recollections (and in later life she unfailingly recollected Strindberg with gratitude, generosity and affection), that moment on stage was
for her part entirely free of black lightning flashes. Yet he was possessed
to such a great degree that he was overtaken wholly. From the start of
the *Occult Diary* we are let into the secret that sex smells to him of celery.
Since Harriet has come into his life, 'Everything tastes and smells of
celery. When I take off my shirt at night it smells of celery. What can it
be? My chastity? My celibacy?'

In January 1901, his obsession takes a demonic turn.

Occult Diary, 13 January, 'I possessed her when she appeared during
the night. Incubus. The whole thing seemed to me quite ghastly and I
begged God to deliver me from this passion.'

The incubus figured large in *fin-de-siècle* dream and literature, a demon
in the form of a bewitching woman who has intercourse with a human,
often in deliriously nightmarish fashion. To induce these visitations and
make them happen more frequently is often a motive for Satanists such
as Przybyszewski, but Strindberg had renounced Black Magic. Visitations
from an incubus were the last thing he desired.

Occult Diary, 12 February, 'I live with only her in my thought. I fear a
catastrophe.'

Now incense replaced celery as the smell of sex.

Scholars of the *Occult Diary* have argued that he was simply masturbat-
ing but the telepathic couplings occur so frequently, often three times
each night, and over so many consequent nights for weeks and months

on end that it is unlikely that any man of fifty-one would be capable, let alone Strindberg who was not *cum laude* in sexual drive.

'What I am going through now is horrible and marvellous', he wrote, recognising that this violent, sustained and uncontrollable spasm of sexual energy was indivisible from the tremendous outpouring of artistic creativity.

During his marriage to Frida he had written *Antibarbarus*, a scientific treatise, and some articles. She had acted as an artistic chastity belt. During the time that his spirit was shackled to Harriet he wrote thirty-one works, all of them worth reading, and during this first year he wrote for her as every facet of woman. He felt, he said, like Faust regretting his youth before this masterpiece of a woman-child.

The night-time incubus did not melt away with the light of day. While awake he would often remain in the unsteady reality of the creative-erotic dream, as he describes in the *Occult Diary* on 26 February 1901. 'Spent an entire day in intoxication of the idea of *Swanwhite*.'

Written in the midst of his incubus possession, *Swanwhite* is the only play in which the modest, prudish Strindberg lifts the skirts on his erotic fantasies, showing them to be Art Nouveau in terms of décor and stuffed with symbols anticipating Freud (who did not publish on dreams until later that year). The heroine Swanwhite is catapulted from nowhere (fairyland?) into an opulent medieval castle described in stage directions that conjure hot-house Symbolist pieces such as Maeterlinck's *Pelléas et Mélisande*, Oscar Wilde's *Salomé* and *Duke Bluebeard's Castle*, all of which were turned into operas which was the natural medium for such pieces. Sibelius composed incidental music for *Swanwhite* but it has yet to be turned into full-blown opera. The stage directions for the piece continue for two pages and it seems incredible that this is the same playwright capable of paring things down to psychology, a couple of chairs and a few pots and pans.

'An apartment in a medieval stone castle', the stage directions begin and they continue with rich and costly garments, mistletoe, a view to the sea, rows of apples, pears and roses, draperies, pumpkins, a well, a clock, a swallow's nest, two gilded tabourets, incense, candles weeping waxen tears, a rose garden with roses of white and pink . . . A lion skin is spread out on the floor near the foreground. At the left, well to the front, stands a white bed with a rose-coloured canopy supported by two columns at the head of the bed (and by none at the foot). The bed-clothing is pure white . . . On the mantel stands a vase with a white lily in it . . . a peacock is asleep on a perch . . . a huge gilded cage with two white doves at rest . . . As the curtain rises, the Duke enters from the rear. After him comes the stepmother carrying in her hand a wire-lashed whip . . .'

Strindberg himself obviously doubles as the grey-haired Duke, her father, who calls Swanwhite the joy of his old age and then a little later hymns her 'little purple snail of a mouth', and he is obviously the virile young prince as well. There is a lot of business about the hair of the men turning white overnight or being restored miraculously to the colour of youth.

A Dream Play, which he wrote in the same year, could not be more different. Indeed, in terms of form it is often considered too abstract both technologically and intellectually. It made a big jump forward from Symbolism weighed down with all its material trappings to his abiding obsession with the unencumbered, feather-light narrative of the subconscious. *A Dream Play* is a 'life's journey' play on the same loose, epic scale as *Lucky Peter's Journey* and *To Damascus*. He originally wanted to use a magic lantern in order to create a set of dissolving images like a dream in which the action takes place but the technology could not be mastered and so he stipulated that the scenery must be stylised, not naturalistic. He did not wish setting obliterated altogether because it is absolutely vital to keep reminding the audience that they are not in fairyland where anything is possible but inside the human condition of being where the physical, the conscious and the unconscious have no life except through and with each other. Another important aspect, notably taken up by Beckett, is the importance of Kirkegaardian repetition, the idea that we as people cannot deviate from our essential selves, and so it is our fate to go back and do things over and over again.

86

The heroine is Indra's daughter (inspired partly by Harriet's 'Javanese' appearance, partly by his interest in the Buddhist idea of reincarnation). She descends to earth to find out about humankind and to solve the riddle of life. Fully human, she is first married to a lawyer, a good man who defends the poor, and she experiences virtue's hardships: married life without money. She then becomes a concierge, a universal listening ear in a large building that recalls the big apartment buildings Strindberg lived in as a little boy. As the concierge, Indra's daughter gathers up people's stories into her shawl. The Officer waits at the door of the Opera House with a bouquet of roses for his beloved but he waits anew every time, in hope and in vain, just as the tramps wait for Godot or Strindberg waits at the brink of expectation for his next wife, always thinking that this time she will be the one to bestow bliss ever after. *Det är synd om människorna*. 'To be human is a tragedy',[11] is the bleak conclusion of the play.

'In this dream play the author has . . . attempted to imitate the inconsequent yet transparently logical shape of a dream', he wrote in the introduction.

> Everything can happen, everything is possible and probable . . . and just as a dream is often more painful than happy, so an undertone of melancholy and of pity for all mortal beings accompanies this flickering tale.
>
> Until recently the notion that life is a dream seemed to us only a figure of Calderon's. But when Shakespeare in *The Tempest* has Prospero say 'We are such stuff as dreams are made on', and employs Macbeth to comment on life as 'a tale told by an idiot', we ought surely to give the matter some further thought . . .
>
> Whoever accompanies the author for these brief hours along the path of his sleepwalking will possibly discover a certain similarity between the apparent medley of the dream and the motley canvas of our disorderly life . . .

In December 1900 he began a very different play with Harriet in mind, *The Crown Bride*. The heroine is a peasant girl who gives her illegitimate child to the midwife to kill and bury so she may wear a virgin's crown at her wedding. It is a straightforward and affecting little play, its plot not unlike Janacek's later and better known *Katyà Kabanovà* (1921) and equally touching.

Harriet opened as the Lady in *To Damascus* on 19 November 1900. Strindberg followed his custom of not attending the premiere but he sent Harriet a bouquet of red roses with this note:

19 November 1900.

Miss Harriet Bosse,

As I am not coming to the theatre tonight I wish to thank you now for what I saw at the dress rehearsal. It was sublime and beautiful, although I had imagined the character a trifle brighter, with little touches of roguishness and a little more expansion.

A touch of Puck! – that was my first word to you – and will be my last.

A smile in the midst of misery suggests the existence of a hope, and the situation does not appear to be hopeless, does it?

And now: Good fortune on the path of thorns and stones – for such is the road! I am merely placing a few flowers on it!

August Strindberg

When the run had finished he sent her another note:

5 December, 1900

Miss Harriet Bosse,

In view of our Damascus journey coming to a close today, I ordered some roses – with thorns, of course – as I believe no others are to be found! And I am sending them to you with this grateful thought: You will be our new century's actress! You have let us hear a new voice – wherever it came from! . . . And give me the hope that I may hear you again – this spring – in *Easter*, as I believe you have promised me!

August Strindberg

During January and February 1901, while her incubus gave him no rest at night, he kept up the courteous, avuncular tone during the day. He gave her books to read: Kipling, Maeterlinck, Zola, Gorki, Emerson. She struggled with French and German and made a timetable for self-improvement, and she must have looked back wryly on this time in 1914 when she became Scandinavia's first actress to play Shaw's Eliza Doolittle. Strindberg also gave her his new plays to read as they flew from the nib of what they now called 'the eagle pen'. In February he was working on the third part of *To Damascus* and he asked her judgement on whether she thought the Unknown One should enter a monastery or go back into the world and live among people again. She knew that she had received a masked proposal and when she went home she wrote a letter that she kept for three weeks before she decided to give it to him.

'I can well imagine', she wrote, 'the little woman's jubilation if the Unknown One – despite all her misgivings – would only quietly take her hand in his and with her wander on towards – the goal. And forget the monastery!'[12]

A few days later she asked if she might call on him to talk about the part of Eleonora.

I went up to Strindberg determined to ask him to give the role to a more experienced actress. This time too, the table was set and decorated with flowers and fruit. Strindberg was as usual amiable and kind. He begged me not to have any anxiety over Eleanora's role – I was bound to overcome any difficulties. He told me how hard and severe life had been to him – how he longed for a ray of light: a woman who could reconcile him to humanity and her sex. Then he placed his hands on my shoulders, looked at me long and ardently, and asked: 'Would you like to have a little child with me, Miss Bosse?' I made a curtsey and answered as though hypnotised: 'Yes, thank you!' – and we were engaged.[13]

On 6 March they bought and exchanged rings and put an announcement in the newspapers that read:

August Strindberg
And
Harriet Bosse

Announced only in
this manner, without
cards or visits.

He was fifty-two; she was twenty-two and nervous of the burden summed up in the congratulatory letter she received from Hjalmar Branting's wife Anna: 'Being August Strindberg's wife is almost like wearing a queen's crown.'

After the engagement, Strindberg made no diary entries until 18 April. He was busy rehearsing his vision for the future. He studied a furniture catalogue. He decided on a five-roomed apartment in a brand new building at 40 Karlavägen in Östermalm, Stockholm's grandest and most moneyed residential area. He planned a Wittenberg gesture of nailing a note to the door of the Gustaf Adolf Church on Master Olof's Day (19 April) announcing their union before the Almighty and All-seeing and exhorting, 'Wanderer, go thou and do likewise!' but he never went through with the plan. Maybe Harriet dissuaded him.

They were married on 6 May with Strindberg's brother Axel and Harriet's brother-in-law Carl Möller as witnesses. Strindberg gave Karl Otto Bonnier's young son Tor five kroner to throw violets at their carriage.

Of the wedding night he wrote,

On our first night H—t had *prolapsus uteri*. I had heard before that she had uterine problems; I was sorry for her and wanted her and tried to comfort her, but then she became angry. Nevertheless, I possessed her twice that night, though with distaste. Next day she pleaded menstruation. After some days we came together again, but now I thought I detected a preventative in her and became angry. I was badly torn and had to bandage myself; thought of going to a doctor but did not. She blamed me repeatedly that she had had no pleasure. I understood nothing but possessed her twice each day, though without the expected pleasure. Often at the climax her uterus fell and pushed me out. It felt as a hand from within slowly drove me back.[14]

Yet the next day, 7 May, he writes simply the word 'Harmony' and on 8 May, 'She says I am the husband she wanted – in every respect! And I am certain she was destined for me. I call her my first "wife".'

He forbade her to bring any furniture to the apartment which he arranged as carefully as a stage production. Colour symbolism reigned. Her bedroom was the pale green of a fragrant spring meadow. At first it included a chaise-longue covered in red material but that soon went as 'nothing was permitted that was likely to lead one's thoughts to anything earthly and material.'[15] His bedroom was yellow, the colour of bliss, with a yellow circle like a halo on the ceiling over the two beds, one blue and one green. There was no Rose Red Room. To furnish the public rooms of the apartment he had ordered a lot of heavy, dark, Renaissance-revival furniture. She thought it 'ghastly' but realised the importance to him of such bourgeois symbols of security and she quietly went about filling her own meadow-green room with the lighter lines and colours of Art Nouveau. Harriet had been self-sufficient, earning her own living, since she was sixteen; she had entered the partnership as an equal, not a victim, but a loving partner, happy to put up with ugly furniture.

She rather expected a honeymoon. One day, to her great delight he told her that they were going to take a trip to Germany and Switzerland. 'We began to plan, ordered round-trip tickets, packed our trunks, and looked forward to the journey. The very morning we were to depart, and just as we were about to leave with all our baggage, he gave forth a groan: "We are not going. The Powers do not wish us to." '[16]

She was left to cancel the tickets and the hotel reservations. She wept. He arranged the wretched neo-Renaissance sideboard with a Germanic tableau of fruit and flowers and a flagon of Rhenish wine, pressed a Baedeker into her hand, told her how much more agreeable it was to take a trip in the mind than to undergo the discomforts of the journey, and retired to work on the current play.

If this was a Rose Room provocation, Harriet was not going to rise to it. A few days later on 26 June she simply took herself off on a honeymoon by herself. Anxious days passed before he received a letter from Denmark. She had found the Red House in Hornbaek, just north of Elsinore, and provisionally rented it for them. Wouldn't he like to join her there?

The bliss of their month by the sea as well as the despair when Harriet left him after their honeymoon was written into the poem *Chrysaëtos* (the Golden Eagle, a reference to the feather she plucked from her hat and gave him at the start of their relationship), a poem about the crows that used to invade the fields round the red-painted cottage. It is one of his very best poems, gathering the melancholia of Poe's *Raven* and Gauguin's *Nevermore* into the nostalgia foretold by a perfect present.

The serpent who ruined their Eden took the shape of a press photographer who took photographs of Harriet bathing in the sea. Strindberg flew at him and beat him with his stick. The resulting debate in the newspapers must have been one of the first concerning the rights of *paparazzi* to invade the privacy of celebrities.

After this there was no staying in Hornbaek. On 1 June they left for Berlin, a city whose very name was glamour to Harriet who anticipated a plunge into the witches' cauldron that had brewed her husband. But Strindberg had just heard the news that Dagny Przybyszewski had been murdered, shot by a lover in Tiblisi who had then shot himself. The last thing he wanted was for Harriet to put her sweet little feet into Dagny's cloven footprints and when she suggested that they take a look at the Café Bauer, then Berlin's apogee of iniquity, he rounded on her furiously and accused her of being a whore. She thought this unfair.

'I wanted to live. Since I was an artist, I thought it part of my work to get out and see . . . It was our great difference in age that separated us. Strindberg had lived his life, had finished with many things which I had not even begun to experience.'[17] But Harriet did not have the energy to riposte in her normal manner by simply going alone to the Bauer to see for herself. She felt weak and ill and this, for some reason, made him happy. She resented him all the more. Strindberg who had seen all this before, suspected she was pregnant. He said nothing and they made their way home where he settled down to work on writing *Englebrecht* and the scene between the Officer and the Lawyer in *A Dream Play*.

Entries in the *Occult Diary*:

August 9th. Visited a doctor. Pregnancy confirmed.

August 20th. She said the child's name was to be Bosse. Tit for tat! Crash! This evening a meteor fell into the constellation of the Waggoner.

August 21st. Fairly quiet but horrible. Did not see Harriet until dinner time. This evening, at the same time, a meteor again fell in the neighbourhood of Capella; later on a shooting star, *Easter* was being performed.

August 22nd. Dinner time arrived and with it a letter from Harriet in which she announced she had 'gone for ever' . . .

August 23rd. Alone. Dismal. Wept a great deal.

Harriet had moved out.

'Can you not understand why I went?' she asked.

I did so to save at any rate the last remnants of feminine modesty and self-respect, that is why. The language you used to me that memorable day in Berlin has been forever ringing in my ears. The things you imputed have so sullied me that the most loving words you could utter would never wash them away or cover them up![18]

The walls, Strindberg wrote, wept. But almost every day they wrote each other letters brimming with love, misery and yearning while also keeping up a running discussion of the parts he was writing. Her opinion was continuing to be central to his development in writing roles of ever increasing subtlety. She was, as he had proposed right at the start, becoming the actress of the new century.

September came and Harriet had not come back to him. He suffered agonies of jealousy.

Occult Diary, 6 September. For the first time in recent years the thought of suicide has risen in my mind. My motive: I am so keenly aware that this woman is going about with my gift to her of all that is finest in my soul, and inviting gatherings of people to partake of me through her. I feel defiled through her. Unknown men defile me by the glances with which they defile her. Through this woman I am sinking into the mire because, even if we are parted, I am sensible of her from a distance. Schopenhauer explains the meaning of *la jalousie légitime* thus: my thoughts are led through my woman to the sexual acts of an unknown man. In certain respects she makes a pervert of me . . . I have never really been able to understand what the not very elegant act of procreation has to do with love for a beautiful female soul. The organ of love is the same as one of the excretory organs. How characteristic that is! (I discovered four years ago that Hegel said the same thing!)

In October she moved back and they spent a calm and happy period waiting for the baby to be born. He painted a great deal, just as he had painted the cottage at Dornach while waiting for Frida's baby to be born, and he encouraged Harriet to take up sculpture. Strindberg was loud in the idiotic theory that childbirth was the greatest physical pleasure a woman could undergo and when Harriet went into labour her sister who had come to help with the birth, kept opening the door to Harriet's room so that Strindberg could hear her cries and Strindberg kept shutting it and Harriet, 'agonised as I was, could not help laughing through my tears.'[19] Their daughter was born on Annunciation Day, 25 March, 1902. She was named Anne-Marie after Harriet's mother.

114

95

Strindberg was once more besotted by his child. In the afternoons he would walk up and down the apartment in specially silent shoes with little Anne-Marie on his shoulder planning his writing for the following day. By September Harriet was ready to return to her stage career. She had a brilliant winter season at Dramaten but this year only one of the plays she performed in, *Karl XII*, was by Strindberg.

For almost two years he had been the darling of the Stockholm stage but his star had fallen. He was hardly performed there again for five years. The rush of nine new plays that Harriet had inspired sat unperformed on his desk. His publisher Ernst Gernandt who was to have published the *Collected Plays* went bankrupt and suddenly Strindberg's main source of income was what he received from German translations of his texts.

The next two years continued in a welter of loving and fighting, separating and coming together while Strindberg was writing fruitfully on the theme of the Flying Dutchman and the next volume of his auto-biography *Alone*.

116   In August 1903 Harriet formally moved to a furnished apartment in Biblioteksgatan. They still ate family lunch every Sunday when they were both in Stockholm and they continued to love each other in every way. On Strindberg's birthday in January 1904 she turned up with a bouquet of red roses for him and later they made love. The next day they quarrelled. So it continued. In May 1904 Harriet suffered a nervous breakdown and spent three weeks in a sanitorium. Preliminary divorce papers were filed. She travelled to Paris on a professional engagement and he took Anne-Marie to Furusund for the summer.

'When life is hard she [Anne-Marie] smiles and has conversations with me', he wrote to Harriet.

95   Her warm little hand guides me across the stones, the way forward. She seems to have come to terms with life and does not fear the awful people. She makes friends herself, preferably with grown-ups. The pharmacist is her good friend, and she introduced herself to a German the other day. Sigrid [the nanny] cannot explain which language they were speaking to each other.[20]

They divorced in 1904 but they continued to love each other in every way throughout the next three years. According to Strindberg's private writings, Harriet was also attuned to the idea of psychic visitations and she would feel his incubus visiting hers and note the time. And so they continued until 20 January 1907 when, to his great sadness, she remained behind in the Yellow Room for the last time.

17 THE INTIMATE THEATRE

In December 1900 the journalist Gustaf Uddgren, long an admirer, received a letter.

> Strindberg wrote me to the effect that I must see him on an important business matter . . . It was the question of starting a Strindberg Theatre. It hurt him terribly to write drama after drama and not see a single one on the stage. This underrating of his capacity as a dramatist must not go on *ad infinitum*. In order to put a stop to it, he wanted me to help him start a Strindberg Theatre.[1]

Uddgren came to call on him in the Red House at 40 Karlavägen.

> The door on the left led into his studio. This was a comparatively small room, oblong in shape, and with a single window facing north. The whole wall on the left was covered with book-shelves reaching from floor to ceiling. On the right there stood a couple of manuscript cupboards and on the highest one of these, an eagle spread his wings. Diagonally by the window there was the writing table full of notebooks, manuscripts etc., and a few trinkets, all arranged in the minute order which Strindberg wanted about himself when he worked. . . . double doors led to the dining room also quite plain, with a dining table in the centre . . . As a rule there was a wealth of flowers, sent by unknown admirers or bought by himself on his early morning walks . . . His bedroom, finally was situated at the rear of the house. It was so plain . . . a narrow iron bedstead, a large photograph of his youngest daughter Anne-Marie, a small table with an old Bible, a couple of old Catholic prayer books – that was all . . . During

the last few years I met Strindberg, his religious life impressed me as an attractive, gentle pose which he desired to assume in order to have the external peace of which he was in need. His battles with himself had been so consuming that when he rose to his feet again he was not able to follow up the syntheses of which he had already found the indications but rather felt the need of embracing almost any doctrine to get out of the chaos of religious brooding . . . his sharpest criticism against Christianity was the dumping of the moral responsibility upon the Saviour . . . a sceptic to the end . . . a puzzler over problems through and through, a believer with whom every church would be glad to have nothing to do, and yet, deeply religious . . . every night he read his old Roman Catholic prayer books, not to acquire a Roman Catholic edification but to become imbued with their peace. The fires that burned within him were so strong that he needed quieting remedies in order to rest at night.[2]

Uddgren asked him what plays they were to put on at the proposed new theatre.

He answered that there was a whole series of short, mystic plays which he had written. It was to be a theatre in the Maeterlinck style, not in the style of the past. We needed only a barn or the like at Djurgarden [the Deer Garden, a park in central Stockholm]. No money need be spent on decorations, we could play . . . in a room with bare walls. The contents of the plays would thus come to the fore much better.

Without in the least suspecting that I might hurt his feelings, I happened, during the course of our conversation to ask him whether I might not read the plays we were to produce.

'No you will not!' he replied in an irritated tone of voice.

'But if I am to stage them, I certainly will have to read them, in order to ascertain that they are not beyond my powers.'

'I never permit anybody to read what I write.'

After this categorical imperative of the author, all the plans proposed came to a sudden stop for the time being.[3]

The dream of a theatre of his own was not to be realised and he became despondent and introspective. 'A feeling has come over me that I have completed my task, and have no more to say. My life often seems as if it has been staged for me, so that I might both suffer and portray it.'[4]

During 1906 he published a book of short stories, *Ny svensk öden* (*New Swedish Destinies*), and a novel, *Taklagsöl* (*The Roofing Feast*), the stream of consciousness of a museum curator who wakes from his slumbers following an accident. Through his morphine-drugged brain stream images from his life, a river without beginning or end until, on the third day, dying,

> propped up on the pillows with his hair in wet drifts across his forehead, his own personality was dissolved, and his inborn character was revealed to be a mask behind which he performed his role, which arose through adaptation to the circumstances of his life. The whole fabric of his upbringing – textbooks, people, and newspapers – frayed into threads, and that little part he had embroidered himself unravelled and disappeared.

The narration of the lonely man asks the questions of the nature of being and appearance that once again had come to the fore in Strindberg's own life. He began to devote much time, again, to experimental photography. He worked with the photographer Herman Anderson[5] on devising new cameras and he was particularly pleased with one that took life-size photographs. He blew up the photograph of Harriet in the role of Puck to life size and kept it behind a curtain. Friends would occasionally describe him disappearing behind the curtain and emerging agitated, 'with his hand pressed tightly against his eyes as though he wished to shut out everything except the picture that had impressed itself on his retina. With difficulty he would control himself and, to calm himself, would dip his hands in a saucer of iced water which always stood to the right of the stove.'[6]

Making music continued to play an important part in his life. Since coming back to Stockholm he had begun musical evenings at home for a group of friends who called themselves *Beethovengubbarna* (the Beethoven Boys). They included his brother Axel who played the cello in the Royal Opera House, the painter Richard Bergh whose friendship dated back to Grez-sur-Loing, Tor Aulin who was the first violinist at the Royal Opera and would become a distinguished conductor and composer, the sculptor Carl Eldh[7] whose dashing and dynamic busts of Strindberg adorned many theatre foyers, and the actor August Palme[8] who both created and consolidated many parts in Strindberg's plays until Palme's death in 1924. The musical evenings would begin on a formal note before ending, often riotously, with food and drink. Strindberg would become neurotically upset if people arrived a minute before or a minute after the allotted hour of seven o'clock. The Beethoven Boys would gather on the stairs with their instruments and there would be a great studying of pocket-watches and listening for the church bells before ringing the doorbell on the dot. The days of the un-tuned guitar were a thing of the past and they played music as written, mostly by Beethoven but Schumann, Schubert, Gounod and Grieg as well. Strindberg's thoughts were turning to opera and it only required the timid but capable Aulin to suggest a collaboration for Strindberg's enthusiasm to spill into long letters setting down his thoughts on where opera should go.

> My response to your suggestion is *The Dream Play*! there you have text which has been tried and tested! But it must be cut as the composer pleases. Brief! A Musical Chamber Play in which all philosophising is omitted. Not a 'sung novel' as in that French thing playing at the Swedish theatre [probably *Manon*] . . . You have an advantage as a composer in not being a pianist because so many figures from piano arrangements remain in pianists' fingers, the conventional forms of harmony and *études*. You know enough of what has been done in the past to avoid academic jingle-jangle, and must sing for the present, for today. That doesn't mean you need give us the noise of tramcars or the ding-a-ling of a telephone as Strauss does, for tone-painting is imitative art, parody theatre, ventriloquism . . . It's crazy! . . .
>
> When an art form has developed over a long period and become complex (Wagner) and turned into a form of higher mathematics, as music has done, there is usually a return to simplicity. I was in Paris when Gluck's *Orfeo* was performed! Mankind caught its breath! Simple but not *too* simple, not clumsy, artistic but not artificial. Seeking new combinations of tones simply to avoid the old ones is affected, not effective! . . . Shall we write a Scandinavian *Midsummer Night's Dream*? I have already mapped it out . . .
>
> *Summa Summarum*: Reflect and sleep on it! Let us then get together in order to try and do something new! light, beautiful! And liberate music a little from its old bonds, just a little![9]

The project never came to anything. His collaborator lacked the energy and the confidence to proceed without Strindberg's full, attentive support which Strindberg did not have the time to give him just now for there was a sudden blooming of interest in his writing. Novels, stories and poems were reprinted in both cheap and lavish editions; his old publisher Bonnier took over the project of publishing the collected works following the bankruptcy of Gernandts. Basking in this moment of approval and prosperity Strindberg sent generous sums to his children and decided to look back on his career and write a novel about the publishing world. The result was *Black Banners*. Had he chosen to disrupt his life by lobbing a bomb, it could hardly have caused a greater explosion.

The book begins with one of his brilliant set-pieces, a meal at the home of Professor Stenkåhl whose glassy mahogany table-top is the sea on which every literary boat in Stockholm is launched. Gathered round the gleaming surface, authors, artists, publishers, journalists and agents spew flattery and mutual loathing. There is only one thing worse than to be here, and that is not to be here. This is the place where careers are floated or sunk; where fees and reputations rise or fall. Ideas are stolen, percentages negotiated, deals done, ideals undone. Each is stealthily intent on pushing the others out of the lifeboat as their pink hands like crawling crabs push bread along the tablecloth's white beach. Strindberg was one of the early subscribers to Stockholm's telephone system, and one of the most enjoyable aspects of the book is the pleasure he is obviously deriving from exploring the new possibilities that the telephone brought to power-play, as well as the new form of language it spawned. He loves the difference between face-to-face speech and telephone talk. Zachris,[10] the main villain, is a master of playing telephone calls against real life: he breaks off a call when he has the caller at a disadvantage by saying someone has just entered the room; he evades an awkward face-to-face discussion by saying he must go and consult on the telephone about a certain point. When the unspeakable Zachris's wife leaves him there is no need of a more elaborate scene than, 'He phoned and said: – This is Zachris. Would you ask Jenny if she wants her fur coat? If so I will send it.' The speedy telephonic speech patterns made this Grub Street satire vastly modern and easy to read. In fact, so taken was Strindberg with the possibilities opened up by the telephone that he wrote a story, 'Half a Sheet of Foolscap',[11] based on nothing more than a list of telephone numbers. The story takes place within the course of a few minutes during the day. A young man is in the process of moving. His apartment is empty. He makes an inspection to be certain he has left nothing behind. He notices half a sheet of paper tacked to the wall by the telephone. The top number is that of Alice, his fiancée. The florist's number follows. The clergyman, the furniture dealer, the box office at the Royal Opera, the midwife, the pharmacist and then a number which he is incapable of reading 'for his eyes began to dim as might be experienced by a person drowning at sea who is trying to see through salt water. But there it was: Undertaker. That speaks for itself. One big and one small. (coffin understood.) And in brackets was written (ashes).'

At first it was difficult to find a publisher for the publishing satire *Black Banners* which languished in a drawer for three years before being accepted by Karl Börjesson,[12] a thirty-year-old radical who shared Strindberg's fury at the mediocrity engendered by back-slapping puff-trade publishing. On 29 May 1907 Björck & Börjesson brought the book out to a howl of anguish from the literary community. Just like *Getting Married* twenty-three years earlier, it became a hot property on the black market. Everyone rejoiced in unlocking the *roman à clef* and it was rumoured that copies could be purchased with the real names inked in. Unfortunately, the novel's main character, the writer Zachris, was taken as a caricature of Gustaf af Geijerstam whose friendship and support had sustained Strindberg over decades. In fact it was as much a self-portrait and an articulation of the writer's own self-disgust. As Strindberg earlier put it when misgivings caused him to give up writing for science: the occupation of flaying your friends and selling their skins in the public marketplace is not an attractive one. Geijerstam was devastated, he died two years later and it was widely believed that the book hastened his death. But apology was never in Strindberg's vocabulary. His old friend Carl Larsson admonished him. A quarrel rumbled on between them, aggravated by Larsson's growing friendship with Harriet Bosse's sister which Strindberg saw as taking sides against him. Larsson was one of his oldest friends, he had stood godfather to Strindberg and Siri's daughter Greta amid much crayfish-eating on Kymmendö in 1881. He had been waiting on the station when Strindberg and Siri began their long exile in France. He had been steady in his friendship but Strindberg could not allow his criticism to rest and Larsson became a target in Strindberg's next book. Larsson was a Utopian, he was also a depressive. His success was built on the illustrations for *At Home* and *My People*, which drew a flawless picture of him and his family leading a perfect life in an enviably furnished and decorated home. The sustained presentation of himself as a sunny paterfamilias effortlessly presiding over an idyll was seen by Strindberg as a sustained untruth. Strindberg denounced Larsson as a 'synthetic person' who in every respect was the opposite of what he pretended to be: an ambitious man who pretended to be modest, a Judas who pretended to be a friend, a depressive who pretended to be happy and a snob who pretended to be humble. There was a degree of truth in this denunciation, but no kindness.

'I sometimes imagine Larsson in Swedenborg's undressing room on the other side of death', his critique of Larsson concluded.

> First coming up to him and peeling off garment after garment; then removing his skin, his muscles, bones, then all the things that are false – and finally there is nothing left of the man at all! Perhaps people in this life, searching for happiness are all like that? Perhaps he has regarded me as being equally false and lacking in character? Just think if I myself were like I have depicted him? Let's be honest, there are many who generally do portray me like that in fact, and hence it is possible that I really am.[13]

Larsson was not the character to allow Strindberg's criticism to shorten his life by a day. Instead he grabbed an ornamental dagger given him by the sculptor Anders Zorn[14] and set off to despatch 'the revolting skunk' Strindberg. The murder did not take place but the long friendship was severed though later, in 1911, Larsson had the grace to write:

> I cannot see him [Strindberg] in the light of Great Vilifier, I just can't. For me he is still the enormously unhappy man, the most unhappy man I have ever known, and moreover something different and more important: the great poet who attacks the material round about him like the Cyclone attacks people and whisks them away in whichever direction the wind is blowing, never pausing to ask what will become of the objects that are sucked into the confusion. In other words I do not believe he made any conscious attempts to wreak vengeance on others. What he wrote should be read as poetry, and seen in the context of his own dark soul.[15]

In June 1906 Strindberg embarked on his largest prose work, *A Blue Book issued to whom It May Concern, and Being a Commentary on 'Black Banners'*.[16] It eventually ran to some 1200 pages, took six years to write, was published in four volumes and he came to refer to it as the latest incarnation of the Green Sack.[17] While it started as an examination of the ethics of what he called this new age of decadence, it developed into a wide-ranging examination of everything that interested him: gold-making, painting, love, food, plants, religion, favourite quotations, even fictitious conversations between himself and Swedenborg whose body, during the writing of the book, was repatriated from England to Uppsala Cathedral.

88, 91   While *Black Banners* had turned the Swedish establishment against him once more, the difficult *Blue Book* now disappointed the expectations of his reading public who had been hoping that he would follow it with another swingeing satire. Initial sales were high but they soon fell off. The dust on his desk grew thicker on the unperformed plays. The home market had once more turned indifferent but interest in his works continued to grow in Europe, particularly in Germany and Russia where Gorky admired his work and Chekhov lamented that censorship precluded the Moscow Arts Theatre staging *Miss Julie*. In 1905 his plays had been staged all over Russia, from St Petersburg, Moscow and Archangel to the Caucasus. In the same year, *The Dance of Death* toured forty German towns while in Berlin the young director Max Reinhardt[18] was progressing the avant-garde in his Kleines Theater which had opened in 1902 and projected the stage into the arena of the small auditorium.

'By its very name', Strindberg wrote, 'the Kleines Theater indicates its real programme: the concept of chamber music transferred to drama. The intimate action, the highly sophisticated motif, the sophisticated treatment . . . No Brussels carpets, lacquered shoes, lacquered motifs . . . no dialogue reminiscent of the question and answers of the catechism.'[19] Strindberg kept up with these developments through the theatre journals and he was delighted that his own chamber plays provided the backbone of Reinhardt's repertoire. He took a great interest in every detail of staging and performance and Reinhardt made the performance of Strindberg's plays, both the intimate battle-of-the-sexes pieces and the allegorical dream plays, an enormously important part of his life's work.

In 1906 Strindberg was approached by a young actor-manager who was brave enough to wish to premiere *Miss Julie* in Sweden. The approach came with an impeccable pedigree for it was signed by August Falck whose father, also August Falck, had premiered *The Father* at the New Theatre in Stockholm.

Strindberg duly granted permission and Falck's *Miss Julie* began by touring the Swedish provinces. Houses were full. Those who had come to be shocked and titillated by an outlandish tale of decadence and lust found themselves, some nineteen years after the play had been written, soberly attending to a play that was relevant to their own time and utterly believable. During the performance at the little coastal town of Varberg, the public prosecutor became so carried away by the realism of the whole thing as he sat in the audience that he leapt onto the stage to demand of the actress playing Julie 'Are you mad, woman, behaving like that?' But such interruptions were the exception; more normally the audience would sit as chastened children in church, recognising their own sins and the sins of their fathers and the evening would often end with 'Three cheers for August Strindberg, Sweden's greatest playwright!'

Falck had not met Strindberg before mounting the tour but he had grown up in the theatre and he had access to his father's long experience of directing Strindberg's plays. He also had a line of communication to the playwright through August Palme whom he had engaged to play the servant Jean. Palme had already acted in many of Strindberg's plays and it was he who had persuaded Strindberg to go and see *A Midsummer Night's Dream* in which Harriet was playing Puck. The part of Miss Julie was taken by Manda Björling[20] whose budding relationship with Falck (which ended in marriage) brought the strong sexual energy that is vital to the part and to the play. When the play was at last brought to Stockholm for the first time on 13 December at the Folk Theatre, it was a triumph for the young director and a vindication for the playwright. Only the ultra-conservative *Nya Dagligt Allehanda* found the play repellent and obscene. Otherwise it was widely praised for its insight, humanity, warmth and understanding. 'Deeply humane', commented Erik Nyblom in *Dagens Nyheter*, going on to observe how far boundaries had moved in the interval between the play's writing and its performance in Sweden. 'The audience was gripped and applauded loudly', reported *Svenska Dagbladet*. Although agreeing that the play was upsetting, the general critical tone was of shamed agreement that things were said and done which everybody knew to be true but which had never been said or seen on a stage before.

Strindberg, as usual, did not attend. 'I cannot stand to see the ghosts of my brain made real',[21] he apologised to Falck, and invited him to come and call on him.

As Falck stood on the threshold preparing to press the door bell, Strindberg flung open the door.

'Your name is August! Your name is Falck! Welcome!' he cried to an astonished Falck who was not yet familiar with the importance Strindberg attached to lucky omens.[22] Falck shared his Christian name August; his surname was the same as the one that Strindberg had given his *alter ego* in *The Red Room*.

Each man brought to the meeting the private intention of proposing the founding of an experimental theatre in Stockholm. No sooner was their common purpose discovered than plans began. Thereafter the two men were in daily contact by telephone, letter and long, long dinners. The first questions to be addressed concerned money and venue. Strindberg was not going to follow Antoine's example of putting on shows in various venues as they came free. He wished to rent his own theatre for a decent few years. Falck was with him on this. As to money, Strindberg was convinced that the project had the blessings of the Powers. Money was raining upon him. His income this year had increased eightfold compared to the previous year. In 1906 he had earned 4,000 kr and as the rent on his Karlavägen apartment alone cost him 800 kr he had been thinking of moving somewhere cheaper. However, in 1907 he received an income of 32,000 kr, mostly from European fees and royalties. By the end of the year, he had spent 19,000 on the Intimate Theatre.

The search for a building ended on 27 June 1907, when they signed a contract on a warehouse at Norra Bantorget (Northern Railway Station). This was a conveniently central location in the north of Stockholm. It would not be difficult for audiences to get to but to do so they would have to enter a political area they might not approve of. This was the neighbourhood where the budding Swedish socialists had followed the Russian example of building a 'People's House', a community centre where the workers could hold meetings without interference from landlords and others opposed to the labour movement. It was at this station that Russian revolutionaries arrived by train; in 1906, the year before Strindberg signed the contract, the Bolsheviks and the Mensheviks had been invited to hold their Fourth Congress here in the People's House and photographs of 1917 show the Menshevik leaders in thin beards and thick overcoats en route for Lenin's famous arrival at Finland Station.

The warehouse site was elbow-shaped, but Strindberg managed an ingenious plan that pushed a cloakroom, ladies lounge, smoking room (gold leather wallpaper, buffalo-hide chairs), toilets, a lobby (overseen by his bust, garlanded on special nights) into the forearm of the elbow

82

shape. The auditorium was angled into the thick joint of the elbow. The stage was tiny, only six meters long and four meters deep. The audience of 160 was half the size of Reinhardt's Kammerspiel theatre but each member of the audience had an upholstered seat and uninterrupted view. Twenty dressing rooms, one for each member of the cast, occupied the upper joint of the arm, as it were. A dressing room for each actor was a tremendous innovation, making the actors feel valued. What immediately strikes the eye is the lack of room for storing any props or furniture but this was a theatre that was going to show soul-play, not interior decoration. When the theatre was up and running, one of Strindberg's joys was to select the one signature prop – a pot-plant, maybe, or a chair or an urn – to shorthand the setting. He recorded his delight when finally the company had sufficiently matured to mount performances with his ideal: two chairs and one table. That would not happen for a few years. Meanwhile there were interminable battles to be fought over City rules concerning sanitation, ventilation and fire regulations. It tried his patience and cost a lot of money. He visited the site every day and when, in November, Intima Teatern (the Intimate Theatre, often known simply as 'Intiman') was ready to open, he had lavished as much care and control over the decorative scheme of the theatre as he always expended over his own domestic surroundings. The auditorium was a subdued harmony of the earth colours yellow, brown and green. The ceiling was draped in yellow silk to diffuse the lighting. The carpet was his favourite dark green and the seats were covered in brownish green. He commissioned the artist Carl Kylberg to make copies of Arnold Böcklin's[23] paintings *The Island of the Dead* and *The Island of the Living* either side of the proscenium arch. Evocative and dreamlike, Böcklin's composition represented yearning towards the sublime for a whole generation – and beyond: Freud had a reproduction in his waiting room, Lenin pinned it up over his bed in Zurich and Hitler, after he came to power, owned one of the five originals. The paintings' subdued greens, beiges and dark greys bled seamlessly into what Strindberg called the colour symphony of the auditorium, heightening the emotional atmosphere before the play had even begun.

While building continued, he paid the company's salaries throughout the summer thanks to the generosity of the Powers who obviously agreed with him that his actors should not go on tour with other people's plays but start working as a company well before the opening date. He attended rehearsals and posterity is fortunate that he found public speaking so

81, 83, 84

118

agonisingly difficult that he simply could not force himself to speak in front of the whole cast. He remained unnervingly silent during rehearsals but sent practically everybody notes on matters great and small, and so we have his *Memorandums to the Members of the Intimate Theatre from the Director*, later published as *Open Letters to the Intimate Theatre*.[24]

The book starts by looking back to his beginnings as a playwright and one realises how far theatre had come in the previous thirty years when he describes that as a young playwright he had to write to a strict formula in order for his plays to stand any chance of being read, let alone performed.

> The play should preferably have five acts; each act approximately twenty-four sheets long or, in all, $5 \times 24 = 120$ folio pages. The division into scenes was not appreciated and was considered a weakness. Every act should have a beginning, a middle and an end. The end of the act should be the place for applause which was aroused by an oratorical figure [a set-piece delivered by a star actor] and, if the play was in blank verse, the last two lines should rhyme. . . . About 1870, when I had written *Blotsven* in five indifferent acts in verse and tried to read it aloud to my fellow poets at Uppsala, I found the whole play unjustifiably extended and uninspired. I burned it (and *Erik XIV*, too). Out of the ashes rose the one-act *The Outlaw*, which, along with its great weaknesses, had the merits of sticking to the subject, being brief but complete. I was undoubtedly influenced by Bjørnson's splendid one-acter *Between the Blows* [*Mellem slagene*, 1857] which I found was my model. The times had, as you see, picked up speed; people demanded quick results and had become impatient . . .
>
> I tried a compromise. In my first version of *Master Olof* I substituted prose for verse, and instead of opera-like blank verse dramas with solos and ensemble numbers, I composed polyphonically, a symphony in which all the voices were interwoven (major and minor characters treated equally). The attempt succeeded but the play has proved too long . . .
>
> If anyone asks what an intimate theatre wants to achieve and what is meant by chamber plays, I can answer like this . . . freedom of treatment which is limited only by the unity of the concept.

Strindberg goes on to refer the reader to his famous preface to *Miss Julie* in which he had already set out his 'naturalist' manifesto against declamatory acting, character make-up, dazzling footlighting, set-pieces for applause and the curtain because 'as soon as a curtain comes down the audience gives itself a shake and rejects what it has seen.'

For the same reason, the preface continues,

> Director Falck broke with the classic tradition of serving liquor in the theatre. That was courageous, for the sale of liquor usually pays at least half the rent . . . but the drawbacks to allowing the audience strong drink in the middle of the drama are well known. The mood is destroyed by talk; the transported spirit loses its flexibility and becomes conscious of what should remain unconscious . . .

He goes on to talk about acting. First, speech:

> Speak effectively! The first requirement is to speak slowly. The beginner has not the slightest notion how exceedingly slowly he can and ought to speak on stage. As a young actor-to-be I imitated our foremost conversational actor, repeating his lines softly. I was amazed, for no one could have made me believe anyone could speak *that* slowly on stage without making what he had to say sound like a sermon.

He abhors the iniquity of trademark mannerisms and stresses the importance of the passive actor whose listening on stage and silent acting deepens the illusion. The next section on directing contradicts any notion that the new theatre is so devoted to the abstract that the smallest physical detail is below notice. Take men's trousers: 'The men have to be careful that their trousers fall attractively and cover their shoes and that they do not creep up revealing garter or sock; moreover, the knee should not have the profile of a pointed angle; the calf or leg should not form a triangle with the foot.'

Next:

> Mastering the role! There are several ways of doing this but the surest is without doubt first a careful reading of the script, which used to be done at the initial group reading of the play, which I consider necessary. I have seen with horror how great artists pick out their roles like grains of sand and leave the rest to its fate as if it did not concern them . . . Since they do not know what other people are saying about them when they are not on stage, they do not know who they are. . . . I have seen a great artist who lost his biggest scene because he did not

understand what it was about. The audience who had heard the preceding scene understood the situation, caught the allusion but could not understand what he was about because he had not understood the play . . .

The following scene, I am told, was acted at a rehearsal:
STAR: Why doesn't he come? Shall I wait for him any longer?
A VOICE: He can't come. He died in the preceding act.
STAR: Died, did he? Well, well!

Again and again Strindberg's advice stresses the importance of company acting, and of the director.

'The director like the orchestra conductor is not a particularly popular person, because he is only there to criticise. He often has to instruct even the mature artist and often gets tit for tat.' Yet the director too must be a receptive instrument; he must direct and not dictate.

> I have seen introspective directors who have drilled and thrashed a play to pieces to impose their own gestures, their own intonation, their own fragile voice, their own mannerisms. We never engage in that sort of thing . . . The director does not have the freedom in selecting plays that actors and authors imagine. Depending on the prevalent taste, the financial or economic situation, or the mood, he is often forced to select a play that people want to see, even if it is not very good . . . Still, following the public's taste can be risky, because taste is forever changing and changes suddenly.

Open Letters to the Intimate Theatre gives no advice to authors, for the good reason that the theatre was to perform only his own plays but even at this late stage in his career, and in a great position of power over his own theatre, he did not regard his words as sacred and he told them that whatever did not work in rehearsal they must feel free to cut or to change.

During the preparations for the opening, Strindberg composed four chamber plays for the theatre, writing at furious speed: *Ovader* (*Storm*), *Pelikanen* (*The Pelican*), *Brända tomten* (*The Burned House*) and *Spöksonaten* (*The Ghost Sonata*).

Storm concerns an old man divorced from a younger wife. He lives in an apartment house. A window shows the comings and goings in the apartment above, which have nothing to do with his story. Much of the action of the play takes place in this connected yet unconnected space. The spoken words take place downstairs. If we allow the upstairs to be the unconscious, the layout on stage resembles the mind. The last speech takes place as the lights are turned off in the upstairs apartment. At the same time, the street-lamps are lit. A different sort of light illuminates his world. The storm has passed.

The Pelican is also easy to trace back to life models. Indeed, he wrote to his brother Axel acknowledging that the portrayal of the mother in the play who, recently widowed, goes all out to seduce her son-in-law, was a further portrayal of their monstrous sister Anna von Philp whose husband Hugo had recently died. This is part two of a portrayal of Anna who had already given him material for the character of Alice in *The Dance of Death*.[25]

The Burned House is about a man who returns from America to visit his childhood home and finds the house has burned down. The story is contained in the ruin. He reads his whole childhood in the ashes, as children read the ashes in the grate and through the simple discovery that the dining table – that great symbol of family unity and pride – was not made of ebony as family humbug had it, but of a cheap wood painted to resemble ebony, the past is undone and the Stranger is free to continue on his journey through the great, wide world unencumbered by the burden of the past.

The fourth and most radical of these chamber plays, *The Ghost Sonata*, is a tale of flirty, evasive complexities which opens with an exchange between a character and a ghost while a cliché is taking place: a student is falling in love with a beautiful girl he sees through the window of a richly appointed house. A sinister character offers an introduction. We glimpse Mephistopheles in the icy handshake. The student enters the house which turns into a surreal, malevolent and macabre world where nothing is as it appears until you realise that time is moving backwards and forwards and you are moving between the conscious and the unconscious, as you are between the upper and lower storey of the houses in *Storm* and, as in *The Burned House*, between the present and the past which is never dead, it is not even past. See the play once, you find yourself disturbed and irritated by the way everything moves just out of reach as you grasp it, like something seen out of the corner of your eye. But if you read it, you see how cleverly it is constructed to reveal the idea that truth is multiple, open, unhierarchical and endless. *The Ghost Sonata* manages to render the concept of truth as frightening as trying to count the stars in the heavens.

While Strindberg was writing these four plays at furious speed, Falck used sometimes to sit outside his study and tiptoe in to pick up the sheets as he threw them to the floor. As usual there was no re-reading, no revision.

The Intimate Theatre opened with *The Pelican*. It was a disappointment. Stockholm's expectations had been raised by their acceptance of *Miss Julie*. They hoped for a play that would extend their newly expanded understanding of modern morals. A portrait of Strindberg's monstrous sister did not answer, however well observed. The theatre was full on the first night and all but empty on the second. After six days, Strindberg wrote to Falck that he thought they would have to close. Falck's reply was to revive *Miss Julie* but both men were well aware that they could not survive on that play alone.

As if to mock his terrible failure, February 1908 saw the grand re-opening of Stockholm's Royal Dramatic Theatre (Dramaten) in a handsome, white neo-Baroque pseudo-palace that seated 949 people and cost 7 million kr. It opened with his early play, *Master Olof*.[26] That year saw the fiftieth birthday celebrations of the man they called the king of Swedish theatre – not Strindberg but Albert Ranft, a theatre manager who controlled seven of the capital's theatres and thousands of its seats.[27]

'O Land! Land! You are sinking!' Strindberg lamented. 'Millions are spent on a palace for – who? – the least worthy who has seven theatres and takes no care of any of them! It's appalling!'[28]

Yet Ranft could not be condemned as a philistine out and out. He was proposing to mount *A Dream Play* at one of his many auditoria, and he had cast Harriet to create the role of Indra's Daughter, the role that Strindberg had written for her in the days of their great love. Strindberg suffered appalling stomach pains. He thought he was suffering the effects of Harriet's psychic betrayal and he fired six housekeepers in the course of a few weeks, each accused of serving him filthy pigswill and trying to poison him. The pain was real. It was not the effect of psychic ill-wishing but the first, ghastly trumpet call of stomach cancer.

With the Intimate Theatre failing and with everything to lose, Falck was inspired to the bold stroke: he approached Prins Eugen, the brother of the reigning monarch King Gustav v. The prince was a fine painter and a man of great culture. He had attended the Intimate Theatre's first night and he put up the money for the coming year.

January of the New Year opened with *The Ghost Sonata*, a prescient play, highly important in terms of the development of Expressionist and Surrealist drama, which would have to wait for the 1920s to come into its own. The critics were divided over whether the play was evidence of the final softening of Strindberg's brain or merely a huge pretentious joke he was playing on them. It was taken off after twelve performances and not played again until four years after Strindberg's death.

In February there was greater success with the twenty-five-year-old *Sir Bengt's Wife* which enjoyed twenty-five performances. Manda Björling played Margit, the title role he had written for Siri. The role of her page boy was taken by a seventeen-year-old girl with a classical profile, masses of wavy brown hair and slightly protuberant eyes.

'Strindberg came up from the auditorium, on his way back to Falck's room', the girl recalled. 'Just inside the door he stopped and looked at me. And then he walked on without saying a word, serious and handsome. Not a word was spoken.'[29]

Her name was Fanny Falkner.[30] Without consulting Falck, Strindberg invited Fanny to his apartment to rehearse the role of Eleonora, the Easter girl in *Easter* opposite the actor Alrik Kjellgren.[31]

Fanny Falkner describes these rehearsals:

> Strindberg himself was terribly moved, tears ran down his cheeks, he was enormously inspiring for both of us. I could hear him sob, it got worse, he burst into tears, his face was completely tear-stained and red. I felt terribly sorry for him. He then turned to Kjellgren and said the following words – which he still remembers – 'What do you think? She is a born artist. Her expressions, her eyes, her hair – her hair!'[32]

After he had coached her for a few weeks he was ready to show her to Falck, who found her voice weak and her movements clumsy. Strindberg lost the battle and on 16 April Anna Flygare opened in the role. The play became one of the Intimate Theatre's successes. It ran for 182 performances and was to be an enduring favourite with the public.

Strindberg arranged for Fanny to have professional coaching and he drew up a list of the basic principles of acting, just as he had for Siri but the slim girl with the pre-Raphaelite hair lost his attention altogether

97

when Harriet sent him a note telling him that she was engaged to be married to Gunnar Wingård, an actor the same age as her. Harriet delivered the note by the hand of their daughter Anne-Marie.

Then began a terribly disturbing period of telepathic communication with Harriet that lasted for three months. He was tormented night and day and his *Occult Diary* records his consuming passion.

Occult Diary, 7 April. Remembered everything beautiful from my first days with Harriet. She is now as though dead. Miss her as one dead.

8 April. In a light-hearted mood all day. Paid Harriet's book bill and had the receipt sent to her.

Letter to Harriet, 9 April. Shall I go away? I think I seem disturbing to you here, and from this apartment invisible wires stretch like inaudible sound waves which yet reach their destination . . . I beg you. Leave me in peace! In sleep I am defenceless like everyone else, not accountable, and afterwards I am ashamed.

Occult Diary, 10 April. I eat little, drink little, and, for whom? I am as though engaged, live 1901 and see Harriet as young, seven years ago, great, glorious, ethereal . . .

Letter to Harriet, 11 April. . . . it is me whom he [Wingård] caresses and therefore I go! Why will you not let me go? What do you want with my old body? Let me go. Take my soul if you will . . . let me go.

Occult Diary, 11 April. During the night Harriet sought me violently twice, and I responded.

12 April . . . Nothing now remains but to ask you, as I did when I proposed: will you have a little child by me, Harriet?

13 April. What is this? She becomes engaged to W and at night she flies to me. We live like newly-weds. We correspond. In the morning I send her flowers . . . Continuous contact with H-t all evening. At 10.30 I had such violent palpitations that I had to put my hand on my heart but when I did so I fancied it was Harriet's heart. It quietened down, then stopped. I thought she was dying but it started to beat again, only more tranquilly. I slept. At 11.30 the feeling of anxiety returned (I believed this time that he was striking her! She told me in her letter that 'she had fought and been struck'). By 12 o'clock she was lying on my arm, calm, friendly! I was woken three times in the night and received her as my wife.

15 April. Harriet came again but without perfume. Towards morning things were different. Ter. [Three telepathic embraces.]

16 April. Maundy Thursday. A dress rehearsal of Easter this morning. Flygare played Harriet's role. Got home at 4.30. . . . Anne-Marie came to see me. She was wearing a bracelet. I asked who had given it to her Uncle W! – Oh God!

17 April. Now the child is his!

On 21 May he buys a revolver and on 24 May Harriet is married to Wingård. Strindberg is inconsolable.

Harriet continued to haunt him through June with her visitations: sometimes in ecstasy with a taste of roses in his mouth and sometimes in torment with a taste of brass and corpses. Pain like two swords came up from his stomach piercing his lungs. Sometimes he thought it was Harriet attacking him through the ether. Sometimes he wrote, 'I am sure I have cancer of the stomach.'

On Midsummer Eve he received a visit from little Fanny Falkner who had developed such a crush on him that she arrived at his door with a bunch of wild flowers but lost her nerve at the last minute and gave them to the housekeeper. His note of thanks invited her to call. She came and played Mendelssohn for him on the piano. He learned that her parents owned a boarding-house in which an apartment had become vacant.

He turned up at her parents' boarding-house at 7.30 one morning to discuss terms, thought about it for a week, and then arrived on the morning of 11 July like the survivor of a shipwreck with nothing but a cloak on his arm and a bag in his hand and announced that he had come to stay.

He left behind his carefully chosen furniture and everything else that could remind him of Harriet. His arrival on foot was followed only by a few cases containing his books, photographs, clothes, Beethoven's death-mask, a coffee-making machine and the now faded laurel wreaths that had been presented to him on notable occasions.

He also closed the *Occult Diary* which he had started in February 1896, shutting the cover in 1908 on two last and utterly exoteric entries:

11 July: Moved to 85 IV Drottninggatan.
Wrote *The Last Knight* 17–27 August.

From now on we are no longer privy to his secret thoughts.

18 THE BLUE TOWER

90, 96 On 11 July 1908 Strindberg moved into three rooms on the fourth floor of the apartment block at 85 Drottninggatan. He could hardly have been closer to the two most important houses of his childhood years and the house in which Siri had lived when he first met her. Every day his morning walk took him through his earliest history, but the home he set out from was a brand new building, high and handsome, with a corner tower, a green-tiled roof and clean, Art Nouveau lines. With an author's love of titles, he named it the Green Tower but a green tower had no mythological significance for him and soon he re-named it the Blue Tower after a famous prison in Copenhagen where many Swedes had found themselves locked up by Danes. There was a grocer's shop downstairs which sold its wares in paper bags ornamented with a blue tower on a white ground and Strindberg sometimes amused himself by cutting the little picture from the bag and pasting it to the head of his letters. Inside the tower, apartments radiated off a handsome stone staircase with pretty Art Nouveau stained-glass windows lighting the stages as you ascended. There was also a lift but he preferred the stairs. His fourth-floor apartment had three small rooms. The tiny bedroom with a narrow iron bedstead could not have been in greater contrast to the sensual colour symphony he had created for himself and Harriet. It was as if he was creating a sentry box against Harriet's incubus, armouring himself against psychic visitations. The writing room was also very small: no more space than to spread the elbows without touching the walls and everything was neat on his desk. There was, of course, a telephone. The living/dining room was the largest room. He arranged it carefully though it was sparse in furniture, much of which was currently at the pawnbrokers to pay for the expenses of the Intimate Theatre but he always filled it with the fresh flowers he loved and he placed candles in front of mirrors to double the effect of space and light. There was the piano and Beethoven's bust and his collection of laurel wreaths and the stuffed eagle who sometimes flew down to the Intimate Theatre when he felt the theatre was in need of special luck. His new home delighted him.

'Come and enjoy yourself in my Green Tower on the hill in Drottning-gatan', he lured his old friends. 'It has a green roof, laurel wreaths and golden horns of plenty, balconies, a shower room – everything – and I have an urge to write, good food, and Beethoven.'[1]

A shower was a novelty which, with his love of cleanliness, he took to immediately. The other novelty, the lift, offered itself as a splendid, new multi-purpose symbol signifying the levels of consciousness, Buddhist reincarnations and stages of spiritual progression on the ascension to Heaven or the descent to Hell: going up, going down. He did not, unfor-tunately, write a whole piece centred on the dramatic possibilities of a lift as he had on the telephone, but it found its way into the next play, *The Black Glove*, which is set in a similar apartment block. He casts himself as the Old Man, an eighty-year-old taxidermist who represents the past with all its old values and its anxieties concerning the new technologies that are superseding it. The Caretaker (*vide* Pinter) is the magician in charge of electricity. He can turn light and enlightenment on and off. He can whizz people up and down to different metaphorical levels via the lift. The play opens with the Old Man and the Caretaker in semi-darkness:

Old Man: Yes, it's me; and I am indeed the preserver of birds, fish and insects, but I cannot preserve myself – if I put arsenic under my skin it wrinkles, and my hair falls out like off a seal-skin trunk, my teeth too are going their way . . .

Caretaker: It's like with all this electricity we've got here, it has to be mended all the time . . .

Old Man: It is unfortunate we should sit here in the dark over Christmas; can't you get it to work?

Caretaker: It seems there's been a short circuit but we'll soon sort that out. – Let's see now. . . . (*He pushes a fuse plug in; the hearth and the coloured window lights up.*)

On the floor above Strindberg's apartment lived his landlady, Fanny Falkner's mother, together with her insuperably selfish alcoholic husband

and their six children.² At seventeen, Fanny was the third child. Strindberg grew very fond of her three younger sisters, the twins Eva and Ada
and the youngest Stella, who was then only four years old. Stella reminded
him of Anne-Marie. She was old enough to manage the stairs down to
his apartment alone and she loved to visit him. For a long time she
believed that he was a magician because once when he asked her what
she wanted for Christmas, she answered a paint box and he, who had just
bought a new one, fetched it and gave it to her.

Life upstairs with their parents was not lighthearted for the girls. The
lodging house that Meta and Frans Falkner ran in the Blue Tower was the
latest in a line of business enterprises that had failed mostly because Frans
drank the money away. As they grew up, the girls had got used to bailiffs
knocking at the door and carting their furniture off. Meta was hardwork-
ing and short-tempered and Frans was tyrannical. There was not much
festivity. When Strindberg had a Beethoven evening or a supper party the
twins Eva and Ada used to creep down and sit outside the door to listen.
Meta arranged the maids to clean his apartment and she cooked his daily
meals which would come down on a tray at set times. They had to arrive
punctually. He wrote her a list of five regulations that would preserve
his peace undisturbed while he was writing:

1. *If* the hall door is bolted, give two short rings, and it will be opened
   at once.
2. Do not disturb me with trivial matters, such as letters or parcels
   that require no answer, nor with magazines, but wait until
   mealtimes.
3. Do not bring down cleaned glasses etc. except at mealtimes.
4. Do not admit strangers (workmen) without permission, so that I
   need not be taken unawares by unknown persons in my rooms.
5. *If* the hall door is bolted, I am not 'angry', I simply do not wish to
   be disturbed!³

Either Meta was a most eccentric cook or his palate was unpredictable,
for sometimes he sent her polite notes thanking her for this or that meal
and sometimes he wrote: 'Are you trying to poison me?' 'Keep your
Danish pigswill' or simply, 'Eskimo food!' Maybe it was his stomach
cancer speaking.

Within a week of moving into the Blue Tower, he received a note from
George Bernard Shaw who was passing through Stockholm on his way

to the Wagner Festival at Bayreuth. Shaw asked if he might call. Strindberg replied with a long letter written in a mixture French, German and English that Shaw took as a refusal. 'I am dying of a mortal disease', Strindberg excused himself, 'I never see anybody. I never go into the streets except at dead of night. I don't know your language. What is the use of a dumb man speaking to a dumb man?'

However, this was merely a ruse, a delaying tactic while Strindberg prepared a surprise for Shaw, a private performance of *Miss Julie*. The lovers August Falck and his leading lady Manda Björling were holidaying in the Skerries when they received an urgent message to return to Stockholm. They ran over their lines on the ferry and when they arrived at the Intimate Theatre they found Strindberg nervous and agitated. He had never actually watched a performance of *Miss Julie* and he asked Manda please to hold back lest the effect be too much for him. He sent a note to Shaw inviting him to come immediately. This was on 15 or 16 July, only four or five days after Strindberg had moved to the Blue Tower; there is some confusion over the date, and this is not the only ground on which accounts differ. In one account, Shaw wrote: 'conversation consisting mainly of embarrassed silences and a pale smile or two by A.S. and floods of eloquence in a fearful lingo, half French, half German by G.B.S., A.S. took out his watch and said, in German: "At two o'clock I am going to be sick." The visitors accepted the delicate intimation and withdrew.'[4]

It makes an excellent story but in a different account Shaw says:

> He [Strindberg] was quite a pleasant-looking person with the most beautiful sapphire blue eyes I have ever seen. He was beyond expression shy. My wife rose to the occasion and talked French to him, and after a time he came to himself, smiled, and we had an extremely pleasant talk. Nothing could have been pleasanter or more charming, and no one could have imagined that he had been the intimate of one of those households that he put on stage.[5]

Shaw does not mention the performance of *Miss Julie* at all, though Falck remembered that Shaw thanked him courteously after the performance.

Another British visitor was Edward Gordon Craig. Strindberg had read Craig's *The Art of the Theatre* shortly after it appeared in 1905. He disagreed with Craig's idea of dethroning the dramatist in favour of the stage manager. What playwright could agree? Mask and mime were further than Strindberg was prepared to go despite the pull of dematerialisation, a word both he and Craig were using frequently at this time.

He seized on Craig's creative ideas on theatre lighting such as coloured spotlights, then only used in vulgar entertainments and variety shows. He was also tremendously drawn to Craig's Wagnerian concept of fusing music, lighting, words, drama, movement and colour in a *gesamtkunstwerk* blurring the borders between straight theatre and light-show, dance and opera which would introduce exactly the elements of a mad, galloping world of esoteric allusion, visual deceit and fantastic surprise that Strindberg had originally hoped to achieve when he thought of setting his ghost plays with the interplay of real actors against magic lanterns. Treated in this way, the post-naturalist plays could become weird laboratories of associative imagery: plays like *To Damascus* '[Where I am] attempting to imitate the disconnected but seemingly logical form of a dream where everything can happen, everything is possible and probable; where time and place do not exist, and where, on the insignificant basis of reality the imagination spins and weaves new patterns into a blend of memories, experiences, free fantasies, absurdities and improvisations.'[6] Craig's phantasmagoria were far more persuasive than any magic lantern. As the lights fell, dancers would move, strange music would be heard and the petals of the play would unfold like a lotus flower held together by the central boss of words while the audience's peripheral senses responded to the audio-visual assault.[7] To try taking over the audience's dream in this way was, as the Sitwells later discovered in 1922 with *Façade*, a good way to hold yourself up to ridicule. But for Strindberg it was irresistible. How could he hold back from such an ambition?

When Craig came to Stockholm in 1906 he was accompanying his mistress, the exotic dancer Isadora Duncan, on her tour of engagements. Craig begged permission to call. Excited, Strindberg filled his flat with flowers and, as the hour approached, peered through the spy-hole. He did not like what he saw. 'Like Oscar Wilde, he was too beautiful for me', Strindberg later commented, adding that Craig dressed not like a person but like a cliché with his long hair and camel coat, the classic outfit of a *teaterbov*, a stage villain. Worse was the shamelessly self-confident Isadora Duncan who bombarded him with flattery, addressed him as 'Master' and presented herself as a great admirer which might or might not have been true. Flattery applied with a trowel was an integral part of her technique.

Isadora invited him to come and see her dance.

He firmly replied, 'I never go anywhere, I hate human beings.'[8]

She countered with an offer to build him a special private box on the stage from which, concealed from sight, he might watch.

This was terrifying. Far too reminiscent of Frida. Convinced that Isadora was a man-eater wishing to seduce him, he wrote to Harriet, who was acting at the Swedish Theatre in Helsinki, asking her to come and save him. Nevertheless, he spent some time sketching out some short dances *à la* Duncan to be inserted into *A Dream Play* and when the Intimate Theatre celebrated its first anniversary with a party on 26 November 1908, 'Isadora dances' were performed by Anna Flygare dressed in purple velvet and Fanny Falkner dressed in green velvet in front of the red velvet curtain. Someone started creating effects with coloured lighting. Strindberg was ecstatic. 'More, more!' he shouted and began calling out the colour changes he wanted.

The party went on till four in the morning and as he left Strindberg paused to bid the company farewell. He raised his hat high above his head. His still-abundant springy, silvery hair, backlit by an electric bulb, haloed his head.

'Long live youth!' he cried, and exited.

* * *

His protégée Fanny Falkner was not a trained actress. Schooldays at the French School in Stockholm had been followed by technical college where she was studying to become an art teacher when she, like many Swedes, travelled to Copenhagen to see Falck's touring production of *Miss Julie* before it finally came to Stockholm. The play had greatly moved her. When Falck's company came to Stockholm, Fanny met Manda Björling who had played Julie; Manda rented an apartment from the Falkners and the two girls became friends. Manda encouraged Fanny to audition for the Intimate Theatre where Falck was looking for people to play small parts. Fanny was accepted and she made her debut in a non-speaking role in *The Ghost Sonata*. This was followed by her role as page boy to Manda's title role in *Sir Bengt's Wife* and her coming to the notice of Strindberg.

While Falck was quite happy for Fanny to take walk-on parts, he persisted in his opposition to giving her any important parts to play. Pay for supernumeraries was laughable, and Strindberg offered her 60 kr a month to act as his part-time assistant. Every day at ten o'clock, when Strindberg had come back from his morning walk and taken his shower, Fanny would appear and sit in front of his desk. She would have to report on the previous evening's performance and audience at the theatre. He expected her to have read the papers and she would give him a digest of the matters that would interest him. He would tell her the programme for the day and she would run little errands here and there. At this point he had no idea that she was falling in love with him. He was, after all, older than her own father. His interest was fatherly but he also felt strongly that she possessed the right elusive quality to play certain ingénue parts. He got his chance to slip her into a starring role when Falck, who was to play the father in a revival of *The Father* in September 1908, relinquished his directing role to Strindberg. Fanny made her debut as Eleonora in *Easter* and even Strindberg had to admit that she was not as good as Anna Flygare in the part but meanwhile he was rehearsing her for *Swanwhite* in the title part he had written for Harriet.

Falck continued to think Fanny Falkner's acting sketchy and her voice weak. He worried lest the theatre be brought down by her anaemic talent. A compromise solution was found by mounting two separate productions with the two leading ladies. One went on tour while the other stayed in Stockholm. With this system of duplicated casting, they managed to put on 150 performances during the 1908–9 season.

Rumour was spreading that Strindberg was in love with the eighteen-year-old Fanny. When she was touring with *Swanwhite* she had mentioned that the weather was very cold and he sent her a fur coat. Tongues wagged.

29 December 1908

Fröken Fanny Falkner,

When you told me how cold and hungry you were on the last tour (3rd Class), I wanted at least to give you a fur coat for the next one. Since you have acted in my plays and there was no Christmas box from the Director, this gift seemed to me both suitable and justified.

But since you tell me that your parents consider it improper, I am sending you instead a gratuity of 120 kr, to be used as seems best.

It is possible my gift was improper.

Therefore, and to avoid anything that might disturb the peace, I must ask you not to visit me again in my room.

Our old agreement, with its weekly remuneration, still stands.

If you have anything to ask or say, then do so by open notes.

As before

Strindberg

On 22 January 1909 Strindberg was sixty. Every newspaper carried a tribute. Seven theatres put on his plays and held tributes.[9] In the Blue Tower the staircase and the lift carried a steady stream of visitors and delivery boys up and down with laurel wreaths, bouquets, telegrams, letters and deputations. Fanny and her sisters arrived at dawn in white dresses, bearing the white narcissi that he loved for the sake of Ovid who too had loved them, long ago. Carl Eldh arrived with a completed bust. Two of the Intimate Theatre's company called to leave a bouquet and the door was opened by Strindberg himself. Over his shoulder they glimpsed the dining room decorated with flowers and pink lights. The table was laid for two. Scenting a romantic tryst, they sought to retreat but Strindberg urged them to stay. It was his daughter Anne-Marie he was expecting to lunch. She was now seven and he had not seen her for the previous two years. When she arrived she flung herself into his arms. Tears poured down his cheeks and the actors left. After that, he left the door ajar with the chain on so that he and Anne-Marie could remain undisturbed while the train of delivery boys pushed presents and bouquets through the gap.

Even on his birthday night he did not attend any of the performances of his own plays. He sent Fanny's small sisters to see *Lucky Peter's Journey* where they sat in the author's box surrounded by laurel wreaths. Strindberg, meanwhile, dined quietly at home with Falck and his old friend Nils Andersson who had come over from Lund. His guests did not stay long, it had been a long and tiring day. As he was preparing for bed he heard the tramp, tramp, tramp under his window of many feet. The Young Socialists had arranged a celebration of his life during the evening in the People's House and it had been full to bursting for his works that had been recited and speeches made in his honour. Enthusiasm soaring for Strindberg, their working-class champion who had pointed out the unfairness of Swedish society in his first novel *The Red Room* and had continued to fight for greater social fairness and universal suffrage in his

95

books and newspaper articles down the years ever since, they marched down the street to wish him a happy birthday and sing the *Internationale* beneath his window. He hastily dressed, and came out onto the balcony to acknowledge their cheers.

The day after his birthday the Intimate Theatre set off on tour with Fanny in the title role of *Swanwhite*. He was still not taking any money out of the Intimate Theatre and his fortunes were not great but then suddenly they soared when a simple little play, *Abu Cassem's Slippers*, was bought for 2,000 kr. The idea for a play about magic slippers came from *One Thousand and One Nights* which he had borrowed for Fanny's little sisters. The play is hardly original or profound but it was a great hit in the provinces. He bought tapestries and furniture and books, forgetting that he owed 775 kr in tax which he then had to borrow to pay off. He wrote a history play, *Bjälbo-Jarlen* (*The Earl of Bjälbo*), and returned to his old interest, the study of language. He burned to read the Old Testament and the Psalms in Hebrew. Realising he needed help, he asked Karl Otto Bonnier if he might find him someone who could teach him 'unpunctuated Hebrew' because 'a year ago I learned a little Hebrew from a Russian Israelite. I imagine the young people read unpunctuated, since their Psalter is unpunctuated.'[10] He amassed a collection of Hebrew books and artefacts that can still be seen in the Strindberg Museum and he began on a new buttonological project to try to prove that Hebrew was the root of all the world's languages, including Latin and Greek.

Fanny now told Strindberg that her father was beating her, stealing her money, taking her clothes and telling her she could no longer expect any support from her family. Strindberg did not wish to get entangled in these family problems. He wrote to her that he would give her money but she must go out into the countryside and find young people to be with; he was no company for a young girl. The Falkners' finances were so bad that there was no question of the three youngest girls getting out of Stockholm over the summer and he felt sorry for them. With their parents' permission, he arranged that they should have a summer holiday staying a few weeks at Lövsta Bruk, a country estate belonging to Baron de Geer, where Strindberg's brother Olle was the head gardener. Now that Strindberg no longer had a garden of his own he used to enjoy plaguing his brother with letters on how to grow the exotic plants that Strindberg himself had so enjoyed failing to grow in Sweden's hostile climate, such as tea and coffee. His letter to the little girls' mother is a model of understanding that is obviously rooted in his own memories of terrible summer holidays when he was sent away to misery and unkindness:

> They will have their own room . . . a big garden with swan lakes and smithies and hammers, a castle, much else to look at and enjoy. Baron de Geer is a youngish man and a kindly soul. My brother is fifty, married, with a daughter of twenty; he is a sound and good person who likes children . . . If the children cannot eat any particular food, we shall warn them, and it can be changed.[11]

Many incidents recorded both in Falck's memoirs and in Fanny's tell of his kindness to little children and the pleasure he took in their company. Falck recalls how if Strindberg saw Fanny's little sisters on the way to school he would join them and buy them sweets. He gave Stella a doll dressed in Sámi costume, telling her, 'Its name is Swanwhite after your sister . . . You don't need to be careful with it. If it breaks, I'll just buy a new head for it.' When he read the children fairy tales, he would explain the puzzling bits and never lose patience. He played shops with them, weighing items, bargaining and handing over the correct money, taking the game solemnly and seriously and never grudging the time. Falck said he had hardly ever seen anyone as kind to children as Strindberg.

Frida had written begging him to take notice of his daughter Kerstin 'who adores you without knowing you.'[12] She wished him to visit Dornach, where the little girl was still being taken care of by her grandmother and her aunt. Frida had been sending him occasional overcharged letters since 1902 and he refused to answer her directly. Since her liaison with Wedekind she had been living a continuation of Der Schwarzen Ferkel in Jung Wien, the circle of literary bohemians of Vienna obsessed with eroticism. Following Wedekind's portrait of her as the suicidally promiscuous heroine in his two Lulu plays Erdgeist (Earth Spirit) and Die Büchse der Pandora (Pandora's Box), Schnitzler drew an equally colourful portrait of her in his play Das Wort (The Word) as Frau Flatterer, an upper-class writer and voluptuary who always carries a tiger skin and a Dionysian thyrsus in her luggage so that she can instantly transform herself into a bacchante should there be an orgy in the offing. She was a mistress of self-publicity and the newspapers of England, France, Germany, America and Austria periodically featured her antics. New Year's Day 1908 carried reports of her behaviour at a reception given by Prince Fugger-Bebenhausen:

Suddenly, greatly agitated, Mrs Strindberg appeared and began to utter a number of threats. When the Prince tried to go into the next room in order to bring a glass of water to the greatly disturbed woman, Mrs Strindberg pulled out a revolver and in the next moment, a shot rang out. In the police investigation it could not be ascertained whether the shot was intended for herself or for the Prince.[13]

Strindberg did not reply directly to Frida's plea that he get in touch with their daughter Kerstin. He was anxious to avoid any contact with her and with Max Friedrich Strindberg, Frida's son by Wedekind. Instead he wrote to Frida's mother in Dornach where she was bringing up the little girl. 'If I now claim my paternal rights,' he wrote to her, 'I shall be suspected of being an inheritance-seeker. This cruel word was once used of me at Mondsee.'[14]

My Child,' he wrote to Kerstin on 5 September 1909,

I have not received a letter from Dornach. I am now so alien to everything that has anything to do with Austria – more than alien. It seems to me like an ancient fairy tale, incredible, and yet it was once true. Is your rich old great-grandmother still alive? She was rich, wasn't she? Your aunt Melanie alive? I know nothing and am not eager to know anything, since everything has become quite alien to me. I am sixty years old and live in a boarding house . . . But I am a writer, and for me life is simply material for plays, mostly tragedies! Adieu! And think of me only as a memory!

Your Father.[15]

The Falkner girls returned to the capital in August, as did Fanny whom he was still paying to run his errands. When rumours reached him that Harriet and Wingård were having marital difficulties, he sent the love-struck Fanny a note instructing her to discover the truth about his ex-wife, with whom he was still in love.

'Use the telephone if necessary! The ? is: Have they separated? i.e. do they live apart?'[16]

His hopes were dashed when Fanny reported back that they were still together. This was in August, the best time for shooting stars. During the summer Strindberg had acquired a new telescope and one evening in September he invited Fanny to come down and look through it. She takes up the tale:

98

I came down at his bidding to look at Saturn. Strindberg stood behind me as I peered into the telescope. It was a cool evening, and he wrapped a shawl around me. He lifted me up a little so I could have a better view. It was the first time he touched me. Then we went inside . . . I said I had a headache.

He said 'Would you like me to hypnotise you?'

I said I had no objection.

Then he came and sat beside me and put his hands on the arm-rest, and I expected he would stroke my forehead or perform some other hypnotic trick. But he did not. Instead he put his hand on mine and said, 'Shall we become engaged, you and I?'

'Yes', I replied, astonished.

We smiled and were happy. After a while I got up and said good night and he kissed me as I left. When the door had closed and I had come to my senses again, I collapsed in despair and tears.[17]

The next day he gave her an engagement ring with a pearl in it and a sapphire ring to thank her for *Swanwhite*.

We stood a long while at his desk and he told me to keep what had happened secret for two weeks. Then he would dress in white tie and tails and ask my parents for my hand. . . . He spoke of how many beautiful things he would write and how lovely it would be for us both to live in the country . . . I liked him awfully and wanted nothing more than to bring him happiness – but I could not get rid of the thought that he was so much older than I. I liked to touch his hair and stroke his cheek, but I could not love him and this was what made it so difficult for I could not be without him. I would gladly live alone in the country with him, I would devote my whole life to him, I would never marry anyone else as long as he was alive – if only I could avoid being married to him . . . He asked me straight, 'Perhaps you would rather I adopted you, so that you can call me uncle?' I replied, perhaps too quickly, 'Oh, yes please!' that made him sad. He had only said it to test me and was expecting me to say no.[18]

After five days she told him she would not marry him.

'My dear child,' he replied, 'I can wait. I am not going to pester you' and he let the matter rest.

He had spent the summer writing *The Great Highway*, his last play. A Wanderer walks the Alps encountering feuding millers, a hermit, a murderer, a Japanese man resolved to burn himself to death to cleanse him of existence and a little girl waiting for her father to return. In the end the Wanderer seeks to justify his life to an unknown woman while coughing blood into his handkerchief. The Devil arrives with a bargain which is no bargain. Finally the Wanderer utters a lamentation that Strindberg had already expressed in his diary and letters:

'I suffered most from not being the man I longed to be.'

Strindberg wanted Fanny to play the Girl in the play, and this caused trouble with Falck who wanted to slim down the Intimate Theatre company to keep expenses down. Fanny was among the actors he wanted to sack. He also wished to put on plays that had been written by other people, specifically Maeterlinck, but Strindberg was strongly opposed to the idea. When Falck began rehearsing *The Great Highway* in February 1910, Fanny discovered herself locked out of the theatre. She ran to Strindberg who saw no other way out than for her to resign which she did, to Falck's considerable relief. Falck put on *The Great Highway* taking the part of the Wanderer for himself and it was not a success. Going against all the acting advice that Strindberg had laid down in his *Open Letters to the Intimate Theatre*, Falck decided to deliver the lines in a slow Maeterlinckian monotone chant which drained the play of any liveliness and his lines of any comprehensible meaning. The critics commented that it was far too big a play for such a small theatre, an epic crammed into a shoebox. After sixteen performances, it came off.

In July Fanny's parents gave up trying to make money from their boarding house and the family moved away from the Blue Tower to live, by ghastly coincidence, in the same apartment block as Harriet and Anne-Marie and Harriet's son by Gunnar Wingård. Harriet and Wingård had separated and Wingård soon committed suicide by shooting himself, in this age of symbolism, through the heart. As Harriet's acting career had reached the heights, his had collapsed. Harriet was rehearsing Electra in von Hofmannsthal's tragedy of that name when Wingård committed suicide.[19] Von Hofmannsthal said that her interpretation of the role was one of the best he had ever seen. Following a stellar career, Harriet married for a third time in 1926. Her husband was fifteen years her junior and this marriage did not last long either. The source of its swift collapse was the cache of Strindberg's letters which her new husband secretly read and suggested she exploit commercially. She smashed a mirror over his head.

Fanny Faulkner's acting career hardly survived her resignation from the Intimate Theatre after which she went back to painting. Strindberg helped further her career as best he could. She was still in love with him and she continued to call on him in the Blue Tower.

'She loved him', wrote her youngest sister Stella, 'because Strindberg's interest in her was the epitome of everything Fanny could not find at home: calm and respect. She looked up to him as to God the Father. She warmed to his presence like a frozen child and humbly served him in any way she could contribute to his comfort.'[20]

Strindberg supported Fanny's efforts as an artist, hanging her paintings in the hall and giving her various commissions including a portrait of him which he paid her for but did not wish to possess and he commissioned her to paint a self-portrait in which she must wear a blue hat with a veil, exactly as Siri, his young lioness, had worn on that day of their first encounter in Drottninggatan.

In September Strindberg's thoughts again turned to marrying Fanny. She was still living at home with her parents who took away her clothes and money, and beat her. She was not very successful as an artist.

Strindberg summoned a friend to take advice on the matter. Fredrik Ström[21] was the coming young man of the publishing world. The two men did not know each other well, and this was the point.

'"What would the public say of a marriage in which the man was over sixty and the woman eighteen or nineteen. You must answer me honestly."'

Ström imagined the question related to some play he was writing.

'I think people would regard such a marriage as unnatural' [I said and] when I had expressed my opinion, Strindberg's face became ashen and he seemed to shrink. For some while he said nothing. I now realised that his question referred not to a play but to some personal matter and that I had unwittingly wounded him. He remained silent; at last he stammered, 'Thank you, I know your feelings. They are also mine. Go now, I need to be alone.'[22]

Another visitor that year was his old friend from Berlin, Carl Ludwig Schleich, now the Professor of Medicine at Berlin University and a vastly distinguished surgeon whose memoirs apparently sold a million copies world-wide.

I climbed the hilly street, and the even steeper four flights of stairs that led to his apartment and rang the bell. I heard his heavy tread in the hall. The letter box was lifted, and looking down I saw his keen, scrutinising eyes. Then I heard a quick, deep-toned exclamation: 'Good God! Schleich!' – And next moment we were hugging each other.

We went upstairs at once to the tower which is known to all Stockholm as Strindberg's watch tower. We entered a very clean, oak-panelled room in which Strindberg did his work. A huge oaken cupboard stood against the wall. He went up to it and opened the double door. 'What's that?' – 'Yes, yes, the green sack!' Innumerable pigeonholes were filled like the shelves of a linen press with manuscripts. 'It's filled out a little, hasn't it, our green sack?' . . . [Later] he accompanied me through the streets of Stockholm, and showed me the places where he had worked. It was astonishing to see how widely he was known and how respectfully he was saluted by almost everyone who met him. He walked through Stockholm like a citizen-king. People would often step off the pavement, sweep off their hats and stand with bowed head, and many would whisper as he passed, 'That's Strindberg!' . . .

He had sought and found the crown of Solitude amidst whose thorns there dwell two stars: Pride and Humility . . . he believed firmly in the immortality of the soul and the higher evolution of the ego after death . . . It must not ever be supposed that Strindberg was ever mentally deranged. He was always lucid, logical and confident and met all objections with the greatest placidity. He was perhaps inclined to give way to ideas of persecution, but these never amounted to an obsession; they were always the expression of a distrust which, as far as my own observation went, was only too well justified. Try to imagine the mental condition of such an all-embracing intellect, and ask yourself what he must have suffered from the almost universal rejection which he encountered, the countless needle-pricks of opposition and obstruction. It needs solid nerves to endure such setbacks without a short circuit![23]

Even now with his semi-mythic status in Stockholm there were further setbacks to be endured. Relations finally broke down between him and Falck in September when Falck staged Maeterlinck's *L'Intruse* at the Intimate Theatre; this was against all the founding principles of the theatre which had been designed to show the work of Strindberg who, after all, had provided the money for it. Strindberg withdrew his financial support and in December 1910 it closed, owing the landlord 9,700 kr. Strindberg had never taken any money out of the theatre. During the three years of its existence, the Intimate Theatre had mounted 124 of Strindberg's plays and given 1,147 performances, besides touring the provinces and abroad. It closed, fittingly, with a final performance of *Miss Julie*.

Once more Strindberg was short of money. Concerned well-wishers organised a Strindberg Exhibition of his paintings, letters, manuscripts, portraits, photographs and even some of his home-made gold at an art dealer's, Hallins konsthandel. He quickly wrote two books, *China and Japan* (his knowledge of these two countries was now very rusty) and *The Roots of World Languages*, as eccentric a book as any he had written. Bonnier published *The Roots of World Languages* and offered to buy his collected works. A spirited exchange took place over money. Eventually, in June a sum of 200,000 kr was agreed to be paid in instalments over four years. 'So that my children may now get a helping hand to start their life', as he wrote to Bonnier. 'I regard it as the repayment of a debt to them.'

Siri's children happened to be in Stockholm where Greta, who was an actress, had an engagement. Karin and Hans were visiting her and they were all invited to the Blue Tower.

The dining table was covered with banknotes, which he had arranged in four piles which gradually became mixed by the air currents caused by Strindberg pacing about the room making certain the doors were shut and locked lest anyone break in to steal his treasure. He took up the money, a pile at a time and gave each child a pile, accompanying it with a little speech on prudent husbandry. We kissed him on the cheek. 'A thousand thanks, little papa', we said. Only the fourth pile remained. He gave the impression he wanted to deal with it as swiftly as possible. He glanced at Karin and said in a low voice, 'This is for Mama.' His voice sank even lower, 'An old debt.'

Karin travelled back to Finland. She gave Siri the whole sum. Siri stared at her as if she thought she was playing a joke.

'For me?' she burst out while a hectic blush suffused her cheeks.

She sat quite still while Karin told the circumstances of the gift and then she said in a voice full of pride:

'Will Karin write to thank Papa from me? I receive it as the payment of the old debt.'[24]

1908 was a turbulent time for Swedish domestic politics. Mayday demonstrators carried placards reading 'Down with the throne, the altar and the purse'. Their demands for universal suffrage and an eight-hour working day were met by sword-wielding police officers. That year there were more than three hundred labour disputes and strikes. Foreign workers were imported as strike-breakers; some English strike-breakers were given lodgings on board the *Amalthea*, a ship at anchor in Malmö harbour. In July a Young Socialist named Anton Nilsson[25] blew up the ship with a small bomb: one strike-breaker was killed and twenty-three injured. Nilsson was sentenced to death by the new guillotine imported from France and the newspapers carried annotated diagrams of the grue-some instrument alongside many bracingly patriotic pictures of the Royal Family on opportune occasions: King Gustav's fiftieth birthday, the Crown Prince's wedding to the Russian Archduchess Maria Pavlovna, state visits by King Edward VII, the Kaiser and the statuesque Queen Emma of the Netherlands. The year 1909 saw the General Strike that forced through real political reforms.

During the period of the General Strike, Strindberg's health was not good but still he continued with his morning walks.

'The day began at seven', began his sister who was staying with him at the time.

> He could never lie in bed after that hour, for then 'the walls began to throb and his bed to burn.' With his hat on his head (so that his thoughts should not fly away) he sat down to make his coffee alone; no one might watch him. Then quickly out for his morning walk . . . about an hour and a half, usually around Djurgården. He seldom looked at the people he met but walked like a somnambulist, starting fixedly ahead . . . On return he would immediately sit down, hot and tired, on a chair in the hall, and change his boots. Once I entered the hall just as he had entered. He simply looked at me and sweated with anxiety. I said nothing and shall never forget his eloquent eyes . . . I had disturbed his train of thought . . . He would then seat himself at his desk and, smoking cigarettes vigorously, work till about noon.[26]

When he had walked too far it would sometimes result in an attack of paralysis down one side. Normally he would take a cab home but during the General Strike there were no cabs and he would go into a shop and buy some small thing so he could rest on a chair until the attack had passed and he could continue homewards.

He thought of writing a play about the General Strike, in the manner of Victor Hugo, to show its crippling effects on society and on the individual but he decided against the idea.

Instead, he decided on direct political action. Unrest in the lower classes had contributed to an unattractive upsurge of right-wing nationalism which came to a head in 1910 with the foundation of the Carolingian Society in honour of King Charles xii, one of Strindberg's *bêtes noires* whose reign between 1697 and 1718 had been characterised either by warfare and glory (as the New Carolingians saw it) or by tyranny and butchery (as Strindberg saw it). The New Carolingians were led by Strindberg's old disciple, the poet von Heidenstam, who now wrote a long lyrical piece entitled *Karolinerna (The Charles Men)* honouring the warrior king. It promptly earned him an honorary degree from the University of Uppsala. Strindberg had never been offered an honorary degree from any Swedish university. The other prominent Carolingian was the famous explorer Sven Hedin whose discoveries in Central Asia were so breathtaking that he was knighted in 1905, the last man in Sweden to receive this honour. His discoveries were legion and his travels enormously impressive but his judgement was unsteady and he later became Hitler's poodle as well as a useful idiot for the Communist Chinese. Hedin claimed to have discovered a region in Tibet which Strindberg knew from his old days as a sinologist in the Royal Library had already been mapped in the eighteenth century. Strindberg pointed this out. He poured mockery and scorn on the New Carolingians, satirically accusing them of importing Russian spies disguised as saw-sharpeners, to frighten the Swedish public into xenophobia and war.

Declaring 'a war of liberation against stupidity and snobbery, and time-serving in literature and government',[27] he walked down the stairs of the Blue Tower with an anti-war article in his hand. He dropped it in to the office of *Afton-Tidning,* a newly founded newspaper conveniently located two doors down the street. About fifty more articles followed, naming names and making fun and pulling no punches where he saw injustice, mediocrity or corruption. In Swedish cultural history these articles and the responses they elicited are known as 'the Strindberg feud'.

91

The feud raged in the newspaper columns between the old and the young, the liberals and the conservatives, the religious and the irreligious. Insults were flung from both sides. Strindberg was called a sexphilosopher, a sphinx, a vampire, a parasite, a volcano who belches not fire but filth. One of Bonnier's female authors appealed 'Who will shoot him?' but on 1 July 1910 a certain Adolf Lundgrehn, a man of whom little is known except that he was a working man, wrote to the newspaper *Afton-Tidning*:

'It is true that we Swedes offer nothing but wormwood and insults to our greatest men while they live, but canonise them once they are safely dead. If this is true of anyone it is true of Strindberg. What has his country offered him, whose writing is more typically Swedish than any man's? Even his outbursts of hatred are typically Swedish.'

Now Lundgrehn came to the point. Strindberg's country had never awarded him an honorific. No honorary doctorates, no state stipend. The Nobel Prize for Literature, by far the greatest honour a writer could receive, was administered by the Swedish Academy, a morally craven panel whose literary judgements were a mystery to any but themselves. The previous year, Lundgrehn's letter reminded, the Nobel Prize had been awarded to Selma Lagerlöf, a minor writer mostly of children's tales who had written one good book and consistently been supported financially by the Swedish Royal Family and the Academy, neither of whom had honoured or supported Strindberg in any way.

'That the Nobel Prize was not given him', Lundgrehn's letter continued, 'was an insult not only to him but to Swedish letters and to the broad mass of the people.'

The idea of an Anti-Nobel prize for literature was born. The idea caught fire. A public subscription was opened and the sum of 50,000 kr was raised. The right-wing press denounced it as a put-up job, a stunt organised by Strindberg's political sympathisers who had come up with the money to make a point. *Social-Demokraten* replied that anyone who cared to check the facts would find that twenty thousand people had contributed to the anti-Nobel. Eleven thousand of those had sent donations of less than 50 öre.

They wished to award it to Strindberg on the same evening as the Nobel itself. Strindberg was against the idea. That year, 1911, the prize for literature was given to Maurice Maeterlinck whose work Strindberg honoured. If Maeterlinck came to Stockholm to collect his prize, Strindberg had no intention of causing a distraction from the honour paid to a talent he respected. It was then mooted that the two great writers might stage a memorable meeting. Strindberg as usual dodged out of celebrity display:

'I admire Maeterlinck's works, and have written some fine things about them – but one should never meet. One can't talk about what is written . . . and the rest isn't worth talking about.'[28]

He postponed the award of the anti-Nobel until after Maeterlinck had received his honour and left Sweden.

Karin, who was living in Helsinki, wrote to tell him that she was engaged to Vladimir Smirnoff, a Russian lecturer at the University of Helsinki.

'Come here and marry. I shall host the wedding of my firstborn!' he replied.

She did. Karin came to stay with her sister Greta, who had settled in Stockholm and was now married to Henry Philp who was Strindberg's physician. Strindberg saw a great deal of him and Greta these days. The wedding festivities lasted most of a week with feasting on duck and crayfish and artichokes and a cake topped by a sugar angel holding two red hearts in its outstretched hands. When his children saw the cake, Strindberg told them with a glint in his eye that the pastrycook had thought she was making it for his own wedding. His stomach was so bad that he could not join in the feasting but he paid for the festivities with pleasure. Vladimir and Karin found him gentle and thoughtful, with that trace of shyness that was characteristic of him even when in the company of those closest to him. He still had big plans. One day he asked Vladimir whether he could expect to be harassed by the Tsarist police if he travelled through Siberia to China and Japan.

The following month he celebrated his sixty-third birthday. He knew that the Social Democrats were planning a torchlight procession to wish him a happy birthday and it made him nervous. It would be impolite not to acknowledge any well-wishers but he was unwell and so he wrote to tell Hjalmar Branting who was organising the event: 'I shall set out my most beautiful lamp to shine a red eye towards Tegnér Square. If I am really ill I will have a message telephoned to the People's House, but shall signal in the windows my appreciation and my gratitude; I may perhaps stand in my living room window.'[29]

When it was dark the procession arrived with torches and banners, waving hats and scarves.

'Long live August Strindberg!' they cried.
'Long live the poet king!'
'The People's Strindberg!'

Strindberg stood at the rail of his balcony, acknowledging them, his top hat in his hand. His little daughter [Anne-Marie] had come out and threw flowers onto the crowd, who bent eagerly to take up these souvenirs. Now and then the writer himself took a handful of long-stemmed roses, which were handed to him from within the room, and as though he, the acclaimed, wished himself to acclaim the torch-bearers, let them fall down upon these men and women who stood cheering up at him. On the pavement opposite a workers' choir had gathered, surrounded by torch bearers and as the workers filed past, they sang. . . . It looked as though a broad river of fire filled Drot-tninggatan. Sometimes there was an interval of darkness and it seemed as though the procession was ending, but then the tones of a new choir were heard and a blaze of fresh torches appeared. The writer still stood on his balcony. His son-in-law had taken a candelabrum and held it so the light illuminated Strindberg's face. He had turned his coat collar up against the night cold, but at each new cheer he bared his head to greet the throngs.[30]

More than fifteen thousand people greeted him that night. Greta says that he was so ill that she had to support him to the balcony where he stood pale as parchment and thin as a skeleton with the sweat sticking his hair to his head and his hand grasping the rail for support.

Not only the workers honoured him. All across Sweden his plays were performed. Fifteen hundred people raised their glasses to him at a banquet in his honour at Berns Salon (where he had set *The Red Room*) and he was honoured by productions of his plays in Germany, Finland, Austria and Chicago where four thousand Swedes celebrated at a staging of *Gustav Vasa*. Falck sent him flowers and he wrote a note back, thanking him. The feud was mended and Falck was both fair and affectionate towards him in his book of memoirs.

The Anti-Nobel prize was presented to him on 2 March by Hjalmar Branting who when he arrived with the prize was greeted by Strindberg with, 'Don't look so damn solemn!'

He received 45,000 kronor because 5,000 had been taken in administrative costs. By the end of the day he had given away 5,000 to a home for the handicapped and soon he had given nearly all of it away. This time his daughter Anne-Marie received 10,000, but it was mostly given in charitable donations, notably to the organisations that helped child victims of polio and the registered unemployed but there are numerous stories of other gifts, small and large.

He sent 1,000 kr to Nathan Söderblom who as Swedish Pastor in Paris had administered Ida Molard's collection to pay for Strindberg's psoriasis treatment in the Hôpital de Saint-Louis. Söderblom was now an archbishop. Soon he would take Strindberg's funeral.

Strindberg wrote to Söderblom:

18 March 1912

Herr Professor,

I had so much to say to you about a great many things, but sick and old, I must put my house in order and settle my accounts.

About 1892 (?) I found myself, through no fault of my own, reduced to poverty in Paris, and by roundabout ways received some 200 francs in assistance from the Swedish Church Relief Fund.

I have tried to console myself with the thought that since then, during these last ten better years, I have given substantial relief to others. But it doesn't help . . .

Since I don't know its Paris address, I am sending the enclosed 1,000 kronor to you, and beg you please to forward it to the Relief Fund for compatriots in need.

As a repayment it can of course in no way be regarded as charity!

One little word is missing from this short letter, that small word which is so hard to say. Thank you! For your help then and for the trouble you are kindly taking upon yourself now.

Yours sincerely
August Strindberg

His mind must have been turning over his time in Paris, for he wrote a warm farewell letter to Charlotte Futterer of Madame Charlotte's *crèmerie* where he and Gauguin, now long dead, had spent so much time together.

The following month, Siri von Essen died in Helsinki. Greta brought the news in a letter from Karin who was with Siri at the end.

When Greta came to the deathly-ill Strindberg who had only three weeks to live, Strindberg asked if he might hear the letter. Utterly emaciated, with his sparse and almost white hair wet from the effort of holding himself upright, he sat in his old brown plaid dressing gown, listening attentively. The letter was factual and impersonal, almost cold in its tone but he sobbed as she read it and blew his nose constantly. When Greta had finished reading the letter he went to the other room and came back a little later in an old black dressing gown and a white opera scarf. In that quiet way he wanted to honour the woman whom he would soon follow into death.[31]

Siri wished to be buried in Stockholm, and her body was sent from Helsinki. The day before her funeral, Strindberg summoned Greta. She found him sitting at his desk with his back to her. He did not turn as he asked her if the children could have anything against him sending a wreath. She told him it could only bring them joy. He sent a wreath of laurels and lilies without a card and it was carried on her coffin.

He could no longer pretend that the stomach cancer was merely psychic warfare aimed at him by those who wished him ill.

7 April 1912 [to his doctor]. Now the pain is with me day and night irrespective of what I eat; sometimes the pain is dull, sometimes more intense, but I am never free of it. Whether I sit, walk or lie down. I go to bed to avoid wearing my clothes, but this no longer helps . . . Sleep may come for an hour or two, then the pain wakes me. The twelve hours of night are endless.

18 April [to his doctor]. In bed, excuse pencil . . . the pains are sometimes eased by morphine since the opium ceased to work (I vomit). No one wishes to operate but I want an end to these agonies.

19 April [to Anne-Marie]. My dear little daughter. Thank you for your red flowers! But you mustn't try to see me. There are so many medicine bottles, doctors and things here that it is no fun.

25 April [to the Editor of Social-Demokraten]. Thanks good friends and colleagues for the beautiful flower. I still had a great deal to say in the paper when my pen fell from my hand – my fountain pen! So forgive the pencil.

During the month he lay dying, Frida sent a telegram from London beseeching him to allow her to come and nurse him. He did not reply.

The news of the sinking of the *Titanic* roused him to his piano to play *Nearer my God to Thee*, the hymn which the papers reported the orchestra had played as the ship was sinking.

To Fanny who came to the door wishing to see him, he sent a message via his maid Mina: 'You must not be sad, for I have been thinking about you.' Fanny replied that she did not mind if he thought about her so long as she could see him. Mina came back with the message 'Herr Strindberg says that if you cry, he will smack you.'[32]

Mina was sent to Harriet with 'an enormous bag' containing a letter to Anne-Marie and 1,500 kr. Harriet describes the contents:

> Strindberg wrote to our daughter that he remembered that when we married he had given me a grand piano but later made me unhappy by changing it for an upright.
>
> 'Perhaps Mummy would now like to buy a grand piano with these fifteen hundred kronor?'
>
> After Strindberg's death I was sent a Chinese chest containing all my letters to him, some small mementoes and my little, withered bridal crown.[33]

He summoned his lawyer and made his last testament in front of two witnesses. His grave was to carry a simple cross with the inscription he had seen so often in the cemetery of Montparnasse: *O Crux Ave Spes Unica* (*O Cross, our only Hope*).

> My body must not be dissected or laid out in state, only shown to my relatives. No death-mask made, no photographs taken. I want to be interred at 8 in the morning, to avoid any curious bystanders. I do not want to be buried in a crypt, much less in a church, but in the new cemetery; not in the section for the wealthy, however. At the grave, there shall be no playing of music, no singing, no speeches. The clergyman should simply follow the words of the ritual.

On 13 May at 10 p.m. his nurse asked him if he would like the morphine:

> 'Yes, a big dose', he said and he rolled up his sleeve.
>
> He slept fitfully, groaning and crying and the nurse sent for the doctor. As the doctor came in he woke, recognised him, and said in an apologetic tone, 'Have you been here all night?' and thanked him, quite

calmly. Then he woke again and asked the nurse for some papers he had been working on. Mina went to search for them while the nurse put his spectacles on his nose. By the time the papers were found he was asleep again. This time it was a calm and settled sleep so the nurse lay down on the floor and wrapped herself in her coat to rest while keeping an eye on him. He opened his eyes and said, 'Has she gone?'

Before she could answer, he saw her on the floor,

and I shall never forget the look he gave me. His eyes were more blue than ever, and he smiled so warmly at me. I half rose but he said, 'No, dear little child, lie still, I am not angry with you. Do not bother about me. I no longer exist.' Those were the last words he spoke and he fell into the sleep before death. If the agonised cries he uttered several times an hour were conscious, his suffering must have been terrible, the morphine no longer had any visible effect.[34]

When he drew his last breath it was 4.30 am on 14 May. Greta placed the Bible and a crucifix on his breast as he had requested.

The funeral took place on 19 May, early in the morning as he had stipulated, to avoid the crowds but long before seven an inky river of top-hats and dark overcoats flowed through the streets of Stockholm. More than ten thousand people followed the horse-drawn hearse to the cemetery. Karin, Greta, Hans and Anne-Marie led the group of family mourners at the head of the long procession. Fanny walked with the actors she had worked with at the Intimate Theatre.

The Royal Family was represented by Prins Eugen. The King himself sent a wreath. Notable by its absence was any sort of acknowledgement by the Swedish Academy. Harriet also stayed away. Instead, she sat on a bench in his beloved Djurgården where he had taken his daily walks. The Social Democrats followed the coffin carrying a hundred red banners. They disobeyed his orders by singing hymns along the way and when the coffin was lowered into its grave the hundred banners were silently dipped.

The following day his grave was plundered by vandals. The tributes were smashed, the gilded wreaths stolen and the wreath from the king had its ribbon cut off. It was not quite as good a rumpus as the orgy held for Victor Hugo but, in its way, maybe a more suitable tribute to Sweden's roaring rebel. Strindberg himself might well have approved, though he could no longer make use of the dramatic experience.

100

NOTES

1 Miss Julie's Kitchen

1　Hotel Leopold was in Hovedvogstgade, Copenhagen. It no longer exists.

2　Strindberg's waxwork figure was added to Bernhard Olsen's Scandinavian Panopticon in 1885.

3　Axel Lundegård (1861–1930). Radical, writer and biographer of Victoria Benedictsson (see n. 6).

4　Axel Lundegård, *Nagrå Strindbergsminnen knutna till en handfull brev*, Stockholm, 1920, pp. 45–8.

5　Karin Strindberg (later Smirnoff, sometimes spelled Smirnov) 1880–1973.

6　Victoria Benedictsson (1850–88). Her play *The Enchantment* is based on her affair with Brandes.

7　Georg Brandes (1842–1927). Important Danish literary critic whose *Main Currents in 19th-Century Literature* expressed the idea that one responsibility of writers was to engage with current issues.

8　*Qvinnans underordnade ställning*, 1869, Georg Brandes's translation of Mill's *Subjection of Women*.

9　Georg Brandes, *Det moderne Gjennembruds Mænd*, Copenhagen, 1883.

10　Georg Brandes to Jonas Lie, 2 January 1888.

11　Karin Smirnoff, *Strindbergs første hustru*, Poul Branners Förlag, Copenhagen, 1948, pp. 124–5.

12　*Ibid.* p. 125.

13　*Ibid.* p. 125.

14　The Teacher says this in the dramatic fragment *The Island of the Dead* (1907).

15　Smirnoff, *Strindbergs første hustru*, p. 126.

16　Now called Tarbæk, approximately 19 km north of Copenhagen on the coast.

17 André Antoine (1858–1943). Actor-manager who founded the experimental Théâtre Libre in 1887, bringing modern, controversial works to Paris such as Ibsen's *Ghosts* and *Miss Julie*.

18 To Lundegård, 28 January 1889.

19 Smirnoff, *Strindbergs første hustru*, p. 127.

20 Skovlyst still stands on Kongvej, near Holte station. It was renamed Geelsgardskolen and is used as a school for handicapped children. The lake is filled in, the pavilion is gone, the big salons are partitioned but one can easily trace Strindberg's life there.

21 To Verner von Heidenstam from Holte, 13 October 1888: *Miss Julie* is also about how fröken Rudbeck seduced her groom. He also relates it to the novel *Fru Marie Grubbe* by J. P. Jacobsen in which the heroine loses caste by sexual relations with a servant.

22 Smirnoff, *Strindbergs første hustru*, p. 127.

23 *Ibid.* p. 127. The account that follows of the adventures at Skovlyst is taken partly from Smirnoff's publication, partly from Harry Jacobsen, *Digteren og Fantasten*, Gyldendal, Copenhagen, 1945, and partly from Strindberg's fictionalised account in the novel *Tshandala*, Schubotes Bokhandel, Copenhagen, 1889.

24 Smirnoff, *Strindbergs første hustru*, p. 128.

25 *Ibid.*

26 Strindberg with Anton Stuxberg, Fahlstedt and other friends, translation of Hartmann's *Philosophy of the Unconscious*.

27 Mind-control featured in *The Father* and found its most popular expression later in du Maurier's *Trilby*, 1894.

28 Jacobsen, *Digteren og Fantasten*, p. 179.

29 August Strindberg, *By the Open Sea*, University of Georgia Press, 1984, p. 67.

30 August Strindberg, *Tschandala*, pp. 384–5.

31 August Strindberg, *Ockulta Dagboken*, facsimile edn, Gidlunds, Stockholm, 1977, p. 2.

32 The overwhelming importance of Skovlyst's garden and greenhouse in the decision to settle there is stressed by Karin and evident from Strindberg's repeated reference to both of them in *Tschandala* and *Blomstermålningar och djurstycken*, Bonnier, Stockholm, 1889. The greenhouse where Strindberg worked has now been removed to Den Gamleby Museum, Denmark, where (in 2010) it remains in use.

33 Carl Willmann, *Moderne Wünder*, then recently translated into Danish as *Moderne Mirakler* (see Jacobsen, *Digteren og Fantasten*, p. 28).

34 To Peter Nansen, 6 March 1889. The cock was named *Himmelsprut*, 'Heavensquirt'. We make of that what we will.

35 For the ancestry of Anna Louisa Frankenau (1848–1922) see Jacobsen, *Digteren og Fantasten*, p. 30 and *Dansk biografi Lexicon*, 1891.

36 Ludvig Hansen interviewed in *Politiken*, 10 August 1928.

37 Unusually, in *Miss Julie*, Strindberg specifies the age of the characters in the cast list. Jean is 30. The gravestone which Hansen himself put up but which is not necessarily reliable, gives his dates as February 15 1859–8 April 1946.

38 Hansen in *Politiken*, 10 August 1928.

39 *Tschandala*, p. 370.

40 Jacobsen, *Digteren og Fantasten*, pp. 36–7.

41 As told to the author by the writer and music therapist Bjørn Mortensen, who lived at Skovlyst in 1983–2004.

42 August Strindberg on himself, essay in the form of a fictitious interview, 1909.

43 Strindberg, *Blomstermålningnar och djur-stycken. Näktergalen*, pp. 18–25. Strictly speaking, not his very first nightingale but his first northern nightingale. Different, as he explains.

44 To Edvard Brandes, 4 September 1888. The resulting book was *Tschandala*. He also uses him in the play *Pariah* but his greatest use of Hansen is as the psychological model for Jean as he analyses him in the introduction to *Miss Julie*.

45 Georg Brandes to Sophus Schandorph, 1 April 1888. The lectures were given every Tuesday between 8 April and 20 May 1888. Strindberg probably received *Twilight of the Idols* later that year in November. (See Strindberg letter to Brandes dated 29 November 1888.)

46 In 1882 Strindberg opened his satirical novel *Det Nya Riket* (*The New Kingdom*), a savage and sustained snarl at the political reforms of 1866, with the epigraph from *Pickwick Papers*, 'You are a humbug, sir . . . I will speak plainer if you wish it. An imposter, sir.'

47 To von Heidenstam, 3 June 1888.

48 Georg Brandes to Romain Roland, 22 February 1922, *Selected Letters*, trans. W. Glynn Jones, Norvik Press, Norwich, 1990, p. 216.

49 Jacobsen, *Digteren og Fantasten*, p. 41.

50 *Tschandala*, p. 448.

51 The bookseller was Henrik Koppel; see Jacobsen, *Digteren og Fantasten*, p. 140. Peacocks appear in the *Occult Diary* (1896–1908), *A Blue Book* (1907–12), *Indigo and the Line of Copper* (1896) and *Swanwhite* (1901).

52 To Edvard Brandes, 4 October 1888.

53 To Edvard Brandes, 4 September 1888.

54 *Politiken*, 9 September 1888.

55 To Siri von Essen, 19 September 1888.

56 To Peter Hansen, 6 September 1889.

57 *Tschandala*, p. 91.

58 To von Heidenstam, 2 October 1888.

59 Strindberg on Jean in his introduction to *Miss Julie*.

60 Interview with Martha Magdalena in *Social Demokraten*, 3 September 1888.

61 Strindberg, Introduction to *Miss Julie*.

62 To Georg Brandes, 3 January 1889.

63 Franz Camille Overbeck (1837–1905). German Protestant theologian.

64 Georg Brandes to Edvard Brandes, 22 July 1888.

65 *Indtryk fra Polen (Impressions of Poland)*, 1888.

66 *Politiken*, 19 September 1888, and *Københavns Posten*, 23 September 1888.

67 *The Son of a Servant*, Anchor Books, New York, 1966, p. 16.

2   *The Son of a Servant*

1 *The Son of a Servant*, p. 16.

2 The members of the First Chamber were elected by the county councils and certain town councils. The members of the Second Chamber were elected by citizens who had property worth at least 1000 *riksdaler* or an annual income of 800 *riksdaler*, about 5.6 per cent of the population.

3 General Armfeld quoted in Herman Lindqvist, *A History of Sweden*, Norstedts, Stockholm, 2002, p. 505.

4 The Karlsborg fortress on Vättern lake on the Göta Canal.

5 King Gustav III, whose assassination at a masked ball is the subject of Verdi's *Un Ballo in Maschera*, planned the transformation employing neo-classical artists such as Johannes Tobias Sergel (1740–1814) and Louis-Jean Desprez (1743–1804).

6 King Charles XII (reigned 1697–1718). *Histoire de Charles XII., Roi de Suède. par M de V**** [Voltaire], Basle, 1731. The biography sold very well.

7 Gas lamps were installed in 1853, some forty years later than London.

8 Statistics taken from Bonnier's *The Traveller's Guide in Sweden and the Most Interesting Places in Norway*, Albert Bonnier, Stockholm, 1871, pp. 6–7.

9 *The Son of a Servant*, p. 34.

10 *Ibid.* p. 31.

11 Two of the more important are the Kansö Quarantine Hospital of 1818 and Stumholmen of the 1830s.

12 Notes for a play entitled *The Sleeping City*. Cited in August Falck, *Fem år med Strindberg*, Stockholm, 1935, p. 82, quoted in Egil Törnqvist, *Strindberg's*

Ghost Sonata, Amsterdam University Press, 2000. See also 'The Dance of Death' and 'The Quarantine Master's Second Story' in *Fair Haven and Foulstrand*.

13   See below, Chapter 16.

14   *The Son of a Servant*, p. 21.

15   Carl Oscar Strindberg (1811–1883); Ulrika Eleonora Norling (1823–1862); siblings: Axel (1845–1927), Oscar (1847–1924), Olle (1853–1943), Anna (1855–1927), Elisabeth (1857–1904), Eleonora (1858–1927); step-mother Emilia Pettersson (1841–1887), half-brother Emil Zacharias (1864–1911).

16   *The Son of a Servant*, p. 18.

17   *Ibid.* p. 14.

18   *Ibid.* pp. 22–4.

19   *Ibid.* p. 15.

20   *Ibid.* p. 26.

21   *Ibid.* p. 27.

22   Famous preachers included Johan Axel Olin (1825–1911), Per Magnus Elmblad (1806–1887) and Carl Olaf Rosenius (1816–1868).

3   Basic Training

1   Lindqvist, *A History of Sweden*, p. 556.

2   Esias Tegnér (1772–1846) quoted in *ibid.* p. 555. Bishop of Vaxjö in 1824, an enthusiast for clarity in all fields, he disliked both mysticism and Gothic architecture, pulled down some of Sweden's oldest churches replacing them with what some called 'barns', the neo-classical basilicas now much admired.

3   *The Son of a Servant*, pp. 48–9. They lived at number 14 Norrtullsgatan.

4   Bonnier, *Traveller's Guide*, p. 13.

5   *The Son of a Servant*, p. 45.

6   *Ibid.* pp. 49–50.

7   He would have read the version of *Robinson Crusoe* written by the German J. H. Campe (1746–1818) that was translated into many European languages.

8   *Miss Julie* between the pantomime and the ballet.

9   *The Son of a Servant*, p. 48.

10   *Ibid.* p. 62.

11   August Strindberg, *The Red Room*, Dent, 1967, p. 174.

12   *The Son of a Servant*, p. 105.

13   'A cat's fur, slightly warmed, is very efficient in electrifying vulcanite or resin', *Chambers Encyclopaedia*, 1879, vol. IV, p. 255, entry on electricity.

14   *The Son of a Servant*, p. 109.

15   *Ibid*. p. 109.

16   *Ibid*. pp. 77–8.

17   *Ibid*. p. 56.

18   Stellan Ahlström, ed., *Ögonvittnen: August Strindberg*, Wahlström & Widstrand, Stockholm, 1959, vol. 1, pp. 18–19.

19   Anna Philp and Nora Hartzell, *Strindbergs systrar berätter om barndomshemmet och om bror August*, P. A. Norstedt & Sönners Förlag, Stockholm, 1926, pp. 31–2.

20   Jacob School was situated where Regeringsgatan meets Brunnsgatan.

21   The Lyceum was on Regeringsgatan. Founded in 1839, in Strindberg's time it had a good proportion of teachers to pupils, 23:200.

22   *The Son of a Servant*, p. 91.

23   *Ibid*. pp. 92–3.

24   Carl Olof Rosenius, minister of the Church of Bethlehem in Stockholm in 1856–68. His congregation consisted mostly of peasants, farmers, soldiers and the working class. His newspaper, *The Pietist*, had a circulation of 7000 whereas the most popular newspaper, *Aftonbladet*, sold only 4000.

25   Carl Johan Bohman (1816–1887). Headmaster of the Stockholm Lyceum.

26   Titles of address were highly important in Sweden. *Fröken* (as in *Fröken Julie*) was used for an unmarried woman of the aristocracy. *Mademoiselle* or *Mam'selle* was used for a woman of social standing while a housemaid would be addressed by her last name.

27   Sixt Karl von Kapff (1805–1879). German Protestant theologian and Pietist.

28   *The Son of a Servant*, p. 116.

29   August Strindberg, *Samlade Skrifter*, ed. John Landquist, 55 vols, Albert Bonniers Förlag, Stockholm, 1912–20, vol. XVIII, p. 138.

30   *The Son of a Servant*, p. 138.

4   The Freethinker

1   Letter dated September 1871 to Johan Oscar Strindberg (1843–1905), Strindberg's cousin. Businessman, father of Andrée who was lost in the tragic balloon expedition to the North Pole in 1897. Johan Oscar, known as Oscar, provided important financial and moral support during August's early days as a writer and during his divorce from Siri von Essen.

2   August Strindberg, *Jäsningstiden* (1886), trans. as *Time of Ferment* or *The Growth of a Soul*, Rider, London, 1913, p. 17.

3 *Ibid.* pp. 7–8.

4 *Ibid.* p. 6.

5 *Ibid.* p. 60.

6 *Ibid.* p. 47.

7 *Ibid.* p. 55. The two daughters of Professor Oscar Sandahl, professor of medicine, who lived at Klara Strandgata 2.

8 Gurli Linder quoted in Michael Meyer, *Strindberg: A Biography*, Random House, New York, 1985, p. 54.

9 *Time of Ferment*, pp. 63–4.

10 *Ibid.* p. 66.

11 Jaqueline Stare and Yvonne Jacobsson, *The Jews of Sweden, their History and Tradition*, Judiska Museet, Stockholm, 2005, p. 9.

12 *Ibid.* p. 15. 95 per cent of articles were hostile.

13 This figure is arrived at from assuming a small increase in the congregation of 588 recorded in 1856.

14 *Time of Ferment*, p. 67.

15 *Ibid.* p. 68. The phial of poison described by Strindberg, like the opium pill soon to be encountered, is taken by some biographers to be fictitious or symbolic or merely self-dramatising. Others (Martin Lamm and Eric Hedén), take it to be literally true. Either way, real or symbol, it is of great significance to Strindberg himself.

16 Quoted in Elisabeth Sprigge, *The Strange Life of August Strindberg*, Macmillan, London, 1949, p. 30.

17 *Time of Ferment*, p. 185.

18 *Ibid.* pp. 121–3.

19 Albert (Bertel) Thorvaldsen (1768–1844). The museum is on Thorvaldsens Plads, Copenhagen.

20 Frans Hedberg (1828–1908). Actor and author of some 100 plays. Features as the director of the 'Limited Theatre Company' in *The Red Room*.

21 Lorenz Dietrichson, *Svunde tider*, Christiania, 1894–1917, vol. II, pp. 247–9.

22 *Time of Ferment*, pp. 199–200.

23 *Ibid.* p. 161.

24 Notably Bjørnson's *Between the Battles* and Ibsen's *The Vikings in Helgeland*. Strindberg refutes the charge in a letter to Eugène Falstadt in May 1872.

25 *Time of Ferment*, pp. 190–91.

26 Samuel Plimsoll (1824–1898). Became an MP in 1868, promoted the Merchant Shipping Act which was passed in 1876. The Plimsoll line was legally enforced 1894.

27 *A Madman's Defence*, p. 43.

28 Bonnier, *Traveller's Guide*, p. 89.

29 When thinking of this paternity thread in Scandinavian literature, it is interesting to remember that Ibsen, when young and poor, fathered an illegitimate son on a maid and abandoned them both.

30 Smirnoff, *Strindbergs första hustru*, p. 7. Much of this account of Siri's youth is taken from this book, a memoir of her mother by Karin.

31 *Ibid.* p. 13.

32 *Ibid.* p. 10.

33 Eivor Martinus, *Strindberg and Love*, Amber Lane Press, Oxford, 2001, p. 28.

34 Carl Gustaf Wrangel (1842–1913), a descendant of Carl Gustaf Wrangel (1613–1676), the Commander-in-Chief of the Swedish forces for a period during the Thirty Years War.

35 Letter from Siri von Essen to Constance Melins quoted in Smirnoff, *Strindbergs första hustru*, p. 30.

36 Ina Forstén (1846–1930). Swedish pianist and writer who became Court Pianist at the Royal Palace in Denmark. She married Algot Lange on 3 January 1876.

37 Algot Lange (1846–1904). Actor and singer from Kalmar, father of the explorer of the same name who took American citizenship and wrote two colourful books on his expeditions to the Amazon.

38 *A Madman's Defence*, p. 57.

39 *Ibid.* p. 30.

40 To Siri, 27 June 1875.

41 *A Madman's Defence*, p. 55.

42 *Ibid.* p. 71.

43 To Carl Gustaf Wrangel dated, dramatically, Thor's Day, i.e. 7 October 1875.

44 Undated letter written that autumn to Rudolf Mauritz Wall (1826–1893), liberal journalist and founder of *Dagens Nyheter*. Wall supported Strindberg with money, encouragement and commissions all his life.

45 *A Madman's Defence*, pp. 99–100.

5 Playing with Fire

1 *A Madman's Defence*, p. 101.

2 *Ibid.* p. 108.

3 Smirnoff, *Strindbergs första hustru*, p. 38.

4 *A Madman's Defence*, p. 143.

5 Hugo von Philp (1844–1906), fellow student at Uppsala. Later a teacher. Married Anna Strindberg in 1875.

6   To Carl Axel Strindberg, Christmas Eve 1876.

7   To Siri, 12 March 1876.

8   Elisabeth von Essen to Strindberg, dated '13 April 5 o'clock in the morning'.

9   *A Madman's Defence*, p. 140.

10   Siri Wrangel to Elisabeth von Essen, some time at the end of April 1876.

11   Augusta Möller, wife of Konsul A. W. Möller.

12   *A Madman's Defence*, p. 176.

13   To Siri, undated, May 1876.

14   *A Madman's Defence*, p. 153.

15   Fredrik Wilhelm Scholander, speech delivered 25 March 1876.

16   *Dagens Nyheter*, December 1876.

17   This and her other reviews are quoted in Smirnoff, *Strindbergs første hustru*, pp. 59–63.

18   *A Madman's Defence*, p. 193.

19   To Johan Oscar Strindberg, 11 April 1888.

20   Berns Salon continues to thrive at Näckströmgatan 8, Berzelii Park, Stockholm. The Red Room is upstairs and, tactfully restored, remains decorated as it was in Strindberg's day.

21   Lindqvist, *A History of Sweden*, p. 600.

22   Founded by Joseph Seligmann (1836–1904) and Hugo Greber in 1878, Seligmann published minor works and translations by Strindberg as well as *The Secret of the Guild* (1880) and *Old Stockholm* (1880–82). Turned down the next big success, the comic novel *The People of Hemsö*, but later published *Miss Julie* when no one else dared.

23   Olof Rudbeck (1630–1702). Another Swedish polymath like Berzelius and Linnaeus who provided role models for Strindberg. Rudbeck put forward his population ideas in *Atlantica*. He studied the lymph glands and their work in the human body and he established the botanical garden in Uppsala which Linnaeus took over.

24   Smirnoff, *Strindbergs første hustru*, p. 70.

25   To Siri, 5 May 1882.

26   Playbill for *Skärtorsdagen* performed on 14 April 1881 at 9 p. m.

27   The voyage of the *Vega* (1878–80) under Adolf Eric Nordenskiöld.

28   Anton Julius Stuxberg (1849–1902). Zoologist and polar explorer. Settled in Gothenburg in 1882, became keeper of the zoological section of the museum. Explored Crimea and the Caucasus in 1897. Translated E. von Hartmann's *Philosophie des Unbewussten* (Philosophy of the Unconscious) with Strindberg.

6   A Short Swedish Honeymoon

1   Ludvig Oscar Josephson (1832–1899). Actor and director. Worked as a bookseller at Bonniers. Acted at the Royal Theatre from 1861, director from 1864. Notable man of vision, director of Shakespeare, Schiller and Byron who bravely premiered Ibsen's *Peer Gynt* and *Brand*. Took over the New Theatre in 1879. Put on *Master Olof* in 1882 and *Sir Bengt's Wife* (1883) with Siri in the title role.

2   Quoted in Meyer, *Strindberg: A Biography*, p. 89.

3   Artur Immanuel Hazelius (1833–1901). Founder of the Nordic Museum and Skansen.

4   August Strindberg, *The Natives of Hemsö*, trans. Arvid Paulson, Paul S. Eriksson, New York, 1965, pp. 4–5.

5   *Ibid*. pp. 14–15.

6   Carl Larsson (1853–1919). Swedish painter and graphic artist.

7   Ahlström, *Ögonvittnen*, vol. 1, pp. 104–6.

8   Carl Ludwig Schleich, *Those Were Good Days!* W. W. Norton, New York, 1936, pp. 202–6.

9   *Blomstermålningnar och djur-stycken*, pp. 10–16.

10   Eva Carlson, nursemaid who remained with the family till 1891.

11   To Siri, 14 May 1881.

12   Elisabeth lived with their father till his death in 1883. Artistic and intelligent, close to Strindberg. In 1898 admitted to Nyköping mental hospital suffering from depression and persecution mania. Moved to Ulleråker asylum in Uppsala. Strindberg came to see her as the scapegoat for the family's sins and drew on her character to create Eleonora in *Easter* and the girl in the asylum in *The Gothic Rooms*.

13   To Elisabeth Strindberg from Kymmendö, 13 June 1882.

14   To Edvard Brandes, 26 July 1882.

15   *Ibid*.

16   Count Carl Snoilsky (1841–1903). After his divorce spent much of his time in Dresden before succeeding Klemming as head of the Royal Library in 1890.

17   *The Newest Kingdom: Characteristic Narratives from the Era of Thoughtlessness and Impudence* by 'Michel Perrin' (W. A. Bergstrand), Stockholm, 1882.

18   Smirnoff, *Strindbergs første hustru*, p. 85.

19   Karl Otto Bonnier (1856–1941). Became a partner in Bonniers in 1886 and its head in 1900–38.

20   To Siri, 12 March 1876.

21   Helga Franckenfeldt, on whom Strindberg drew for the silent Fru Y in *The Stronger*. Strindberg and Stuxberg were not reconciled until 1892.

22   Quoted in Meyer, *Strindberg: A Biography*, p. 99.

7   Rabble Rouser

1   To Pehr Staaff, 18 September 1883.

2   Larsson's painting was entitled *At the Court Painter's*. On a narrow strip he kept for himself he added two figures, and this is the painting now called *Little Suzanne* (1885).

3   Ville Vallgren (1855–1940). Made a bust of Strindberg that was exhibited at the Paris Salon of 1884.

4   'Spada' was the *nom de plume* of Johan Janzon (1853–1910), Paris correspondent of *Stockholm's Dagblad*.

5   To Rudolf Wall, 7 October 1883.

6   Bjørnstjerne Bjørnson (1832–1910). Writer and nationalist.

7   Jonas Lie (1833–1908). Writer who corresponded with Strindberg and supported him.

8   Bjørnstjerne Bjørnson to Ludvig Josephson, 4 January 1884, cited in Meyer, *Strindberg: A Biography*, p. 122.

9   Published 1883. See Strindberg's letter to Erik Thyselius, 11 January 1884.

10   Nikolay Chernyshevsky (1828–1889).

11   To Bjørnson, 25 January 1884.

12   To Bjørnson, 4 May 1884.

13   To Carl Johan Thyselius, 11 January 1884.

14   Hjalmar Branting (1860–1925). Politician and writer. In 1886 became the editor of *Social-Demokraten*. Won the Nobel Peace Prize in 1921.

15   To Hjalmar Branting, from Ouchy, 12 May 1884. *Underground Russia* (1882) by the Russian dissident, Sergius Stepniak.

16   To Oscar Strindberg, 4 May 1884.

17   Hélène Welinder's memoir published 1912 after Strindberg's death, quoted in Olof Lagerkrantz, *August Strindberg*, trans. Anselm Hollo, Farrar Straus Giroux, New York, 1985, pp. 123–4.

18   To Carl Larsson from Genoa, March 1884.

19   *Getting Married*, ed. and trans. Mary Sandbach, Quartet Books, London, 1977, p. 146.

20   Queen Margareta of Denmark, Sweden and Norway (1353–1412).

21   *Getting Married*, preface.

22   *Getting Married*, p. 71.

23   To Carl Larsson from Geneva, 7 October 1884.

24   Mikhail Constantinovich Elpidin (1835–1908).

25   To Carl Larsson from Geneva, 7 October 1884.

26   Bjørnson to Strindberg, 7 October and 10 October 1884.

27   Strindberg to Bjørnson from Geneva, 14 October 1884.

28   Bjørnson to S. A. Hedlund, 18 October 1884, quoted in Meyer, *Strindberg: A Biography*, p. 137.

29 To Isidor Kjellberg, 1 November 1884.

30 Smirnoff, *Strindbergs første hustru*, p. 100.

31 *Ibid.* p. 101.

32 Reports of the size of the crowd vary but *Dagens Nyheter* and *Aftonbladet* both mention the figure of a thousand.

33 Smirnoff, *Strindbergs første hustru*, p. 101.

34 *Aftonbladet*, October 1884, quoted in Meyer, *Strindberg: A Biography*, p. 139.

35 Axel Lundegård in *Dagens Nyheter*, 24 October 1884.

36 To Albert Bonnier, 4 October 1884.

37 Letter from Gustaf af Geijerstam to Siri dated Stockholm, 30 October 1884.

38 Passage in *The Sequestration Journey*, quoted in Lagerkrantz, *August Strindberg*, p. 131.

39 To Albert Bonnier, 15 November 1884.

40 To Albert Bonnier, 28 November 1884.

8   Under the Ice

1 To Georg Brandes, June 1885.

2 To Albert Bonnier, 4 January 1885.

3 *Sequestration Journey* was published in instalments by *Budkaflen*, a newspaper that had supported him through the trial; they paid him 1,000 Swiss francs.

4 Letter from Albert Bonnier to Strindberg, 30 December 1884.

5 'My Anti-Semitism', *Tiden*, December 1884, quoted in Meyer, *Strindberg: A Biography*, p. 144.

6 To Albert Bonnier, 4 January 1885.

7 To Jonas Lie from Geneva, 2 December 1884.

8 The Federation was founded in England in 1875 and in Sweden in 1878 with the abolition of prostitution as its main goal.

9 Letter from Gustaf af Geijerstam to Siri, 30 October 1884, cited in Smirnoff, *Strindbergs første hustru*, pp. 102–3.

10 To Jonas Lie from Geneva, 2 December 1884.

11 Verner von Heidenstam (1859–1940). Poet, novelist, essayist; won the Nobel Prize for Literature in 1916.

12 To Albert Bonnier, 25 May 1885.

13 February 1886, quoted in Meyer, *Strindberg: A Biography*, p. 154.

14 Now usually published in the same volume as the first stories.

15 To Georg Brandes, 3 January 1887.

16 *Ur Dagens Krönika*, January 1885.

17 *Le Plaidoyer d'un fou*, p. 274.

18   To Albert Bonnier, 21 June 1886.

19   Gustaf Steffen (1864–1929). Sociologist, politician and mineralogist.

20   To Gustaf Steffen, 5 August 1886.

21   To Gustaf Steffen, 9 August 1886.

22   To Hjalmar Branting, 6 December 1886.

23   To Jonas Lie, Christmas Eve 1884.

24   Emil Hillberg (1852–1929). Actor and editor of the Saturday newspaper *Stockholm*.

25   To Axel Strindberg, 19 December 1885.

26   Ibid.

27   Hugo Nisbeth, *Figaro*, December 1885.

28   To Isidor Kjellberg, October 1885.

29   To Gustaf af Geijerstam, 20 January 1886.

9   Madness and Modernity

1   To Verner von Heidenstam, 22 November 1885.

2   Karl Nordström (1855–1923). Impressionist and, later, Symbolist painter. Loyal friend to Strindberg who helped in 1911 to organise the anti-Nobel prize awarded to Strindberg.

3   Nordström to his fiancée Tekla Lindeström, quoted in Lagerkrantz, *August Strindberg*, p. 148.

4   Smirnoff, *Strindbergs første hustru*, p. 110.

5   To Albert Bonnier, 3 August 1886.

6   To Edvard Brandes, April 1886.

7   To Albert Bonnier from Grez, 25 April 1886.

8   *Ibid.*

9   To Alexander Kielland, 26 November 1886.

10   To Oscar Levertin, 1 June 1885.

11   To Albert Bonnier, 9 June 1886.

12   To Albert Bonnier, 21 June 1886.

13   *Ibid.*

14   Laura wields the power of suggestion over the Captain in *The Father*, Jean over Julie in *Miss Julie*, Gustav over Adolf in *Creditors*, Biskra over Guimard in *Simoom* and the Physician over the Unknown in *To Damascus*. At this time Strindberg was writing *Vivisections*, a book of seven short stories exploring Bernheim's theories of suggestion. It found a publisher in Vienna's Neue Freie Presse, Austria being more interested in psychology than Sweden at the time.

15   To Verner von Heidenstam, 5 October 1886.

16   According to her daughter Karin who said that, though the name

sounded like Oltramar, she was not certain this was the correct spelling. Smirnoff, *Strindbergs første hustru*, p. 121.

17 *Ibid.* pp. 106–8.

18 To Albert Bonnier, 31 December 1886.

19 The subjects of the projected plays are laid out in a letter to Edvard Brandes dated 3 January 1887.

20 To Verner von Heidenstam, January 1887. The anti-feminist book he refers to is *La Légende de la femme emancipée* by Firman Maillard, 1886.

21 *Ibid.*

22 To Albert Bonnier, 3 February 1887.

23 His name, it transpires, is Adolf but we only learn this during the play as his intimates have to address him in some way other than 'Captain'.

24 Johan Personne, *Strindbergslitteraturen och osedligheten bland skolungdomen: Till föräldrar och uppforstrare samt til de styrande*, Stockholm, 1887. Personne (1849–1926), Bishop of Linköping 1910–26, author of numerous articles and books.

25 Letter from Oscar Levertin to Edvard Brandes, 23 July 1887, cited in Meyer, *Strindberg: A Biography*, p. 173.

26 Personne, *Strindbergslitteraturen*, pp. 58–9, quoted in Meyer, *Strindberg: A Biography*, pp. 172–3.

27 Letter from Georg Brandes to Alexander Kielland, 21 September 1881.

10 Experimental Theatre

1 Karin Strindberg quoted in Per Hemmingson, *August Strindberg som fotograf*, Kalejdoskop Förlag, Göteborg, 1989, p. 155.

2 To Georg Lundström, 4 March 1887.

3 Smirnoff, *Strindbergs første hustru*, p. 122.

4 In *Plaidoyer d'un fou*, p. 283, he specifically mentions using the techniques of Bishop (whom he misspells Bishof), a mesmerist and mind-reader popular with the Court and upper classes in Sweden.

5 Staaff's replies to Strindberg's letters make it clear that there had been gossip about Siri's unfaithfulness during 1882–3 but gossip is of course no proof. Eivor Martinus deals with it in her analysis of Strindberg's wives and loves in *Strindberg and Love*, pp. 91 and 102–3.

6 To Pehr Staaff, 21 August 1887.

7 *Ibid.*

8 To Pehr Staaff, 5 September 1887.

9 Letter from Albert Bonnier to Strindberg, 25 July 1887.

10 Claës Julius Looström (1846–1916). Publisher. Looström & Co published *The New Kingdom*, *Sir Bengt's Wife*, *Swedish Destinies and Adventures*.

11 To Karl Otto Bonnier, 6 June 1886.

12 To Axel Strindberg, 28 June 1887.

13 For Strindberg's analysis of this moment in theatre see *On Modern Drama and Modern Theatre* (1889).

14 August Lindberg (1846–1916). Actor and director who commissioned Strindberg to make a dramatic version of *The People of Hemsö*.

15 To August Lindberg, 3 June 1887.

16 Hans Riber Hunderup (1857–1902). Staged *The Father* at the Casino Theatre, Copenhagen, in 1887.

17 To the Editor, *Dagens Nyheter*, 15 August 1887.

18 David Norrman, *Strindbergs skilsmässa från Siri von Essen*, Stockholm, 1953, pp. 26–7.

19 Knud Pontoppidan (1853–1916). Danish physician and pioneering psychiatrist who aroused such controversy that he finally retired from the field to become professor of forensic medicine at Copenhagen University. He treated Amalie Skram who drew a picture of him as Professor Hieronimus in her autobiographical novel of that name published 1895.

20 To Axel Lundegård, 12 November 1887.

21 Karin Smirnoff, *Så var det i verkligheten*, Albert Bonniers Förlag, Stockholm, 1956, p. 205.

22 Edgar Allan Poe, *The Fall of the House of Usher and Other Writings*, Penguin, Harmondsworth, 1986, p. 194.

23 To Johan Oscar Strindberg, 20 March 1888.

24 *Dagens Nyheter*, Stockholm, 18 March 1889.

25 To Siri, 5 May 1889.

26 Smirnoff, *Strindbergs förste hustru*, p. 164.

27 To Karl Nordström, 30 January 1891.

11 The Black Piglet

1 Adolf Paul, *Min Strindbergsbok*, Norstedt, Stockholm, 1930, p. 39.

2 Ola Hansson (1860–1925) married to Laura Marholm (1854–1928). Following the acrimonious break in their relationship, Hansson portrayed Strindberg as the painter Ödmann in his novel *Mrs Ester Bruce*.

3 Carl Ludwig Schleich, *Those Were Good Days!* p. 202.

4 Adolf Paul (1863–1943). Finnish-Swedish pianist and writer whose work was influenced by Strindberg. During their short association in Berlin, Paul seems to have been conflicted between pride at his association with the great man and resentment, masochistically enjoyed. In 1914, with the subject safely dead, he published his memoirs of this time in *Min Strindbergsbok* (*My Strindberg Book*) and expanded it in the edition of 1930.

5 Paul, *Min Strindbergsbok*, p. 53.

6   Stanislaw Przybyszewski, *Erinnerungen an das literarische Berlin*, Winkler Verlag, Berlin, 1965, p. 190.

7   See Strindberg's essay 'New Directions in Art! Or Chance in the Creative Process' written in French and first published in *Revue des revues*, 15 November 1894. Frequently re-published since.

8   Stanislaw Przybyszewski (1868–1927). Polish novelist and playwright, author of *Chopin and Nietzsche* (1891), *Ola Hansson* (1892) and *Totenmesse* (1893). Later, leader of the New Poland movement and author of *Homo Sapiens* (1894–6), a trilogy of novels on the Berlin period in which Strindberg figures as the painter Iltis. Painted by Edvard Munch several times.

9   August Strindberg, *The Cloister*, p. 20.

10   Carl Ludwig Schleich (1859–1922). Medical doctor, professor at University of Berlin 1889 and later director of the department of Surgery at Gross-Lichterfelde. Introduced infiltration anaesthesia by cocaine solution. Wrote numerous books including a treatise on hysteria, novels and memoirs.

11   Otto Erich Hartleben (1864–1905).

12   Schleich, *Those Were Good Days!* pp. 204–5.

13   *The Cloister*, p. 118.

14   Friedrich Nietzsche, *Die fröhliche Wissenschaft*, III.108(1882), Wilhelm Goldmann, Munich, 1994.

15   Knut Hamsun, *The Unconscious Life of the Soul*, Samtiden, Oslo, 1890.

16   Dr Max Asch (1863–1944) met Przybyszewski when they were both studying medicine in Berlin. See Munch, *Dr Max Asch*, drypoint on copperplate, in the Meier-Graefe portfolio published in 1895.

17   Edvard Munch (1863–1944). Norwegian Expressionist artist and writer.

18   Strindberg, *Inferno*, p. 82.

19   To Per Hasselberg from Dalarö dated 15 August and 10(?) September 1892.

20   Ernst Haeckel (1834–1919). Visionary natural historian, anthropologist and philosopher whose philosophy was set out in illustrated books.

21   *Inferno*, p. 10.

22   Edvard Munch, *The Scream*, 1893, tempera and crayon on unprimed cardboard. Nasjonalmuseet for kunst, arkitektur og design, Oslo. Annotated upper left in pencil: 'Can only have been painted by a madman'.

23   Munch, *Stanislaw Przybyszewski*, 1894, casein and distemper on canvas, Munch Museum, Oslo.

24   Adolf Paul, *Berliner Tagblatt*, 15 April 1927. Munch, *Vampire*, 1893, oil on canvas, Göteborgs Konstmuseum. There are several later versions.

25   The same actors who had played in *Miss Julie* at the Freie Bühne also played in *Creditors*. Rosa Bertens played Julie and Tekla, Rudolf Rittner played Jean and Adolf. Josef Jarno played Gustav.

26 Stanislaw Przybyszewski, *Totenmesse*, Berlin, 1893, p. 17.

27 Maria Friederike Cornelia Uhl (1872–1943). Strindberg's second wife. Their daughter Kerstin was born in 1894. Frida Strindberg wrote an entertainingly unreliable account of her marriage to Strindberg in *Marriage with Genius*, Jonathan Cape, London, 1937.

28 *Ibid.* p. 244.

29 Romain Coolus (1868–1952).

30 André Antoine, *Memories of the Théâtre Libre*, trans. Marvin Carlson, University of Miami, Miami, 1964, p. 216. Also Edmond de Goncourt, *Journal*, Oxford University Press, 1978, entries for 16 and 19 January 1893.

31 Antoine, *Memories*, p. 216.

32 *The Cloister* p. 34.

33 *Ibid.* p. 35.

34 *Ibid.* p. 38.

35 Frida Strindberg, *Marriage with Genius*, p. 43.

36 Severin Segelcke (1867–1940). Norwegian painter who studied in Paris. Undistinguished naturalist who painted landscapes and portraits.

37 Frida Strindberg, *Marriage with Genius* p. 316.

38 Julius Meier-Graefe quoted in Ragna Stang, *Edvard Munch*, Abbeville Press, New York, 1977, p. 84.

39 Paul, *Min Strindbergsbok*, p. 92.

40 *Ibid.* pp. 95–9.

41 Rudolf Weyr (1847–1914). Viennese sculptor.

42 Mitzi Wehr quoted in Meyer, *Strindberg: A Biography*, pp. 269–71.

43 The Heligoland-Zanzibar Treaty of 1890.

44 Paul, *Min Strindbergsbok*, p. 101.

45 Frida Strindberg, *Marriage with Genius* pp. 154–63.

12 Frida, No Stranger to Drama

1 *The Fortnightly Review*, September 1892.

2 William Heinemann (1863–1920). Established the publishing house in 1890.

3 Jacob (Jack) Grein (1862–1935). Dutchman naturalised in England in 1892. Began as a critic. Wrote five interesting volumes, *Dramatic Criticism*, covering the years 1898–1903. Launched the Independent Theatre in 1891.

4 George Bernard Shaw, *Widowers' Houses*, staged in 1891.

5 *The Cloister*, p. 66.

6 Frida Strindberg, *Marriage with Genius*, p. 163. Frida says that the famous Green Sack was of flannel but Strindberg describes it as being made of canvas.

7 They stayed at 12 Pelham Road, Gravesend.

8   Letter dated 1 July 1893, concerning the pirated Swedish publication, to Fritz Kjerrman (1858–1896), a journalist at *Dagens Nyheter* which had announced that *Budkaflen* would be publishing the book.

9   *The Cloister*, p. 71.

10   Then 84 Warwick Street, Eccleston Square, London S.W., now Warwick Way.

11   To Marie Weyr, 22 July 1893.

12   To Frida, 7 August 1893.

13   Karl August Tavastjerna (1860–1898).

14   Bengt Lidforss (1868–1913).

15   To Birger Mörner, 9 May 1893.

16   *The Cloister*, p. 104.

17   This is a theory advanced by Torsten Ecklund, who edited Strindberg's letters.

18   It is often called Dornach Castle but this is wrong. The towers and battlements are later than Strindberg's day, as is the blinding yellow paint. There is a castle: Burg Clam, fine and ancient, on the hill above the Reischl Manor House, about 20 minutes walk up the gorge at Clam.

19   Two reproductions of Turners were found among his papers on his death and once, in an interview published in *Svenska Dagbladet* on the day of his funeral, 19 May 1912, he said that Turner was his favourite artist. During this time at Dornach he painted *The Danube in Flood*, 1894, oil on panel, private collection; *The Verdant Island I & II*, 1894, oil on cardboard, Strindberg Museum, Stockholm; *Wonderland*, 1894, oil on cardboard, Nationalmuseum, Stockholm.

20   To Leopold Littmansson, 14 August 1894.

21   Leopold Littmansson (1847–1908). Son of a cantor in the Jewish community in Stockholm. Spent summer 1872 with Strindberg on Kymmendö. Married a wealthy Frenchwoman, lived in Versailles and supported Strindberg during his time in Paris.

22   To Littmansson, 15 July 1894.

23   The piano can now be seen and played in the Strindberg Museum in Grein, on the Danube.

24   Ola Hansson in *Fru Ester Bruce* (1893).

25   To Adolf Paul, 14 May 1894.

26   Lidforss to Strindberg, 20 December 1892.

27   *Strindberg and Science*, published in *Dagens Nyheter*, 13 April 1894.

28   To Adolf Paul, 14 May 1894.

29   See Lagerkrantz, *August Strindberg*, p. 253.

30   *The Cloister*, pp. 129–31.

31   Smirnoff in Eklund and Björn, *August Strindbergs brev*, vol. x, pp. 49–50n.

32 To Littmansson, 14 July 1894.

33 To Richard Bergh, 9 July 1894.

34 To Littmansson, 14 August 1894.

35 To Frida, 11 September 1894.

13 French Vivisections

1 Edmond de Goncourt, *Journal*, entry for 20 December 1894.

2 From the introduction to *Somnambulist Nights*, 1884.

3 Albert Langen (1869–1909). German publisher specialising in Scandinavian literature. Founder of the satirical journal *Simplicissimus*.

4 Henri Becque (1837–1899). French dramatist.

5 To Frida, 29 August 1894.

6 Willy Pederson or Peterson, alias Grétor (1868–1923). Danish painter, rogue and confidence trickster.

7 To Frida, 9 September 1894.

8 Martinus, *Strindberg and Love*, p. 177.

9 'Césarine' in *Le Figaro*, 30 September 1894.

10 *Horizon*, London, November 1942, p. 127. Augustus John, *Chiaroscuro*, London, 1952, p. 116. Richard Cork is the authority on the Golden Calf. See his article in *The Times*, 31 December 1998 and *Wild Thing: Epstein, Gaudier-Brzeska, Gill*, Royal Academy of Arts, London, 2010.

11 Georg Brandes quoted in Martinus, *Strindberg and Love*, p. 187.

12 *Inferno*, pp. 119–20.

13 Frederick Delius (1862–1934). Composer born in England of Scandinavian-German descent. After 1890 lived almost entirely in France.

14 Gérard Encausse (1865–1916). Physician, hypnotist and occultist. The book was *Anatomie et physiologie de l'orchestre*, Paris, 1894.

15 To William Molard, 27 January 1910.

16 Paul Gauguin to Mette Gauguin, from Martinique, August 1887.

17 Reviews quoted in Meyer, *Strindberg: A Biography*, pp. 310–12.

18 Professor Henri Hallopeau (1842–1919). Eminent dermatologist who probably coined the word 'anti-biotic'.

19 His psoriasis can be dated from a letter written on 19 June 1891 to Vult von Steijen: 'To my children's guardian. The skin complaint affecting my hands which Dr Anton Nyström has treated for three years can in no way be described of a syphilitic nature.'

20 *Inferno*, p. 257.

21 *Ibid.* p. 125.

22 To Paul Gauguin, early February 1895. Gauguin's reply is dated 5 February.

23   Knut Hamsun to Adolf Paul, 19 March 1895.

24   Strindberg to Hamsun, 6 April 1895.

25   Jung quoted in Anthony Storr, *The Essential Jung*, Princeton University Press, 1983, p. 284.

26   *La Paix*, 19 January 1883 quoted in Meyer, *Strindberg: A Biography*, p. 334.

27   Johannes Jörgensen (1886–1956). Danish poet quoted in Jan Verklade, *Le Tourment de Dieu*, Paris, Librairie de L'Art Catholique, 1926, pp. 83–4.

28   To Torsten Hedlund, 11 July 1896.

29   'L'Iode comme un dérivé de houilles', reprinted in *Le Moniteur industriel*, 8 June 1895.

30   Denis Brian, *The Curies: A Biography of the Most Controversial Family in Science*, John Wiley and Sons, Chichester, 2005, p. 91.

31   Sir William Crookes (1832–1919). Improved vacuum tubes, electric lighting and invented the radiometer (1873–6). Founded *Chemical News* (1859). Wrote on Spiritism and joined the Society for Psychical Research.

32   Sir Oliver Lodge (1851–1940). Professor of physics at Liverpool. First Principal of the new University of Birmingham. Demonstrated that radio frequency waves could be transmitted along electric wires. Known for his efforts in reconciling the ideas of science, religion and the paranormal.

33   Taken from Frederick Delius, 'Recollections of Strindberg', *The Sackbut*, December 1920.

14   *Inferno*

1   Mathieu Orfila (1787–1853). Sometimes called the father of toxicology. Published copious studies of poisons.

2   *Inferno*, p. 134.

3   The Hôtel Orfila was owned and run by M. and Mme Ginguet. Room and service cost 40 fr a month. Strindberg was served breakfast for 66 fr a month and he took his evening meal at Mme Charlotte's *crèmerie*. All this was paid for by August Röhss (1836–1904) who donated 1,200 kr in monthly instalments from March to July 1896, through Strindberg's Swedenborgian admirer Torsten Hedlund.

4   The recipe and the cigar advice are both contained in a letter to Anders Eliasson of 23 April 1896.

5   Some, led by the Symbolist painter Emile Bernard, were striving towards the foundation of a modern, occult school of Athens. Unpublished letter to Emile Schuffenecker from Bernard, 6 October 1891.

6   Strindberg called Huysmans 'Zola's great successor' in a letter to Eliasson, 1 December 1896.

7   Shah Nasreddin (1831–1896) was killed by an anarchist. Oskar von Vegesack (1837–1896) died while visiting Paris with the Swedish king.

8   To Torsten Hedlund, 20 August 1896.

9   Anna Philp quoted in Lagerkrantz, *August Strindberg*, p.274.

10   Munch's exhibition ran from 19 May 1896 and included 12 paintings, 6 drawings and 42 prints.

11   Siegfried 'Samuel' Bing (1838–1905).

12   1 April – 31 May 1896, catalogue in the Munch Museum, Oslo.

13   To Georg Brandes, in Eklund and Meidal, *Strindbergs brev*, vol. x, pp. 107–8, cited in *Eros and Psyche*, ch. 11, n. 14.

14   Strindberg's review of Munch's exhibition in *La Revue blanche*, vol. x, 1 June 1896.

15   *Les Etats profonds de l'hypnose* (1892) and *L'Extériorisation de la sensibilité* (1895) both by Albert Rochas d'Aiglun (1837–1914), French military administrator.

16   Madame Charlotte interviewed in *Verdens Gang*, 29 November 1898.

17   *Peer Gynt*, Act IV Scene in Gizah, lines 5–8. This interesting connection through the word *stind* is pointed out by Reidar Dittmann in *Eros and Psyche*, p. 138. Though speculation, it seems worth including as both the lithograph and the break between Strindberg and Munch are important.

18   Munch, *Strindberg på hospitalet*, 1896, lithograph.

19   *Inferno*, pp. 194–5.

20   Eklund and Meidal, *Strindbergs brev*, vol. xi, p. 278.

21   To Torsten Hedlund, 26 June 1896.

22   Max von Pettenkoffer (1818–1901). Bavarian chemist important in the establishment of scientific hygiene by his study of the movement of air through permeable clothing, walls and floors.

23   August Strindberg, *In the Cemetery* (1896) and *Jardin des Plantes* (1896).

24   To Hedlund, 19 July 1896.

25   *Ibid.*

26   Frits Thaulow (1847–1906). Norwegian landscape painter.

27   Anders Eliasson (1844–1900). Swedish doctor.

28   *Inferno*, p. 206.

29   *Ibid.*

30   *Ibid.* p. 221.

15   Out of Inferno

1   At this time Strindberg took particular note of Swedenborg's *Arcana Coelestia* and *Apocalypsis Revelata*.

2   The gorge at Clam was renamed Strindberg Weg in 1949. It can be

walked. The castle holds an exhibition of alchemists' paraphernalia in his honour, and the houses in which he lived in the village of Saxen can still be seen.

3   Marie Uhl in Ahlström, *Ögonvittnen*, vol. II, pp. 113–15.

4   To Torsten Hedlund, 26 September 1896.

5   To Hedlund, 20 July 1896.

6   Dr Lars Nilsson (1855–1933). They had first met in Skurup in 1891.

7   To Kerstin Strindberg, 4 May 1897.

8   Marcel Réja (1873–1957). See Munch's woodcut of Réja (1896–7), Munch Museum, Oslo.

9   Marcel Réja's reminiscences of Strindberg are 'Strindberg genom franska psykiaterögon' ('Strindberg through the eyes of a French Psychiatrist'), *Göteborgs Handels- och Sjöfartstidning*, 1 May 1914, and *Souvenirs de Strindberg* in the French edition of *Inferno* (1966).

10   Eugène Fahlstedt (1851–1935). Member of the Runa society founded by Strindberg in 1870, he was familiar with Strindberg's literary style from university days. He also translated *Fables*, *Legends* and *Getting Married II* into Swedish and *Tschandala* back into Swedish from Danish when the Swedish original was lost.

11   Henrik Ibsen on *Inferno* in *Aftonbladet*, 13 April 1898.

12   Salomon August Andrée (1854–1897) led an expedition by hydrogen balloon to reach the North Pole. He and his companions Nils Strindberg (1872–1897) and Knut Fraenkel (1870–1897) were all killed.

13   To Karin, Hans and Greta, 26 December 1898.

14   To Karin, 20 June 1898.

15   To Axel Herrlin (1870–1937), philosopher and psychologist. Letter dated 31 January 1898.

16   To Herrlin, 10 March 1898.

17   To Gustaf af Geijerstam, 8 March 1898.

18   To Kerstin, 29 August 1898.

19   To Emil Scherring, January 1898.

20   Albert Ranft (1858–1938). Actor and theatre manager, director of the Royal Theatre, 1908–11.

21   To Karin, Greta and Hans, 19 December 1899.

22   Harriet Bosse, introduction to *Letters of Strindberg to Harriet Bosse: Love Letters from a Tormented Genius*, ed. and trans. Arvid Paulson, Grosset and Dunlap, New York, 1959.

16   Harriet Bosse

1   The entry reads '31, Besök af Fröken Bosse, 1ste gangen.' The line is cramped in between the entry for 30 May and 1 June and the words *1ste gangen*

(the first time) may imply that he put in the entry later when he realised the significance of their relationship, or he might have written it there and then in knowledge or hope that there would be a second.

2   *Occult Diary*, September 1901.

3   To Harriet Bosse, c.20 October 1901. To Emil Scherring, 5 March 1901.

4   Arvid Paulson, *Letters of Strindberg to Harriet Bosse*, p. 41.

5   Johan Fahlström. After Harriet left Oslo (Kristiania)' she never visited her sister and brother-in-law again and when, many years later, she returned as a famous actress to Norway, she was not invited to their home.

6   Maurice de Féraudy (1859–1932). French actor and songwriter.

7   Paulson, *Letters of Strindberg to Harriet Bosse*, p. 15.

8   *Ibid.* p. 17.

9   Harriet says that they did not see each other again until December but Strindberg's *Occult Diary* marks an entry in July when she calls on him to say she will play the part in *To Damascus*. It is the briefest of visits, with her sister waiting in the carriage.

10   *Occult Diary*, 15 July 1900. He used this later in the novel *Ensam (Alone)*, 1903.

11   Literally, 'It's sad about human beings', but this word-for-word translation goes no way at all to translate the grandeur of the sentiment in the original language.

12   Harriet Bosse to Strindberg, 4 March 1901.

13   Paulson, *Letters of Strindberg to Harriet Bosse*, p. 26.

14   *Occult Diary*, 2 June 1904.

15   Paulson, *Letters of Strindberg to Harriet Bosse*, p. 41.

16   *Ibid.* p. 42.

17   *Ibid.* p. 46.

18   Harriet Bosse to Strindberg, 27 August 1901.

19   Paulson, *Letters of Strindberg to Harriet Bosse*, p. 81.

20   To Harriet Bosse, 8 June 1904.

17   The Intimate Theatre

1   Gustaf Uddgren (1865–1927). Author of the memoir *Strindberg the Man*, Four Seasons Press, Boston, Mass., 1920, p. 106.

2   *Ibid.* pp. 109–17.

3   *Ibid.* pp. 106–7.

4   To Emil Schering, 2 April 1907.

5   Herman Anderson (1856–1909). Photographer.

6   August Falck, *Fem år med Strindberg*. Wahlström & Widstrand, Stockholm, 1935, pp. 74–5.

7   Carl Eldh (1873–1954). Sculptor. Executed four busts of Strindberg and the Strindberg monument at Tegnérlunden, close to the Blue Tower. While studying in Paris, Eldh had frequented Madame Charlotte's *crèmerie*.

8   August Palme (1856–1924). Actor.

9   To Tor Aulin, 20 and 28 January 1908.

10   'Little Zachris, called Cinnober' alludes to E. T. A. Hoffmann's story 'Klein Zaches, gennant Zinnober' (1819) and the popular song from Offenbach's *Les Contes de Hoffmann*.

11   'Ett halvt ark papir' published in *Midsummer Day and Other Tales* (1903).

12   Karl Börjesson (1877–1941). Publisher and bookseller. Published *Black Banners, A Blue Book, Open Letters to the Intimate Theatre, The Last Knight, The Regent, The Earl of Bjälbo, China and Japan* and *The Origin of the Chinese Language*.

13   *A Blue Book* (1907).

14   Anders Zorn (1860–1920). Swedish painter and sculptor.

15   Carl Larsson to Richard Bergh, 5 November 1911.

16   Written over 1906–12 and eventually published in four volumes.

17   To Karl Börjesson, 20? November 1908.

18   Max Reinhardt, born Max Goldmann (1873–1943). A shy actor before turning to theatre direction at the Kleines Theater in Berlin in 1902. Co-founder of the Salzburg Festival (1920), he left Germany in 1933 for Hollywood.

19   From Strindberg's introduction to *Open Letters to the Intimate Theatre* (1907–8).

20   Amanda (Manda) Björling (1876–1960). Married August Falck in 1909 and appeared in numerous productions at Strindberg's Intimate Theatre between 1907 and 1911. Roles included Queen Kristina, Miss Julie, Laura in *The Father*, Tekla in *Creditors*, Alice in *The Dance of Death*, Henriette in *Crimes and Crimes*, Mélisande and the title role in *Hedda Gabler*.

21   To August Falck, 14 November 1907.

22   Falck, *Fem år med Strindberg*, p. 20.

23   Arnold Böcklin (1827–1901). Swiss symbolist painter.

24   Published in 1907 and 1908 as a series of brochures. Since reprinted in many languages.

25   In a letter to his brother Axel, dated 29 November 1907, Strindberg acknowledges Axel's understanding that the mother in the play is based on their sister Anna von Philp. The daughter's marriage to a man with whom the mother is conducting an affair probably refers to his niece Märta Philp's marriage later that year to Hugo Fröding.

26   Strindberg had not met the actor Ivar Nilsson who played Master Olof

but he wrote to him: 'Play the role as I have written it and you will succeed! He is no elegiac Hamlet, but an angry man. His speech is always arrogant . . . Master Olof has been called our Luther and like the latter, he was a bear on every path . . . why won't you call on me?' the letter ends, 'Or at least let me know whether you have received my letters.' Nilsson did call, became a friend and an occasional Beethoven Boy. He also played the officer in Reinhardt's celebrated 1921 production of *A Dream Play*.

27   Kunglige Teatern, Svenska Teatern, Oscars-Teatern, Vasa Teatern, Sodra Teatern, Östermalms Teatern and Djurgårds Teatern. At this time, Ranft was widely tipped to take control of Dramaten as well.

28   To Falck, 30 March 1908.

29   Fanny Falkner, *Strindberg i Blå Tornet* (*Strindberg in the Blue Tower*), quoted in Martinus, *Strindberg and Love*, p. 265.

30   Fanny Falkner (1891–1963). Painter and actress.

31   Alrik Kjellgren (1883–1964). Actor. Played Benjamin in *Easter* opposite Anna Flygare as well as Fanny Falkner at the Intimate Theatre.

32   Stella Falkner-Söderberg, *Fanny Falkner och August Strindberg*, Stockholm, 1970, pp. 21–2.

18   The Blue Tower

1   To Nils Andersson, July 1908.

2   Fanny's parents Meta and Frank Nilsson, singers. Meta was Danish, Frans was Swedish. They changed their name to Falkner some time in the 1890s.

3   Memo headed *Regulations*, August 1908, in Robinson, *Strindberg's Letters*, vol. II, p. 797.

4   Postcard from George Bernard Shaw to William Archer cited in Meyer, *Strindberg: A Biography*, p. 514.

5   Shaw interviewed in the *Baltimore Sun*, 4 March 1928, cited in *ibid.*

6   Author's Note to *A Dream Play* published together with the play about 1 June 1902.

7   Edward Gordon Craig interviewed in *The Listener*, 1956.

8   August Strindberg quoted in Isadora Duncan, *My Life*, London, 1966, p. 203.

9   Kunglige Dramatiska Teatern, *Siste riddaren*; Svenska Teatern, *Gustaf Vasa*; Östermalmsteatern, *Lycko-Pers resa*; Intima Teatern, *Brott och brott*; Viktoriasalen, *Strindbergsafton*; Socialist-Demokraten Ungdomsklubbarnas, *Strindbergsfest*; Stockholms Socialistiska Ungdomsklubbar, *Strindbergsdikter*.

10   To Karl Otto Bonnier, 6 July 1909.

11   To Meta Falkner, 12 June 1909.

12   From Frida to August Strindberg, n.d. 1907.

13   *Neues Wiener Journal*, 26 January 1908.

14   To Marie Uhl, 20 December 1909.

15   To Kerstin Strindberg, 5 September 1909.

16   To Fanny Falkner, August 1909.

17   Falkner-Söderberg, *Falkner och Strindberg*, pp. 116–17.

18   *Ibid.* pp. 122–4.

19   Wingård shot himself a few months after Strindberg's death in 1912.

20   Stella Falkner in Falkner p. 106, quoted in Meyer, *Strindberg: A Biograghy*, p. 540.

21   Fredrik Ström, director of the Young Social Democrats' publishing house Fram.

22   Ström quoted in Meyer, *Strindberg: A Biograghy*, p. 541.

23   Schleich, *Those Were Good Days!* pp. 220–22.

24   Smirnoff, *Strindbergs første hustru*, p. 221.

25   Anton Nilsson (1887–1989). Political agitator, later a Communist. His fellow bombers were Algot Rosberg, also sentenced to death, and Alfred Stern, given life imprisonment.

26   Philp and Hartzell, *Strindbergs systrar*, p. 90.

27   Letter dated some time in June 1910, to Valfrid Spångberg (1871–1946). Founder of *Afton-Tidning*.

28   To Birger Mörner, 7 December 1911.

29   To Richard Bergh, 17 January 1912, suggesting that Bergh approach Branting.

30   *Dagens Nyheter*, 23 January 1912.

31   Smirnoff, *Strindbergs forste hustru*, p. 223.

32   Fanny continued to live with her family and make a living as an artist, painting porcelain and miniatures. An affair with an army officer ended in tragedy when they made a suicide pact. He succeeded in shooting himself but she survived taking poison. After a failed marriage she settled in Copenhagen where she made a shrine to Strindberg. In 1920 she wrote *Strindberg i Blå Tornet*. In 1957 she was present at the fiftieth anniversary of the opening of the Intimate Theatre. In 1963 she committed suicide. 'He's a person you'll never be free from. He is always present', she said in 1957 on the occasion of the Intimate Theatre's anniversary.

33   Bosse in *Strindbergs brev til Harriet Bosse*, Stockholm, 1932, p. 311.

34   Account by his nurse Hedvig Kistner, cited in Ahlström, *Ögonvittnen*, pp. 293–5.

SELECT BIBLIOGRAPHY

Ahlström, Stellan, ed., *Ögonvittnen:August Strindberg*, vols I and II, Wahlström & Widstrand, Stockholm, 1959 and 1961.

—, *Strindbergs erövring av Paris*, Almqvist & Wiksell, Stockholm, 1956.

Antoine, André, *Memoires of the Théâtre Libre*, trans. Marvin Carlson, Miami, 1964.

Bergquist, Lars, *Swedenborg's Secret*, Swedenborg Society, London, 2005.

Brandell, Gunnar, *Strindberg in Inferno*, trans. Barry Jacobs, Harvard University Press, Boston, Mass., 1974.

Brandes, Georg, *Selected Letters*, trans. W. Glynn Jones, Norvik Press, Norwich, 1990.

Breidbach, Olaf, *Visions of Nature: The Art and Science of Ernst Haeckel*, Prestel, Munich and London, 2006.

Buchmayr, Friedrich, *Wenn nein, nein! August Strindberg und Frida Uhl briefwechsel 1893–1902*, Bibliothek der Provinz, Austria, 1993.

Carlson, Harry G., *Out of Inferno: Strindberg's Reawakening as an Artist*, University of Washington Press, 1996.

Champion, Jean-Loup, ed., *The Perfect Medium: Photography and the Occult*, Yale University Press, New Haven and London, 2005.

Cork, Richard, *Wild Thing: Epstein, Gaudier-Brzeska, Gill*, Royal Academy of Arts, London, 2010.

Dahlbäck, Lars, ed., *Samlade Verk*, 72 vols, Almqvist & Wiksell, Stockholm, 1981–.

Didi-Huberman, Georges, *Invention of Hysteria*, trans. Alisa Hartz, MIT Press, 2003.

Eklund, Torsten, and Björn Meidal, eds, *August Strindbergs brev*, 22 vols, Albert Bonniers Förlag, Stockholm, 1948–2001.

Falck, August, *Fem år med Strindberg*, Wahlström & Widstrand, Stockholm, 1935.

Granath Olle, ed., *August Strindberg, Painter, Photographer, Writer*, Tate, London, 2001.

Hamsun, Knut, *Selected Letters*, trans. Harald Naess and James MacFarlane, Norvik Press, Norwich, 1990.

Hedström, Per, ed., *Strindberg: Painter and Photographer*, Yale University Press, New Haven and London, 2001.

Hemmingson, Per, *August Strindberg som fotograf*, Kalejdoskop Förlag, Göteborg, 1989.

Jacobsen, Harry, *Digteren og Fantasten*, Gyldendal, Copenhagen, 1945.

Kossowski, Lukasz, ed., *Totenmesse: Munch − Weiss − Przybyszewski*, Muzeum Literatury im. Adama Mickiewicza, Warsaw, 1995.

Lagerkrantz, Olof, *August Strindberg*, trans. Anselm Hollo, Farrar Straus Giroux, New York, 1985.

Lalander, Agneta, ed., *Strindberg og Fotokunsten*, Jydsk Centraltrykkeri, Aarhus, 1996.

Lamm, Martin, *August Strindberg*, trans. and ed. Harry G. Carlson, 2 vols, New York, 1971.

Landquist, John, ed., *Samlade Skrifter*, 55 vols, Albert Bonniers Förlag, Stockholm, 1912−20.

Leblanc, Georgette, *Souvenirs: My Life with Maeterlinck*, E. P. Dutton, New York, 1932.

Lindqvist, Herman, *A History of Sweden*, trans. Roy Bradbury, Norstedts Förlag, Stockholm, 2002.

Lishaugen, Roar, *Dagny Juel: Tro, håp og undergang*, Andreson & Butenschøn, Oslo, 2002.

Lundegård, Axel, *Några Strindbergsminnen knutna till en handfull brev*, Tidens Förlag, Stockholm, 1920.

Martinus, Eivor, *Strindberg and Love*, Amber Lane, 2001.

Meidal, Björn, *Goddag, mit barn!* P. P. Förlag, Copenhagen, 2003.

Meyer, Christian, *Strindberg, Schönberg, Munch: nordische Moderne in Schönbergs Wien um 1900*, Arnold Schönberg Center, Vienna, 2008.

Meyer, Michael, *Strindberg: A Biography*, Random House, New York, 1985.

Paul, Adolf, *Min Strindbergsbok*, Norstedt & Sonners Förlag, Stockholm, 1930.

Paulson, Arvid, ed. and trans., *Letters of Strindberg to Harriet Bosse: Love Letters from a Tormented Genius*, Grosset and Dunlap, New York, 1959.

Philp, Anna, and Nora Hartzell, *Strindbergs systrar berätter om barndomshemmet och om bror August*, P. A. Norstedt & Sonners Förlag, Stockholm, 1926.

Robinson, Michael, MHRA Bibliographies (4), *Strindberg Studies 1870–2005*, *Volume One: General Studies; Volume Two: The Plays; Volume Three: Prose and*

Miscellaneous, Modern Humanities Research Association, London, 2008.

—, *Strindberg and Autobiography: Writing and Reading a Life*, Norvik Press, Norwich, 1986.

—, *Strindberg's Letters*, vols I and II, University of Chicago Press, 1992.

—, ed., *The Cambridge Companion to August Strindberg*, Cambridge University Press, 2009.

Schleich, Carl Ludwig, *Those Were Good Days!* W. W. Norton, New York, 1936.

Smirnoff, Karin, *Så var det i verkligheten*, Albert Bonniers Förlag, Stockholm, 1956.

—, *Strindbergs første hustru*, Poul Branners Förlag, Copenhagen, 1948.

Sommar, Carl Olov, *Strindberg på Östermalm*, Billbergs, Stockholm, 1980.

Strindberg, August, *Ockulta Dagboken*, facsimile edition, Albert Bonniers Förlag, Stockholm, 1977.

Strindberg, Frida, *Marriage with Genius*, Jonathan Cape, London, 1937.

Swerling, Anthony, *Strindberg's Impact in France 1920–1960*, Trinity Lane Press, Cambridge, 1971.

Wennberg, Kåa, *Strindberg på Brevik*, Bohuslaningens Boktrykeri, Sweden, 1994.

STRINDBERG'S PRINCIPAL LITERARY WORKS

Plays

Fritänkaren (1869) The Freethinker
Den sjunkande Hellas (1870) Greece in Decline
Hermione (1870) Hermione
I Rom (1870) In Rome
Den fredlöse (1871) The Outlaw
Mäster Olof (1872–7) Master Olof
Anno fyrtioåtta (1876–7) The Year '48
Gillets hemlighet (1880) The Secret of the Guild
Lycko-Pers resa (1882) Lucky Peter's Journey
Herr Bengts hustru (1882) Sir Bengt's Wife
Marodörer/Kamraterna (1886–7) Marauders/Comrades
Fadren (1887) The Father
Fröken Julie (1888) Miss Julie
Fordringsägare (1888) Creditors
Den starkare (1888–9) The Stronger
Paria (1889) Pariah
Hemsöborna (1889) The People of Hemsö
Samum (1889) Simoon
Himmelrikets nycklar (1892) The Keys of Heaven
Debet och kredit (1892) Debit and Credit
Första varningen (1892) The First Warning
Inför döden (1892) Facing Death
Moderskärlek (1892) Motherly Love
Leka med elden (1892) Playing with Fire
Bandet (1892) The Bond
Till Damaskus I, II, III (1898–1901) To Damascus parts I, II and III

Advent (1898) Advent
Brott och brott (1899) Crimes and Crimes
Folkungasagan (1899) The Saga of the Folkungs
Gustav Vasa (1899) Gustav Vasa
Erik xiv (1899) Erik xiv
Gustav Adolf (1900) Gustav Adolf
Midsommar (1900) Midsummer
Kaspers Fet-Tisdag (1900) Casper's Shrove Tuesday
Påsk (1900) Easter
Dödsdansen I, II (1900) The Dance of Death, parts I and II
Kronbruden (1901) The Crown Bride
Svanevit (1901) Swanwhite
Karl xii (1901) Karl xii
Engelbrekt (1901) Engelbrekt
Kristina (1901) Queen Christina
Et drömspel (1901) A Dream Play
Gustav iii (1902) Gustav iii
Holländaren (1902) The Flying Dutchman
Näktergalen i Wittenberg (1903) The Nightingale of Wittenberg
Moses (1903) Moses
Sokrates (1903) Socrates
Kristus (1903) Christ
Oväder (1907) Storm
Brända tomten (1907) The Burned House
Spöksonaten (1907) The Ghost Sonata
Toten-Insel (1907) The Island of the Dead
Pelikanen (1907) The Pelican
Siste riddaren (1908) The Last Knight
Abu Cassems tofflor (1908) Abu Cassem's Slippers
Riksföreståndaren (1908) The Regent
Bjälbo-Jarlen (1909) The Earl of Bjälbo
Svarta handsken (1909) The Black Glove
Stora landsvägen (1909) The Great Highway
Homunculus (1918 posthumously) Homunculus
Starkodder Skald (1918 posthumously) Starkodder the Skald

On Drama and Acting

Öppna brev till Intima teatern (1907–8) Open Letters to the Intimate Theatre

Preface to *Miss Julie* (1888)
Author's Note to *A Dream Play* (1902 and addition 1907)

Autobiographies

Tjänstekvinnans son (1886–7) The Son of a Servant
Jäsningstiden (1886) Time of Ferment *or* The Growth of a Soul
I Röda rummet (1886, published 1887) In the Red Room
Författaren (1886, published 1909) The Author
Han och hon (1886, published 1919) He and She
Le Plaidoyer d'un fou (1887–8) A Madman's Defence
Inferno (1897) Inferno
Legender (1898) Legends
Jakob brottas (1898) Jacob Wrestles
Klosteret (1898, published 1966) The Cloister
Karantänmästarns andra berättelse (1902) The Quarantine Master's Second
Story
Ensam (1903) Alone
Ockulta dagboken (1896–1908, published 1977) The Occult Diary

Novels and Short Stories

Röda rummet (1879) The Red Room
Det nya riket (1882) The New Kingdom
Giftas I (1884) Getting Married
Giftas II (1885) Getting Married II
Utopier i verkligheten (1885) Utopias in Reality
Svenska öden och äventyr (1882–91) Swedish Destinies and Adventures
Hemsöborna (1887) The People of Hemsö
Skäkarlsliv (1888) Life in the Skerries
Tschandala (1888) Tschandala
I havsbandet (1890) By the Open Sea
Silverträsket (1898) The Silver Marsh
Sagor (1903) Fairy Tales
Götiska rummen (1904) Gothic Rooms
Historiska miniatyrer (1905) Historical Miniatures
Svarta fanor (1904–7) Black Banners
Taklagsöl (1906) The Roofing Feast
Nya svenska öden (1906) New Swedish Destinies

Syndabocken (1907) The Scapegoat
Armageddon (1908) Armageddon

Poetry

Dikter på vers och prosa (1883) Poems in Verse and Prose
Sömngångarnätter på vakna dagar (1884) Somnambulist Nights in Broad Daylight
Ordalek och småkonst (1905) Word Play and Minor Art

Non-fiction

POLITICAL

Om Det Allmänna Missnöjet: Dess Osaker och Botemedel (1884) On the General Discontent: Its Causes and Cures
Lilla katekes för underklassen (1884) A Little Catechism for the Underclass
Mitt Judehat (1884) My Anti-Semitism
Bland franska bönder (1886, published 1889) Among French Peasants
Sista ordet i kvinnofrågan (1886) Final Word on the Woman Question
Kvinnans underlägsenhet under mannen (1888) Woman's Inferiority to Man
Tal till svenska nationen (1910) Speeches to the Swedish Nation
Folkstaten (1910) The People's State
Religiös renässans (1910) Religious Renaissance
Tsarens kurir (1912) The Tsar's Courier

ALCHEMY, HISTORY, LINGUISTICS, NATURAL HISTORY, SCIENCE

Gamla Stockholm (1880–1) Old Stockholm
Kulturhistoriska studier (1881) Studies in Cultural History
Svenska folket (1881–2) The Swedish People
Vivisektioner (1887) Vivisections
Blomstermålningar och djur-stycken (1888) Flower Paintings and Animal Pieces
Antibarbarus (1893) Antibarbarus
Le soufre est-il un corps simple? (1895) Is Sulphur an Element?
L'Avenir du soufre (1895) The Future of Sulphur
Om Ljusvärkan vid fotografering (1896) On the Action of Light in Photography

Un Regard vers le ciel (1896) A Glance into Space
L'irradiation et l'extension de l'âme (1896) The Irradiation and Extension of the Soul
Synthèse d'or (1896) The Synthesis of Gold
Sylva Sylvarum (1896) Sylva Sylvarum
Jardin des Plantes (1896) Jardin des Plantes
Synthèse de l'iode (1897) The Synthesis of Iodine
Världshistoriens mystik (1903) The Mysticism of World History
En blå bok (1907) A Blue Book
En ny blå bok (1907) A New Blue Book
En blå bok, avdelning III (1908) A Blue Book, part III
Bibliska egennamn (1910) Biblical Proper Names
Modersmålets anor (1910) The Origins of our Mother Tongue
Världsspråkens rötter (1911) The Roots of World Languages
En blå bok, avdelning IV (1912) A Blue Book, part IV

ART

'Des arts nouveaux! Ou le hazard dans la production artistique', *La Revue des revues*, 15 November 1894 (1894) 'New Directions in Art! Or the Role of Chance in Artistic Creation'
Preface to the catalogue for Gauguin's auction at the Hôtel Drouot, 18 February 1895
'L'exposition Edvard Munch', *La Revue blanche*, 1 June 1896 (1896) 'Edvard Munch's Exhibition'

Letters

Some 10,000 letters are published in *August Strindbergs brev*, ed. Torsten Eklund and Björn Meidal, 22 vols, Albert Bonniers Förlag, Stockholm, 1948–2001

A wide selection of the letters may be read in English: *Strindberg's Letters*, vols I and II, selected, ed. and trans. Michael Robinson, Chicago University Press, 1992

CHRONOLOGY

1849   22 January Johan August Strindberg born at Riddarholmen, Stock-
            holm.

1856–67   Attends Klara school, 'a preparation not for life but for Hell', Jakob
            School and the Stockholm Lyceum.

1853   Father declared bankrupt.

1862   Mother dies.

1863   Father marries housekeeper, Emilia Charlotte Petersson.

1866   Tutoring. Reads Byron and Dickens. Religious thinking influenced
            by the American evangelical Theodore Parker. Ibsen writes *Brand*.

1867   To Uppsala University. Reads aesthetics and modern languages.
            Begins painting. Leaves university after a term. Ibsen writes *Peer
            Gynt*.

1868   Returns to Stockholm. Works as a teacher. Haeckel publishes *History
            of Creation*.

1869   Lives with Dr Lamm's family. Studies to become a doctor but fails
            chemistry examination. Takes up acting. Given a few walk-on parts
            at Dramaten. Writes first plays: *A Name-Day Gift* and *The Free-
            thinker*.

1870   Returns to Uppsala. Writes *Greece in Decline* (later called *Hermione*)
            and *In Rome*. Reads Kirkegaard.

1871   Writes *The Outlaw*. King Charles xv enjoys it and gives him a small
            grant. First Impressionist exhibition in Paris.

1872–3   Leaves Uppsala University with no examinations. Takes up journal-
            ism in Stockholm. Stays on the island of Kymmendö and completes
            first version of *Master Olof*. Studies telegraphy. First known painting,
            The Ruins of Tulborn Castle. The Red Room at Berns Salon becomes
            meeting place for intellectual circle. Darwin's *On the Origin of Species*
            translated into Swedish. Reads Georg Brandes's *Main Currents in
            Nineteenth Century Literature*. Interested in the nature of the uncon-

scious. Assists in translating Eduard von Hartmann's *Philosophy of the Unconscious*. R. L. Stevenson's *Dr Jekyll and Mr Hyde* published.

1874 Assistant librarian at the Stockholm Royal Library. Studies sinology and cartography.

1875 Meets Baron Carl Gustaf Wrangel and his wife Siri (née von Essen).

1876 First visit to Paris. Reports on Impressionists for Swedish newspaper. Rewrites *Master Olof*, this time in verse. It is once more rejected. Final quarrel with his father. Siri divorced.

1877 Siri's debut as an actress in January soon after the death of her daughter by Baron Wrangel. Marries Siri von Essen, 30 December. Ibsen writes *The Pillars of Society*.

1878 Daughter born 21 January. Dies two or three days later.

1879 Files for bankruptcy. Writes *The Red Room*, the first modern Swedish novel, a romp through Stockholm's bohemia. Widely read and enjoyed. Praised by Georg Brandes. Awarded silver medal of the Imperial Geographical Society in St Petersburg for cultural studies. Elected member of La Société des Etudes Japonaises, Chinoises, Tartars et Indo-chinoises in Paris for studies in the Royal Library. Ibsen writes *A Doll's House*.

1880 Daughter Karin born 26 February. Writes *The Secret of the Guild* which is put on at Dramaten with Siri as Margaretha.

1881 Daughter Greta born 9 June on Kymmendö. Close friendship with Carl Larsson who is illustrating Strindberg's two-volume history *The Swedish People*. It offends Sweden's establishment on publication. *Master Olof* staged at last (prose version). Ibsen writes *Ghosts*.

1882 Publishes *The New Kingdom*, a satire on Swedish society and institutions. Establishment further offended. Writes plays *Lucky Peter's Journey* and *Sir Bengt's Wife*, his answer to *A Doll's House*. Siri has rare stage success in title role of *Sir Bengt's Wife*. Ibsen writes *An Enemy of the People*.

1883 Leaves Sweden with family. Joins artists' colony in Grez-sur-Loing, France. Friendship with Bjørnstjerne Bjørnson and Jonas Lie in Paris. Travels in Switzerland, Bavaria, Denmark. Publishes *Poems in Verse and Prose*.

1884 Son Hans born 3 April. Stays in or near Geneva. Interest in Rousseau and Chernyshevsky. Contact with Russian anarchists. Writes long poem *Somnambulist Nights* and socialist essays. Visits Italy for the first time, Pegli and Genoa. *Getting Married* prosecuted for blasphemy. Returns to Sweden to stand trial. Acquitted. Returns to Switzerland. Ibsen writes *A Wild Duck*.

1885   Visits Venice and Rome with Verner von Heidenstam. Writes rabidly anti-feminist *Getting Married II* and idealistic political essays *Utopias in Reality*.

1886   Writes four volumes of autobiography, *The Son of a Servant*, *Time of Ferment*, *In the Red Room* and *The Author*. Photographic self-portraits. Travels France for *Among French Peasants*. Interested in psychological naturalism, hypnotism and suggestion. Reads Henry Maudsley, Théodule Ribot, Hippolyte Bernheim and Jean-Martin Charcot. Writes play *Comrades*, which later became the play *Marauders*. Théâtre Libre opens in Paris. Ibsen writes *Rosmersholm*.

1887   Writes 'battle of the brains' play *The Father* and comic novel masterpiece *The People of Hemsö*. Writes *Vivisections*, essays on psychological states. En route to Copenhagen consults Knud Pontoppidan on his sanity. 14 November *The Father* opens at Casino Theatre, Copenhagen, with Georg Brandes directing. Victoria Benedictsson attempts suicide. The future bishop John Personne accuses Strindberg of corrupting youth in *Strindbergian Literature and Immorality among Schoolchildren*.

1888   To Taarbeck. Marriage under strain. Writes *Le Plaidoyer d'un fou* novelising his disintegrating marriage. Writes essay *Woman's Inferiority to Man*. Brandes introduces Strindberg to Nietzsche's philosophy. They correspond. Victoria Benedictsson kills herself. Nietzsche loses his mind. Strindberg and family move to Skovlyst where Countess Frankenau and her steward Ludvig Hansen inspire *Miss Julie* (written July/August). It is rejected by Bonnier. Writes *Creditors*. Prosecution for under-age sex with Martha Magdalena collapses but earns him unpleasant publicity. Enthusiasm for Edgar Allen Poe leads him to play with the idea he is Poe reincarnated. Writes Nietzschean novel *Tschandala*. Ibsen writes *The Lady from the Sea*.

1889   *Creditors*, *The Stronger* and *Pariah* staged in Copenhagen. Siri creates the part of Julie in *Miss Julie* which is performed privately to overcome the censor. Writes play *Simoon*. *Among French Peasants* published. Returns to Sweden.

1890   Suspects Siri of lesbianism. Publishes *By the Open Sea*. *Master Olof* staged at Dramaten to wide acclaim. Ibsen writes *Hedda Gabler*.

1891   Sued for libel concerning lesbianism by Siri's friend Marie David. Paints and sculpts.

1892   Legally separated from Siri, 21 March. Found guilty of assault on Marie David. Sculpts and exhibits paintings. Tries to invent colour photography. Writes plays *The Keys of Heaven*, *Debit and Credit*, *The First Warning*, *Facing Death*, *Motherly Love*, *Playing with Fire*, *The Bond*.

Marriage dissolved in September. To Berlin. Zum Schwarzen Ferkel circle of artists, physicians and promiscuous women. Paints with Edvard Munch. During their close friendship Munch paints Strindberg's portrait as well as *Madonna*, *Jealousy*, *Vampire*, *Self-portrait with Cigarette*, *Dagny Przybyszewska*. Ibsen writes *The Master Builder*.

1893   French premiere of *Miss Julie* at the Théâtre Libre. German premiere of *Creditors*, with *Facing Death* and *The First Warning* at the Residenztheater, Berlin. World premiere of *Playing with Fire* at Lessingtheater, Berlin. Meets Austrian journalist Frida Uhl. They get engaged. Brief affair with Dagny Juel. Marries Frida in Heligoland on 2 May. Possibly sees Turner's paintings during their London honeymoon. Leaves London for Rügen. Reunited with Frida at her family's estate in Dornach. Pursues alchemy and painting. Takes Celestographs, photographs of the night sky taken 'without camera or lenses'. Writes *Antibarbarus*, four essays on the transmutation of matter. Ernst Haeckel holds lecture 'Der monismus als Band zwischen Religion und Wissenschaft' ('Monism as connecting Religion and Science'). Strindberg calls himself a Monist. Munch paints *The Scream*.

1894   Daughter Kerstin born at Dornach, 26 May. Interest in Strindberg in Paris. *Creditors* staged at Lugné-Poë's Théâtre de l'Oeuvre. The astronomer Flammarion puts celestographs on show in Paris and discusses them at the Société Astronomique de France. Corresponds with Haeckel. Writes 'Des arts nouveaux! Ou le hazard dans la production artistique'. Promised a career as an artist in Paris, leaves for that city. Hoodwinked by conmen Willy Grétor and Albert Langen. Briefly joined by Frida before she returns to Austria. Frida and Strindberg never see each other again. Contact with French occultists Jollivet-Castelot, Papus *et al.* Ibsen writes *Little Eyolf*.

1895   Inferno crisis begins. Retires into alchemy, magic and self-analysis. Friendship with Paul Gauguin. Writes introduction to catalogue of Gauguin's Tahitian paintings. Circle of friends including Frederick Delius and Alphonse Mucha at Madame Charlotte's *crèmerie*. Hospitalised for psoriasis. Writes for French occultist publications. Scandinavians in Paris organise a collection of money for him. Gauguin leaves for Tahiti. Przybyszewski arrested for murdering his mistress. Munch executes lithograph of Strindberg who accuses Munch of trying to murder him.

1896   Moves to Hôtel Orfila. Height of Inferno crisis. Studies Swedenborg's doctrine of correspondences. Spends time in the Cimitière de Montparnasse. Begins *Occult Diary*. Reads *Séraphita*. Summer at Clam in Austria with Frida's mother and his daughter by Frida but not

Frida who is already pregnant with Frank Wedekind's child. Writes speculative scientific pieces, *On the Action of Light in Photography*, *A Glance into Space*, *Sylva Sylvarum*, *Jardin des Plantes*, *The Synthesis of Gold*, *The Irradiation and Extension of the Soul*. Plans a completely new type of novel, *Inferno*, through which he intends to become 'the Zola of the Occult'. Ibsen writes *John Gabriel Borkman*.

1897   Marriage to Frida annulled in February. Summer in Lund, Sweden, where he writes *Inferno* in French. Friedrich Strindberg born 21 August. To Paris in autumn to seek publisher. Writes *Inferno II* better known as *Legends* and *Jacob Wrestles*, describing his inability to desert God.

1898   Writes plays *To Damascus I* and *II* (eventually a trilogy) and *Advent*. *The Quarantine Master's Second Story* (later called *The Cloister*) deals with his time in Berlin and his marriage to Frida. Leaves Paris for Lund. Renounces alchemy and occultism though still reading Sâr Péladan. Bowled over by Maeterlinck, particularly *Pelléas et Mélisande*.

1899   Summer in Furusund with sister Anna von Philp. Writes play *Crimes and Crimes* and the history plays *The Saga of the Folkungs*, *Gustav Vasa* and *Erik XIV*. *Quickborn* publishes tribute edition to Strindberg and Munch. Carl Larsson pencil portrait of Strindberg. Moves to Stockholm. Ibsen writes *When We Dead Awaken*.

1900   Writes plays *Gustaf Adolf*, *Midsummer*, *Casper's Shrove Tuesday*, *Easter*, *The Dance of Death I* and *II*. Meets the actress Harriet Bosse. Details 'astral' relationship with Bosse in the *Occult Diary*.

1901   Marries Harriet Bosse, 6 May. Hears of Dagny Juel's murder. Honeymoon in Denmark and Berlin. Harriet becomes pregnant. Writes plays *The Crown Bride*, *Swanwhite*, *A Dream Play*, *To Damascus III*. History plays *Karl XII*, *Engelbrekt* and *Kristina* about Queen Christina. Paints *The Child's First Cradle*, *Yellow Autumn Painting* and *Inferno*.

1902   Daughter Anne-Marie born 25 March. Writes history play *Gustaf III*, poem *The Flying Dutchman* and publishes collected writings *Fair Haven and Foulstrand*. Max Reinhardt opens Kleines Theater, Berlin.

1903   Harriet leaves with Anne-Marie to live in separate accommodation though they continue to see and love each other. Writes *Alone*, *Fairy Tales*, 'The Mysticism of World History', plays *The Nightingale of Wittenberg*, *Moses*, *Socrates* and *Christ*.

1904   Divorce from Harriet. Writes satirical novel *Gothic Rooms* and social critique *Black Banners*.

1905   Models for sculptor Carl Eldh and painter Richard Bergh. Ernst Thiel adds three canvases by Strindberg to his collection of Nordic painting. Strindberg ceases to paint. Publishes poems *Word Play and Minor Art* and book of essays on historical subjects, *Historical Miniatures*. Max Reinhardt takes over Deutsches Theater in Berlin.

1906   Publishes *The Roofing Feast*, a stream-of-consciousness novel. Works with photographer Herman Anderson. Builds camera that can take life-size photographs. Draws clouds. Thinks about opera. Begins *A Blue Book*. *Miss Julie* first performed in public in Sweden: a great success. Ibsen dies and is given a state funeral.

1907   Founds the Intimate Theatre in Stockholm with August Falck. Writes chamber plays *Storm*, *The Burned House*, *The Ghost Sonata*, *The Island of the Dead* and *The Pelican* for the Intimate Theatre which opens on 26 November. Publication of novel *The Scapegoat*. Publication of *Black Banners* causes furore.

1908   Rehearsals at the Intimate Theatre crystallise his thoughts on acting which he sets down in *Open Letters to the Intimate Theatre*. Harriet Bosse marries the actor Gunnar Wingård. Strindberg concludes 'astral' relationship with Harriet. Ceases to write the *Occult Diary*. Moves to final residence in Stockholm, the Blue Tower, now the Strindberg Museum. Musical evenings with the Beethoven Boys. Visits from George Bernard Shaw and Edward Gordon Craig give new ideas for staging plays. Writes plays *The Last Knight*, *Abu Cassem's Slippers*, *The Regent*. Essays on Goethe and Shakespeare as playwrights. Coaches Fanny Falkner in acting.

1909   Sixtieth birthday. Parades and honours. Briefly engaged to Fanny Falkner. Writes plays *The Earl of Bjälbo*, *The Black Glove*, *The Great Highway*. Swedish General Strike.

1910   'The Strindberg Feud' fuels popular idea of awarding Strindberg a people's anti-Nobel prize. Strindberg studies Hebrew, collects Judaica. Intimate Theatre closes. Publishes *Biblical Proper Names* and *The Origins of our Mother Tongue*.

1911   Publishes *The Roots of World Languages* and *China and Japan*.

1912   Honoured on 63rd birthday with a torchlight procession. Awarded the anti-Nobel prize of 45,000 kronor raised by public subscription: fifteen thousand subscribe. 21 April, Siri von Essen dies. 14 May, August Strindberg dies. Ten thousand follow his coffin.

1939   Ban on public performance of *Miss Julie* lifted in England.

1984   *Miss Julie* published uncensored in Sweden for the first time.

2002   US $4,168,160 paid for *Alplandskap I* at Sotheby's, a world-record price for a painting by Strindberg.

INDEX

painting and deception in 200–2, 228, 346

performance of plays in 161, 175, 197, 205–6, 207, 346

protracted attempts to publish *Inferno* 239–40

psoriasis treatment 208–9, 305, pl. 69

stay with Siri 106–10

Strindberg's impressions of 199–200

Théâtre de l'Oeuvre 197, 346

visit as journalist 81–2

see also Théâtre Libre

Parker, Theodore 343

Paul I, Tsar of Russia 25

Paul, Adolf 165–6, 173, 181, 187, 195

peacock thefts 17–18

People's House, Stockholm 274, 291

Personne, Bishop John pl. 46

    Strindbergian Literature and Immorality 144–5, 345

Petersson, Emilia Charlotte (stepmother) 49–50, 51, 52, 77, 343, pl. 4

Pfaeffinger, Baroness Rosa 201–2

Philp, Anna von (*née* Strindberg, sister) 47, 77, 221, 247, 313*n*.15, 347

    rift and merciless portrayal in work 252, 279

    on Strindberg's health late in life 300

Philp, Henry 303

Philp, Hugo von (brother-in-law) 77, 221, 247, 252, 279

phrenology 165

Picasso, Pablo ix

Pietism 37–8, 48, 50, 51–2, 58, 124, 234

Pirandello, Luigi x

Plimsoll, Samuel 66

Poe, Edgar Allen 10, 158–9, 219, 345

Pontoppidan, Knud 157, 345

Poor Laws 39

Pound, Ezra 204

Prussian militarism 142–3

Przybyszewski, Stanislaw 171

    appearance 169

    Dagny Juel as mistress and wife 189, 191, 223, 225

    libertarian views and libertine lifestyle 168–9, 178–9, 180

    Munch's portraits 173, pl. 57

    murder charge 224, 225, 346

    musical evenings with Strindberg 166

    Requiem 195

    and Strindberg's paranoia 217, 224, 225–6

    and Strindberg's work 169, 245

psychomancy 9

quarantine hospitals 30

Quickborn (magazine) 244–5, 347

Ranft, Albert 248, 280

Rée, Paul 20–1

Reinhardt, Max x, 272, 347, 348

Reischl, Cornelius and Marie (Frida's grandparents) 191–2, 194, 197, 211, 233, 293, 294

    Strindberg's portrayal in work 243

Reischl, Melanie (Frida's aunt) 233–4, 293, 294

Réja, Marcel 240

Residenztheater, Berlin 174, 346

Revue blanche, La 223

Ribot, Théodule 139, 345

Riddarholmen, Stockholm 33

Röhss, August 219, 328*n*.3

Roman Catholicism

    of family 192, 241–2

    Strindberg's engagement with 241–2, 244, 266–7

Rousseau, Jean-Jacques 40, 110, 126, 344

in Berlin and Schwarzen Ferkel
164–75, 178–81, 187, 188–9,
192–3, 195–6, 237, 345
compartmentalisation and clubs 63–4,
86, 89–90, 95, 166
and financial support 66, 131–2, 136,
208, 210–11, 299, 305, 328n.3,
346
and Siri's drinking problem 103, 127
sparring with Steffen 130–1
'vivisections' and demands of 96
German sojourn 142
health
decline in Siri's absence on
Kymmendö 98
downturn after trial 128, 132–3
fear of madness 140, 157, 158, 196,
345
paranoid episodes 217, 222–8,
230–1, 235
psoriasis and hospital treatment
208–9, 305, 346, pl. 69
Schleich's assessment of mental
soundness 298
stomach cancer 280, 283, 303, 304,
306–7
stress and discord in life 198, 208
homesickness in exile 125, 161
homosexuality in work 242
honours and awards 65, 88, 344
Academy indifference x–xi, 302, 308
Anti-Nobel prize 302–3, 304–5, 349
birthday tributes 244–5, 291–2,
303–4, 348
hostility towards 120, 131–2
damage of Personne's moral crusade
144–6, 154, 345
friends' accounts of Strindberg 195–6
reviews of *Miss Julie* 161
impressions of Paris 199–200

interests
Asian studies 88, 90, 344, 348
chance and artistic creation 166, 167,
173, 229
classification and 'buttonology' 44,
92, 112, 292
cycling 237–8
gardening 11, 22, 96–7, 228–9, 292
genius and madness 158–9, 165, 170,
182, 240
guitar playing 55, 64, 165, 166,
pl. 55
Hebrew in later life 292, 348
monkeys and humans 215
paranormal and occult 9–10, 16, 192,
211–32, 235, 346
Prussian militarism 142–3
psychology and madness 137–8,
139–40, 143, 165–71, 170, 212
snake-charming 162
as student 55, 64
telephone and incorporation in plays
269
see also scientific interests *below*
Jews and anti-Semitism 58, 101, 123–4,
154–5
as journalist 66–7, 74–5, 81–2, 91–2,
125–6, 343
art criticism 82, 344
article on children's rights and
obligations 128
'My Anti-Semitism' article 123–4
war correspondent proposal 142
kindness to children 286, 291, 293
language skills 48, 64, 88, 165, 287,
292, 348
marriages *see* Bosse, Harriet; Essen,
Countess Siri von; Strindberg, Frida
musical evenings with friends 267–8,
348

masturbation and religious
condemnation 50–1
mistresses after divorce from Siri 181
pressures of return to single life
153–4
pressures of Siri's unavailability 127–8
sexual frankness of work 116, 127
sexual insecurities and Siri's infidelity
153
and staging of plays
Craig's influence 288, 289, 348
directions on 161, 276–8, 296, 348
Strindberg Theatre project 265–6
student days and youth pl. 10, pl. 15
acting aspirations 60–1, 277, 343
insight into happy families 57, 58, 60
lack of means 52–3, 54, 56
literary criticism 56–7
medical studies under Lamm 58,
59–60, 343
opium pill and gift of poetry 61–2
reading preferences 56–7
royal bequest 65
Uppsala University 52–3, 54–6,
63–6, 343
writing experiments and early works
55, 61–3
suicidal thoughts and preparations
59–60, 137, 157, 158, 207
and provisions for corpse 229
suicide attempt in Dalarö 76–7
teaching jobs 52, 56–7, 343
on water-closets abroad 105
will and provisions for funeral 307
writing routine 15, 300
AUTOBIOGRAPHICAL WRITINGS 29, 57,
61–2, 340
Alone (Ensam) 264, 347
analysis of self ix, 137–9, 158,
239–40

The Author (Författaren) 141, 154, 345
The Cloister (Klosteret) 242, 347
He and She (Han och hon)) 73, 139
In the Red Room (I Röda rummet) 139,
345
Inferno and contributing experiences
68, 218–32, 239–40, 346–7, pls
65–9, pls 73–8, pl. 77
Jacob Wrestles (Jakob brottas) 215, 240,
347
Legends (Legender, formerly Inferno II)
240, 347
Occult Diary (Ockulta dagboken) 11,
220–1, 224, 250–1, 253–5,
262–3, 282–3, 346, 347, 348, pl.
102
Le Plaidoyer d'un fou (A Madman's
Defense) 6, 158, 159, 179, 185,
190–1, 194, 345
The Son of a Servant (Tjänstekvinnans
son) 24, 28–9, 33–7, 41, 43–4, 45,
46–7, 48, 50, 51–2, 68, 137–8,
345
Time of Ferment (Jäsningstiden) 138, 345
use of third person 29
HISTORY PLAYS AND WRITINGS viii, 62–3,
246–9, 338, 339, 341, 342
The Earl of Bjälbo (Bjälbo-Jarlen, play)
292, 348
Engelbrekt (play) 347
Erik XI (play) 62–3
Erik XIV (play) 246–8, 276, 347
Gustaf Adolf 347
Gustaf III 347
Gustav Vasa (play) 246, 248, 347
Karl XII (play) 263, 347
Master Olof see Master Olof (history
play)
plans for history of German people
141

The Rise and Fall
of the House of Windsor

A. N. WILSON

The Rise and Fall of the House of Windsor

W·W·NORTON & COMPANY
New York   London

The author and publisher wish to thank the following for use of illustrations: 1b, 2b, 4a, 6b, 7, 9, 11a, 12a, The Camera Press; 12b, 15, 16, Tim Graham; 1a, 5, The National Portrait Gallery; 8, 11b, Popperfoto; 14, Rex Features; 2a, 3, 4b, 6a, 10, Topham Picture Source.

The House of Windsor

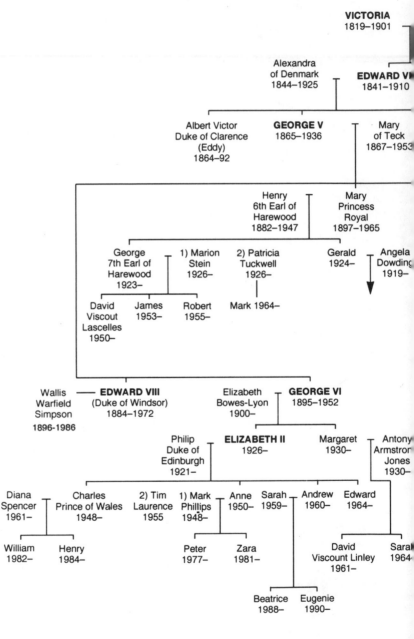

VICTORIA
1819–1901

Alexandra
of Denmark
1844–1925 — **EDWARD VII**
1841–1910

Albert Victor
Duke of Clarence
(Eddy)
1864–92

GEORGE V
1865–1936 — Mary
of Teck
1867–1953

Henry
6th Earl of
Harewood
1882–1947 — Mary
Princess
Royal
1897–1965

George
7th Earl of
Harewood
1923– — 1) Marion
Stein
1926–   2) Patricia
Tuckwell
1926–   Gerald
1924– — Angela
Dowding
1919–

David
Viscout
Lascelles
1950–   James
1953–   Robert
1955–   Mark 1964–

Wallis
Warfield
Simpson
1896-1986 — **EDWARD VIII**
(Duke of Windsor)
1884–1972

Elizabeth
Bowes-Lyon
1900– — **GEORGE VI**
1895–1952

Philip
Duke of
Edinburgh
1921– — **ELIZABETH II**
1926–   Margaret
1930– — Antony
Armstrong
Jones
1930–

Diana
Spencer
1961– — Charles
Prince of Wales
1948–   2) Tim
Laurence
1955   1) Mark
Phillips
1948– — Anne
1950–   Sarah
1959–   Andrew
1960–   Edward
1964–

William
1982–   Henry
1984–   Peter
1977–   Zara
1981–   David
Viscount Linley
1961–   Sarah
1964–

Beatrice
1988–   Eugenie
1990–

The House of Windsor

Albert of
Saxe-Coburg-Gotha
1819–61

8 others

| Louise 867–1931 | Alexander Duff Duke of Fife 1844–1912 | Victoria 1868–1935 | Maud 1869–1938 | Haakon VII of Norway 1872–1957 |

Henry
Duke of
Gloucester
1900–74

Alice Montagu-
Douglas-Scott
1901–

William
1941–72

Richard
Duke of
Gloucester
1944–

Birgitte
van Deurs
1946–

Alexander
Earl of Ulster
1974–

Davinia
1977–

Rose
1980–

George
Duke of Kent
1902–42

Marina
of Greece
1906–68

John
1905–19

Edward
Duke of Kent
1935–

Katharine
Worsley
1933–

Alexandra
1936–

Angus
Ogilvy
1928–

Michael
1942–

Marie
Christine
von Reibnitz
1945–

Helen
1964–

Tim
Taylor

Nicholas
1970–

• Frederick
1979–

Gabriella
1981–

James
1964–

Marina
1966–

Paul Mowatt

Sylvanna
Tomaselli
1957–

George
Earl of
Saint Andrews
1962–

Zenouska
1990–

Edward
1988–

Contents

Photographs appear between pages 116 and 117.

The Rise and Fall
of the House of Windsor

ONE

The Curse
of the Coburgs

'I know this sounds crazy, but I've lived before.'

Lady Diana Spencer
on the 'Squidgygate' tapes

'Then verily shall I pray to the Lord Almighty to
visit the sins of the fathers upon the children to
the third and fourth generation of the Coburg line.'

Brother Emericus Kohary

On November 23, 1992, speaking at a banquet to celebrate forty years on the throne and forty-five years of her marriage, Queen Elizabeth II admitted that the previous twelve months had been an *annus horribilis*. Three days before, her childhood home, Windsor Castle, had suffered a major fire. But this was only one of the calamities to befall the British Royal Family in this disastrous year. The Royal Family's claim, until recently, had always been that it represented an ideal of family stability to which the British people could look for an example of Christian home life. In March, Prince Andrew, the Queen's favourite son, announced that his marriage to Sarah Ferguson was over. A few months later, his sister had divorced her husband, Captain Mark Phillips. By the end of the year, 'Fergie', otherwise known as Her Royal Highness the Duchess of York, had been photographed in the South of France having her toes sucked by a 'financial adviser' from Texas; Charles and Diana had announced their separation; the Queen had been forced to pay income tax; and, even in the most conservative quarters, the unthinkable question was being asked: could the Monarchy survive?

No one could doubt that the Royal Family, as individuals, had had a bad year – three marital separations and a major fire is more than most families have to endure in a single twelve-month period. But does this mean that there is actually a crisis in the institution of the Monarchy itself? No one could fail to see that there had been a change in the Monarchy's relations with the Press during the forty years that Queen Elizabeth II had been on the throne. At the beginning of this period, there were many conventions governing the way in which journalists spoke of royalties; little by little, these conventions (which were, in any case, of very recent vintage) began to be discarded, not only by newspapers but by the royalties themselves. In 1953, it was 'not done' to repeat what was said to you by a Royal Personage, let alone reprint it in the newspapers. By 1992, members of the Royal Family were themselves 'leaking' the most intimate details of their private lives to the Press.

The relations between the Royal Family and the Press are of obvious importance: without the Press and television, how would any of us know about these people? And there can be no doubt that there have been many crises in the relations between these two institutions which feed off, and to a large degree encourage, one another.

These 'crises', or scoops, depending on your point of view, can be exciting for a few days. When the Duchess of York was photographed in the South of France, everyone might have deplored the intrusion into her privacy. It would, however, have been an austere figure who would not have turned the pages of *Paris-Match* or the *Daily Mirror* during that week, had the opportunity to do so arisen. By a similar token, most people have enjoyed reading the transcripts of a telephone conversation in which the Prince of Wales declared that he would like to be reincarnated as Mrs Parker-Bowles's Tampax, just as, some months earlier, they enjoyed accounts of his wife being sick and having tantrums. One does not have to be of a very vindictive temperament to savour the essentially comic misfortunes of a talentless and, it has to be said at the outset, largely charmless family who, by the accidents of birth and marriage, happen to be the custodians of the British monarchical system. It is they who have chosen to behave like characters in a Feydeau farce, and they cannot be surprised when the audience laugh. Figures such as the Princess Royal who have not chosen to tell the newspapers about their marital secrets, have been highly esteemed. (In Princess Anne's case, while her abrasive manner might have been noticed from time to time, she is largely regarded as a sportswoman and charity organiser: rumours about her private life, in general circulation among journalists, never, to my knowledge, saw print.)

Entertaining as the Feydeau-esque interludes might be, it remains to be seen whether they are damaging to the institution of Monarchy as such. Journalists like to believe that they have power and influence, and so it is not surprising that they should declare that such incidents as the Royal toe-sucking or the Royal Tampax pose 'serious constitutional questions'. In the seemingly interminable journalistic debates about the subject, there has been an interesting class division, perhaps because the British always try to resolve questions of politics or religion by reference to class.

Andrew Neil, the Editor of the *Sunday Times*, which first published extracts from the book *Diana: Her True Story*, is a lower-middle-class Scot. He believes that the institution of Monarchy should go or be changed, and while he is about it he would like to shake up all the snobs and toffs who run what he believes to be the Establishment in Britain today. There probably still is an Establishment, and it probably bears some hazy resemblance to the Establishment of Mr Neil's worst nightmares, but it has not been this 'Establishment' which has responded to him. Rather, it has been the more middle-class, public-school-educated of his fellow-journalists who have enjoyed baiting him by adopting a pro-monarchical position.

At the right-wing extreme there have been High Tory journalists with an aristocratic point of view who believe that the country has now become unworthy of the Monarchy. Sir Peregrine Worsthorne, the Highest Tory of them all, as well as being the noblest and most aristocratic journalist at work in Britain today, has proposed that republicanism is the only true faith that a monarchist can now adopt. The almost equally aristocratic Mr Auberon Waugh, who for years in his journalism has excoriated and insulted members of the Royal Family, was turned by the indiscretions of the Princess of Wales in the *Sunday Times* into an adherent (more or less) of the Worsthorne school, believing that the classless New Brits, as he calls them, have become entirely unworthy of our excellent Royal Family. 'The Windsors have served this country well,' he now writes (though you would not have guessed it to read his journalism for the last quarter-century); his advice is 'that they should be allowed to return to Germany with dignity and decorum, the plaudits of a grateful people ringing in their ears, and leave Princess Monster* behind on her own to receive the cheers of her adulatory fans,

* Mr Waugh's unkind way of referring to HRH the Princess of Wales, *vide Spectator*, January 30, 1993.

Madonna-like, until they grow bored and decide to tear her to pieces'.

Behind such journalistic rough-and-tumble, there exists one possible reason for believing that the Royal House of Windsor is in difficulties. That is, that Britain has changed so much since the Queen's Coronation that it is in some way no longer appropriate for it to be governed by a monarch and by a system which is inherently monarchical – a non-elective Second Chamber in Parliament, a system of patronage extending to many areas of public life, in the Armed Forces and the Civil Service, and an established Church. No political institution survives if it is not flexible in the face of change, and one of the reasons that the British Monarchy survived so comparatively vigorously after the First World War, when so many other European dynasties collapsed, was, precisely, its constitutional flexibility.

But equally, no institution, political, religious or social, can survive if it has no function, and if the conditions in which it flourished have altered so fundamentally that it has nothing to sustain it.

This book is an attempt to examine whether the House of Windsor – and with it the British Monarchy – is indeed in a state of crisis. I shall examine various aspects of the Crown's function – its relations with the Press, its symbolic role as a guardian of pure home life and monogamy, its traditional Christian function, embodied in the Queen's claim to be Defender of the Faith, and its constitutional role. In the first three areas, I believe that the Royal Family are in desperate trouble. Their relations with the Press have been disastrous; their claim to be symbols of a Christian happy family look, to say the least, hollow in the light of their real marital history; and the Sovereign's role as Supreme Governor of the National Church appears harder and harder to sustain, for two powerful reasons: most English people are not Anglicans, and most Anglicans do not want their unique status as an Established religion to continue.

It is in the fourth, and most crucial, area – the constitutional area – that I believe the Monarchy to be much stronger than the journalists would have us suppose. When the British (Old Brits as well as New Brits, I fear) have all finished laughing at the Royal Family in the newspapers; and when they have reflected how few of them – less than two-and-a-half per cent – share their Sovereign's religious faith, there remains an overwhelming majority of British people who wish the Monarchy to continue. This is not merely for sentimental reasons, important as those are: it is because they dislike the idea of an elective presidential system. In the years which follow, there will indubitably be calls by British politicians to have such a system, not least because some British politicians would no doubt like to be President themselves. As Britain moves towards closer and closer political as well as economic union with the other European nations, it will seem advisable to some of the keener 'Europeans' that Britain should have an elected president, like the Italians, the French and the Germans. This is not an argument which will be easily won, however, when the British remind themselves of the constitutional history of those three countries in the last sixty years.

The House of Windsor is not composed of interesting people: few of them, except the Queen herself, are even very remarkable. From 1936 to the present time, they would seem to be able to capture the public imagination only when dying or committing adultery. Their dullness might make them unappealing to newspapers, but it might be a large part of their political strength. For the paradox is that the British Monarchy has actually gained in political strength and importance during the reign of Queen Elizabeth II, though this partly has to do with the popular reaction against Margaret Thatcher and the phenomenon known as Thatcherism.

Before tackling my four great issues, therefore – the Press, Royal marriages, religion and the Constitution – it will be necessary to assess the recent history of the House of Windsor, and I have chosen to do so not in a strictly chronological framework but by sketching very briefly the *dramatis personae*. There are, I think, four crucially important figures in this story: Margaret Thatcher, Lady Diana Spencer, Prince Charles and Queen Elizabeth II, and it would not be possible to discuss the generalities without paying some attention at first to these particular individuals. Only when we have done so can we decide whether there is a future for the House of Windsor, or whether the noise of tumbrils is soon to be heard on the cobblestones of the stable courtyards of Buckingham Palace.

Before that, however, we must remind ourselves that the House of Windsor is not really 'of Windsor' at all. During the First World War, the British were embarrassed by the fact that their Sovereign, though speaking like a Cockney and dressing like a minor English country squire, should be of purely Germanic origin. 'I may be uninspiring,' King George V remarked, 'but I'll be damned if I'm an alien.' Like many persons of foreign origin who have settled in Britain, he decided to change the family name to something impeccably British. The House of Saxe-Coburg-Gotha (as the Royal Family has been called since Queen Victoria married Prince Albert of Saxe-Coburg) would be renamed the House of Windsor.

'The true royal tradition died on that day in 1917 when, for a mere war, King George V changed his name,' said the distinguished Bavarian nobleman Count Albrecht von

Montgelas. The Kaiser, more good-humouredly, asked if he could attend a performance of *The Merry Wives of Saxe-Coburg-Gotha.**

What is perhaps less generally discussed is the Royal Family's entitlement even to the Saxe-Coburg inheritance. This would perhaps be of interest only to pedantic genealogists, were it not for the curious story of the Curse of the Coburgs.

Both Albert and Victoria came of the Coburg line. Albert's father was the brother of Victoria's mother (the Duchess of Kent). Their brother, Ferdinand, married Antoinette de Kohary, the only child of Prince Joseph Kohary, Chancellor to the Austrian Emperor and a member of one of the richest families in Hungary. The Coburg estate was entailed in favour of the male line, but Prince Joseph persuaded the Emperor to issue a 'filiation' order, which bestowed on Antoinette the benefits of a son. The male members of the Kohary family resisted in vain, and one of them, the monk Brother Emericus Kohary, went to a churchyard in Darmstadt at midnight and solemnly read out the curse according to the ritual of the *Manuale Exorcisorum.*† 'Then verily shall I pray to the Lord Almighty to visit the sins of the fathers upon the children to the third and fourth generation of the Coburg line.'

The efficacy of this malediction may be assessed if we pause to follow the Coburg line through the four prescribed generations and see how they fared. One could fill a book with the names of the descendants of the House of Saxe-Coburg, which was in effect the nursery for most of the Royal Families of Europe in the nineteenth century. But, even allowing for the selectivity of the following account,

---

* Kenneth Rose, *King George V* (1983) p.174.
† David Duff, *Hessian Tapestry* (1967) p. 46.

which traces only the more immediate relations of the present Duke of Edinburgh, the reader will feel compelled to acknowledge that the breed has been singularly unfortunate since the monk uttered his curse.

In the first generation, Prince Albert died of typhoid fever at the age of only forty-two. His wife and cousin, Victoria, had unknowingly inherited haemophilia from her Coburg mother, also called Victoria, and therefore passed on this fatal disease (which is 'carried' on the X chromosome and therefore can be borne quite unconsciously by females) to the Royal Families of Spain, Bulgaria, Greece, Germany and Russia. The Portuguese Royal Family, also inheritors of the Coburg line and of the monk's curse, were almost entirely wiped out by the same disease which killed Prince Albert, typhoid fever.

But let us limit our pursuit to the line which eventually produces Prince Philip. The next generation – the second generation of the monk's curse – is that of Princess Alice, who married Louis IV, Grand Duke of Hesse and the Rhine, in 1862. Like her father, she was destined to die young (only thirty-five) of diphtheria, caught from the lips of a dying infant daughter. She did not die, however, before producing a good crop of children, all of whose lives would have surely gratified the malicious Kohary monk, had he lived to witness them. Most famous of them was Alix (Aleksandra Feodorovna), last of the Tsarinas, who perished with her husband, Tsar Nicholas II, and all her children at the hands of the Bolsheviks at Ekaterinaburg in 1918. Her sister, Ella Feodorovna, a Grand Duchess of Russia, also died at the hands of the Bolsheviks – she was thrown live down a mineshaft at Alapevsk in Siberia, her husband having been assassinated in Red Square thirteen years before, during the Russo-Japanese war. Their other siblings included Frederick ('Frittie'), who died at the age of three by falling out of his mother's bedroom window (not before his haemophilia had been diagnosed), and their sister little Princess Marie, who died of the black diphtheria which also killed her mother. There was also Princess Victoria of Hesse and the Rhine, who in 1884 married Louis Prince of Battenberg, who changed his name to Mountbatten in the same year, 1917, that George V changed the Royal House to that of Windsor and was granted the reassuringly British-sounding title Marquess of Milford Haven. The former Princess Victoria of Battenberg, later the Marchioness of Milford Haven, Prince Philip's grandmother, lived to see the birth of her great-grandchildren, Prince Charles and Princess Anne, before dying in 1950. It might therefore be supposed that she had bypassed the curse of the monk.

But presumably, for a curse to be fully satisfying to the malice of its perpetrator, there must be some unfortunates who survive in order to witness the calamities and misfortunes befalling its most direct victims. The Marchioness of Milford Haven lived long enough to see the disastrously unhappy marriage of her daughter Alice (mother of Prince Philip) to Andrew, Prince of Greece and Denmark. She also witnessed one of the most extraordinary consequences of the monk's malice, which wiped out most of the adolescent Prince Philip's relations at a stroke and which left a permanent scar on his nature. In 1937, Prince Louis of Hesse announced his engagement to the Hon. Margaret Campbell-Geddes; the wedding was to be held in England. Prince Philip of Greece, aged sixteen, went down to London for the wedding, and awaited the arrival of his Hesse relations at Croydon airport. November 16 was a clear sunny day as their aeroplane took off from the Continent, and it was only when they approached Croydon that a freak mist gathered. The plane crashed into a chimney and was smashed to pieces. All the crown jewels were lost, as were many members of the family – Hereditary Grand Duke George Donatus, his wife, his two young sons, Louis and Alexander, the Dowager Grand Duchess Eleonore, and so forth.* Only the baby of the family, Johanna, was left behind. She died of tubercular meningitis two years later, aged three. Some weeks later, while Prince Philip was still reeling from the shock of this multiple bereavement, his favourite sister Cecile was killed in another air crash, this time over Brussels, aged twenty-six.

The Kohary monk extended his curse to the 'third and fourth generation' of the Coburg line. If we take it that Victoria and Albert were the first generation, then the fourth (limiting our studies specifically to the direct ancestors of Prince Philip) comes to an end with his mother, Princess Alice, a melancholic nun who was to be seen drifting sadly about the corridors of Buckingham Palace dressed in her religious habit. Perhaps her piety and prayers were offered in reparation for the Curse of the Coburgs. If so, they could not prevent the monk's little *coup de grâce*, the assassination of her brother, Earl Mountbatten of Burma, in the summer of 1976 on a yacht off the coast of Ireland.

It might be supposed, as readily as it is to be hoped, that the curse of the Kohary monk has now spent its force. The four generations specified in his ritual commination have now been born, and even those who are unable to believe in such things on rational grounds must concede

* The young couple were married wearing full mourning, with Lord Mountbatten as best man and Von Ribbentrop, the German Ambassador in London, signing the register. Princess Margaret Mountbatten (the former Miss Campbell-Geddes) returned to Germany with her young husband and five coffins. 'Everybody was crying,' she recalled, 'even when they were doing the Nazi salute, they were still crying.' Tim Heald, *The Duke. A Portrait of Prince Philip* (1991) p.49.

that, since the churchyard utterance, the descendants of the House of Coburg have had immoderate ill fortune.

Some will have wondered, when they read – or heard – the claim by the Princess of Wales that she had 'lived before', whether by some cruel quirk of destiny she had walked the earth before in the person of the Kohary monk, and whether, in her falling-out with her husband, she threatened to undermine what had appeared, until she married Prince Charles, to be an institution of unshakeable durability. Others will dismiss all talk of curses or reincarnation as mere fantasy: but they will think that monarchs, like maledictory monks, belong to a vanished age. To such as these, the march of historical change is not to be resisted.

The gradual dissolution of the class structures in modern Britain and the undermining of its Parliamentary sovereignty and independence by European federalism perhaps make the notion of a constitutional Monarch seem a trifle anachronistic. In time, and given a crisis – so such forward-looking minds would conceive – the House of Windsor will have to go. Just as the huge proportion of their cousins among the royalties and high nobilities of Old Europe have been swept away by history, so, it is imagined, will they. If France elects a President and Germany elects a President – why shouldn't Great Britain? In which case, without the violence which disposed of their cousin the Tsar, the House of Windsor might – like so many of their German cousins – retreat to their large houses and their obscure lives, and allow history to march on without them.

Those who believe this moment of history to have arrived are still very much in the minority in Britain, but they have gathered in numbers and momentum. Even a decade ago, the only British people who regarded themselves as republicans were almost all recognisable eccentrics – the sort of people who would also believe in reforming the English spelling system, or who would doubt the authorship of Shakespeare's plays. Something happened during the 1980s which changed all that. A carefully thought republicanism is still a minority fad in Britain, but it has gained ground and *gravitas*. And one of the people responsible for that is the woman who cast her personality so forcefully on the decade between 1979 and 1989: the Right Honourable Margaret Thatcher.

TWO

Margaret Thatcher's Legacy

'We have enjoyed ourselves immensely.'

Margaret Thatcher
in the Soviet Union

The removal of Margaret Thatcher from political office, after nearly eleven years as the Prime Minister of Great Britain, was accomplished with remarkably little fuss. Once it had happened, it was accepted on all sides with a certain degree of incredulity. For many people in the world – Russians, Americans, Japanese, Europeans of the EC and of the former Warsaw Pact (perhaps particularly for this category) – it was simply incomprehensible that the British Conservative party should have chosen to remove from power a leader of such outstanding qualities. Mrs Thatcher had been more than a politician, she had been an icon. Wherever she went in the world, she was recognised and – a scarcely English phenomenon – what she stood for was recognised. This was particularly marked in her visits to Eastern Europe. Her early expression of confidence that she could 'do business' with Mikhail Gorbachov meant that she believed that she could abolish world communism. Together with her political ally and close personal friend President Ronald Reagan of the United States, she believed herself to have done this, and she spoke openly of the part she had played in *glasnost*, the collapse of the Berlin Wall and the gradual undoing of Soviet power. Her 'values' – a belief in self-determination, in personal freedom, in a reduction of State interference and the promotion of *laissez-faire* economics, a hatred of left-wing tyrannies, a willingness to 'do business' with right-wing tyrannies (most notably in South Africa), and an uncomplicated belief in Bible Christianity – all seemed much more American than British, which is one of the reasons for her continued and immense popularity in the United States.

At home in Britain, the picture was rather different. A small number of right-wing ideologues rejoiced in her as a revolutionary who had reversed (as they hoped, for ever) the march of the liberal consensus. A much larger group – the electorate who returned her to office in three successive general elections – saw, like the rest of the world, that she 'stood for' things, and they were things which they liked. She was unashamedly belligerent in her attitude to foreigners. When General Galtieri invaded the Malvinas in 1981, she immediately sent a task force of British servicemen to boot him out again. Liberals watched askance, but this action won her enormous popularity, not merely with the vulgar newspapers ('GOTCHA!' said the headline of the *Sun* newspaper on the morning the Argentinian ship the *Belgrano* was sunk by Her Majesty's Navy) but with the electorate at large. So did her clever trick of persuading the electorate that under her they paid less tax. (In fact they paid more, but she reduced direct taxation and increased indirect, thereby greatly benefiting the New Rich and increasing the gap between rich and poor.)

15

According to the Thatcherite way of viewing history, Britain, which had been a bumbling, decaying little island, controlled first by an Aristocratic Oligarchy (1689–1939), then by a Government of National Unity (1939–1945), then by a Socialist Experiment (1945–1951), and at last by the Liberal Consensus which was the heir to the Whig Consensus of Aristocratic times (1951–1979), suddenly found itself proclaimed as a 'share-owning, property-owning democracy'. Those who were unable to afford to do so were encouraged to take out mortgages and buy their own homes. Nationalised industries were sold off, and a high proportion of the holdings were sold to small private investors. The Trades Unions, most notably the National Union of Mineworkers, who were seen to have held the country 'to ransom' for forty or fifty years, were seen off with crippling legislation and an even more crippling miners' strike, which the miners lost and which weakened British manufacturing industry, particularly in the North.

There could be no doubt, in the shared minds of Mrs Thatcher and her supporters in the popular right-wing press, of who was in charge. Everyone knew, when they considered the matter rationally, that Mrs Thatcher was not really 'in charge' any more than any previous Prime Minister had been. The economy was still, in fact, controlled by forces over which Government had very limited power. The European Community, in spite of Mrs Thatcher's rudeness to the French and Belgians and Germans when she went abroad, continued to extend its influence; and when she was presented with legislation such as the Single European Act, Mrs Thatcher signed up to it without a murmur. Educational standards, on which as Minister of Education Mrs Thatcher had appeared to set such store (she abolished nearly twice as many grammar schools as her socialist predecessor Mrs Williams), continued to decline catastrophically, and the crime rate soared. What was more, Mrs Thatcher was the least 'Thatcherite' Prime Minister when it came to public spending, which she increased with liberal gusto every year she was in office – on transport, defence, the police, on health and social services.

The reality, however, was far less important than the propaganda; and nearly everyone believed in a part of themselves that this little woman, with her firm blonde hair-do, and her handbag, and her dark blue and white suits, was a Leader such as Britain had never known in peacetime. This was particularly true of the Opposition parties, Liberal and Labour, who attributed nearly all the evils of the age – increasing crime and unemployment, a tendency towards British isolationism in Europe, etcetera – less to the general policies of the Conservative Party than to the personal will of Mrs Thatcher. In consequence, when they went to the polls and tried to persuade the electorate to return a Liberal Government or a Labour Government, the electorate voted for the little woman with the handbag. Far from being an electoral liability as her enemies within the Conservative Party claimed, she had a genius for winning elections.

Margaret Thatcher had pulled off the trick – achieved in the past by Bismarck, among other great political leaders – of appearing on one level to be quite independent of her party or movement. While in any poll only forty per cent of the electorate thought the Conservatives were a worthy party of Government, eighty to ninety per cent believed that Margaret Thatcher was not merely the most eligible Prime Minister, but, little by little, the natural Prime Minister. She was in 'a class of her own', and it was imaginatively impossible to replace her.

On this irrational, gut level, Mrs Thatcher had become

something much more than the Prime Minister, and certainly much more than the Parliamentary Leader of the Conservatives. She had become a grand national icon, frequently depicted by cartoonists as Britannia, the emblem of Britain itself. On one level she had achieved presidential, almost monarchical, status.

Relations between Mrs Thatcher and that other little woman with a handbag, Her Majesty Queen Elizabeth II of Great Britain and Northern Ireland and her dominions beyond the seas, were known to be frosty, if not positively glacial. The Queen is known to favour the 'Liberal consensus' by which Great Britain was governed throughout the first thirty years of her reign. She had famously enjoyed harmonious relations with all her previous Prime Ministers. After Sir Winston Churchill there had been that firebrand Whig Anthony Eden, followed by the Whig of Whigs, Harold Macmillan. (Throughout this period, incidentally, the Labour Party had decided that they disliked the socialist experiment of 1945–50 as much as the British electorate had done, and they had elected as their leader Mr Gaitskell, who in all important areas – defence and public spending – thought roughly the same as the Conservatives.) The collapse of Sir Alec Douglas-Home's Government of 1963–4 meant that the Whig Consensus had to be dressed up in slightly more plebeian clothes. Harold Wilson and Edward Heath became successive Prime Ministers, speaking with plebeian accents and boasting of their low social origins, but both fundamentally upholders of the old status quo – the power of the Civil Service, the power of the Foreign Office in foreign affairs, a Keynesian economic outlook, a generous view of social services. No wonder the Queen had liked them all, for these were all policies in which she had been brought up to believe, and, much more importantly, they were the policies which underpinned the Monarchy.

The British Monarchy since 1689 has had a peculiarly bloodless history when compared with the other Royal Houses of Europe. This is because, after James II was forced from his throne in 1688 by the Whigs, it has always been perfectly apparent who actually exercised power in Britain. Kings and Queens only need to have their heads chopped off when they exercise power – as happened to James II's father, Charles I. The Hanoverian compromise after the death of James II's last surviving sister, Anne, in 1702, was for the ruling upper class to put in a monarch of their own choosing, and this was done when they found the Elector of Hanover, an obese divorced German who knew almost no English, and proclaimed him as George I. Ever since then, the British Monarchs have known who called the tune, and, with the defeat of any attempts to put the 'rightful' Stuart Monarch on the throne (the so-called Jacobite rebellions of 1715 and 1745), something stronger than mere alliance grew up between the British Monarch and the governing class. It was symbiosis; the one fed the other, was dependent on the other for its life.

So while all real power was exercised by the governing class – who returned the Members of Parliament from their pocket boroughs, and formed Cabinets and elected Prime Ministers largely from the Upper House, the House of Lords – the ultimate sanction for this power rested, technically speaking, with the Crown. This had an extraordinarily stabilising effect throughout the nineteenth century, when other European countries were convulsed with revolutions and counter-revolutions. The gradual extension of franchise – first in 1831 and 1832 with the Great Reform Bill, leading inexorably much later in the century (with the Reform Act of 1867) to the possibility of 'universal suffrage', that is, 'one man, one vote', then in the twentieth century to votes for men and women over the age of majority – all happened not merely with the Monarch's consent but, crucially, with the Monarch's involvement. No one believed that William IV would have been able to stop the Reform Bill of 1831; but his involvement (and he was no political genius) did actually ensure the passage of the Bill without a threat to the status quo. A very similar thing happened in 1910, shortly after the accession of George V, when the 'left wing' of the Liberal Party threatened to create 500 peers to force through the abolition of the House of Lords unless Lloyd George's radical Budget was accepted. George V was able to intervene and save the situation in rather the same way that William IV, another dim-witted sailor king, had intervened in 1831. When it came to the point of decision, the governing class did not want to lose the Monarchy any more than the Monarchy wished to lose the governing class. As the governing class changed, the Monarchy adapted, but both continued to depend upon one another until the arrival of Margaret Thatcher.

In all her public pronouncements about the Queen, in particular since her own fall from grace, Margaret Thatcher has been deferential to the point of oiliness. This hardly disguises the fact that, throughout her years in office, the Queen and Mrs Thatcher were perceived as being not merely at odds over individual political questions, but also in a sense rivals for the same job. Almost the only area of public debate where the Queen has allowed her personal views to be known is in the future of the British Commonwealth.

It is possible that the Queen is the only person in the British Isles who is interested in the British Commonwealth. Most of her subjects have some difficulty in remembering what exactly it is. The Commonwealth is sometimes described by Her Majesty as 'a family of nations', the nations in question being those which used to comprise the former British Empire. For someone whose mother was the last, self-styled, Empress of India, it is hardly surprising that the Queen should have grown up with a strong sense of her Imperial responsibilities. The wireless broadcast which she made as Princess Elizabeth, on her twenty-first birthday, was not to the nation but to the Empire. It was delivered not from London but from Cape Town.

She told her Imperial father's subjects that she saw her coming-of-age as a self-dedication. 'I should like to make that dedication now. It is very simple. I declare before you that my whole life, whether it be long or short, shall be devoted to your service and the service of our great Imperial Commonwealth to which we all belong. But I shall not have strength to carry out this resolution unless you join in it with me, as I now invite you to do; I know that your support will be unfailingly given. God bless all of you who are willing to share it.'

These words, spoken on April 21, 1947, were sincerely meant at the time, and the Queen has gone on sincerely meaning them, long after the political reality to which they referred – Great Britain an Imperial power in the world – has evaporated. The unity of the Commonwealth is always something upon which Her Majesty has set much store, and successive British Prime Ministers have paid lip-service to this idea, largely for reasons of politeness, and have entertained the Commonwealth leaders to annual dinners and functions. Whenever the leaders sat down together to discuss politics, there were clashes and disagreements, since they did not in fact represent any cohesive entity beyond the fact that, historically, their countries were all former British dominions or dependencies. This was never more sharply apparent than in the attitude of the British Commonwealth Conference to the country where Princess Elizabeth first made her moving self-dedication:

South Africa.

Well trained in the art of political flannel, and believing the liberal consensus to be almost as sacred as her Coronation Oath, Her Majesty very naturally sided with the Commonwealth leaders in their desire to impose economic sanctions on South Africa (an ex-member of the Commonwealth!) as a means of putting pressure on the all-white Government to abolish the apartheid laws.

Mrs Thatcher took a notoriously different view, and stood up to the various Commonwealth leaders with characteristic robustness. When accused of the immorality of not imposing sanctions on South Africa, she said, 'I find nothing moral about people sitting in comfortable circumstances, with good salaries, inflation-proof pensions, good jobs, saying that we, as a matter of morality, will put x hundred thousand black people out of work, knowing that this could lead to starvation, poverty, unemployment, and even greater violence.'

It was at the Commonwealth Conference of 1986 that these issues were to be debated by the different nations who attended. Two days before the opening of the conference, the *Sunday Times* claimed that there was now a breach between Margaret Thatcher and her Sovereign.* Most of the story was subsequently admitted by the editor of that newspaper to be untrue. It had claimed that the Queen differed from Margaret Thatcher over a whole range of issues, ranging from the Libyan bombings to the miners' strike and the poverty of the inner cities. Their 'clash' over Africa was merely the latest example of the Queen being 'worried to the point of outrage' by the Iron Lady.

There had been plenty of occasions in history where Prime Ministers and their sovereigns had had personal

* July 20, 1986.

disagreements: Gladstone disapproved of Queen Victoria's attitude towards the Ottoman Empire, for example; George V disliked Lloyd George's Bismarckian Social Welfare schemes; there were clashes, particularly in the early days, between Winston Churchill and George VI. What was entirely new in the disagreement between Mrs Thatcher and the Queen* was its public nature. The *Sunday Times* article, like so much journalism, was an example of something where 'everything was true except the facts'. While it was obviously untrue that the Queen wished to express her views about the Prime Minister by 'leaking' them to one of Mr Rupert Murdoch's newspapers, there was a perceptible public difference of style between the two women. While there was no reason to suppose that they did not conduct themselves with perfect politeness at their weekly meetings, there was no secret made by the Prime Minister that she thought such encounters 'a waste of time'. And over the African question, they plainly did take different sides – the Queen holding the view that the Commonwealth must be held together at all costs, and Margaret Thatcher regarding the Commonwealth with increasing impatience.

The *Sunday Times* article, inaccurate as it was in substance, was believed, and this was a symptom of the fact that the British public thought of Margaret Thatcher and the Queen as rivals.

This was understandable, given the fact that Mrs Thatcher appeared, as time went on, to adopt a manner which was increasingly regal. Her adoption of the royal

---

* Or 'Buckingham Palace', as the Queen is usually called on such occasions. Throughout her *annus horribilis*, it was noticeable that whenever the Queen expressed disgust, astonishment, disagreement or outrage with her subjects she was referred to as if she were this substantial work of architecture. ('Buckingham Palace said last night that . . .') When things go right, the Queen is referred to in her own person.

'we' in her speech was only a symptom of this. 'We are a grandmother', said to the waiting reporters after the birth of a son to her son Mark and his wife, is the most famous of these utterances. The biographers include many other examples: 'We are in the fortunate position in Britain, of being, as it were, the senior person in power.' And again – having visited some block of flats in Moscow – 'We have enjoyed ourselves immensely.'

Whether, at the height of her power, Mrs Thatcher regarded herself as regal, we shall have to wait for history to decide. Certainly she more and more took upon herself roles which had traditionally been fulfilled by royalties, rather than by politicians. The Queen is a naturally diffident person, and when disasters occur, she is frightened that her immediate appearance on the scene to comfort the survivors will distract the rescue-workers, nurses and such people from the job they are wishing to do. 'I shall only be in the way,' she is quoted as saying.* Nevertheless, she has been unobtrusively faithful in turning up at scenes of calamity to offer comfort to those left behind; it was a tradition which went back to the Second World War, when the Queen's father, King George VI, and her mother, Queen Elizabeth, were tireless in visiting bomb-sites and hospitals. The only peacetime occasion on which the Queen has deliberately stayed away from a disaster, delaying her visit by a few days – Aberfan, where a slagheap collapsed on a primary school, killing many of the children in the Welsh mining village in October 1966 – is privately regarded by Her Majesty as the greatest mistake of her reign.†

It was noticed by the Royal Family that the longer the

* Douglas Keay, *Elizabeth II* (1991), p.256.

† Douglas Keay, p.247.

Prime Minister was in office, the more she seemed to be taking upon herself this role of the national figurehead. In the spring of 1987 a British cross-Channel ferry sank outside the Belgian port of Zeebrugge. Mrs Thatcher set out at once, but not before telling her staff that the Palace presence – in this case the Duke and Duchess of York – was not to be allowed to upstage her own. If this story by Hugo Young* is true (and there is no particular reason to doubt it), it implies that by this stage of her Premiership Mrs Thatcher had risen above the rule that Prime Ministers do not travel abroad without the consent or at least the knowledge of the Monarch, since she rapidly flew off to Belgium.

While Mrs Thatcher was still Prime Minister, most people in Britain felt that they had more to think about than her effect on the Royal Family. As the country lurched from one drama to the next – now a war, now a great national strike, now an artificially created boom which gave everyone the impression that their homes had doubled in value (by which they meant that their houses had doubled in price) – the Queen was not to the forefront of anyone's attention. It was only after Mrs Thatcher's removal from office by the *coup d'état* of 1990 that the British people began to absorb the imaginative effect of her years of power and to sense that one of her legacies has been a weakening of the importance of the Monarchy. Those who disliked Mrs Thatcher helped to create this impression even more strongly than those who cheered on 'the Leaderene', and this is for two very simple reasons.

The first is that everyone felt that they had passed through more than a decade of all but monarchy in the reign of Margaret. With her upstaging of the Royal Family themselves, her use of the royal 'we' to describe herself,

* *One of Us*, (1990) p.492.

her immense appeal at election time, her genius in front of television and film cameras, Margaret Thatcher had begun to displace the Queen and to demonstrate that the British could have a very plausible national leader who was not a Monarch but an elected representative.

The second anti-monarchical legacy of Mrs Thatcher is that she is a democrat. It is not exactly clear at what stage of her career she became one, but there can be no doubt of her democratic credentials now that she has been released from the shackles of power. Her objections to the British ratification of the Maastricht Treaty have taken a singularly democratic turn for one who, in the days of her power, rejected any notion of a referendum as a way of determining the destiny of events. Because all three major political parties in Britain support the Treaty, Lady Thatcher takes the democratic view that Parliament is no longer capable of representing the wishes of those British people opposed to it. Therefore, by one of those paradoxes by which political truth only seems visible by being turned on its head, she supports a referendum to defend the sovereignty of the Westminster Parliament, even though a majority of the Members of the Westminster Parliament do not want such a referendum.

Not that this is a pure volte-face. There has always been a democratic tendency in Margaret Thatcher's political thought, visible in her wish that every British family should, if possible, own their own home; visible in her willingness to make a recording of the Gettysburg address; visible in her cheering on the collapse of Eastern Bloc communism slightly before it actually collapsed.

The British constitutional Monarchy is not a democratic institution. At General Elections the British people elect men and women to represent them in Parliament. Thereafter, they have never asked for any say in the way these representatives ran their affairs (though they reserve the right to grumble about the inefficiency of politicians and to rejoice in their downfall), and until the advent of Mrs Thatcher it is questionable whether they wanted such a say. The underlying principle of the British system, until twenty or so years ago, was deference. This did not necessarily mean the same thing as subservience. People were able to hold politicians in contempt while recognising that it was the function of Parliament to draw up and control the legislation which affected their lives. By the same token, people could make (usually pretty mild) jokes about the Queen or the Duke of Edinburgh without losing sight of the principle of constitutional Monarchy: which is that the Monarch has the ultimate power to ratify the legislation which Parliament decides. Of course, in the event of a Monarch choosing to block Parliamentary legislation the system would break down, but there had been no serious clash between a Prime Minister and a Sovereign for sixty or more years until the Queen's disagreement with Mrs Thatcher about South Africa.

The principle of deference is that one group of individuals literally defers to another group for political purposes. The people, having made their electoral choice, defer to Parliament's decisions. Parliament, both in the matter of law and the matter of patronage, defers to the Crown, and so does the Civil Service. The bishops, the Regius professors in the older universities, the nobility, all owe their authority to the Crown and swear allegiance to the Crown. This is not a democratic system, though when it operates well it provides checks to the possible abuse of power which might surprise a true democrat.

Margaret Thatcher's democratic revolution was only a partial success, but she did succeed in eliminating the concept of deference from many individual lives. This was most noticeably successful in her reform of Trade Union law. No system so much depends on deference and is so undemocratic (in simple terms) as the old Trades Union movement. In order to speak on behalf of its individual members a Union must make collective decisions. When this came to the exercise of a block vote at Labour Party Conferences and at its own Trades Union Congresses, it was increasingly unacceptable to its own rank and file. The idea had got abroad that democracy meant not the freedom to ask someone more engaged or better informed to make decisions on your behalf, but the freedom to make those decisions for yourself (of course, Mrs Thatcher had not invented it, she was merely one of its more colourful champions). This spelt anarchy in the Trades Unions and delivered their death blow.

How long can it be before Parliamentary democracy, based on the principle of constitutional monarchy, goes the same way as the old dinosaurs of the Labour Movement? And what will take their place? Populism is politics for the non-thinker. Fifty million people cannot all make a joint decision about the level of inflation, or the level of income tax, or about whether to go to war. These decisions have to be made for them. In the past they have been made by the Prime Minister in Cabinet, answerable on the one hand to the Sovereign and on the other to Parliament. Take away the check of Monarchy, and how long before you have removed the check of Parliament also? The British might find they have dismantled more than the Royal Household if a republican mood caught fire. But in my view there can be no doubt, if such a mood were to spread, that one of its principal authors, for all her protestations of loyalty to the Queen and to the Crown, is Margaret Thatcher.

The democratic populism on the left in Britain – represented by such figures as the former Lord Stansgate, Tony

Benn – never took hold because it sounded cranky. (This was because Benn has always appealed to logic, and human affairs are seldom run on logical lines.) Mrs Thatcher's demagogic populism made appeals to the purse and the family hearth, and to the idea that grocers' daughters and simple folk had as much right as anyone else to run the affairs of a great nation. She brought to pass what Harold Wilson, with his sauce bottles and his cheap mackintoshes, had dangled in front of the electorate as a mere dream. She would probably be horrified in one part of herself to realise the Frankenstein's monster which she has brought to birth; in another part of herself – the demagogue – she would be very far from horrified since, in the event of Britain adopting an elective Presidency, there is small doubt in anyone's mind who would consider herself most eligible for such a role. But populist whims can be difficult to extinguish. Five years ago Mr Auberon Waugh seemed a lone voice among British journalists complaining about the damage done to Britain by Mrs Thatcher and her 'New Brits'. His father, Evelyn Waugh, was asked what he would be voting in a General Election, and said that he would not presume to advise Her Majesty on the choice of Her Ministers. Things have now swung so far in an opposite direction that son Auberon can write that 'we are no longer a fit country to have a monarchy, being eaten up with rancour, hatred, aggression and envy'.* These are all good Thatcherite qualities, but if I were the Monarch, surveying the drizzly view from the windows of Buckingham Palace, I should take the words of Waugh *fils* very seriously indeed.

* *The Oldie*, December 25, 1992.

THREE

Lady Di

If the position of the Monarchy was significantly weakened by Mrs Thatcher's rise to power in 1979, she was
not the only lady who was to have a profound effect –
some would say a profoundly weakening effect – on the
House of Windsor. It was in the first year of Mrs Thatcher's
premiership that Prince Charles decided that he wanted to
marry Lady Diana Spencer.

She was a nineteen-year-old infant-school teacher, living
at the time in Coleherne Court in Earls Court, West London.
She came from an ancient aristocratic lineage: the Spencers had received their earldom from Charles I, and they
are distantly related to the poet Edmund Spenser, author
of *The Faerie Queene*, a fact which caused the historian
Edward Gibbon to remark: 'The nobility of the Spencers
has been illustrated and enriched by the trophies of Marlborough; but I exhort them to consider *The Faerie Queene* as

the most precious jewel in their coronet.'* Had he been able to see into the future, Gibbon might have revised his judgement. The eighth Earl Spencer was to father a fairy princess who far outshone *The Faerie Queene* of his poetical collateral.

Lady Diana was his third daughter. She was born on the Sandringham estate in Norfolk at her father's residence there, Park House. The story is told that when, as a young child, Lady Diana was informed that they were all driving over to nearby Sandringham to visit the Royal Family, she protested. Diana hated the 'strange' atmosphere there and kicked and screamed, and refused to go until her father told her it would be considered very bad manners if she did not join the Royal children. A strange precedent! Not much more than a dozen years later she was eagerly accepting invitations to Sandringham, and married the heir to the British Crown, His Royal Highness Charles, Prince of Wales, in St Paul's Cathedral on July 29, 1981.

Many people supposed that the marriage had been concocted by the grandmothers. The Queen Mother's friend and lady-in-waiting, Lady Fermoy, was Lady Diana's maternal grandmother, and nothing could have seemed more probable than that the old ladies had arranged the match between them. If the chronicles of Andrew Morton are to be believed, however, this would appear not to have been the case, and we learn that, before Lady Diana committed herself to Prince Charles, Lady Fermoy warned the girl strongly against marrying into the Royal Family. 'You must understand,' said Lady Fermoy, 'that their sense of humour and lifestyle are very different. I don't think it would suit you.'

---

* As the allusion shows, they are also related to the Dukes of Marlborough.

The differences between the Prince's famous sense of humour and that of Lady Diana did not make themselves sufficiently apparent during the summer of 1980: indeed, it was only a few days before her wedding day that Lady Diana discovered the notorious bracelet engraved with the initials 'F' and 'G' entwined – Fred and Gladys being the pet names used by His Royal Highness and his friend Mrs Parker-Bowles. While hindsight has persuaded Lady Diana that she wished at this juncture to cancel her wedding (a very usual sensation in brides two or three days before the ceremony, whether or not they discover F and G bracelets), there are those who take a different view of the Princess's approach to marriage. For such as Lady Colin Campbell, the marriage which took place in St Paul's Cathedral was the fulfilment not merely of Diana's ambitions, but of the monarchical ambitions of a whole dynasty of Spencers. Lady Colin even traces back this supposed family ambition to the lesbian love affair conducted between their ancestress Sarah, Duchess of Marlborough, with her sovereign lady Queen Anne. Not content with seducing the Queen, Duchess Sarah also bribed the Prince of Wales (later George II) with £100,000 to marry her granddaughter, Lady Diana Spencer. The bribe was not accepted, and it was not, according to Lady Colin's view of things, until 200 more years of rollicking, bodice-ripping history had passed before this voraciously ambitious family achieved their desire.* No doubt many girls who are in a position to have such dreams wonder what it would be like to marry the Prince of Wales. What makes Diana Spencer special is not merely that she achieved this aim, but that she herself turned, in consequence of her position, into a figure who eclipsed, and threatened to destroy, the Royal Family.

* Lady Colin Campbell, *Diana in Private* (1992) p.45.

*

Throughout his twenties, the Prince of Wales must have excited hopes in many young women that they might one day wear the Crown of England on their heads. Many of them, no doubt, were happy to have brief affairs with the Prince; but there must have been others who laboured under the belief that, having surrendered to him their virtue, he would surrender to them his name. The opposite was true. The very fact that they were prepared to go to bed with the Prince proved to him that they were not the virginal woman he was seeking as his bride.

We do not know how or where this obsession with virginity developed. There can be no doubt, however, that, by the time Prince Charles was thirty years old, the mood had reached fever-pitch: that he must find himself a wife, and she must be a virgin. Given the strength of his desire, the obvious place to look for such a bride was among his mother's former dominions – for example in Pakistan, where the observance of Islam (unlike the practice of Roman Catholicism, it is no barrier to marrying a British Monarch) has ensured a higher standard of sexual propriety among young females than obtained in the post-Christian Britain of the 1970s. Apart from guaranteeing for himself a wife who would observe the proprieties and know her place, the Prince could have formed an important *entente cordiale* with the Islamic world had he married a rich young Muslim. Nor, probably, would he have scorned the money and treasures brought in her dowry, which could have been greater than anything that the third daughter of a divorced English peer could possibly have secured.

It has generally been assumed – not least by those closest to the throne – since the Prince could only marry with his mother's permission, that she would choose his bride for him. It might have been better if this had been the case. (As Samuel Johnson sagely observed, 'Marriages would in general be as happy, and often more so, if they were all made by the Lord Chancellor.' How much truer for royalties than commoners.) In fact, Prince Charles did have his future bride chosen for him; but the arbiter of his destiny was neither his Sovereign nor her Lord Chancellor, but the Prince's old friend Camilla, now Mrs Parker-Bowles.

Perhaps Mrs Parker-Bowles is one of the many women in England, Wales, Scotland, Northern Ireland and the Duchy of Cornwall who believed that she might have become Queen in return for favours rendered. So indeed she might have been, if our chroniclers tell the truth, but we learn that she tired of waiting for him while he was serving in the Royal Navy, and married instead the Roman Catholic Army officer Andrew Parker-Bowles.

Though we must assume that most of what is written about the Parker-Bowleses in the newspapers is fiction, there does seem to be substantial evidence that Mrs Parker-Bowles helped the Prince choose a wife when it became apparent that this was what he needed or thought he needed. There was in reality no need for the Prince of Wales – one of nature's bachelors – to marry at all. Thanks to the fecundity of nearly all the Queen's family, there has never in recent times been a shortage of perfectly suitable heirs to the throne. A former member of his household, recalling the Prince's bachelor existence, said, 'It's very sad, really. He would never have got married, of course, because he was happy with his bachelor life. If he had his fishing tackle ready, his polo ponies saddled and a £5 note for the church collection, he was perfectly content. It was great fun. You could wake him up at six in the morning and say: "Right, Sir, we are going here"; and off we would go.' Moreover, as we are informed by one of the chroniclers, 'His friendship with Mrs Camilla Parker-Bowles, who eagerly adapted her life to his diary, dovetailed perfectly with his lifestyle.'*

Nevertheless, by the time he was thirty, people were wondering why he had not got married: the Press were wondering, politicians were murmuring about it, and his parents were worried. Any foreign Princesses deemed passable on other grounds were ruled out by the Royal Marriages Act because they were Roman Catholics. English aristocrats were unlikely to be virgins unless minors; and even a very young age was no guarantee of purity. He was on one level the most eligible bachelor in the world; but in the event, the choice of a bride seems to have been almost haphazard and clumsy, like a man who has left all his shopping for presents until Christmas Eve and dashes into the nearest department store for an armful of trinkets, however unsuitable.

It had been back in 1977 that he started to woo Lady Sarah Spencer, the eldest daughter of Lord Spencer. One of her friends at the time (presumably no longer a friend, unless Lady Sarah is very long-suffering) told Lady Colin Campbell, 'Sarah now says ... that she didn't fancy Prince Charles and that she was never interested in him as anything but a friend ... If you believe that, you'll believe anything. Of course she was interested. And she would have hung in there for as long as it took to get him, but for the fact that her emotions got the better of her. She wasn't strong-minded like Diana ... and the strain reached her. You have to understand the way the Prince treated his girl-friends to see why she wasn't up to the job – of waiting, I mean. He blew hot and cold, not only with her, but with all of them. One minute he'd be very caring, and the next it would be as if she didn't exist. After you'd seen him steadily for several days, you might not hear from him

*Andrew Morton, *Diana: Her True Story* (1993 version) p.48.

for weeks. And Sarah Spencer was not tough.'

It was on a shooting party at Althorp during his affair with Sarah Spencer that Charles had renewed his acquaintanceship with the youngest sister, Diana, then a sixteen-year-old schoolgirl. Two years and several girlfriends later, he started to invite Diana for visits, first to Sandringham and then to Balmoral. It was at Petworth, sitting on a bale of straw, that we are told Lady Diana first really captured his heart by expressing sympathy for his demeanour at Lord Mountbatten's funeral: 'You looked so sad when you walked up the aisle at the funeral. It was the most tragic thing I've ever seen. My heart bled for you when I watched it. I thought: "It's wrong, you are lonely, you should be with somebody to look after you." ' Charles consulted with the appropriate authority, and Mrs Parker-Bowles, after a few inspections of the young woman, pronounced her marriageable. In October 1980 Charles and Camilla extended the honour to Lady Diana of showing her Highgrove, the house which he had lately acquired in Gloucestershire to be near the Parker-Bowleses.

Whether Lady Diana was indeed too naïve to understand the nature of the relationship between Prince Charles and Mrs Parker-Bowles – and what, indeed, the nature of that relationship has been – is not to the purpose here. Whether we believe, with Mr Morton, that she went up the aisle of St Paul's Cathedral as a lamb to the slaughter, or whether, with Lady Colin Campbell, that Lady Macbeth hardly seized a crown with more ambitious alacrity, the wedding changed everything for the House of Windsor.

On the surface of things, it would seem that the crisis in the House of Windsor was caused by the very public break-up of this marriage. In a step which was completely unprecedented, the Princess of Wales chose to make known to a journalist the details of her grievances against

Prince Charles. They were all published in a book, *Diana: Her True Story*, by Andrew Morton. This author claimed to have derived his information from the 'friends' of the Princess, but there could be no doubt that many of the most astonishing and damaging claims came direct from Lady Diana herself. 'I can *hear* my wife saying those words,' remarked Prince Charles as he read the newspaper extracts from the book.

Morton was able to reveal to the world that, a few days before the ceremony in St Paul's Cathedral, Lady Diana considered calling off the wedding when she discovered that her husband had no intention of abandoning his 'friendship' with Mrs Parker-Bowles. Sympathetic readers were able to discover that, throughout her supposedly idyllic marriage, Lady Diana had suffered from the eating disorder bulimia nervosa, that she had made suicide attempts which were in reality 'cries for help' on four or five occasions, that she persistently resented the cold and unloving attitude of her husband both towards herself and towards his two sons, and that she heartily detested his family. As soon as these disturbing details had been revealed, it was only a matter of months before the separation between the unhappy pair was announced formally from Buckingham Palace. It came at the end of an appalling year for the Queen.

The publishers of Andrew Morton's book, and in particular the Editor of the *Sunday Times*, who had paid large sums for the serial rights, were insistent that the details revealed in it would change the Monarchy forever, and possibly bring it to its knees. They and their readers were in danger of missing a point which was difficult to see because it was so obvious. Plenty of royal wives have been unhappy – Queen Alexandra's misery at the infidelities of her husband Edward VII, for example, was no secret to the world. Many women (perhaps most) have considered calling off their wedding a few days before the ceremony; and many, we are informed, overeat, vomit, hurl themselves downstairs, weep at the sight of their mothers-in-law and pour out their sorrows to unreliable 'friends'. The remarkable thing about Lady Diana Spencer is not what was revealed about her by Mr Morton; it was what she had visibly and publicly become from the very moment she walked down the aisle of St Paul's Cathedral: an object of fantasy and love for millions of people throughout the world.

The Editor of the *Sunday Times* thought that he had uncovered secret things about Lady Di which posed a great threat to Constitutional Monarchy. In fact he had only uncovered painful tittle-tattle, and the really dangerous thing about her, from the point of view of the Queen, had been staring newspaper editors in the face for more than a decade. It was not Lady Di's secret life, nor even her marriage problems, which had posed a threat to the future of the Monarchy; it was her public life, and the consequent changed attitude on the part of the Royal Family towards the Press. More than any film star in the history of Hollywood, this woman could captivate huge crowds wherever she went. She has probably been photographed more often than anyone in history, including Churchill, President Kennedy and Marilyn Monroe. And all this was apparent before her more recently developed talents as a healer and comforter of the sick – what her husband has unkindly called her 'Mother Teresa act'.

All this was new, and the Royal Family were perhaps slower than the Press to realise how damaging it was to the Crown. Before the arrival of Lady Diana Spencer as the Royal Family's star turn, the attitude of the British public to the Crown was oddly sophisticated. The huge majority of British people, as every survey has shown, wished to retain a monarchical system. They revered the Crown, and they were capable of being carried away by periods of enthusiasm for one or another member of the Royal House. But 'loving' the Queen did not mean the same as being interested by her. Continental newspapers throughout the 1950s and 1960s would carry stories about the Queen's private life and her supposedly unhappy marriage. These stories were never repeated in the English newspapers, and while that is partly because of the atmosphere of deference which unquestionably existed in those days, and which has now disappeared, it was also because, although people would have wanted to know the intimate details of the Queen's married life, they might not have wanted to read such things in a newspaper.

Editors and newspaper proprietors, even in London, were never noted for their altruism. They knew what their readers wanted. And nobody wanted the Royal Family to be like film stars, their mood swings, marital rows and favourite restaurants made into the subject of newspaper articles. People revered the Crown, but they were not really interested in the Queen, for the very simple reason that she is not really interesting.

The time for the Queen to grow worried was when the public began to respond to Lady Di in a very different manner. Her first visit to Australia, in 1982, was to set the tone for many such tours. In a country of seventeen million people, one million people were actually on the move, following the Royal couple as they journeyed from city to city. Not even the Pope was attracting crowds like this, and certainly such numbers had never massed to see the Prince of Wales in his bachelor days. Lady Di was an entirely new phenomenon in the Royal story. With the possible exception of Queen Elizabeth the Queen Mother, no member of the Royal Family had ever been so popular on a personal level.

Lady Di was loved first of all for her extraordinary photogenic beauty. Although she found the huge crowds daunting, she adapted to the role of a megastar with remarkable speed. Soon enough she was herself becoming dependent on the adulation of her fans. She was eventually to discover within herself great gifts of sympathy for those in need, for the sick and the dying; but, rather more dangerously for the family into which she had married, she had a taste for publicity. This meant that very early on she learnt that she could to a certain extent manipulate and control the Press; but only to a certain extent. If the world's newspapers and television companies made Lady Di into a star, they were to exact a price for it. The relationship between Lady Di and the Fourth Estate was comparable to the old relationship which existed between the Hanoverian Kings and the Whig Aristocracy. The one was the creature of the group; but in time each came to depend upon the other.

Up to this time, the Royal Family had viewed the Press warily and with extreme caution. Some individual members of the Royal Family, such as Prince Philip and Princess Anne, exhibited a hostility towards journalists which bordered on the paranoid. They were all, from the Queen downwards to the remotest Royal cousin, entirely unprepared for the 'new relationship' with the Press established by Prince Charles's young bride. Because of Lady Di, they all now stood in a new relationship with the Press. New rules applied, and they were not prepared for them; new newspaper proprietors such as Mr Murdoch had appeared on the scene, with none of the old attitudes of respect and decorum towards English institutions. The potential chemistry of this mixture was deadly.

Lady Diana had many qualities which remained hidden

from the world on her wedding day. From an early stage, Royal-watchers were beginning to make the comparison with another non-Royal Aristocrat, Lady Elizabeth Bowes-Lyon, who had married into the Royal Family, and made it supposedly more popular, on April 26, 1923.

Whatever one's views of either lady, both Lady Diana and the present Queen Mother are possessed of an impressive capacity to mythologise themselves and to project this personal myth* on to a credulous world. This is not to suggest that either lady is in the smallest degree either dishonest or dishonourable. But it is no inconsiderable gift to persuade the world to see oneself in one's own particular way.

From her early twenties, Lady Elizabeth Bowes-Lyon showed ambition to be the Queen of England. She was humiliated by the then Prince of Wales, and had to make do by marrying his brother, the Duke of York. She was nevertheless able to persuade herself and her children – and therefore to persuade the world – that it was the most tremendous grief to her when her 'Bertie' inherited the throne. In spite of being a very rich woman who all her life has been pampered by servants and enjoyed everything handsome about her (and nothing wrong with any of that), Queen Elizabeth has also managed to be 'the Queen Mum', supposedly never happier than when condescending to East Enders and sharing the humble plight of her loyal subjects.

Lady Diana Spencer has similar powers of self-mythology, similar abilities to make the public see her in her own terms. This is obviously not to the Royal Family's advantage. Whereas Lady Elizabeth Bowes-Lyon saw herself as the

---

* I do not imply, by the use of the words 'myth' or 'mythologise', to impugn the sincerity of Her Majesty or of Her Royal Highness. I am discussing the distinctive way in which they are able to share their own highly developed idea of themselves with their joyous admirers.

saviour of the Monarchy, rescuing it from the clutches of Wallis Simpson and restoring the homely family values which she herself exemplified, Lady Diana had a more confused self-image, which included the icon of Diana the Martyr. In this mythology of events, the carefree, innocent tomboy of Coleherne Court was snatched by an older and more cynical man, who did not love her and who forced her to be his smiling bride, however cruel and cold he was towards her. Bravely, because this experience (added to the trauma of her parents' divorce) had taught her to understand suffering as few people did, Lady Di was able to stretch out healing hands to sufferers the world over. A tireless charity worker, whether for marriage guidance or care for AIDS victims, our Saint was there in the midst. As she said herself to the Bishop of Norwich during her mysterious telephone call – later unkindly ridiculed as the 'Squidgygate' tapes – '"I understand people's suffering, people's pain, more than you will ever know." He said, "That's obvious by what you are doing for AIDS." I said, "It's not only AIDS, it's anyone who suffers, I can smell them a mile away."'* Not since Queen Anne had touched and allegedly healed the sick, had such claims been made by a Royal personage.†

This is not to say that Lady Di has invented the qualities for which people love her. She is quite patently and genuinely concerned with the sick and the suffering; she is exuberant, enlivened by her encounters with people, humorous

---

* *Sun*, August 25, 1992.
† Charles II, at his Restoration in 1660, revived the old custom of 'touching' the sick for 'the King's Evil'. The idea was that, because anointed Kings were divinely chosen, they had special healing powers. The practice continued throughout the reigns of James II, William and Mary, and Anne, but was discontinued by the Hanoverians. One of the last persons to be touched for the evil was the scrofulous infant, Samuel Johnson.

and extraordinarily beautiful. When her admirers speak of being in love with her, this is quite seriously meant: she has attracted genuine and heart-wrenching love from her followers.

Whether the cult of Lady Di will survive the break-up of her marriage remains to be seen. The commentators have not been reticent. At the end of 1992, Paul Johnson, the wise Nestor of newspaper columnists, told readers of the *Daily Mail*: 'What the public will not tolerate is the kind of vendetta against Diana which the family pursued against the Duchess of Windsor, and for which, in Diana's case, there is no justification. If Diana is seen to be ill-treated, public sympathy will swing violently in her favour. The republicans will rejoice, the enemies of the Royal Family will rub their hands with fiendish glee, and those MPs and journalists who never miss an opportunity to undermine the institution of the Monarchy will move swiftly into action.'*

Julie Burchill, writing in the *Mail on Sunday*, took the view that it did not particularly matter any longer what the Royal Family thought of Lady Di. Burchill's message was that the Princess had, in effect, taken over already as the member of the Royalty in whom most people were interested. 'With the Windsors as they were, Britain was nothing more than a tatty tourist trap. Diana replaced its hackneyed mystique with the magic of good works and glamour. A few thousand tourists watched the Changing of the Guard at Buckingham Palace; the whole world watched the changing of Diana's clothes.'†

This, for traditionalist aristocrats like Sir Peregrine Worsthorne, was just the trouble. When Lady Diana took her two sons on a Caribbean holiday after the first Christmas of her

* December 31, 1992.

† December 13, 1992.

marital separation, Sir Peregrine allowed it to be known that 'I was by no means impressed by the many pictures of the Princess of Wales romping in the Caribbean, and if she had set out to convince me that she was a wildly unsuitable person to have custody of a boy born to be King of England, she could not have thought of a better way than to take him and his younger brother to that notorious playground of the world's rich white trash, even arranging to have the world's Press present to celebrate her deplorable taste in Christmas holiday locations.'*

Journalists are even more fickle than the public whose appetite for comment and tittle-tattle they attempt to satisfy. At the beginning of 1992 Lady Di had few critics in the Press, and by the end of it she had few friends.† That was because she had taken an enormous gamble, which the journalists called 'manipulating them'. Trapped in the misery of a marriage which had become intolerable, Lady Di would appear to have offered her husband an ultimatum. Either he let her go, or she would go in her own way. It would seem that he did not believe her, and the idea of indiscretion on this scale would not have been something which the Queen would not have believed possible until it happened. Whatever other peculiar or egotistical motives Lady Di had for revealing her unhappy story to Mr Morton, the indiscretion had its desired effect. Not surprisingly, the more stuffy commentators recalled Cosmo Gordon Lang's sermon to the exiled King after the Abdication in 1936: 'By his own will he has abdicated – he has surrendered the trust. With characteristic frankness he has told us the motive. It

---

*Sunday Telegraph, January 10, 1993.
† For a fuller discussion, the reader is referred to Chapter Six.

was a craving for private happiness.'*

The moralisers will continue to attack her, not always aware of why there should be an alternative to their way of thinking, sometimes known in Britain as the Princess's party. The members of this group, together with their fellow-travellers and sympathisers, are not all silly men, droolingly in love with their 'Fairytale Princess'. They are people who have taken the trouble to think out the implications of what has happened in the last year, and above all to think out the implications of what has happened to the constitutional monarchy since the separation of Lady Diana from her husband.

Now that she has become a creature of the media, Lady Di's reputation will be decided by journalists. But the journalists, powerful as they might wish to be or consider themselves to be, cannot decide who is to be the future King of England. Unless the hereditary laws are radically altered,† the Crown will one day pass to Lady Diana's son William. Little as the fastidious might enjoy her tastes in friends or holiday venues, no one is going to be able to wrest her from her own children. She has shown, by her independence of spirit, that she is prepared to defy all conventions and bring a Royal Marriage to a public and painful end. One can have no doubts at all that if she is antagonised by the Royal Family in the discussions relating to the separation, she would exercise her rights to go and live abroad, taking her sons with her. That would probably spell the end of the Monarchy, or at any rate the end of the House of Windsor (which is not the same thing).‡

Throughout the summer of 1992, as the increasingly

* J.G. Lockhart, *Cosmo Gordon Lang* (1949) p.405.
† For some further suggestions on this, see Chapter Ten.
‡ Again, see Chapter Ten.

embarrassing stories unfolded in the newspapers, the Prince and Princess's lawyers, in close consultation with the Queen herself, played their dangerous poker game. There were threats to separate Diana from her children, which were scotched by Diana's apparent willingness to give the public details of Prince Charles's behaviour as a husband. There were petty discussions about the Princess's titles – whether or not she would be allowed to call herself Her Royal Highness. There were discussions, which were less petty, about cash, and about who should live where. All the time the Queen was trying to smooth things over and persuade the Prince and Princess of Wales to patch up their differences, for the sake of the Royal ideal and the future of the Crown. Their disastrous joint visit to Korea in the autumn was undertaken solely to fulfil an agreement with the Queen that they would have a three-month trial period of shamming. When they came home, the Prince's party lost no time in letting the world know that Diana had let down her husband by showing how miserable she was. It was at this time in London that I first began to hear the ominous calls for Lady Di's removal from the scene. Sometimes these were mock-jocular – as when the Prince's party's more puerile members called for her to be beheaded on Tower Green like the unfortunate wives of Henry VIII. Sometimes they took the form of knowing predictions – that she would 'commit suicide' by the end of 1993.

The Prince's followers seemed to have allowed a curious delusion to settle in their brains: that if the Princess could be removed from the scene, all the problems of the House of Windsor would be removed. But if this was what they thought, they were overlooking one glaringly obvious and unhappy fact: that the greatest 'problem' faced by the House of Windsor was not Lady Diana; it was her husband, His Royal Highness Prince Charles. And this would have been the case whether he had married or not.

46

FOUR

The Prince of
Wales

'My will henceforth is, If it ever chance that my particular interest and the general good of my Countries
should seem to go against each other, in that case,
my will is, That the latter always be preferred.' This
is a fine dialect for incipient Royalty.

Thomas Carlyle, *The Life of Frederick the Great*

Throughout November 1992, the world watched in sus-
pense to see whether the delicate GATT (General Agreement on Tariffs and Trade) negotiations would succeed,
or whether the disagreement between the United States
and France about agriculture would be irreconcilable. The
particular nub of the dispute concerned the sale of oil seed
and the respective share of the world market claimed by
French and American farmers. The more general area of
dispute concerned the Common Agricultural Policy of
the European Community. Here, not merely the United
States, but also the New Zealanders, the Canadians and the
Australians, felt that they could not be expected to open up
their markets to British and other European competitors if
the huge subsidies awarded to the French farmers by the
CAP continued to weight trade so heavily in favour of
France.

No one appeared to doubt that if the GATT talks broke

down, the world would be plunged into a trade war. The White House economic advisers suggested that the world economy would be $1,000 billion worse off if the talks collapsed. Rather than moving towards global free trade, the world would have broken down into three aggressive and highly protectionist trading zones – those dominated by Japan, the United States and Europe. The effects on the 'developing' nations would have been catastrophic. Desperate poverty, possible starvation and probable armed combat would have been the consequence of French intransigence. Since then there have been further developments, caused by the new administration in the White House, but, for the purposes of our present discussion, all that matters is to recognise the delicacy of *that particular phase* of GATT talks.

It was seen to be in everyone's interest that these talks succeeded. It was even in the French interest, as M. Jacques Delors eventually conceded after three or four weeks of international shadowboxing on the issue. It was therefore with some dismay that the world leaders read reports on December 5, 1992, of a speech delivered in French by the Prince of Wales to the Académie des Sciences Morales et Politiques in Paris.

'Because of the imperatives of trade and the unyielding rigours of "comparative advantage", do we really need to compress the traditions and vitality of rural life and culture into the straitjacket of an industry like any other?' he asked. 'One of the joys for me of being in France is that you have a particularly strong sense of those traditions – and of the ultimate cost to the human spirit of the unrelenting migration from the countryside to the big cities.'

The Prince's words were heard with especial dismay at home in Britain. Whatever his own personal views, he was surely aware of the views of the British Government and the British Foreign Office, which were fundamentally opposed to his ideas? 'I do not always do what I'm told,' he was reported as boasting to the French philosophers and academics.* The question at issue here was not whether the Prince was right or wrong about the value of rural life in France, but whether he spoke with the same voice as his mother's Government; and he clearly did not. This was not some harmless issue – such as his supposed wish that more English children studied the plays of Shakespeare or his belief that Hebridean islanders had a better 'lifestyle' than city-dwellers. It was a highly delicate political issue which his intervention could very easily have upset, for he was in danger of placing the British Government in the embarrassing position of seeming to contradict the potential Head of State. Had Charles been King when he made this speech he would actually have been the Head of State, and we should have witnessed the strange spectacle of the King taking one view of the GATT agreement and his chief Ministers taking another.

In passing, it might be worth asking what prompted Charles to make this strange outburst. One Conservative Member of Parliament said when he had read the speech, 'The Prince of Wales should be defending the people of this country, who have to pay £16 a week per family extra on average to support the French farmers and their food mountains.' What this Parliamentarian, Dr Robert Spink, perhaps did not realise was that the Prince was speaking to a very recognisable political agenda. While most of the mainstream political parties in the free world were committed to the success of GATT, there was one group, the Greens, who were committed with equal vigour to the failure of the world governments to reach economic accord.

Daily Telegraph, December 5, 1992.

The Friends of the Earth had explained ten days before the Prince's speech in Paris why they were opposed to GATT. It was because of the commitment of GATT signatories to a Multilateral Trading Organisation. In a dispute between the USA and Mexico, for instance, over 'dolphin-friendly tuna', the Organisation had ruled that individual countries did not have the right to apply 'extraterritorial environmental measures' to their problems. In the Prince's words, 'do we really need to compress the traditions and vitality of rural life into the straitjacket of an industry like any other?'

The question which arises here is not whether the Prince happens to be right or wrong over the matter of French agriculture. Nor is it entirely a question – though this is a very important matter – of whether he directly contradicts Her Majesty's Government in areas which could affect the peace and stability of mankind. It is also the question of whom he speaks *for*. Perhaps he thinks that he speaks for himself, though there is abundant evidence that all the famous speeches which he has delivered to the world – about architecture, the environment or cheese – have been written for him by someone else. In the case of the GATT speech to the Académie, he was being used as a pawn by a powerful international pressure group. At a time when the French were feeling particularly belligerent towards Britain and when the French farmers especially were ready for a trade war, it was in the interest of such pressure groups to wish to embarrass the British. A British Prime Minister was on the point of hosting the meeting of the European leaders in Edinburgh. The Greens and the pressure group Friends of the Earth were committed to crippling the GATT talks. Prince Charles's speech in Paris in fact failed to wreck GATT, but it had a better chance than most such utterances. To some observers, the speech may have displayed his famous intellectual daring and independence.

To others he seemed simply like a ventriloquist's dummy mouthing the ideas of cranky pressure groups.

Prince Charles is not notably cleverer than his mother, grandfather or great-grandfather, but he entirely lacks their intellectual humility. At his father's disastrous insistence, Prince Charles was not given a conventional education; he was sent to Gordonstoun, not a noted centre of intellectual excellence. The combination of bullying and toadyism which he encountered at this German educational establishment set in the rigours of the Scottish Highlands will hardly have given him an accurate idea of his own capabilities, and indeed he left the school and went up to Cambridge with a wholly inflated sense of his own cleverness. Had he been sent to a school such as Eton where there are some genuinely clever boys and masters, he might have come to understand his actual level. He is not, as his sycophantic followers have been assuring him for twenty years, 'an intellectual'. Unlike first-rate minds he does not always understand what he is saying. For example, inspired by his mentor Sir Laurens van der Post, the Prince decided that the 'simple life' is preferable to the unspiritual existence pursued by most city-dwellers in the West. This inspired the Prince, most unwisely, to make a television documentary film about the Hebridean island of Berneray.

At the sight of the Prince arriving on this island by aeroplane and car, and having an abundance of extremely expensive luggage carried for him by underlings, it was hard to restrain a smile – particularly when he began to lecture the local inhabitants about the beauty of the simple life. Accompanied by one of the best-paid British television 'personalities', Miss Selina Scott, Prince Charles visited a turf-roofed hovel which had been deserted by its miserable inhabitants; the Prince said how sad he found it that people no longer lived in such dwellings. Miss Scott enthusiastically agreed. On this particular island, there are gale-force winds for much of the year. During the week of the Prince's visit we saw that it was with the greatest difficulty that the children were able to open the door of the school, such was the force of the wind. Quite understandably, their parents wished to live in windproof bungalows with metal-framed draught-excluding windows with double glazing. The Prince wished they could see that the old turf-roofed hovels were much more in tune with the environment.

Having delivered himself of this view, the Prince flew home to Highgrove, the substantial country house which he bought for himself in Gloucestershire from his income as Duke of Cornwall.* The Duchy comprises 126,000 acres of property in twenty counties, though most of its real estate is to be found between the Isles of Scilly and Dorset. There is probably no reason to suppose that Prince Charles is a better or worse landlord than the other great property-holders in Britain, such as the Oxford and Cambridge Colleges or the Duke of Westminster. His critics would point to the fact that he did nothing to save the Cornish tin mines which had been in operation since Roman times, and that he had been a hard taskmaster to the tenants. In 1984, the Prince was persuaded to have a change of investment policy. Assets were sold off, and the policies of agricultural expansion and 'conservationism' were sacrificed to considerations of the highest possible investment income. Three years later, the Secretary of the Duchy was able to say, 'The Duchy is stronger today than twenty years ago. Its investment is better spread.' Cynics noted that this had been achieved by exorbitant rent rises for the Duke of Cornwall's tenants and

*His income from the Duchy of Cornwall makes him the fourteenth richest man in Great Britain. See Anthony Holden, *Charles* (1988) pp.42 ff.

the closing down of such pet schemes as the 'model farms', which, one might have thought, would have appealed to the Prince's traditionalist approach to the countryside.

No reasonable person would object to a landlord wishing to get as much out of his property as possible and to manage his investments wisely. They might only begin to feel dissatisfaction at being lectured by such a landlord on the beauties of old-fashioned agriculture and the simple life. Likewise, only the strictest puritan would expect the Prince of Wales or any other Royal personage to have a blameless sexual career. It was his persistent sermonising, the explicit claim that his views of life – on farming, on architecture, on the environment – would bring people not merely closer to peace but closer to God which made malicious ears so willing to listen to the so-called 'Camillagate' tapes, transcripts alleged to be of recorded telephone conversations between the Prince and his friend Mrs Parker-Bowles.

Charles:	One has to feel one's way along, if you know what I mean.
Camilla:	Mm. You're awfully good at feeling your way along.
Charles:	Oh, stop! I want to feel my way along you, all over you and up and down you and in and out . . .
Camilla:	Oh.
Charles:	Particularly in and out . . .
Camilla:	Oh . . .
Charles:	The trouble is, I need you several times a week.
Camilla:	Mm. So do I. I need you all the week. All the time.
Charles:	Oh, God. I'll just live inside your trousers or something. It would be much easier.

Camilla:	(Laughs) What are you going to turn into, a pair of knickers? (Both laugh) Oh, you're going to come back as a pair of knickers.
Charles:	Or, God forbid, a Tampax! Just my luck!*

It is cruel to quote these words. On the other hand, it would not be entirely fair to omit them either. They have become part of the story, whether any of us likes it or not, and if one were to consider the recent history of the Royal Family without alluding to the notorious tapes (however they were obtained, by whom they were obtained, and for what purpose – that is all another story) it would be exhibitionistic to leave them out, just as it is distasteful to remember them. After forty years of earnestly trying to do his best, and after ten or fifteen years of very public service in which the Prince has offered us his opinions on everything from gardening to global warming, from Shakespeare to Jung, from the language of architecture to the future of the Third World, it must be dismaying for him to realise that the public at large can probably only remember two of his utterances: his comparison of a proposed scheme to modernise the National Gallery to a 'monstrous carbuncle'; and his wish to be reincarnated as Mrs Parker-Bowles's Tampax.

The British royalist who contemplates the career of the Prince of Wales must sing the National Anthem with a particular fervour: – '*Long* to reign over us – God save the *Queen!*' Not only would the Prince of Wales's marital status make it difficult for him to become the Supreme Governor of the Church, it would also make a nonsense of the Windsor

---

*New Idea, January 23, 1993 pp.22–23.

tradition that the King should have an exemplary domestic life. Though wisdom might be granted him with age, it has to be said that many of his public utterances to date have come perilously close to being 'unconstitutional'; and, far from appearing to mind all this, the Prince positively relishes it.

If we were concerned in this book in passing judgement on the personages of the Royal Family, it would be necessary to say in the Prince's defence that he has had a life which would have taxed many others in his position. On the one hand he has been trained (with considerable lack of wisdom) by his parents for the position of being King. On the other hand, since his mother was a very young woman when he was born, it was obvious from the first that no one wished Prince Charles to inherit the throne – or, at least, not until he was advanced in years. Since the Queen was generally acknowledged to be an exemplary monarch, no one could wish Prince Charles to be King without wishing dead his highly esteemed and wholly admirable mother.

Charles's training was all, therefore, of a contingent character. His life has been one large 'AS IF!' He was never allowed, as most young people might be, to find his *métier* and then pursue it, for the *métier*, if he found it, would have involved the death of the one person supremely capable of keeping the British Monarchy flourishing in the mid-twentieth century. Thus it was, from the moment he was sent to his appalling boarding school to the blunder about the GATT talks in December 1992, that Prince Charles has been a tinkerer, a potterer, a dabbler with this and that. After school, a visit to Timbertop, the Bushland annexe of Geelong Grammar School, Australia. Presumably, the bright idea behind this experience (Prince Charles was said to hate it) was that he should acquaint himself with the Commonwealth of which he might one day be Head.

Then, since he was the Prince of Wales, he was sent to the University of Aberystwyth for a few weeks to acquire a smattering of Welsh in a language laboratory. Then off to Cambridge, where he changed course several times. Then a spell in the Army. Then a spell in the Navy. And after that – there has been no fixed career, no obvious role for him to follow.

Of course, there is no reason why Princes should have 'jobs'. Had he not been brought up from an early age to believe that he was being trained to be King, Charles might have been perfectly happy tending his country house, Highgrove, where he is said to be a keen gardener, playing polo, hunting, and mixing with his loyal circle of slightly eccentric friends. But how would anyone feel if they were trained for a specific role, only to be told, when that 'training' was nearly done, that they could not start the job until they were seventy years of age? Would not a young doctor emerging from medical school feel some sense of frustration if he or she were told they could not practise until they were old; and a lawyer who could not be called to the Bar until they were past the age when most people retire? The then Prince of Wales (Bertie), during the celebratory service at St George's Chapel, Windsor, for the Diamond Jubilee of Queen Victoria, remarked in an audible voice to an equerry, 'I have no objection to praying to the Eternal Father, but I have heard enough about the Eternal Mother.'

It would seem very likely that Prince Charles's irresponsible old great-uncle, Lord Mountbatten, had led the boy to understand that 'Lilibet' would stand down as soon as her son was ready to take over the reins of office. Nothing could have been further from the Queen's mind, and, as her son's unfortunate life unfolded, she was hardened in her resolve not to abdicate. In her Christmas Broadcast in 1991, she even took the unprecedented step of reminding listeners and viewers all over the world that she was ever-mindful of her Coronation oath to be Queen *for life*. Prince Charles was furious, and the coldness led to a period when mother and son were not on speaking terms.

He is in fact one of the very few people in the world who has never had to 'prove himself', and yet, perhaps for that very reason, his life has been one long attempt at self-justification. All the public speechifying, all the patronage of worthy charities, his concern for British cities – both their architectural heritage and the lives of the urban poor – have an air of strain about them. It is as though, like a constipated man at his stool, he is struggling and forcing himself to bring to pass what, in happier circumstances, might be expected to follow quite naturally. During a coast-to-coast tour of the United States in 1977, an arduous itinerary of public speaking engagements, visits, banquets, receptions, an American journalist remarked, 'My God! That guy works so hard you'd think he was running for office!' His biographer, Anthony Holden, quoting this remark, added, 'In a way, he is.'*

But of course he isn't running for office, he is merely marking time, and since that remark was made and Mr Holden's first book about the Prince was published we have seen the sad effects of the Prince's boredom and self-doubt.

In Mr Holden's second biography of Prince Charles, published nine years later, we read of a fascinating encounter between Margaret Thatcher and the Prince of Wales, which took place at Kensington Palace on March 25, 1988.

There had been considerable feelings of dismay from the Conservative wing of the House of Commons about Charles's intervention in political questions – such as his

*Anthony Holden, *Charles, Prince of Wales* (1979) p.272.

concern for the unemployed and the plight of the homeless in inner cities. Mr Norman Tebbit (now Lord Tebbit) had said on television, 'I suppose the Prince of Wales feels extra sympathy towards those who've got no job because in a way he's got no job, and he's prohibited from having a job until he inherits the throne . . . He's forty, yet he's not been able to take responsibility for anything, and I think that's really his problem.' Another Conservative MP, Tony Marlow, had decided, on the strength of Charles's moderately expressed concern for those less well-off than himself, that he was a dangerous pinko, 'unfit to be king'. Since Mrs Thatcher had reformed the Trades Unions, the Health Service and the Nationalised Industries, why should she not – asked her right-wing 'radical' followers – set about reforming the Monarchy?

On that sad morning, Lady Day, 1988, it was the Prime Minister who, in physical terms, called on the Prince; but in actual terms, it was he who came to her, 'cap in hand'. He had arranged the meeting in the hope that he could work himself back into the Government's favour, and even get some concessions from the Prime Minister which had been hitherto denied him by his mother: a few pathetic little things to do. Would it be possible, he asked the Prime Minister, for him to preside over the State Opening of Parliament in his mother's absence? The Prime Ministerial answer to this question was a modified Yes, but if he did so it would only be as a 'Lord Commissioner', and he would only be allowed to read the Queen's Speech (written of course by the Prime Minister) from a bench in the Chamber rather than from the Throne.

Then Charles raised the delicate question of whether he might assume some title which gave him a greater significance in the running of State affairs. Might he not be declared Prince Regent? The making of this request is one of the odder things done by Prince Charles; a Regent, after all, is only necessary if the Monarch has ceased to be able to perform her functions, and Queen Elizabeth II was still very much in control of things when this request was made. So, unsurprisingly, the Prime Minister turned him down.

There was, however, one task for which she considered him to be eligible: the Governorship of Hong Kong. In the event, this task was seen to be too delicate for someone as insensitive as the Prince. After the Tianamen Square massacre in Peking in 1989, the Governorship of Hong Kong and the task of handing over the colony to the Chinese when the British Lease expires in 1997 were given to a professional politician. For a sad interlude, however, Charles had been under the impression that he was going to have what he had for so long coveted: a real job, a position in the world.*

In the aftermath of the Prince's separation from his wife, it was inevitable that outside observers should 'take sides'. Those who felt that his wife had treated him shabbily by making public so many of her private marital discontents were perhaps tempted to overemphasise Charles's many good qualities – his famous sense of humour, his fondness for the old 1950s radio *Goon Show*, his wish to do well by 'his people', his harmless pursuits such as foxhunting and painting in watercolours. It was emphasised, and this could hardly be denied, that he was one of the best-dressed men in the Western world. All these undoubted merits would need to be placed in the balance if we were conducting a judgement of Prince Charles's character, but we are not.

Our subject is the Royal crisis – whether there is one, whether there would be one if the Queen were to die. And

*Anthony Holden, *Charles: a Biography* (1988) pp.212 ff.

from that point of view, one has to say that Prince Charles does not merely contribute to the difficulties of the Royal House, he is the difficulty. The rest – the fact that some parts of the population wish the Queen were not so rich, or that the Patronage system should be reformed or abolished, or that certain newspapers have published certain photographs of the Duchess of York, or that an American biographer may be unkind enough to spill the beans about the Duke of Edinburgh's alleged indiscretions – all this is in a sense irrelevant to the central concern. That concern can be summarised in one sentence: can the British Monarchy survive? And the only thing which could seriously make it difficult for it to survive is the survival of Prince Charles.

There are quite simple reasons for this. The House of Windsor, under the tutelage of George V, George VI and Elizabeth II, has evolved a very distinct and a very workable role for the Monarchy. It is a symbol of family values; it is religious; it is constitutional. Because of the way that Charles has led his life, he is now woefully unsuited to fulfil any of these three functions. He has separated from his wife, and so can hardly provide the sort of icon of virtuous domesticity which was given to the world by his parents. He inherits peculiar difficulties in the religious field,* but he has compounded these difficulties by allowing his marriage to collapse. It was over the question of divorce that Edward VIII was sent into exile, and (less importantly) it was because she was 'mindful of the Church's teachings' that Princess Margaret, the Prince's aunt, was unable to follow her own inclinations and marry Group Captain Townsend, whom she loved. Moreover, as I have shown, Prince Charles has made life very difficult for himself by consistently speaking out on delicate public issues, to the point where Ministers

*See Chapter Eight.

of the Crown can make very slightly threatening jokes about his being unemployed.

Given the way in which Charles has lived in the last forty years, it would be necessary, were he to inherit his mother's throne tomorrow, to revise the traditional relationship between Church and State, to amend the Coronation Oath and to think very seriously about the Monarch's constitutional role; for if the Prince's intervention in the GATT dispute were a harbinger of things to come, no British Prime Minister could risk having him as King without curbing his constitutional role almost to the point where he was purely decorative.

This is the reality of the thing, and it is the reason that Charles himself will almost certainly be persuaded to stand down in favour of his son William and to renounce any claim which he might still have to the throne. If he could not be persuaded to do this, however, the British people would simply have to live with the fact. That it would provoke a crisis, there cannot be any doubt. But the Monarchy has survived crises before, and there is no particular reason for supposing that it could not survive crises again. It is not as though Prince Charles were entirely devoid of king-like qualities.

Indeed, it could be said, without straining after paradox, that the crucial flaw in the House of Windsor was their desire to be good monarchs. The strength of a constitutional Monarchy such as has evolved in Britain over the last two centuries is that the system works perfectly well, whether the Monarch is 'good' or 'bad' at their task. By most of the hard-working standards established by the House of Windsor, Queen Victoria could be seen as deplorably 'bad' at her job. 'Anything to please' – Edward VIII's highly ironic and oft-repeated little catch-phrase – had never been Victoria's rule of life. Unlike Queen Elizabeth II or Prince Charles, she seldom undertook public duties, she made no attempt to disguise her feelings about individual politicians, she was unashamedly partisan in constitutional questions and idle in her discharge of the minimal duties required of her. (She even refused, for many years of her widowhood, to take part in the State Opening of Parliament ceremonies.) Yet it could be argued that there was never a period when the British Monarchy was stronger than in Queen Victoria's reign.

True, Prince Charles's faults are very different from Queen Victoria's. She was indolent, where he is 'workaholic'. She was unabashed by personal unpopularity; he is neurotically hypersensitive about his reputation in the Press. But the history of Victoria's reign triumphantly demonstrates that a successful constitutional Monarchy can be maintained for decades without a markedly competent Monarch at the head of it. No one can predict how long Queen Elizabeth II will live, but there is every possibility that Charles's reign, if it happened at all, would be of extremely short duration. If the future of the Monarchy depended upon him alone, it would be sad indeed. But the office is larger than the individuals who succeed to it. He would no doubt try to be a conscientious and dutiful King. There is a great poignancy in the fact that the elaborate 'training' he has received for this office is precisely what makes him such an unsuitable candidate for it. But, if he were to succeed to the throne, the public could wait for better days; and in the short duration of his reign – who knows? – they might in some small areas be pleasantly surprised.

Things would never be the same, however, as in the palmier days of his mother's reign. Even supporters of the Prince would feel that there were only very limited areas where he could be expected to shine. They would hope that he would fulfil his constitutional functions, but they would fear, every time that he made a public speech, that he would say either something tactless or something foolish. They would have to play down his religious role, and, when he stood on the balcony of Buckingham Palace, he would either be there alone or in the forlorn company of his two sons. As the Victorian critic who had seen a production of *Antony and Cleopatra* remarked, 'How unlike the home life of our own dear Queen.'

FIVE

The Queen

When I broke the news to Margaret and Lilibet
that they were going to live in Buckingham Palace,
they looked at me in horror. 'What!' Lilibet said. 'You
mean forever?'

Marion Crawford, *The Little Princesses*

When the Queen was in her early teens, it was decided
that she should be instructed in the mysteries of the British
Constitution, and she was sent off to Sir Henry Marten,
the Vice-Provost of Eton College, just down the road from
Windsor Castle. Sometimes Princess Elizabeth attended
upon Sir Henry in his study – he had an endearing habit of
chewing on sugar lumps as he expounded the thoughts of
Walter Bagehot, the Victorian editor of the *Economist*, whose
views on constitutional matters are seldom questioned by
any modern advisers to the Royal Family.

Bagehot wrote at a time when franchise was being extended to all males, for the first time in British history. The
Reform Act of 1867 allowed a parliamentary vote to the
unskilled labouring class. 'What I fear', Bagehot wrote in
the Preface to the second edition of *The English Constitution*,
'is that both our political parties will bid for the support of
the working man: that both of them will promise to do as he

likes if he will only tell them what it is.' Bagehot, in other words, saw democracy, in the popular sense of the word, rearing its Gorgon head, and he feared the consequences. In these circumstances, he saw the Monarchy as an institution of crucial importance. Monarchy, in his view, is strong government because it is 'intelligible'. Unlike the democrats of fourth-century BC Athens, the Victorian English did not have a slave class. 'But we have whole classes unable to comprehend the idea of a constitution – unable to feel the least attachment to impersonal laws. Most indeed do vaguely know that there are other institutions besides the Queen and some rules by which she governs. But a vast number like their minds to dwell more upon her than upon anything else, and therefore she is inestimable.'

Bagehot appears to be reducing the Monarchy to the role of a sideshow, useful for distracting the ignorant multitudes while the actual business of government continues, as it has done before, in the hands of the statesmen. But, within the Parliamentary system, he believed that the Sovereign did have some function – as an emblem of family life, as a religious figurehead, as the 'head of society', as a moral example; and, in her dealings with ministers, as an adviser. Successive generations of modern Prime Ministers have piously repeated Bagehot's view that the function of a constitutional Monarch was to warn, to encourage and to advise.

When one examines Bagehot's 'sketch', as he calls it, of the constitution, and compares it with the original from which he was taking a likeness, one is arrested by the distortion of his view. 'We shall find', he wrote, 'that it is only during the present reign that in England the duties of a constitutional sovereign have ever been well performed.' One would not have expected a Victorian journalist of Bagehot's standing to have been positively insulting about Queen Victoria, but the compliment here is distinctly double-edged. Bagehot knew perfectly well that Queen Victoria's relations with her ministers were initially stormy, but ultimately docile and acquiescent. After *The English Constitution* was published, as the Queen sank further and further into introspection and depression, she all but abandoned the responsibilities of office for decades, though losing no opportunity to interfere with matters of foreign policy when they affected either her far-flung family or her whim. If Bagehot wished to claim that Queen Victoria was the great example of how to perform the roles of a constitutional Monarch, he might have been taking the same view of the sovereign as W. S. Gilbert took of the House of Lords, which 'did nothing in particular, and did it very well'.

The person who could, however, be said to be a Monarch cast in Bagehot's mould, and who has followed his injunctions most slavishly, is Elizabeth II. She has been a Monarch who was always prepared to seem useless and busy at the same time. For, if Bagehot is her guide, her parents are her role model.

George VI and Queen Elizabeth (now the Queen Mother) occupied the monarchical role at a peculiar period in British history. While 'Lilibet' sat with Sir Henry Marten, hearing him crunch sugar lumps and expound the works of Bagehot, the King and Queen were playing a crucial part in Churchill's war leadership. Sir Winston Churchill had been a leading light in the 'King's Party' – the small group of people who believed that King Edward VIII should not be forced to abdicate in 1936. As such, Churchill was viewed with deep suspicion by the Royal Family, and by Queen Elizabeth in particular. When Churchill became the wartime Prime Minister in 1940, however, Queen Elizabeth was prepared to put her hostility to Wallis Simpson beneath her duties as Queen-consort. It did not take long for feelings of close friendship to develop between Churchill and the new King.

Nearly all British people who lived through the Second World War felt that the King and Queen did immeasurable good. The King wore uniform throughout the war. Even when Buckingham Palace was bombed, the King and Queen refused to leave London, though this meant that (like many poor London families) they had to be separated from their children. (For their safety, the Princesses Elizabeth and Margaret Rose were immured in Windsor Castle.) Queen Elizabeth's famous comment after the bombing of Buckingham Palace – 'Now we can look the East End in the face' – was rightly seen as characteristic of her, and the King's, plucky approach.

The Second World War was, in fact, a godsend to the British Royal House. Only three years before the outbreak of the war, the Abdication crisis looked as if it might bring the Monarchy to an end. The war made the British feel that they needed the Monarchy, and the King and Queen could not have presented a better image of themselves during the years of hostility. They used ration books. They visited hospitals and battlefields and bomb-sites. They gave meaning to the cliché that the Monarchy could provide a 'focus of national unity' during a time of crisis. 'This war', wrote Churchill to the King, 'has drawn the Throne and the people more closely together than was ever before recorded, and Your Majesties are more beloved by all classes and conditions than any of the princes in the past.' This sounds like pure flattery, but it was simply true.

Urged on by her parents' example, Queen Elizabeth II, when she inherited the throne, continued to visit her people as often as her parents had done during the war. In wartime there was some obvious value in the King appearing in urban areas devastated by bombs. The habit survived into peacetime. Hospitals, factories, old people's homes, shopping malls, motorways, railway stations – it did not seem possible for any of these places to be rebuilt or to extend themselves without receiving a Royal visit. Ever anxious to oblige, the new Queen visited them all, as well as keeping up a taxing programme of world travel and being far more conscientious than Queen Victoria would ever have been about the political aspect of her functions: the signing of papers, the consulting with Prime Ministers, and so forth. Because the Queen did all these things with such alacrity and such professionalism, and such lack of fuss, it was assumed that this was a necessary part of her job; and when her children were old enough they were taught to do the same. Many of her subjects could be forgiven for believing that it was the Queen's 'job' to travel constantly, unveiling plaques, making visits and shaking hands with lord mayors. None of these journeys was necessary, and it is certain that none of them was constitutionally necessary. But they have been highly characteristic of the reign, and it would probably be difficult now for them to stop altogether.

Given the tireless service which the Queen has given to her country, the attitude of the British Press to her famous year of misfortunes in 1992 was, to say the least, surprising.

When the fire broke out in Windsor Castle on November 20, 1992, there were unforgettable sights of the Queen, pacing about among the firemen and helpers in her wellington boots and her headscarf, visibly distressed and yet trying to offer what help she could. It was her forty-fifth wedding anniversary, and her husband was abroad. She was at Windsor again the next day, still in the headscarf and wellingtons. Although she is a woman in her mid-sixties, she seemed like a resourceful but unhappy child, a Christopher Robin-like figure.

It must have been with some astonishment that many British people opened their newspapers that morning and discovered that the more oafish elements of the Press were choosing to continue their onslaught on the House of Windsor. If ever there was a morning to 'lay off' the Queen, this was surely it. And yet on they went, asking who was going to pay for the repair of the castle, estimated at £60 million. The Queen, of course, had had no chance to say anything about the matter, and nobody knew whether she intended to make a contribution to the restoration of Windsor. It was just assumed that she would not. The arguments about whether the taxpayer or the Sovereign should bear the cost of official residences were perfectly legitimate. The fact that the newspapers were choosing to have such arguments on such a day, however, looked like sadism. When, the following day, nursing a heavy cold, the Queen went to the Mansion House and made her by now famous speech about 1992 having been an *annus horribilis*, she had become an object of pity, at least in some circles. Even this was something which could be held to her charge. When the Monarch has become an object of pity, said Sir Peregrine Worsthorne, it is time for loyal monarchists to declare for a republic.

Certainly, the unsympathetic – some would say ungallant – newspaper coverage of the Queen and the Windsor fire was very surprising. I at least believed that most people in England had some respect for the Queen and – though it sounds absurdly sentimental to say so – some love. Could I have been wrong? What had this woman ever done to make her an object of such cruelty? From childhood, she had been thrust into the role of a public servant. She had helped her father George VI with running what he called 'The Firm' until his early death, when she was only twenty-five. Since then, she has been a full-time Head of State. Unlike Queen

Victoria, Elizabeth II has been excessively conscientious in the fulfilment of all her duties. No President in the world has ever held office for so long, or worked so hard or served their country so faithfully. How could it be, on the simple level of natural gratitude, that the British could not have contrived to be a little kinder to the Queen in her hour of sadness?

Having reflected on the matter, I think I have come up with some possibly plausible answers. Perhaps – who knows? – they throw some light on the part the Queen has played in the decline of the House of Windsor. For it is customary to say that 'for forty years the Queen has not put a foot wrong'. If that were true, there would be no crisis. But a crisis there certainly is, and the Queen must have played some part in causing it, though I suspect that her fault might, paradoxically, be in her near-faultlessness. The British have very understandably come to take her for granted; and, in a mood which is not justifiable, but understandable, they have come to feel that she is such a hard act to follow that maybe the act itself should be wound up. Is that a possible view of events?

It is very difficult to classify the Queen or to write about her intelligently. Most historians of the Royal Family or experts on such matters can only fall back on the language of worship and sycophancy when they attempt to do so; and, understandably, that provokes those who find it nauseating into wholly unfair assaults on the Queen herself. One possible reason for the Royal Family's current 'image problems' with the media is that, although the Queen has been admired and loved, I think it would be a mistake to suppose that the British Royal Family had ever, strictly speaking, been popular. At the time when it was arguably strongest, during the reign of Queen Victoria, the Monarch was actively hated by the majority of her subjects.

Certainly, no one has ever admired Queen Elizabeth II because they thought she was interesting in herself. Virtuous, bright-eyed, surprisingly good-looking when met 'in the flesh'; all these things might be said about the Queen, but she has not been revered so much for her personal qualities as for what she represented and what she was. At the time of her Coronation, a reverence was felt for her office which was quasi-religious, which would account for the extraordinary hostility meted out to any who ventured to criticise her in any degree. In 1956, Malcolm Muggeridge, writing in the *New Statesman*, had coined the phrase 'the Royal soap opera' and pointed out that while the Queen was popular with her lower-class subjects she was held in some derision by those better born. 'It is duchesses, not shop assistants, who found the Queen dowdy, frumpish and banal,' he wrote. The article was syndicated and sold to the United States, and was republished to coincide with a Royal visit to America in 1957. Reprinted with the headline 'Does England Really Need a Queen?', the article caused enormous offence. Muggeridge himself was accused of calling the Queen 'dowdy, frumpish and banal'. British Empire Loyalists posted excrement through Muggeridge's door, daubed his house with paint and wrote to express their pleasure that his teenage son had been killed in a skiing accident. ('One Muggeridge the less!') Lord Altrincham, at about the same time, writing in the *National and English Review*, expressed comparably moderate reservations about the Monarchy. He ventured to say that, in the Queen's speeches, 'the personality conveyed by her utterances which are put into her mouth is that of a priggish schoolgirl, captain of the hockey team, a prefect and a recent candidate for confirmation'. Lord Strathmore, the Queen's cousin, said that if he had a gun, he would have shot Lord Altrincham for writing these words; and some loyal member of the public struck Altrincham in the face.

But just because Altrincham and Muggeridge excited public outrage, it would be wrong to suppose that the public attitude towards the Royal Family was one of slavish interest. True, there were those who collected mugs or biscuit tins emblazoned with the faces of Prince Philip, Queen Elizabeth II and their relations. But nearly all royal jokes of the last forty years – on television, stage, or radio – have been gentle meditations on the Queen's essential dullness. The supposedly 'satirical' mood of the 1960s produced jokes about the essentially bourgeois qualities of the Queen and her family, the fact that they were unfashionably dressed, dowdy and intellectually limited. When she visited the Emperor Hirohito of Japan, she had an hour or so of private conversation with the divinely born potentate. When she emerged, she is supposed to have remarked, 'That man can talk of nothing except tropical fish'; he, for his part, was remarking testily to his entourage, 'That woman can talk of nothing except horses.' It is on this scarcely exciting level that the Queen was perceived. 'Loving' the Queen did not mean, for her average subject, being interested by her.

Throughout the 1950s and 1960s, the British public would be periodically amused by rumours that some continental newspaper, usually an Italian one, was running the story of some royal 'scandal' – usually the marital difficulties of the Queen or her sister, or both. British newspapers, partly for reasons of politeness and deference to the Crown, never published such stories. But editors and newspaper proprietors, even in London, were never as high-minded as all that. They knew what their readers wanted. And nobody wanted the Royal Family to be like film stars, their mood-swings, marital rows and favourite restaurants made into the subject of newspaper articles. People revered the Crown, but they were not really interested in the Queen for the very simple reason that she is not really interesting. Her uninterestingness is a positive asset.

Her husband and her son had both, in their slightly poignant ways, attempted to capture the public interest as figures 'in their own right'. Prince Philip did this by occasional ill-judged speeches on the nature of British industry, expressing the wish that workers and management would 'pull their finger out'. Even before his famous outbursts about modern architecture or the environment, Prince Charles let it be known that he held a number of deeply sincere 'views' on issues of the day. We have already discussed the political implications of some of Prince Charles's public outbursts, but in general what these speeches by Prince Charles and his father revealed was what we had all suspected before they made them: that there was nothing interesting about Royal personages at all. Indeed, there was always something extremely embarrassing about men of clear intellectual limitations attempting to form sentences which would impress the average newspaper reader. In a world of real industrialists, real intellectuals, real naturalists, they could not compete. When they opened their mouths, it was time to shuffle and look hard at one's feet.

While it probably did not do to say this too loudly, and while it might have grieved the Queen when she realised that this was what people thought of her and her family, it was not necessarily a drawback. If the Royal Family had been cleverer or more interesting, people might have been tempted to suppose that they were there because of their own merit, rather than simply because they were royal; and as soon as anyone supposed that the Monarch deserved to be the Monarch, that would be the end of the Monarchy. One would have replaced the whole concept of hereditary monarchy for an elective meritocracy.

Having been drilled in the Bagehot mould, the Queen has faithfully made herself into the Monarch of that constitutionalist's famous essay. But was Bagehot right? And, even if he was right in the 1860s and 1870s, do his words still make sense when applied to the Britain of the mid-1990s?

Bagehot, who viewed with such misgivings the extension of political suffrage to the labouring classes, would hardly have felt at home in the age of television and popular culture – a world to which, willy-nilly, the Queen belongs. He would have been unable to conceive (as would anyone in the pre-cinematic age) the importance of visual – filmed or televised – images for the mass culture. At the opening of his discussion of the Monarchy he wrote, 'Most people when they read that the Queen walked on the slopes at Windsor – that the Prince of Wales went to the Derby – have imagined that too much thought and prominence were given to little things. But they have been in error . . .' To read a newspaper report in Victorian England which described the Queen walking in her garden or her son at the races might, indeed, have run the danger of making too much of 'little things'. In the age of mass culture, the little things are in danger of seeming as if they are the only things. The Queen has always been willing to use the popular media. With the marriage of her son, however, the Royal House became, as we have seen, something different: almost an extension of Hollywood, with many of the inevitable attendant calamities.

So Bagehot's praise for the 'little things' would probably now have to be modified. If the medium of television has emphasised the 'little thing' above the great and unseen virtues of the monarchical system, then might not that system itself have been trivialised out of existence?

Bagehot also seems questionable in his assumption that a Monarch's only function in a modern political context is to warn, encourage or advise. Just as he wrote before the age of mass culture, he wrote before the political exploitation of mass culture and those great political movements which were only made possible because of radio and newsreel: Stalinism and Nazism. The political dangers which face even so conservative (with a small 'c') a country as Britain in the twentieth century would have been quite inconceivable to anyone living in the nineteenth century. True, Bagehot contemplates the tempestuous European events of 1848, just as he was to contemplate the turbulent history of France in and around 1870, and he found that he preferred the House of Lords and the House of Commons. But no nineteenth-century demagogue had the resources which were to be placed at the disposal of twentieth-century demagogues: the microphones, the film camera and the weapons of destruction.

Even if one does not fear the ultimate calamity in Britain, the arrival of some fascist or Stalinist dictator – and it seems, on the face of things, a rather unlikely eventuality – one is compelled to recognise that our world is a much nastier world than Bagehot's, and one in which politicians have far more opportunities of wrecking societies and individual lives through the abuse of power. In such a world as this, one has to notice, observing the political scene in Europe over the last half-century or so, that it is in apparently free and apparently elective systems that the worst abuses of power have taken place. Once elected, the despot receives no check on his or her power. It is in such a dangerous world as ours that one begins to see the virtues of the British monarchical system, where the Head of State (there through no merit of her own, solely through birth) has the right and duty to check the abuse of Parliamentary power; and where the Cabinet and Parliament exercise a perpetual check on the power of the Monarch. One can be quite sure that, were Britain to have an elected president, no such restraints would operate.

The political role of the Monarchy has therefore become more important, and not less, since Bagehot's day. While the more bright-eyed and unthinking of our Parliamentarians might believe that it would suit their careers better if they had a system more like that of the French or the Germans or the Italians, there are many (not least, Germans, Italians and French) who would dispute their cosy view of democratic systems and see virtues in the British system which are perhaps not apparent to those who have come to take it for granted.

The virtue of the system and the fact that everyone takes it for granted are very much part of Elizabeth II's manner of conducting herself. She has been unobtrusive and conscientious for so long that people suppose that the 'machine' of Monarchy works smoothly almost as an act of nature. This is not so. We only notice machines when they begin to malfunction. The smoothness with which the monarchical machine has operated is a measure of the Queen's tremendous skill.

There are now two major threats to the smooth running of the machine; for the sake of shorthand one could describe them as her mother and her children.

Not, of course, that Her Majesty the Queen Mother has been anything but a pillar of the Monarchy, nor that the Queen's children, as individuals and in their own sphere, are not all perfectly decent individuals. But the Queen Mother's way of being a Queen, which in some measure Queen Elizabeth II has tried to imitate, while appropriate for wartime Britain, is out of step with the times. As a matter of habit, lord mayors, lords-lieutenant, chairmen of companies and managers of hospitals will continue to bombard Buckingham Palace with requests that the Queen should come to open this, unveil that; a scurrying parody of her parents, who moved from bomb-site to bomb-site during the Second World War to rally the spirits of their people. People in modern Britain do not need their spirits rallying in quite this way, and the programme of Royal visits (which, candidly, few would miss if they stopped) has set up in the public mind the wholly false idea that this is the Queen's 'job': going round and unveiling things and opening things. It is also deemed in some journalistic quarters to be the 'job' of other members of the Royal Family too, and individuals such as Princess Margaret, who has quite understandably played down this aspect of life as much as possible in recent years, are taken to task if they do not perform these useless and rather ridiculous functions.

The Queen does not have a 'job', though the Crown has a function. Now that they have nearly all been removed from the Civil List,* none of the Queen's relations is obliged to perform any public functions whatsoever. This is something which the Queen Mother would go to her grave misunderstanding. Edward VIII caused mortal offence on September 23, 1936, by sending the Duke and Duchess of York (the future George VI and Queen Elizabeth) to open a hospital in Aberdeen. The local dignitaries had hoped that the King would open the hospital, but he went instead, quite publicly, to the railway station to welcome Mrs Simpson on her visit to Balmoral.† To show that she was never to be accused of putting pleasure before duty,

*See Chapter Nine.
†Philip Ziegler, *King Edward VIII* (1990) p.288.

the Queen Mother spent the next sixty years of her life opening hospitals, and she groomed her children to do the same. But no one felt as strongly as she did about her brother-in-law's alleged offence, and those who did feel strongly have forgiven him by now. Royal personages do not have to be visible all the time; they do not even have to be seen doing good. Bagehot was right to say that it cheers us all up to read of Princes going to race meetings.

To be so much in public has done the Queen no harm, but hers has been a discreet and largely blameless life. Unfortunately for her children, they have all survived into an age where newspapers believe that public personages deserve perpetual public scrutiny, even on occasions when they would prefer to be private.

The longer her reign has continued, the more forceful have seemed the criticisms of Lord Altrincham in 1957. While she has continued to be a conscientious Monarch, cast very firmly in the mould of her father and grandfather, she has allowed herself to be advised and surrounded by persons whom Altrincham castigated as 'tweedy'. In times when everything is progressing smoothly, there is nothing wrong with these 'tweedy', slightly stuffy courtiers. But, because they were presumably so much out of sympathy with the social and political developments of the twentieth century, they have been powerless to protect the Queen against the cruellest assaults of the Press. Her Press Secretaries have tended to be gentlemen when they should have been bruisers, poachers turned gamekeepers who knew the world of tabloid journalism from the inside. While Mrs Thatcher appointed Bernard Ingham as her Press Secretary – a bruiser if ever there was one – the Queen, at the darkest hour of her *annus horribilis*, had Sir Robert Fellowes, a man who was bamboozled by his sister-in-law the Princess of Wales simply because he was too nice.

At the same time, because she is so unmodern that she does not even know what it is to be modern, the Queen has allowed herself to be guided by those who suggested that the Royal Family should 'modernise' itself. Her late mentor, Lord Mountbatten, was the chief offender in this area, but Prince Philip, Mountbatten's nephew, must probably shoulder some of the blame too. One of Prince Philip's most devoted biographers, Tim Heald, congratulates his subject for 'nursing the Royal Family into the twentieth century'.* That Prince Philip has made this part of his life's work is not in question, but it remains questionable whether the late-twentieth century is a very good habitat for any Royal Family, let alone the House of Windsor. As a conscientious (but always, one suspects, slightly stiff) mother – one recollects the occasion when she flew home from some foreign tour to greet the six-year-old Prince Charles by shaking his hand – she has wanted to involve her children in 'The Firm'. This idea of 'The Firm' was manageable when it consisted merely of the King, the Queen, Lilibet and Margaret Rose. It is a little less easy to see what possible Royal functions could be found for four children, their spouses, their children and all the cousins. Many of them, even remote relations by marriage such as the Duchess of Kent, have done their best, opening hospitals as if there was no tomorrow. But the price paid for all this dutifulness is that any member of the Queen's family seems like fair game to the tabloid papers; and when taken as a whole, the Royal Family are seen (from a strictly constitutional perspective) to be so useless that the institution of Monarchy itself is useless.

*Tim Heald, *The Duke* (1991) p.253.

It has to be said – not as a value judgement but as a matter of fact – that none of the Queen's children makes a very obvious heir to the throne. The position of Prince Charles has already been discussed. The Princess Royal has done sterling work as the President of the Save the Children Fund, but her marital position makes it impossible that she could ever be the Supreme Governor of the Church of England, and she has made it very clear, by moving out of Royal residences even when in London and renting a flat in Dolphin Square, that she does not wish to be considered as an active member of 'The Firm'. At the time of writing, Prince Andrew's marital position would also make it very embarrassing for him to inherit the Throne – which only leaves Prince Edward, who has so far had no marital difficulties, perhaps because nature has blessed him with a disinclination towards matrimony. There is no reason to suppose that he would make a bad King, but it has seemed for the last few years as though he would prefer a career in the theatre.

Sir Henry Marten had a conscientious young pupil. She learnt how to be a Monarch, and she has performed the role so flawlessly that anyone who comes after her will seem second-rate. But the position is rather more serious than that. Because of what has happened in the last few years, there can never be a Monarch quite in Elizabeth II's mould. The Bagehot formula will not work for any of her children, however they contort themselves and try to fit themselves into it. They can never be regarded as exemplars, nor as religious icons, nor as ideals of daily life, and none of them looks exactly the sort of which sage political counsellors are made. The Queen's last function must be to live a very long time, until some new Bagehot arises to advise her successors how the Monarchy might survive. Otherwise, we must feel ourselves close not merely to the decline, but to the end, of the House of Windsor.

SIX

The House of Windsor
and the Press

'Most journalists just want the shot
where you're seen picking your nose.'

Prince Philip in Douglas Keay, *Elizabeth II*

Relations between the House of Windsor and the British
Press have, until a decade ago, been distant and polite.
It was traditionally left to the foreign newspapers and
broadcasting stations to intrude or to criticise. From 1910
until 1980, most journalistic comment on the Royal House
in Britain bordered on the sycophantic, and newspaper
coverage of Royal events was little better than an extended
or illustrated version of the Court Circular, published each
day by the various courts and households of the Royal
Family, chronicling their public doings and arrangements,
the appointments of lords and ladies-in-waiting, the attendance at receptions, the representation of Royal personages
by the attendance of someone else at memorial services.
'KENSINGTON PALACE, February 17th, The Princess Margaret,
Countess of Snowdon, was represented by The Lady Sarah
Armstrong-Jones at a service of thanksgiving for the life of

Sir Kenneth MacMillan in Westminster Abbey today . . .'
'BUCKINGHAM PALACE, February 8th, The Lady Elton has succeeded the Lady Susan Hussey as Lady-in-Waiting to the Queen.' And, stop press!, 'CLARENCE HOUSE,* February 17th, Queen Elizabeth the Queen Mother, Honorary Colonel, The Royal Yeomanry, this evening opened Cavalry House, the new Regimental Headquarters at the Duke of York's Head-quarters . . .' Can there be anything more reassuring for a conservative-minded Briton than these daily bulletins from the Royal Palaces? Can there be anything more calculated to make him or her feel that the world is as it was, and as it should be?

Even in the 1930s, however, the deference felt for the Crown by the Press was matched by the fear and respect shown by the Crown for the Fourth Estate. Presumably the most extreme example of this is the death of George V itself, which the family arranged very largely with the newspapers in mind. When, on January 20, 1936, it became apparent that the King was dying, a concern was expressed that he might struggle through the night and die after the morning papers had 'gone to bed'. It would therefore have fallen to the evening newspapers in London to convey the news of the King's death to the world. To spare his Royal master this indignity and to ensure that his sovereign's demise should first be reported in *The Times*, Lord Dawson of Penn, Chief Physician to His Majesty, administered a lethal dose of chloroform to George V some time before dinner at Sandringham. He picked up a menu-card from the household dining-room and wrote on it what the royal biographer describes as 'a farewell of classic simplicity': 'The King's life is moving peacefully to its close.' After

---

* The official residence of Queen Elizabeth the Queen Mother.

eating dinner with Queen Mary and her children, Lord Dawson was able to announce the King's death to the Editor of *The Times*. Earlier in the day, when the King was still conscious and a few members of the Privy Council had stood around in his bedroom, Dawson had suggested to His Majesty that, were his health to improve, he might benefit from a visit to his beloved Bognor Regis. This provoked the highly characteristic reply, 'Bugger Bognor!' Since the Royal Household were able to engineer the exact hour of their Sovereign's departure from this world, it is not surprising that they should have also chosen to offer to the world an amended version of George's last words. 'Bugger Bognor' became, in the official version, 'How is the Empire?' Only the most rigorous pedants or seekers after historical exactitude would deny that this was an ingeniously pleasing emendation.

Those who know how highly King George V was regarded by his subjects in the closing years of his reign might be surprised by his wife's caution in the timing of his death and the breaking of the news. But Queen Mary was old enough to remember when relations between the Royal Family and the Press were very much less cordial, and when newspapers contained regular attacks on the institution of Monarchy itself, demands that the Queen be paid less money, and prurient inquiries into the marital troubles of the Prince of Wales. In April 1871, for example, Gladstone remarked gloomily to Lord Palmerston, the Foreign Secretary, that he had been reading *Reynolds's Newspaper*, a popular imprint with a circulation of over 300,000. One item in the paper described the Prince of Wales losing a fortune in the gambling salons of Homburg; another complained of Queen Victoria's parsimony and hoarding of money 'obtained from the toil and sweat of the British working man'. 'Things go from bad to worse,' said Gladstone. 'I see *What Does She Do*

With It? on the walls of the station at Birkenhead.'*

Throughout the nineteenth century the British Press attacked the Monarch and her family for their idleness and greed. Queen Victoria herself formed the view that the institution was so unpopular that it would not outlast her lifetime by more than twenty years. She failed to understand that it was she herself who was unpopular, not the Crown; and as soon as Bertie (whom she considered such a disgrace to the family) became King, the Royal Family became extremely popular, not merely in Great Britain but in the rest of Europe as well.

Queen Victoria's family learnt other lessons from her hostile treatment at the hands of the Press. They knew that they were only protected and kept in their position of privilege by 'the Establishment'. The very undemocratic nature of England meant that no institution could be directly answerable to 'the People' by democratic means. The Members of Parliament are not, in the British system, obliged to reflect the views or wishes of their constituents. They are the representatives of the people, not their unthinking mouthpiece. As figures who to some extent are part of the Establishment, and to some extent depend upon it, they are very unlikely ever to criticise the Crown. There are always one or two Members of Parliament in any one generation who take it upon themselves to do this, but they almost instantaneously become 'joke' figures (if they were not joke figures to start with). Until the present Parliament (that convened after the 1992 election), those who intended to have a serious political career in Britain have not dared to criticise the Monarchy. Things are beginning to alter now, but until recently it has meant that when criticism of the Monarch or the institution of Monarchy has been made,

*Christopher Hibbert, *Edward VII* (1976) p.111.

it has been left to the Press alone to fulfil this democratic role; and, given the nature of matters in Britain, it is not a role which, historically, the Press has fulfilled with any great relish. Indeed, for the greater part of the twentieth century, the English newspapers, when compared with their Victorian or Regency counterparts, have been almost incredibly diffident and mealy-mouthed.

The year which followed the death of King George V was perhaps the most dramatic in the history of the British Monarchy, but not a whisper of what was taking place was ever reported at the time to the British people. Newspaper readers in the United States and on the European continent were kept abreast – with the degree of journalistic inaccuracy which was to be expected in such a situation – with the King's Matter. Edward VIII was enamoured of Mrs Simpson; he intended to marry her; this was regarded by the Prime Minister, by the Archbishop of Canterbury and by the Prime Ministers of the Dominions as entirely unacceptable. Abdication was an inevitability. And yet it was not until a week before the Abdication occurred that the story of Edward and Mrs Simpson appeared in the English Press. Journalists are rightly mocked for repeating the cliché that the public has 'the right to know' this or that; G. K. Chesterton, that great journalist who died in the same year as the Abdication, was probably closer to the truth when he said that journalism was the art of interesting people in the fact that Lady Jones was dead who had not heard that Lady Jones had ever been alive. But, in the case of the Abdication, there surely was a case for saying that the People had 'a right to know'.

The reason for the silence of the papers was that the proprietors had been frightened off by the Establishment – at this date it still made sense to speak of such a thing. The Establishment had decided, long before the 'Abdication crisis', that they would get rid of the King, and they did not wish their plans – for the coronation of the Duchess of York and their tame King-candidate, her husband – to be interfered with by a popular upsurge. Had the Abdication crisis happened in the atmosphere of 1992, with a free Press all commenting on the situation and influencing events as they unfolded, it is difficult to know what would have happened, but it is easy to picture how some of the newspapers would have reacted. Some would have sided openly with Mrs Simpson. Others would have adopted the 'Hands off our King!' approach. In any event, it is hard to suppose that the Abdication would have happened quietly and behind closed doors. Apart from anything else, Edward VIII's frequent cross-Channel telephone calls with his future Duchess would have been intercepted by the Intelligence services and sold to the highest bidder. There might have been a surge of republicanism which would have led to the abolition of the Monarchy. There might, instead, have been a populist movement to crown Queen Wallis in Westminster Abbey: a consequence which traditionalists might have abhorred more than the abolition of the Monarchy itself. But the Press was muzzled in 1936, and so neither thing happened. Instead, King George VI and Queen Elizabeth were crowned, and their elder daughter Lilibet was groomed for becoming the Queen of England.

There were by now quite a lot of skeletons hanging in their family cupboard; by the end of the war, during which a high proportion of the King's German relatives had been active and keen Nazis, there were even more. So it is not surprising that Queen Elizabeth and King George developed an attitude to the Press which was almost paranoid. Anything except 'official' reporting was frowned upon. Queen Elizabeth, an adept at inventing new Royal traditions, coined the idea (unknown to Pepys, Horace Walpole, Greville, Creevey,

Disraeli et al.) that no loyal subjects ever repeated what was said to them by a member of the Royal Family. The price paid for indiscretion was immediate ostracism from the Royal circle, as any ex-friend of Queen Elizabeth's (there are many) could attest.

The legend of the Forbidden Fruit is habitually repeated in life, as in folk-tale. The tree from which you must not eat, the cupboard which you must never open – these are the ones which prove too tempting for the unfortunate protagonists of any tale. The employees of Queen Elizabeth enjoyed many freedoms, except the freedom to repeat what was said by their Royal employers. It was a restriction which the governess to the Little Princesses, Marion Crawford, found intolerable.

Crawfie, as the girls called her, was not a seditious communist intent upon bringing down the government. Nor was she motivated by greed, though there is no doubt that she made some money out of her written account of the childhood of Lilibet and Margaret Rose, *The Little Princesses*. Friends and courtiers of the Queen Mother believe that Crawfie wrote *The Little Princesses* out of pique because she was not made a Dame Commander of the Victorian Order for her services to the Royal Household.* To Queen Elizabeth, who has been so dominated by a desire for revenge,† this might seem a plausible motive for writing a book, but to those of a more equable disposition it will be obvious how seldom human beings outside the walls of Clarence House, or the more lurid pages of literature, are ever motivated purely by a desire for revenge. Crawfie was not Prince Hamlet or the Count of Monte Cristo: she was that much more innocent and dangerous thing, a compulsive

---

* Elizabeth Longford, *Elizabeth R* (1977) p.117.
† i.e. revenge on Wallis Simpson for marrying King Edward VIII.

blabbermouth. She had been the witness to the upbringing of the future Queen of England and her sister. She retained for them the toadyish worship, entirely devoid of irony, without which it is impossible to endure the company of any Royal personage for more than an evening. But her tongue was stronger than her heart. She could not resist *telling*.

Like the real village gossip she was, Crawfie could not resist bringing everything in: the Emperor of India dies, and it is an occasion for Crawfie to remember her own toothache. But, buried in the artless, syrupy prose, there are unforgettable vignettes of both the little girls – prophetic snapshots of what they were and what they were to become.

'I had a telegram almost immediately asking me to return to Royal Lodge, Windsor, where the children were. I had had a tooth out the day before. Cocaine never goes through my face; it sat there like an apple on my cheek, and I looked as though I had been crying my eyes out. I can still remember the sort of hush that had fallen over England. All the way down south the stations were strangely silent and empty, and everyone looked sad. People had not realised how much they loved the old King until he was dead.

'At Royal Lodge two little figures were waiting for me. The Duke and Duchess had gone to town and left a message for me: "Don't let all this depress them more than is absolutely necessary, Crawfie. They are so young."

'I kept them in Windsor until all arrangements had been made for the funeral, then I took them to London. Margaret was much too young to pay attention to what was going on. She was intrigued by the fact that Alah [their nurse] from time to time burst into a flood of tears.

'Lilibet in her sensitive fashion felt it all deeply. It was very touching to see how hard she tried to do what she felt was expected of her. I remember her pausing doubtfully as she groomed one of the toy horses and looking up at me for a moment.

' "Oh, Crawfie . . . ought we to play?" she asked . . .

'I remember I was very bothered at the thought of Lilibet going to the lying-in-state. She was so young, I thought. What could she possibly know of death? But she had to go. She drove off with the Duke and Duchess, in her black coat and black velvet tammie, looking very small and, I thought, rather scared . . .

' "Uncle David* was there," she told me afterwards, "and he never moved at all, Crawfie. Not even an eyelid. It was wonderful. And everyone was so quiet. As if the King were asleep." '

And so on, and so on. There is nothing in *The Little Princesses* which is not profoundly respectful towards the Royal Family and gushingly affectionate about Crawfie's young charges. But to have published it at all was regarded as an act of unpardonable sedition, and for ever afterwards the repetition of family intimacies was known as 'doing a Crawfie' – the unpardonable sin in Queen Elizabeth the Queen Mother's eyes.

Writing in 1983, Elizabeth Longford claimed – on the scarcely reliable evidence of her friend and neighbour Malcolm Muggeridge – that *The Little Princesses* had in fact been written by the biographer of George V, Harold Nicolson. This is quite a good joke about Nicolson, who had his governessy side, but it is not to be taken seriously. In real life, the Royal Family had no doubt at all about the authenticity of *The Little Princesses*, and Crawfie was cruelly ostracised. That peculiarly harsh and unforgiving streak in the Queen Mother, which allowed her brother-in-law to be banished for a lifetime, moved equally swiftly to destroy

*The future Duke of Windsor.

Crawfie. Lilibet and Margaret Rose were never to see or speak to their old governess again.

'Royal control on memoirs has been decidedly tightened since the Crawford best-seller,' Lady Longford wrote. This was a polite understatement. The Royal Family exercised an iron control over what was written about them; their capacity for censorship would have been the envy of Stalin's Politburo; and this applied not merely to what journalists or others said about the *living*, but to what scholars said about the dead. Any serious historian wishing to write books which touch on Royal history is obliged to use the Royal archives at Windsor. Access to this archive is far from free. It has to be worked for. If the archivist and her assistants suspect a scholar of any mischievous intent, he or she will certainly be excluded from the archives.

Any Royal biographer will tell you that fierce censorship is operated by the Royal archives, even if the material relates to events which happened a hundred or more years ago. An acquaintance of mine, researching the Royal family in the nineteenth century, was astonished to discover in the archives at Windsor the draft of a letter written by Prince Albert in 1861 to the Privy Council. It was written shortly after the death of his mother-in-law. Queen Victoria had in effect taken leave of her senses and was hysterical much of the time. Life with her had become unendurable. The letter was asking, should the Queen become permanently insane, whether the Prince Consort could be granted a separation from her.

The scholar who told me of this document's existence implored me not to say anything about it, since, if it ever came out that he was the person who had spoken of it, his entire professional future as a Royal biographer would be jeopardised; he would certainly be forbidden any further access to the archives at Windsor. I asked another royal scholar first whether his fears were justified, and second whether such a document as the Prince Albert letter might not conceivably exist. I received the reply that first he was right – to tell the world that the dear Prince Consort was not happily married would constitute 'doing a Crawfie', even though the parties concerned had all been dead for nearly a century. The Queen did not like her family linen being washed in public – even the antique linen. On the second question, the scholar whom I approached said that such a document could conceivably have existed but, once I had written about it publicly in a newspaper (which I had done), it was almost certain that some discreet hand at Windsor would have found the offending piece of paper and consigned it to the flames.

Some years ago I asked Lady Longford, herself an esteemed historian, biographer and friend of the Royal Family, why they were quite so fearful. After all, I said, the Vatican itself, which had (one would have supposed) far more dangerous secrets to hide, is more liberal than Windsor Castle. When Owen Chadwick wished to investigate the Papal archives for that most delicate of periods, the Second World War, he received no opposition at all. The then Pope, Paul VI, had not read all the documents in the files of his predecessor Pius XII. It was being widely suggested, on no evidence, that the wartime Pope had behaved discreditably during the war, either by not doing enough to speak out against the Nazis or even by nursing secret sympathy for them. No one knew, until the files were open, the truth or otherwise of these highly damaging allegations. And yet no restrictions whatsoever were placed upon Owen Chadwick. Though Chadwick was not a Catholic, he was allowed to read anything he liked and to draw any conclusions which he chose.

When I said this to Lady Longford, who is a devout

Catholic, she admitted that there was a difference of approach between the Roman Pontiff and the English Monarch. 'But then, you see,' she said, 'the Pope really does believe that he has been given the keys of the kingdom, and that the gates of hell cannot prevail against him. No such assurance has ever been given to the English Kings and Queens. It is understandable that they should be a little more cautious.'

Some would think that they took caution to the point of mania. Certainly, in the post-Crawfie era, there was such an atmosphere of reverence surrounding the Royal Family and household that the merest breath of criticism, however mild, was treated in Great Britain with some of the horror which is aroused by blasphemy in countries of the Islamic world. The case of Lord Altrincham is a good example.

The 1960s certainly changed the atmosphere of stultifying sycophancy which surrounded the Queen. The satirical magazine *Private Eye* reverted to robustly eighteenth-century satires on the Monarch and her family. The Queen was referred to as Brenda, and her sister as Yvonne – somehow, these appellations are perfect. 'True-Life Romances' in the manner of cheap women's magazines were composed (allegedly by the author Sylvie Krin) about the emotional lives of Brenda's children. *Love in the Saddle*, about Princess Anne, was a personal favourite of mine, though the one which achieved classic status was the story of the Prince of Wales and his marriage – *Heir of Sorrows* – which eventually had to be discontinued since life so doggedly continued to imitate art, and the Prince in particular began to behave more and more in the way that *Private Eye* depicted him, rather as if he were a puppet, mouthing lines written for him by Sylvie Krin.

Addicts of a crueller form of Royal satire will treasure the fantasies of Auberon Waugh in his famous Diaries.

His physical revulsion against Princess Anne is perhaps one of the most savage things about these productions. On January 23, 1978, he noted that 'the Queen was most interested in some photographs which I showed her from today's *Daily Express*: of a Saudi-Arabian commoner being beheaded after his wife, a princess, had been shot for daring to marry him. But she was not in the least bit amused when I started making pointed remarks about her own son-in-law Captain Mark Phillips and his bride, Princess-Dame Anne Phillips.' The diary pretends that Waugh is on intimate terms with all the Windsors. 'For over a month now I haven't heard a squeak from any member of the Royal Family. I was beginning to wonder why they were avoiding me, but today everything is explained. Prince Michael of Kent (whom I have not seen since he was a reasonably attractive junior boy at Eton) announces his plans to marry the Catholic wife of poor old Tom Troubridge. No wonder they are trying to make themselves scarce.' In the diaries, Waugh adopts the persona of a Catholic squire, very much the Royal Family's social superior (Prince Charles calls him 'Sir'), and the Queen is constantly asking his advice. Indeed, in the fantasy world of the Diaries, Auberon Waugh occupies the same sort of position in the Queen's life as was occupied by Lord Melbourne or the Duke of Wellington in the life of Queen Victoria, only with the difference that between the present Queen and Waugh there is rather more physical intimacy. Though they are not lovers, they enjoy stroking each other's feet while he offers her his advice on issues of the day.

Perhaps the most prophetic entry in the Diaries concerning the Monarchy and the Press is that for November 28, 1980. It was at the time of Prince Charles's courtship, and a story had appeared in the *Sunday Mirror* to the effect that the Prince had spent the night in a railway siding, alone in a deserted Royal train with Diana Spencer. 'I never thought I would find myself jumping to the defence of Bob Edwards, curly-headed editor of the *Sunday Mirror*, but things are getting serious. Bob's resignation from the Kennel Club may be at stake if senior stewards have their way after his clash with Buckingham Palace over whether or not Prince Charles was romancing late at night with his beloved on the Royal Train. I was not there and so have an open mind on the crucial point of whether or not any romancing took place. But nobody can sit back idly and see a respected public figure like Bob Edwards – whose position does not allow him to hit back – have his name dragged through the mud by such proven liars as inhabit Buckingham Palace . . . If the Queen is tired of "press lies" as she informed the *Daily Telegraph*, then it is plain she is tired and ought to abdicate.'

By the time *Private Eye* had been in production for ten or fifteen years, television had developed its 'satirical' view of Royalty to a position where gentle mockery gave place to scabrous lampoon. The puppets on *Spitting Image* showed the Royal Family as ugly and contemptible. The Queen Mother was portrayed as a gin-sodden old Cockney, frequently applying the bottle to her lips. The Duchess of York was even seen in a recent episode undergoing colonic irrigation. That such programmes have appeared on television and gradually been accepted as part of the common hoard of mass-culture 'jokes' makes the older style of reverence for the Royal Family seem almost unthinkable today. I noticed this in a very minor way when Her Majesty the Queen Mother was ninety years old and I published (in a small weekly magazine) an account of meeting her at dinner some years before. Perhaps a few more copies of this small-circulation paper were sold in consequence, but it did not really produce outrage (except

95

in my host on the occasion of the dinner) that I had broken with Royal protocol and repeated what was said to me by the Queen Mother. It was all harmless stuff – but then, so had Altrincham and Malcolm Muggeridge been harmless. Older journalists, when I printed my conversation with the Queen Mother, said that I would receive the same sort of treatment and could expect a few brickbats to come my way. They could not have been more wrong. It was a small sign of how things had changed. My article made very little more impact than if I were describing a meeting with a famous film star who did not normally give interviews.

One of the great changes which I have noticed personally in the last few years in London is the nature of Royal tittle-tattle among journalists. Until very recently – the last couple of years – rumours and stories about the Royal Family have been very distinctly 'at one remove' from the principal participants. A few Royal gossips have always been in the habit of chatting to some of their journalistic friends, but none of this information was 'authorised', and therefore none of it ever appeared in the newspapers. In 1982, at least ten years before the Princess of Wales had announced her desire to be separated from Prince Charles, Nigel Dempster, the Diarist for the *Daily Mail* and a close personal confidant of 'the Royal moles', had disclosed in his column that all was not well with the Waleses' marriage and that the Princess's displays of distress and bad temper had earned her the title of a 'fiend and a monster' among the more staid courtiers and royalties. In the years which followed, one heard a whole string of stories, about Prince Charles, his wife, his brothers and his sister, not one of which appeared in the newspapers.

Then came the *annus horribilis*. When the 'revelations'

began to appear in the newspapers, there was a predictable outcry from such figures as back-bench Tory MPs, calling for a gag to be put upon the newspapers which printed them. Largely as a result of the 'intrusions' into the Royal Family, a special Commission was established to investigate the extent to which the Press were abusing their freedoms and to explore the possibility of new legislation which would limit the power of journalists to intrude into private lives. At the same time as the *Sunday Times* began its serialisation of Andrew Morton's book, *Diana: Her True Story*, the Press Complaints Commission issued a condemnation, stating that the book was 'dabbling in the stuff of other people's souls'. This was in June 1992.

What surprised me about Morton's book, when it first appeared, was that there was nothing in it which my expert friends, such as Nigel Dempster, had not been openly discussing over the lunch-table for years. In other words, for anyone 'in the know' it was not the contents but the timing which were a puzzle; and the protests by the Press Complaints Commission did not quite seem to hit their target. Like most people, however, the real answer to the mystery – 'Why now?' – had not dawned on me because it was so completely improbable, namely that the book had in effect been 'ghosted' by Mr Morton at the Princess of Wales's dictation.

In fact, for a year or so previous to Morton's book, something quite new had been happening in the newspapers. At the time of the Princess's thirtieth birthday, for example, there was widespread criticism of Prince Charles because he had not left his country house in order to be with his wife in London. On July 2, 1991, the *Daily Mail* carried the headline CAUSE FOR CONCERN, and a story by Nigel Dempster which revealed that the Prince had in fact offered his wife a birthday celebration, and she had turned him down. The next day, in the *Sun*, Andrew Morton had a story in which the Princess supposedly said that she had not wished to have a grand ball with her husband's 'stuffy friends'. 'I had hoped my husband knew me well enough to understand that I don't like that sort of thing,' she said.

Reading this at the time, one assumed that, like the majority of 'Royal' stories to appear in the newspapers, it was, if not straight fabrication, at least a creative reconstruction of the kind of thing the Princess might have said. By the time Mr Morton's book had been published, a year later, one realised that something much odder was at work. The initial 'leak' – that the Prince of Wales had wanted to give a party for his wife – had come direct from the Prince himself. The explanation for her refusal had come direct from the Princess herself. From now onwards, an extraordinary war was waged in print between the Prince and his wife, each using journalists whom they felt they could trust to bring the other into ridicule and contempt. Nearly all the stories printed in the British Press about the Prince and Princess of Wales – stories about the Prince's supposed intimacy with his friend Mrs Parker-Bowles, about the Princess's eating disorders, about the quarrels which they had, with each other and with the Queen and Prince Philip – were printed, not because of the indiscretion of some eagle-eyed reporter, but because of their own conscious decision to 'go public'. And this was a game which they both played. It was not the Princess alone who did it, and at this distance it would be rather difficult to establish which of the royal pair 'started it'. Auberon Waugh's *Private Eye* joke-fantasy, in which royalties treat journalists as confidants and the Royal Family bamboozle the innocent tabloid journalists with their devious lies, began to look perilously like the truth (though of course this was a story in which there were no innocent parties).

As early as May 1991, at a private dinner in Luxembourg, Lord Rothermere, the Chairman of Associated Newspapers, which publishes the *Daily Mail* and the *Evening Standard*, told Lord McGregor, the Chairman of the Press Complaints Commission, that the Prince and Princess had taken this course of action. His words were that 'the Prince and Princess of Wales had each recruited national newspapers to carry their own accounts of their marital rifts'.*

Now, what is of interest about this confession by Lord McGregor is that, in spite of his knowing the facts of the case, he continued to behave, as Chairman of the Press Complaints Commission, as if the 'intrusions' into the Royal marriage came from journalists alone, rather than being orchestrated by the Royal pair themselves. His reason for doing this was that he had confronted the Queen's Press Secretary, Sir Robert Fellowes (brother-in-law to the Princess of Wales), with what Lord Rothermere had said, and it was categorically denied by Sir Robert. McGregor told Fellowes that he, on behalf of the Royal Family, should send a list of the inaccuracies in Morton's book to the Press Complaints Commission, and each inaccuracy could then be dealt with in turn.

It was clear to any journalist who knew how these things worked that the Morton book, and all the subsequent journalistic 'intrusion' into the Waleses' marriage, could not have happened without authorisation from some Royal quarter. Something new had happened in the course of 1991 which enabled the journalists to print the stories which were beginning to emerge. That new development had to be that Prince Charles and his wife were authorising journalists to tell their stories, since no journalist, no editor and no proprietor would dare to publish

*Letter by Lord McGregor in the *Guardian*, January 12, 1993.

stories of such magnitude unless they had been substantiated.

This fact, obvious to any jobbing journalist, is less obvious to the reading public (however sophisticated), and this was why the Palace was able for so long to represent this seedy episode in Royal history as a sudden invasion of the citadels of civilisation by the barbarian hordes. Everyone in Royal circles knew that Mr Morton's book was substantially true, but this did not prevent them all from attempting to pretend that it was false. One of the known sources for Mr Morton's stories was Carolyn Bartholomew, the Princess of Wales's friend and former flatmate. When the denunciations of Morton were at their height, Lady Diana staged a very public visit to Carolyn Bartholomew's house and k issed her openly as she was greeted on the doorstep. On this occasion, the newspapermen and photographers, sensing that it was a moment of some intimacy between the two friends, held back. Lady Diana, however, surprised them all by driving her car twice round the block, to make sure that her public display of friendship with Mr Morton's sources was immortalised on camera.

The fairly unsubtle code of this occasion was not difficult to crack, either for the Press or for the Palace. Thereafter, it was open war between the official Royal Press Secretaries (including Sir Robert Fellowes) and Lady Diana. When the extent of Palace hypocrisy was finally rumbled in January 1993, and Lord McGregor was forced to admit that both sides in the Waleses' marriage rift had fed the press with stories, it was no surprise that the Prince's party put all the blame on to the Princess. The Princess of Wales had, the public were informed, 'in practice been invading her own privacy'.

This is perfectly true, but it is not, of course, the whole truth. As someone who became an idol of the world's Press from the moment she was engaged to be married, Lady Diana showed an exceptional gift for self-promotion. If the Palace thought that they were able to beat her at her own game, they were disastrously wrong. She quickly mastered the power of the visual image. Outside the complicated realm of economics, nearly all the great twentieth-century news 'stories' have in fact been photographs. When things went right for Lady Diana, she learnt how to be the 'smiling Princess'. But when she felt the Court and her husband's friends and family were conspiring against her, she knew that she could – at least for a time – promote a picture of herself to the world which told its own story, long before any of us necessarily knew about her husband's alleged emotional involvements elsewhere.

One of these was the famous photo opportunity at the Taj Mahal in February 1991. Her husband, on a previous visit to India, had famously said that he would like to take his affianced bride to this monument to married love. Eleven years after he had made this declaration, he was on an official visit to India in the company of this same wife. She chose a day when he was delivering a speech in Delhi – an engagement which he could not possibly cancel at short notice – to travel to the Taj Mahal to be photographed alone. All her aides and staff were banished from the picture, and she was photographed there, a solitary figure, neglected by her indifferent husband. The photographic message was clear, and it had the added amusement value that once again she had 'upstaged' her husband. His speech in Delhi received scant attention in the next morning's newspapers.

She staged a similar photographic message to the world in May, when she posed alone at the Pyramids during an official visit to Egypt. Charles had come out to Egypt with her, but then left her there alone to travel on to Turkey where, as we subsequently learned, he met up with Mrs Parker-Bowles. (When this fact was disclosed by Charles's biographer Anthony Holden in the February 1993 edition of *Vanity Fair*, it was vigorously denied by the Prince's representatives, speaking through the medium of Nigel Dempster in the *Daily Mail*. But Charles did in fact go to Turkey on that occasion in order to be with Mrs Parker-Bowles.)*

In general, men tend to like – or besottedly to adore – Lady Diana, and for that very reason women tend not to like her. Since journalism is one of the few professions in which there is a more or less equal proportion of men and women working at a high level, it is not surprising that a diversity of views have suggested themselves to the commentators about Lady Diana's so-called 'manipulation' of the media. Some journalists have felt inclined to comment upon its morality. What is not in doubt is its boldness.

It certainly seems as if Lady Diana may have connived at the 'press intrusions into her private life' as a means of releasing herself from her husband. This is a measure of how powerful the Press had become in the Royal Story. Until the arrival of Lady Diana in the family, the Royals – even the indiscreet ones – behaved with tremendous circumspection in relation to their journalist 'contacts' or friends. Any journalist who abused the trust of a member of the Royal Family knew that he or she would never be admitted into Royal circles again, so it simply was not worth the while of any seasoned Royal-watcher or Court Correspondent to quote Royal stories unless they were supplied 'on the record'. This meant that almost all Royal news and almost all Royal books, with the exception of Crawfie's, were stultifyingly boring, because they only told us what the Royal Family wanted us to know.

*Private information.

Lady Diana saw that, by 'doing a Crawfie', she could exercise enormous power over her husband and his family. Only they would know fully how much of Andrew Morton's book was true. The rest of us could only guess. This left her in a position of great strength when her lawyers came to approach her husband's lawyers, in the summer of 1992, to discuss the possibility of a marital separation.

While these negotiations were in progress, 'The Redhead', as Lady Diana contemptuously called the Duchess of York, had decided that she too would like to clamber aboard the bandwagon. If Diana could tell the story of her marriage to the Press, why shouldn't she? With the help of her friend, the Texan millionaire John Bryan, she entered into negotiations with the *Daily Mail* with a view to publishing her 'story'. Realising that they were on to a very hot thing, the *Mail* had been deliberately restrained about its reporting of the Duchess's marital troubles, and had never made use of its knowledge that John Bryan was extremely close to the Duchess.

Unfortunately for both the *Mail* and the Duchess, events were to pass out of their hands. Though estranged from her husband Andrew, she accompanied him up to Balmoral with their two daughters. And it was during the week that they were there that the *Daily Mirror* published what must be some of the most remarkable Royal portraits ever to appear in a British newspaper. *Paris-Match*, which bought the rights in these interesting glimpses of a Royal holiday, have subsequently paid a substantial sum of money in legal damages both to the Duchess and to her financial adviser. Everyone agreed that it was morally insupportable that such photographs should be in circulation, and everyone in Great Britain bought the *Daily Mirror* on the morning that they were published. The scene at Balmoral on the morning when the newspaper was published may only be imagined. It would certainly need another pen than mine to reconstruct the conversations, if any, which took place between the Duchess and her husband's family before she took a speedy flight to London on an ordinary shuttle from Aberdeen that day. Her position is irrecoverable, the more so since the revelations of Miss Player, concerning that lady's love affair with Her Royal Highness's father, Major Ferguson. But the Duchess of York and her sordid life, though of entertainment value in the cheaper newspapers, does not have a serious part to play in this story, except in so far as she contributed to the general cheapening of the Royal House in the eyes of the Press. And, doubtless, whenever she pops up in the tabloids, she will continue to do so for many entertaining years to come.

But what of the serious implications of the last few years? Does the present relationship between the Press, particularly the British Press, and Buckingham Palace represent a threat to the institution of Monarchy itself?

In a leader of December 19, 1992, the Conservative newspaper the *Daily Telegraph* asked whether the Monarchy had a future. Having rehearsed the marital troubles of the Prince of Wales, it claimed that 'the future of the Prince of Wales and of the Monarchy as a whole will depend upon the behaviour of those concerned *and the public response to them* [my italics] over the next generation, rather than upon any narrow technical interpretation of the constitution'. The leader continues, 'The most serious threat to the Monarchy's future stems not from the few who are directly hostile to it, but from the growing number who are indifferent. Vociferous critics have argued in the past week that the Royal Family is irrelevant to modern British life. Many of the young, especially, do not feel the awe and respect which the Royal Family has traditionally attracted. They simply do not care. It is this generation whose support and enthusiasm are needed to secure the Monarchy's future in the 21st century.'

This article would appear to be seriously meant, and the 'arguments' which it advances are frequently heard on British lips at the present time. The argument is that the Monarch is only there on sufferance. This, historically speaking, has been true. But what is new is the name of the supposed master calling the Monarch's tune. James II and Edward VIII were both fired, as William III and George I had been hired, by the same master – the oligarchy who ruled Britain at the time – which could variously be described as the aristocracy, the Establishment or both. Now that the Establishment has been dissolved in real terms, it is very hard to see who has the power to hire and fire Monarchs. But we can see who think they have this power: the Press barons and, beneath the barons, the newspaper editors.

This is surely the new development in the life of the Royal Family, and the one which is, from everyone's point of view except that of the journalists, the most damaging to the Monarchy. Examine the *Telegraph*'s argument in more detail: it is one which one hears repeated week in, week out, in any editorial conference in London where newspaper editors freely and grandly speak of which members of the Royal Family they will 'allow' to continue, and which they will 'get rid of', 'destroy', etc.

The Royal Family is 'irrelevant to modern life' – whatever this is supposed to mean. Certain members of it are in danger of failing to behave in a way which 'society' will accept. The future of the Monarchy apparently depends upon the support of the younger generation of uneducated people with no sense of the past. 'Part of the Monarchy's problem is that the Monarchy is strongly associated with the past, with an historical legacy about which young people ignorant of the dates of Trafalgar and Waterloo know and care less and less.'

Historically, the *Daily Telegraph's* view is complete nonsense, as any survey of English history would show. Not since the most primitive times of tribal Saxon kingship in the sixth or seventh century has English or British Monarchy been elective, or dependent upon a common consensus. During the last two hundred years there have been two huge constitutional crises when the Crown appeared to be heading for a clash with Parliamentary processes – in 1831–2 and in 1910. In both cases, remarkably enough, the crisis was largely averted by the Sovereign himself. In neither case was the King concerned a clever person in ordinary worldly terms, but both William IV and George V had a basic instinct of common sense and a firm idea of what the constitutional position of the Monarchy was. It existed, and exists, in symbiotic relation to the Houses of Parliament, and it used to exist in a similar symbiosis *vis-à-vis* the upper class or the oligarchy which actually controlled those two institutions of Lords and Commons. What it never did was exist by common consent or democracy. A democratic Monarchy is probably a contradiction in terms. Whether it is or it isn't, no foresight is required in today's world to see who would step forward as the Tribunes of the People, declaring when or whether the monarch must *go*.

The Royal Family's view of the Press until very recent times has tended to be wary, if not paranoid. Prince Philip – with his frequent cry, if the Press cameras come too close, of 'Don't jostle the Queen!' – has been the most outspoken enemy of the popular journalists, whom he describes as the apes of Gibraltar. Reporters approaching Prince Philip in a spirit of polite deference have frequently been told to 'Fuck off' – and this robust attitude to the Press has been inherited by his daughter Princess Anne. It is surely no coincidence that, through all the vicissitudes of the Royal Family's reputation, these two members of it – Prince Philip and Princess Anne – are the ones to whom journalists in general concede a grudging respect. Those who have attempted to woo the Press have had a rougher ride. Dean Inge remarked that he who set out to woo the spirit of the age would soon find himself a widow. This has almost literally occurred with the principal actors in the younger Royal generation, as the separate households and broken marriages of Prince Andrew and Prince Charles both testify. Consequently, the future of the Monarchy is seen to depend neither on parliamentary consensus nor upon constitutional principle, but on the whim of newspaper editors and their journalists. Whether this is a good or bad thing, it certainly changes the function of the Crown as it has been traditionally understood. Disregarding the question of whether it is proper, it also changes the time-scale by which such matters can be considered.

Monarchy is by its nature an old and slow institution. Its place in the scheme of things has been worked out slowly. Prime Ministers and their administrations come and go; the Monarchy remains in place. Its customs, ceremonies and constitutional function provide continuity with the nation's history in a way which no politician could ever do. When Ho Chi Minh was asked whether the French Revolution had brought benefit to the human race, he said that it was too early to say. A similar judgement could be made of the British Monarchy. Its value and function can only be understood on a very long time-scale.

The Press, by contrast, is by definition ephemeral. There is the world of difference between news and history. Most 'news' has a dragonfly life which is dead within a day. Its attitude to everything, including the Royal Family, is instantaneous. It looks for 'stories' which can be hurried on to the front page and which will encourage people to buy newspapers. 'Queen works her way through red boxes for the forty-second year' is hardly a very exciting headline. Nor is: 'Queen meets Prime Minister, as she has done each week for the last forty-odd years, and discusses the future of Canada/Europe/the House of Lords, drawing on a lifetime's constitutional experience.' In the world of hurry and headlines, 'John Sucks Fergie's Toe' or 'Lady Di Throws a Tantrum' make more instantly appealing stories, even though these events, dramatic as they must have seemed at the time, are perhaps of less moment in historical terms.

But this 'perhaps' looks as if it is going to require some readjustment. The new development in the relationship between the Royals and the Press is that, instead of regarding journalists as their enemy, or at the very best a necessary evil, to be kept at arm's length, the Royal Family have decided to woo the media, offering them leaks and stories in the manner of politicians.

Although all this might be seen as 'doing a Crawfie' on a big scale, it has to be admitted that the first person who started on the slippery path of 'publicity' for the Royal House was none other than Her Majesty the Queen. When she had completed her first televised Christmas broadcast, the Queen sighed and said to the producer, 'It's no good, I'm not a film star.'* Unfortunately she, or those who advise her on these matters, had forgotten this fact, and in July 1969 BBC television showed a film called *Royal Family*. It was supposed to be an intimate, behind-the scenes, family snapshot sort of programme. Some indication of the level of public interest shown in the Royal Family may be given

*Douglas Keay, *Elizabeth II* (1991) p. 221.

by the viewing figures: 23 million British people watched it, compared with 30 million who watched the World Cup football final three years earlier, and the 26 or so million people who regularly watched a weekly comedy show called *Steptoe and Son*, about a rag-and-bone merchant.* David Attenborough, a noted BBC film-maker who special-ises in the capturing of endangered species on celluloid, was surely right when he said to the producer, 'You know, you're killing the Monarchy with this film you're making. The whole institution depends on mystique and the tribal chief in his hut. If any member of the tribe ever sees inside his hut, then the whole system of the tribal chieftain is dam-aged and the tribe eventually disintegrates.'† These words sound very wise when read twenty years later.

The point is not merely that the viewing public had been shown inside the hut, but, in allowing themselves to appear on television in this light, the Windsors had become the mere creatures of television. There is no political theory, no *realpolitik*, no system of religious self-abnegation which is more humiliating for individuals than to make them into television 'personalities'. Television is the great lev-eller, and it quite indiscriminately devours those whom it attracts. Journalists, comedians, orators, great actors might be tempted, by avarice or vanity, to make appearances on it. However brilliant they might be, they become in the shortest possible time indistinguishable from the air-heads on the chat shows, and even from the puppets and cartoon creations of children's TV. The Queen's children did not help matters, when they grew up, by appearing on tele-vision fairly frequently. Prince Charles has made two or three documentary films. His brothers and sister-in-law

---

* Keay, Ibid. p. 224.
† Ibid. p.125.

starred in what must be the most embarrassing Royal appearance in history, including raucous team games in which they wore supposedly funny mediaeval costumes, and Prince Edward, the organiser of the event, flying into a tantrum with the audience for laughing in the wrong places.

Since the Windsors had become 'television personalities', albeit minor ones, it was not surprising that tabloid newspapers should have begun to think that the private lives of the Queen and her family were fair game. Journalists, who had hitherto been forced to make do with the love-life of starlets and stand-up comedians, could now legitimately contemplate the heirs to the throne; and sometimes it was not always easy to tell the difference between them.

In Britain, by the end of 1992, there was a perceptible air of satiety in the reading public. The year concluded with the *Sun* 'leaking' the Queen's Christmas broadcast and printing its contents on the front page two days before Christmas. The Queen was said to be furious, and authorised her solicitor, Sir Matthew Farrer, to sue the newspaper for breach of copyright.

This action was very widely welcomed, because it was felt that the Murdoch press in particular had gone too far in their sadistic and intrusive attacks on the Royal Family. Murdoch or his minions had orchestrated what seemed to be an attack on the Monarchy itself. The *Sun*, edited by Kelvin McKenzie, had published the contents of the 'Squidgygate' tapes. The *Sunday Times* had serialised the Andrew Morton book. In the early months of 1993, Murdoch's Sky TV screened a mini-series based on the break-up of the Waleses' marriage. Few people of the educated class in Britain are able to watch Sky TV since, in order to do so, you have to append a satellite dish on the side of your house. In the still class-ridden society of Britain in 1993, the possession of such a dish would write its owner down as a plebeian. Those sophisticates who did see the film at a private viewing-theatre, sometimes drowned the noise of the characters speaking (or, in the case of the actress playing the Princess of Wales, the noise of being sick) with their contemptuous laughter.

It was still widely believed that Murdoch had not sufficiently received his come-uppance. When accused of megalomania recently, Murdoch is said to have replied that the editor of the *Sun* was more powerful than the Queen. Probably true in modern Britain, but this did not stop a few loyalists from hoping that Her Majesty would fight back. Newspaper magnates could fall as well as rise. Had not Robert Maxwell's empire collapsed about him in ignominy, and was it not true that Murdoch's enterprises were supported by huge borrowing? 1992, with its high interest rates and a continuing world recession, had been an *annus horribilis* for him too. This placed him in a position of some weakness when it came to the flagrant breach of copyright involved in printing the Queen's speech three days early, as if it were an article which she had penned at the behest of that powerful man Kelvin McKenzie. There was talk in Royal circles about the need to hire a tough lawyer, and to pursue Murdoch to the High Courts, taking from him 40 or 50 million pounds.

Unfortunately, the Press got wind of this, and the story appeared in the *Sunday Telegraph*'s 'Mandrake' column, perhaps contributed by that close friend of the Royal family and distinguished royal biographer, Mr Kenneth Rose. Murdoch was on the telephone to his underlings the moment the 'Mandrake' article appeared. The next day, the *Sun* offered a rather perky apology to the Queen, saying that since she had been so kind as to offer to pay income tax they would offer to pay £200,000 to charity. Needless to say, Her Majesty was urged to settle at once.

Many loyalists felt that a great opportunity had been missed. It would obviously have been possible throughout the *annus horribilis* to sue any number of the tabloids for criminal libel. Even the broadsheets spoke openly of Mrs Parker-Bowles in a way which was clearly defamatory, not only of herself and of the Prince of Wales, but of her husband and her children. But no one sued for libel, because no one dared. In a world where bullyism of that kind rules, the Commissions for this and that give advice, and even help draft laws, but the tabloid editors know that they have the Queen and her family on the run. By suing for breach of copyright, the Queen would have avoided any of the embarrassment of a libel case, but could still have exacted punitive damages; but, as always, she was badly advised, and so she will remain the permanent victim of the situation.

Like the stars of proletarian soap operas, the Windsors are doomed to appear in the pages of the cheap papers whenever the editors of those papers cannot think up any proper news; and that will be often. The self-importance of newspaper editors is not to be underestimated, nor is their capacity for self-deception. As someone who works quite happily in the world of newspapers, I have no idea whether or not they are 'influential' or, if so, in what ways they are influential. I should not wish them silenced, even though one might rejoice when the Citizen Kanes have mighty falls. The Royal obsession with the newspapers has become every bit as obsessive as the newspapers' interest in Royalty. Indeed, as we have seen, the Princess of Wales's escape from matrimony was orchestrated by means of the Press. The day-to-day tittle-tattle is not very likely to undermine the constitution. But what Lady Di has done could have wholly destructive effects, for, by publicly humiliating her husband and forcing him to acquiesce in the idea of a divorce, she cuts at the very *raison d'être* of the House of Windsor. For if no one in that family minded about divorce, then the Queen Mother could have remained the Duchess of York all her life (as she claims she would like to have done), bending her knee in gracious curtsies whenever she met her rightful Sovereign Lady, Queen Wallis of Baltimore.

SEVEN

The Merry Wives
of Saxe-Coburg

'We are not supposed to be human.'

Queen Elizabeth (quoted by Crawfie)

'No feeling could seem more childish than the enthusiasm of the English at the marriage of the Prince of
Wales. They treated as a great political event what,
looked at as a matter of pure business, was very small
indeed. But no feeling could be more like common
human nature as it is, and as it is likely to be . . . All
but a few cynics like to see a pretty novel touching
for a moment the dry scenes of the grave world. A
princely marriage is the brilliant edition of a universal
fact, and, as such, it rivets mankind.'

Walter Bagehot, *The English Constitution*

It was a sad day for the Royal Family when Prince Albert
decided that they were meant to be custodians of the
nation's morals. The House of Windsor, the unhappy heirs
of this novel viewpoint, is more than usually haunted by
the difficulties of the married state. In matters of sexual
conduct, it would seem, upon a survey of the last 200 years
of Royal history, as though English Kings and Queens have
veered excessively between extremes of puritanism and
profligacy. Prince Albert, the child of a syphilitic rake and
an adulterous mother who died when he was only twelve
years old, determined to bring up his children with cruel
and puritanical severity. Queen Victoria, the child and
niece of roués and rakes, was only too eager to encourage

him to make the Royal Nursery into the severest of penitentiaries. But, although they made the Prince of Wales (Bertie) work for hours each day on uncongenial book-learning, and although they beat him black and blue in an attempt to inculcate within him the principles of Christian chastity, he turned out to be just as fat and lewd and sensual as his grandparents and his obese great-uncles.

Bertie's son, by contrast, was something of a puritan. Having watched Queen Alexandra, whom he called Mother-dear (*sic*), suffer as a result of her husband's repeated adulteries, George V was only too happy to marry Queen Mary, a figure who was so emotionally buttoned-up that it is scarcely believable that she was able to proceed with the necessary preliminaries to pregnancy. That George V's married life was emotionally or sexually fulfilled, we may rather doubt – 'marvellous' though Queen Mary was, as a semi-comic, heroic figure, as a Queen Consort, as a friend to her husband. Like many puritans before and since, George V took refuge with the occasional prostitute discreetly arranged for him in seaside towns such as Bognor – renamed Bognor Regis because of the happy hours he had spent there. For the rest of the time he was a rigid upholder of old-fashioned morality. He insisted that divorced persons should never be admitted to any Royal function. A Scottish nobleman who had been divorced and had remarried once pleaded during King George V's reign with a court functionary at Holyroodhouse in Edinburgh that his remarriage in church had 'purged' the errors and sins of the past. 'That may well get you into the Kingdom of Heaven,' he was told, 'but it will not admit you to the Palace of Holyroodhouse.' Equally strong was the rule that divorced persons should not be admitted to the enclosure at Royal Ascot, an injunction which held good until the divorce of Princess Margaret in 1978. As for other expressions of human sexuality, they were, in the simple-minded world of George V and Queen Mary, unthinkable. When told that a member of the House of Lords had been involved in a homosexual scandal, George V remarked, 'I always thought people like that shot themselves.' This statement is all the more touching when we remember the emotional complexion of such close relations of the King as his son, the Duke of Kent, and his cousin, Lord Louis Mountbatten.

With innocents like George V and Queen Mary for parents, it was hardly surprising that Edward VIII should have decided to be completely different and to reject what he conceived of as their stodgy values. After that experiment had landed the Royal Family so spectacularly 'in the soup', it was still less surprising that Edward VIII's brother, George VI, and subsequently his niece Elizabeth II, should have been rigid upholders of the George V approach to these matters.

It is no longer any secret that the Queen's own marriage has been far from 'happy' in any of the conventional senses of that term. At the end of her *annus horribilis*, on her forty-fifth wedding anniversary, a substantial part of Windsor Castle burst into flames. Two of her sons, Prince Edward and Prince Andrew, helped to clear the Palace of its art treasures. Her other children got in touch either that day or the next day. The notable absentee on this occasion was her husband, the Duke of Edinburgh, who was in South America and did not fly home until a day or two later, in time for the banquet at which the *annus horribilis* speech was made. It is no secret that the Queen and her husband lead separate lives, and have done for years. To what extent it was an 'arranged' marriage we shall perhaps never fully know, but she had certainly considered him as an eligible partner from her early teens, and there is no evidence that in these early adolescent years she ever seriously consid-

1a Queen Victoria, Prince Albert and their children at Osborne, Isle of Wight. Prince Albert left his descendents the difficult legacy of being an 'ideal family'.

1b Queen Victoria with 'Bertie' and his Danish wife Princess Alexandra. Bertie's repeated adulteries provided the public with entertainment and did much to revive the popularity of the Monarchy which had plummeted during Queen Victoria's widowhood.

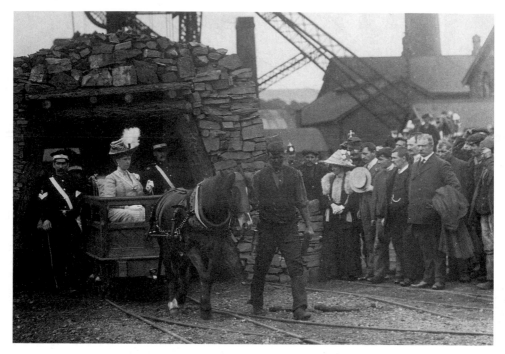

2a Queen Mary visits a Welsh coal-mine.
Her bolt-upright posture seldom varied.

2b George V making the first Royal Christmas broadcast in 1934.

3a The former King, Edward VIII, commits the crime of marrying for love, 3 June 1937. At the new Queen's insistence, Duchess Wallis was never allowed to be Her Royal Highness.

3b How the news of the Abdication reached the streets of London.

4a The new Queen's 'homely' appearance helped to create her 'virtuous' image with the public. Here she is pictured with her daughters, the future Queen Elizabeth II, and Princess Margaret Rose.

4b 'Now we can look the East End in the face.' The King and Queen, when their own palace had been hit by enemy bombs, built up a particular rapport with bomb victims.

5 Sir James Gunn's 'Conversation Piece at Royal Lodge, Windsor, 1950', is
one of the most successful pieces of royal iconography. The Queen holds the
teapot ('Who'll be mother?') as the princesses lean forward, perhaps
wondering whether their father will speak. A corgi snoozes beneath his chair.

6a Princess Elizabeth makes a 21st birthday speech to the Empire – significantly, it is made in Cape Town, South Africa, 22 April 1947.

6b Prince Philip, the handsome Duke of Edinburgh, was a serving officer in the Royal Navy until his wife became the Queen.

7a The coronation of
Queen Elizabeth II in
Westminster Abbey.

7b Coronation
photograph of Queen
Elizabeth II and Philip,
Duke of Edinburgh.

8 The Queen's devotion to her father's Empire, now re-named the British Commonwealth, never diminishes. This photograph shows Her Majesty's visit to the spice island of Grenada, 13 February 1966.

9a Not everyone would consider the influence of 'Uncle Dickie' (Lord Mountbatten of Burma) to have been a happy one. He tried to persuade the Queen to change the name of her family to Mountbatten Windsor — a proposal which led to a major rift between the Queen and Mountbatten's nephew Philip.

9b Corgis and the indomitable mother have been a constant feature of the Queen's grown-up life.

9c Sisters. The Queen's unchanging gum boots and headscarf never looked fashionable and therefore never dated. Princess Margaret's modish outfit, worn at Badminton 1971, already looks like an exhibit in a museum of costume.

9d The familiar sight of the Queen Trooping the Colour is one which most British people would miss if the Monarchy were modernized or abolished.

10a Prince Charles being welcomed to Trinity College, Cambridge (where he studied for three years) by the Master, Lord Butler.

10b Charles at his Investiture in Caernarvon, North Wales, 1 July 1969. This ancient ceremony was invented by David Lloyd George to gratify his Welsh constituents and was first enacted by the future Edward VIII.

11a Prince Andrew on his twenty-first birthday. He later went on to serve as a Royal Navy helicopter pilot in Margaret Thatcher's war against the Argentine.

11b Margaret Thatcher's known hostility to the British Commonwealth was one of the many areas where she differed from her sovereign.

12a Happy in love — the famous engagement photograph taken at Buckingham Palace, 24 February 1981.

12b The Royal pair on one of their first visits abroad together — here pictured in Bunbury, near Perth, Western Australia.

13 Before long Lady Diana Spencer had flowered into the Fairy Princess — a figure who was poised to do more damage to the British Monarchy than anyone since Oliver Cromwell.

14a Skiing in Klosters. At first Lady Di and the Duchess of York were friends, but they soon became rivals for public attention.

14b Meanwhile, the Prince of Wales continued to see his friend Mrs Parker-Bowles, seen here after a polo match.

15a Fire at Windsor Castle nearly destroys the Queen's childhood home.

15b Her Majesty delivers her famous 'annus horribilis' speech at the Mansion House, November 1992.

16 The Princess of Wales, on holiday in Austria
with Prince William and Prince Harry, April 1993.

ered an alternative partner, though two Dukes were both suggested to her as possibilities.

Partly because the Queen has been held in very great affection by the British people, and partly out of fear, it was only in recent times that anyone would have dreamed of writing openly about such matters. The Queen and Prince Philip often eat their meals apart, and they spend their evenings, if they do not have company, in separate apartments, the Queen watching television or struggling with the *Daily Telegraph* crossword by her electric fire with only her corgis for companionship, the Duke otherwise engaged. To all outward appearances, the Royal pair are represented as ideal figures. To those of a younger generation this would seem like hypocrisy, but the truth is that nearly all systems – political, religious, social – depend to a very large degree on what could be called hypocrisy, or could equally well be called keeping up appearances.

Speculations about the Royal Marriage were frequent in its early days, but there were certain things which were Never Written, though they might have been gossiped about by courtiers and by those who took an interest in such matters.

One example was the supposed mistresses of the Duke of Edinburgh. This was a fact noted by Fiametta Rocco in a major interview with Prince Philip in the British newspaper the *Independent on Sunday*.* With extraordinary candour, Ms Rocco confronted the Duke with the rumours of his infidelities over the years, to receive the reply, 'Have you ever stopped to think that for the last forty years I have never moved anywhere without a policeman accompanying me? So how the *hell* could I get away with anything like that?' There are plenty of answers to that. But the remarkable

*December 13, 1992.

thing about this conversation is not whether you believe Prince Philip's answer; the remarkable thing is that such an exchange should have been happening at all. In the inconceivable event of King George V having granted an 'interview' to a journalist,* you can guess his response if the said journalist had quizzed His Majesty about jaunts to boarding houses in Bognor.

'The papers continually accuse Philip of having been a harsh father,' the Queen Mother once remarked to a dinner-companion. 'If they only knew the truth . . .' her voice trailed away, and she gave a little shrug. 'It was always Lilibet who was too strict, and Philip who tried to moderate her.'† No one outside the immediate family circle could test the truth of this highly subjective judgement. In any event, it would seem to have been easier to be born a daughter than a son of the House of Windsor. Princess Anne shows fewer signs of emotional scarring than her brothers, but this is partly because she has chosen to reveal herself much less to the prurient view of television cameras and newspapers. There also remain the facts of her divorce and her many un-happy dependencies on such figures as Royal bodyguards and policemen. If it is true that children learn how to be married by watching their parents, then the young Wind-sors will have had some distinctive role models. One cannot fail to admire the pluck and constancy of Prince Philip and the Queen, who undoubtedly have a strong partnership of

---

* Though George V never gave an interview, it is an
interesting historical fact that the first modern royalty to
grant an 'interview' to the Press was King George's cousin the
Kaiser, while staying at Osborne House on the Isle of Wight after
the death of Queen Victoria.
† Private information.

sorts as they begin to face old age; but it is a partnership based on much separation, and it is not what a bourgeois person would recognise as a 'happy' marriage. Certainly the modern idea that married people should contrive to do everything, including sleeping, together has never been part of Prince Philip's or the Queen's idea of how a Royal couple should conduct themselves. They themselves had some distinctive role models to follow. Queen Elizabeth was a notoriously 'devoted' wife to George VI, but his last hours were spent alone, drinking chocolate and smoking a cigarette in bed, and it was left to a servant to find him dead some time the next morning. Philip's parents brought him up in an extraordinary way – with no fixed home. His parents separated when he was young, and by Royal standards there was very little money. His mother, a constant figure in his life (she lived in Buckingham Palace in latter days), was, as we have already mentioned, a nun.

Whatever contemporary psychiatrists might consider the perfect school for 'normal' or 'happy' marriage, this cannot have been it. And if this is the background to the marriages of Prince Charles's parents and grandparents, the emotionally unsatisfactory nature of Lady Diana Spencer's background is equally well known. The beautiful but emotionally brittle Frances Roche 'bolted' after thirteen years of marriage to Johnnie Spencer. No family therapist or marriage guidance counsellor would imagine, when they saw the wedding of Prince Charles and Lady Diana Spencer, that they were going to have an easy time.

The marriage of 'the Waleses' was from the first the subject of stupendous, unimaginably intense observation: 600 million people watched it on television. What would Hitler or Stalin not have done to achieve audiences of this size and scale?

Lady Diana Spencer chose as her wedding-hymn 'I vow to thee, my country', a religious air more associated in England with times of war and periods of national emergency than with nuptial celebration. Until pacifism became the prevailing fad in the Church of England, it was sung annually at Armistice Services. In that hymn she prayed to be inspired with the love that asks no questions, the love which asks no price, but lays upon the altar the final sacrifice; and all this was done in a spirit of simple patriotism. For those watching the solemnities, it gave new meaning to the old phrase about lying back and thinking of England.

Since almost every male in Great Britain had fallen in love with Lady Diana, there was inevitably some ambivalence in the national response to this act of supreme sacrifice. Auberon Waugh had observed, shortly after their engagement, 'We must all decide that 19-year-old Lady Diana Spencer is innocent, truthful, sweet and entirely delicious. What has Wales done to deserve her? More particularly, what has she done to deserve such a hellish fate?'* Few of the professional 'Royal-watchers' understood that this was what she was letting herself in for – a 'hellish fate'. Even so, after her honeymoon, Lady Diana confided to reporters: 'I never thought it was possible to be so happy'†, though she did not say whether the cause of her happiness was what had happened during the previous two weeks, or the fact that the honeymoon was now over.

Certainly, to all outward appearances, it seemed as though Lady Diana, in the first years of marriage, was defying her grandmother Lady Fermoy's advice and submitting with great fortitude to the final sacrifice. Rumours

---

Private Eye, November 29, 1980.
†Elizabeth Longford, *The Royal House of Windsor* (1984 revised edition) p.281.

that all was not well with the marriage in those early years, when she had slept with her husband with at least enough frequency to produce a couple of fine sons, only added to the general feeling that she was doing a good job, as she accompanied her husband on his tours of duty and, with increasing frequency, appeared as a patroness in her 'own right' of various charitable, cultural or public concerns. True, it was less than eighteen months after Lady Diana's marriage that, in December 1982, in his column in the *Daily Mail*, Dempster revealed that Lady Diana was 'a very wilful and spoiled girl. Suddenly, getting this enormous power, having people curtsy and bow to her, doing everything she wants, she's become a fiend. She has become a little monster.'

Ten years later, the Princess's biographer, Andrew Morton, revealed that this criticism had caused Lady Diana particular pain. Morton's version of what had happened to her since she married makes compulsive reading. While she suffered from post-natal depression as a result of Prince William's birth (June 21, 1982), Lady Diana had not been cheered up by the continuing closeness of her husband's relationship with Mrs Parker-Bowles. After the birth of his son, the Prince was frequently away from home. 'Whatever happens, I will always love you,' he said on one of the evenings he happened to be at Kensington Palace. But his wife did not find the words particularly reassuring; they were said into a portable telephone (presumably to Mrs Parker-Bowles, perhaps to one of his other attachments), while his wife whimpered and eavesdropped in an adjoining room.

Not only was he, as we now learn, entirely unsympathetic to his wife's eating disorder, bulimia nervosa, but he was also dismayed by her extremely modern, not to say middle-class, attitude to the marriage conventions. 'During a ferocious argument with Diana, Charles made clear the Royal Family's position. He told her in no uncertain terms that his father, the Duke of Edinburgh, had agreed that if, after five years, his marriage was not working he could go back to his bachelor habits. Whether those sentiments, uttered in the heat of the moment, are true or not was beside the point,' adds Andrew Morton. 'They had the effect of placing Diana on her guard in her every dealing with her in-laws.'

Some of Mr Morton's readers might decide that it matters very much indeed whether these words 'were true or not' – first, whether they were uttered, and second, whether they represent the Royal Family's attitude to marriage.

One's answer to the first question must depend upon a whole bundle of irrational things, which include how one feels about Lady Diana herself. ('Diana Spencer,' said the vicar's wife in Norfolk all those years ago, 'if you tell one more lie like that I am going to make you walk home.')* Those with an experience of giving, or receiving, confidences about marital feuds will know how much 'editing' takes place, often quite unconsciously, on the teller's part.

Certainly, as a supposed statement by Prince Charles, it is extremely odd – so odd, some would say, that it would have been difficult to invent. Some would think it odd to consult one's father about the permissibility or otherwise of committing adultery, but we now all know enough about Prince Charles to know that he is an extremely odd man. Historians cannot at this juncture pronounce with any certainty whether he said it or not, and whether or not Prince Philip introduced a 'five-year rule', whereby the Prince of Wales had to endure a further three years after making the alleged statement before feeling able to philander with a free

*Morton, op. cit. p.21.

conscience. But whether or not these exact words were said at this exact juncture, the general view expressed of the married state is surely one which has operated in the House of Windsor throughout its history.

What has contributed in such large measure to the difficulties of the Royal Family in the present generation is that the wives of the two Princes – Lady Diana Spencer and Sarah Ferguson – expected their husbands to behave like modern middle-class husbands rather than Edwardian aristocrats.

One of King Edward VII's most devoted mistresses – so close to him that Queen Alexandra invited her to attend the King's deathbed – was Mrs Alice Keppel. Some sixty years after Mrs Keppel took her touching farewell of her Sovereign and lover, her great-great-granddaughter, Camilla, met the great-great-grandson of Edward VII. Having informed Prince Charles of the tenuous ancestral connection between them, Camilla is supposed to have said, 'How about it then?' – the beginning of a fond attachment.

It would be quite wrong to suppose that Victorian and Edwardian upper-class marriages, with their high incidence of 'contained' adultery, caused no pain. The biographers of Edward VII and of Queen Alexandra do not tell a story of smiling indulgence on the wife's side, nor of guilt-free sensuality on the husband's. Even *The Times* said in 1890 that it would be 'affectation to conceal' the reason why such huge crowds had attended a production of *She Stoops to Conquer* at the Haymarket Theatre. It was because the Prince of Wales insisted on bringing his wife to see his mistress perform in the part of Kate Hardcastle. In 1891, for example, we read of poor 'Alix', unable to bear the humiliation of the very public knowledge of her husband's adultery with Lady Brooke – known because of her indiscretions as

The Babbling Brooke. In consequence she refused to attend his fiftieth birthday party, and went off to the Crimea with her sister, the Empress of Russia. All this seemed like a mirror of what was going on in Kensington Palace in 1992.

Yet those who have studied the period, or those old and grand enough to recall it, have assured us that Edwardian marriages survived because of the existence of a code. The observance of this code meant that, on the surface of things at least, the institutions and great houses which these marriages cemented were unthreatened by the frailty of those who were born to uphold them. Divorce took place – inevitably – among the upper classes in early-twentieth-century England; but the vigorous families, and the ones which survived most triumphantly as political powers, were not necessarily those where no infidelity was known, but where wives and husbands were tolerant and prepared to 'weather the storm'.

Diana belonged to a generation where you hoped to marry for 'love'. When 'love' dies or fades, or changes into something else, you consult a therapist – either a psychotherapist, a sex therapist or some other kind of therapist. If that fails, and you are both sufficiently young and vigorous, or sufficiently optimistic, to suppose that happiness might be found with a different partner, you decide that the marriage is over and you file for a 'civilised' divorce, trying to hide from yourself the devastating effect this is having on your children. Such is modern marriage, European- and American-style. One of the strange facts about modern life, in spite of its supposedly more relaxed attitude to sexual morality, is that adultery *per se* should be seen as grounds for a divorce. The 'old' view of marriage is perfectly encapsulated in an exchange between the great eighteenth-century moralist Dr Samuel Johnson and his biographer James Boswell: 'I mentioned to him a dispute between a friend of mine [in fact Boswell himself] and his lady, concerning conjugal infidelity, which my friend had maintained was by no means so bad in the husband, as in the wife. *Johnson*: 'Your friend was in the right, Sir. Between a man and his Maker it is a different question: but between a man and his wife, a husband's infidelity is nothing. They are connected by children, by fortune, by serious considerations of community. Wise married women don't trouble themselves about infidelity in their husbands . . .'

Unappealing as this might be to modern feminist sensibilities, it is hard to see how a Royal Family (or, come to that, an American Presidential family) could be sustained unless it took this attitude. Added to the naturally conservative approach to divorce which any person might wish to share, the Royal Family are obliged to embody in their own weak persons an office of State. It was with irony, but truth, that George VI and Queen Elizabeth spoke of their little family unit – themselves and the two princesses – as 'The Firm'. Those who have since married into 'The Firm' have, as the Queen and her subjects might have hoped, undertaken to promote the values and purposes of 'The Firm'. Without such intentions on both sides, irreparable damage was bound to be done to the young people involved, to their marriages and to 'The Firm' itself.

Had the present Queen been a character built in the Edward VII mould, it might have been much easier for anyone wishing to marry her children to be cynical and to realise what they were letting themselves in for. As it happens, she was the child of George VI and Elizabeth Bowes-Lyon, a couple who did not always observe the borderline which exists between a seemly desire to keep up appearances and a crippling hypocrisy.

*

One of the most potent images which they wished to present of themselves was enshrined by Sir James Gunn in his beautiful group portrait of the King, the Queen and the two Princesses at Royal Lodge. It greets any visitor to the National Portrait Gallery in London, and it is one of the most potent visual declarations of what the New Monarchy (by contrast with Edward VIII) so firmly stood for. Nothing could more confidently and primly have proclaimed the difference between Elizabeth Bowes-Lyon, her reassuring plumpness, her sweet smile, her dear young daughters, her hand stretched out to be 'mother' with the teapot – and the exiled Duchess of Windsor, fast, worldly, beautiful, childless, thin, jewel-bedecked. In spite of the beautiful Gothick interior in which they sit, there is something essentially middle-class about this icon. They are the perfect mid-twentieth-century, classless nuclear family, who have struggled through the Second World War with their ration books and their austere simple tastes, and will continue through the peace to be emblems of happy family virtue.

Since the despised David, the Duke of Windsor, and Wallis had been honest enough, selfish and naïve enough, to marry for love, whatever it cost them, Queen Elizabeth (later the Queen Mother) never lost the opportunity to emphasise to the public that the new proprietors of 'The Firm' stood firm for Family Values. The last thing any of those four round the table would ever contemplate would be a horrible divorce, such as That Wallis Woman had allowed herself – not once, but twice.

If that is the message of James Gunn's picture, and of thousands of comparable royal icons put out during the 1940s and 1950s, we can now see that the King and

Queen were piling up trouble for the future. One figure in that group of four – Princess Margaret – fell in love with one of her father's equerries, Group-Captain Peter Townsend, who was divorced from his wife in 1952. It was of course unthinkable, only twenty years after her mother had become Queen of England on the 'No divorce please, we're Royal' ticket, that Princess Margaret should have married this man. The King was told that, if they married in such circumstances, Princess Margaret would not be eligible for a Civil List pension. Since the King was only worth several million pounds, it would obviously have been beyond his own capacities to provide his daughter with any such allowance. Group Captain Townsend has subsequently, a little ungallantly, told friends that he might have married the Princess in defiance of the conventions had they had enough money to live on. These pecuniary considerations were swept to one side, however, when – with what some of their friends considered nauseating humbug – a statement was issued to the Press indicating that 'I would like it to be known that I have decided not to marry Group Captain Peter Townsend. I have been aware that, subject to my renouncing my rights of succession, it might have been possible for me to contract a civil marriage. But, mindful of the Church's teaching that Christian marriage is indissoluble, and conscious of my duty to the Commonwealth, I have resolved to put these considerations before any others.' Conscious of her duty to the Commonwealth, the Princess then married a charming photographer called Tony Armstrong-Jones. The marriage ended in 1976. (Decree absolute 1978.)

The other young figure in James Gunn's icon, the future Queen Elizabeth II, has not, at the time of writing, sought a divorce, but it is noticeable that, out of her four children, three have been married and three have had marriages which came unstuck. In other words, from that first ideal 'nuclear family' of George VI and Elizabeth Bowes-Lyon, which was supposed to be so much more reassuring than the (in fact devotedly happily married) Wallis and David Windsor, not one marriage has survived. It seems that the Queen's is a polite shell of which it has only recently been possible for people to speak. Princess Margaret's ended; Prince Charles's has ended, Prince Andrew's has ended and Princess Anne has lately demonstrated the triumph of hope over experience by divorcing one nonentity and marrying another. One does not need to parody Lady Bracknell by saying that to have had one unhappy marriage in the family may be deemed a misfortune, but to have had five begins to look like carelessness.

What Lady Fermoy, in her delicate warning to Lady Diana, should have said was: 'It is not difficult to be married to any member of this family. It is impossible.'

Lady Fermoy was in a better position than most of us to recognise that British Royal personages are actually different from the rest of mankind, different even from the rich and the aristocratic who live in comparably large houses and employ a comparable number of servants. Being Royal is itself a kind of selfishness. It would take a saint born into the Royal Family to draw a border between respect which was owing to the Crown and slavishness owing to their Royal personages. Anyone who has ever had to do with the Royal Family has their own tale to tell of capriciousness which in a private individual would be insupportable. King George VI, for example, like his daughter after him, seldom found himself sitting at the same dinner-table as his wife. He was often left alone in the evenings, and he did not like it. In consequence, he would habitually telephone an equerry and demand his presence. Group Captain Townsend was not the only Royal equerry at this period whose marriage ended in divorce. Single people are better equipped than the married to be Royal servants.

There is of course a distinction between being a Royal servant and being a Royal friend, but it is not always one which the Windsors know how to observe. Princess Margaret's friends are devoted to her, but one seldom meets any of them, after they have had the Princess to stay, without hearing a tale of woe – how she has kept the company up until four in the morning (it is supposedly not allowed to withdraw from a room until a Royal personage has done so); or insisted on winning at parlour games, even those such as Trivial Pursuit which require a degree of knowledge which she simply did not possess; how she has expected her hostess to act as a lady-in-waiting, drawing back the curtains in the morning, and so forth.

Prince Charles is no less lordly in his own way, and his brother Prince Andrew, a rather sadly friendless figure, thought nothing in his bachelor days of commanding the presence of young people whom he barely knew at Buckingham Palace to make up parties. This is the sort of behaviour which all four children of the Queen grew up as believing to be normal. Their parents might have been 'severe' with them, but no one in the family questioned their inherent superiority to the rest of mankind, an idea which was inextricably tied up with reverence for the Crown itself. 'From his childhood onwards,' said Keir Hardie about the birth of the future Edward VIII in 1894, 'this boy will be surrounded by sycophants and flatterers by the score.' Nothing much has changed since 1894 – except the world, a fact which the House of Windsor has been slow to notice. A friend of mine had grown-up children who objected to lining up and bowing, morning and evening, when they had a member of the Royal Family to stay in their house. They were wrong to object, said this loyal hostess: if you have a Royal Family you have to retain the idea that the Crown is to be reverenced, and you have to try to befriend the person trapped inside the royal carapace; 'because', said this kind lady, 'they need friends'.

Like Richard II in Shakespeare's play, the Windsors live with bread, feel want, taste grief and need friends. This does not mean that it is particularly easy to be their friend, and if ordinary friendship is seen to be impossible one begins to see why marriage in these circumstances is next to impossible. Those on the outer reaches of the Royal Family – such as the Kents, both the Duke of Kent and his brother Prince Michael, or the Duke of Gloucester – have managed to combine a life of public service with a relatively 'normal' way of life. Their spouses have obviously had strains which are not placed on the shoulders of wholly non-Royal personages,* but by and large they are able to lead private lives. Their marriages and their careers or their functions in life have been somehow distinct. But for those who have married the Queen's children or her sister, this has not been the case. In taking on their marriage partner they have also taken on that partner's career. Marriage has almost been a 'job' for them – a job from which there has been no vacation.

The role-model for this 'job' has been the Duke of Edinburgh. All his biographers, and all the perceptive journalists who have ever studied Prince Philip, have noticed that he had a very hard time as a young man adjusting to his marital status, particularly after his wife

---

*The strains include persistent and open malice from the 'hard core' Royals such as the Queen Mother, who never misses an opportunity to denigrate Princess Michael, the Duchess of Kent, et al.

became the Queen of England. Michael Parker, Prince Philip's former Secretary, has said, 'He told me the first day he offered me my job that *his* job, first, second and last, was never to let her down.' He has fairly heroically fulfilled this function – and one says that knowing full well that he has always been as discreet and as publicly loyal as any human being could have been. No one could expect in their youth that their actions might one day be subject to the searchlight of Kitty Kelley's investigative glare; and no human life would survive such scrutiny. Having your life written by Kitty Kelley is like appearing before the judgement seat of an unmerciful Deity; most of us are able to live in this world without such exposure, knowing that it would only be in the world to come, if at all, that 'the secrets of all hearts shall be revealed'. Nevertheless, the burdens of being a Royal spouse have been visible in Prince Philip's manner and demeanour ever since his father-in-law the King died prematurely of lung cancer. Someone who was present in Kenya when the news of the King's death came remarked, 'I remember seeing her moments after she became Queen – moments, not hours – and she seemed almost to reach out for it. There were no tears. She was just there, back braced, her colour a little heightened. Just waiting for her destiny. It was quite different for Philip. He sat slumped behind a copy of *The Times*. He didn't want it at all. It was going to change his whole life: take away the emotional stability he'd finally found.' Another person who watched the Royal couple at this time said, 'I'll never forget it. He looked as if half the world had fallen on him.'*

The first thing to happen to Philip was that he lost his naval career. He was perhaps not the most brilliant officer who had ever served in the Royal Navy, but he

*Quoted by Fiametta Rocco, *Independent on Sunday* December 13, 1992.

was perfectly adequate and a good deal better liked than
his popinjay uncle, Lord Mountbatten, had been when he
was in the Senior Service. Speaking forty years later to a
journalist, Prince Philip said, '"It wasn't my ambition to be
president of the Mint Advisory Committee. I didn't want
to be president of the World Wildlife Fund. I was asked to
do it" – he says, staring out of the Palace windows, his face
set. "I'd have much rather stayed in the Navy, frankly."'*

It was shortly after the Coronation that Philip, who
felt his very identity was being eroded by the experience
of being the faithful Royal spouse, attempted to persuade
the Queen to take his surname. There was some pathos in
this, since it was only a surname which he had adopted
on his marriage. His father's name – if it makes sense to
speak of royalties possessing surnames – was Schleswig-
Holstein-Sonderburg-Glucksburg. When he married, Philip
chose to take the name Mountbatten, the name adopted by
his grandfather Prince Louis of Battenberg in 1917 when the
Royal House of Saxe-Coburg became the House of Windsor.

To the idea of calling her children 'Mountbatten', the
Queen was most adamantly opposed. It had been a feature of Lord Mountbatten's insane ambition and desire to
stamp his ego on everything he touched that, as well as
persuading the gullible young Philip to adopt his name, he
should impose it upon the entire future dynasty of the Royal House. The compromise was suggested that the Queen's
children should bear the surname 'Mountbatten-Windsor'.
Churchill, the Prime Minister, urged the Queen to stand
firm and to call them merely 'Windsor'. At this point Philip
exploded with wrath and walked out of the room shouting,
'I'm just a bloody amoeba! That's all!' A secretary who was
present at the time says, 'I've always taken it to mean that

*Ibid.

he was just there to deposit semen.'*

It was following this row that an estrangement came – years in which the Queen and Prince Philip were only notionally and publicly 'together'. Prince Philip usually travelled abroad on his own. All this was handled with the utmost discretion, and it is only right to say courage, by Prince Philip, and probably by the Queen herself. But it would be foolish to pretend that this heroic charade – the marriage of Queen Elizabeth II and Prince Philip – provided an ideal role model for their children to follow, and it would be equally foolish to believe that anyone other than Prince Philip would be able to stay the course.

The pressure on Royal spouses is made so much worse by the notion that they should be 'ideal'. And yet, considering the way in which George VI and his Queen came to the throne, it was not entirely unreasonable of them to stress this aspect of Monarchy as so important. No one chose George VI as King because he was cleverer than his brother, or more handsome or more dynamic. In dismissing Edward VIII the Establishment had made it abundantly clear that the King was totally powerless politically, and that the idea of him actually exercising any of his Royal prerogative was laughable. (George VI did indeed try to do so when Churchill became Prime Minister. He objected to Beaverbrook becoming a member of the Cabinet. Relations between George VI and Churchill had been strained since 1936, when Churchill was the most eloquent supporter of the King's Party and Beaverbrook its most energetic propagandist. When George VI made his objections, Churchill ignored them, and when the King summoned Churchill to the Palace to explain himself, this command too was ignored. Not for nothing did Churchill

*Rocco; *Independent on Sunday* December 13, 1992.

choose 'The Battle Hymn of the Republic' as one of his funeral hymns.) Given then the neutered position of the Monarchy after 1936, what else could it be except a religious and moral figurehead to the nation? And, since the notional reason for sending his brother into exile had been a dispute about the doctrine of marriage, the least George VI could bequeath to his heirs was the wholly new and disastrous concept that Royal marriages should be perfect.

In the course of 1992, it became clear how extremely unhappy the marriages of the Queen's children had been. Unhappiness is impossible to quantify. There is no reason to suppose that Charles and Diana, Anne and Mark, or Fergie and Andrew, were any more or less unhappy than their parents. For Elizabeth II, the concept of divorce has not, to date, been a possibility. Her father became King with the words of Archbishop Cosmo Gordon Lang ringing in his ears: 'From God he [Edward VIII] had received a high and sacred trust. Yet by his own will he has abdicated – he has surrendered the trust. With characteristic frankness he has told us his motive. It was a craving for private happiness. Strange and sad it must be that for such a motive, however strongly it pressed upon his heart, he should have disappointed hopes so high and abandoned a trust so great.'

This broadcast – one is tempted to write broadside – by Archbishop Lang was given to speed the departing Edward VIII on his way in 1936, and it was universally condemned at the time as the unjust sport of 'kicking a man when he is down'. ('What is the point in kicking a man,' Lang is alleged to have replied, '*unless* he is down?') It was strange in 1992 to find that some of the stuffier English papers revived the sermon and preached it to the 'younger Royals' – in particular to the Princess of Wales. This was what appeared to give the publication of Andrew Morton's book its significance in the six months or so after its publication. It was one thing for the

Royal couple to be unhappy, and for everyone to infer, from their appearances and non-appearances together in public, that they were unhappy. It was another altogether for their 'craving for private happiness' to threaten the very foundations of the Monarchy itself. For so long as the marital troubles of the Queen's children were merely matters of rumour – even though the whole country might be teeming with such rumours – there was no danger to the Crown. As soon as they openly decided to bring their marriages to an end, the situation radically changed. Since Charles's great-uncle had actually been sent on his way because of the Church's teachings on marriage, how could Charles ever hope to become King? Who could look to Charles as a model of domestic virtue as they had looked to King George VI, and to Elizabeth II in the first forty years of her reign?

If the House of Windsor is to owe its future survival to its record of marital happiness, then it is almost certainly doomed. Its more optimistic supporters have put forward the enterprising notion that this family should not be ideal, it should be representative. This has even led to enthusiastic speculation among the gay lobby about Prince Edward's reasons for choosing a career in the theatre and delaying the announcement of his own wedding.

Whatever the truth of Royal fairy stories, it is unlikely that homosexual propaganda will ever succeed to the point where homosexuality in a Royal man is considered positively desirable. This is probably a mistake. With a plethora of heirs from the minor royalties, and the built-in difficulties which any of the Windsors and their partners were bound to meet in marriage, it might have been better for all concerned if none of the Queen's children had been allowed to marry.

For in the end, the strain of being married to a royal personage was too much – for Anthony Armstrong-Jones; for Diana Spencer; for Mark Phillips, and for Sarah Ferguson. Whatever the individual reasons for the collapse of these marriages, the collective effect of these four failures has been devastating. No doubt Monarchy is one of those things which is best not examined in too strictly utilitarian a manner. If the attempt is made too rigidly to define its functions, these very functions begin to seem insubstantial. Monarchy is really one of those areas of life which justifies the saying that 'the heart has its reasons . . .'

This has not prevented defenders of the Monarchy advancing the view that the domestic virtue of the Royal Family was an essential part of the Crown's role in national life. Had the Bourbons or the Borgias or the Hapsburgs taken this line, many of the greatest Monarchs in European history would have been forced to resign their thrones. Frederick the Great, arguably the most distinguished Monarch of the eighteenth century, would hardly have passed the Bowes-Lyon 'respectability' test, and even Lady Di might have been forgiven for wondering whether he was heterosexual.

In the past it was one of the prerogatives of royal personages that they could behave more sinfully than their subjects. In twentieth-century Britain they are for some reason expected to be more virtuous. In his very Abdication speech, Edward VIII had contrasted himself with his good, monogamous brother, the Duke of York: 'He has one matchless blessing, enjoyed by so many of you, but not by me – a happy home with his wife and children.' The 'happy home' image was exploited for rather more than it was worth by King George VI's Queen, and it was something which their daughter, Elizabeth II, was prepared to go along with – though one suspects that among the things which made her 'happy' marriage and motherhood probably came rather low down on the list of preferences. (Grandmotherhood is evidently a different matter, but she never gave the impression of liking any of her children except Andrew more than she liked horses and dogs.)

At the time of the Silver Jubilee, the Queen made a speech at the Guildhall. 'I think everyone will concede that today, of all occasions, I should begin my speech with "My husband and I".' This was not a bad joke – her habitual use of the cliché in broadcasts and speeches had been lampooned for so long. Then, with one of those leaden pleasantries which are presumably believed by royal speech writers to 'lighten' the tone, she quoted the bishop who, when asked for his opinion of sin, replied, 'I am against it.' The Queen went on to say that if asked her opinion of family life, she would say, simply, 'I am for it.'

Clearly none of her immediate in-laws was able to echo her. Whatever else the British Monarchy will be in the coming decades, it will hardly be able to represent itself as an emblem of happy, unified, Christian family life. Of course, there was never any reason why it should. Some of the most impressive Monarchs in British history have either been unmarried, like Queen Elizabeth I, or figures who scarcely represent 'family values' at their best. (One thinks of Charles II or George IV.) The self-righteous way in which the House of Windsor advertised themselves as the ultimate Happy Family was their excuse not merely for exiling King Edward VIII, but also for refusing so much as to be on terms with his wife. The feud which the Queen Mother kept up with the Duchess of Windsor for over forty years was no doubt conducted with the highest of Christian motives. The monogamous principle could not have been more fiercely underlined than in Queen Elizabeth's insistence that her sister-in-law must be denied even the title of Her Royal Highness.

Not long ago, in defiance of the laws of trespass, I stood beside the Duchess's modest little grave at Frogmore, in the shadow of the enormous mausoleum built by Queen Victoria to the memory of her sainted husband Prince Albert. When I thought of the emaciated body which they had lowered into that grave with such maimed rites, I momentarily hoped that the dead can witness our doings here; for in the 'scandals' of Fergie, Di, Mark Phillips and Princess Margaret, Wallis surely would have read the visitation of Nemesis.

EIGHT

The House of Windsor and the Church

The King's Majesty hath the chief power in this
Realm of England, and other of his Dominions,
unto whom the chief Government of all Estates
in this Realm, whether they be Ecclesiastical or
Civil, in all causes doth appertain ... The Bishop
of Rome hath no jurisdiction in this realm of
England.

Articles of Religion, Book of Common Prayer

On one of the few occasions when I met Princess Margaret,
the Queen's sister, I was arrested by the seriousness with
which she took the Queen's religious role. 'She is God's
representative in this realm,' the Princess said to me,
in language which might have made very good sense if
spoken about an English Queen in 1588 or even, if you had
a sympathetic audience, in 1888, but which sounded odd
in 1988. Why should it have sounded odd? Not because
the Queen is anything but a good Christian woman. In a
nebulous, indefinable sense, one feels not merely that she
exercises a religious function, but that this could perhaps
be seen as the most important part of her role. But when we
come to examine the legal and practical implications of the
Queen's religious role, you realise that she is locked into a
number of very deep difficulties. These are not difficulties
of her making; perhaps they were always inherent in the
Erastian idea (the control of religion by the State), but they

have greatly increased because of the changes which have happened in England since she was a young woman. And this has less to do, strangely enough, with the secularisation of British society than with the growth of religions other than the Queen's.

If all the non-Anglicans in the United Kingdom were agnostics or atheists, the ceremonies of the Coronation and the orotund phrases of the Prayer Book concerning the Queen's Most Excellent Majesty would probably be lovingly preserved. But it is difficult to maintain a religious establishment in a country where most religious people do not share the religion of the Monarch. England today – with its abundance of devout Moslems, Roman Catholics, Hindus, Sikhs, Mormons – is not the England of which Elizabeth II was crowned Queen in 1953. The attempt to maintain a religious establishment in a country where more people than not have a religion different from that of the Queen does not work; and anyone who doubts that should read the history of nineteenth-century Ireland. But if the Establishment is broken, does that not mean that one of the most important functions of the Queen has been abandoned and that one of the most potent reasons for maintaining a Monarchy has been dissolved?

The Crown has a religious, as well as a political, significance in British history. It might be truer to say it has a religious function. It is not merely a nebulous 'spiritual' function, teaching us that all power is ultimately from above* (though monarchists might derive comfort from such thoughts). Part of the actual, and practical, role of the King or Queen is to be the Supreme Governor of the Church of England. All bishops of the Church of England and the deans of the Cathedrals are technically speaking appointed by the Crown. So, too, are the Regius Professors of Divinity at the older universities, and the Prebendaries and Canonries of the various 'Royal Peculiars'. It is, of course, the Prime Minister's task to find suitable candidates for vacant bishoprics – hence Lord Melbourne's famous 'Damn it, another bishop is dead', and Lord Salisbury's 'I believe they die to spite me'. Although in practice neither the Monarch nor the Prime Minister alone is responsible for selecting all these clergymen today (they are chosen by the Prime Minister's Patronage Secretary in consultation with various ecclesiastical advisers), every one of them, before accepting his office in the Church of God, has to take an oath of secular allegiance to the Crown. This quite inevitably means that only believers in, or tolerators of, the idea of Religious Establishment can serve the Church of England in this way. Those who believe in the principle of 'Render to Caesar the things that are Caesar's and unto God the things that are God's' are obliged either to stay out of the Established Church or to take their Erastian vows to the Monarch in bad faith.

For many historical reasons, the Church of England has grown unhappy with its position as the Established Religion, and most members of it would not wish the Establishment to continue. This has less to do with the role of the Monarch in ecclesiastical life and more to do with the possibility of the secular Parliament having control over ecclesiastical affairs. The Anglican folk-memory of 1928 is

*Vide the Book of Common Prayer: 'ALMIGHTY God, Whose kingdom is everlasting, and power infinite; Have mercy upon the whole Church; and so rule the heart of Thy chosen servant ELIZABETH our Queen and Governor, that she (knowing whose minister she is) may above all things seek Thy honour and glory: and that we, and all her subjects (duly considering whose authority she hath), may faithfully serve, honour and humbly obey her . . .'

141

bitter: that was the year in which the Church's attempt to revise its own liturgy was prevented by the alliance of Protestants and Anglo-Catholics in the Church with Members of Parliament; and a House of Commons substantially composed of Jews, Agnostics, Roman Catholics and other Nonconformists refused to make legal the Revised Prayer Book. Such a débâcle is unlikely to repeat itself – especially since the Church of England has its own General Synod in which it can debate and to a large extent decide its own destiny. But for any major change in its laws – for example, in its decision to ordain women to the priesthood – it is still beholden to the secular Parliament at Westminster. Women cannot become priests in England until the matter is ratified by Parliament and by the Monarch. Predictably, those opposed to women's ordination hoped to use the Royal Prerogative as a means of blocking the legislation, even after it passed the General Synod, and even if it were approved by Parliament. 'MY SISTER WOULD NEVER ALLOW WOMEN PRIESTS', said one hopeful headline, purporting (rather plausibly, I thought) to quote the words of Princess Margaret.

As it happens, Queen Elizabeth II is a very devout Christian and a believer in the Establishment of the National Church. The great majority of practising worshippers in the Church of England feel a personal affection for her, quite regardless of what they might believe concerning 'Establishment' or the question of 'whose authority she hath'. But the feelings of unease expressed by senior churchmen and ordinary churchgoers about the future cannot be ignored. What would happen if they were to have a Monarch who was not in good faith with the Church? For example, what would happen – which looks all too likely – if Prince Charles were to be divorced? The Church of England forbids the remarriage of divorced persons. This would surely put the Church and the Crown in an impossible position if a divorced King were to inherit his mother's throne.

This is a real conundrum, and it could certainly put paid to Prince Charles's chance of inheriting the throne, just as his great-uncle's wish to marry a divorced woman in 1936 cost him the throne. The situation in 1936, however, was very different from the situation today. Prince Charles's dilemma only serves to highlight the much more drastic division between the Monarch's defined role in law and the actual reality of the situation in Britain today. It is the widening gap between the Sovereign's idea of herself and the reality of things which poses the crisis here. How can the Queen continue to be the Supreme Governor of a Church which, in general, does not wish to continue the Establishment? And even if it did, how could such an Establishment be continued, with its bishops in the House of Lords, and its claims – for example in the language of the Coronation Service – that the Queen is the religious representative of her people, when so few of her subjects share her religious beliefs?

Fidei Defensor, Defender of the Faith, is one of the British Monarch's oldest titles. It was granted to Henry VIII by the Pope for writing a tract on the Seven Sacraments, and for denouncing Luther. The 'Faith' in this august title is the Catholic and Roman Faith. Thereafter, Henry VIII declared himself to be the Supreme Governor of the Church *in* England, and during the reign of Elizabeth I, his daughter, the Church *of* England was brought into being as part of the so-called Elizabethan Settlement.

After the Revolution of 1688, the ruling class were determined that there should be no repetition of the James II fiasco. Since James was a Catholic convert and his particular offences had taken a very Catholic form – in the matter of suppressing the Heads of Houses at Oxford and putting the Seven Bishops on trial – a new doctrine was invented: that the British Monarch might neither be, nor marry, a Catholic. This rule applies not merely to those in the likely running for the Crown, but to any of the Sovereign's heirs. Prince Michael of Kent (fourteenth in line to the throne) in our own day had to seek the Queen's permission before marrying his Catholic spouse; he also had to renounce any claim to the throne.

The days have long since passed when British Catholics felt a conflict of loyalty between their allegiance to the Pope and their allegiance to the Crown. Guy Fawkes, who attempted to blow up the King and Parliament with gunpowder and to place the Catholic Lady Arabella Stuart on the English throne, has been dead for nearly 400 years. The idea that Catholicism might pose a threat to the State was abandoned by the Houses of Parliament in 1829, when they passed the Catholic Emancipation Act, allowing Catholics to attend Universities and Inns of Court, to enter the professions, and to stand for Parliament. Only the Monarch and her family are still stuck in penal times over this question.

As a young man, Prince Charles used to take this extremely seriously, and there were a number of likely brides, of a variety of nationalities, who had to be rejected on the grounds that he would one day be the Supreme Governor of the Church of England. As Supreme Governor, he would be legally entitled to marry a Hindu, a Quaker, an Atheist, a Parsee. The one category of being whom he could never marry would be someone who remained loyal to that Faith of which he was supposed to be the Defender. This ruled out the daughter of the Duke of Wellington – Lady Jane Wellesley – who was dabbling with Catholicism at the time when the Prince was dabbling with her, as well as such Continental princesses and eligible brides as the Princesses of Liechtenstein.

The Queen's position as Supreme Governor of the Church of England is comparable to her position as Head of the Commonwealth. That is to say, an impartial observer could be forgiven for thinking that she was presiding over something which in most palpable terms had ceased to exist. The Church of England, almost by definition, is, or was, a National Church, one of the most distinctive features of Renaissance nationalism. We can now see, from a perspective of 400 years, that the evolution or creation of the Church of England was all of a piece with England's development as a highly independent, belligerent island nation. It is no accident that it evolved in the century in which English sea-power established supremacy even over the mighty maritime empire of Spain, and in which Shakespeare showed himself the Lord of Language.

Plenty of potentates have quarrelled with Rome, and Henry VIII's row with the Pope over his divorce from Katherine of Aragon, and even his despoiling of the monasteries, would not necessarily have led to the establishment of a National Church in a different age. The idea of the Church of England really got under way in the reigns of his children. Under his son Edward VI, there emerged two Prayer Books – vernacular liturgies: the first, of 1549, closely based on the old Roman Mass, and the second, of 1552, much more Protestant. Under Edward VI's sister Queen Elizabeth, the Settlement of the Church of England became more fixed, a liturgy closely based on that of 1552 was established as the Common Prayer of the Realm, and the Church was increasingly seen as an essential part of the self-confident independent nation-state which England had become. Crown and Church were inextricably linked. Not merely did the Queen appoint the bishops, but Queen and bishops between them shared a view of what the Church was, and what its place was in the life of the nation.

Those Christians who dread Erastianism would have a particular horror of the Elizabethan Settlement and the subsequent development of the Church of England. Viewed from another perspective, however, the Church of England could be seen as a sanctifying thread, woven through the entire texture of national life. The whole of England was divided into parishes. Every soul in that parish was the responsibility of the parish priest – even if as individuals they expressed beliefs which were quite different from those of the established faith. Morning and evening, the parson would ring the bell to read Morning and Evening Prayer, with, or on behalf of, his people. The Church of England ideal was an inclusive, not an exclusive, ideal. The doctrinally scrupulous attacked it, Calvinists because it retained too much of the old Catholic structures – for example, the threefold ministry of bishop, priest and deacon; Roman Catholics likewise attacked it for its doctrinal vagueness, its lack of apparently Catholic intention in its ordinal, its apparent lack of Eucharistic theology in the Thirty-Nine Articles.

Yet the Church of England took root and, though perhaps it never was quite what its early defenders, such as Richard Hooker, desired, it did remain deep into the nineteenth century a unique part of national life. Enthusiasts for it, such as Gladstone, seem like bigots to us today, with their unwillingness to grant emancipation – the franchise, a career at the Bar, or a University degree – to Nonconformists and Roman Catholics and Jews. Their ideal was in one sense intensely narrow-minded and in another extraordinarily wide: they believed that to be English, and to believe in God, naturally qualified you for membership of the national Church. Why go elsewhere, when you were already, under God, a member of this 'blessed company'; when you already, whether or not you recognised it as a fact, belonged to a parish; there was already a font to baptise your children, a register in which your marriage and death would be recorded, an altar from which you could be sacramentally fed, and a churchyard in which you could be buried? This ideal, in a way which was not logical but empirical and factual, had little by little been bound tightly to the concept of Monarchy.

When James VI of Scotland became James I of England in 1603, and summoned the Hampton Court Conference to debate the future of the national Church, it was put to him by a Protestant representative that they should abolish the episcopate. He made his famous exclamation: 'Thus, I take it – no bishop, no king!' The phrase was much on everyone's lips a generation later, when the extreme Protestants of the victorious Parliamentary side, led by Oliver Cromwell, insisted upon the execution of Charles I. Whatever his faults as a King and as a war leader, there can be no doubt of Charles's piety. He was the first English Monarch to be brought up from the cradle as a member of the Church of England, and he certainly saw his own death as a form of martyrdom. Among other things, he died for the Book of Common Prayer and for the bishops. When, after eleven years of republicanism, the English restored the Monarchy, it was automatically, and correctly, assumed that the Church of England would be also restored, together with its bishops, priests and deacons. Thereafter, the Monarchy and the Church were inextricably linked, and it has been a curious fact that on the two occasions since, when it was found necessary to get rid of the Sovereign, the instrument for doing so was religious: both James II and Edward VIII had to go because of their unwillingness to conform to the Church of England.

Many of those who watched the Queen's Coronation on television in 1953 would have been struck by the intensely religious nature of the occasion. After the great officers of State – the Archbishop of Canterbury, Garter King of Arms, the Lord Chancellor, the Lord Chamberlain and the Earl Marshal – had presented the Queen to her people, and the fanfare of trumpets had blasted out, the Queen took her Coronation Oath. She promised in that oath to govern her peoples in all their lands according to their respective laws and customs; to cause law and justice in mercy to be executed in all her judgements; and then, more controversially, she promised to 'maintain the laws of God and the true profession of the Gospel, to maintain in the United Kingdom the Protestant Reformed Religion established by law, to maintain and preserve inviolably the settlement of the Church of England and the doctrine, worship, discipline and government thereof'.

There then followed the Communion service, and what – to some eyes – must have seemed the highly un-Protestant ceremony of anointing, in which the Queen was consecrated wearing sacred vestments – the *colobium sindonis* (a white, sleeveless surplice), the *supertunica*, a close-fitting surcoat almost indistinguishable from a deacon's dalmatic. When she had been thus arrayed, the Queen had a sword placed in her right hand by the Archbishop and he spoke to her these words: 'With this sword do justice, stop the growth of iniquity, protect the holy Church of God, help and defend widows and orphans, restore the things that are gone to decay, maintain the things that are restored . . .'

It is a beguilingly conservative picture of the Monarch's religious and civil functions. It is a little more difficult, looking at Great Britain forty years after the Coronation, to see the reality to which these symbolic gestures were supposed to correspond. There are more practising Moslems in Great Britain than there are Methodists. Among the Christian denominations, by far the most flourishing is the Roman Catholic Church, which accounts for about half the church-going population of the country.

Among Anglicans (as members of the Church of England almost always seem to call themselves nowadays, as though they were merely, like other English Christians, members of a 'denomination') there are many who question the value or morality of Establishment. Since 1970 the Church of England has had its own Parliament, known as the General Synod. With this Parliament they have thrown out the Prayer Book which was the sign and focus of unity in the national Church. They replaced it with a new 'Alternative Service Book' (1980) but, in reality, there is no more 'Common Prayer' in the English Church. Some follow the Alternative Book; many make up their own rites or follow the missals of Rome. The Church of England is in a state of liturgical anarchy since it chose to manage its own affairs, and since its decision to ordain women to the priesthood (1992) it would appear to have lost its semblance of unity. Both the Archbishops of Canterbury and York have said that the Coronation Oath must be changed, and they have hinted that they are not really happy that the Church of England (if it may still be said to exist) should be the Established Religion. Princess Margaret and a few of her friends might choose to believe that the Queen derives her authority from God, and that the Church of England derives its deserved supremacy over all other religions directly from the Queen. But in reality it is hard to see how the Established Religion can retain any sort of plausibility when fewer than five per cent of the population claim to adhere to it.

When the Prime Minister rose to tell the House of Commons on December 9, 1992, that the Prince of Wales was to separate from his wife, he caused considerable astonishment by stating that this would not stop the Princess being crowned Queen at some future date. Gasps were heard in the Chamber. The astonishment was partly caused by the sheer unlikeliness of such a ceremony ever taking place – the new King arriving at the Abbey in one carriage, the new Queen in another, before departing, presumably, to their separate palaces to receive the adulation of separate crowds. But the idea of the Prince of Wales and his wife ascending the throne awakened memories of Edward VIII who, because of his honest desire to marry the woman he loved, a woman who had been married before, was prepared to abandon the throne. Of course, Mr Major had not said that if the Prince divorced his wife she could still be the Queen; but the idea of a 'legally separated' King and Queen came close to this unthinkable ideal.

Surely the marital status of the new King or Queen – whoever they turn out to be – is only a small part of what makes us gasp if we actually contemplate any future Coronation ceremony. Can the Head of State of a country which is eighty per cent irreligious, five per cent non-Christian religions and five per cent Roman Catholic persist in holding a sword in his or her hand and promising to maintain the 'Protestant Reformed Religion established by law'? In all probability, by the time of the next Coronation it will not be established by law. Quite possibly a large section of those who dislike the ordination of women to the priesthood will, on this ground alone, have separated themselves from the Established Church and either joined the Roman Church or formed a new sect of their own. In these circumstances in which 'things fall apart', it is hard to see how the monarchical 'centre' can hold.

Or is this another case, like the political sphere, where the Monarchy can survive without any function or status whatsoever? It is actually quite hard to see how this could be. Even if they are meaningless to the majority of those who hear them, the words of the Coronation Oath still have to be spoken, and in the multi-cultural, multi-ethnic, multi-denominational Britain in which the Sovereign now finds herself it is hard to see how they could be spoken, for the more sincerely they were spoken, the more offensive they would seem.

There is of course no need to have Coronation Services at all. The Queen became the Queen automatically on the death of her father, and when the appropriate proclamations and oaths had been made that day, on her return to London from Kenya, she did not have to wait fifteen months – from February 1952 when the King died, to June 1953 when she was crowned – to call herself Queen. Her ancestor William IV wanted to forgo a Coronation Service altogether; this was because he believed the ostentation of his brother's Coronation only ten years before had been shocking. In spite of his irregular habits, William IV was a devout man who died with the mysterious words 'The Church! The Church!' on his lips. One can have Kings without Coronations, and one can have Anglican Churches without the Establishment, as the Anglican Churches all over the world – in Wales, Ireland, the United States, Australia and Africa – have shown.

Nevertheless, when these facts come to be recognised on the Statute Book and the appropriate changes are made by the Westminster Parliament, there is no doubt that they will be seen as a further weakening of the House of Windsor. Bagehot believed that Queen Victoria exercised a religious role in society, and in her strange way she probably did. (Not that she was a very keen Anglican;

when Archbishop Benson told her that he did not like her receiving the Sacrament in the Scottish Church while she was north of the border in Balmoral, she reminded him that, while the Church of England was the Established Church in England, the Church of Scotland (Presbyterian) was the established Church there. The Archbishop had no authority in Scotland, and the Queen had. Henceforth she excommunicated herself from the Church of England and, though she continued to be its supreme Governor, she did not receive its sacraments.

Probably, Queen Elizabeth II, with her taste for unfussy ceremonial and her simple, Bible-based Christianity, is happier to worship at Crathie parish church, near Balmoral, than she would be in some of the more exalted Anglo-Catholic fanes in London, such as Holy Trinity, Sloane Street, favoured by her racier sister. If the Queen visited the Shrine of Our Lady of Walsingham, much favoured by the Duchess of Kent, she might respond as her grandfather George V did when he saw it – 'Is this *my* church?' Prince Philip, who has done his best to be a loyal Anglican since his marriage, and has befriended such figures as the Dean of Windsor, the Very Reverend Michael Mann, has now reverted to the Greek Orthodoxy which was his parents' religion.

It looks increasingly unrealistic to insist that the Royal Family should be the upholders of the Church of England. But it leaves them with a problem. For if they are not, as George V and George VI would have maintained, the firm upholders of monogamous, Church of England faith and life, what is their function? If the Monarch's connection with the Church does not matter, and if the Establishment of the Church can be discarded without shaking the fabric of things, why was it necessary to send Edward VIII into exile? The Queen Mother might have an answer to this, but few others would. If the Windsors are no longer fit to be icons of happily married life – because of their unhappy marital history – and if their religious beliefs are not even upheld within their own household – let alone shared by more than five per cent of the population of Great Britain – does it not follow that their function, if they have one at all, is diminished? No longer Defenders of the Faith, and no longer Ideals of Family Virtue, the Monarchs of the future – if such there be – will exercise a purely constitutional role.

NINE

Constitutional Monarchy

'What must the king do now? Must he submit?'
Shakespeare, *Richard II*

In his recent book on the Constitution, Ferdinand Mount*
noted a perceptible change in the way that the Royal Family
appeared to regard their public role. They have begun to
speak out about issues of the day in a way which would have
been regarded as 'undue' interference in the days, let us say,
when Edward VIII said that 'something must be done' about
the plight of the unemployed in South Wales in 1936. Mr
Mount lists the Princess Royal lamenting the shortage of
services for the under-fives and urging the Government
to match the level of facilities available on the Continent,
and Prince Philip deriding the environmental ignorance
of 'the cloistered precincts of the schools of monetary
economists'. And there has been a whole series of comments on public matters by the Prince of Wales: his protest
against inadequate Government spending on the care of the

The British Constitution Now (1992).

154

elderly, and his attacks on modern architects. Mount says, 'The really remarkable thing is that nobody – nobody at all, whether on the constitutionalist right or the socialist left – seems to have felt like uttering a peep of protest. The sort of royal opinion which only ten or twenty years ago would have had the media clucking about a constitutional crisis is now taken for granted as a natural element in public debate.'

Those words appeared in 1992, and they already seem very slightly out of date. Since Mr Mount's book was published, there has been the crisis of the GATT talks, in which the quarrel between the United States and the French farmers over the subject of rape-seed oil threatened the future economic stability of the world. As was explained in Chapter Three, at the most delicate moment of the negotiations the Prince of Wales, on a visit to France, declared himself wholeheartedly on the side of the French farmers.

Mr Mount offers two justifications for Royals speaking out on public matters, or at least an explanation for why the public might tolerate such outbursts. In the first place, he says, 'self-expression has become an article of faith. Virtually everyone now seems to be in a position to answer back.' In the second place, Royal persons are merely exercising in public the right they used to exercise in private, 'to be consulted, to encourage, to warn' – the old 'rights' attributed to Queen Victoria by Bagehot.

While this might conceivably apply to the Princess Royal wishing that there were better nursery facilities in English towns, it all begins to look rather different in a case such as the Prince of Wales's intervention in the GATT dispute. Here we have a case of the British Government, its Foreign Office and its Treasury, taking one view, and the Prince of Wales (son of the Head of State, and potential Head of State) taking another. Supposing he had made his intervention when he was actually King, which would have constituted the view of His Majesty's Government? Is this the taste of things to come – a Monarch who will not be content to be consulted, to encourage and to warn? Are we entering another phase of British history when, to use Bagehot's memorable phrase to describe George III, 'we have the case of a meddling maniac'? In constitutional terms, all this matters much more than whether the Prince of Wales has 'talked dirty' on the telephone with the wife of a brother officer. 'George III interfered unceasingly, but he did harm unceasingly' – Bagehot again.

No one questions that the Prince of Wales is perfectly within his rights to make comments about any matter which he chooses. Not only is he a free individual, but, as Duke of Cornwall, he is a member of the House of Lords, and he is every bit as entitled as any other peer of the realm to make pronouncements about the important issues of the day. Moreover, this is an area where, surprisingly enough, the Royal Family have neither declined nor fallen in public esteem.

British politicians are held by the public at large in a derision and contempt which it would be impossible to overestimate and difficult for a foreigner to comprehend. Bagehot wrote at a time when politicians enjoyed a measure of public esteem, and when some of them, such as Gladstone and Disraeli, were extremely popular. Parliament was vigorous, and franchise was still a recent privilege for the majority of the British male population; for the female population it was still an unrealised dream. It was small wonder, then, that he should have supposed that the glory of England was its Parliament and that 'when we look at history, we shall find that it is only during the period of the present reign that in England the duties of the constitutional sovereign have ever been well performed'. What he meant by this was that the politicians of the high Victorian era were giants who entirely overshadowed their Monarch; and that though Queen Victoria did make periodic attempts to interfere in political life, especially in the area of foreign affairs, she was generally much too lazy to follow in the footsteps of her grandfather, the 'meddling maniac'.

After more than a decade with a Prime Minister who belonged very decidedly to the Meddling Maniac school, the British people have had a surfeit of politicians. The present Prime Minister, Mr Major, is said by the opinion polls to be the least popular since such information was first collected, and the same would undoubtedly be true whoever occupied this office and whichever party were in power. In such a circumstance there is undoubtedly a vacuum in British political life, and in different circumstances this vacuum could obviously be filled by some members of the Royal Family.

This is not to indulge in royalist fantasy. Few would wish for an absolutist Monarchy in Britain. But there is a basis of ill will (against politicians) in Britain upon which the Royal Family could certainly have capitalised. At the beginning of this book it was suggested that the overwhelming presidential style of Margaret Thatcher left the British public winded, and the Monarchy somewhat overshadowed. But in the right climate this would have counted, eventually, to the benefit of the Royal Family. It may do so yet. But the *annus horribilis* was the one year in the family's history when they could have done without any breath of scandal.

This was a year in which scandals of one sort or another clung to the Government. Cabinet Ministers were exposed in the Press for the seedy lot they are: one of them inadvertently rented his basement to a prostitute, and no one except himself could see why it had been necessary for him to borrow over £20,000 from public funds for having her evicted. Another Minister of the Crown confessed to having a steamy affair with an actress on a mattress in Earls Court. The newspapers made much of the fact that toe-sucking had formed part of this strange liaison. If ever there were a year in which the Royal Family could have been well advised not to indulge in toe-sucking, it was this one. Unfortunately, the Duchess of York could not resist allowing her feet to be kissed by her financial adviser, thereby giving the tabloid Press the chance to make all these public figures – royalties and politicians – equally clownish, equally base in the eyes of the public. But when the toe-sucking has stopped or been forgotten, when Prince Charles's extremely embarrassing telephone calls to the wife of Silver Stick in Waiting have been consigned to oblivion, are the British still capable of taking the Monarchy seriously? Does the idea of a constitutional Monarchy still have a place in modern Britain – multi-cultural, multi-ethnic Britain, Britain the somewhat grudging member of the EC, Britain the not-so-popular satellite of the United States? What does the Queen do? Why do the English in particular, and the British in general, retain a monarchical system of government? How much is the Queen still a serious part of the political scene, and how far is she merely a decorative figure?

There are no easy answers to these questions. How you answer them depends on the angle from which you are looking. Rather than attempt a definition, it would probably be better to look at the Monarchy from several angles, just as one might study different elevations of a single building. One way of exploring the constitutional position of the British Monarchy is to answer the question: how might it be abolished? Not 'How could you get rid of one Monarch and replace them with another?', but 'How could you get rid of the Monarchy?' I do not posit this question in an emotive manner, and I do not suggest that it *should* be abolished. I am asking the question as a way of discovering what part is still played by the Crown in British national life. It will be found when one asks this question that Monarchy, and the concept of Monarchy, is interwoven with the fabric of British life at many levels, and one could not merely get rid of the Monarchy without changing many other things as well. The Monarchy is not just a golden bauble on the top of a stone pyramid; it is more like the golden thread running through an entire tapestry. Unpick it, and much more than the thread itself would be lost.

Or such would have been the case until fifty years ago. Another way of viewing the whole matter would be to suggest that Monarchy was an inherent and inextricable part of a structure of society and a *realpolitik* which has already changed; that as the British wrestle with, or discard, the old class structures of society and the parliamentary tradition of government, it is inevitable that the Monarchy itself will be threatened. Whichever way you regard it, the Crown is very much more than simply the person who happens to be wearing it, and its significance transcends the personalities of the Royal Family.

Viewed from the most extreme monarchist position, the idea of abolishing Monarchies is self-contradictory. No one possesses such authority, since the power of Kings comes from God. When Charles I was put on trial in Westminster Hall in January 1649, he protested against the very legality of the proceedings with the words, 'If it were my own particular case, I would have satisfied myself with the protestation I made the last time I was here against the legality of the Court, and that a King cannot be tried by any superior jurisdiction on earth. But it is not in my case alone, it is the freedom and the liberty of the people of England; and do you pretend what you will, I stand for their liberties. For if power without law may make laws, may alter the fundamental laws of the kingdom, I do not know what subject he is in England, that can be sure of his life or anything that he calls his own.' In the course of the trial, Bradshaw, the President of the Court, asserted that 'the King is but an officer in trust, and he ought to discharge that trust'. It was Charles's failure to discharge that trust to the Court's satisfaction which led to the King's condemnation and beheading.

The debate about the function of the Monarchy was to continue during the next thirty years until the Revolution of 1688–9 which sent Charles I's son James into exile. Cromwell in the Protectorate had never sufficiently answered the King's fundamental question – how is it possible outside a Monarchy to maintain an independent judiciary and legislative system and to protect individual citizens, by means of the law, against the encroachments of power? Charles maintained that the Crown and the judiciary between them were a safeguard, which a Republican government could never be. Cromwell might have seen himself as King in all but name, as 'an officer in trust', to use Bradshaw's definition of kingship. But the eleven-year Republican experiment in England from 1649 to 1660 was an illustration of how true Charles I's words had been at his trial. Ruling sometimes by overt military means – as during the spell of government by the Major-Generals – and sometimes by covert military power, Cromwell replaced monarchy with dictatorship. After the Restoration of Charles II in 1660, there were tensions between a monarchist perception of the Divine Right and a Parliamentary stressing of the civic duty of Kings. The Revolutionary settlement of 1689 was very largely a compromise between these two positions. It would seem illogical, but it has gradually evolved into a workable system. Those who look askance at the inequalities which are an essential part of any monarchical system must face the conundrum contained in Charles I's protest to his prosecutors. Power in the political sphere, like energy in the physical sphere, is not something which will vanish. If it is not harnessed in one way, it will be harnessed in another.

Monarchy is one such check on the unlimited power of Parliaments or of Cabinets, or of juntas or of autocrats. Since this check has been an inbuilt part of the system in Britain since 1689, there are only two ways in which the Monarchy could be abolished. The first – more or less unthinkable in the present political climate – is a revolution or *coup d'état* such as deposed Charles I in 1649 or Louis XVI in 1789. The only other way in which the British Monarchy could be abolished would be if it were to abolish itself, by ratifying a Parliamentary Bill which brought the Monarchy to an end. This would involve the Prime Minister coming to the dispatch box of the House of Commons and proposing the motion that Great Britain should be a republic. In the present climate, this would be so profoundly unpopular, both in the House and in the country at large, that it would be very unlikely to happen; but if such a proposal were to be passed through the House of Commons and be drafted as a Bill, it would then have to be sent to the Upper House for approval. In the very unlikely event of such a Bill being approved in the House of Lords and passing all the various Committee Stages in both Houses, it would then be sent to the Sovereign to be ratified. He or she would then discharge his or her last office of State by abolishing the Crown. Such an Alice-in-Wonderland fantasy would be extremely unlikely to come to pass in any foreseeable British Parliament.

But let us imagine that the Republic were established. By so doing, Parliament would also abolish the system of patronage, it would abolish the system of Royal prerogative whereby the Queen can exercise power outright, and it would abolish the Monarch's ability to ratify Bills. It would be unrealistic to suppose, merely because the Crown had been removed from Elizabeth Windsor's head, that the network which thrives upon and feeds the system of patronage would disappear overnight. We are not here talking just about who gets particular awards in the Birthday Honours list. Patronage as an idea runs through the whole of British public life, which is why thoroughgoing democrats and republicans like Mr Tony Benn wish to abolish it. Administrative tribunals, advisory bodies, the Civil Service, the judiciary, justices of the peace, the major ecclesiastical appointments, some of the more prestigious academic appointments, are all tied up with the system of patronage, and they all depend, at least notionally, upon the Crown. Such a system cannot be abolished overnight; it can merely be handled more or less corruptly.

Idealists would like to believe that, once the Crown and the class system and the 'old-boy network' were done away with, the system would become freer, more honest, more accountable. Such an optimistic view would not seem to be justified by a study either of human nature or of the systems of government which obtain throughout the world. The laborious manner in which new administrations come and go (not always without corruption) in the United States would have to provide the British with a role model. It is hard to see why they would be tempted to substitute their creakingly archaic, but workable, system for one which, however it were devised, would not necessarily be any more efficient or more just.

The existence of a Royal Prerogative dismays some democrats. For example, while Members of Parliament were debating the Maastricht Treaty, it was pointed out to them that it did not require the yea or nay of Parliament to ratify a treaty. It was only a courtesy that they were being consulted at all. Treaties with other nations are ratified not by Parliament, but by the Sovereign. There was an outcry at this, but there should not have been. It was a reminder of how responsibly and sensibly the Royal Prerogative has been exercised over the last fifty years, and what a useful check it has placed on potential power-maniacs in No. 10 Downing Street. When the Prerogative is in the hands of an hereditary Monarch, there can exist the principle that Parliament must be consulted on matters of national importance. This is partly a democratic principle, partly a looser thing, based on that notion of 'consensus' which has been at the basis of the Windsors' political education. Imagine what use Margaret Thatcher would have made of Presidential Prerogative had she been the head of a British Republic in the days of her fullest power and vigour!

Such a comparison might make us suppose that the Queen has no power. But the Sovereign is devoid of power only in the sense that the Queen herself is not a dictator. She is not devoid of power if you imagine this power being transferred from her hands to those of anyone else. Constitutional Monarchy provides, as the Spanish have found, an extremely effective non-democratic means of controlling the power of the State. It is as different as possible from dictatorship, since its power is used to check and to control rather than to tyrannise.

The Constitutional Sovereign occupies a position as Head of State which is comparable to that of a leaseholder of real estate. The leaseholder purchases the right to occupy a particular property for a fixed period but, when the lease is finished, the ownership of the property reverts to the freeholder. This analogy does not fit the case in every particular, but it is truer, as a picture of things, than to suppose that the British Sovereign exercises a purely independent authority. Had they been absolute Monarchs (as perhaps they would have liked to be), James II would not have been dispatched from his realm in 1688, and Edward VIII would not have been sent to France in 1936.

The principles of 1689, when William of Orange and his wife Mary (sister of James II) were offered the Crown by the Lords and Commons of England, held strong for 250 years. There was no need for a written 'lease' agreement between Sovereign and people, because everyone knew the rules. Britain was governed by an oligarchy, and this ruling class remained dominant from 1689 until the outbreak of the Second World War. This is not to say that during the nineteenth century there had not been a gradual extension of franchise. But, when you look at the composition of successive British Governments during this period, no one can be in any doubt where the real power in Great Britain actually resided. It resided with the oligarchy – or the upper class. The great landed and monied families ensured that the Establishment ran the country – beneath the aristocracy, the Civil Service and the professional classes, most of whom were educated at private schools, who spoke and dressed in a manner which differentiated them from the rest of the people. Into this scheme of things, the Constitutional Monarchy fitted very well, and it was when the Constitutional Monarchy came under threat that two other views of Monarchy resurrected themselves: the spirit of 1649 and the spirit of 1715.

In 1649, Charles I, having lost the Civil War against the Parliamentarians, walked to his death on a scaffold which had been set up outside the Banqueting Hall in Whitehall. For the next eleven years England was a Republic, for most of this period under the Protectorate of Oliver Cromwell. Republicanism of this out-and-out character –

known to its adherents as the Good Old Cause – knew some fine defenders: the poet John Milton was perhaps its most eloquent spokesman in the seventeenth century; Tom Paine in the eighteenth century. After the aristocratic *coup* of 1689, however, which neutered both the power of the people and the power of the Monarch, and kept power firmly in the hands of the oligarchy, there was little hope that republicanism would take root in England.

The case altered in the twentieth century with the arrival of universal suffrage, but strangely enough the British Labour movement, though it has always carried republicans in its midst, was never strongly republican in flavour in its purer socialist days. The former railwayman J. H. Thomas, the first Labour Colonial Secretary, became one of King George V's best friends. When one reads accounts of Ramsay Macdonald, it is striking how afraid the first Socialist Cabinet were of the corruption of snobbery; rightly, as it turned out. A Labour 'incorruptible' asked the Prime Minister why he could not go to Buckingham Palace, and Macdonald replied, 'Because its allurements are so great that I cannot trust you to go.'* He meant it. No doubt snobbery, which is no less prevalent on the left wing of the political spectrum than on the right, has saved the British people from more sinister alliances between the Sovereign and forces of the extremes. For snobbery is one of the small things in life which inspires even political ideologues to want the system to continue much as it is; and this desire has always been strong, even in the parties of reform – whether Whig, Liberal, or Labour.

The opposite of Constitutional Monarchy would be the extreme right-wing wish that British Monarchs should be absolute rulers in the Bourbon mould. '*L'état, c'est moi.*' The

*Kenneth Rose, *George V* (1983) p.331.

two major attempts in the eighteenth century to restore
the Stuart dynasty – the rebellions of 1715 and 1745 –
were the most romantic expressions of this view. In the
first three decades of the twentieth century, those on the
extreme right came to believe that an Absolute Monarchy
was the only system of government which protected the
people from the ravages of the Money Power (a euphem-
ism in most such writings for the Jews). The most eloquent
English (or half-English) exponent of such an opinion in the
1930s was perhaps Hilaire Belloc; Maurras in France took a
comparable view. They saw the new dictators, such as Dr
Salazar, General Franco and Signor Mussolini, as absolute
monarchs come again to wrest power from the plutocrats
and hold it, in sacred trust from on high, on behalf of
their people. It was perhaps harder to take quite such
a neo-mediaeval view of Herr Hitler, though there were
those, such as G. K. Chesterton's cousin, A. K. Chesterton,
who tried. There would seem to be some evidence, in spite
of his protestations of belief in the constitutional principles
of George V, that Edward VIII inclined to this view of the
Monarch's rule. Certainly Hitler and his immediate associ-
ates were given to understand by von Ribbentrop that, in
the event of a German victory in 1940, Edward VIII and
his Duchess would be installed as the Nazi puppet King
and Queen; we do not know whether they would have
accepted such a role had it been offered to them. No
doubt the Fascist sympathies of the King and his friends –
such as the Metcalfes, the Mosleys et al. – helped to alarm
the Establishment, and it was convenient when he fell in
love with a divorced woman for them to get rid of him on
non-political grounds. But the Jacobite or Absolutist idea
of Monarchy has never had many adherents in England
since 1649, and probably not in Scotland since the Battle
of Flodden in 1513. Like the Good Old Cause, the devotion

to the King Over The Water has been the luxury of a few eccentrics.

The principle of 1689 was what kept the Monarchy alive and made it plausible. Those who still believe in the Good Old Cause and wish to get rid of the Monarchy's power would point to the fact that the British Sovereign exercises more than a purely symbolic function. As we have seen, every Member of Parliament, every civil servant, every bishop, must make an oath of obedience to the Sovereign.

It is true that all legislation passed through the Houses of Parliament has to be signed and ratified by the Royal Assent. And the Monarch spends much of her time with 'boxes', signing documents. But (and this is the fact to which Mr Benn and the Good Old Causers perhaps give insufficient attention) she would be gravely mistaken if she thought that her 'assent' could be withheld from any item of legislation without a major rumpus, and she would almost certainly find if she chose to oppose some law or act that the Houses of Parliament made her think again. A deliberately orchestrated clash between the Crown and the Commons over a serious matter of public policy is now, in the reign of Elizabeth II, so unthinkable that it would never actually happen. To that extent she is a rubber stamp, just as the Queen's Speech is a semi-farcical ritual in which she announces from the throne a set of policies which have been written down by whichever politicians have just won the General Election.

The system, however, began to break down long ago with the dissolution of the old governing class, and it was really a series of accidents which disguised from the British people – and, one suspects, from the Sovereign herself – the fact that she is a leaseholder whose landlord no longer exists. The symbiosis of monarchy and aristocracy which insured that the system worked properly has now gone.

This has had the effect of neutering the Monarchy. It also means that since there is no one truly empowered to sack the Monarch, so there is no one usefully empowered to advise or counsel or support the Sovereign. One very obvious fact about the present Royal Family, when you compare them with, let us say, the children of George III, is how few people they really know. This was made worse by Prince Philip's desire to educate his sons at an eccentric German school in Scotland rather than sending them – if they were sent to school at all – to Eton. True, they have met people since, in the Navy and in hunting parties. But had Prince Charles been at Eton, he would have known half London. Eton would have provided him with ready-made links, just like the old aristocratic houses in London in which George III's sons, the wastrel Royal Dukes, 'knew' people. To this extent it has been of more importance, politically, for the Prince of Wales to make friends than for the Queen. It is to be hoped that more care is taken over his sons' education than was taken over his own. It is simply essential that they be sent to Eton, for it is only by 'knowing people' on a wide scale that the Sovereign's power can be exercised usefully in the future.

There are those who would say that the Maastricht Treaty represents a neutering of the power and function of the Crown. For example, it would be by no means clear, were anyone to attempt to put this treaty into effect, whether the Sovereign was still head of the Armed Forces or whether she retained the power to make or unmake laws. Such powers as these would seem to have been deferred to Brussels Eurocrats or passed to the European Parliaments. How much this would matter in practice will remain to be seen. There are so many other imponderables about Maastricht that this might be thought to be the least of the difficulties of those attempting to put it all into effect. Taking the Foreign Office line, the Queen went to the European Parliament and said that she was wholeheartedly in favour of the Maastricht Treaty. The frivolous reason for this might be supposed that she was bored by having to sign all those State papers, and was perfectly happy to pass the chore to a Eurocrat. The emotional reasons are probably much deeper and stronger. No British family has so many continental (and particularly so many German) connections, and she might well feel that this is a matter close to her personally. It is very much the sort of thing Prince Albert and Edward VII would have approved.

If Sovereignty itself technically passed to Europe, and the religious significance of Monarchy was changed or eradicated – what would be the function of the Crown in British life? By curtailing the Sovereign's power yet further by Maastricht, it is harder than ever to be a Jacobite. The men of 1649 (many of them opposed to Maastricht for different reasons) would nonetheless say that this is the moment for Britain to become a republic. If politics were ever decided according to logical principles, this would quite possibly take place. But there is of course nothing logical about these matters, and the Sovereign might well survive without having a reason to survive.

The new development has been the call from serious Westminster Parliamentarians for a reform of the Monarchy. Hitherto, as we have seen, republicans or radicals who dared to criticise the Royal Family were always relegated to the status of clowns by the Parliamentary Labour Party because it was known that to allow the party as a whole to be tarred with the republican brush would be electorally disastrous. In the recent Parliament, however, even though the Leader of the Labour Party has tried to restrain them there have been a considerable number of

Labour MPs supporting the calls by such as Mo Mowlem and Roy Hattersley (no Marxists they) for a 'reformed Monarchy'. These views have also been echoed in some of the more killjoy areas of the Liberal benches.

Perhaps the most senior politician to support the call for reform is Mr Hattersley, the former deputy leader of the Labour Party. In a long article in the *Observer*,* he opined that 'it is preposterous that, in the last decade of the twentieth century, Parliament should be regaled with assurances about the rights of succession'. It is hard to see why the late twentieth century should be a better or worse time than any other to discuss the rights of succession to the British Crown. But, according to Hattersley, 'the whole idea of inherited authority is innately unreasonable'. It is based on what Bagehot called 'mystic reverence' and 'religious allegiance'. Needless to say, Hattersley feels the need to repeat that 'neither of these emotions is appropriate to the last decades of the twentieth century'. His article concludes that, however much 'reform' the Queen introduces, 'a republic is one day inevitable'. The paradox is, of course, that even after its most disastrous year since the Abdication, the British Monarchy is infinitely more popular than the Labour Party. Given the democratic choice, whether to choose a President like Mr Hattersley or to continue with the present system, the British would vote in droves for the Queen. It is for this reason – the rather self-contradictory fact that the British Monarchy is democratically popular – that it remains politically important. Because most British people wish it to continue, it is essential that it continues to adapt itself to the political, social and religious realities of the day. If it needs to change and adapt, and to be quarrelled about and debated, that is precisely because it is alive, not because,

*December 13, 1992.

as Hattersley implies, it is moribund. Meanwhile, of course, Hattersley and his like will bring before Parliament all kinds of plans to 'streamline' or 'modernise' the Monarchy, and, since they are politicians, the subject uppermost in their minds will be money.

TEN

Royal Money

'What does she do with it?'
Graffito seen by Gladstone

When Norman Hartnell, the Queen's dressmaker, died, there was a flurry among all the grand couturiers in London. Was this, I asked one of them, because they were all so anxious to make dresses for the Queen Mother and the Queen? Not at all. They all dreaded the commission. When I asked why, I was told that the Queen Mother had seldom been known to pay a bill in her life. 'The Queen, of course,' said my informant, 'pays on the nail. But we have not had the heart to tell her that prices have risen somewhat since 1947.'

If the House of Windsor has aroused envy and rancour in the populace at large, one has to concede that it is partly because of their greed and their meanness. Any formal public analysis of the riches of the Queen or her family fails to take account of what they claim by way of expenses. In this regard, they could give a lesson to the most cynical of journalists or lawyers. Every time the

Queen or her husband travels abroad, a bill for travelling expenses is sent to the British Embassy of the country which she or he happens to be visiting. This bill will include the price of Prince Philip's suits and ties and shirts, the Queen's outfits and the clothes worn by all their equerries and ladies-in-waiting. No ambassador ever questions the bills, which are often enormous. They are sent back to the Foreign Office in London, and paid by the taxpayer. Since the Queen and the Duke of Edinburgh spend a substantial part of each year travelling, they could be said to live on 'expenses'. These vast sums never appear in any account of what the Royal Family costs the British taxpayer.

At a time when many British people have been feeling poor, the Royal Family has not hesitated to flaunt its great personal wealth. The most glaring, and ugly, example of this is the ranch-style dwelling, built for a sum in excess of £5 million on the edge of Windsor Great Park, for Prince Andrew to live in with his unfaithful wife. Since that marriage lasted less than five years, this hideous dwelling may be said to have cost the Queen a million pounds a year.

One could write a lengthy and tedious catalogue of the greed of the Windsors. The Queen Mother's gambling addictions, and the high sums she has wasted on injudicious wagers, would alone fill a book. The question remains, however, whether a discussion of Royal money should hinge upon the Windsors' moral failings or whether it should try to ask the more delicate question of what, and whose, the Royal money is. What principles, if any, govern the thinking of politicians and journalists about this matter? Is it simply envy of the Windsors' wealth and distaste for the way they spend it? If so – bring on the tumbrils! Or is it a confused sense of contract? A muddle about what Royal ownership – let us say of a palace or a castle – means?

Nearly all the quarrels which the English people have had with their Kings and Queens have been to do with money. In the past, a Monarch's revenue was raised through taxation. Charles I, for example, did not, like a modern rich man, have an 'investment portfolio' to help him indulge his taste for fine paintings. He bought all those Rubenses and Van Dycks and Titians out of taxpayers' money – because this, apart from rents on Royal lands, was the chief source of his income. The modern distinction between 'private wealth' and 'State wealth', between the personal property of Charles Stuart and the property of 'the Crown', would have been meaningless to the Royal Martyr. Parliament wished to keep to itself the right to grant the King money through tax revenue – one of the great causes of dispute between them when the King exercised his ancient privilege of raising Ship Money without reference to Parliament. In the days when English Kings aspired to absolute power, they were dependent on their people to supply that power to give them the money to raise armies and to build their palaces. Paradoxically, it is in the twentieth century, when the Royal House is almost devoid of political power, that the Kings and Queens have enjoyed enormous independent wealth. If the Queen's Civil List payment were stopped tomorrow, she could survive on a personal basis – but of course it would remain open to question whether the Monarchy could survive.

Many seemingly wise words are written nowadays about the Queen and her money. Lawyers and tax experts and politicians pontificate wisely about property which belongs to 'the State' and property which belongs to Her Majesty in a private capacity, but their words do not make much sense. The great difference between the House of Windsor and the House of Stuart is that the Windsors are indeed extremely rich in a private capacity. This notion of the 'private capacity' was developed during the reign of Queen Victoria, who managed to cream off a tidy fortune from her income from the Civil List and the Privy Purse. She learnt this trick from her Uncle Leopold, later King of the Belgians: he was briefly husband of Princess Charlotte, 'Prince Consort', a role for which the British Parliament voted him £1 million annually for life, and which he continued to draw long after the demise of his beloved Princess. Balmoral was built with what Victoria and Prince Albert regarded as 'our own money'. And, from the same source, Sandringham House in Norfolk, with a fine estate, became the personal property of her son, the Prince of Wales.

Nineteenth-century newspapers habitually carped at the money which the Royal Family spent on their houses. The extravagance of George IV is something for which posterity is grateful – since it gave us, among other glories, Brighton Pavilion, the remodelled Windsor Castle and the renovated Buckingham Palace. At the time, the Press and Parliament only minded about the money – £1 million spent on the refurbishment of Buckingham Palace alone! When Prince Albert, only twenty years after the death of George IV, tried to restructure the Palace and to make 'a new east front to the Palace, clear out and rearrange rooms in the south wing, make alterations in the north wing, new kitchen and offices with ballroom over, take down the Marble Arch, redecorate, paint and alter the drains', he asked for a mere £150,000 from the public purse.* The humorous periodical *Punch* depicted Prince Albert addressing an audience of the London poor. 'Such is our distress,' he pleads, 'that we should be truly grateful for the blessing of a comfortable two-pair back, with commonly decent sleeping-rooms for our children

---

*Bruce Graeme, *The Story of Buckingham Palace* (1928) p.250.

and domestics.' Class envy and money envy are not new in Britain.

Nevertheless, while the British people have always resented giving any money to their Sovereigns, the degree of rancour and envy which has crept into the discussion of Queen Elizabeth II's finances has become ugly to behold. For that reason I do not want this to be a long chapter, even though its subject – money – might turn out to be the one single factor which brings about the fall of the House of Windsor.

Throughout 1992, the calls for the Queen to pay income tax became increasingly strident, and it was in the summer of that year, while the Prime Minister was staying with her at Balmoral, that she confided in him her decision that she *should* pay tax. They agreed to delay an announcement of this until the scandals about the Royal marriages had died down, possibly until the Spring Budget of 1993. Then came the Windsor Fire, with the disclosure that none of the Royal palaces is insured, and that Governments undertake to pay for their refurbishment and upkeep. The idea that the bill for repairing the damage at Windsor might cost the taxpayer £60 million, at a time of profound recession and high unemployment, could not have been more unfortunate from the royalist point of view. In the event, to allay further speculation about the matter and to quieten the critics, the announcement was made in February 1993 that the Queen would pay tax.

The *Daily Mirror* on February 12 carried a full-length cartoon on the front page, depicting the Queen in a tiara and a row of pearls staring avariciously at a pocket calculator. The headline was H. M. THE TAX DODGER. It was the cruellest picture of the Queen ever to be printed outside the underworld of 'satirical' journalism. Rather than welcoming the fact that the Queen was to pay some tax, the paper took an abrasive line. 'The Queen's astonishing tax "dodge" was branded an insult to the ordinary punter last night' – by whom? By some 'sub' on the *Daily Mirror*, presumably. 'Top accountants' – two telephone calls to friends in accountants firms? – 'said nobody else could wriggle out of paying tax on so many perks. And MPs protested the whole deal stank of one law for the rich and another for the poor. Under the "save as you reign" arrangement, the Queen won't pay inheritance tax.' Presumably not, since when her heirs inherit she will be dead, but go on. 'Nor will she pay tax on her palaces, her art collection, jewels, and private use of the yacht *Britannia*, royal flights and royal trains . . .' And so on.

The radio in Britain that morning seemed obsessed by the royal train, and Parliamentarians, full of reforming zeal, who claimed that such 'luxuries' as a royal train or the royal yacht could no longer be supplied by the taxpayer and it was time to 'streamline the monarchy', get rid of the State coaches, reduce the staff at Buckingham Palace and Clarence House, or wear slightly cheaper crowns at a cut-price Coronation ceremony.

Rather than weary the reader with details and statistics, I should like to discuss the essential principles by which decisions could be reached concerning the wealth of the House of Windsor.

First, let us be clear that whether or not she is the richest woman in the world, as is sometimes claimed, or the fourteenth richest (as I saw claimed in a newspaper recently), the Queen is a very rich woman. Since Great Britain has an hereditary Monarchy, I fail to see how any distinction can be made between her public and her private wealth. The only category of person to whom she could be compared in Britain is the higher rank of aristocrat – figures like the Dukes of Devonshire and Buccleuch, who own vast estates, great houses, huge art collections. Ownership in these contexts becomes a notion different in kind from the ownership by a bourgeois of his house, car and portfolio of investments. In an egalitarian society, wealth on a ducal scale might provoke gasps of envy. Many of us would like to be as 'rich' as the Duke of Westminster – said to be the richest man in England – or the Duke of Devonshire. But there is a sense in which these immensely wealthy Dukes, as well as being affluent individuals, are almost in the nature of being institutions. It would be extremely difficult for them to cash in all their 'wealth', and even if they did so – if, for example, the Duke of Devonshire sold Chatsworth and Bolton Abbey and Eastbourne and the Burlington Arcade in London and all his other 'possessions', and went to live in Palm Beach with a bank account worth several billion dollars – these vast chunks of real estate would still need to be 'owned' and administered by some other person or body. If such a thing were to happen, 'the taxpayer' would be no better off. On the whole – there are exceptions – the Dukes have been good landlords, and experiments in the public 'ownership' of land or of great houses do not suggest that committees or government departments or private bodies such as the National Trust make better or more responsible custodians of paintings, houses, forests or coastlines than do individuals and families.

The Queen's 'wealth' is, like the wealth of Dukes, huge. If the Monarchy were abolished and she were allowed to keep, say, Sandringham, Balmoral and the private investments in her portfolio, she would be a very rich private individual. But, of course, she has no intention of abandoning the Monarchy, and it is fanciful to make these distinctions. Since she embodies in her own person the institution of the Monarchy, and since she is the Head of State, she is the custodian, for her lifetime, not merely of Balmoral and

Sandringham and two studs of racehorses and a roomful of jewels – but also of Windsor Castle, Buckingham Palace and all the other, now disused, Royal palaces, such as Hampton Court and the Tower of London. She also 'owns' the State coaches, the royal yacht, the royal train and the royal parks in London. In so far as she is the Head of State, there is a sort of absurdity about her having to pay tax to herself. It is often pointed out that earlier Monarchs paid income tax, but this was in the days when income tax was a penny or little more in the pound, and because they did so it does not mean that they were right to do so.

The reasons given for Queen Elizabeth II paying tax are purely cosmetic. Politicians wish to see her as an immensely rich woman who is not 'contributing' to an expensive Welfare State of Parliament's devising. Before her decision to pay tax on a regular basis, she was in fact making a substantial contribution to State revenues from her income from the Duchy of Lancaster, just as Prince Charles, before the new arrangements came into force, used to pay to the Inland Revenue a considerable portion of his income from the Duchy of Cornwall.

Any rich landowner of even remotely comparable substance could not survive in modern Britain, with its confiscatory levels of taxation and its punitive inheritance tax, without all sorts of clever arrangements, which the *Daily Mirror* would call tax dodges. Without such arrangements, however, there would be no 'stately homes' in private ownership, and all houses like Chatsworth, and most of the English countryside, would be in the hands of public bodies. If one wants to see what this would be like, one only has to visit those parts of Scotland formerly in private ownership and now handed over to the Forestry Commission. All the great estates in England would be a forest of

Christmas trees within a generation without some form of 'tax dodging' by their landlords.

Most landlords and rich men, however – that is, the very rich, but not those in the Duke of Devonshire league – will be paying less tax than the Queen for the simple reason that they do not pay tax at all. Levels of taxation in Britain are so high that the huge majority of the rich long ago put all their wealth 'offshore' and tied up their houses, furniture, paintings and properties in a variety of 'dodges' which keep them safe for their heirs. One can imagine how the *Daily Mirror* and Mr Hattersley would respond if the Queen behaved like a real 'tax dodger' – making her mother into a registered charity or placing the bulk of her loose cash in offshore securities. In the sudden demand for the Queen to pay tax, she is being victimised in a way which no other great landowner or art-collector would find tolerable. For example, any other great landowner who found himself faced with a huge tax bill would feel himself entitled to raise the revenue by charging entry to all his properties. Tourists at the moment have to pay to visit the Queen's Picture Gallery in London, the Tower of London and Windsor Castle and Hampton Court. It would be interesting to see the public reaction if the Queen charged motorists a toll every time they drove through Regent's Park or charged dog-owners for walking Fido in Kensington Gardens. Advocates of taxing the Queen would probably say that these Royal Parks (which were not always open to the public) are now 'public property'. But the same people would have no difficulty in describing a State coach or a royal train – only used for the purpose of serving or entertaining the public – as a 'tax perk'.

So it is necessary to 'clear the mind of cant', as Dr Johnson would say, before discussing the question of Royal money; and it is also necessary to clear the mind of distaste, either for the greed of individual members of the Royal House or for the vulgar envy of wealth in any form which is part of the British character.

The Queen's income derives from four main sources. The first – the most obvious 'drain on the taxpayer' – is the Civil List, which was last fixed in 1990. This grants Her Majesty £7.9 million a year for her official expenditure. Seventy per cent of this is devoted to the (usually quite modest) salaries of those who work directly for the Queen in her official capacity: those, in fact, whom any Head of State would have to employ, whether she were a Queen or an elected President: secretaries, clerical workers, civil servants who help with the State papers, organisers of public engagements, meetings and functions. There are also entertainment expenses which would probably be as great, if not greater, whoever were the Head of State – such things as garden parties. The Queen entertains over 40,000 people each year. Her stationery bill is £139,000 each year, and in 1990 she spent £123,000 on computers. One might consider this an absurd waste of money, but it needs to be seen in context. The computers on almost every British Rail platform announcing from a barely readable screen the times of train arrivals and departures cost £20,000 each – there must be thousands of them in Britain. Any large corporation or company would consider the Queen's expenditure on computers as modest, though one must observe that the Monarchy got on perfectly well without computers for hundreds of years.

If a surge of public opinion led to the collapse of the Monarchy and the election of Mr Roy Hattersley as President, it is doubtful whether he would be able to manage on as little as £7.9 million from the Civil List. Doubtless, he would try to cut down here and there, and have fewer footmen – perhaps even fewer computers. But then he would still need secretaries and paper and envelopes, and presumably, even in the austere rule of President Hattersley, there would be the occasional Presidential garden party or State banquet.

The second source of the Queen's income is the Grant in Aid, and this is the area which is most likely to be attacked by the reforming politicians. These are annual funds which are granted by Parliament for the upkeep of the Royal Palaces and those 'grace and favour' residences given to the Queen's family, favourites or servants of high or low degree: Buckingham Palace, St James's Palace, Clarence House, Marlborough House, the residential office and the general areas of Kensington Palace, Frogmore House and Hampton Court Mews and Paddocks. The Royal Palaces Agency looks after the unoccupied palaces. Three-quarters of the money for these buildings is spent on maintenance. It is again hard to see how the sum would be reduced in the event of President Hattersley taking control. If these buildings, nearly all of them of great historic interest, were to be maintained, it would still cost the same to maintain them whether there were a Queen or not.

The debatable area here is how much the Queen should be expected to make a contribution from her other areas of income towards the maintenance of her palaces. Had the question of her paying tax never arisen, this might have seemed perfectly reasonable. Why should not one part of the Queen's income – whether you call it 'private' or not – be used to finance her houses? But as soon as the Government has said that it regards some of her wealth as 'private', then there seems no reason why she should dip into this to pay for essentially 'public works', like the restoration of the State Banqueting Hall at Windsor: is anyone pretending that if she were a private individual she would have State Banquets? And if it is conceded that the restoration at Windsor is a public work, then it surely falls into the same category as the building of roads or the repair of any other public monument. We should not ask the Queen, merely because she is very rich, to pay for Nelson's Column if it fell down. No doubt, however, the Parliamentarians and the newspapers will want to have things both ways and claim that the Queen ought to pay for Windsor because she lives there. But this is a circular argument which could go on for ever. She lives there not because she is a plutocrat who got out her cheque-book one day and decided she would like to buy a luxurious castle within easy reach of Heathrow. Airport. She lives there because she is Queen. The reformers are in danger of persecuting Elizabeth Windsor as an individual because of their muddled ideas of the monarchical function.

The third source of the Queen's income comes from revenue designated by the Privy Purse. Nearly all of this comes from the Duchy of Lancaster; a much smaller part comes from estate revenue from Sandringham. In the year 1992 the net surplus was £3.6 million, most of it from rents. The Privy Purse pays for the estate workers at Sandringham and those who administer the Duchy of Lancaster, which owns 11,800 acres of Staffordshire, Cheshire and Shropshire; 10,700 acres in the Fylde and Forest of Bowland; 8,000 acres of Yorkshire near Scarborough, and 3,000 acres in Northamptonshire and Lincolnshire. These estates are administered in the same way as the estates owned by Oxford and Cambridge Colleges, or by the Duchy of Cornwall, or by the great landowners like the Duke of Westminster. There is no evidence that the Queen creams off crippling profits from the Duchy of Lancaster. If it is proposed by the reformers that the Duchy of Lancaster be administered by the Government, the saving to the taxpayer would be the equivalent of what was wasted in approximately two minutes on 'Black Wednesday', when the Treasury was vainly trying to defend the value of the pound sterling before its ignominious retreat from the ERM.

These, then, are the three chief areas of the Queen's income. And what the Hattersleys are slow to recognise is that almost none of this money would be saved if the Queen were to be replaced by an elected President. We should still need someone to clean the windows at Buckingham Palace, whether it was the Queen's face or President Hattersley's looking out of them. It must also be said that, compared with some of the other things on which the politicians are prepared to spend the taxpayers' money, the Monarchy is not ludicrously expensive.

The fourth area of the Queen's income is what is known as her personal wealth – such things as her investment portfolio and her private income. No other taxpayer is obliged to disclose their annual income, but this does not stop even the more respectable newspapers speculating about the Queen's private wealth and imagining how much or how little she will have to pay to the Inland Revenue. I have already intimated my own view, that it is difficult to distinguish between what is owned by the Queen as an individual and what is owned by her as Head of State. To have made the distinction implies, on her part, a lack of confidence that the House of Windsor will go on forever. It seems like the equivalent of a packed suitcase or a foreign bank account. As such, her ill-advised decision to pay tax has weakened the Monarchy.

The reformers who pine to make the British Monarchy more like the simple, bicycling monarchies of Northern Europe have been vociferous lately in expressing their wish that much of the ostentation and ceremony of the Monarchy be reduced. I began this chapter with some harsh words about the personal greed and ostentation of some members of the Royal Family – a fact which, in prosperous times, the British people have overlooked, but which in times of hardship will make them hated. But I should not like to end this discussion of Royal money on a carping or a cheese-paring note. Of all the most ridiculous suggestions which I have heard in the endless discussions of these matters on television and radio, the prize for the most absurd must go to the Member of Parliament who felt it would be 'appropriate' for the Queen to get rid of the State coach and to travel to the Palace of Westminster in a car. The one aspect of Royal life to which only the most dogged killjoys would object is its pageantry. The Queen owns a great number of coaches: let her ride in them. No photograph ever taken of her in private life suggests that she is the sort of person who would be remotely tempted to wear ostentatious jewels at home. She is not the Duchess of Windsor. Tweeds and twinsets and headscarves are her style at Sandringham and Balmoral. But when she is in London opening Parliament, please do not let us have her doing it on her bicycle. We want crown, robes and State coaches. When she entertains visiting Heads of State and gives them a banquet, as she owns tiaras by the score: let her wear them. Her cupboards are groaning with gold plates, bought by George IV. It costs us nothing for her to have them laid on her table. What possible service will have been performed to anyone by putting these things in a museum and never using them? Though the Royal Family, like all rich people, excite envy when they flaunt their wealth, they are also unlike any other wealthy people. When she wears the crown, the Queen reminds us that the crown itself is greater than the head that wears it. George V used to wear a crown each day while signing State papers, to remind himself of this fact. Very odd it must have looked, with his pepper-and-salt Norfolk jacket and his plus-fours.

This matter of the Royal money will not, of course, die down. Motivated by muddle and malice, the politicians and the journalists will go on and on carping, and the Queen, as she always does, will bow to their requests and demands. 'Anything to please': that was the phrase that Edward VIII kept repeating. Only, now she has made the first concession and chosen to pay tax, nothing will please. It will be a sad day when they persuade her to put all her jewels and all her coaches in a museum, for the Royal pageantry is very much the best part of the Royal act, and certainly the most popular. There are few finer spectacles in the world than the Queen in her uniform taking part in the ceremony of Trooping the Colour, or the Queen in her robes of State processing through the House of Lords at Westminster to open Parliament. Inappropriate, though, as Hattersley would want to remind us, for the last decade of the twentieth century. Highly inappropriate in John Major's 'classless society'.

ELEVEN

A Modest Proposal

> My friends, it is not good to be without a servant
> in this world; but to be without master, it appears,
> is a still fataler predicament for some.
>
> Thomas Carlyle, *Essays*

Let us rehearse very briefly the position of the British Monarchy today. We find an ancient, much-valued institution under violent assault from the Press for very largely frivolous reasons (some Punch-and-Judy marital quarrels, a 'dirty' telephone call). In a time of recession and economic hardship, the personal wealth of the Windsors has awoken a particularly nasty outbreak of money-envy, a disease endemic in Britain.

But we have also seen that there are serious causes for concern that the House of Windsor is no longer in a position to fulfil the traditional functions of constitutional kingship. We have taken those functions to fall under three general headings. The Monarch is the Defender of the Faith and the upholder of the Church of England. This position has been made very difficult for the present Queen, not because of anything which has happened to her or her family, but because the religious 'map' of Britain has changed radically since her accession. The clergy might quarrel about the exact numbers whom it is possible to describe as 'practising Anglicans', but it seems beyond doubt that only a tiny proportion of the Queen's subjects are practising members of her Church, compared with the high proportion who are religiously indifferent, and the significant number of Muslims, Hindus, Sikhs and Roman Catholics. Given this change in Britain since 1953, and given the changes in relations between the Christian Churches and the growth of the ecumenical movement, it is no longer deemed suitable by the Church of England itself and by its two primates, the Archbishops of Canterbury and York, to ask any new Sovereign to swear an oath at the Coronation to uphold the Protestant religion. The Church of England has itself changed, and the schism following the Synod's decision to authorise the ordination of women to the priesthood makes it all the harder to speak of Anglicanism as the official or the given, still less the Established, religion of England.

If all these difficulties would face Elizabeth II, a devout woman in good standing with her Church, what difficulties would be added were she to be succeeded by Prince Charles! His marital status would make it extremely hard for him to become the Supreme Governor of a Church which still forbids divorce. And it now looks certain that he and his wife will be divorced. It was the impossibility of Edward VIII marrying a divorced woman which forced him to renounce the throne. If the House of Windsor is true to its own rule of life, it is hard to see how Prince Charles could claim to be the Defender of the Faith. The difficulty caused by his marital status is this: if or when the Coronation Oath is changed (for the reasons which we have discussed), it would *look* as if the Church were fudging its principles in order to accommodate Prince Charles. Either way he cannot win, whether the Church and State alter their relations or remain the same. The Evangelical wing of the Church of England have said that they would not be able to support the Church if the Protestant Promise were removed from the Coronation Service; nor, say they, would they be able to accept an apparent adulterer as the Supreme Governor of the Church, though this stringent proviso, it must be said, would have eliminated all previous Defenders of the Faith from being crowned, with the possible exceptions of Charles I, George III, Queen Victoria and George VI.

It would seem, then, as though the House of Windsor has reached a crossroads over the religious question. Either it abandons its own religious 'Windsor rules', those rules which led to the destruction of Edward VIII and the Coronation of the virtuous George VI, or it vetoes Charles III.

The second great function of the British Royal Family has been to serve as figureheads of happy family life. Prince Albert laid particular stress on this, which was why the libertine behaviour of his eldest son Bertie caused him such heartbreak. George V and George VI were both in their slightly different ways puritans in the Prince Albert mould. Queen Elizabeth emphasised the differences between her own wholesome, aristocratic friends and the 'fast set' favoured by Edward VIII. The Little Princesses were the very types and embodiments of wholesomeness. And it was a similar image of family life which the present Queen was encouraged to display in her television film *Royal Family*. It could be argued here, as in the case of the specific question of religion, that the world had changed since 1953. In those days, when divorced persons were not allowed in the Royal Enclosure at Ascot, it would not have been thinkable that all the immediate Royal Family who had attempted marriage would have failed in it: Princess Margaret, divorced; Princess Anne divorced and remarried; Prince Andrew, soon to be divorced; Prince Charles, on the road to divorce and legally separated. Attitudes to sexual morality in Royal circles have now relaxed to the point where homosexuals may now bring their partners to Buckingham Palace garden parties. Considering the loyal service given to all the Royal Households by homosexuals, this is nothing more than justice.*

In these circumstances, as we have suggested, it might be said that with its high incidence of divorce and its smattering of homosexuality, the Royal Family are now a more representative figurehead to a nation where there are so many broken homes and where there is a high incidence of homosexuality. It is doubtful whether King George V and Queen Mary would have seen things in quite this way. Once again it would seem as if the House of Windsor were faced with a choice: either it abandons 'Windsor Rules' or it abandons Prince Charles – and, indeed, all the Queen's children. Many people would find it extremely distressing that the Royal Family had cynically relinquished its claim to represent 'family values' just so that it could hold tenaciously to the Crown.

The third function of Monarchy which we have examined in this book is its constitutional role in the narrowly political sense. Bagehot saw the Sovereign's role as 'to be consulted, to encourage, and occasionally to warn'. For

---

* For obvious reasons, the unmarried make happier Royal servants than the married since Kings, Queens and Princes tend to be so demanding. The story of the Queen Mother's telephone call to her butler's pantry, while she sat impatiently in her drawing-room, can bear repetition: 'I don't know about you old queens, but this Old Queen wants a drink.'

this system to work, it presupposes a willingness by the Prime Minister to acknowledge the Sovereign's traditional place in the scheme of things, and we suggested that it was in part Margaret Thatcher's abrasive attitude to the Queen which helped to precipitate the present difficulty.

But since Prince Charles is still the heir to the throne, we must ask whether his career to date inspires confidence. When asked how he had learned his role, Prince Charles once replied, 'As monkeys learn, by watching their mothers.' One can only conclude, a little sadly, that he has not watched his mother carefully enough. There is only one occasion – her disagreement with Mrs Thatcher over South Africa – in his mother's reign where she was seen openly to clash with her Prime Minister. In the case of Prince Charles and the GATT talks, it was he who shot his mouth off with potentially calamitous results, not merely for his country but for the world. Deprived of any real function, Prince Charles would appear to relish the headline-grabbing potential of adopting 'controversial' attitudes, and this could be of the greatest possible danger in the years ahead, particularly if, as we argued in Chapter Nine, the Monarchy is moving into a phase where it is more politically necessary, and where the situation in Britain (poised between Island Fortress Nationalists and Federalist Fanatics) is much more sensitive than it has been for decades. There never was a time when a potential Monarch more needed to imitate the examples of George V and Elizabeth II, for there could so easily come a time when they need to do slightly more than encouraging or warning the politicians. The Royal Prerogative is still potentially a real political power. Only a very experienced or a very wise Monarch will know how to prevent a Prime Minister from abusing this Prerogative to sidestep the wishes of an elected House of Commons or the interests of the British people.

We seem to have reached the position of saying that the British people and the House of Windsor have a choice. Either they choose to continue the monarchical system (with the necessary emendations to the religious part of the Coronation Oath), that system which has been held in trust by the House of Saxe-Coburg since 1837 (renamed Windsor in 1917); or they abandon the 'Windsor Rules' and have a new sort of Monarchy with Prince Charles at the head of it – with no Established Church, no sense of the Monarch as a family emblem, and his only function being political – with the possibility of a future punctuated by policy clashes between the Head of State and the Prime Minister, as happens from time to time in France. It would not be long, if we had such a system, before people began to ask why – since the Monarch's only function seemed to be political – we could not elect a President.

This is a dilemma indeed. It is not an invented problem. It will not go away so long as Prince Charles remains the heir to the throne. But Constitutional Monarchy is by its nature conservative. Its strength is that it provides continuity with the past which could never be offered by recurrent Presidential elections. Not only is it useful to have a Head of State (as the British do now) with a long political memory stretching back to the time of Churchill; it is appreciated on the deepest level by the people that, in an ever-changing world, the Monarchy should remain the same because the persons of the Royal Family also remain the same.

The British Monarchy is seen at its best on ceremonial occasions. During the *annus horribilis* of 1992 we might have forgotten this, because it probably seemed as though we never saw a Royal personage in a newspaper unless they were committing adultery or conducting a lawsuit or making some crassly foolish speech about the way the rest of us should live. But, even during that year, Trooping the Colour took place on Horseguards Parade in June: the Queen in her uniform reviewed her brightly arrayed troops, providing something infinitely more than a pageant, an important national ritual which linked together tribal feelings of belonging, ideas of the past and feelings of intense loyalty. At the Cenotaph in November, the Sovereign is the first person to lay a wreath in memory of those who died in the World Wars. Once again it is of immense symbolic significance that it should be a Monarch who does this, rather than some politician. Of course, politicans are there, and the heavens would not fall if politicians alone attended the ceremony; but most of the old airmen and soldiers and sailors would say that they wanted to see the Queen there. The Monarch is able at such moments to stand for a whole nation, not because of her character or her 'qualifications' but purely by virtue of the fact that she is the Queen.

It is on such occasions of national mourning or rejoicing that one sees the point of having a Monarch who is a 'figurehead'. Nations have these feelings, whether or not sophisticated people might smile at or mock them. They are most easily focused on individuals. One wonders whether the history of Germany might not have been different in the 1930s had the Kaiser not been forced to live in exile. When, today, one objects to the garish or immoral behaviour of the younger members of the Royal Family, it is less on puritanical than on constitutional grounds. The best constitutional Monarch would be one, like Queen Elizabeth II, who was, in all public senses of the word, slightly colourless, and who had the humility and the dullness of nature not to draw attention to herself. It would be a figure whom the country at large might plausibly reverence as Sovereign, but not a 'personality' whom the people should be asked to admire as if she were a politician or a film actress; it should perhaps be someone like the present Queen, about whom not very much (in the last resort) is really known.

The misbehaviour and misfortunes of the young Windsors provide amusing copy for newspapers, but the best sort of royalties would be the sort of people whose lives were so blameless and so discreet and so dull that we never really wanted to read about them unless we were addicted to reading the Court Circular. If Prince Charles were to become King in the near future, it is not difficult to imagine the response of the Press. Hardly a month would pass without a story of one of his alleged mistresses; and this would provoke his wife, or ex-wife as she would be by then, into newer frenzies of self-advertisement. A fine way for the young Princes, and in particular the Heir Presumptive, Prince William, to grow up and be prepared for the office of Monarchy!

It might well finish off the British Monarchy if Prince Charles were to attempt such a 'bumpy ride'. Institutions can only survive if they can be demonstrated to have a function within the real world and Prince Charles's position and personal history sadly disqualify him from embodying those values and exercising those duties which were so faithfully fulfilled by the three great Windsor Monarchs – George V, George VI and Elizabeth II.

The solution proposed in the Press by the Princess's party, as it came to be known, was that Prince Charles should stand down in favour of his son, and that his wife should, in the event of the Queen dying before Prince William reached his majority, be Princess Regent. The Princess's party was not, as some people supposed, governed by a childishly besotted love of Lady Di; it was attempting to find a serious answer to the crisis in the House of Windsor. It grieves me to write these words, as a stalwart of the Princess's party, but Lady Di no longer looks like a plausible Princess Regent. Her disloyalty to the Royal Family, her hysterical nature, her indiscretion with journalists and her ludicrous friends really make the prospect of her being a suitable guardian of the constitutional Monarchy seem wholly implausible.

The House of Windsor, one must recognise this, has reached the end of the road. One should not be surprised. If one counts their tenure of the throne as dating from 1837, then they have been serving their country for close on 160 years. The Tudors, the last great dynasty of comparable longevity, lasted 126 years, and the Hanoverians 123 years. There is every reason for thinking that, while the Monarchy should continue, it could benefit from a new dynasty, or at least from a different one. The disadvantage of this idea, of course, is that one of the great strengths of an hereditary Monarchy should be the continuity which it provides with the nation's past. Merely to shove in, arbitrarily, some other family and put a crown on the head of its most eligible male would be to institute a presidency or a dictatorship in kingly regalia. This would be Bonapartism not Monarchism.

What Britain needs is an ancient Monarchy with strong family links to the House of Windsor; and what the Monarchy needs is a release from the impossible prospect of King Charles III, or Queen Anne Laurence, or King Andrew, separated from Queen Fergie and her daughters. If we were right to suppose that the ideal constitutional Monarch would be of a quiet disposition, uninterested in the allure of 'fame' and bored by the prospect of 'stardom', then the Princess Regent, however much we may love her, seems equally unsuitable for the role.

As it happens, a solution is to hand.

If we consult the history books, we discover that the claims of both the Stuarts and the Hanoverians to the

English throne from the late-seventeenth century onwards were in the highest degree questionable. On April 9, 1649, barely two months after the execution of Charles I, a son was born in Rotterdam to Charles II and one Lucy Walter. Both the parents were under twenty years of age – after a rackety career, Lucy was to die in Paris, in 1658, of 'a disease incidental to her manner of living'; the aspersion is that of James II, Charles II's brother. James, who inherited the Crown from his brother, had every reason to cast as many slurs as possible upon Lucy Walter and her son, the Duke of Monmouth. Certainly, as early as 1662 Pepys had heard the rumour that Charles II intended to make the Duke of Monmouth his legitimate heir. The King doted upon his son, heaped honours upon him and allowed him to bear the Royal Arms. It was said that the King and Lucy Walter had been married, which would have meant that the Duke of Monmouth was in fact the legitimate heir to the English Crown. The rebellion of Monmouth and his Protestant supporters against the Catholic James II was not successful. The matter was settled after Charles's death by the Battle of Sedgemoor, the last battle ever fought on English soil, on July 5, 1685. Having lost this battle, Monmouth was brought to London to be beheaded. The axeman bungled his work. According to one eyewitness, he struck the Duke five blows and 'severed not his head from his body till he cut it off with his knife'. According to the entry for the Duke of Monmouth in the *Dictionary of National Biography*, 'not a tittle of real evidence exists in favour of the supposed marriage between Charles II and Lucy Walter', but Monmouth always maintained that he possessed the proof of his legitimacy. The marriage certificate of Lucy and Charles II was said to be contained in a black box entrusted by Bishop Cosin of Durham to his son-in-law Sir Gilbert Gerard. It was claimed that Lucy Walter had been a penitent of

Cosin's when he was living in Paris before the Restoration.

Years later, when Queen Victoria was on the throne, it is said that the Duke of Buccleuch, the heir and descendant of Monmouth, produced this marriage certificate and showed it to his Sovereign. Then, as a gesture of his loyalty to the House of Saxe-Coburg, he tossed it into his grate and burnt it in front of the Queen.

It might have been more prudent had he kept it, for this would have enabled the whole question of Monmouth's legitimacy, and his claim to the English throne, to be rehearsed all over again. In an article in the *Spectator*,* the magazine's deputy editor Simon Courtauld put forward the case for maintaining the Monarchy and disposing of the services of the House of Windsor. Having recognised the unsuitability of Jacobite claimants to the English throne, such as Albrecht, Duke of Bavaria,† who at eighty-seven might be thought a little old to make a lively contender, Mr Courtauld resurrects the Monmouth claim and suggests that on the Queen's death the Crown should pass to the Dukes of Buccleuch.

'The Buccleuchs', he writes, 'would now be admirably suited to succeed to the British throne. The present Duke ... is a larger landowner than the Queen. If the Windsors wanted to hang on to their rather dreary piles at Sandringham and Balmoral, the Buccleuchs are happily seated at Dalkeith Palace near Edinburgh, Bowhill in Selkirk, Drumlanrig Castle in Dumfriess & Galloway and Boughton in Northamptonshire – where they have one of the finest art collections in Europe. When the time comes, they should be ready to step into the breach.'

*January 2, 1993.
†The Duke is descended, through the House of Savoy, from Henrietta, Duchess of Orleans, sister of Charles II and daughter of Charles I.

The Courtauld scheme is very nearly, but not quite, the right answer. The drawback is its oddness. The public, unaware of the story of the Duke of Monmouth and probably largely unaware of the Duke of Buccleuch, would feel that someone was trying to pull a fast one. There would be a 'Hands off our Charlie' movement if you tried to persuade people that the King's residence was Bowhill, not Buckingham Palace. Courtauld's sympathies are too aristocratic.

But all good Monarchists owe him a debt of gratitude for reviving the Monmouth claim, since it points us in the right direction. The reader will remember that what we are looking for is someone to carry on the Monarchy in the honest, dull tradition of George V, George VI and Queen Elizabeth II. We are looking for someone who is not a vulgarian whose wife likes posing for the television cameras, but is a decent, quiet sort, preferably someone in whom it would be impossible to take very much interest, even if we tried. We are looking for a man or woman who would provide some continuity with the Royal past, but who would also draw a firm *finis* upon the claims of the poor Queen's unsuitable children to inherit the throne. Ideally, therefore, we should be looking for someone who is descended both from King George V and – to satisfy the Monmouth legitimists – from the Dukes of Buccleuch.

Such a man there is: Richard, Duke of Gloucester. It is true that some of the Duke's known opinions – such as that Richard III did not kill the Princes in the Tower, or that cigarettes are bad for your health – suggest that he is not a person of complete common sense. But we are looking for a constitutional Monarch, not a paragon. His father, Henry, Duke of Gloucester, was the fourth child of George V and Queen Mary. Prince Henry was an unsophisticated man with an endearing weakness for the bottle. For much of his life he was a professional soldier. His heir, the present

Duke's brother William, was sadly killed in an air crash in 1972. Prince Richard, who had never expected to inherit the Dukedom, trained as an architect, but since he became Duke has largely devoted himself to running the family estates at Barnwell in Northamptonshire. He is married to an attractive Dane, Birgitte van Deurs, and they have three fine children. His mother, Princess Alice, believes them to be pitiably poor – 'they cannot afford a chauffeur, a lady's maid or a valet'.* It is the same Princess Alice, of course, who provides the Duke with his Monmouth connection, since she was the third daughter of the seventh Duke of Buccleuch.

For the Queen to declare that the Duke of Gloucester and all his legitimate descendants were henceforth to be the heirs to the British Crown would certainly be better than doing nothing, if she wishes to guarantee the future of the Monarchy. That she would ever make such a declaration is, unfortunately, unlikely; and that the mild-mannered bespectacled Duke would himself, like his ancestor Monmouth, take up arms to assert his right to the throne is even less likely. Anyone who hopes that the Monarchy has a future must await the Queen's demise with some trepidation and hope that it is a long time off. What this book has tried to show is that it is not so much a question of whether Prince Charles would make a passable King or a good King, but whether – as that role is at present defined – he could possibly be King at all. And once an heir to the throne is seen to be ineligible, it becomes inevitable that there will be talk of a republic.

In Britain in the last forty years many good, old things have passed away, less because there was widespread enthusiasm for the new than that there was not sufficiently

*Kenneth Rose, *Kings, Queens and Courtiers* (1985) p. 136.

articulate expression by the mass of people in defence of
the old. Prince Charles, about whom some harsh things
have been said in this book, surely deserves praise for
his attempt, since a famous speech in 1984, to speak up
for what the huge majority of people have felt about the
modernistic style in architecture. Only a handful of architects and aesthetic fanatics ever liked the modern style,
and most city-dwellers in Europe hate what this style has
done to their cities. And yet nearly all the towns in England
were spoilt during the 1960s, because everyone took the
old style for granted and so few people voiced any protest
at the wreckage. A comparable thing happened in the
Church. Few people except cranks could have preferred
the hideous modern liturgies to the ancient time-honoured
words of the old. Certainly in the English Church, the *Book
of Common Prayer* and the Authorised Version of the Bible
were cast aside almost without discussion. Wherever one
went in England, anguish was expressed about this, but the
anguish got nobody anywhere. It seemed slightly 'cranky'
to join any society or action group to save the old Prayer
Book.

The English have a fear of seeming odd by sticking
their necks out and complaining at change. They will
grumble quietly among themselves when changes have
taken place and agree that they were changes for the worse,
but it is seldom that they will take action before a change
has become irrevocable and say that it is not a change
which they want. It is this indifferentism in the English
which is the republicans' strongest weapon. A republican
newspaper proprietor, Rupert Murdoch, has made it quite
clear that he intends to continue to fill his newspapers,
especially the vulgar ones like the *Sun* and the *Sunday
Times*, with as much filth as he can muster about the House
of Windsor. Any sexual indiscretion they might commit will

find its way on to Murdoch's front pages. Nor will his editors miss any chance to attack the wealth and privilege and position of the Monarchy, so that matters will reach the point when the Parliamentarians can say that there is now a 'popular' groundswell against the Monarchy itself. When they attack the Queen, her defenders can say that these attacks are contemptible, since she is peerless and as nearly perfect as it is possible for a constitutional Monarch to be. It is a very different matter when they attack the Queen's children, or when those children themselves use the newspapers to attack one another. It looks perilously as if the Monarchy is going to be one of those things, like the architecture of the older English cities and the language of the old English Church, which is simply allowed to go because no one can think of a good word to save it.

When it has gone, there will be grumbling. More than the House of Windsor will fall if the Monarchy is allowed to be hounded out by bullies and brutes. It will be a symptom of the general coarsening of life in Britain today, in which the brashly new inevitably defeats the old, in which the ugly always overcomes the beautiful, and everything of which the British used to be proud is cast down and vilified. It is too much to hope in modern Britain – filthy, chaotic, idle, rancorous modern Britain – that sweetness and light could ever triumph over barbarism. The Queen is the only individual in British public life who has held out some hope that decency might survive. By failing the trust which she put in them, her children have failed us all. The lights have not quite gone out. But they are guttering in their sockets.

INDEX